MW00852282

A BEACHCOMBER'S GUIDE TO FOSSILS

Bob Gale | Pam Gale | Ashby Gale

Photography by Ashby Gale

A BEACHCOMBER'S GUIDE TO Fossils

The University of Georgia Press | Athens

Athens, Georgia 30602
www.ugapress.org

Designed by Mindy Basinger Hill
Set in Skolar Latin
Printed and bound by
Martin Book Management.
The paper in this book meets the guidelines forpermanence and durability of the Committee on Production Guidelines for Book Longevity of theCouncil on Library Resources.

Most University of Georgia Press titles are available from popular e-book vendors.

Printed in Korea

24 23 22 21 20 P 5 4 3 2 1

Library of Congress Cataloging-in-Publication Data
Names Gale, Bob, 1951 March 1– author.
Title A beachcomber's guide to fossils / Bob Gale, Pam Gale, Ashby Gale ; photography by Ashby Gale.
Description Athens : The University of Georgia Press, [2020] | Series: Wormsloe foundation nature book | Includes bibliographical references and index.
Identifiers
LCCN 2020013383
ISBN 9780820357324 (paperback)
Subjects
LCSH: Fossils—Collection and preservation—Atlantic Coast (U.S.)—Identification. | Fossils—Collection and preservation—Gulf Coast (U.S.)—Identification.
Classification
LCC QE746 .G35 2020
DDC 560.975—dc23
LC record available at https://lccn.loc.gov/2020013383

This book is dedicated

to all the beachcombers

who stand out from the crowd

and pick up the shiny black “rocks,”

along with the shark teeth.

Contents

Foreword

A naturalist is a person who studies the world of nature and marvels at it. Everyone is a naturalist to one degree or another. We are all curious about the world around us. That curiosity leads to two questions: "What is it?" and "How does it fit into the rest of the world?" Identification comes first. We like to know the names of things. Then we want to know about connections and relationships between organisms and their environment. We delight in finding order in nature. It helps us make sense of the world.

When I began picking up and studying fossils on South Carolina beaches in the early 1960s, I compared them to skeletal material and other remains of modern animals and found many correlations. But there were things that didn't match anything I had seen before. How was I going to figure out what they were? In those days, the M. C. Thomas book, *Fossil Vertebrates: Beach and Bank Collecting for Amateurs* (1968), was the best book available. It was filled with black-and-white photographs of common fossils with captions and basic information about collecting. The book was a great help to me, but I wanted more photographs and more in-depth information. Over time, I was able to gather what I needed from a variety of other sources. The authors of this book have done all that work for you. I wish I had had this book when first starting out!

A Beachcomber's Guide to Fossils is written for the amateur collector who wants as much information about the subject as possible. It covers fossils found along the Atlantic coast from New Jersey to Florida, as well as those found along the Gulf coast from Florida to eastern Texas. This book is a unique presentation; I know of nothing else quite like it. It contains hundreds of excellent color photographs with common and scientific names, and a great deal of information that is easy to understand. An up-to-date list of references allows access to even more information. It helps the reader answer the two questions posed earlier. This book lets you know what to look for and how to look for it. Fossils are clues to the past. The following pages will teach you how to be a detective, read the clues, and make discoveries on your own. That thrill of discovery is something you will never forget. Share what you learn with museums in the area. You can learn from them, and they can learn from you. Learning has always been a combination of information and experience. This book will give you the information you need.

I challenge you to walk the beach and experience the joy of fossil hunting for yourself. You never know what you will find until you look, and the tides give you a new beach to explore every day. Now would be a good time to start.

Rudy Mancke

RUDY MANCKE is a past curator of natural history at the South Carolina State Museum, founder of the South Carolina Association of Naturalists, host of the award-winning television series *NatureScene*, and naturalist in residence at the University of South Carolina.

Preface

Do you enjoy a good mystery? How about leisurely walks along the beach? Are you fascinated by mammoths, mastodons, or other giant creatures that once roamed the earth? If you answered yes to the above, then this book was written for you!

Most people look forward to a vacation trip to the beach to soak up the sun's rays, bounce among the buffeting waves, or cast their rods into the surf in hopes of landing some tasty fish fare. Many adventurous beachgoers spend their time combing the sandy shoreline in search of seashells. The ocean holds an incredible diversity of many-colored shells in a wide range of shapes and sizes that were once the protective homes and skeletons of unusual creatures. Searching for these treasures can involve many happy hours of fun.

But other riches along the sandy shores are waiting to be discovered—even more unusual and harder to find than seashells. These discoveries offer a real prize for those who love to scour Gulf Coast beaches from Texas to the Florida peninsula, and the Atlantic beaches north to New Jersey. These treasures, ranging from ten thousand to millions of years in age, reflect life on earth long before, and soon after, man appeared. They are the fossil remains of mammals, reptiles, birds, and fish species from an earlier era of history. Some of these were giant versions of animals that are common today. Glyptodonts and giant armadillos up to nine feet in length were contemporaries of giant sloths, giant tortoises, tapirs, and alligators. Other fossilized remains awaiting discovery include intricately patterned teeth and mouthparts of the ancestors of manta rays, puffer fish, and drum fish. Finely toothed stingray spines and beautifully

above Sunrise on the beach at Botany Bay, South Carolina.

Toe bone from an extinct giant ground sloth.

colored shark teeth can be found, as well as an amazing variety of bones. These include fish skulls, whale vertebrae and inner ear bones, and huge pieces of leg joints or toe bones of the mammoths and mastodons that commonly grazed in the prehistoric environment. Surprisingly well-preserved teeth and tusk parts of these early elephant relatives can also be found.

Perhaps you think that such fossils could be found only by joining a paleontology dig at a highly restricted site, under the supervision of a college professor. In fact, the good news is that you are not disturbing any paleontological site by collecting them, because these fossils are often available on beaches and inlets that are open to the public. They naturally erode out of ancient soils along coastal plain rivers or get churned up from long-buried ocean sediments. Then they are washed up onto beaches by tidal currents and left behind as the tides retreat. Thanks to the gravitational pull of the moon, this happens twice in every 24-hour cycle. Even more fossils are brought to light by churning waves accompanying offshore storms or hurricanes.

These treasures are out there for you to discover. This book was written as a user-friendly guide to quickly give you the knowledge and skill to identify them. Your finds will excite you and bring the life of these creatures into a very real, present-day focus. They will fuel your imagination.

So start searching. We wish you the best of luck!

Acknowledgments

We are indebted to many who helped provide inspiration, references, and review during the writing of this book.

First and foremost, we are grateful to Rudy Mancke, naturalist in residence at the University of South Carolina, for first opening our eyes to the fossil treasures that lie within reach of anyone who visits a beach. Thanks to his experience as curator of natural history at the South Carolina State Museum, his extensive knowledge of coastal plain fossils, and his skill at communicating to the public all things natural, we (Bob and Pam) became proficient at fossil identification. We were able to transfer Rudy's excitement to Ashby, who has quickly become an expert in his own right, providing much additional research and many fossil additions for this book.

We also thank Ken Carman for helping us find our first megalodon teeth through his knowledge and gracious sharing of favorable locations, and to Duane Jackson for allowing us to feature his intact mammoth molar. Our appreciation goes to Mark Bunce for helping fill faunal gaps in our shark tooth collection and for treating us (Bob and Pam) to our first inland site after 30 years of beach collecting. In addition, we thank Bess Kellett, with the South Carolina Department of Natural Resources, for allowing Ashby to photograph a *Cuvieronius* molar and mammoth phalanx featured in this book. We also thank Justice Rozic for allowing us to feature his dire wolf canine. And our thanks to Todd Knaperek of Bydand Graphic Solutions for his excellent graphic design work and for being patient with a bunch of design-illiterate people. We are also appreciative to Laura, Jack, and Evalyn Telford for allowing us to photograph them at the beach for our closing image on page 521.

Besides our collective gratitude as the team that wrote and illustrated this book, each of us has individual acknowledgments to make.

BOB I wish to express deep thanks to my friend Todd Ballantine, principal of Ballantine Environmental Resources, Inc. (BER) and a widely published nature illustrator and author. Todd was an inspiration over many years as I became a published nature writer and photographer. He was also a valued collaborator on environmental restoration projects and scientific data analysis while we worked together at BER. I also extend my thanks to Vince Schneider, research curator of paleontology with the North Carolina Museum of Natural Sciences, for helping me with the identification of specimens in the early stages of this book's preparation.

PAM I express gratitude to Andy Cox and Sara Setzer for providing me with the artistic foundation to critically reflect on and create the drawings for this field guide. Thanks also to Megan Tichy for her assistance with drawing the human form. I also give credit to the experiences and lessons gained from thousands of adults and youth to whom I have given drawing instruction over a 35-year teaching career.

ASHBY I thank Matthew Gibson, curator of natural history at the Charleston Museum, for identifying many fossil fragments that I brought to him during the early stages of working on this book. Much gratitude also goes to Robert Boessenecker, adjunct lecturer at the College of Charleston, for identifying the whale fossils in this text and correcting the many false statements about whales that once proliferated across the amateur community in South Carolina. Appreciation is also extended to Sarah Boessenecker, collections manager at the College of Charleston, for curatorial assistance with the specimens photographed. Thanks also to Richard Hulbert, collections manager of the Division of Vertebrate Paleontology at the Florida Museum of Natural History, for identifying some tricky Pleistocene fossils; both Stephen Godfrey, curator of paleontology at the Calvert Marine Museum, and Giorgio Carnevale, professor of earth science at Università degli Studi di Torino, for identifying some of our fish fossils; Dana Ehret, assistant curator of natural history at the New Jersey State Museum, for discussions on the megatoothed shark lineage; and Alex Hastings, Fitzpatrick Chair of Paleontology at the Science Museum of Minnesota's Paleontology Department, for identifying some of our reptile fossils. I also thank Kevin May for showing me to the Calvert Cliffs on the shores of Maryland and the Potomac River, and John Owen for his excellent and informative fossil trips among the beaches of Florida through Coastal Fossil Adventures. I also express gratitude to Jason Thompson for helping fill faunal gaps in our ever-growing shark tooth collection, and to Nick Rose, who helped me find our first *Carcharocles angustidens* tooth through his knowledge of accessible sites. I am grateful to Greg Whitman for his excellent tooth restoration work with our *Otodus obliquus* and *Parotodus benedeni* shark teeth. Of course, my deepest gratitude to Tabytha Walls for her constant supports and encouragements on all of those long days of manuscript writing.

Finally, we wish to give special thanks to the staff at the University of Georgia Press for their expertise and guidance as we made our first journey through the book-publishing experience. We are grateful to Patrick Allen, Jon Davies, Katherine La Mantia, and Nathaniel Holly for their personal, informal manner and their continual, helpful communications throughout. Thanks also go to the rest of UGA Press staff—Jordan Stepp, for financial and contractual expertise; Steven Wallace, for marketing guidance; Christina Cotter, for assembling the marketing catalog; David Des Jardines, for help with the marketing guide and online promotion; and to the members of the design team who helped assemble the cover graphics. Additional thanks go to Kip Keller, for his editing skills; to Mindy Hill, for her expertise in composing the layout of such a lengthy guide; and to the anonymous peer reviewers, for their comments on an earlier draft.

INTRODUCTION

How to Use This Book

Fossils found in the beach environment are different from those freshly dug near riverbanks or from roadside cuts, quarries, and construction sites. The difference lies in the fact that beach fossils have been exposed to physical weathering from waves and repeated collisions with shells and other fossils. They therefore often appear as remnants of more intact fossils of the kind typically found in excavated sites. Nevertheless, beach finds contain clearly definable features and often are surprisingly complete. The photos and descriptions in this book reflect these characteristics, including small details, remarkably well. This guide is purposely designed to aid in fossil identification rather than to provide specific locations in which to search for them. (A number of publications offering that kind of information are listed in the Suggested Reading section on pages 491–492.) The book begins with a general description of how fossils form, before proceeding to accounts of specific fossils you might find.

The Geologic History section provides background information on dynamic physiographic events that occurred on Earth before and during the time line of animals whose fossils are featured in this guide. This background is given to provide a basic understanding of the conditions that made prehistoric life possible.

Following this history, the Process of Fossilization section describes how those early animals became preserved in forms that can be identified, often to the species level, today.

The next section, Fossils and the Beach Profile, provides an informative series of "classroom" lessons that show the beginning collector how and where to look for fossils on the parts of the beach where these treasures occur. Included are helpful diagrams and photographs of each area of the beach profile.

How and Where to Find Shark Teeth is a special section focused only on these teeth, which are unique when compared with the fossil hard parts of other animals.

The heart of *A Beachcomber's Guide to Fossils* occurs within the fossil Identification Page entries. Section headings include Shark Teeth, Bones, Osteoderms, Mouthparts, Teeth, Vertebrae, Miscellaneous, and Look-Alikes. Differing colored backgrounds and icons representing these features on the upper outside page corners help readers quickly locate the desired identification section. The Miscellaneous section includes fossils that cannot be neatly grouped in the other sections, as well as some Native American artifacts. Look-Alikes includes objects that are not fossils but that are easily confused with them. Each identification section is preceded by a two-page Overview explaining the general characteristics of the items in that section.

The major focus of *A Beachcomber's Guide to Fossils* is on high-quality photographic images that can be used to facilitate immediate comparison and identification of your fossil samples. Because the photos are close-ups intended to show minute details, small fossils may appear larger in the book than their actual size. It is therefore important to compare a fossil's size with the measurements given under the photos.

Immediately below the photos, a title space lists the anatomical part of the fossil shown, followed by its scientific name. Generally, we provide the genus and species names. For fossils that cannot be accurately identified to species, or even to higher classification levels, we provide the scientific name of the level that is known. Thus, a title may list the anatomical part, such as a bone, followed by "*Genus species*," or "*Genus* sp.," or "Family," "Order," "Class," and so on. Scientific names follow the standard nomenclature rule of listing the genus (capitalized and in italics), followed by the species (lowercase and in italics), with other levels noted in standard font beginning in uppercase. Prehistoric species often lack common names, but we provide these when known.

Most fossils are part of a given species' bone or tooth structure, and these have anatomical names, but again, do not always have common names. For this reason, many of the descriptive paragraphs necessarily contain technical anatomical terms. Their definitions are found in the Glossary of Terms and the Illustrated Glossary.

We indicated the geologic age of specimens in two ways. First, in the Shark Teeth section, the age provided reflects the entire geologic age range during which the species represented by the tooth was alive. If a shark species is still

SPECIMEN PHOTOS

Multiple angles provide a detailed look at all angles of a single specimen.

IDENTIFICATION TITLE

Anatomical part followed by the most precise taxonomic identifier; in some cases, only a taxonomic identifier is given.

SECTION ICON

An icon representing the section is located in the corner of each page for quick visual access.

SECTION TITLE

Every Identification Page has the corresponding section title displayed at the top of the page, along with a unique color header.

SHARK TEETH

Ln Lb L

Palaeohypotodus rutoti

Lower anterior tooth from the extinct sand tiger shark *Palaeohypotodus rutoti*. This tooth, from an early Paleocene site, has lateral cusplets (occasionally double) and broadly tapers from the crown tip to the base. The roots are relatively thick, with prominent centers and distinct nutrient grooves. The tooth margins are unserrated. It is similar in appearance to modern sand tiger (*Carcharias* sp.) teeth. *P. rutoti* teeth do not occur in deposits younger than the Eocene. Note that this tooth has double lateral cusplets, the second cusplet being extremely reduced.

SIZE
22 × 12 × 7 mm
0.9 × 0.5 × 0.3 in

GEOLOGIC AGE
Paleocene–Eocene
66–37.2 Ma

IDENTIFIERS
Lateral cusplets
Broad taper
Prominent root

DENSITY

DID YOU KNOW? Sharks, rays, sea turtles, eels, fish, whales, and dolphins are believed to have a bit of lodestone, or magnetite, in their bodies. Particles of this mineral aid their navigation and long-distance migrations around the world, just as magnetized compass needles help humans in their travels. Imagine that—a compass inside sea creatures!

45

ANATOMICAL VIEW

Each specimen photo has a corresponding circular label noting the anatomical position from which the specimen is being viewed. See page 461 for a listing of the positions corresponding to these abbreviations.

CHARACTERISTICS

Concise information about the fossil.

Size: Listed in metric and U.S. units.

Geologic Age: Epoch from which the specimen originated.

Identifiers: Three quick identifying features, explained in the description.

Density: Graphic showing the object's relative density, from lightest, at left, to densest, at right.

ITEM DESCRIPTION

Explanation of the anatomical features of the specimen, and features to look for in identifying other fragments.

DID YOU KNOW?

Fun, informative write-ups on the animal associated with the pictured fossil or on a broader topic.

alive today, that range extends into the Holocene and is listed from the first geologic epoch (of that shark species' existence) to the present. For all other sections, only the geologic age of the pictured fossil is presented, even if the specimen is from a species still alive today. This age correlates with the date of the rock layer (usually an entire epoch) from which the featured fossil originated. The photos in this guide depict fossilized remains, even if some of these species live on today.

Finally, a series of twelve animal Species Highlights are spaced throughout the guide. Each provides background on the featured animals' earliest known appearance in the fossil record and the evolutionary paths they followed from ancestral development to their modern descendants. Included are artistic renderings and photos relating to the extinct species. Each animal group has its own fascinating story, and these stories are intended to be interesting and informative.

We hope that the unique format provided in *A Beachcomber's Guide to Fossils* helps you come quickly up to speed in beach fossil recognition. When you are first starting, picking out the seemingly indistinguishable shapes of many fossilized animal parts may be difficult. But be assured that you will soon develop expertise in recognizing the often subtle patterns that define these interesting fragments of prehistory.

Geologic History

LAYING THE BEDROCK FOR TODAY'S FOSSILS

We know from fossils found today that incredible, giant creatures roamed the earth in prehistoric times. Such intriguing finds lead to questions about early life. How did these animals evolve into the vast number of species revealed by those fossils, and what conditions led to their populations being found in the southeastern U.S. coastal plain?

To gain an understanding of this, it is helpful to look at the shifting "jigsaw puzzle" of Earth's continents and oceans. This geologic process, commonly known as continental drift, is described by the theory of plate tectonics. Dynamic geologic activity, along with climatic changes caused by this random continual continental movement, influenced prehistoric plant and animal life and contributed to a subsequent explosion in diversity of species around the world.

The material that makes up Earth is in constant motion, both within the planet's interior and on its surface. This unrest is caused by the movement of molten material at Earth's core, and the more solid but still plastic, that is, pliable, rock within the thick mantle, which lies between the core and Earth's outermost layer, or crust. Convection currents within the mantle form as hotter material rises toward the surface and cooler rock sinks back toward the core. In some parts of the world, this extensive cyclical activity causes the outer crust to split open in places where fresh new rock is pushed up from the mantle. Correspondingly, in other regions, the existing crustal rock is forced back downward into the mantle.

The openings formed by this activity appear roughly as linear seams that extend throughout the earth's crust, dividing it into a series of plates that "float" on the mantle. These crustal plates support the continents and oceans. The plates

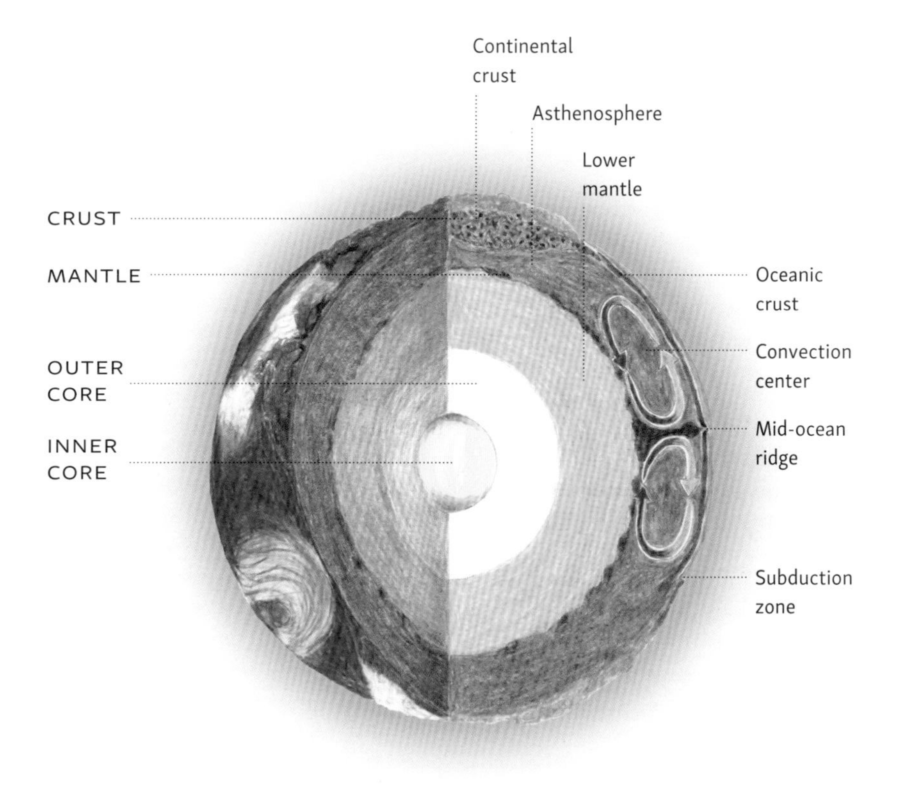

move away from each other along the boundaries where the mantle material is pushed up. Conversely, where continental and oceanic plates collide with each other, the underlying crustal rock of one of those plates pitches downward into the mantle.

This continental drift shapes Earth's topography, which in turn directly impacts climate. As the global plates have shifted through time, oceans have opened up, shrunk, or completely disappeared, and mountain ranges have been built, eroded, and rebuilt. During such changes, extensive ocean currents are formed, and these in turn transport massive quantities of warm and cold water around the continents, influencing long-term global atmospheric temperatures.

In a similar vein, mountain ranges influence precipitation. When moving air currents are forced to rise with mountain elevations, the moisture within these air masses cools and condenses out as rain or snow. If the mountains are high enough, there can be a "rain shadow" effect in which all the moisture occurs on one side of the range, while the other side remains virtually dry, sometimes resulting in deserts.

These diverse topographic and climatic conditions directly influence the formation of plant communities and give rise to the kinds of animals that thrive in particular environments. Many wildlife populations became separated when the continent on which they evolved split into two plates that moved away from each other. Similarly, species moved onto new continents when crustal plates came together or when land bridges created by newly lowered ocean levels connected two formerly separate continents.

Examples of this occurred when the Bering Land Bridge formed between Asia's Siberian region and what is now Alaska. For the first time, animals and humans were easily able to enter North America. Similarly, the appearance of the Panamanian Land Bridge led to a massive species movement known as the Great American Biotic Interchange, during which animal groups moved from South America to North America, and vice versa. Interestingly, the species shift northward was much larger than the reverse.

As a result of this dynamic geologic shifting, animals similar to one another, along with their ancestors' fossilized remains, can be found on continents now distant from each other. One example of this can be seen in the similarity between today's elephants, found in Africa and Asia, and the mammoths and mastodons that roamed North America over 10,000 years ago. Early elephant ancestors migrated across the Bering Land Bridge and spread south to most of the lower 48 states and Mexico.

Fossils dating back to earlier geologic periods and epochs provide a tantalizing and rich history of the past. Many plant and animal species became extinct, in part because of cataclysms arising from the restless motion of Earth's crust. Other species, however, benefited from the opportunities brought by these ecological changes and the resulting biological pressures, to which they were able to adapt; some of these species went on to flourish under the new conditions. These changes also led to random but periodic increases in diversity. New fossils of species previously unknown are constantly being discovered around the world in buried or unstudied rock layers that originated far from their present positions.

CENOZOIC ERA

PERIOD	EPOCH	AGE*
		0.01**
Quaternary	Pleistocene	2.6
Neogene	Pliocene	5.3
Neogene	Miocene	23.0
Paleogene	Oligocene	33.9
Paleogene	Eocene	56.0
Paleogene	Paleocene	66.0

* Ma ** Holocene Epoch: 11ka to Present

Shards of pottery from a 4,000-year-old group of Late Archaic Indians.

GEOLOGIC TIME SCALE

The animals whose stories are told in this book lived long after the formation of the earth, 4.5 billion years ago; well after the supercontinent Pangaea split into the Laurasia and Gondwanaland land masses; and even long after the Euro-African and North and South American plates collided and separated, creating the current oceans and continents. Included here are fossils from creatures that walked the earth or swam in its waters as far back as the Cretaceous period. Most, however, lived after the Oligocene epoch, which dates from 33.9 to 23 million years ago (Ma). The greatest focus is on those that lived during the Pleistocene epoch, which extended from 11 thousand years ago (ka) to 2.6 Ma. Some samples are from the Holocene (11 ka to the present), including artifacts from prehistoric Native American clans or tribes.

TIME LINE OF EVENTS AND SPECIES OCCURRENCE AND RESPONSE

The right-hand column denotes occurrences simultaneous with the events at left. Some but not all of these occurrences may have been in response to those events.

Event	*Species Occurrence/Response*
PALEOCENE EPOCH (66–56 million years ago)	
Seas retreating; South America, previously detached from Antarctica, still isolated from North America; fluvial (riverine) and coastal plain sediments deposited	Expansion and diversification of marine life, including foraminifera, shellfish, finfish, and shark species
Proliferation of flowering plants, including tree and shrub species	Dominance of mammals; appearance of early primates, rodents, large flightless birds; increase in herbivore and carnivore species.
EOCENE EPOCH (56–33.9 million years ago)	
Climate warming and rising seas; flooding of coastal and low-lying inlands; sand deposition in upper coastal plain; limestone deposition in middle and lower Atlantic coastal plains	Return of terrestrial species to the sea as mammals; evolution of early species of whales and seals
Separation of European and North American crustal plates; mountain building and resultant erosion; fault-zone activity	Continued increase in terrestrial mammals; first appearance of early horses and other odd-toed ungulates
OLIGOCENE EPOCH (33.9–23 million years ago)	
Climate cooling; continents increasingly covered with woodlands and grasses	Proliferation and diversification of grazing species; appearance of canids, giant sloths, and even-toed ungulates, such as pigs
Continued continental movement; separation of Australia and Antarctica; further separation of North America and Europe; influence of marine arches and embayments on coastal plain deposits; continuation of carbonate deposition	Evolution of primitive whales into toothed whales, which replace the former

Event	*Species Occurrence/Response*
MIOCENE EPOCH (23–5.3 million years ago)	
Falling sea levels	Appearance of browsing horses and species with teeth adapted for grazing
Blanketing of polar regions by ice sheets	Diversification of species of grazing ruminants as grasslands spread
Mountain building in the Himalayas, Rockies, and Andes; continued erosion of eastern U.S. mountains and piedmont, with coastal sedimentation	Extensive diversification of mammals; appearance of saber-toothed cats; early primates (apes, monkeys)
Bering Land Bridge flooded, separating North America and Asia	Mastodont elephant species well established in North America before separation from Asia
Formation of modern circular ocean currents (gyres) as global circulation changed after the closing of the Tethys Ocean	Extensive diversification of marine species, including such mammal species as baleen whales, seals, sea lions, walruses, and sea cows
Seasonal climatic cycles established in the Northern Hemisphere	Giant white shark (*Carcharocles megalodon*) a common marine predator
PLIOCENE EPOCH (5.3–2.6 million years ago)	
Present position of continents	Diversification of horses and even-toed herbivores; mammals approaching present-day diversity
North and South America linked by Panamanian Land Bridge	Great American Biotic Interchange (movement of species between North and South America)
Climatic cycling from cool and dry to warm and wet and then to cool and dry again	Appearance of early human ancestors in Africa

Event	*Species Occurrence/Response*
PLEISTOCENE EPOCH (2.6 million–11,000 years ago)	
Reign of ice ages: at least 20 climatic cycles of glaciation with warmer interglacial periods	Major megafauna extinctions in North America, including ground sloths, llamas, camels, saber-toothed cats, mammoths, and mastodons
Expansion of continental shelves due to falling sea levels; southeastern U.S. coast extends out to current Gulf Stream	Migration of humans out of Africa; appearance of *Homo sapiens*
HOLOCENE EPOCH (11,000 years ago–present)	
Climatic warming after the end of the last ice age	Human civilizations; human expansion to every continent
Increasing rate of glacial melting	Shifting of plant communities in response to warming climate
Increasing levels of atmospheric carbon dioxide	Beginning of human-caused pollution of air and water by extracting and burning fossil fuels and by developing and disposing of synthetic chemical compounds
Rising sea levels	Rapidly increasing extinctions of animal species
Alteration of landforms, rivers, and climate by human activities	Humans attempt first environmental restoration of species and ecosystems

A snapshot of the fossilization process. This *Turitella* snail shell dissolved away, leaving behind a phosphatic steinkern—an internal cast of the original creature's shell.

Processes of Fossilization

Fossils are remnants, impressions, or traces of plants and animals from past geologic ages that have been naturally preserved within the earth's crust.

Fossilization is the process by which these organisms turned into fossils through time. This process can occur in a number of ways depending on the conditions occurring immediately or soon after an organism's death, the type of sediments surrounding the organism, and the presence or absence of moisture during the period of fossilization.

The odds that a living organism will become fossilized are extremely small. For this to happen, a plant or animal must start the fossilization process before significant decomposition occurs. This can happen if the organism is covered by water or sediments shortly after its death. Submersion in water, for example, on the floor of an ocean, lake, or slow-moving tidal river near the coast, is essential for preserving plant and animal tissue, since it ensures that aerobic (oxygen-requiring) animals and microorganisms won't be able to break down the dead specimen's tissues.

PERMINERALIZATION, REPLACEMENT, AND PETRIFICATION

Such environments provide suitable conditions for one of the most common fossilization processes, permineralization. All organisms have pores and spaces that, during their living years, are filled with water or air. In permineralization, the water in the sediments surrounding the dead plant or animal becomes supersaturated with minerals dissolving out of those sediments. The three most commonly found minerals in this process are silica, calcite, and iron, which are present to varying degrees in groundwater. This hard water fills the dead

Will this raccoon skeleton decompose or become fossilized?

organism's pores, empty spaces, and even areas within cell walls. Eventually, as the water is driven out through time, the minerals crystallize, in much the way that as saltwater evaporates out of a glass, salt crystals are left at the bottom. The minerals that remain solidify in the form of an organism's original structure, creating the fossils we know today.

Sometimes the minerals in the surrounding sediments replace the minerals present in the dead organism, a form of permineralization called replacement. When all the empty spaces and all the organic matter of an organism have been replaced by new minerals, the organism has literally become stone. This is known as petrification, the most extensive form of permineralization. Depending on which minerals replace which parts of the organism, very detailed fossils can result, and these aid in identification. Petrified wood, for example, can sometimes be identified to its original tree species.

CHEMICAL PROCESSES OF PERMINERALIZATION

Permineralization can be broken down into three categories, namely carbonate mineralization, pyritization, and silicification.

The main fossils formed from carbonate mineralization are coal balls, which result from the formation of multiple plant and animal species into balls. These primarily date to the Carboniferous period, about 359 to 299 million years ago.

Pyritization of fossils occurs in many marine deposits, where iron, sulfates, and organic carbon are readily available. Some of the most famous specimens include ammonites that were either partially or wholly pyritized, leaving behind beautiful golden specimens.

Silicification is the most common form of permineralization, which is understandable, since silicon and oxygen combine to form silicon dioxide, the most abundant mineral in the earth's crust. Silicon dioxide is the primary mineral found in Pleistocene bones and teeth.

ADDITIONAL PROCESSES OF FOSSILIZATION

The following are other ways that plants and animals can become fossilized under particular environmental conditions that in some cases were also the causes of their deaths. Some of these are not fossils in the truest sense, but rather are well-preserved animals or structures. Nevertheless, they are included here because they are (or were parts of) extinct prehistoric creatures, and paleontologists consider these structures and remnant body parts as important as fossils in providing clues to previous life-forms.

AMBER When ancient conifers oozed resin from wounds in their tree limbs, hapless insects crawling into the resin became stuck. Further oozing caused them to become fully encapsulated, and the hardened resin perfectly preserved the insects.

BURROWS Many species of burrowing animals living on the ocean bottom secreted fluids that cemented the walls of their tunnel homes, preventing their collapse. These reinforced burrows eventually underwent permineralization, and their hardened structures can be dug out of prehistoric sediments. See pages 403–404

MOLDS AND CASTS Organisms can be covered in sediments that later dissolve away, leaving empty cavities or mold impressions of the organisms. Such cavities can then fill with sediments that eventually harden into casts (steinkerns). The external and internal impressions and structures are reflected in the resulting stone surfaces. See pages 412 and 422.

View down a tube cast.

COPROLITES Prehistoric animal excrement can become preserved in sediment, just like the organisms that produced it, resulting in a fossilized (but not odoriferous) facsimile of the original feces. Many coprolites form within animal intestines, thus preserving the shapes and patterns of those intestines. See page 405.

CARBONIZATION Under the right conditions, the soft parts of animals and leaves can decompose in water where oxygen, nitrogen, and hydrogen are driven off, but carbon remains. Dark impressions of the original organisms are then left in the rocks formed from the original sediments.

PEAT BOGS Many organisms of more recent times are preserved within peat bogs, which, because of their anaerobic environments and high levels of tannic acid, prevent decomposition.

FREEZING Mammoths and rhinoceroses have been found in permanently frozen ice in Alaska, Siberia, and Canada. These animals, which were rapidly frozen in catastrophic circumstances, remained perfectly preserved until their modern discovery. Even the hair of these creatures survived intact.

DRYING Fossil mummies of animals including camels and giant ground sloths have been found in caves in the southwestern United States, where dry conditions remained sealed off from the atmosphere. Amazingly, these species' hair and skin, and even their colors, were preserved.

TAR PITS Countless animal species became stuck in the Rancho La Brea Tar Pits of Los Angeles. Many other animals attacking these hapless creatures also became mired down, leaving scientists with a treasure trove of well-preserved specimens and a history of their predator-prey relationships.

Fossils and the Beach Profile

The world of beach fossils is as exciting as going on a paleontological excavation or engaging in a thrilling game of hide-and-seek. As with many games or missions, there are a few "rules of play." In this section, you will travel back to lessons in science, art, geometry, and geography to become acquainted with these rules of the beach. You can use them to your advantage in successfully searching for fossils.

BACK TO THE SCIENCE CLASSROOM

When you are combing the beach for fossils (and other artifacts), one of the most important factors to keep in mind is that objects on the beach are sorted by two factors: size and density. Loosely defined, size is generally measured in three dimensions, expressed commonly as length, width, and height. Density is another story. Scientifically speaking, density is defined as the mass of an object per unit volume. Many people use the terms "mass" and "weight" interchangeably, despite their differences. Mass is defined as the quantity of matter, whether in an object or in the universe; mass remains constant in the entire universe. Weight, on the other hand, is defined as the gravitational force applied to an object. The classic example is to compare your weight on Earth with what it would be on the moon. While your mass does not change, you would "feel lighter" on the moon because of its weaker gravitational pull, and a scale would show you weighing less (about one-sixth as much as on Earth).

In this book, density is expressed as a relative value. For example, a slice of chocolate cake is "heavier" or denser than a similarly sized slice of angel food cake, and a piece of fudge is denser than the slice of chocolate cake. To maintain

COMMON FOSSILS DEPICTED IN THEIR USUAL LOCATIONS ON A BEACH PROFILE.

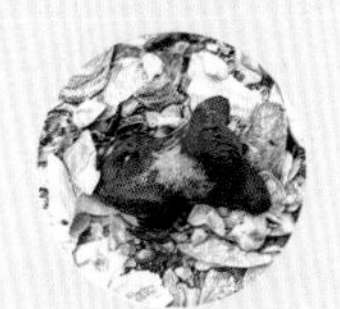

HIGH-TIDE LINE

Though few and far between, fossils at the high-tide line are large: bones, larger turtle shells, and complete molars and vertebrae are frequently found here.

MID-TIDE LINE

Large to medium bones, turtle shell elements, and larger mammal tooth fragments are common here. Fossils are often isolated, exposed from shell clusters and mounds.

MID-TIDE TAILINGS

Medium-sized fossils such as fish skull elements, large ray teeth, small mammal molars, and burrfish and porcupinefish teeth can be found here.

LOW-TIDE AND SURF LINES

Small fossils such as shark, ray, and fish teeth can be collected from the low-tide line, although large bones can occasionally be uncovered in a patch of bare sand.

DENSITY SCALE

the ease of use of this book, no numbers are assigned to the density of a fossil. Instead, a sliding scale with five categories is used, each represented by a shaded box of varying darkness (above). Inside the box on each identification page is a shark tooth to indicate how dense the specimen is.

Evidence of wave action that sorts objects by size and density is apparent each time you walk on a beach, regardless of locality. Small dense objects are the most common items found at the surf and low-tide lines. Conversely, large light objects are found at the mid- to high-tide lines. Of course, there are always exceptions to this rule; you might find a large molar at the high-tide line, demonstrating that one factor can occasionally overrule another. But whether you are on a shelly beach in the lower Atlantic states or on a gravelly beach near the northern cliff faces, these factors remain true.

BACK TO THE ART ROOM

Once you have a handle on where certain fossils are most commonly found, it is time to retrain your knowledge of colors. Fossils obtain their colors from the matrix (surrounding sediment) they were in while they fossilized. This is predominantly the case in permineralized fossils, since groundwater bearing dissolved minerals seeps into bones and other hard structures. Many hunters will pick up gray fragments of oyster, whelk, or ark shells and pronounce them "black." And yet in the world of fossils, even some of the darkest shells are not the black color described in this book. Also to keep in mind: items appear darker when wet.

Specimens collected on the beach that appear to be fossils or are darker in hue may lighten as they dry and prove to be a shell fragment or a piece of rock. One of the common mistakes that early fossil hunters make is in their perception of what fossilized objects look like. Many concretions can trick the inexperienced (and occasionally veteran) fossil hunter into thinking an item is a fossil. For this reason, a Look-Alikes section near the end of this book provides many of the common pseudofossils and detrital fragments found on beaches.

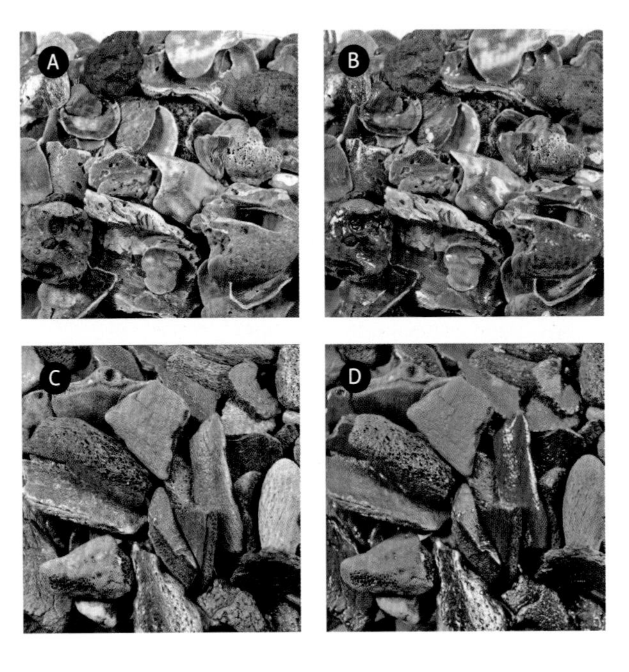

Comparison of shell and fossil material both wet and dry: *A*, dry shells; *B*, wet shells; *C*, dry fossils; *D*, wet fossils.

BACK TO GEOMETRY CLASS

Now that we have a good handle on the colors of fossils, we can continue to build our mental glossaries of images by adding common shapes, patterns, and textures found in the fossil realm. Having a proper understanding of the textures of bone, turtle shell, tooth enamel, or ivory (to name a few) can help turn a mediocre day of fossil hunting into one of your best. These patterns and textures are key to identifying even the smallest fossil fragments.

Common Fossil Textures

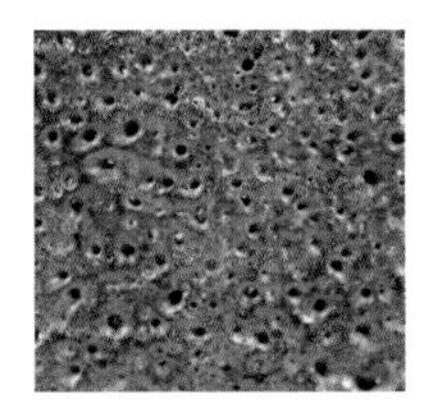

Armadillo osteoderm
Page 194

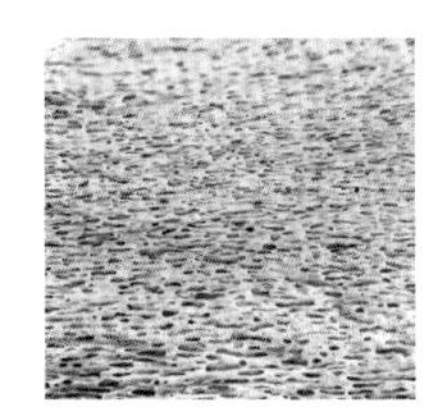

Spongy inner bone
Page 463

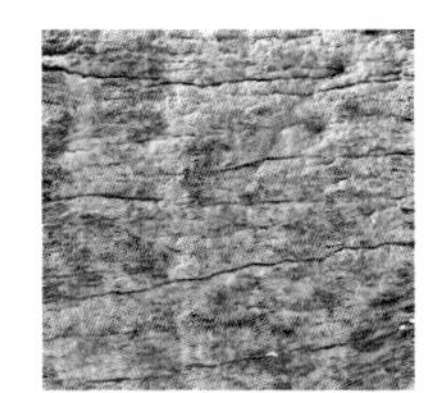

Worn outer bone
Page 463

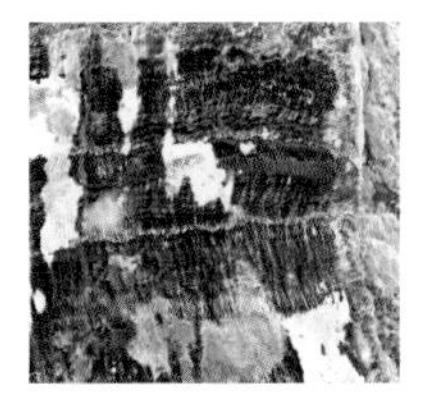

Mammoth tooth enamel
Page 318

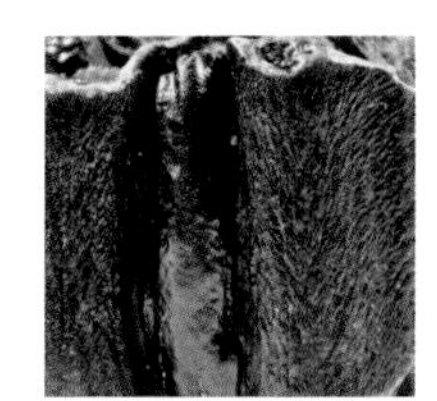

Bison tooth enamel
Page 293

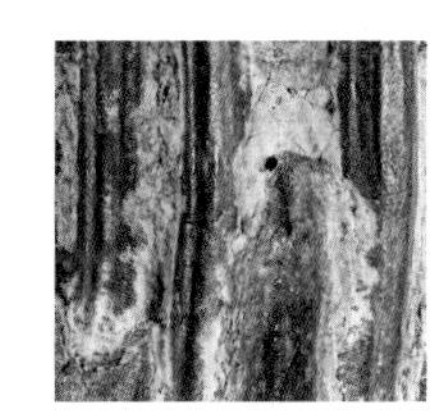

Horse tooth enamel
Page 283

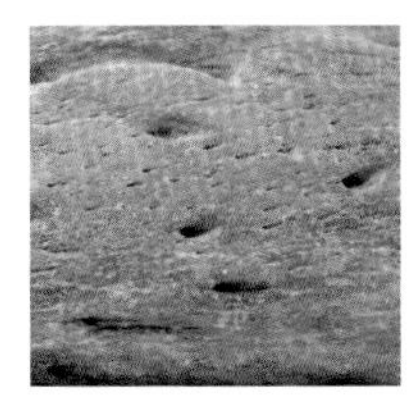

Alligator mandible
Page 242

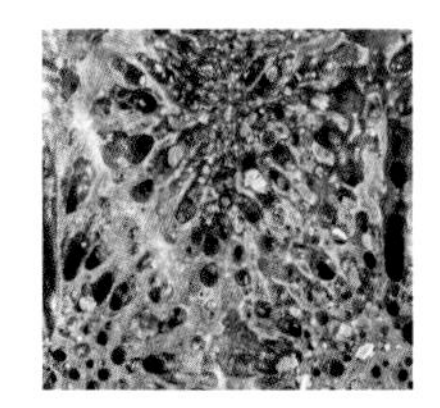

Sea robin skull
Page 389

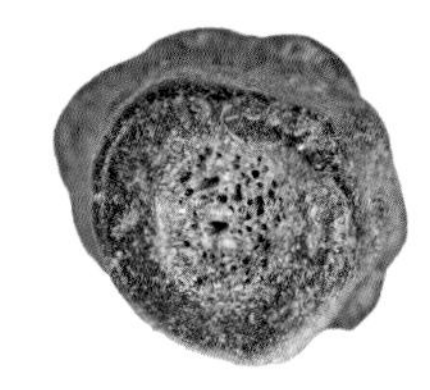

Deer antler
Page 409

Common Fossil Shapes

Drum fish teeth
Page 322

Gar fish scales
Page 206

Armadillo osteoderms
Page 196

Carpals and tarsals
Page 174

Stingray teeth
Page 231

Shark teeth
Page 43

Turtle neural bones
Page 211

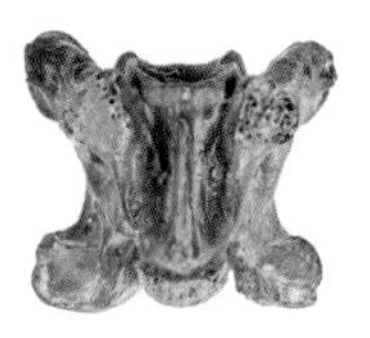

Vertebrae
Page 347

Tortoise leg spurs
Page 200

Common Fossil Patterns

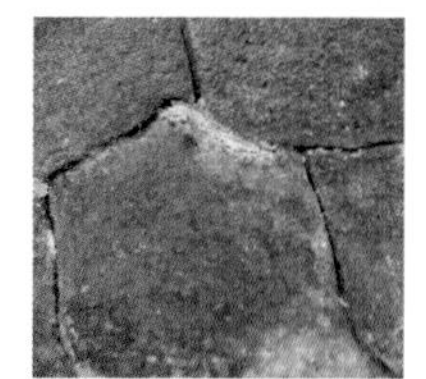

Turtle scute lines
Page 208

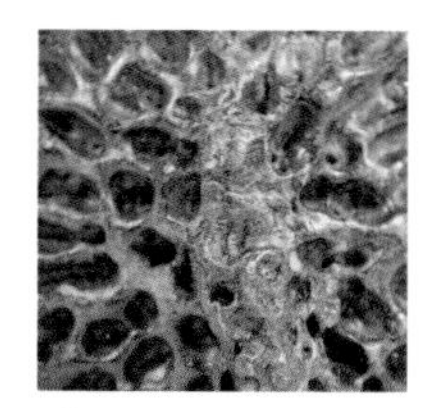

Alligator osteoderm
Page 191

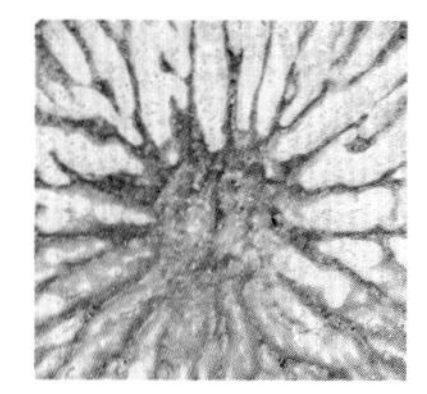

Vertebra epiphysis
Page 376

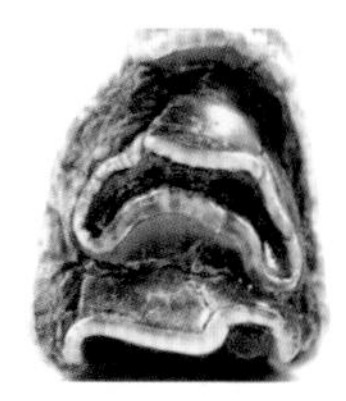

Bison tooth enamel
Page 292

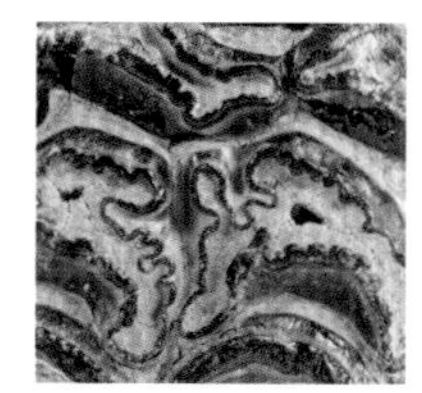

Horse tooth enamel
Page 284

Ivory Schreger pattern
Page 399

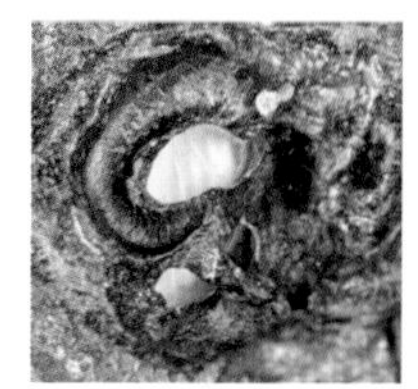

Petrosal canals
Page 124

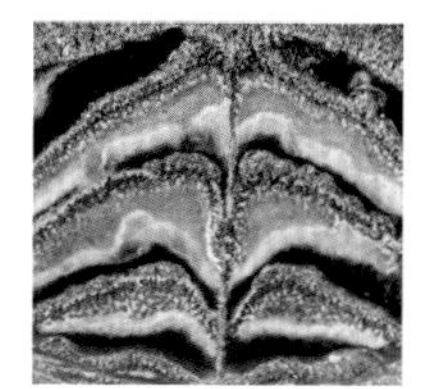

Chilomycterus teeth
Page 238

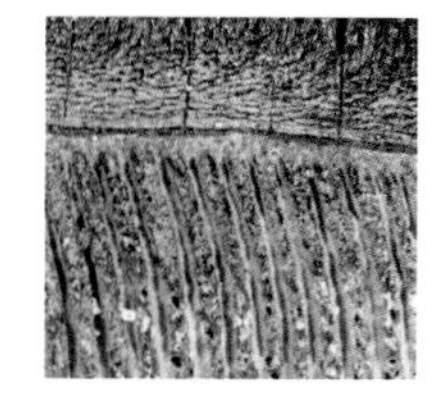

Eagle ray teeth
Page 229

BACK TO GEOGRAPHY CLASS

Our last stop is geography class. Keeping in mind all the factors and tips discussed in the science, art, and geometry lessons, we are able to analyze a beach anywhere in the world and locate fossils if present. The following are images from representative fossiliferous beaches in the eastern United States, displaying their profiles, and the fossils found on them.

Florida

Low tide on the shores of Fernandina Beach, Florida.

Sorted beach material at low tide.

Characteristic coquina shell hash found on many Atlantic Coast Florida beaches.

Chilomycterus (burrfish) teeth at the high-tide line.

Baleen whale tympanic bulla found along Ponte Vedra Beach, Florida.

left Sand tiger shark tooth uncovered after a receding tide.

right Turtle rib bone in shell hash at the high-tide line.

middle Native American pottery shard from Late Archaic Indians.

bottom Bone fragment stranded at the mid-tide line.

Predominantly oyster-shell beach, typical of beaches near Charleston, South Carolina.

High-tide line filled with oyster, quahog clam, whelk, and ark shells.

Maryland

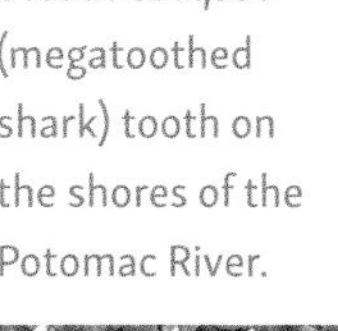

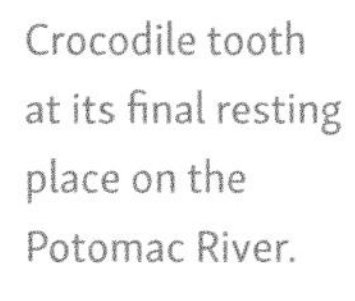

Otodus obliquus (megatoothed shark) tooth on the shores of the Potomac River.

Crocodile tooth at its final resting place on the Potomac River.

Galeocerdo aduncus (extinct tiger shark) tooth on the shelly shore beneath the Calvert Cliffs.

Sunrise on the clay-strewn profile of Bayfront Beach, along the Calvert Cliffs.

above left *Hemipristis serra* (extinct snaggletooth shark) tooth hiding in the clay balls and detritus at Bayfront Beach, Maryland.

above right Cliff faces along the Potomac River in Charles County, Maryland.

left Beaches on the Potomac River with widespread gravelly patches.

How and Where to Find Shark Teeth

Many fossil hunters and tourists alike often come to the beach with the same questions: How do I find shark teeth? and Where do I find them? These questions have a number of answers. Some collectors hunt strictly at low tide, while others search between tides; some search only at the tide line, where the waves crash onto shore, and others hunt by digging a hole in the sand and sifting material until they come across a tooth. It seems as if no matter where you go or whom you ask, someone is always willing to offer advice on techniques—with varying degrees of success.

Despite all the speculation, superstition, and individual preferences, tooth hunters share some common threads in their search for shark teeth:

They look for fossilized teeth.

They search in similarly sized material.

They use water to aid in the search.

They use mental glossaries to identify teeth.

They are passionate about the search.

First of all, the shark teeth washing up on the beach (and portrayed in this book) are fossilized. These are teeth that have been preserved in marine muds and fossilized over thousands and millions of years. Depending on the substrate, or surrounding mud, the color of the teeth may vary. In Maryland, some sandy, tan sediments create beautiful yellow-orange fossil teeth! Along much of the East Coast, however, shark teeth washing in to shore are black from phosphate-rich sediments on the continental shelf.

One of the greatest misconceptions about searching for shark teeth on the beach is that the teeth will be white. From this mistaken belief, tourists often walk away from the beach with a handful of oyster shell fragments and spines from knobbed whelks, proclaiming that they have found real shark teeth. In fact, the teeth lost by today's sharks are being slowly dissolved by compounds and organisms in the ocean. Shark teeth are made of apatite (a mineral composed of calcium phosphate), which becomes weathered and eroded down over time in the ocean if it is not deposited in conditions ideal for fossilization. Thus, beachcombers rarely find the white teeth lost by extant shark species.

Beach material stratified by wave action.

Have you ever shaken a jar of mixed nuts to bring the pecans and walnuts to the top for you to eat, leaving the peanuts for everyone else? Then you have re-created the simple sorting process that occurs on every beach, every minute of every day. Items on the beach are sorted by two main factors: size and density. When ocean waves crash against the shore, currents remove smaller sand particles from between larger objects. Generally speaking, most shark teeth found on beaches are somewhere in size between rice grains and cereal flakes.

More importantly, this sorting is a direct result of water dynamics. Even if searchers are not consciously aware of water patterns, they are actually unknowing experts on fluid dynamics. By searching in rivulets and gullies, fossil hunters display their understanding of how important water is in classifying and uncovering shark teeth. Even after tidally driven waves retreat to their farthest point at low tide, groundwater continues to flow out to the ocean, creating gullies where larger items, including shark teeth, accumulate.

For many, half of the battle is in knowing what to look for. As with all hobbies, searchers have to build their mental glossaries to improve their proficiency. For instance, if the mental image you recall for a shark tooth is a white triangle, your glossary needs a little updating. When we search on the beach, our brains are constantly flipping through thousands of images of fossils and shark teeth. Once you have numerous hours of searching under your belt, your glossary of images will contain an incredible number of depictions of broken teeth, buried teeth,

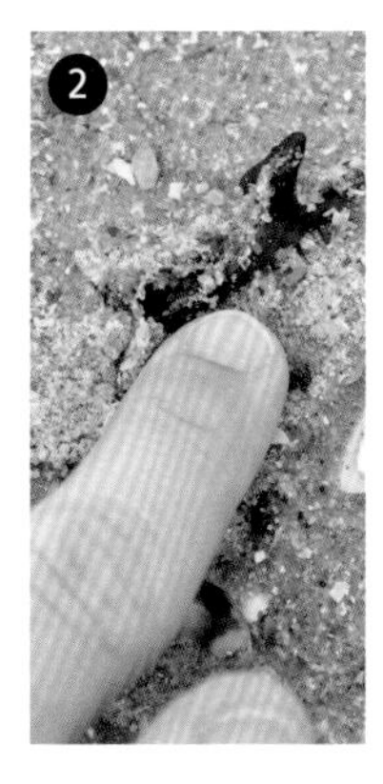

Beachcombers must be familiar with all parts of a shark tooth. Only the root was visible on this sand tiger tooth (1), but careful searching and a sharp eye (2) revealed a complete specimen (3).

and covered teeth, along with multiple species of shark teeth. Then, when you spot a familiar image on the beach, bingo, you can instantly identify it as a shark tooth.

Finally, you have to be passionate and patient in your search for that perfect shark tooth. People who give up easily or are quickly discouraged often walk away from the beach empty-handed. Time, effort, and an understanding of how items on the beach are distributed arc vital to succeeding in the search for shark teeth. Try not to get dispirited if you don't find a tooth in your first fifteen minutes on the beach; accustom your eyes to looking for those small black triangles and stay hopeful.

METHODS OF SEARCHING

While many enthusiasts have a self-proclaimed "best method" of looking for shark teeth, the following approaches can yield good quantities of teeth.

Debris and Tide-Line Scanning

One of the easiest and most productive ways of finding teeth is to walk the tide lines laid out on the beach and scan the shell and rock debris for teeth. This method allows you to cover a large amount of ground, and the more beach area you look over, the greater the chance you will come home with a handful of teeth. Remember: just as in the jar of mixed nuts, material is grouped by size. So if you focus your search efforts in material the size of rice grains, the odds are that the shark teeth you find will be fairly close to the same size. Many of these teeth may include lemon, hammerhead, dusky, and small sand tiger shark teeth—no megalodons here. The best time to use this method is in the hours just before, during, and after low tide; that way, you can inspect the most surface area for the longest amount of time.

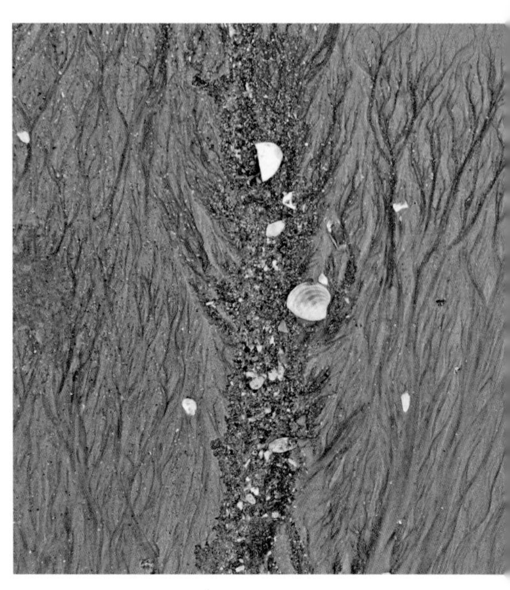

above Giant thresher (*Alopias grandis*) tooth at the high-tide line.

right Gully and rivulets formed by water draining out to the ocean at low tide.

Scattered between the mid- and low-tide lines are occasional piles of shells and bits of debris isolated in larger expanses of bare sand. Here, some of the larger teeth tend to fall out, such as those from sand tiger, tiger, and some mako sharks. As you walk down the beach, try to follow a meandering path in order to find that zone parallel to the surf where the most teeth are located. Once that area is located, you can concentrate your efforts on raking in the teeth. This method is the one used most often by the authors.

Scanning the Surf Line

Searching right along the surf line, another highly preferred method, is best used when the tide is coming back in—anytime between low and high tide. The advantage of this approach is that you get to observe the ocean in action as it reclassifies the material deposited during low tide; all the mid to large shell fragments congregate at the edge of the surf.

Material that may have spanned the beach for 100 feet from the water's edge now covers only a few feet, and any shark teeth present are included in that collection. Additionally, the ocean continuously uncovers new material via the tides, and what was covered at low tide may now become visible. Collectors can search along the same path of surf line, a few hundred feet apart, and walk away with a comparable number of teeth.

Scanning Gullies and Rivulets

Primarily at low tide, areas of exposed, seeping groundwater create gullies and low areas of sand worn away by the retreating water. As with the surf lines of retreating and advancing tides, these channels isolate similarly sized material and reveal many shark teeth. It is important to note that these are smaller teeth—from small dusky, hammerhead, lemon, and sand tiger sharks. Most gullies occur where the slope of the beach changes from steep to less steep.

Digging in Wet Sand

Should you happen to arrive at the beach at high tide or when gullies and rivulets are not present, fear not. There are other methods for recovering shark teeth. Digging in the wet sand near the surf allows you to create your own gullies by exposing the groundwater table. Start by digging a large hole, preferably in an area showing a decent size range of shell hash. Once your hole has filled with water, sit down and splash water against the sides of the hole and watch for any teeth falling down to the bottom. You will occasionally have to scoop searched material out of the hole—but don't fling this load too far. There is always a chance you may have missed a couple of teeth in your initial search. Spread the sand out around you and allow the waves to wash over it. Note: When you are finished, be sure to fill in your hole; many states have laws against leaving unfilled holes on the beach, in order to protect nesting and hatching sea turtles.

Exposed Sandbars

Sandbars are perhaps among the least visited treasure sites hidden along the shorelines of the coastal states. The key to the sandbar's productivity stems from a few factors: these expanses are generally uncovered twice a day; heavier objects don't have to work their way onto the beach; and not very many people take the trouble, or are able, to search them.

Beachcombing a sandbar on a winter day.

A nice snaggletooth shark (*Hemipristis serra*) tooth uncovered on a sand bar.

Sand sifters: homemade floating sifter at left, commercial sifter at right. Note the differently sized material caught in each sifter, based on mesh size.

The sandbar hunter must be willing to get a little wet when crossing onto a sandbar and to vacate the sandbar quickly before becoming stranded by the incoming tide! Because these features are exposed at low tide, they can be searched for a limited time, sometimes for only thirty minutes. The constant wave action passing over sandbars allows heavier objects to congregate there, and those objects are accessible when uncovered at low tide. Here, the searcher can find larger, more complete teeth—maybe even a megalodon or two.

Sand Sifters

If covering great distances on foot is not possible at your beach, or if there are only pockets of hot spots, then sifting might be the most productive method of searching for you. (Provided that state laws allow such activity. Check the local state or municipal regulations before heading to the beach with a large sifter.) Of course, the advantage of using a sand sifter is that you can concentrate material, eliminating all the sand that obscures shark teeth. A few types of sifters are on the market—many are available at beachfront gift shops—and some you can make yourself.

One type of sifter is available in a scoop form. It has a screened bucket affixed to the end of a long pole. Called "sand flea rakes" and marketed to fishermen for catching mole crabs in the intertidal zone, these scoops are especially handy for pulling material from under the water's surface in hopes of finding teeth not yet uncovered. Once material has been collected in the scoop, dump it out just within reach of the breaking waves to allow some water to run over the material.

Keep a sharp eye out for any teeth and be ready to pick them up before a wave carries them away. With all sifters, it is important to pay attention to the screen size of your scoop; if you enjoy finding small lemon and hammerhead teeth, make sure the mesh size is small enough to catch them.

Another popular sifter design is the floating sifter—this is one that can be made very easily. The materials needed are the following:

- HARDWARE CLOTH—any dimension ranging from 12 by 12 inches to 12 by 18 inches works well
- 2 INCH BY 2 INCH LUMBER OR PVC—the perfect size for a frame that will be both sturdy and lightweight
- HOLLOW FOAM POOL NOODLE—since it is buoyant enough to keep people afloat, using it to hold up sand is not a problem
- BRASS SCREWS—it is best to avoid iron or steel screws, which rust
- ZIP TIES—simple and cheap but sturdy enough for attaching the pool noodle

Decide on the size of sifter and the material for the frame. The authors use one made from a lumber frame that has withstood many trips to the beach and creeks.

Once the frame is assembled, use a heavy-duty staple gun or thin metal wire to attach the hardware cloth to the frame. To prepare the pool noodle, cut a lengthwise slit in the noodle deep enough to reach the hollow core, and then cut segments to fit each side. After that, zip-tie the noodle in place, and you are set. A handy finishing touch is to use a carabiner clip and length of rope to secure the floating rig to your body.

River Collecting and Diving

For the adventurous searcher, a whole new world awaits in the rivers and estuaries carving away at fossil-bearing sediments. Some rivers and creeks are shallow enough to allow wading, but many are deep enough that a search for shark teeth means scuba diving. In Florida and the Lowcountry of South Carolina, many teeth-bearing rivers are blackwater rivers, stained dark from the tannins present in oaks and pines. Here, searchers battle low visibility, strong, tidally driven currents, and large predators such as alligators and sharks. Despite all the dangers, the teeth unearthed speak for themselves—the risk can be worth the reward. A few reputable publications describe river searching and locations to hunt. (See the reference material in the back of this book.)

Many states and municipalities have laws about the removal of fossils and other

A pristine sand tiger shark tooth uncovered by a receding tide.

artifacts from waterways, so check state and local regulations before collecting from these areas. Many states require collectors to obtain an artifact collection permit first.

BEFORE YOU LEAVE THE HOUSE

Keep in mind that the techniques listed in this chapter are merely some of the most commonly used methods. There is no right or wrong way to search for teeth, simply more or less efficient techniques. The productivity of particular hunting methods can vary by location. It may also take some time to train your eyes to pick out shark teeth from the shell hash or pebbles on a beach. Again, be patient; you will develop your own method or variations on those listed above.

Some people claim that the availability of fossil teeth corresponds to the new and full moons. This is partially true; but fossil abundance is not linked with celestial occurrences. The presence of fossil material on beaches is correlated with the height of tides (which are driven by lunar cycles—hence, the moon's involvement), the roughness of the surf, and whether a large number of collectors were on the beach that day. If you live at or visit the coast long enough, you will be able to schedule your visits during opportune times. For instance, beach renourishment can have a positive or a negative impact on the quantity of fossils that washes up, depending on how a particular dredge site is operated. Unfortunately, more times than not, renourishment has a negative impact on beach fossil material. (See page 412 for a positive impact of renourishment.)

Finally, while all the above techniques will increase your chances of finding fossils, remember that they are randomly distributed among beach detritus. An element of luck is involved, too, so be persistent; the more you search, the more you will find. Being in the right place at the right time, or simply glancing in the right direction, will ultimately net you a big reward.

You now have all the essential technical knowledge for a trip to look for shark teeth. Remember the five points discussed at the beginning of this chapter and equip yourself for success. Put on a pair of sandals or waders, grab a collection container, and hit the beach!

IDENTIFICATION PAGES

SHARK TEETH

TRAITS OF SHARK TEETH

With the exception of some sharks that lived more than 65 million years ago, most sharks have teeth comprising two distinct sections: the root and the crown. The root generally consists of two lobes that merge to provide the foundation for the enamel crown. The highly variable nature of teeth and their position in the shark's mouth is called heterodonty; dignathic heterodonty designates differences in upper and lower teeth; and monognathic heterodonty describes variation along the jaw (anterior to posterior teeth).

COMMON TERMS

Anterior, bourlette, crown, cusp, cusplets, dental band, distal, enamel, foramina, labial, lateral, lingual, mesial, notch, nutrient foramen, nutrient groove, posterior, root, root lobe, serrations (extra fine, fine, medium, coarse, extra coarse), shoulder, symphyseal

COMMONALITY

Shark teeth are perhaps the most prevalent fossils found along the North American coastlines. When visiting a fossiliferous beach, determine the age range of the geologic deposits to aid in the proper identification of recovered teeth. For example, many Paleocene sand tiger teeth can be confused with extant sand tiger (*Carcharias taurus*) teeth.

INCLUSIONS AND EXCLUSIONS

This section offers fairly thorough coverage of shark teeth from the Oligocene through the Pleistocene. Some Paleocene teeth are included, but they are by no means a complete representation. Because of tooth heterodonty, many posterior, intermediate, and symphyseal teeth are highly variable and therefore not included in this section. Only some of the most common shapes and positions of shark teeth are shown here. Shark teeth easily warrant a field guide of their own.

The geologic age is listed as the time range for the existence of a species, not just the specimen's age.

MEASUREMENTS

All shark teeth have measurements displayed in a three-part system:

(diagonal tooth length × root width × root height)

The diagonal tooth length, or slant height, is measured on the longest side, from the base of the root to the tip of the crown or main cusp. Likewise, the root width spans the longest distance between the two root lobes, and the root height is measured at the thickest location. (Dashed lines indicate the third dimension.)

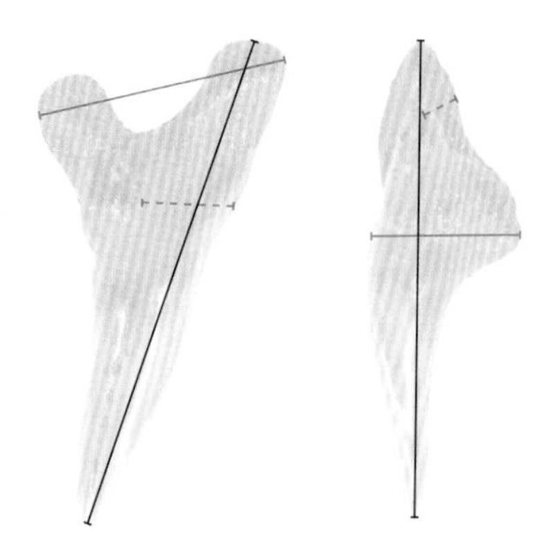

SUPPLEMENTARY IMAGES AND TERMS

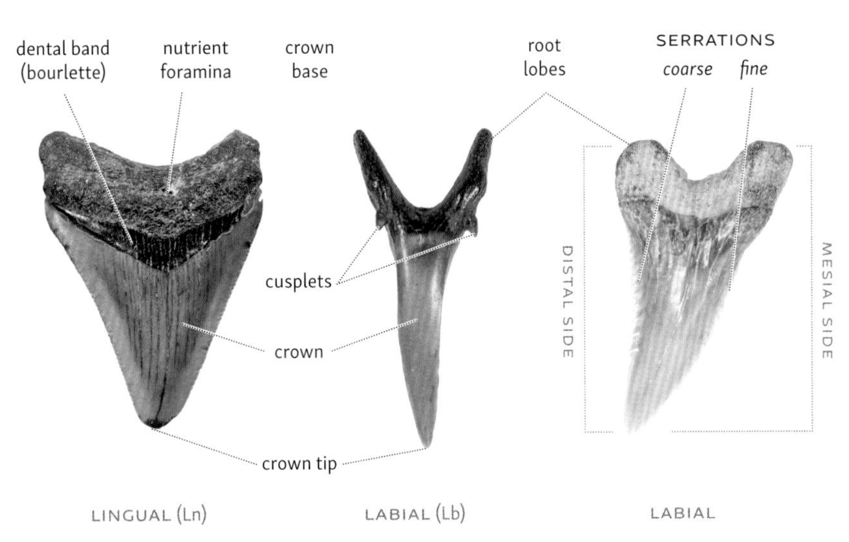

Ln

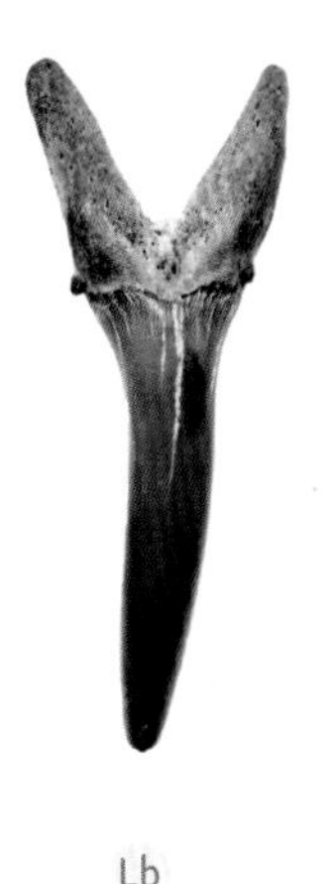
Lb

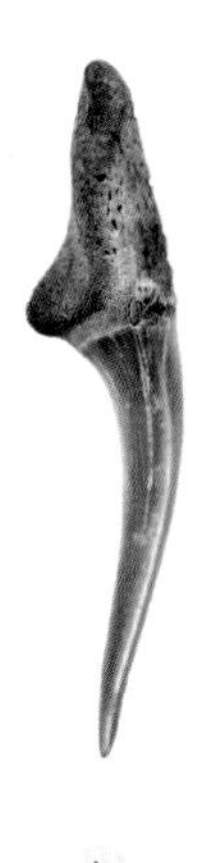
L

Striatolamia striata

Anterior tooth from the extinct mackerel shark *Striatolamia striata*. Restricted to the Paleocene, *S. striata* is similar in appearance to the Eocene species *S. macrota*. Teeth of *S. striata* bear fine striations along the lingual side of the crown, extending from the crown base to the tip. Cusplets are present on all *S. striata* teeth, but are rounded nubs on the anteriors. Compare the above specimen to the vastly different lateral teeth.

SIZE

35 × 14 × 8 mm

1.4 × 0.5 × 0.3 in

GEOLOGIC AGE

Paleocene

61.7–56 Ma

IDENTIFIERS

Lingual striations

Round cusplets

Lack of serrations

DENSITY

DID YOU KNOW? The extinct *Striatolamia* shark lived from the Paleocene epoch through the Miocene. In Latin, the shark's genus name, *Striatolamia*, means "striations," which form the texture found on the lingual face of the elongated tooth of this shark. Lines, ridges, peaks, and valleys on the tooth surfaces create this pattern. Three species of *Striatolamia* occurred worldwide in low-salinity marine and estuarine habitats.

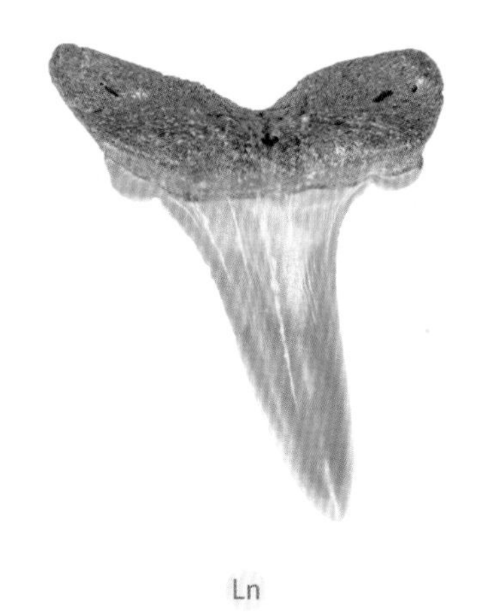

Ln

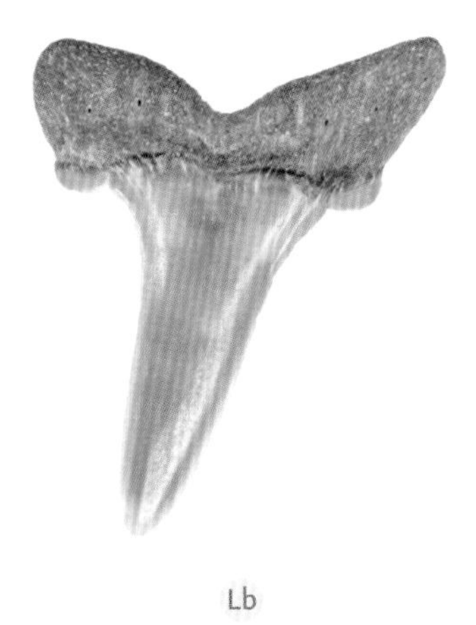

Lb

SIZE

23 × 17 × 5 mm

0.9 × 0.7 × 0.2 in

GEOLOGIC AGE

Paleocene

61.7–56 Ma

IDENTIFIERS

Striated enamel

Round cusplets

Raised lingual ridge

DENSITY

Striatolamia striata

Lateral tooth from the extinct mackerel shark *Striatolamia striata*. The teeth of *S. striata* exhibit marked monognathic heterodonty, or differences in shape between anterior and lateral teeth found on separate locations within the jaw. The enamel has fine longitudinal striations on the lingual side and is unserrated along the margins. Lateral cusplets are blunt and rounded. The root is wide, with a raised ridge along the lingual side of the crown base, and contains visible foramina.

DID YOU KNOW? Male sharks have two reproductive organs called claspers, which are attached to their pelvic fins. After a female accepts his intentions (following some sharky foreplay), he approaches one side of the female, grasps her pectoral fin, and, arching his back, inserts his right or left clasper, depending on the side he approached, into her vent. He holds on by unfurling spikelike clasper spurs, and mating begins.

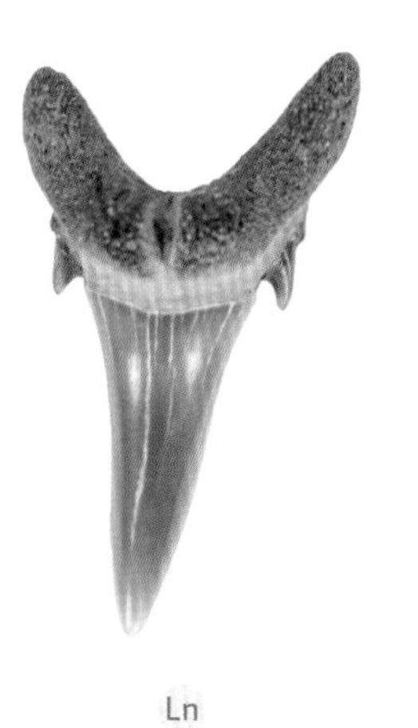
Ln

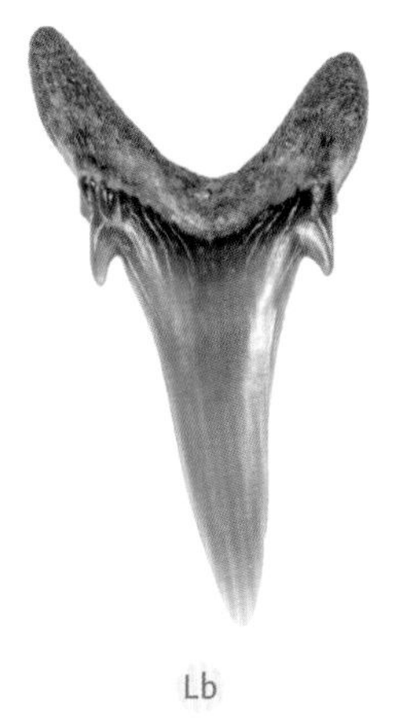
Lb

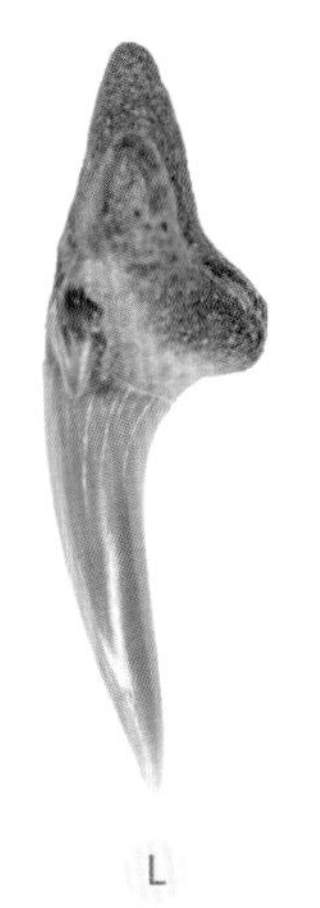
L

Palaeohypotodus rutoti

Lower anterior tooth from the extinct sand tiger shark *Palaeohypotodus rutoti*. This tooth, from an early Paleocene site, has lateral cusplets (occasionally double) and broadly tapers from the crown tip to the base. The roots are relatively thick, with prominent centers and distinct nutrient grooves. The tooth margins are unserrated. It is similar in appearance to modern sand tiger (*Carcharias* sp.) teeth. *P. rutoti* teeth do not occur in deposits younger than the Eocene. Note that this tooth has double lateral cusplets, the second cusplet being extremely reduced.

SIZE

22 × 12 × 7 mm

0.9 × 0.5 × 0.3 in

GEOLOGIC AGE

Paleocene–Eocene

66–37.2 Ma

IDENTIFIERS

Lateral cusplets

Broad taper

Prominent root

DENSITY

DID YOU KNOW? Sharks, rays, sea turtles, eels, fish, whales, and dolphins are believed to have a bit of lodestone, or magnetite, in their bodies. Particles of this mineral aid their navigation and long-distance migrations around the world, just as magnetized compass needles help humans in their travels. Imagine that—a compass inside sea creatures!

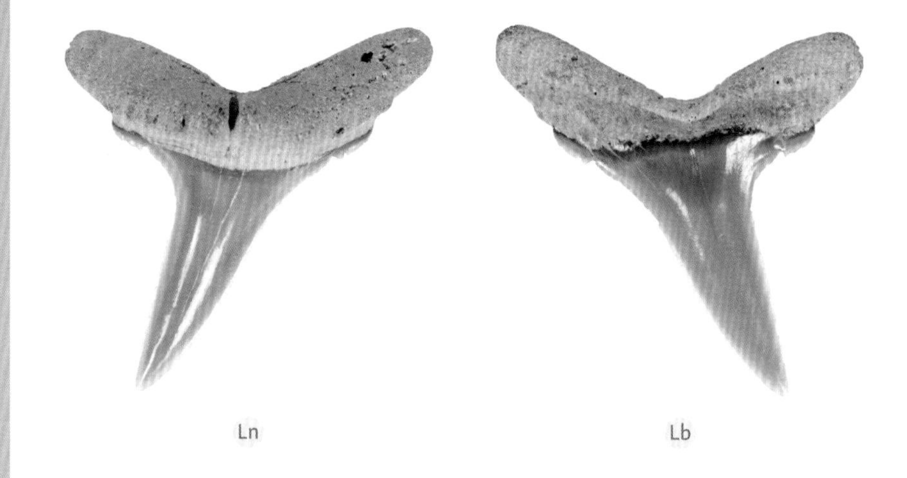

SIZE

25 × 20 × 5 mm

1.0 × 0.8 × 0.2 in

GEOLOGIC AGE

Late Cretaceous–Pliocene

70.6–2.6 Ma

IDENTIFIERS

Nutrient groove

Wide flat cusplets

Smooth crown

DENSITY

Carcharias cuspidatus

Lateral tooth from the extinct sand tiger shark *Carcharias cuspidatus*. These teeth are similar in appearance to those of the modern sand tiger shark, *Carcharias taurus*, with a long thin crown, wide root, and moderate nutrient groove. *C. cuspidatus* teeth differ in having wide flat cusplets as well as double lateral cusplets. In contrast with modern sand tiger teeth, *C. cuspidatus* enamel is smooth on both the lingual and labial sides of the crown. While there is an observed overlap in the geologic time spans of *C. taurus* and *C. cuspidatus*, the prevalence of *C. cuspidatus* in geologic deposits diminishes greatly after the Early Miocene.

DID YOU KNOW? Do sharks sleep? Maybe, but not with their eyes closed. At least four species of sharks are known to visit caves at Isla Mujeres off the Yucatán Peninsula. Scientists have observed tiger, lemon, blue, and bull sharks lying motionless and apparently resting, but with their eyes open. They intently watch any divers moving around the cave. They might be sleeping, but best not to disturb.

Ln

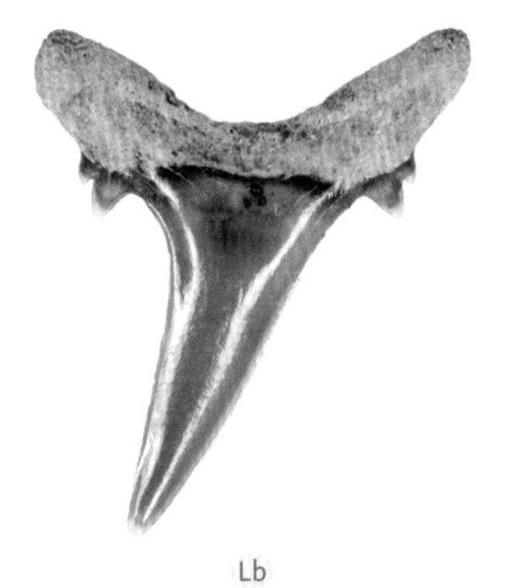

Lb

Carcharias cuspidatus

Lateral tooth from the extinct sand tiger shark *Carcharias cuspidatus*. These teeth are similar in appearance to those of the modern sand tiger shark, *Carcharias taurus*, with a long thin crown, wide root, and moderate nutrient groove. *C. cuspidatus* teeth differ in occasionally having double lateral cusplets and also wide flat cusplets, as seen on page 46. In contrast with modern sand tiger teeth, *C. cuspidatus* enamel is smooth on both the lingual and labial sides. While there is an observed overlap in the geologic time spans of *C. taurus* and *C. cuspidatus*, the prevalence of *C. cuspidatus* in geologic deposits diminishes greatly after the Early Miocene.

SIZE

20 × 15 × 5 mm

0.8 × 0.6 × 0.2 in

GEOLOGIC AGE

Late Cretaceous–Pliocene

70.6–2.6 Ma

IDENTIFIERS

Nutrient groove

Double cusplets

Smooth crown

DENSITY

DID YOU KNOW? Bluntnose sixgill sharks are extremely sensitive to light and to the lower water pressure near the ocean surface. They typically range from a maximum depth of 6,150 feet to a minimum of 300 feet. But at times during fall and winter along the coast of British Columbia, these rare sharks come to within 70–90 feet of the surface, allowing scuba-diving scientists a chance to observe their behavior.

Ln

Lb

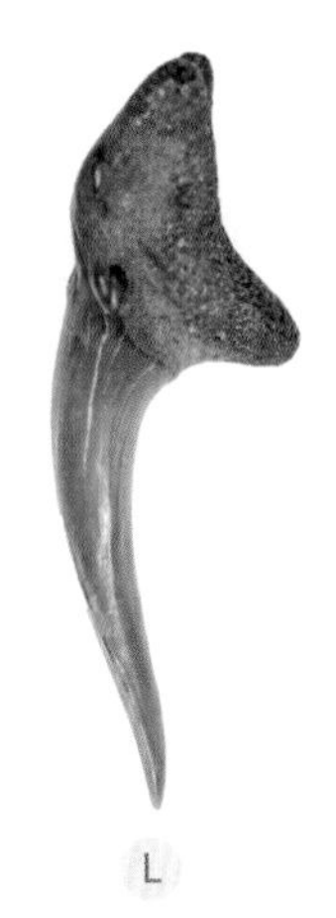

L

SIZE

28 × 15 × 8 mm
1.1 × 0.6 × 0.3 in

GEOLOGIC AGE

Miocene–Holocene

23 Ma–present

IDENTIFIERS

Long thin crown

Wrinkled enamel

V-shaped root

DENSITY

Carcharias taurus

Anterior tooth from the extant sand tiger shark, *Carcharias taurus*. Reflecting the sharks' piscivorous diet, sand tiger teeth are long, thin, and sharply pointed. Upper and lower teeth appear similar, with V-shaped roots on the anterior teeth. Weak wrinkles run the length of the crown, but are much subtler than the striations of *Striatolamia* teeth. Each tooth bears a single lateral cusplet that tends to bend toward the lingual side of the crown. The narrow roots are relatively prominent, with a strong nutrient groove.

DID YOU KNOW? Sharks are known for having ominous dorsal fins that appear above the waves as they circle their prey. But they also use their caudal (tail) fins effectively when hunting. Working as a group, sand tiger sharks whip their tails to generate waves and loud sounds that confuse and stun their prey, making for an easier catch. Females also use tail whipping as a defense against other sharks, and possibly humans.

Ln

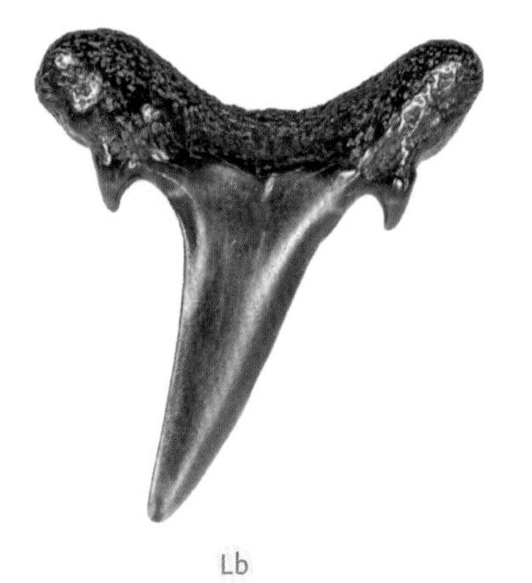

Lb

Carcharias taurus

Lateral tooth from the extant sand tiger shark *Carcharias taurus*. Upper and lower laterals, which are similar in appearance, have wide roots, and a nutrient groove is visible on unworn specimens. Weak wrinkles run the length of the crown, but are much subtler than the striations of *Striatolamia* teeth. Each tooth bears a single lateral cusplet that tends to bend toward the lingual side of the crown. The cusplets are conical.

SIZE

21 × 17 × 4 mm

0.8 × 0.7 × 0.2 in

GEOLOGIC AGE

Miocene–Holocene

23 Ma–present

IDENTIFIERS

Long thin crown

Wrinkled enamel

Conical cusplets

DENSITY

DID YOU KNOW? Sharks are often thought of as lone hunters, but some species exhibit teamwork and altruistic behavior. In 1915, Russell Coles observed a pack of 100-plus sand tiger sharks off Cape Lookout, North Carolina, circle a school of bluefish and systematically guide them toward shallow waters. He watched as individual sharks would then attack, grab a meal, and back out so that other sharks could take a turn.

Carcharoides catticus

SIZE

16 × 13 × 3 mm

0.6 × 0.5 × 0.1 in

GEOLOGIC AGE

Oligocene–Miocene

28.4–5.3 Ma

IDENTIFIERS

Extremely small

Thin root and cusp

Broad lateral cusplets

DENSITY

Upper lateral tooth from the extinct mackerel shark *Carcharoides catticus*. These teeth are rare and small; 16 millimeters is around their maximum size. The crown and the cusplet margins are unserrated. The root is moderately flattened, with a lingual protuberance around the slight nutrient groove. Both root and crown are very flat, much more so than other similarly sized teeth.

DID YOU KNOW? Megalodon sharks and large predatory whales were able to coexist in prehistoric oceans because of the diversity and fecundity of available prey. Changing climatic conditions, lowered sea levels, and restricted ocean currents contributed to a reduction of this plentiful food supply, causing both of these gigantic species to slowly die out.

Ln

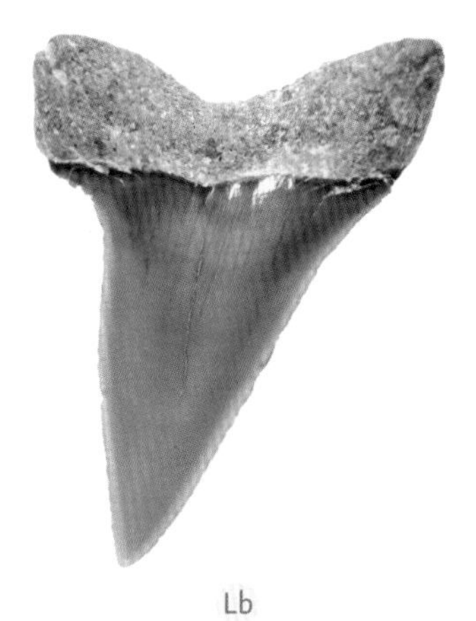

Lb

Macrorhizodus praecursor

Upper tooth from the extinct Eocene mackerel shark, *Macrorhizodus praecursor*. Though the teeth of *Isurus* (mako shark) species are similar in morphology, *M. praecursor* belongs to an extinct group of mackerel sharks. The crown is wide, with a sharp curve at the base on the distal side; this identifier is positional, being more apparent on lateral teeth than anterior teeth. The crown tip is curved slightly toward the labial side. Roots are relatively thick, with a moderate nutrient foramen visible on some (obscured above by matrix).

SIZE

36 × 25 × 7 mm

1.4 × 1.0 × 0.3 in

GEOLOGIC AGE

Eocene

40.4–33.9 Ma

IDENTIFIERS

Lack of serrations

Tip labially curved

Moderate foramen

DENSITY

DID YOU KNOW? Imagining what life might have been like 485 million years ago is unfathomable. Some of us can't remember what we did last week. Nevertheless, the earliest evidence of sharks is known from the latter part of the Ordovician period (485–444 Ma). Since then, sharks have undergone much evolutionary diversity, including two major periods of upheaval. Some early ancestors lacked scales, while others had spiny fins. But modern sharks have retained the most beneficial features for surviving today.

Ln

Lb

SIZE

29 × 17 × 6 mm

1.1 × 0.7 × 0.2 in

GEOLOGIC AGE

Eocene

40.4–33.9 Ma

IDENTIFIERS

Lack of serrations

Tip lingually curved

Moderate foramen

DENSITY

Macrorhizodus praecursor

Lower tooth from the extinct Eocene mackerel shark, *Macrorhizodus praecursor*. The crown is narrower than those found in the upper teeth, and the crown tip is lingually curved. Root lobes are relatively thick and pointed, with a moderate nutrient foramen visible on some (obscured above by matrix). *M. praecursor* was historically assigned to the line of mako sharks (*Isurus* spp.), but such assignments relied solely on tooth design and did not acknowledge the earliest Miocene occurrences of formal mako sharks. This problematic published record requires further scrutiny to resolve questions regarding the lineage.

DID YOU KNOW? For humans, proper manners call for generally keeping one's mouth closed. Not so for many sharks, however, which often bare their teeth with open mouths. Mako sharks couldn't win the manners game even if they tried: their teeth show even when their mouths are closed. They can't help it. Some of their lower teeth are long and protrude from their bowl-shaped mouths.

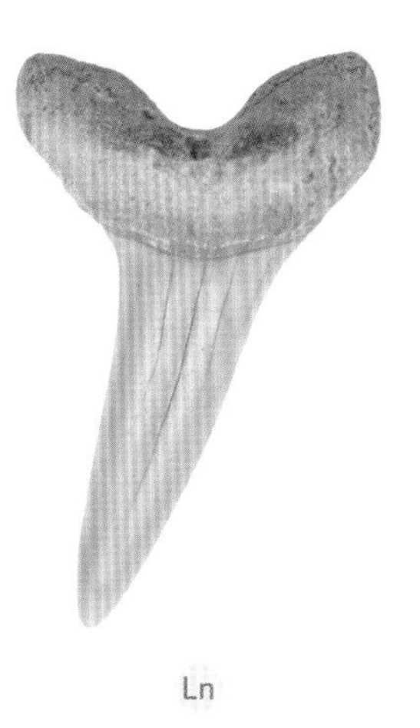

Ln

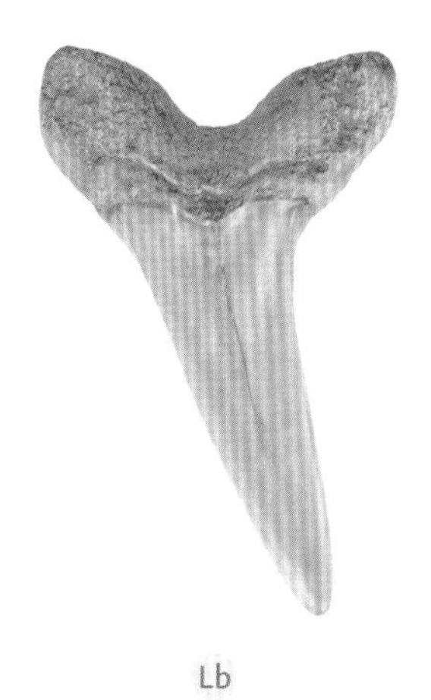

Lb

Isurus oxyrinchus

First upper anterior tooth from the shortfin mako, *Isurus oxyrinchus*. More slender than upper teeth from other mako species, *I. oxyrinchus* teeth are narrow, bend labially, have broad root lobes, and lack nutrient grooves. The primary characteristic that sets *I. oxyrinchus* teeth apart from those of *Carcharodon hastalis* (an extinct great white shark) is the crown width; those of *C. hastalis* are much wider. These teeth are unserrated and rather large, averaging over one inch (25 mm) in slant height.

SIZE

34 × 22 × 6 mm

1.3 × 0.9 × 0.2 in

GEOLOGIC AGE

Miocene–Holocene

23 Ma–Present

IDENTIFIERS

Thin crown

Labial bend

Lack of serrations

DENSITY

DID YOU KNOW? The smooth hammerhead shark lives in warm shallow waters off the Atlantic and Pacific U.S. coasts. Its numbers are declining because of commercial fishing; some overseas operators target the shark for its valuable fin. In Asia, shark fin soup is a delicacy signifying wealth, and shark fins fetch $400 per pound. Hammerhead sharks declined in the U.S. Atlantic region by 90% from 1986 to 2000, and these sharks are nearing extinction in the eastern Pacific. In 2011, California passed a law prohibiting the sale, possession, or trade of shark fins, and further efforts are under way nationally to protect the shark under the Endangered Species Act.

Ln

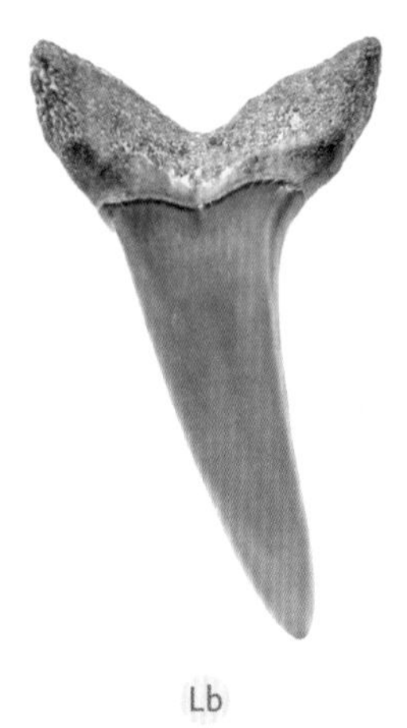

Lb

SIZE

43 × 24 × 8 mm

1.7 × 0.9 × 0.3 in

GEOLOGIC AGE

Miocene–Holocene

23 Ma–present

IDENTIFIERS

Long, slender teeth

Pointed root lobes

Lack of serrations

DENSITY

Isurus oxyrinchus

Upper tooth from the shortfin mako, *Isurus oxyrinchus*. Similar to other mako teeth, *I. oxyrinchus* teeth are slender, used for grasping prey. Root lobes are pointed, and the nutrient foramen lacks a groove. At the base of the crown, these teeth are sharply skewed to the distal edge (at left above, in lingual view). *I. oxyrinchus* teeth are unserrated. As can occur in other teeth exceeding one inch in height, occasional longitudinal hydration cracks in the enamel are present on the lingual side of the crown.

DID YOU KNOW? Miocene shark fossils show evidence of the early development of gill slits, through which sharks pump water to absorb oxygen. Gills save on energy by freeing sharks from having to continually rise to the surface for air. Another big evolutionary change occurred as sharks were forced to adapt to colder water temperatures during the Pliocene epoch. These adaptations have enabled sharks to survive from prehistoric times to the present.

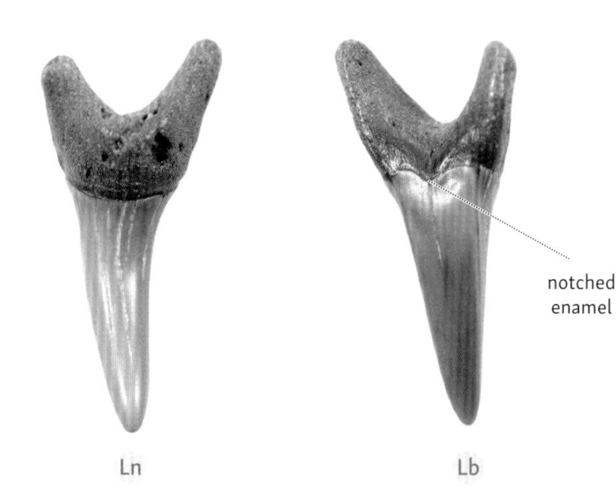

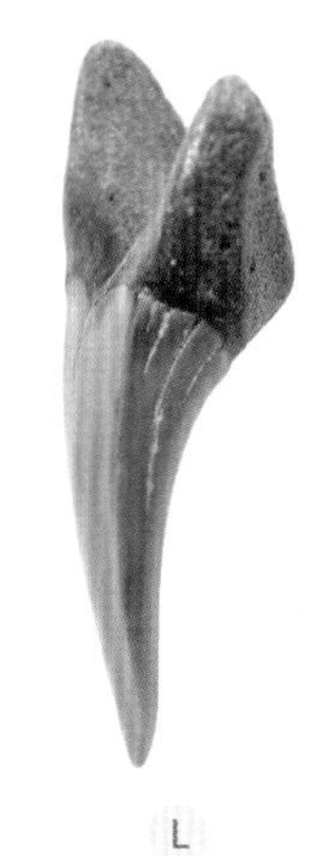

Isurus oxyrinchus

Lower tooth from the shortfin mako, *Isurus oxyrinchus*. Contrasting with the lower teeth of the extinct great white shark (*Carcharodon hastalis*), those of the shortfin mako are much more slender and thinner at the crown base. Root lobes are fairly pointed and protrude lingually (seen above in lateral view). The junction of the labial and lingual sides of the crown is abrupt, creating a nearly 90-degree angle on the edges. On the labial side, a dip or notch in the enamel is present in the center of the crown base (indicated).

SIZE

48 × 22 × 14 mm

1.9 × 0.9 × 0.5 in

GEOLOGIC AGE

Miocene–Holocene

23 Ma–present

IDENTIFIERS

Long, slender teeth

Prominent root

Lack of serrations

DENSITY

DID YOU KNOW? Are you a super swimmer? Think you can swim faster than a mako shark? Humans can swim about 4 miles per hour, while mako sharks can swim at 60 miles an hour when hunting and migrating. When out for a leisurely swim, they propel themselves at only 35 miles per hour.

Ln

Lb

Isurus oxyrinchus

SIZE

26 × 18 × 5 mm

1.0 × 0.7 × 0.2 in

GEOLOGIC AGE

Miocene–Holocene

23 Ma–present

IDENTIFIERS

Bladelike teeth

Labially hooked teeth

Delicate form

DENSITY

Tooth from the extant shortfin mako, *Isurus oxyrinchus*. Smaller and more delicate than other mako teeth, those of *I. oxyrinchus* are razor-sharp, unserrated, and bladelike. *I. oxyrinchus* teeth are hooked labially, a trait seen in modern makos, whose lower teeth protrude from their closed jaws. Some lateral and most posterior teeth of *I. oxyrinchus* possess lateral cusplets—a feature previously noted in the avocational community as one unique to *I. retroflexus*. Note the razor-sharp edge on the specimen above, seen as the translucent rim of enamel around the crown of the tooth.

DID YOU KNOW? Beware of the adaptable, warm-water-loving, cold-water-loving, shallow-water-loving, and deep-water-loving mako shark! Makos are found worldwide in diverse saltwater habitats. The largest population of makos is found around Tahiti.

Ln

Lb

Isurus retroflexus

Upper tooth from the extinct longfin mako, *Isurus retroflexus*. The best identifier of *I. retroflexus* teeth is found labially on the crown as a shelf that extends across the crown base. This shelf, which is broad and intermittently covered in enamel, often results in callosities mesially and distally. Teeth crowns are broad and spatulate, with exceptionally broad roots. Lower anterior teeth are the most symmetrical teeth of any position; however, even lateral and posterior teeth lack the asymmetry found in similar positions of other mako species.

SIZE

28 × 22 × 7 mm

1.1 × 0.9 × 0.3 in

GEOLOGIC AGE

Miocene–Pliocene

23–2.6 Ma

IDENTIFIERS

Labial shelf

Cusplets

Broad crowns

DENSITY

DID YOU KNOW? Endangered Species International (ESI) has tracked the precipitous drop in shark populations, many of which are at dangerously low levels. Of the 1,044 shark species, ESI has seen declines by over 50% in almost all species except the mako. ESI predicts that one-third of the world's shark populations are threatened with extinction from commercial fishing, including as bycatch. The popularity of Asian delicacies such as shark fin soup adds to such pressures.

Ln

Lb

SIZE

46 × 35 × 7 mm

1.8 × 1.4 × 0.3 in

GEOLOGIC AGE

Miocene

23–5.3 Ma

IDENTIFIERS

Lack of serrations

Broadly triangular shape

Labiolingually thin crown

DENSITY

Carcharodon hastalis

Upper lateral tooth from the extinct great white shark, *Carcharodon hastalis*. The crown is wide and thin, with occasional longitudinal cracks on the lingual side. The tips of the upper teeth dip slightly toward the labial side, while the tips of the lowers dip toward the lingual side. Crown margins are unserrated, and the roots bear a shallow notch with squared-off root lobes. *C. hastalis* teeth are similar in width to those of its successor, *C. carcharias* (the modern great white), and are abundant in Miocene deposits.

DID YOU KNOW? Great white shark teeth have the dual purposes of grasping and cutting. The first and second teeth emanating from the anterior hollow in the upper and lower jaws act as awls, or punch-like tools, which assist in grasping prey. The other teeth, referred to as laterals and posteriors, sit toward the back of the mouth and slice up prey as it is being held.

Ln

Lb

Carcharodon hastalis

Upper lateral tooth from the extinct great white shark, *Carcharodon hastalis*. In comparison to anteriors, lateral teeth of *C. hastalis* are asymmetrical and distally inclined, with a longer cutting edge on the mesial side and a shorter edge distally. *C. hastalis* root surfaces, which were removed by water wear on the above specimen, have a cluster of nutrient foramina on the basal, downslope side of the lingual protuberance. Crown edges are smooth and unserrated.

SIZE

51 × 34 × 9 mm

2.0 × 1.3 × 0.4 in

GEOLOGIC AGE

Miocene

23–5.3 Ma

IDENTIFIERS

Lack of serrations

Broadly triangular shape

Clustered foramina

DENSITY

DID YOU KNOW? The extinct white shark *Carcharodon hastalis* wasn't always white. Or rather, "white" wasn't always part of its name. Before recent discoveries, scientists had placed this shark in the genus *Isurus*, grouping *C. hastalis* with the mako sharks. It wasn't until researchers analyzed an associated set of fossil teeth and vertebrae from Peru showing the transition of smooth to serrated teeth in white sharks that the "foster child" *C. hastalis* was placed with his true biological family.

Ln

Lb

Carcharodon hastalis

SIZE

54 × 32 × 11 mm

2.1 × 1.3 × 0.4 in

GEOLOGIC AGE

Miocene

23–5.3 Ma

IDENTIFIERS

Thick crown base

Longitudinal cracks

Lack of serrations

DENSITY

Lower anterior tooth from the extinct great white shark, *Carcharodon hastalis*. Broad and massive, *C. hastalis* lower teeth are triangular and unserrated, and can have multiple longitudinal cracks running along the length of the lingual side of the crown—a common feature of larger shark teeth. (The dehydration of dentine and enamel results in surface cracking during taphonomic processes.) At the crown base, lower teeth are extremely thick, much more so than the upper teeth, and protrude lingually. The root lobes of anterior teeth are symmetrical and U- or V-shaped, while those of the lateral teeth are much broader (page 61).

DID YOU KNOW? How do you disguise 1,000 pounds of mako shark? By coloring it like the ocean and sky. The beautiful azure color on top of the fish closely matches the color of the water, and the pure white underbelly, seen from below, blends with the light-colored sky. This camouflaging helps these predators stealthily approach their prey.

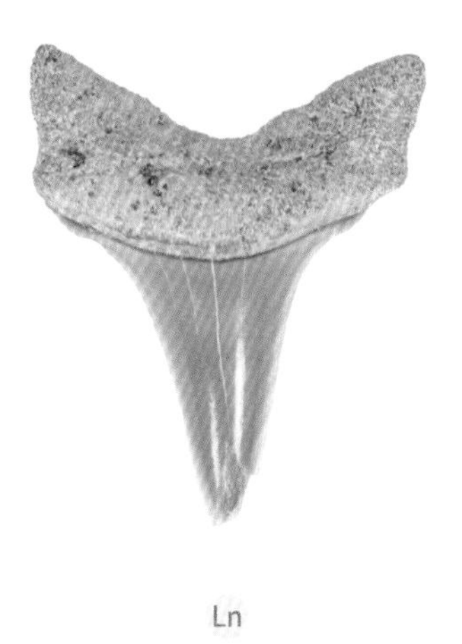

Ln

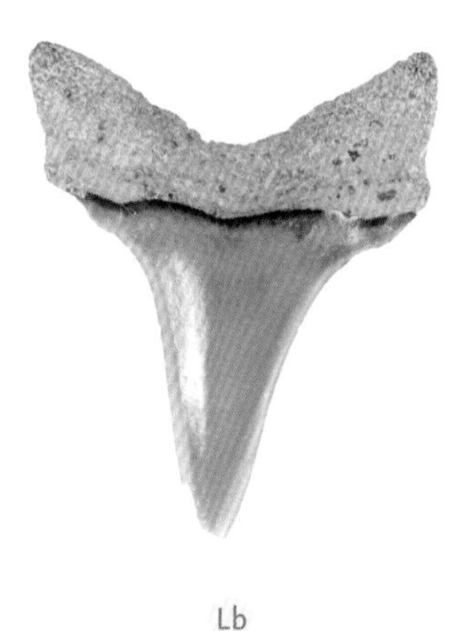

Lb

Carcharodon hastalis

Lower lateral tooth from the extinct great white shark, *Carcharodon hastalis*. Smaller and thinner than the anterior teeth, lower laterals are fairly symmetrical; other shark species have distally skewed laterals. Root lobes are pointed and broadly Y-shaped. The crown is unserrated, as in the uppers, and is relatively thick at the crown base.

SIZE

21 × 16 × 5 mm

0.8 × 0.6 × 0.2 in

GEOLOGIC AGE

Miocene

23–5.3 Ma

IDENTIFIERS

Symmetrical form

Y-shaped root lobes

Lack of serrations

DENSITY

DID YOU KNOW? Mako sharks aren't picky about their food. They eat most species of fish, although their favorite is tuna. They also seek out fish that have gone to school, meaning those that are swimming in schools. It is much easier to hunt prey that is found in a group, and mako sharks are well "schooled" on this fact.

Ln

Lb

Carcharodon carcharias

SIZE

50 × 39 × 7 mm

1.9 × 1.5 × 0.3 in

GEOLOGIC AGE

Miocene–Holocene

6 Ma–present

IDENTIFIERS

Coarse serrations

Wide flat root

Lack of bourlette

DENSITY

Upper tooth from the extant great white shark, *Carcharodon carcharias*. Easily identified by their large size, great white teeth also have coarse serrations—much coarser than those of *Carcharocles megalodon*. On the lingual side, these teeth lack the broad dental band, or bourlette, found in megatoothed sharks. Despite their great size, the roots are relatively thin and break easily. The tips are frequently missing on these teeth because of feeding damage resulting from the bony-fish and mammal diet of the great white. Adult *C. carcharias* teeth do not have lateral cusplets. Nutrient foramina are present in the middle of the root on the lingual side.

DID YOU KNOW? Scared of great white sharks? Here is another reason to fear them. Their jaw muscles are loosely attached below the skull, enabling them to stick their jaws far out and grab prey while sucking it in. Their jaws are made of cartilaginous material, which offers extra flexibility for this movement. So don't get sucked in. Stay a little farther from these sharks than you do from other shark species.

Ln

Lb

Carcharodon carcharias

Lower tooth from the extant great white shark, *Carcharodon carcharias*. In comparison with the upper teeth, lowers are much thicker anteroposteriorly, with a raised root and a more rounded, thicker crown. The crown is coarsely serrated and much narrower laterally than on the upper teeth. A nutrient foramen is located in the center of the root on the lingual side. Functionally, the lower teeth of the great white serve to hold the prey, and the upper teeth are used for slicing.

SIZE

31 × 20 × 7 mm

1.2 × 0.8 × 0.3 in

GEOLOGIC AGE

Miocene–Holocene

6 Ma–present

IDENTIFIERS

Coarse serrations

Prominent root

Lack of bourlette

DENSITY

DID YOU KNOW? Raise your hand if you think all sharks are large. In fact, of the 465 shark species in the class Chondrichthyes, only 10 reach a length greater than 13 feet. The epaulette shark, *Hemiscyllium ocellatum*, measuring only 2–3 feet, is but one example of the many smaller species that make up the majority of the class of sharks.

Ln

Lb

Palaeocarcharodon orientalis

SIZE

16 × 15 × 3 mm

0.6 × 0.6 × 0.1 in

GEOLOGIC AGE

Paleocene

61.7–55.8 Ma

IDENTIFIERS

Coarse serrations

Lateral cusplets

Thin, broad crown

DENSITY

Lateral tooth from the extinct pygmy white shark, *Palaeocarcharodon orientalis*. This rare tooth was found along the shores of the Potomac River in Paleocene sediments. In unworn specimens, these teeth have extremely coarse serrations (page 474). Crowns are thin and flat, and the roots are angled sharply to the labial side. All teeth have coarsely serrated lateral cusplets. The above specimen is so worn that the cusplets are almost imperceptible. Because of their rarity, many *P. orientalis* teeth sold in the United States are imported from Morocco.

DID YOU KNOW? *Palaeocarcharodon orientalis* may be closely related to *Carcharocles megalodon* or *Carcharodon carcharias*. Family relations are confusing in the shark world. *P. orientalis* has two cusplets at the base of its main teeth, while cousins *C. megalodon* and *C. carcharias* do not. Yet these species all have similar serrations on their tooth edges. The presence of such shared features among different species is known as convergent evolution.

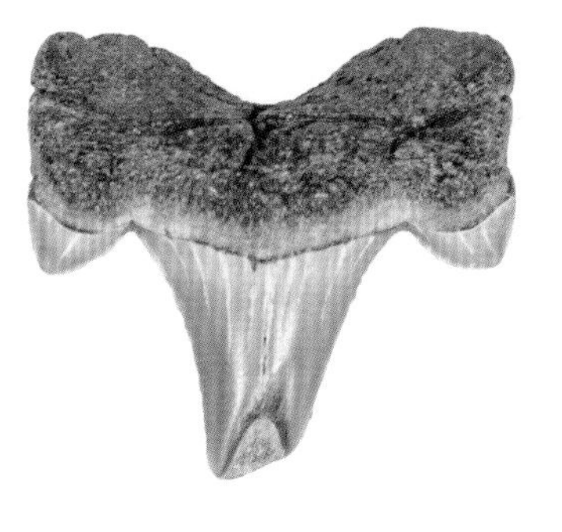

Ln

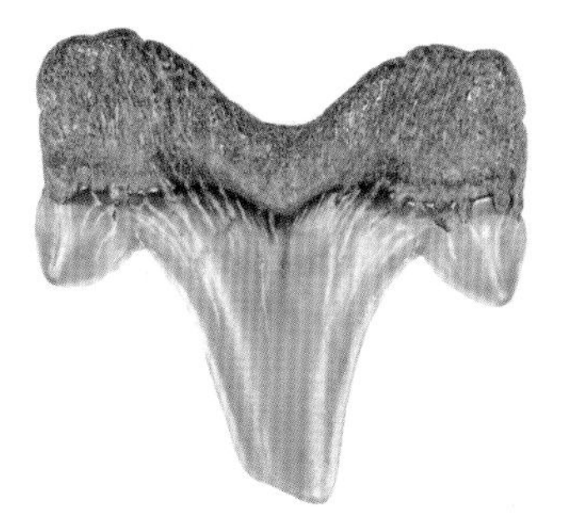

Lb

Cretalamna appendiculata

Tooth from the extinct mackerel shark *Cretalamna appendiculata*. Known from the Late Cretaceous through the Early Eocene, *C. appendiculata* teeth are identifiable by an unserrated triangular cusp with two broad lateral cusplets. The bilobate U-shaped root protrudes lingually and has a detectable foramen. Note the potential feeding damage on the above tooth, whose main cusp was broken off.

SIZE

18 × 18 × 6 mm

0.7 × 0.7 × 0.2 in

GEOLOGIC AGE

Late Cretaceous–Eocene

99.7–40 Ma

IDENTIFIERS

Lack of serrations

Broad lateral cusplets

Prominent root

DENSITY

DID YOU KNOW? Sonic telemetry for tracking sharks involves ping-emitting devices that are bolted to the dorsal fin, inserted into the body cavity, or hidden within bait that the shark swallowed. This method's shortcomings are that humans must follow by boat to stay within transmitter range, and this proximity can alter a shark's natural behavior. Archival tags improve on this by detaching themselves from the shark after collecting data, and then signaling for retrieval.

Ln

Lb

Otodus obliquus

SIZE

35 × 26 × 7 mm

1.4 × 1.0 × 0.3 in

GEOLOGIC AGE

Paleocene–Eocene

66–38 Ma

IDENTIFIERS

Lack of serrations

Triangular cusplets

Thick root

DENSITY

Lateral tooth from the extinct giant mackerel shark *Otodus obliquus*. Crowns are broad and triangular, bordered by large triangular lateral cusplets. Teeth occasionally bear more than one set of cusplets. On the lingual side, the root has one or more foramina, and the base of the crown has a distinct bourlette. Root lobes are rounded and large, becoming fairly thick in some anterior teeth. Enamel on the crown is smooth, and the edges are unserrated. Note the minor restoration on the above specimen's root lobes.

DID YOU KNOW? A new method for the archival tagging and tracking of sharks involves the placement of motion-sensing monitors in their underwater hangouts. When tagged sharks swim by the monitors, the sleeping monitors wake up and receive information from the sharks' tags as the creatures go merrily about their business. Future plans involve adding video cameras to the monitors to collect visual information on the sharks' activities.

Ln

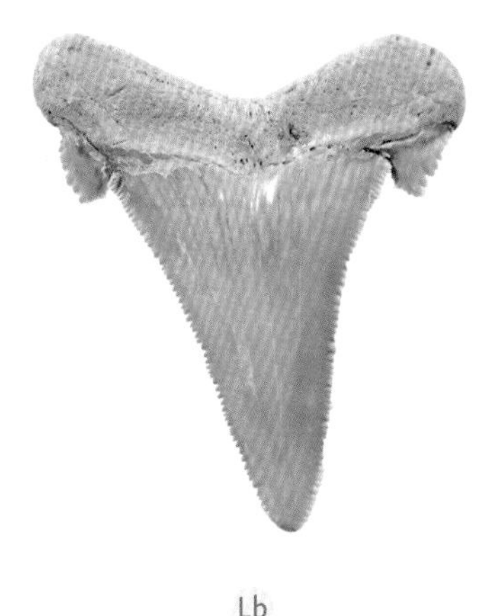
Lb

Carcharocles auriculatus

Tooth from the extinct megatoothed shark *Carcharocles auriculatus*. Compared with teeth from *C. angustidens*, those from *C. auriculatus* have larger lateral cusplets, which are more coarsely serrated than the main crown. The root lobes are large and rounded. *C. auriculatus* was the Eocene ancestor of *C. angustidens*, which progressively lost the lateral cusplets, culminating in the evolution of *C. megalodon*. Knowledge of local stratigraphy aids in differentiating the Eocene teeth of *C. auriculatus* from those of the Oligocene *C. angustidens*.

SIZE

62 × 50 × 11 mm

2.4 × 2.0 × 0.4 in

GEOLOGIC AGE

Eocene

55.8–33.9 Ma

IDENTIFIERS

Serrated cusplets

Medium serrations

Rounded root lobes

DENSITY

DID YOU KNOW? *C. auriculatus* was one of the megatoothed sharks, nicknamed for their triangular teeth, which are huge compared with those of today's species, including great whites. Fossilized teeth from *C. auriculatus* have been found in the lower Piedmont of South Carolina and beyond. The fossil record shows this species' range covered a wide expanse of the Northern Hemisphere's middle latitudes. Because when you are 27 feet long, you can pretty much swim anywhere you want.

Ln

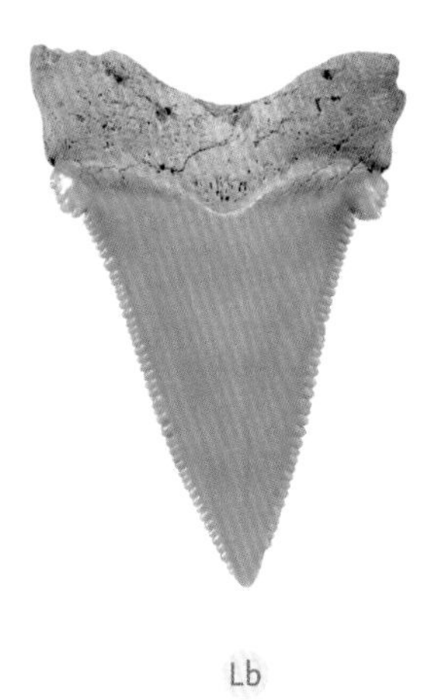
Lb

Carcharocles angustidens

SIZE

47 × 30 × 10 mm

1.8 × 1.2 × 0.4 in

GEOLOGIC AGE

Eocene–Oligocene

37.2–23 Ma

IDENTIFIERS

Serrated cusplets

Medium bourlette

Medium serrations

DENSITY

Anterior tooth from the extinct giant white shark *Carcharocles angustidens*. This shark is the Oligocene ancestor of *Carcharocles megalodon*. Its teeth are large, with medium serrations and a medium bourlette. All teeth have lateral cusplets, which are equally serrated and can range from rounded to triangular. The roots are thick, with pointed to squared-off lobes. *C. angustidens* teeth can be distinguished from those of *C. auriculatus* by the geologic age of the deposit.

DID YOU KNOW? It has been difficult to track where sharks live and forage. For several decades, sharks that were captured, tagged, and released were eventually recaptured after roaming free. This provided useful information about their movements. The U.S. National Marine Fisheries Service, which conducted this research, found one blue shark (*Prionace glauca*) that traveled an astonishing 3,740 miles, from New York to Brazil, in a year and a half.

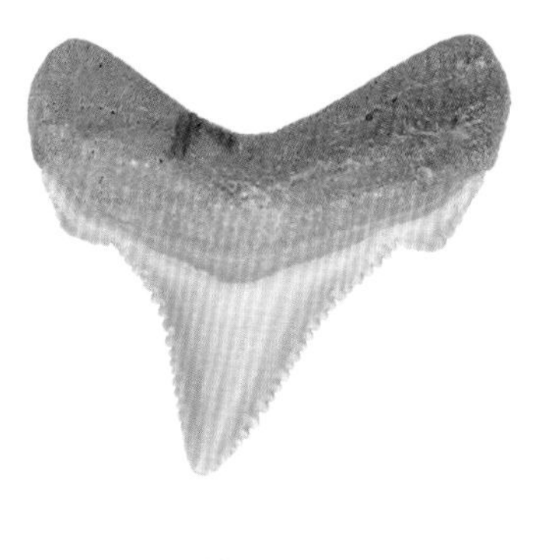
Ln

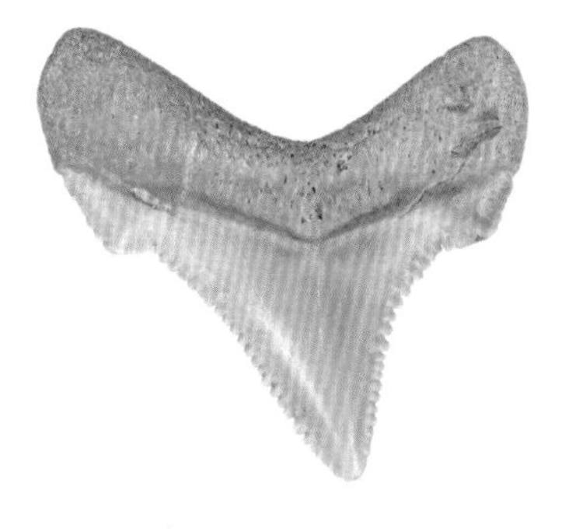
Lb

Carcharocles angustidens

Posterior tooth from the extinct giant white shark *Carcharocles angustidens*. Similar to the anterior teeth, posteriors have medium serrations, triangular serrated cusplets, and a thin bourlette. Regardless of position (anterior, lateral, posterior), all *C. angustidens* teeth have serrated cusplets, which aids greatly in identification. Root lobes are fairly pointed when intact.

SIZE

25 × 23 × 6 mm

1.0 × 0.9 × 0.2 in

GEOLOGIC AGE

Eocene–Oligocene

37.2–23 Ma

IDENTIFIERS

Serrated cusplets

Thin bourlette

Medium serrations

DENSITY

DID YOU KNOW? A nearly complete *Carcharocles angustidens* fossil skeleton unearthed in New Zealand included 35 vertebrae and 165 teeth, which, scientists believe, all came from one individual. The shark was estimated to be over 27 feet long, and its diet likely included small to medium dolphins and whales. Imagine eating a whale because it is "small."

Ln

Lb

SIZE

71 × 47 × 12 mm

2.8 × 1.8 × 0.5 in

GEOLOGIC AGE

Miocene

20.4–15.9 Ma

IDENTIFIERS

Medium serrations

Broadly triangular shape

Serrated cusplets

DENSITY

Carcharocles chubutensis

Tooth from the extinct megatoothed shark *Carcharocles chubutensis*. Teeth of *C. chubutensis* are distinguished from those of *C. megalodon* by having serrated cusplets that are weakly separated from the main crown. The root lobes have shallow concavities on the mesial and distal sides, giving the root a pinched appearance. Lateral cusplets are more developed on posterior teeth, occasionally becoming as deeply notched as those from *C. angustidens*.

DID YOU KNOW? How would you like living with a big cousin like *Carcharocles megalodon*? For 23 million years, *C. chubutensis* did so, but competition among numerous gargantuan sharks required enormous amounts of food, and the supply was apparently inadequate. One by one, the megatoothed sharks—*C. auriculatus*, *C. angustidens*, *C. chubutensis*, and *C. megalodon*—disappeared from the world's oceans.

Ln

Lb

Carcharocles megalodon

Lower anterior tooth from the extinct giant white shark *Carcharocles megalodon*. Perhaps the most famous of all shark teeth, megalodon ("meg") teeth are the most massive, robust teeth of any shark. Specimens have tall, prominent roots, a wide V-shaped dental band (bourlette) between the enamel and the root, and medium serrations. Teeth are wide, thick, and extremely dense. They cannot be mistaken for any other teeth. The largest specimens are recorded at just over seven inches tall.

SIZE

123 × 93 × 25 mm

4.8 × 3.6 × 1.0 in

GEOLOGIC AGE

Miocene–Pliocene

15.9–3.6 Ma

IDENTIFIERS

Medium serrations

Prominent root

Wide bourlette

DENSITY

DID YOU KNOW? Living on a remote Polynesian island in the early 1800s allowed for the creative use of commonly found items. Surrounded by coastal waters and abundant marine life, islanders developed efficient methods of shark fishing. They then constructed spears, daggers, and swords that incorporated shark teeth. Teeth were fastened to a wooden shaft with coconut fibers (and sometimes human hair!) and arranged in rows to create these ominous weapons.

Ln

Lb

Carcharocles megalodon

SIZE

29 × 28 × 5 mm

1.1 × 1.1 × 0.2 in

GEOLOGIC AGE

Miocene–Pliocene

15.9–3.6 Ma

IDENTIFIERS

Medium serrations

Prominent root

Bourlette

DENSITY

Posterior tooth from the extinct giant white shark *Carcharocles megalodon*. Posterior teeth are found in the back corners of the shark's mouth, indicating why this "small" tooth belongs to a shark as large as *C. megalodon*. Posterior teeth in most shark species are smaller than the anterior teeth. Such a decrease in size allowed the shark to close its jaw. While the above specimen is water-worn, the medium serrations are still visible, as is the bourlette.

DID YOU KNOW? How many fish could a megalodon munch if a megalodon could munch fish? In one day, a megalodon could eat up to 2,500 pounds of fish. Which is how these prehistoric "megasharks" could grow to be up to 59 feet long.

Ln

Lb

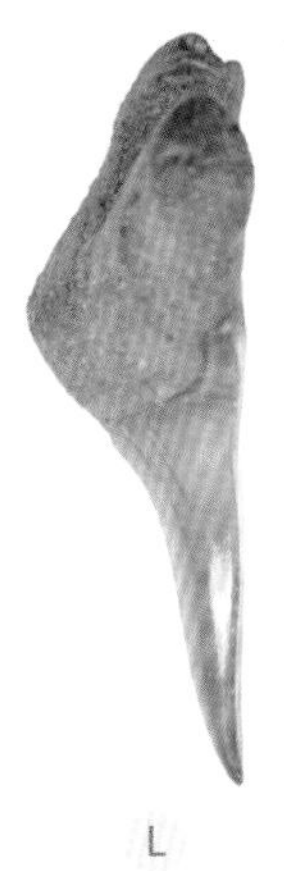
L

Parotodus benedeni

Tooth from the extinct "false mako" shark, *Parotodus benedeni*. The teeth are robust and have erect, parallel root lobes, a thin dental band, and distally skewed crowns. The root protrudes significantly on the lingual side, with a cluster of foramina. It is generally accepted in the scientific literature that the *Parotodus* lineage dates back to the Oligocene. Most of these early teeth are smaller than shark teeth from the Miocene–Pleistocene (neighboring page), with some occasionally bearing cusplets. These cusplets are a point of contention among shark paleontologists; some scientists suggest that such teeth came from juveniles, while others propose new species as the source.

SIZE

32 × 20 × 8 mm

1.3 × 0.8 × 0.3 in

GEOLOGIC AGE

Oligocene–Pleistocene

30–1.1 Ma

IDENTIFIERS

Curved crown

Lingual protuberance

Lack of serrations

DENSITY

DID YOU KNOW? Mackerel sharks come in all shapes and sizes, swimming all over the oceans. Some species prefer shallow coastal waters and reefs, while others, such as the goblin sharks (Mitsukurinidae), hang out in chilly waters 4,000 feet deep. The smallest members of the mackerel shark order (Lamniformes) include the crocodile sharks (Pseudocarchariidae), measuring 3.5 feet in length, while the largest members, the basking sharks (Cetorhinidae) come in at 33 feet long.

Ln

Lb

SIZE

75 × 46 × 16 mm

2.9 × 1.8 × 0.6 in

GEOLOGIC AGE

Oligocene–Pleistocene

30–1.1 Ma

IDENTIFIERS

Curved crown

Lingual protuberance

Lack of serrations

DENSITYDENSITY

Parotodus benedeni

Tooth from the extinct "false mako" shark, ***Parotodus benedeni***. Teeth from ***Parotodus*** are extremely wide, with remarkably thick crowns; this tooth structure was well suited for punching through prey with great force. The distal edge is sharply hooked, continually curving from crown tip to crown base, and the whole crown is unserrated. The roots of lower teeth protrude more lingually than the roots of uppers. Most roots of ***P. benedeni*** teeth are situated at acute or right angles to one another. There has been some restoration work on the root lobes of the above specimen.

DID YOU KNOW? True or false: *Parotodus benedeni* teeth are welcome finds for shark tooth hunters. The answer is true, although the common name for these sharks is false mako shark. The teeth of these extinct sharks are large and have thick U-shaped roots. A 30-foot-long shark would need big teeth in order to catch enough prey to maintain its body weight. False mako sharks inhabited the open ocean, which may be why their teeth are rarely found in coastal deposits.

Ln

Lb

Alopias grandis

Tooth from the extinct giant thresher shark, *Alopias grandis*. Giant thresher teeth, which are relatively rare, are robust, with distally skewed crowns and wide U-shaped roots lacking a nutrient groove or foramen. On the labial side, the enamel crown covers a significant portion of the root, especially when compared with the gum line present on the lingual side.

SIZE

38 × 27 × 7 mm

1.5 × 1.1 × 0.3 in

GEOLOGIC AGE

Miocene

15.9–13.7 Ma

IDENTIFIERS

U-shaped root

Sickle-shaped cusp

Lack of serrations

DENSITY

DID YOU KNOW? Lamnoid sharks include many of the best-known sharks, including the goblin, sand tiger, thresher, megamouth, and great white. This group's sturdy teeth have been preserved well over time, leaving a rich history. But very few specimens came from an articulated, or fully intact, individual. Teeth give only one side of the story, leaving paleontologists wanting more information about other parts of shark evolution.

Ln

Lb

Alopias cf. *A. superciliosus*

SIZE

14 × 10 × 5 mm

0.6 × 0.4 × 0.2 in

GEOLOGIC AGE

Oligocene–Holocene

30 Ma–present

IDENTIFIERS

Mesial root longer than distal root

Thin, gracile cusp

Lack of serrations

DENSITY

Tooth from a male extant bigeye thresher shark, *Alopias superciliosus*. Crowns are distally inclined, bent labially, and unserrated, with incomplete-to-complete cutting edges that are restricted apically. The rounded roots are broadly concave; labially, callosities and enameloid shoulders are frequently present, with occasional nubbed cusplets. The mesial root lobe is longer than the distal lobe, and one or two foramina are present lingually within a nutrient groove. Thresher teeth are highly variable, and the fossil lineage has been poorly studied. The problem of species designation is compounded by sexual dimorphism in thresher teeth—that is, the teeth of males and females differ. Given these complications, the authors leave the assignment of this tooth as *A.* cf. *A. superciliosus*, the senior synonym.

DID YOU KNOW? "A, B, C, F, D, E, G"—That is how the alphabet song goes, right? Well, at least for scientists of taxonomy. Taxonomists, who classify organisms, have ways of indicating uncertain attributions. They use the abbreviation "cf.," from the Latin word *conferre*, which means "compare to," when they are unsure of an exact genus or species and recommend comparing it to a very similar one. Now, when you spot "cf." written in a scientific name, you can knowingly sing this alphabet song!

Ln

Lb

Alopias vulpinus

Narrow tooth from the extant common thresher shark, *Alopias vulpinus*. Tooth crowns are broad and triangular, unserrated, complete, and compressed. Anterior teeth are erect, at times equal in length and width, while laterals are distally hooked. The rounded roots arch lingually with one nutrient foramen; they are broadly concave and bear labial callosities with infrequent plications. *A. vulpinus* teeth exhibit a wide range of shapes and sizes, including the "broad form" seen on the following page.

SIZE

10 × 11 × 3 mm

0.4 × 0.4 × 0.1 in

GEOLOGIC AGE

Oligocene–Holocene

30 Ma–present

IDENTIFIERS

Single foramen

No nutrient groove

Lack of serrations

DENSITY

DID YOU KNOW? Humans have five senses—touch, taste, sight, hearing, and smell. Sharks are thought to have those senses plus others. Most notable is electroreception, the ability to sense and distinguish the electric fields around other species in the ocean. Many prehistoric marine mammals used this form of detection, and certain extant shark species have maintained this ability, giving them at least six senses.

Ln

Lb

Alopias vulpinus

SIZE

21 × 22 × 4 mm

0.8 × 0.9 × 0.2 in

GEOLOGIC AGE

Oligocene–Holocene

30 Ma–present

IDENTIFIERS

Single foramen

No nutrient groove

Lack of serrations

DENSITY

Broad tooth from the extant common thresher shark, *Alopias vulpinus*. Tooth crowns are broad and triangular, unserrated, complete, and compressed. Anterior teeth are erect, at times equal in length and width, while laterals are distally hooked. The rounded roots arch lingually with one nutrient foramen; they are broadly concave and bear labial callosities with infrequent plications. *A. vulpinus* teeth exhibit a wide range of shapes and sizes, including the "narrow form" seen on the previous page.

DID YOU KNOW? Would you swim with sharks? No? Because they eat people? Well, thresher sharks don't. This species enjoys dining on bony fish such as menhaden, herring, Atlantic saury, sand lance, and mackerel. Their favorite prey are bluefish and butterfish, with bonito and squid as close seconds. So go ahead and take a plunge with an inoffensive thresher shark the next time you go for a swim.

Ln

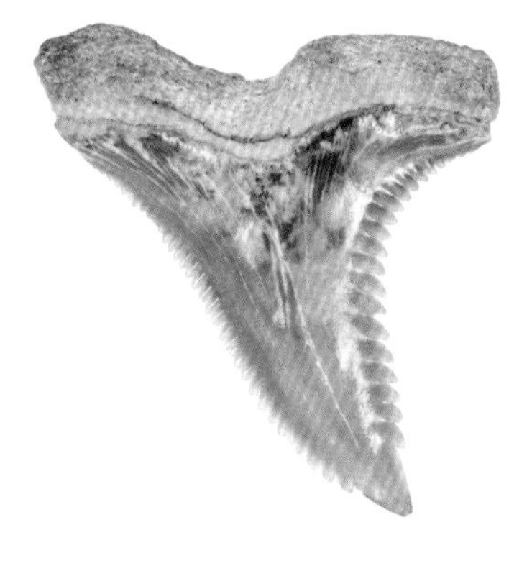

Lb

Hemipristis serra

Upper lateral tooth from the extinct snaggle-tooth shark, *Hemipristis serra*. This species has curved, serrated teeth, with the serrations usually coarser on the distal side than the mesial side. Serrations run from the crown base almost to the tip. The roots are irregularly shaped, curving up to the lingual protuberance in the middle of the tooth. While the above specimen has a relatively narrow crown, many lateral teeth are broader and more distally inclined.

SIZE

37 × 29 × 8 mm

1.4 × 1.1 × 0.3 in

GEOLOGIC AGE

Oligocene–Pleistocene

33.9–1.1 Ma

IDENTIFIERS

Coarse serrations

Unserrated cusp tip

Broad root

DENSITY

DID YOU KNOW? Snaggletooth sharks hold the distinction of having different-looking upper and lower teeth. The upper teeth are broad triangles with serrations on both cutting edges. Many of the lower teeth, however, look similar to sand tiger shark teeth: long and pointed rather than triangular, with fewer and less distinct serrations than upper teeth.

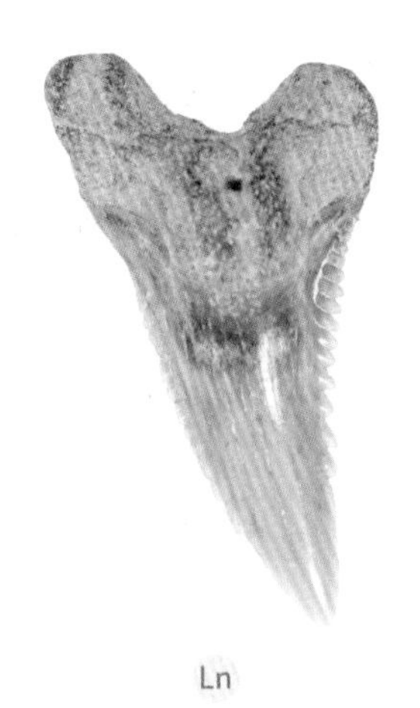

Ln

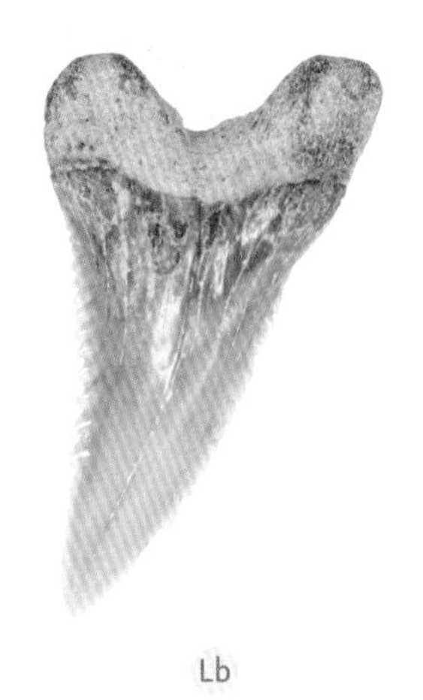

Lb

SIZE

31 × 18 × 9 mm

1.2 × 0.7 × 0.4 in

GEOLOGIC AGE

Oligocene–Pleistocene

33.9–1.1 Ma

IDENTIFIERS

Nutrient foramen

Coarse serrations

Bladelike cusp

DENSITY

Hemipristis serra

Upper anterior tooth from the extinct snaggletooth shark, *Hemipristis serra*. Coarse serrations extend from the crown base both mesially and distally, but are lacking on the apical tip. Distal serrations are coarser than the mesial ones, but both sets are angled obliquely off the tooth. The root has a large lingual protuberance with a broad nutrient groove and at least one nutrient foramen. Anterior teeth differ from laterals in being narrow, compressed, and erect.

DID YOU KNOW? Family names carry history, and many people love to trace their personal ancestry. *Hemipristis* is a genus within the Hemigaleidae, or weasel shark, family. The Greek root "hemi" means "half," and "pristis" means "saw"; therefore, the literal translation of "hemipristis" is "half saw," referring to the shark's jagged teeth. Speaking of families, did anyone in your family call you "snaggletooth" as a kid when your permanent teeth were emerging?

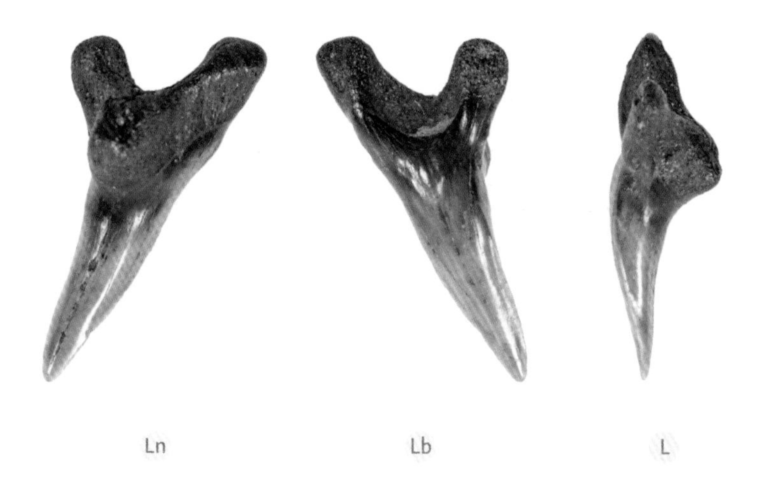

Hemipristis serra

Lower tooth from the extinct snaggletooth shark, *Hemipristis serra*. Drastically different from the upper teeth, lowers are long and pointed, with occasional slender serrations at the crown base. The roots protrude lingually, with a faint nutrient groove in the middle of the root. To the untrained eye, it would be easy to mistake a lower tooth from a snaggletooth for a sand tiger tooth. Some older texts mislabel *H. serra* lowers as "extinct sand tiger" teeth.

SIZE

24 × 13 × 8 mm

0.9 × 0.5 × 0.3 in

GEOLOGIC AGE

Oligocene–Pleistocene

33.9–1.1 Ma

IDENTIFIERS

Prominent root

Serrations at base

Unserrated cusp tip

DENSITY

DID YOU KNOW? Considering a home improvement project? Better include a paleontologist in your planning—just in case you dig up a 15-million-year-old shark. This happened to a family near Calvert Cliffs, Maryland, when their children discovered a vertebra in the construction excavation. Further work unearthed 79 more vertebrae, plus a whole mouthful of teeth from a fossilized *Hemipristis serra*.

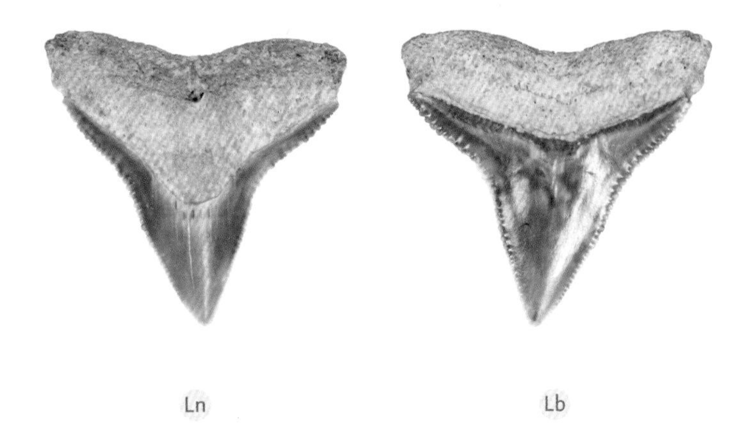

Carcharhinus leucas

SIZE

28 × 26 × 4 mm

1.1 × 1.0 × 0.2 in

GEOLOGIC AGE

Miocene–Holocene

15.9 Ma–present

IDENTIFIERS

Nutrient foramen

Fine serrations

Bladelike cusp

DENSITY

Upper tooth from the extant bull shark, *Carcharhinus leucas*. This species has some of the most distinctive upper teeth of the *Carcharhinus* sharks, with fine to medium serrations, usually coarser toward the base. The distal edge is bent inward laterally, and the overall tooth appears pinched on both sides. The main cusp is oblique and skewed distally. Roots are wide and relatively thin, with a nutrient foramen.

DID YOU KNOW? Whitetip sharks swim to the surface and "sniff" for interesting scents and food. The shark's nostril-like slits, or nares, are acutely developed to distinguish which side, right or left, an interesting smell is wafting from. This may help the whitetip get to the dinner table before nearby competitors. And as the saying goes, "The early bird gets the worm" (or fish)!

Ln

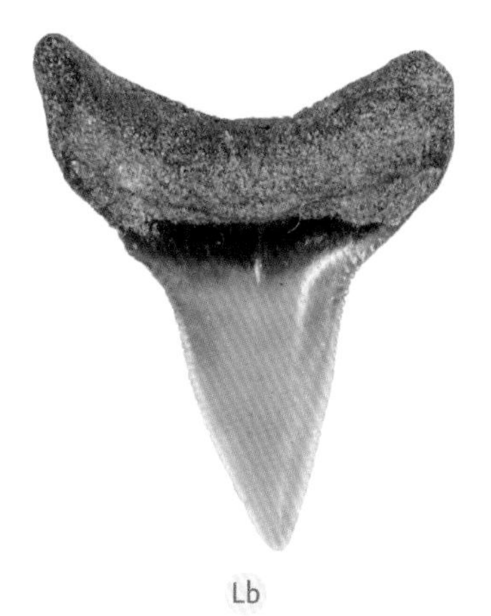

Lb

Carcharhinus leucas

Lower tooth from the extant species of bull shark, *Carcharhinus leucas*. Lower teeth bear fine serrations from the crown tip to the base, although depending on wear, serrations may be visible only closer to the tooth base. As with the upper teeth, lowers have a prominent nutrient foramen. These teeth are frequently confused with teeth of the lemon shark (*Negaprion brevirostris*), but have a more deeply notched root and usually lack an enamel shoulder on the root.

SIZE

21 × 16 × 5 mm

0.8 × 0.6 × 0.2 in

GEOLOGIC AGE

Miocene–Holocene

15.9 Ma–present

IDENTIFIERS:

Nutrient foramen

Light serrations

Thin cusp

DENSITY

DID YOU KNOW? Sharks are a mysterious lot. They live their lives in secret spaces, prompting humans to wonder about, and sometimes fear, these large creatures that might appear and attack suddenly. But interest in their watery lifestyles is growing. Scientists are purposefully seeking them out so that more two-legged water-loving creatures will appreciate sharks in their environment.

Ln

Lb

SIZE

19 × 16 × 4 mm

0.7 × 0.6 × 0.2 in

GEOLOGIC AGE

Miocene–Holocene

15.9 Ma–present

IDENTIFIERS

Curved distal edge

Medium serrations

Square root lobes

DENSITY

Carcharhinus obscurus

Upper tooth from the extant dusky shark, *Carcharhinus obscurus*. Of the *Carcharhinus* sharks, the dusky have teeth that are some of the easiest to distinguish. The distal edge is curved, as opposed to the notched distal edge on *C. leucas* teeth. Medium serrations are present and increase in coarseness closer to the root. A nutrient foramen is visible on the lingual side, and the root lobes are blunt-to-square in shape. *C. leucas* teeth, by comparison, have smaller serrations and notched crowns.

DID YOU KNOW? Dusky sharks, *Carcharhinus obscurus*, range widely among warm waters in open coastal regions. Hard to track, and even harder to keep alive when caught, dusky adults have been declining in number in recent years. They take time to reach adulthood and sexual maturity, and females have long gestation periods, traits that increase the species' susceptibility to extinction.

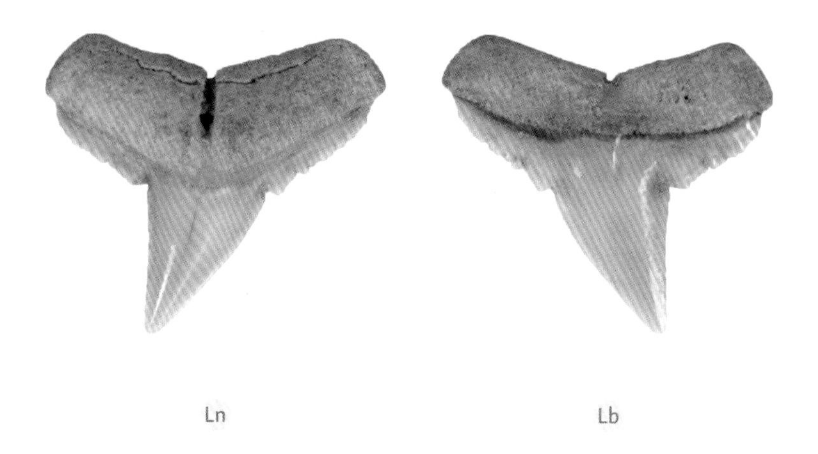

Carcharhinus gibbesi

Upper tooth from the extinct requiem shark, *Carcharhinus gibbesi*. These teeth are distally skewed and bear serrations primarily along the shoulders, though some specimens have serrations extending farther down along the crown. Since the crowns are oblique, some teeth may have a notch on the distal side. The roots are simple, with a prominent nutrient groove on the lingual side.

SIZE

12 × 12 × 2 mm

0.5 × 0.5 × 0.08 in

GEOLOGIC AGE

Eocene–Miocene

37.2–16 Ma

IDENTIFIERS

Distally skewed crown

Serrated shoulders

Nutrient groove

DENSITY

DID YOU KNOW? A requiem is a ceremony for the soul of a dead person. "Requiem" is therefore a fitting common name for *Carcharhinus gibbesi*, since sharks of this genus often attack humans. These streamlined predators move swiftly through water to find fish, mollusks, marine mammals, and sea birds to satisfy their appetites. And they occasionally bump into a few humans along the way.

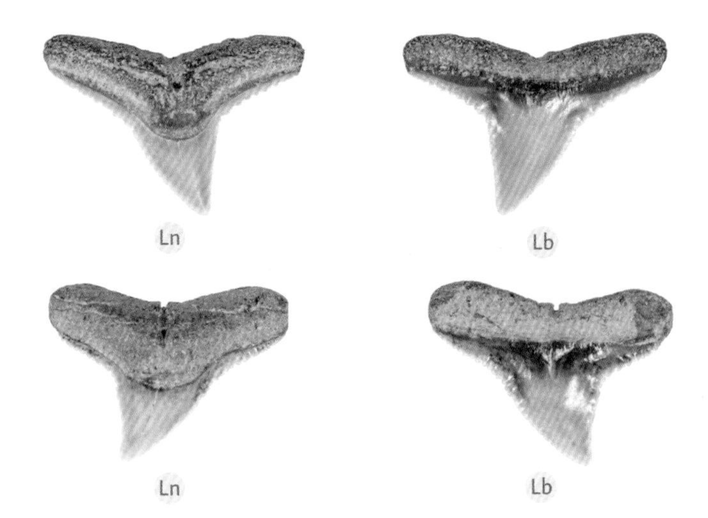

SIZE

15 × 18 × 3 mm

0.6 × 0.7 × 0.1 in

GEOLOGIC AGE

Eocene–Holocene

40.4 Ma–present

IDENTIFIERS

Variable serrations

Variable nutrient groove

Rounded root lobes

DENSITY

Carcharhinus spp.

Two teeth from extinct requiem sharks in the genus *Carcharhinus*. Teeth belonging to members of the *Carcharhinus* genus are notoriously hard to identify to the species level. There are morphological similarities across many species (both extant and extinct), adding to the difficulty in specific identifications. Generally, *Carcharhinus* dentitions are of the cutting-clutching design, with medium serrations on the broad "cutting" upper teeth, and finer serrations on the slender "clutching" lower teeth.

DID YOU KNOW? Imagine swimming and grazing the open waters in search of plankton to swill, along with other filter-feeding species such as some sharks. There are about 13 modern species of such sharks and rays. These species became filter feeders rather than the fearful predators that literature and Hollywood have promoted; basking sharks, megamouth sharks, whale sharks, manta rays, and some devil rays are among these.

Ln

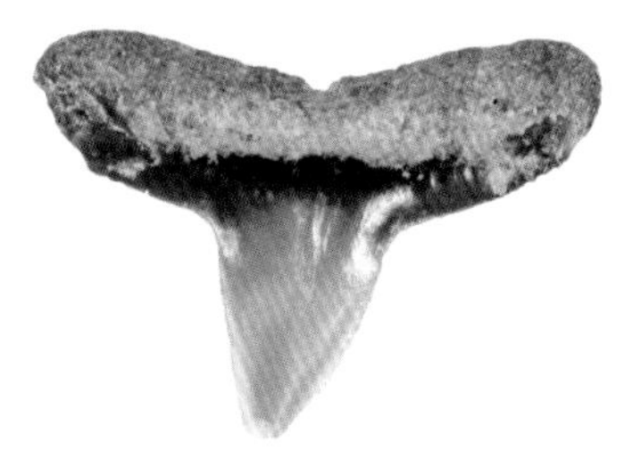
Lb

Carcharhinus sp.

Lower tooth from a requiem shark in the *Carcharhinus* genus. Similar in form to teeth of the hammerhead sharks (*Sphyrna* sp.), the lower teeth of the requiem sharks can have both nutrient grooves and a nutrient foramen. The short crowns are usually both lingually and distally curved. Crown margins have serrations, distinguishing these teeth from those of hammerheads and the lower teeth of lemon sharks. Lower teeth from requiem sharks are some of the most common teeth found along southeastern U.S. beaches.

SIZE

13 × 15 × 3 mm

0.5 × 0.6 × 0.1 in

GEOLOGIC AGE

Eocene–Holocene

40.4 Ma–present

IDENTIFIERS

Nutrient groove

Nutrient foramen

Fine serrations

DENSITY

DID YOU KNOW? Scientific classification begins with the kingdom name and narrows down to phylum, class, order, family, genus, and species. Carcharhinidae, the requiem shark family, includes *Carcharhinus*, its "type genus." The type genus generally defines a family: its name usually forms the root of the family name, and it contains most of the family's species. Common names of *Carcharhinus*'s 35 species include blacktip, sandbar, bull, copper, requiem, and dusky sharks.

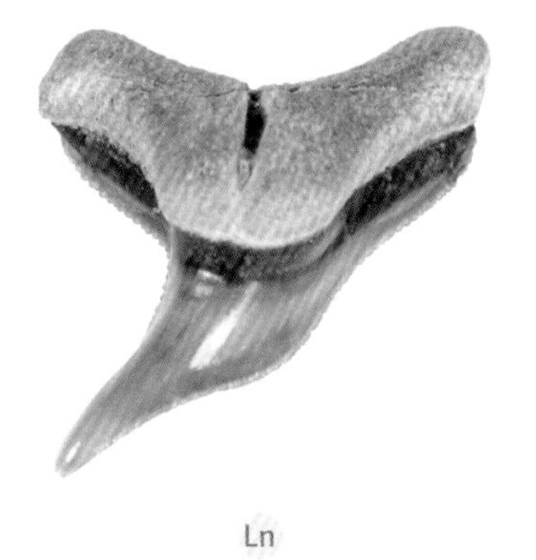
Ln

Lb

SIZE

21 × 17 × 5 mm

0.8 × 0.7 × 0.2 in

GEOLOGIC AGE

Oligocene–Miocene

30–5.3 Ma

IDENTIFIERS

Twisted mesial edge

Weak serrations

Protruding root

DENSITY

Physogaleus contortus

Tooth from the extinct longtooth tiger shark, *Physogaleus contortus*. Upper and lower teeth appear identical, with long, twisting crowns and a centrally raised root. The crown is twisted, or contorted, on the mesial edge (page 475); in some cases, this feature can be very pronounced. The root protrudes significantly above the crown, with a noticeable nutrient groove. Serrations are fine across most of the crown and usually coarser on the distal edge, especially along the shoulder. Note: In older texts, this tooth was assigned to the *Galeocerdo* genus, with the same species epithet.

DID YOU KNOW? The National Geographic Society funded research to learn why sharks sometimes lie motionless. Scientists observed that Caribbean reef sharks resting inside the caves of Isla Mujeres were respiring at the rate of 20–28 times per minute. Analysis of upwelling freshwater there revealed a high concentration of oxygen, which may have a recharging or even a narcotic effect, causing sharks to visit often and stay for long periods.

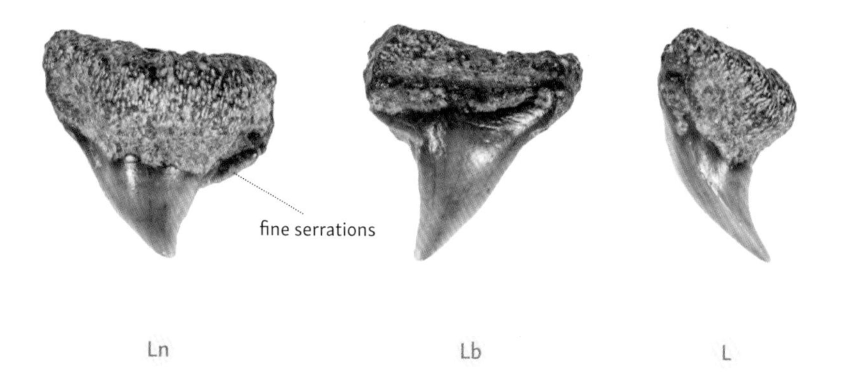

Physogaleus contortus

Symphyseal (middle) tooth from the extinct longtooth tiger shark, *Physogaleus contortus*. Symphyseal teeth of *P. contortus* are similar in appearance to megamouth shark (*Megachasma* sp.) teeth; however, the base of the crown is finely serrated (seen above in lingual view, indicated). The roots of symphyseal teeth are usually asymmetrical, with the raised or larger end closer to the symphysis, or middle of the jaw.

SIZE

10 × 9 × 5 mm

0.4 × 0.4 × 0.2 in

GEOLOGIC AGE

Oligocene–Miocene

30–5.3 Ma

IDENTIFIERS

Serrated base

Prominent root

Curved crown

DENSITY

DID YOU KNOW? The ability to feel pain depends on sensory neurons in the body. Group C fibers, which are thin neurons that lack a myelin sheath, respond when tissue damage occurs. Humans have lots of these neurons, but sharks have a much lower number. This suggests that they feel little surface pain, which explains why sharks will continue feeding even when mortally wounded.

Ln

Lb

SIZE

10 × 11 × 2 mm

0.4 × 0.4 × 0.08 in

GEOLOGIC AGE

Eocene

48.6–33.9 Ma

IDENTIFIERS

Coarse serrations

Wide root

Unserrated crown

DENSITY

Galeocerdo latidens

Tooth from the extinct Eocene tiger shark *Galeocerdo latidens*. Though very coarsely serrated on the shoulders, the crowns of *G. latidens* teeth are unserrated. Upper teeth appear similar to lowers. The roots are usually wider than the diagonal tooth length, setting them apart from other tiger shark teeth. A strong nutrient groove is present on the lingual side. Compare these teeth to the doubly serrate teeth of *G. aduncus* and *G. cuvier*.

DID YOU KNOW? "Tiny Bubbles" was the Hawaiian singer Don Ho's theme song, but "Tiny Teeth" might be more appropriate for *Galeocerdo latidens*. Their teeth measure on average about one-half inch long.

Ln

Lb

Galeocerdo aduncus

Tooth from the extinct tiger shark *Galeocerdo aduncus*. Similar in appearance to modern tiger shark teeth (*G. cuvier*), those of *G. aduncus* are much smaller, reaching only around three-quarters of an inch (20 mm) long. The root lobes are rounder than those of *G. cuvier*, and a broad nutrient groove is detectable. The serrations on the distal shoulder are considered doubly serrate, which, with the geologic age difference, distinguishes these teeth from those of *G. latidens*.

SIZE

19 × 19 × 2 mm

0.7 × 0.7 × 0.1 in

GEOLOGIC AGE

Oligocene–Pliocene

28.4–4.9 Ma

IDENTIFIERS

Doubly serrated shoulders

Broad nutrient groove

Round root lobes

DENSITY

DID YOU KNOW? People are excited to see large shark teeth, but many smaller teeth have fascinating features, too. *Galeocerdo aduncus* teeth are dime-sized and have serrations on the distal edge that are hard to see without a magnifying loupe. Magnification reveals that there are "teeth within teeth" on these teeth. Between each serration are smaller points, making the teeth "doubly serrate."

Ln

Lb

SIZE

29 × 28 × 6 mm

1.1 × 1.1 × 0.2 in

GEOLOGIC AGE

Oligocene–Miocene

33.9–5.3 Ma

IDENTIFIERS

Broad main cusp

Shallow distal notch

Complex serrations

DENSITY

Galeocerdo mayumbensis

Tooth from the relatively rare Miocene tiger shark, *Galeocerdo mayumbensis*. Similar to the teeth of *G. cuvier*, these bear complex serrations. Other main identifiers include the broad main cusps, which are much wider than those of the modern tiger shark, and the shallow notch between the main cusp and the complex serrations on the distal side. *G. mayumbensis* teeth are also slightly concave on the distal heel; this is a variable feature that is not reliable as an identifier.

DID YOU KNOW? Who do you think would win if the largest shark ever to have lived faced a *Tyrannosaurus rex* in a "bite off" contest? The bite of the 60-foot *Carcharocles megalodon* is estimated to have exerted 182 kilonewtons, or 40,960 foot-pounds, of force. This force is five times greater than the force that could be delivered by *Tyrannosaurus rex*!

Ln

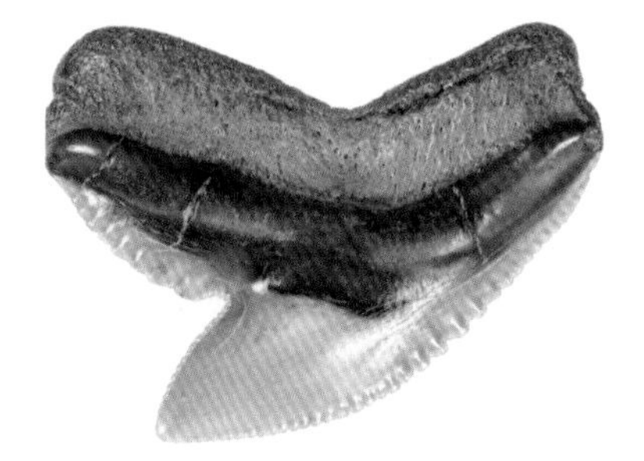

Lb

Galeocerdo cuvier

Tooth from the extant tiger shark, *Galeocerdo cuvier*. These teeth have complex serrations (also known as secondary serrations), in which the larger serrations can have their own serrations. This feature is similar to doubly serrate leaf margins in botany. *G. cuvier* teeth have a distinct notch on the distal edge that other tiger shark teeth do not have. The root lobes are squared off; for comparison, *Galeocerdo aduncus* lobes are rounded.

SIZE

30 × 30 × 7 mm

1.2 × 1.2 × 0.3 in

GEOLOGIC AGE

Miocene–Holocene

23 Ma–present

IDENTIFIERS

Square root lobes

Oblique cusps

Complex serrations

DENSITY

DID YOU KNOW? Did you know that sharks love teeth? They have lots of them, with backup replacements stored in rows called "files." When a worn tooth is ejected, another takes its place. Special symphyseal teeth grow at the front and center, or symphysis, where the right and left jaws are joined. Sharks usually have only one symphyseal tooth, located in the lower jaw, but some species have a second one in the upper jaw as well.

Ln

Lb

SIZE

22 × 16 × 6 mm

0.9 × 0.6 × 0.2 in

GEOLOGIC AGE

Miocene–Holocene

23 Ma–present

IDENTIFIERS

Straight crown

Medium serrations

Asymmetrical root

DENSITY

Galeocerdo cuvier

Upper symphyseal tooth from the extant tiger shark, *Galeocerdo cuvier*. Symphyseals, found at the midpoint of the lower and upper jaws, are straighter and less distally skewed than the anterior and lateral teeth. Serrations are fine toward the tip of the crown and become increasingly coarse as they progress toward the base. The roots of symphyseal teeth are usually asymmetrical, with the raised, or larger, end closer to the symphysis (middle of the jaw). Lower symphyseal teeth are significantly smaller than the upper ones.

DID YOU KNOW? "Know your enemy," the saying goes. Bottlenose dolphins can distinguish between shark species, knowing which ones to avoid. In the 1960s, the U.S. Navy trained bottlenose dolphins to attack sharks. The dolphins instinctively focused on sandbar, tiger, and nurse sharks, butting them in their sensitive gill areas. They would not, however, attack bull sharks, their natural enemies.

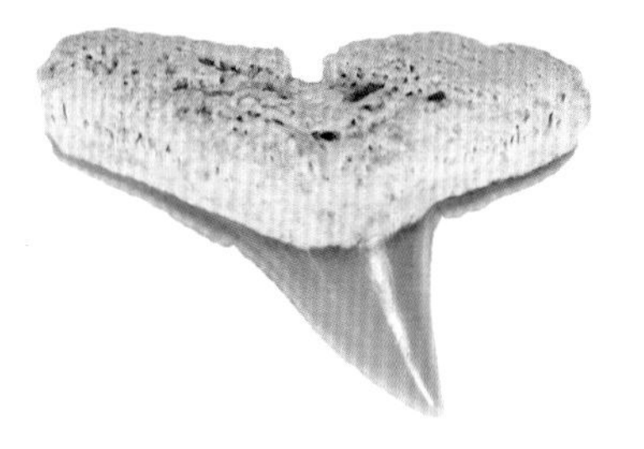

Ln

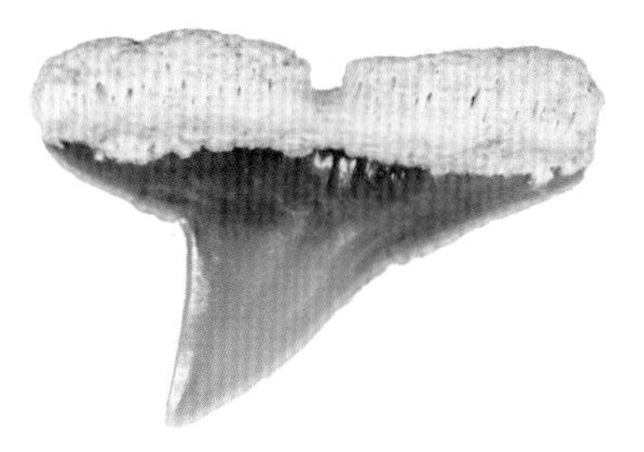

Lb

Sphyrna laevissima

Tooth from the extinct hammerhead shark, *Sphyrna laevissima*. Hammerhead teeth, which are relatively small, are most easily found by screening material. The most distinct features of a hammerhead tooth are the distal notch (page 465) and deep nutrient groove. On the mesial edge, the tooth curves in slightly or can appear dented (as above). Despite their size, the root and crown are quite robust. Serrations can occasionally be found on the distal shoulder; however, most teeth lack serrations.

SIZE

14 × 14 × 3 mm

0.5 × 0.5 × 0.1 in

GEOLOGIC AGE

Miocene

23–11.6 Ma

IDENTIFIERS

Deep nutrient groove

Distal notch

Wide root

DENSITY

DID YOU KNOW? Hammerhead sharks are famous for their unusually shaped heads. Why do these sharks have such a feature? Scientists list several possible reasons, including greater electroreceptivity sharpness for locating prey in a "metal detector" fashion (as when the sharks sweep over stingrays buried in ocean floor sediments); enhanced scent capability, thanks to their widely spaced nostrils; and better maneuverability and increased lift from the airplane-wing shape of their heads.

Ln

Lb

Rhizoprionodon sp.

SIZE

9 × 9 × 2 mm

0.4 × 0.4 × 0.1 in

GEOLOGIC AGE

Eocene–Holocene

40.4 Ma–present

IDENTIFIERS

Concave mesial cusp

Nutrient groove

Small size

DENSITY

Lateral tooth from the extant genus of sharpnose sharks, *Rhizoprionodon*. Teeth of *Rhizoprionodon* are relatively small, with the 9-mm-long example shown here at the larger end of the range; most specimens are around 6 mm in length. Tooth crowns are long, weakly concave, and distally skewed. The distal heel is convex and prominent. The roots are broad, approximately the same length as the crowns, and bear a deep nutrient groove. *Rhizoprionodon* teeth are similar in morphology to some hammerhead (*Sphyrna*) teeth, but occasionally are found with weak serrations (seen above on the distal shoulder in labial view).

DID YOU KNOW? You might not think of sharks as feeding on worms, but the Atlantic sharpnose shark does. These diminutive sharks are known for eating small fare, including worms, shrimp, crabs, and small fish. Measuring a maximum of 32 inches long, the sharpnose shark may not be as fearsome as the great whites of *Jaws* fame, but it isn't a shark that small creatures would want to mess with.

Ln

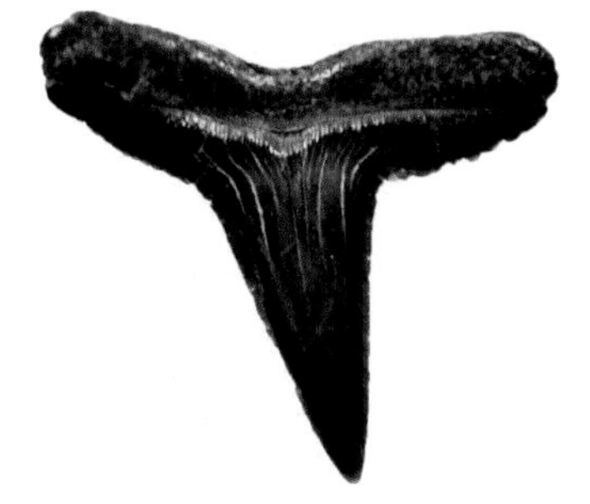

Lb

Negaprion brevirostris

Upper tooth from the extant species of lemon shark, *Negaprion brevirostris*. Note the serrations on the shoulder of the crown, indicating that the above specimen is an upper tooth. Lower teeth are not serrated on the shoulders. The overall form of lemon shark teeth is T-shaped, and when viewed laterally on a flat surface, the crown on upper teeth is horizontal and does not curve up. Weak to moderate nutrient grooves are present on the roots, being more pronounced on lower teeth. At smaller sizes or in lateral positions, lemon teeth can be misidentified as hammerhead or *Carcharhinus* lower teeth.

SIZE

20 × 20 × 3 mm

0.8 × 0.8 × 0.1 in

GEOLOGIC AGE

Miocene–Holocene

16 Ma–present

IDENTIFIERS

Unserrated crown

Tall, narrow cusp

Broad roots

DENSITY

DID YOU KNOW? To determine whether marine organisms use Earth's magnetic field, Adrianus Kalmijn, of the Woods Hole Oceanographic Institute, experimented with lemon sharks. He set up electromagnets in their foraging area and documented their movements under a normal magnetic field. Kalmijn then switched the magnets on, changing the local magnetic field by 90 degrees. Remarkably, the sharks responded, altering their routes by 90 degrees to match the new field.

Ln

Lb

SIZE

17 × 14 × 4 mm

0.7 × 0.5 × 0.2 in

GEOLOGIC AGE

Miocene–Holocene

16 Ma–present

IDENTIFIERS

T-shaped form

Enamel on roots

Lack of serrations

DENSITY

Negaprion brevirostris

Lower tooth from the extant lemon shark, *Negaprion brevirostris*. Like the upper teeth, lowers are T-shaped, with a long skinny crown perpendicular to the roots. The crown and shoulders are unserrated, though enamel covers part of the root on the labial side. The crown curves lingually, in contrast with the flat crowns of the upper teeth. Roots are skinny, with a visible nutrient foramen above the crown on the lingual side. Lower teeth of the extinct Miocene lemon shark (*Negaprion eurybathrodon*) have nutrient grooves.

DID YOU KNOW? The name "lemon shark" refers to the fishes' unusual yellow dorsal skin, and not to the flavor of their meat. Lemon sharks are relatively small, 10 feet long at most, so this coloration serves a purpose. It helps them blend in with the sandy sediments of the shallow waters they inhabit, offering them some protection against larger, predatory sharks. These predators might be thinking, "Wouldn't it be nice if the meat came preseasoned?"

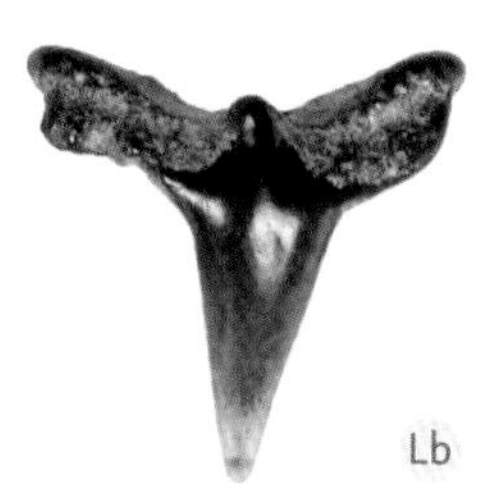

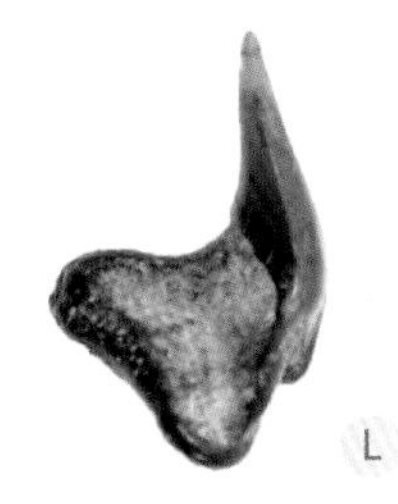

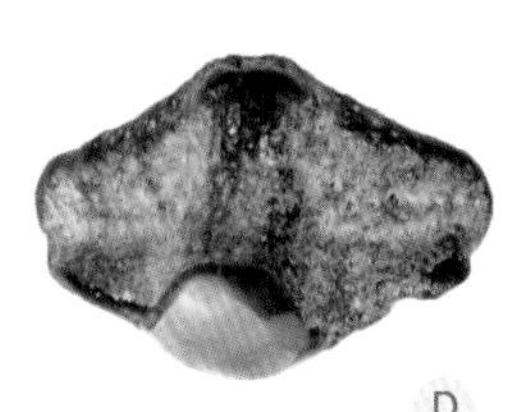

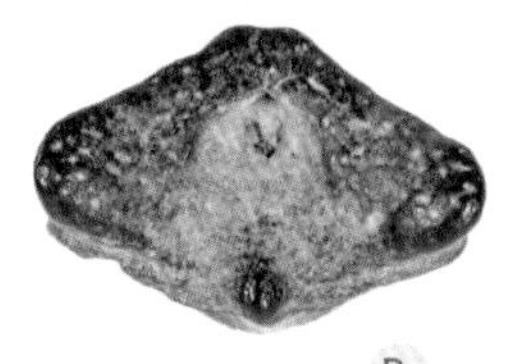

Squatina subserrata

Tooth from the Miocene angel shark, *Squatina subserrata*. These oddly shaped teeth have thin conical crowns and wide flat roots nearly perpendicular to the crown. The root is diamond-shaped with a deep depression in the middle (seen above in labial view). Teeth from *S. subserrata* are larger and have taller roots than those of *S. prima*, and are from the Miocene, while *S. prima* is from the Paleocene and Eocene.

SIZE

8 × 7 × 5 mm

0.3 × 0.3 × 0.2 in

GEOLOGIC AGE

Miocene

23–5.3 Ma

IDENTIFIERS

Conical crown

Wide, flat roots

Lack of serrations

DENSITY

DID YOU KNOW? Sharks have been on Earth for over 420 million years, evolving and adapting to the planet's changing climate and habitats. Around the Cretaceous period (145–66 Ma), the sharks made their biggest leap in growth, because of an increased abundance of food. As marine organisms diversified and moved around the vast oceans, sharks followed, adapting to new fish species as well as to shellfish such as clams and other kinds of mollusks.

Ln

Lb

SIZE

23 × 19 × 5 mm

0.9 × 0.7 × 0.2 in

GEOLOGIC AGE

Miocene–Pliocene

23–3.6 Ma

IDENTIFIERS

Labiolingually thin roots

Single root lobe

Prominent cusp

DENSITY

Notorynchus primigenius

Upper anterior tooth from the extinct sevengill cow shark, *Notorynchus primigenius*. As in the lower teeth, the upper teeth have laterally broad roots that are squared at the edges and taper to less than 1 mm thick. Anterior teeth bear a single prominent cusp, with multiple lateral cusplets. Lateral teeth may have up to five cusps, with one remaining significantly longer, whereas in the lower teeth, cusps become progressively smaller.

DID YOU KNOW? Some shark teeth differ between the jaws. The male cow shark uses the longer anterior cusp on his upper teeth to hold the female during mating. That gives a whole new meaning to a bite on the neck. Thankfully, there is no such thing as a vampire shark!

Ln

Lb

Notorynchus primigenius

Lower lateral tooth from the extinct sevengill cow shark, *Notorynchus primigenius*. These lower teeth have seven main cusps, which taper toward the distal end. *N. primigenius* teeth have curved serrations on the mesial edge; *Hexanchus griseus* teeth, with which they are often confused, have extremely fine serrations. *H. griseus* teeth also have up to 13 cusps, whereas *N. primigenius* teeth never exceed 7 cusps. While the above specimen is mostly complete, intact teeth have rectangular roots approximately 10 mm tall and only 2–3 mm thick, which break or wear easily.

SIZE

11 × 22 × 3 mm

0.4 × 0.9 × 0.1 in

GEOLOGIC AGE

Miocene–Pliocene

23–3.6 Ma

IDENTIFIERS

Serrated mesial edge

Up to seven cusps

Thin square roots

DENSITY

DID YOU KNOW? Sharks are among the oldest predators on Earth, having survived five mass extinctions dating back to 439 Ma. Sharks' skeletons, which are made up of soft cartilage rather than bone, are mostly dissolved by saltwater after a shark dies. A shark's enamel teeth, however, persist beyond death and are soon covered by sediment on the sea floor. There they become fossilized, a process that changes their color from white to shades of gray, brown, or black.

A Note on the Megatoothed Shark Lineage

What's in a name? That which we call a *Carcharocles megalodon*
by any other name would smell as sweet.

Maybe Shakespeare's Juliet didn't say it exactly that way. But the family dispute in *Romeo and Juliet* couldn't have been much more intense than that of three groups of scientists who disagree over the proper genus of the megatoothed shark lineage. The modern argument began in 1960 with a hypothesis by the French ichthyologist Edgard Casier, prompting the genus-classification question that many paleontologists yearn to solve: should it be *Carcharodon, Carcharocles,* or *Otodus/Megaselachus*?

Scientific nomenclature stipulates that genus is the level within which one or more species are grouped. Popular discussion of which genus to assign megatoothed sharks has narrowed the choice to the above generic names for the species *megalodon*. We have analyzed this issue and the justifications forwarded by proponents of the three perspectives. It should be noted that many renowned paleontologists support each hypothesis, and that science is a dynamic system, constantly accepting new data and working to support or disprove former theories and hypotheses. Below are the arguments in support of each perspective:

CARCHAROCLES HYPOTHESIS

The megatoothed sharks are more closely related to the extinct otodontids (*Otodus* and *Parotodus*) than to any extant genus.

1. The large teeth of the megatoothed sharks more closely resemble the large teeth of *Otodus* than those of any other Cenozoic era shark species.
2. There are differences between the teeth of *Carcharodon* and *Carcharocles,* signifying that their lineages do not derive from a shared ancestor. Instead, these species represent the ends of two separate lineages.
2. *Carcharodon hastalis* is the unserrated ancestor of *Carcharodon carcharias*.
3. The coarse serrations of *Carcharodon* teeth, in contrast to the fine serrations of megatoothed sharks' teeth, support the idea that the two lineages developed independently.
4. The presence of serrations in both *Carcharodon* and megatoothed sharks is not diagnostic. Tooth morphological similarities are driven by convergent evolution (homoplasy); both genera filled comparable ecological niches and used similar feeding strategies.

5. The teeth of *Otodus* and other megatoothed sharks have a large bourlette, while teeth of *Carcharodon* do not.
6. The loss of lateral cusplets in adult teeth is not unique to *Carcharodon*. It has occurred in other shark lineages and therefore does not serve as a link between *Carcharodon* and advanced megatoothed sharks.
7. *Carcharocles* root shape and foramina are more similar to those of *Otodus* than those of *Carcharodon*.

The *Carcharocles* hypothesis supports the idea that megatoothed sharks are related to *Otodus*, along with the hypothesis that the great white shark (*Carcharodon carcharias*) evolved from the extinct white shark (*Carcharodon hastalis*) via *Carcharodon hubbelli*.

OTODUS/MEGASELACHUS HYPOTHESIS

The megatoothed sharks represent a linear series of chronospecies, showing gradual changes from the ancestral *Otodus obliquus* through successive megatoothed species.

1. All species with cusplets are assigned to the genus *Otodus*.
2. The final species, *chubutensis* and *megalodon*, are placed in a separate genus, *Megaselachus*, to differentiate them from *angustidens* and earlier species.
3. *Otodus* and *Megaselachus* are placed into the Otodontidae family, while *Carcharodon* is placed in Lamnidae.
4. *Carcharodon hastalis* is the unserrated ancestor of *Carcharodon carcharias*.
5. The last common ancestor between lamnids and otodontids lived in the Cretaceous period.

The *Otodus/Megaselachus* perspective uses subgenera in the lineage, showing the transition as *Otodus* (*Otodus*) *angustidens*, *Otodus* (*Megaselachus*) *chubutensis*, and *Otodus* (*Megaselachus*) *megalodon*. Some scientists question the delineation of subgenera and subspecies in the fossil record, since there is currently no clear way of determining whether species interbred or shared similar DNA.

CARCHARODON HYPOTHESIS

The megatoothed sharks are closely related to *Carcharodon carcharias*, the modern great white shark.

1. Fossil white sharks (including *C. hastalis*, *C. hubbelli*, *C. carcharias*, and the *C. megalodon* lineage) all belong to one genus, *Carcharodon*, and share a single common ancestor (monophyly).

2. Extinct megatoothed sharks and *Carcharodon* are placed in the family Lamnidae.
3. *Carcharodon* vertebrae are closer in appearance to megatoothed shark vertebrae than they are to those of *Isurus* sharks.
4. The intermediate tooth of both *Carcharodon* and megatoothed sharks is inclined toward the mesial position, as opposed to the distal inclination in lamnids such as *Isurus* and *Otodus*.
5. In megatoothed sharks and in *Carcharodon*, the first anterior upper tooth is the largest tooth. But the largest tooth in *Isurus* is in the second anterior lower position.
6. Large *Carcharodon* teeth take on the appearance of megatoothed shark teeth in root shape, serration size, crown proportions, and bourlette size (large). This leaves size relationship as the only similarity between *Otodus* and megatoothed shark teeth.

The *Carcharodon* perspective, though it is used in many older texts and museum displays, is now widely dismissed by scientists. Multiple aspects of this hypothesis depend on dentition and tooth positions. An articulated *C. megalodon* dentition has not been found, and reconstructions are based on *Carcharodon*, thereby resulting in "similar dentitions." Several sets of associated *C. megalodon* teeth are known, but none were found articulated, and so tooth positions cannot be definitively determined. Further, isolated lamniform vertebrae are indistinguishable among genera without tooth associations. The inclusion of this perspective is to acknowledge the history of the debate.

Based on all the above, we side with the *Carcharocles* hypothesis, using this genus in all assignments of serrated megatoothed shark teeth throughout the book.

Megatoothed lineage displaying the loss of lateral cusplets. *Left to right*: specimens from *Cretalamna appendiculata, Otodus obliquus, Carcharocles auriculatus, C. angustidens, C. chubutensis, C. megalodon*. A tooth from *Otodus sokolovi*, which should follow *O. obliquus*, is not shown.

The *Otodus/Megaselachus* hypothesis is a relative newcomer to the discussion, and many points that it raises need further research and resolution.

Because of the nature of marine fossils, the discovery of articulated dentitions is quite rare. Other problems confounding the assignment of a genus include shared traits in teeth that can be traced to a common ancestor, and conclusions based on tooth morphology. Tooth shapes and serrations are driven primarily by diet and therefore don't show a direct correlation with family groups. Sharks that eat primarily fish have narrow, conical teeth (sand tiger and lemon sharks), while those that eat larger prey such as dolphins, small whales, and turtles have larger, more robust teeth (tiger, great white, and mako sharks).

Many scientific papers take up the debate over megatoothed generic assignments, and they are well worth taking the time to read before forming one's own conclusions. Science is a beautiful system that constantly updates itself and seeks to support or disprove existing work. Even if you're not much interested in the "family drama" surrounding the history of megatoothed sharks, it is a sure bet that a three-inch-long tooth lying on the beach will catch your eye.

A 6-foot-tall human in comparison with a 60-foot-long *Carcharocles megalodon* shark (bottom) and a 20-foot-long great white shark (*Carcharodon carcharias*).

SPECIES HIGHLIGHT

Chondrichthyes | Cartilaginous Fish

Spineless creatures? Don't throw a barb like that at sharks and rays!

Sharks are among the best-known fishes. They have evolved over hundreds of millions of years to become the top predators in the world's oceans, feared by some people but loved and respected by others.

The first fish species looked nothing like the fish (or sharks) of today. In fact, they were neither true fishes nor vertebrates. These creatures lacked bony structures and looked more like worms.

But *Pikaia* species, which are known from fossils of the Middle Cambrian period (530 Ma), contained several traits that led to the diversity of modern fish species. First, *Pikaia* had a distinct head that was differentiated from its tail. Second, it exhibited bilateral symmetry—its right side resembled its left. Third, *Pikaia* muscles were layered rather than bundled, as they are in vertebrates. Each layer, or myomere, was separated by light-colored connective tissue and exhibited a V-shaped or W-shaped pattern when seen from the fish's side. This unusual musculature allows for a side-to-side swimming motion. Last, and perhaps most importantly, the species had a nerve cord running the length of its body. Though this cord was unprotected by a bony spine, it is a trait shared by all the chordates that followed.

The next leap in fish evolution was seen in the jawless fish, so named because they lacked a lower jaw. Though this prevented them from being able to prey on large creatures, these bottom-feeding organisms had developed a bony head plate that offered a form of protection from the more dominant arthropods of the Ordovician period (485–444 Ma). The 6-inch-long species of *Astraspis* and *Arandaspis* resembled tadpoles and lacked fins, but their early skeletal plates apparently were effective against sea scorpions and other predators.

During the Silurian and Devonian periods, a class of chordates called placoderms had evolved. These organisms reached up to 30 feet in length and had upper and lower jaws, plus plated skin as a form of early armoring. Placoderms had disappeared by the end of the Devonian, but gave way to two classes we know today. One is Osteichthyes, which includes all fish species with bony skeletons. The other, Chondrichthyes, includes fishlike creatures that have cartilaginous frameworks rather than bony skeletons.

Within this second class is the subclass Elasmobranchii, which includes two superorders, Selachii (sharks) and Batoidea (rays and skates).

The cartilaginous endoskeleton of an extinct skate from the Green River Formation. Specimen number CCNHM-5552, housed in collections at the Mace Brown Museum of Natural History in Charleston, South Carolina.

Sharks, the larger of the two groups, contain eight extant orders: angel sharks, saw sharks, ground sharks, mackerel sharks, carpet sharks, bullhead sharks, cow sharks, and dogfish sharks. These orders are divided into 34 families, which contain numerous species.

Sharks' predatory skills are well known to most people, thanks to such classic media productions as the television series *Sea Hunt* (1958–1961), the novel *Jaws* by Peter Benchley, its movie adaptation directed by Steven Spielberg, and cable TV science docudramas such as those aired during the Discovery Channel's Shark Week.

The trait that sharks are best known for is their teeth. Remarkably, sharks have several rows of teeth, called files. A shark's tooth is used for a few weeks and then replaced by another from one of its files. Since countless shark teeth have been shed over millions of years, they are abundant in fossil form. Searching for them on coastal beaches can provide hours of enjoyment.

Though there are many species of sharks, the shapes of fossilized shark teeth come in three general forms: long, pointed, and rounded in cross section; broadly triangular and flat on the inner (lingual) surface; or multiple but inseparable tooth cusps (usually six) making up a single tooth. Examples of the first kind come from sand tiger sharks and lemon sharks. The second type may be from a variety of species, including nearly two-inch-long great white shark teeth or those in excess of five inches that come from the monstrous extinct predator *Carcharocles megalodon*. The teeth exhibiting multiple cusps are much smaller and come from sharks in the Hexanchiformes order, commonly known as cow sharks.

One other fairly common type of fossil tooth has a broad (though not triangular) shape, and its cusp is slanted sharply toward the back of the jaw and serrated along both edges as well as along the edge that transitions into the rear root. These fascinating teeth are from the tiger sharks.

Though shark spinal columns are made of cartilage, their vertebrae are often preserved in fossil form, and since they are distinctly different from other fish vertebrae, these fossils are readily recognizable. Other parts of sharks, such as denticles and rostral nodes, rarely survive long enough to go through fossilization, though many are pictured in scientific literature.

Stingrays, manta rays, and other members of the superorder Batoidea, are distinct from the sharks in that they lack dorsal and caudal fins, have greatly elongated pectoral fins, and have gill slits located on the ventral (underside) portion of the body rather than on the sides. Also, unlike sharks and most other fishes,

Cartilaginous endoskeleton of the extinct megalodon shark, *Carcharocles megalodon*, on display at the Calvert Marine Museum, Solomons, Maryland. This view may be disorienting, since the branchial, cranial, and rostral cartilage is rarely observed intact in fossil or modern specimens.

rays generally have mouths positioned ventrally instead of at the front. Whereas other fish propel themselves by moving their caudal (tail) fins from side to side, rays "fly" through the water by flapping their pectoral fins much like birds.

There are four orders of rays: Myliobatiformes, which includes stingrays, butterfly rays, and manta rays; Rajiformes, containing the skates and guitarfishes; Torpediniformes, which are electric rays; and Pristiformes, within which sawfish are listed. Each order has unique characteristics.

The stingray species of Myliobatiformes have one or two saw-toothed barbs, or spines, on the first third of their tails, and these barbs have two grooves containing venomous glands. The venom makes up a coat under a thin skin that covers the spine. When a would-be predator is stung by a stingray's spine, this skin folds back and venom is transferred to its enemies. Such wounds are rarely fatal to humans, but often cause an infection; in addition, the spine may break off, requiring minor surgery for removal. Some rays have small (2- to 3-millimeter-long) teeth, but these are rarely found as fossils. The fossilized flat grinding teeth of rays are those most commonly found on southeastern U.S. beaches.

Manta rays and most devil rays do not have spines, venom, or bony mouth

Depiction of a fossilized skate and *Knightia* fish from the Green River Formation, western United States.

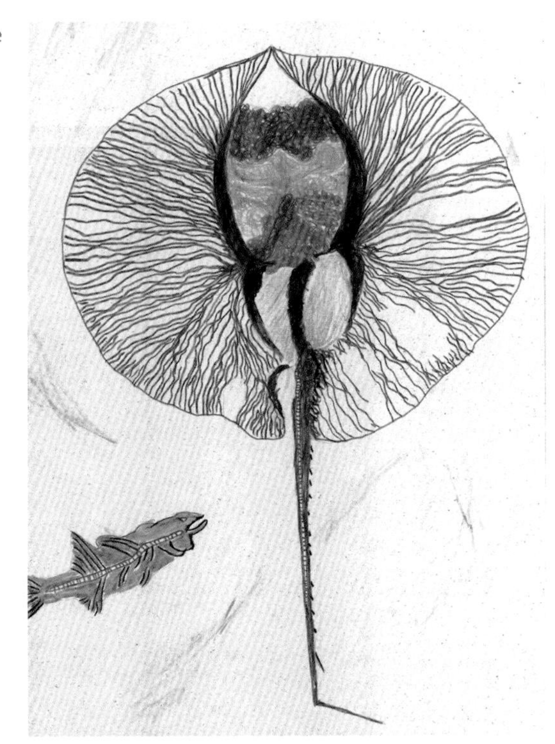

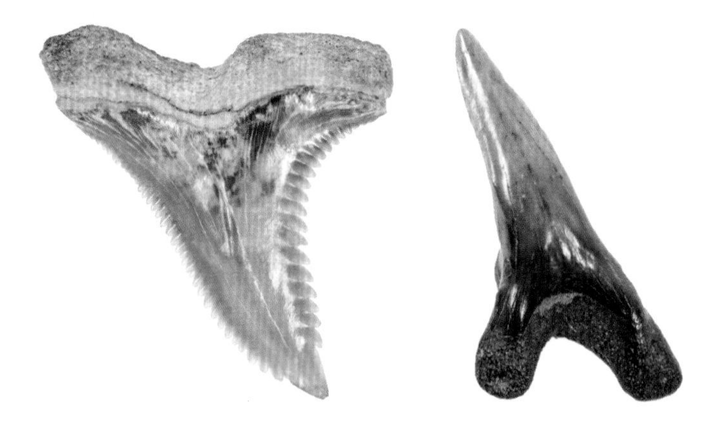

Upper and lower teeth of the extinct snaggletooth shark, *Hemipristis serra*.

plates. They lack bony plates for crushing shellfish, feeding instead on plankton taken in as they swim, so their mouths are located at the front of the body. Mantas have two cephalic fins, which they maneuver to funnel plankton into their mouths. Manta and devil rays both exhibit breaching behavior—they burst from the ocean surface and briefly glide through the air on their winglike fins. Some rays can reach heights of 6.5 feet above the water before diving back in headfirst or tail first, or spectacularly somersaulting before reentering.

Electric rays are similar to stingrays and manta rays, but can transfer an electric charge from their pectoral fins to predators and prey. They can produce enough voltage to stun a human.

Sawfish look like a cross between a shark and a ray. They have the typically elongated pectoral fins but also a caudal fin for propulsion. Their most interesting trait, however, is a long flat snout that can reach up to six feet in length. These structures are lined with toothlike projections along both edges and around the front of the snout. Sawfish use this structure to slash back and forth when swimming through a school of prey; they then pursue the injured victims. Their rostral "teeth" are not actually enamel or teeth, but are adaptations of dermal ossicles normally found within the skin.

The Chondrichthyes are an amazingly diverse collection of creatures. Their fossil record reveals what humans might call a "rags to riches" evolutionary story. But in the case of cartilaginous fishes, it is perhaps better termed a "lowly worm to monster shark" journey. Why not take your own journey? Head over to a beach and sink your teeth into some shark tooth fossils!

SPECIES HIGHLIGHT

Osteichthyes | Bony Fish

Fins, feet, scales, parrots—something sounds fishy!

At the end of the Devonian period (359 Ma), the prehistoric fish ancestors known as placoderms had become extinct. This left two superclasses: Chondrichthyes, made up of sharks and other cartilaginous fish (see page 107), and Osteichthyes, comprising fish with bony skeletons. These two superclasses contain about 30,000 species of fish today. Virtually all are in the bony fish group, which is broken down into two classes, the lobe-finned fish and the ray-finned fish.

Lobe-finned fish (class Sarcopterygii) have stiff fleshy fins that are controlled by muscles and bones where they join to the body. They have two dorsal fins as well as strong pectoral and pelvic fins, which help these bottom feeders work their way through plants and corals. Lobe-finned fish have both gills and lungs. Their bodies are covered with elasmoid scales. These scales are similar to the

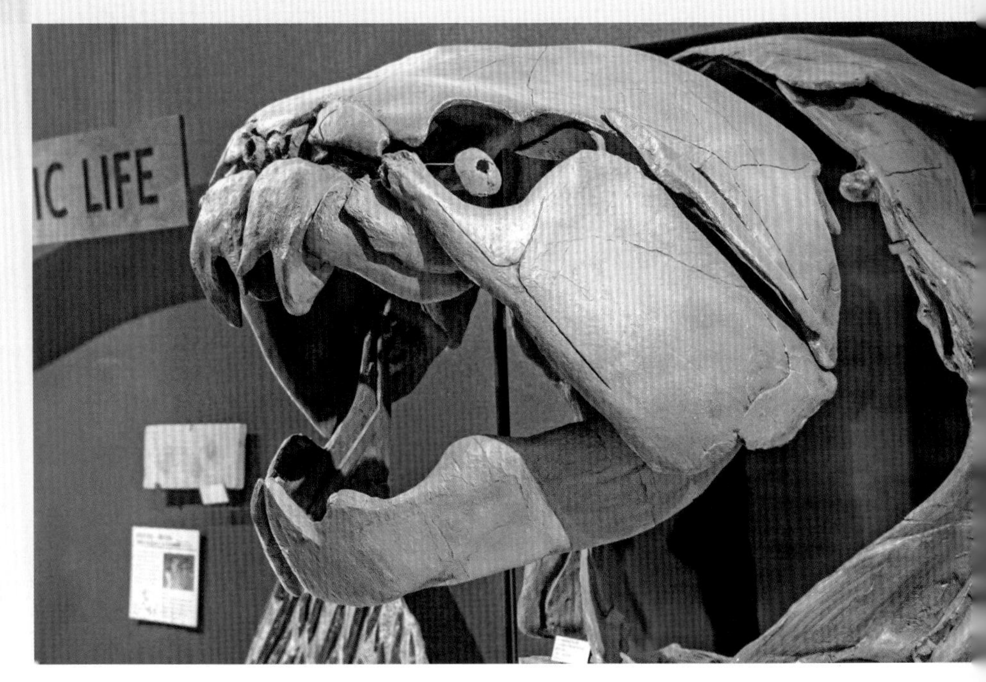

The fierce, bony maw of *Dunkleosteus*, an extinct arthrodire placoderm fish that lived during the Devonian, over 350 million years ago. Specimen on display at the Mace Brown Museum of Natural History in Charleston, South Carolina.

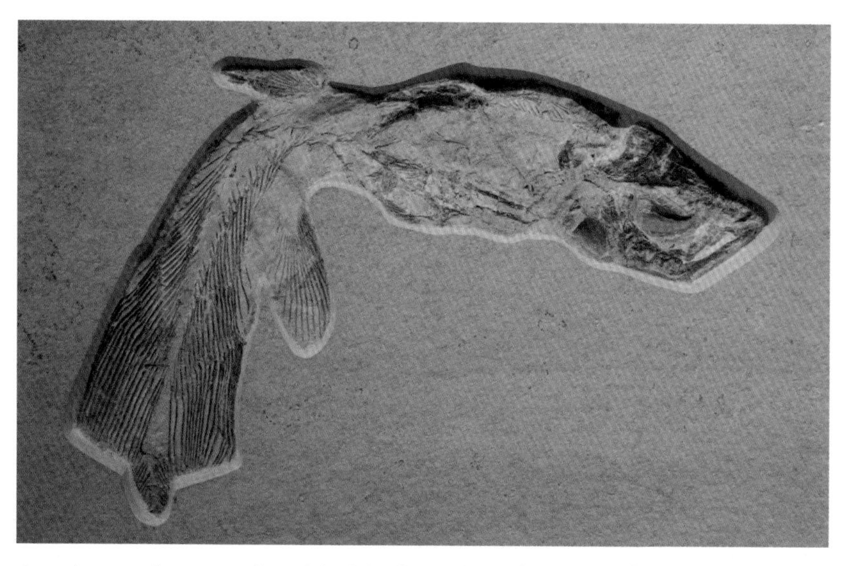

Coccoderma nudum, a member of the lobe-finned fishes (coelacanths), from the Late Jurassic Solnhofen Limestone of Germany, on display at the Mace Brown Museum of Natural History in Charleston, South Carolina.

prehistoric cosmoid scales of early lungfish, which had two thin layers of bone covered by a layer of cosmine (similar to dentine) and a surface of keratin. In most lobe-finned fish, the elasmoid scales lack the cosmine layer.

The only extant Sarcopterygian species are the lungfish and the deep-ocean-dwelling coelacanths. The latter were thought to have been extinct since the late Cretaceous period (roughly 100 Ma) until an individual was caught in the waters around South Africa in 1938. Coelacanths are still extremely rare; only two species exist today, and they are considered critically endangered.

Lobe-finned fish are the closest relatives to fishes called tetrapods, which include both extinct and living species. Their name is derived from Greek roots meaning "four feet." This group evolved from early aquatic species into semi-aquatic amphibians, reptiles, and, eventually, all other terrestrial animals. Tetrapod fins are homologous to the limbs of present-day land animals. Their pectoral fins contain bones that correspond to arms, wrists, and fingers (humeri, ulnae, radii, carpals, and phalanges), which are joined to the shoulder in all modern vertebrates. Similarly, their pelvic fins correspond to the legs, ankles, and toes (femur, fibula, tibia, tarsals, and phalanges), which are joined to the pelvis in modern vertebrates.

Ancestral tetrapods, with their specialized fins, were the first fish to develop

Stripped of scales and muscle, the skeletons of bony fish can appear almost alien-like. This skeleton of *Pachyrhizodus caninus* is no exception, displaying multiple interlocking bony elements. On display at the Mace Brown Museum of Natural History in Charleston, South Carolina.

a walking ability in their bottom-dwelling marine environment. Around 400 million years ago, more advanced tetrapods used this ability to crawl out of the sea onto land, giving rise to early amphibians and reptiles. They were followed, about 200 million years later, by the appearance of land mammals. Remarkably, the mammals of the order Cetacea (whales, dolphins, and porpoises) later returned to the sea. DNA analysis indicates that these mammals evolved from even-toed ungulates, sharing a common ancestor with the modern hippopotamus. Equally fascinating, a group of bear-like mammals also returned to the sea about 23 million years ago, forming the Pinnipedia suborder, made up of present-day seals, sea lions, and walruses.

Ray-finned fish (class Actinopterygii) form an extensive group that includes 99% of all fish species. These fish have fins that are basically skin membranes stretched over a series of spines, or rays. They have only one dorsal fin, rather than two, and while earlier species had caudal (tail) fins with lobes that were longer above than below, modern species increasingly developed symmetrical caudal lobes.

Ray-finned fish evolved swim bladders, which can expand or contract by inflating or deflating with gas, allowing these fish to swim at an amazing variety of depths while maintaining equilibrium as the water pressure changes. Because the swim bladders are positioned near the dorsal portion of the fish, above the center of gravity, they also help keep the fish in a stable, upright position.

Another feature of the Actinopterygii relates to their mouth structure. Ancestral fish species had relatively weak and narrow mouths that developed for grabbing at aquatic plants and slow-moving organisms. Later, bony fishes evolved mouthparts that, upon opening, could widen suddenly, creating suction to draw prey into their mouths. This is important for predatory fish that quickly lunge at their prey, since such thrusting action actually pushes objects away in the water, the same way a mosquito often escapes with the air that is compressed between a pair of hands clapping around it.

Lastly, most ray-finned fish developed leptoid scales, as opposed to the placoid scales found in cartilaginous sharks and rays or the elasmoid scales of lobe-finned species. Leptoid scales grow larger through time by adding concentric rings, a feature that makes it possible to determine the age of such fish. These scales overlap like shingles on a roof, which reduces drag when the fish are swimming. Leptoid scales come in two forms, cycloid and ctenoid.

Cycloid scales are smooth-textured and are found on primitive species such as salmon and carp. Ctenoid scales have a rougher texture and contain tiny comblike teeth on the trailing edge. They are found on more highly evolved ray-finned fishes such as bluegills, bass, and perch. Within the flatfish group, which includes flounder, sole, and halibut, ctenoid scales occur on the eye side of the fish, above, and cycloid scales are found on the blind side, below. In other

Skeletal X-ray of a modern sheepshead, *Archosargus probatocephalus*. Specimen courtesy of Edisto Beach State Park, South Carolina.

species within the flatfish group, the males are covered in ctenoid scales, while females have the cycloid type.

An additional type of scale is found on gar fish and sturgeons. Ganoid scales are composed of spongy bone covered with dentine and a layer of an enamel-like substance called ganoine. These diamond-shaped scales do not overlap, but fit together with one another in a peg-and-socket-like arrangement. On sturgeons, they form large armor-like plates on the sides and back of the fish.

Fish scales offer protective armor and have continued to evolve in many species. The increased flexibility and lighter weight of scales on modern fish have improved their speed and versatility, enhancing both predatory and escape abilities.

Fish fossils of many forms can be found on beaches today. Common fossils include gar fish scales, sea robin skulls, vertebrae, and dorsal spines. Beautiful sapphire-like surfaces can be seen on drum fish teeth, and porcupinefish and burrfish fossils have unique and intriguing shapes and patterns. Train your eyes for these and have fun collecting them!

BONES

TRAITS OF BONES

Bones, classified as the individual parts of vertebrate skeletons, form the framework for most vertebrate bodies and are, unsurprisingly, the fossils that wash up on beaches most often. In general, there are two types of bone: cancellous (spongy) and cortical (hard). Cancellous bone is generally found at the ends of limb bones, around joints, and inside the centrum of vertebrae. Cortical bone is the type of bone that we are most familiar with, covering all elements of the axial and appendicular skeletons. Bones are shaped according to their purpose—locomotion, digging, protection—which occasionally enables the identification of fragments; however, most bone fragments are either too broken or too worn to allow for a determination of their bodily placement or animal origin.

COMMON TERMS

Anterior, articulate (articulation, articular), astragalus, calcaneum, carpal, cranial, distal, dorsal, femur, fibula, humerus, lateral, medial, metacarpal, metatarsal, phalanx (phalanges), posterior, proximal, radius, tarsal, tibia, ulna, ungual, ventral

COMMONALITY

Bones are undoubtedly the most abundant fossil fragments on fossiliferous beaches, and second only to shark teeth on the entire coastal range.

INCLUSIONS AND EXCLUSIONS

Since the axial and appendicular skeletons have many bone components (domestic dogs, for example, average 319 bones), the following elements are included in this section: ear bones (petrosals, periotics, and tympanic bullae), cranial fragments, phalanges, all limb bones, carpals and tarsals, ankle bones, and some rib bones. Excluded are jaw fragments and vertebrae; they can be found in the Mouthparts and Vertebrae sections. Bony elements from some fish are also excluded, and these can be found in the Osteoderms and Miscellaneous sections.

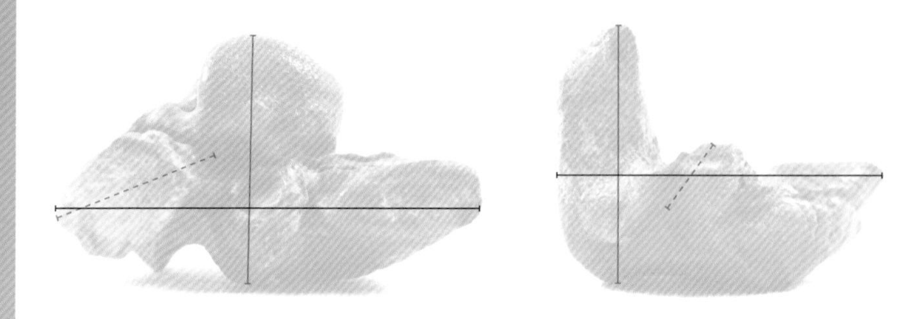

MEASUREMENTS

All bones have measurements displayed in a three-part system:

(longest side × next longest × shortest side)

The longest side is always given first, regardless of position. If this side is ambiguous in the photos, it is explained in the Item Description. The second-longest side is measured perpendicular to the longest side and in its thickest part; the shortest side is similarly perpendicular. (Dashed lines indicate the third dimension.)

SUPPLEMENTARY IMAGES AND TERMS

See page 461 for a graphic of the positional terms in relation to the body.

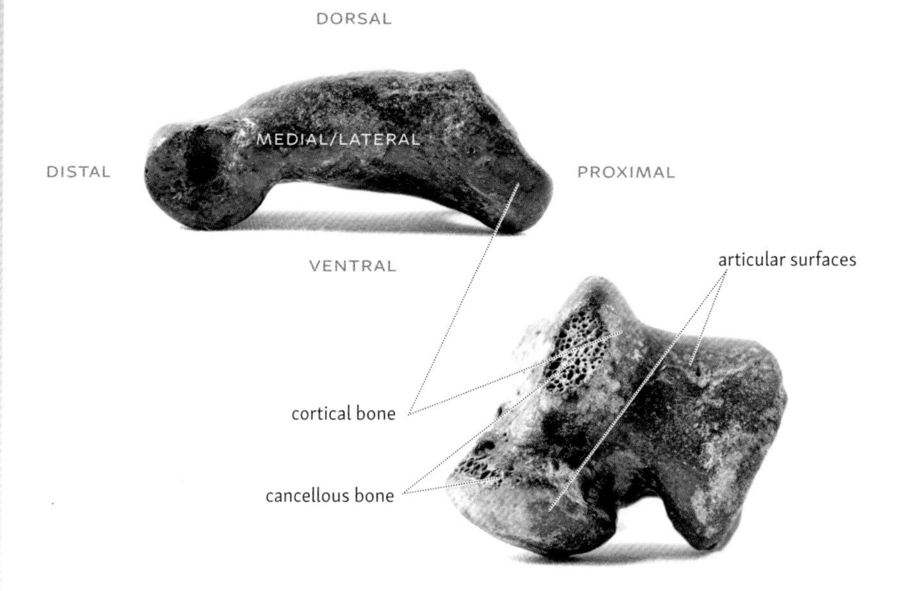

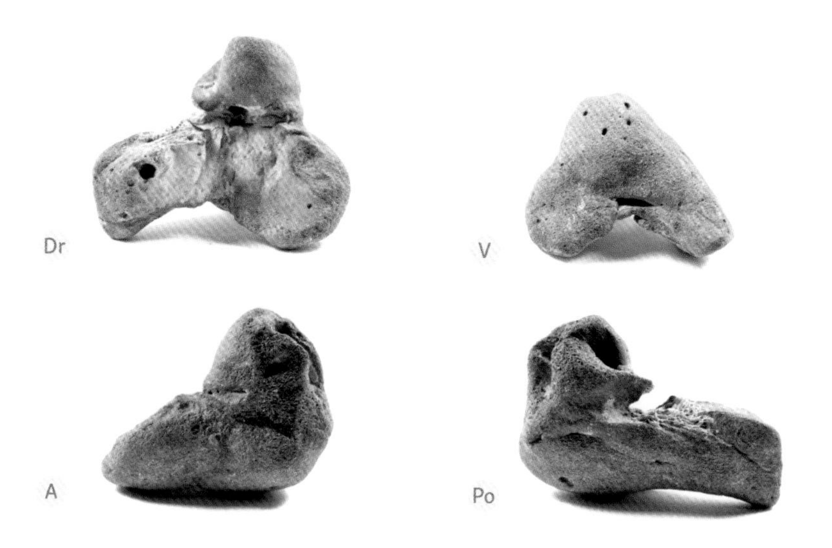

PERIOTIC Balaenidae

Ear bone from a mysticete, most likely a juvenile right whale (*Eubalaena* sp.) or bowhead whale (*Balaena* sp.), based on the size of the specimen. This periotic, unusually complete for a beach find, shows the characteristic water wear from tumbling in the surf. Note the intricate ear canals in the center (dorsal view), slightly obscured by tubeworm casings.

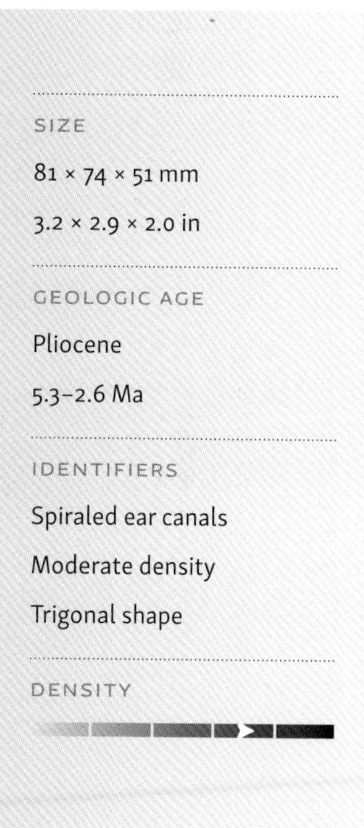

SIZE

81 × 74 × 51 mm

3.2 × 2.9 × 2.0 in

GEOLOGIC AGE

Pliocene

5.3–2.6 Ma

IDENTIFIERS

Spiraled ear canals

Moderate density

Trigonal shape

DENSITY

DID YOU KNOW? Whales were known to be a significant food source for *Carcharocles megalodon*, the largest shark to inhabit the prehistoric ocean. When *C. megalodon* became extinct, about 3.6 million years ago, the baleen whale population began to rise.

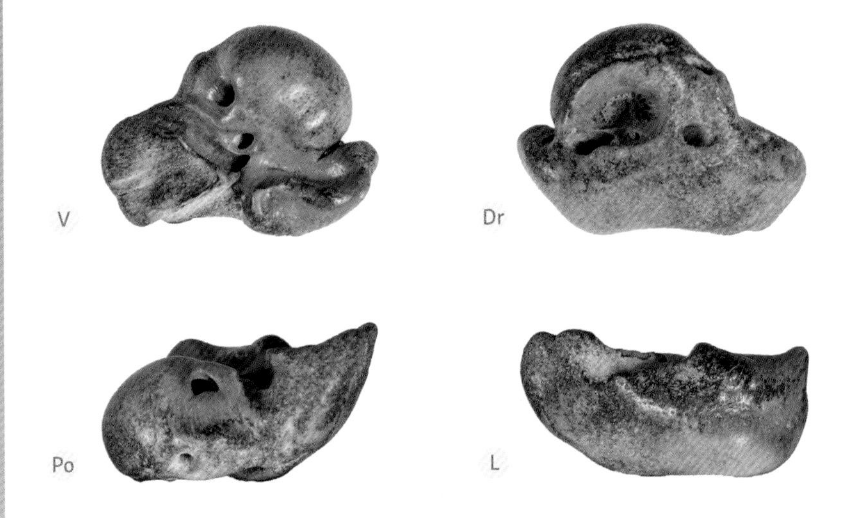

PERIOTIC cf. *Astadelphis*

SIZE

30 × 23 × 12 mm

1.2 × 0.9 × 0.5 in

GEOLOGIC AGE

Pliocene

5.3–2.6 Ma

IDENTIFIERS

Bulbous shape

Spiraled ear canals

Faceted processes

DENSITY

Ear bone from a dolphin in the *Astadelphis* genus. Along with the tympanic bullae, periotics are dense bones of the ear that fossilize exceptionally well. Note the spiraling canals on both the dorsal and ventral sides. These canals (known as the cochlea) aid in hearing the high-frequency sounds produced by echolocation. Opposite the canals, one or more large holes are present on the ventral side. A wide facet is present on the posterior process, indicating the point of attachment for the other ear bone, the tympanic bulla.

DID YOU KNOW? What do wrinkles and being smart have in common? The more wrinkles or folds there are in your brain, the smarter you might be. Human brains have lots of folds, but dolphin brains have even more, and dolphins have been around for millions of years longer than *Homo sapiens*. Could this mean that dolphins are smarter than people?

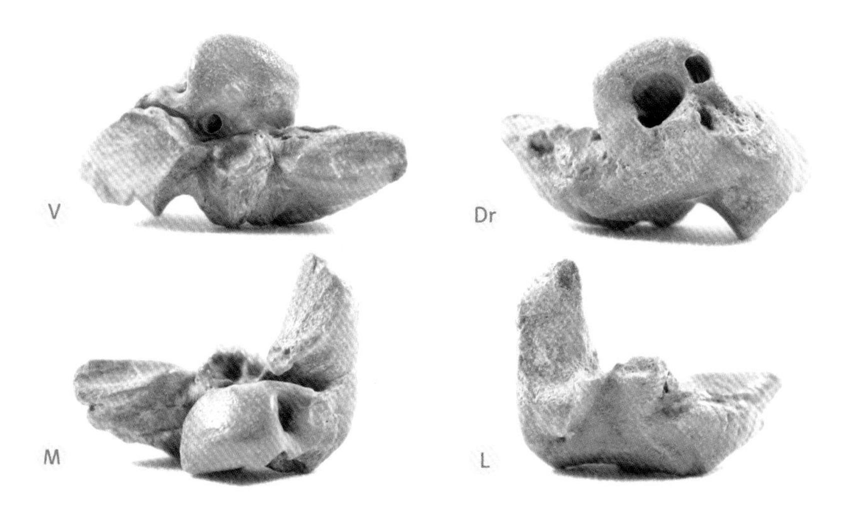

PERIOTIC Pomatodelphinae

Ear bone from an indeterminate platanistid dolphin found in the Calvert Cliffs exposures of Maryland. Periotics are relatively dense bones that fossilize well, making them common finds in marine deposits. Similar to modern dolphin periotics, this specimen contains intricate ear canals on its ventral and dorsal sides; fewer canals are present on the dorsal side. Note the larger hole (internal acoustic meatus). This particular odontocete had angular attachments on the anterior and posterior processes (seen in the medial view).

SIZE

39 × 28 × 23 mm

1.5 × 1.1 × 0.9 in

GEOLOGIC AGE

Miocene

23–5.3 Ma

IDENTIFIERS

Bulbous shape

Spiraling ear canals

Faceted processes

DENSITY

DID YOU KNOW? The bullae are attached in different ways for different species of animals. In mammals, each bulla is affixed to the base of the cranium. In some mammals, especially rodents, the bullae are enlarged, allowing for more acute hearing in wide-open spaces. In whales, the bulla is attached outside the cranium, positioning that aids in hearing separate sounds in a watery environment.

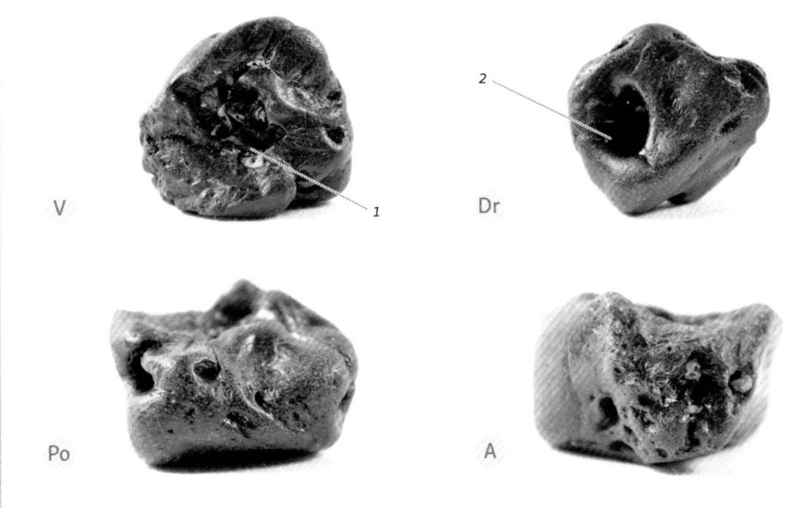

SIZE

35 × 32 × 19 mm

1.4 × 1.2 × 0.7 in

GEOLOGIC AGE

Pleistocene

2.6 Ma–11 ka

IDENTIFIERS

Spiraling ear canals

Large, single canal

Angled form

DENSITY

PETROSAL Mammalia

Ear bone from an undetermined species of Pleistocene land mammal. Isolated and severely worn, the above specimen retains enough features to be identified as a mammalian petrosal. Compare it to cetacean periotics, pages 121–123. Note the intricate, spiraling canals of the external auditory meatus and the large facial canal on the other side of the specimen, indicated by 1 and 2, respectively.

DID YOU KNOW? Humans and reptiles are related through their ears. Paleontologists analyzed the bones of prehistoric lizards and documented the connection between reptilian and mammalian jaw and ear bones. As baby lizards develop within their eggs, two bones in their skulls grow into jaw and ear bones. As baby mammals develop from conception to birth, these same two bones develop into the hammer, anvil, and stirrup ear bones.

AUDITORY BULLA Balaenopteridae

Ear bone from an indeterminate baleen whale species, possibly one from *Balaenoptera*. The Balaenopteridae family includes the large baleen whales, identified by collectors from isolated bullae, periotics, and, occasionally, mandible fragments found on beaches. As in dolphins, bullae in whales are hollowed out on the dorsal side and bear a thickened portion on the ventral side. Bullae are generally oval in shape and relatively dense. Note the large size.

SIZE

90 × 46 × 41 mm

3.5 × 1.8 × 1.6 in

GEOLOGIC AGE

Pleistocene

2.6 Ma–11 ka

IDENTIFIERS

Oval shape

Hollowed-out interior

One thick side

DENSITY

DID YOU KNOW? Cetaceans and land mammals have similar hearing mechanisms. But each has specific adaptations. For land mammals, hearing is based on airborne sound waves hitting the eardrum, which transmits its vibrations via three small bones to the cochlea, where they are converted to neural brain impulses. For whales, waterborne sound is captured by acoustic fat and transferred to the hollow bulla, which sends its vibrations through a pathway similar to that found in land mammals.

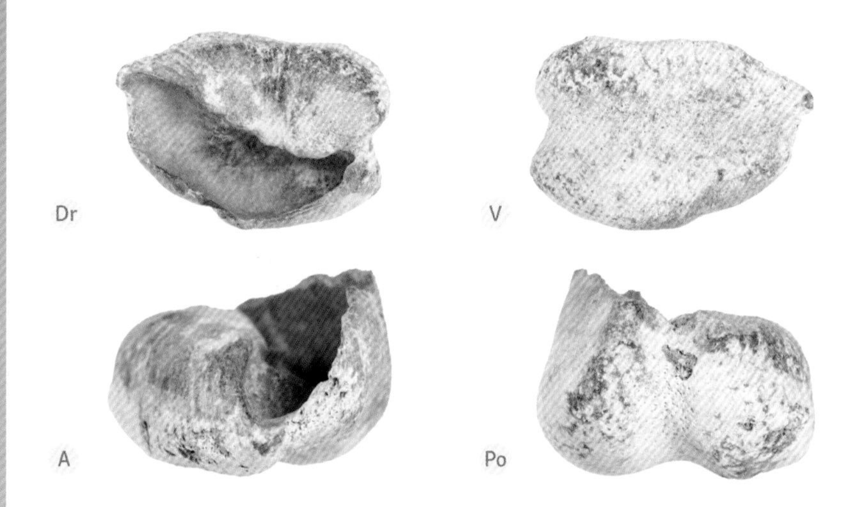

SIZE

43 × 27 × 20 mm

1.7 × 1.1 × 0.8 in

GEOLOGIC AGE

Oligocene

33.9–23 Ma

IDENTIFIERS

Lobed posterior end

Pointed anterior end

Hollowed-out interior

DENSITY

AUDITORY BULLA Platanistidae

Ear bone from an extinct species of dolphin in the Platanistidae family. Note the spine on the anterior end that hooks up slightly and projects off the main body of the bulla; also note the lobed posterior margin and shallow depression running the length of the ventral side. Ear bones having this appearance are readily identifiable as coming from a member of Platanistidae.

DID YOU KNOW? The auditory bulla in most mammals is a bone that encloses the middle- and inner-ear structures and keeps them safe from damage. Generally rounded and hollow, the bulla includes the tympanic bone, which works in concert with the other bulla structures to transfer sound waves for interpretation by the brain.

Po

A

OCCIPITAL CONDYLE Proboscidea

Left occipital condyle from a Pleistocene proboscidean species. The occipital condyles are the points of articulation between the back of the skull and the first vertebra in the spine. While not all bone fragments are readily identifiable, this specimen was included to demonstrate how some are recognizable. Using an online resource of three-dimensionally scanned skeletons, we compared the point of articulation with that of a mastodon, measuring between several prominent points in common. Note the large sinuses inside the skull, which lighten the brain casing.

SIZE

178 × 173 × 55 mm

6.9 × 6.7 × 2.1 in

GEOLOGIC AGE

Pleistocene

2.6 Ma–11 ka

IDENTIFIERS

Interior sinuses

Main articulation

Large size

DENSITY

DID YOU KNOW? Clues to prehistoric animals' diets can be obtained from carbon isotopes in their fossilized skeletons. Most plants are C3 plants, which begin photosynthesis by using a 3-carbon compound. C4 plants, which begin the process with a 4-carbon molecule, can tolerate arid conditions. Carbon isotopes in fossils show that mammoths living in Florida ate mainly C4 plants—warm-temperature grasses and drought-resistant plants.

SIZE

65 × 45 × 23 mm

2.5 × 1.8 × 0.9 in

GEOLOGIC AGE

Pleistocene

2.6 Ma–11 ka

IDENTIFIERS

Dorsal surface pitted

Grooved ventral side

Layered cortical wall

DENSITY

CRANIAL ELEMENT

Alligator mississippiensis

Skull element from the extant American alligator, *Alligator mississippiensis*. Though badly water-worn, this cranial bone is readily identifiable by the wide pitting visible in the dorsal view as coming from the American alligator. As seen in their osteoderms, alligator skull elements have a pitted surface dorsally, giving the bone a broken appearance. Another identifiable trait of reptilian bone includes a layered cortical wall (seen ventrally above). The lateral view shows the elongated sutures where this bone was connected to another distinct element within the skull.

DID YOU KNOW? Alligators are "conservationists" at heart. They dig large holes or wallows in swampy habitats such as the Everglades. During droughts and dry seasons, the deep pits collect and retain water throughout wetland landscapes. During such times, many aquatic life-forms seek refuge in these wallows, so the alligators' actions help maintain a sensitive ecosystem.

M

L

SKULL FRAGMENT Chordata

Skull (cranial) fragment from an undetermined Pleistocene vertebrate. Cranial bones, especially those of larger animals, are pitted with large pockets and structural buttresses to lessen the weight of the skull (see proboscidean fragment, page 127). Certain mammoth skull fragments can be positively identified based on a unique diamond-shaped pattern formed by the buttresses within the bone.

SIZE

63 × 42 × 17 mm

2.5 × 1.6 × 0.7 in

GEOLOGIC AGE

Pleistocene

2.6 Ma–11 ka

IDENTIFIERS

Pitted interior

Large hollow spaces

Generally thin walls

DENSITY

DID YOU KNOW? Ear ye! Ear ye! Paleontologists can tell a mammal from a reptile by the presence or absence of three small ear bones, or ossicles, which are found inside mammalian skulls. A *Liaoconodon hui* fossil dating from the Cretaceous period is believed to be a transitional stage from reptiles to mammals. It contains three ossicles that are separate from the jaw structure, a characteristic found in most mammals today.

SIZE

123 × 21 × 17 mm

4.8 × 0.8 × 0.7 in

GEOLOGIC AGE

Pliocene

5.3–2.6 Ma

IDENTIFIERS

Linear grooves

Elongated pores

Conical tapering

DENSITY

ROSTRUM Istiophoridae

Rostrum from an undetermined species of Pliocene billfish. To the untrained eye, these fragments may appear to be indistinguishable bits of bone, but the long grooves running the length of the bone (indicated) identify these as billfish rostral fragments (page 463). The bone texture is similarly coarse, with elongated pores and trabeculae where marrow and nutrients moved. The fragments are generally conical and uniformly tapered. Lower rostra are short and triangular in some species.

DID YOU KNOW? Modern billfish (swordfish, sailfish, and marlin) have much longer upper rostra (jaws) than lower rostra. These swordlike bills are used to slash and stab prey. Fossils reveal that the rostra of some extinct billfish were equal in length. How did they manage these extensions? With both bills stuck in their prey, how would they have withdrawn from, much less eaten, their prey?

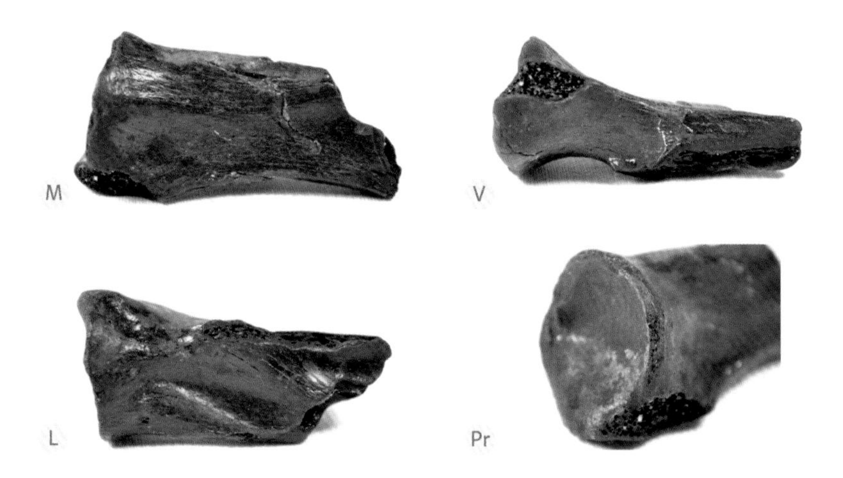

SCAPULA Ungulata

Proximal end of a shoulder blade from a small Pleistocene ungulate. The ungulate group comprises horses, camels, deer, pigs (peccaries), tapirs, and other relatives. Fragments of scapulae are identifiable by the concave articular surface seen above at right. On intact specimens, the distal end fans out into a broad flat bone. Between the proximal and distal ends are angled ridges of bone where muscles attached.

SIZE

59 × 24 × 16 mm

2.3 × 0.9 × 0.6 in

GEOLOGIC AGE

Pleistocene

2.6 Ma–11 ka

IDENTIFIERS

Concave proximal articular surface

Fan-shaped distal end

Muscle attachments

DENSITY

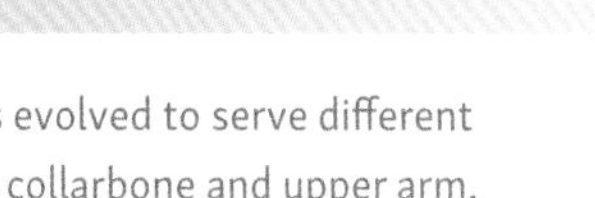

DID YOU KNOW? The scapulae of Pleistocene tetrapods evolved to serve different functions. In humans, the shoulder blades connect to the collarbone and upper arm. In frogs, the scapula is paired with the coracoid and muscles to allow for the repetitive action of jumping and landing. In turtles, the scapula and coracoid connect to the carapace. In birds, scapulas form two ends of the coracoid in supporting wing movement.

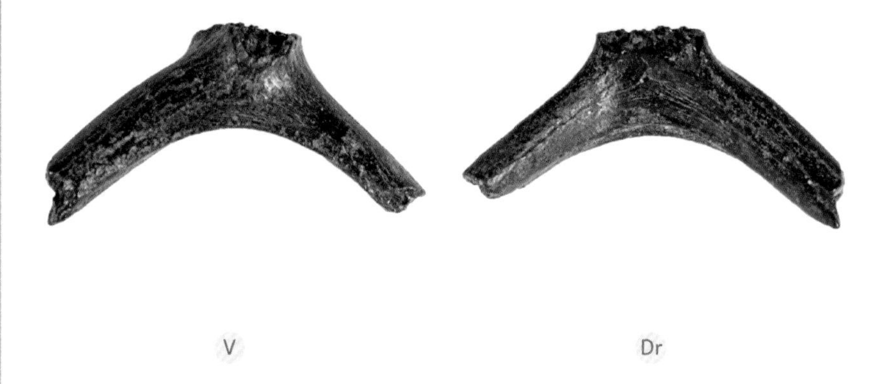

V Dr

SCAPULA Testudines

SIZE

18 × 4 × 3 mm

0.7 × 0.2 × 0.1 in

GEOLOGIC AGE

Pleistocene

2.6 Ma–11 ka

IDENTIFIERS

V shape

Thin shafts

Circular socket

DENSITY

Scapula (shoulder blade) from an undetermined Pleistocene turtle species. This V-shaped bone articulated with the coracoid, which is missing at the top of both views. A complete specimen would show the circular socket of articulation between the junction of these two bones. In turtles, two other elements of the shoulder are modified into components of the shell, the clavicle and the interclavicle, which become the epiplastron and entoplastron, respectively.

DID YOU KNOW? Clavicles, commonly known as collarbones, connect the scapulas (shoulder blade) to the sternum (breastbone). In birds, the clavicles are fused to form the furcular, or wishbone. This configuration gives these bones the springlike flexibility necessary for flight. "Clavicle" means "little key" in Latin, reflecting the resemblance of human collarbones to skeleton keys.

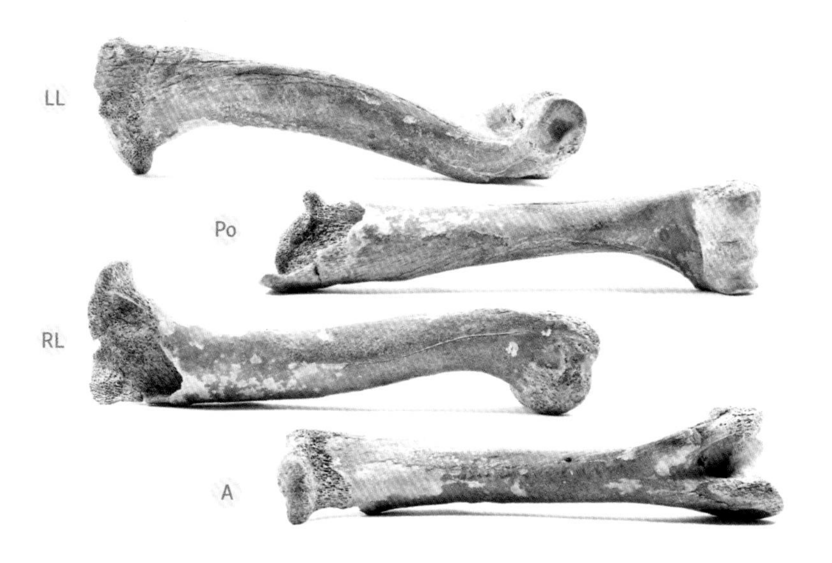

HUMERUS

Odocoileus virginianus

Upper-arm bone from the extant white-tailed deer, *Odocoileus virginianus*. The proximal articular surface has been greatly worn away, but the diagnostic distal end (at right) is intact. The humerus articulates with the radius and the ulna in the front legs, which work in concert with the hind limbs and ankle bones to allow the deer to specialize in running at great speeds for long distances.

SIZE

186 × 40 × 46 mm

7.3 × 1.6 × 1.8 in

GEOLOGIC AGE

Pleistocene

2.6 Ma–11 ka

IDENTIFIERS

Grooved distal end

Elongated form

Curved shaft

DENSITY

DID YOU KNOW? The phrase "can't see the forest for the trees" can be modified to apply to white-tailed deer. Deer are masters of camouflage, having tawny brown coloration that closely matches the forest background. When deer stand perfectly still, predators often "can't see the deer for the forest." Their top predators, deer-hunting humans, employ their own camouflage—specially colored clothing—in an effort to prevent deer from seeing *them*.

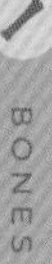

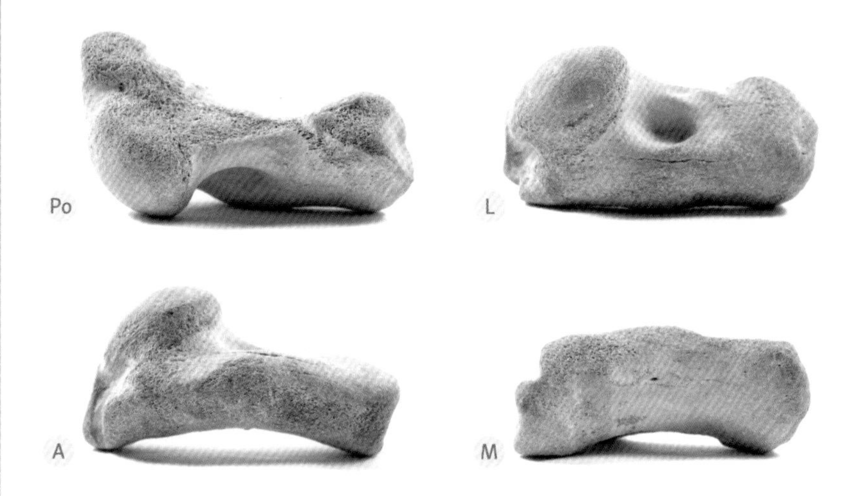

SIZE

113 × 60 × 43 mm

4.4 × 2.3 × 1.7 in

GEOLOGIC AGE

Miocene

23–5.3 Ma

IDENTIFIERS

Proximal head

Compact form

Arched structure

DENSITY

HUMERUS Eurhinodelphinidae

Humerus from a eurhinodelphinid dolphin found in the Calvert Cliffs exposures of Maryland. In contrast with the more elongated humerus of a seal (*Phoca* sp.), the humeri of dolphins and other odontocetes are compact. The proximal head (seen at left in the anterior and lateral views) is well developed for articulation with the scapula. For distal and proximal views, see page 465.

DID YOU KNOW? Consider how similar your arms are to a dolphin's fore flippers. Dolphins' fore fins, or pectoral fins, are shortened versions of three bones in our arms—the humerus, ulna, and radius—firmly connected by cartilage and muscle tissue to form the powerful flippers. The dolphin's flipper uses all these bones in swimming, steering, and touching.

M

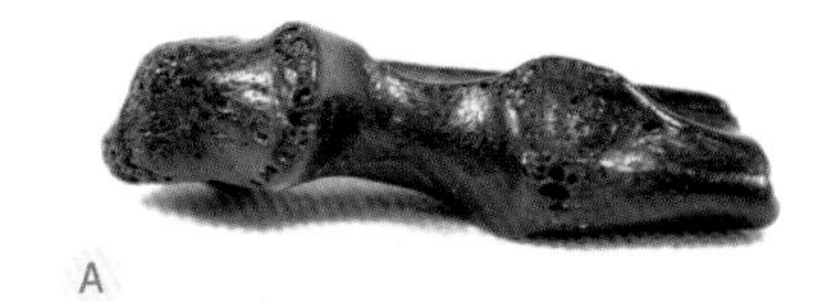

A

L

Po

ULNA *Procyon lotor*

Proximal half of an ulna from the extant raccoon, *Procyon lotor*. Modern specimens and size comparisons enabled the identification of this fragment as belonging to a raccoon. This specimen shows the classic identifier of an ulna—the trochlear notch. Ulnae are more commonly known as elbow bones, since that is where they join with the radius to articulate with the humerus. The trochlear notch faces anteriorly.

SIZE

29 × 5 × 10 mm

1.1 × 0.2 × 0.4 in

GEOLOGIC AGE

Pleistocene

2.6 Ma–11 ka

IDENTIFIERS

Articular surfaces

Size comparison

Trochlear notch

DENSITY

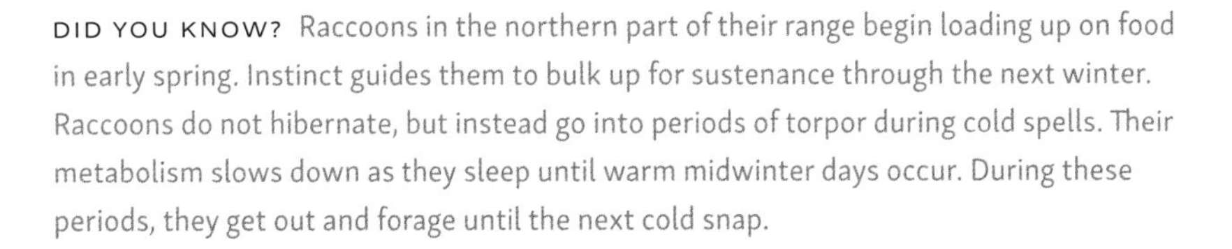

DID YOU KNOW? Raccoons in the northern part of their range begin loading up on food in early spring. Instinct guides them to bulk up for sustenance through the next winter. Raccoons do not hibernate, but instead go into periods of torpor during cold spells. Their metabolism slows down as they sleep until warm midwinter days occur. During these periods, they get out and forage until the next cold snap.

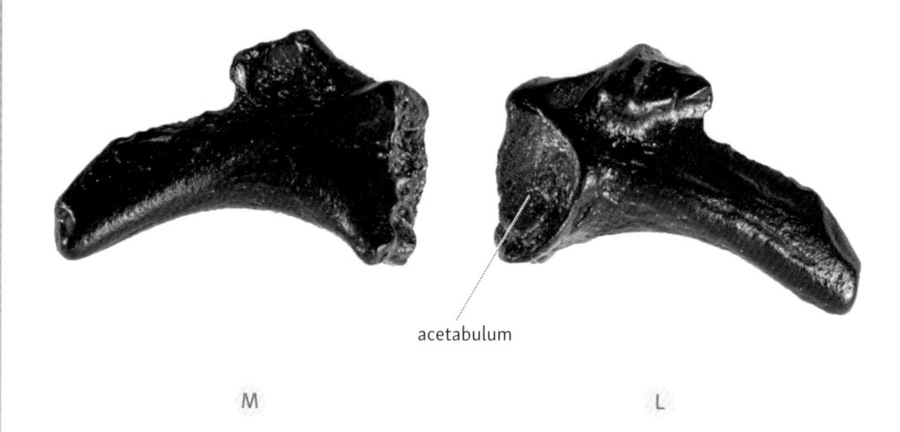

SIZE

15 × 7 × 4 mm

0.6 × 0.3 × 0.2 in

GEOLOGIC AGE

Pleistocene

2.6 Ma–11 ka

IDENTIFIERS

Acetabulum

Small size

Anterior shaft

DENSITY

ILIUM Anura

Hip bone element from an undetermined Pleistocene anuran, that is, frog or toad, species. It is rare to find fossils from amphibians and other small creatures washed up on beaches, because of their fragility, size, and the distance they travel from the original deposit. Note the circular acetabulum, or "hip bone" socket (indicated). Of the anuran pelvic girdle fossils, the ilium is one of the most commonly found elements, since the ischium and the pubis are extremely reduced and would require screening to collect. The three elements are not fused during the animal's lifetime, so finding them together would require an in situ discovery.

DID YOU KNOW? Huey Lewis and the News sang, "It's hip to be square," and for dinosaur hunters, hips are big news. Three hip bones—the ilium, ischium, and pubis—form a diagnostic tool for paleontologists trying to determine whether a dinosaur belongs to the group of lizard-like creatures or to the birdlike creatures. Saurischian (lizard-hipped) dinosaurs have a downward-pointing pubis that is forward of the ischium. Ornithischian (bird-hipped) dinosaurs have a rearward-pointing pubis parallel to the ischium.

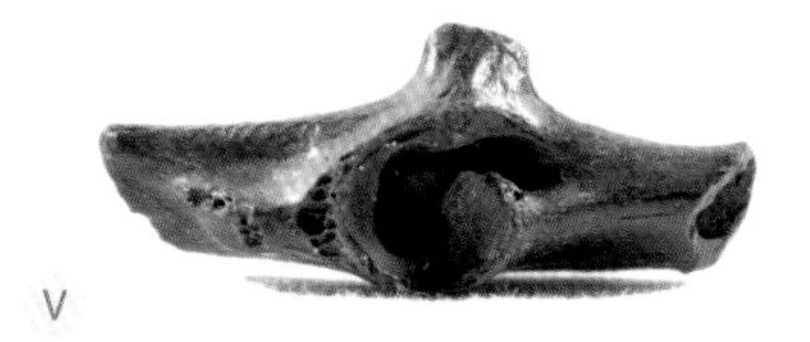

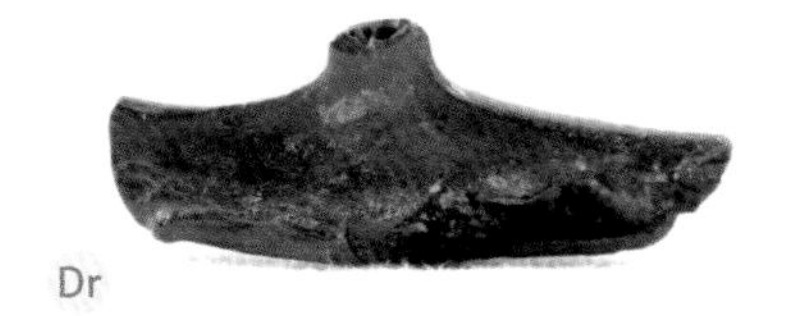

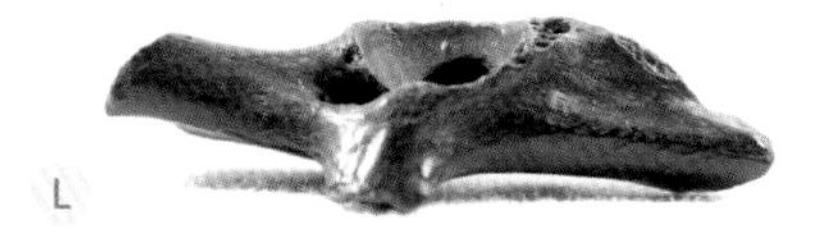

PELVIC ELEMENT Aves

Isolated pelvis fragment from an undetermined Pleistocene bird species. In the middle of the specimen is the acetabulum, the articulation where the femoral head sat, allowing movement of the leg. As with other bird bones, the above element is hollow, lacking the cancellous bone found inside the bones of most terrestrial vertebrates.

SIZE

28 × 10 × 7 mm

1.1 × 0.4 × 0.3 in

GEOLOGIC AGE

Pleistocene

2.6 Ma–11 ka

IDENTIFIERS

Hollow bone

Acetabulum

Light in weight

DENSITY

DID YOU KNOW? Reptiles, amphibians, birds, and mammals have ilia. In humans, the ilium is the largest of the three bones making up the pelvis. Four areas on the ilium are points of attachment for muscles and ligaments. The ilium is also important because it is easily reached, which allows surgeons to obtain bone-grafting material for reconstructing other bones or to extract its bone marrow for use in the treatment of leukemia.

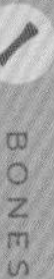

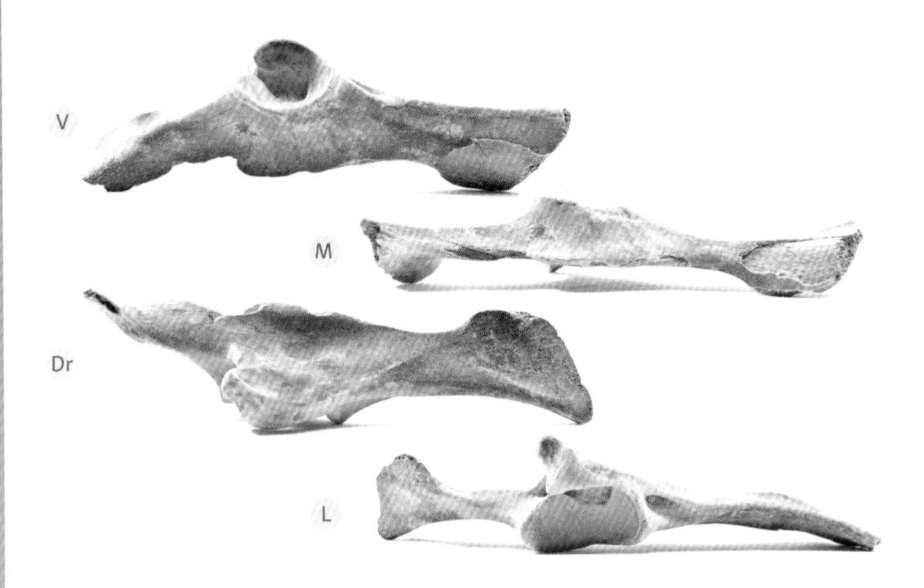

SIZE

190 × 54 × 36 mm

7.4 × 2.1 × 1.4 in

GEOLOGIC AGE

Pleistocene

2.6 Ma–11 ka

IDENTIFIERS

Femoral socket

Sutured proximal edge

Thin form overall

DENSITY

PELVIS

Odocoileus virginianus

Pelvic fragment from the extant white-tailed deer, *Odocoileus virginianus*. Fragments from the pelvis of an animal are best identified when the acetabulum, the articular surface for the femoral head, is intact. For the above specimen, the femoral articulation is best visible in the center of the ventral and lateral views. Unlike the scapula, which has a similar socket for articulation on its end, the pelvis bears a similar articulation in the middle.

DID YOU KNOW? Meriwether Lewis and William Clark relied on their hunters to supply them with nutritious deer meat during their expedition (1804–1806). The explorers made deer jerky, which preserved the meat through drying and smoking; that food helped ensure the explorers' survival. Without it, the expedition might not have weathered a difficult Oregon winter.

METATARSAL

Megalonyx jeffersonii

Isolated metatarsal from the extinct giant ground sloth *Megalonyx jeffersonii*. Sloths are members of the xenarthran group, which translates to "strange joints," referring to extra processes on their vertebrae. Such strange joints are also apparent in the metatarsals, which articulate with the proximal phalanges (page 161). Note the many points of articulation and the angled distal articulation (at right in the ventral and right lateral views).

SIZE

88 × 44 × 53 mm

3.4 × 1.7 × 2.1 in

GEOLOGIC AGE

Pleistocene

2.6 Ma–11 ka

IDENTIFIERS

Skewed distal end

Multiple articulations

Irregular form

DENSITY

DID YOU KNOW? Modern slow-moving sloths seem an unlikely group to have evolved from over 100 different species through time. During the Pleistocene epoch, 19 species were present; 6 survive today. The earliest record of a sloth comes from fossils found in the Antarctica-Patagonia region that date back to the Eocene epoch. Time may wait for no man, but it has been very patient with today's lethargic creatures!

SIZE

233 × 26 × 26 mm

9.1 × 1.0 × 1.0 in

GEOLOGIC AGE

Pleistocene

2.6 Ma–11 ka

IDENTIFIERS

Long and slender form

Distal taper

Phalanges articulation

DENSITY

METATARSAL

Odocoileus virginianus

Rear leg bone from the extant white-tailed deer, *Odocoileus virginianus*. Similar in appearance to the front leg (metacarpal), the metatarsal is approximately one inch longer. Note the double areas of articulation on the distal end (at right), where the proximal phalanges articulate (page 158).

DID YOU KNOW? Modern white-tailed deer mate in the fall. Males choose several females, while the females are more selective. Females produce 1–3 fawns every year. Yearling bucks are ready to be on their own and mate with females. A yearling doe, however, may stay with its mother and start an extended family unit.

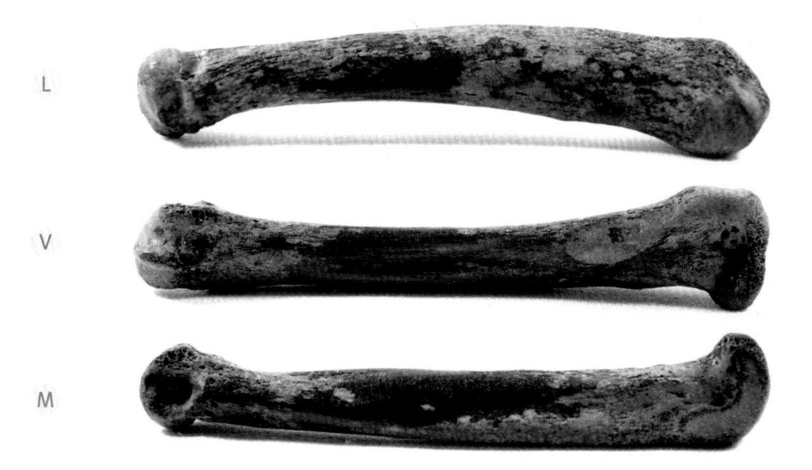

METAPODIAL *Canis dirus*

Metapodial from the extinct dire wolf, *Canis dirus*. Because of the isolated nature of this limb element, it is difficult to determine whether it is a metacarpal or metatarsal, that is, from the front or hind limb. Thus, the term "metapodial" acknowledges its location as a bone between the ankle or wrist and the phalanges. *C. dirus* metapodials are slimmer than those of *Smilodon* and other large cats.

SIZE

85 × 10 × 8 mm

3.3 × 0.4 × 0.3 in

GEOLOGIC AGE

Pleistocene

2.6 Ma–11 ka

IDENTIFIERS

Slender form

Articular surfaces

Arched ventral side

DENSITY

DID YOU KNOW? The ranges of the extinct dire wolf and the extant gray wolf overlapped for about 100,000 years. The gray wolf is smaller than the dire wolf, and it is believed that the two fed on different food sources. The lightweight gray wolf preyed on fast-moving elk (and still do today), while the larger and stronger dire wolf hunted peccaries, deer, and weak young animals such as baby mammoths and mastodons.

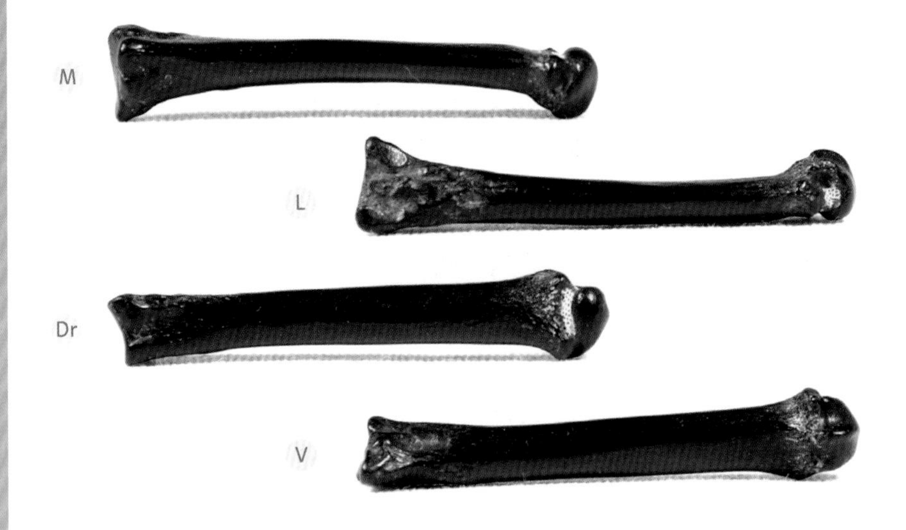

SIZE

41 × 5 × 7 mm

1.6 × 0.2 × 0.3 in

GEOLOGIC AGE

Pleistocene

2.6 Ma–11 ka

IDENTIFIERS

Flat proximal end

Grooved distal end

Long slender form

DENSITY

METAPODIAL *Procyon lotor*

Metapodial from the extant species of raccoon, *Procyon lotor*. Either a hand bone (metacarpal) or foot bone (metatarsal), the above metapodial is long and slender, characteristic of digit bones from raccoons. Note the flattened proximal side at left; note also the grooved distal end for articulation with the proximal phalanx.

DID YOU KNOW? Raccoons are considered nocturnal, but not all of these "masked bandits" do their marauding after dark. Southeastern coastal raccoons time much of their activity to the tidal cycle. They are often found in salt marshes long after daylight, preying on tasty mussels along the receding water's edge. Mussel shells close slowly, so crafty coons "stick their foot in the door" while they have the chance!

METAPODIAL *Equus* sp.

Fragment of the second or fourth metapodial from the extant genus of horses, *Equus*. The second and fourth metapodials in modern horses are significantly reduced—vestigial remnants of *Equus*'s three-toed origins. The main cannon bone is the retained and enlarged third metapodial, flanked on each side by a splint bone such as the one shown above. Places for muscle attachment are visible at the proximal ends of these specimens.

SIZE

98 × 22 × 11 mm

3.8 × 0.9 × 0.4 in

GEOLOGIC AGE

Pleistocene

2.6 Ma–11 ka

IDENTIFIERS

Wide proximal end

Thin shaft

Tendon attachments

DENSITY

DID YOU KNOW? And the award for Best Performance by Supporting Bone in the Leg goes to . . . the fibula! Although quietly playing backup to the larger tibia, the fibula nonetheless takes on numerous roles. Its proximal and distal joints permit the tibia to have a greater range of movement. The hamstring's attachment to the fibula facilitates movement of the knee, and eight flexor and extender muscles connect the lower fibula to the heel, arch, and toes. Congratulations, fibula! (Wild applause.)

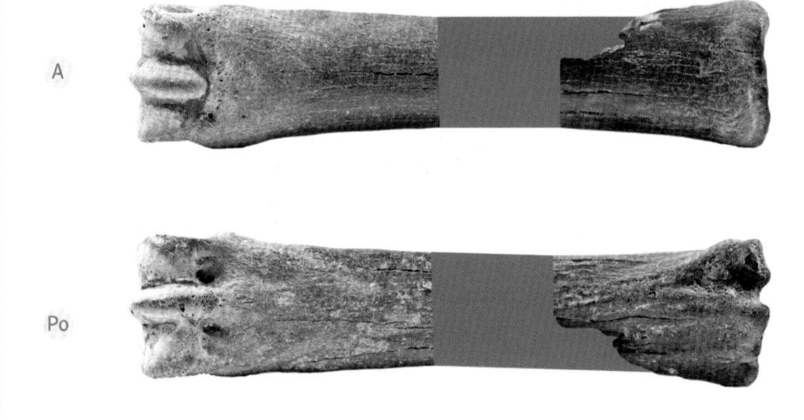

SIZE

290 × 53 × 40 mm

11.3 × 2.1 × 1.6 in

GEOLOGIC AGE

Pleistocene

2.6 Ma–11 ka

IDENTIFIERS

Lobed distal end

Flat proximal end

Posterior grooves

DENSITY

CANNON BONE *Equus* sp.

The cannon, or metatarsal, bone from the extant genus of horses, *Equus*. The above specimens are two composite ends of a metatarsal, with the total length at left provided by an intact specimen. The anterior side of a metatarsal is smooth, while the back is grooved where the small metatarsal bone is located. For a view of the proximal end, see page 469.

DID YOU KNOW? The Lascaux Caves of southern France are home to the earliest-known artistic depictions of horses, bulls, and deer, painted approximately 17,000 years ago. Many horses can be seen walking along a line of light and dark limestone, which the paleo artists used to symbolize the ground. In these detailed paintings, the horses closely resemble the modern species known as Przewalski's horse, the only wild horse living today, which is limited to a small population in Mongolia.

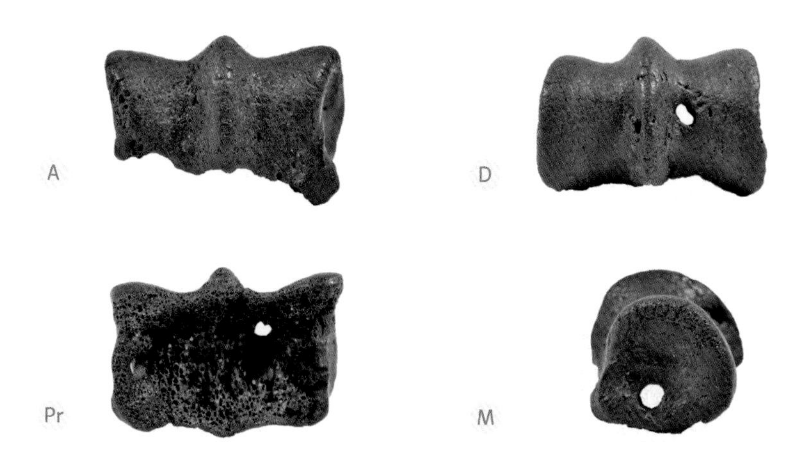

METATARSAL *Equus* sp.

Fragment of the distal end of a metatarsal belonging to the extant genus of horses, *Equus*. Compare this fragment to the metatarsal on page 144. Note how the proximal view shows the cancellous bone where this fragment joined to the rest of the bone. The dimensions of the intact lateral width aided identification to the genus *Equus*.

SIZE

50 × 32 × 30 mm

2.0 × 1.2 × 1.2 in

GEOLOGIC AGE

Pleistocene

2.6 Ma–11 ka

IDENTIFIERS

Lobed distal end

Cancellous bone

Lateral width

DENSITY

DID YOU KNOW? The horse's cannon bone extends from the knee to the fetlock. It is among several leg bones that reflect the human hand. Being the third metacarpal bone in the horse's leg, it correlates with the third digit of a hand. A wide circumference of the cannon bone is desirable in horses that are bred for carrying weight.

SIZE

25 × 20 × 10 mm

1.0 × 0.8 × 0.4 in

GEOLOGIC AGE

Pleistocene

2.6 Ma–11 ka

IDENTIFIERS

Grooved articulation

Circular form

Pulley-like shape

DENSITY

JOINTS

Odocoileus virginianus

Fragments from the distal end of a Pleistocene vertebrate's metapodial, most likely a white-tailed deer, *Odocoileus virginianus*. The joints pictured would have articulated with the proximal phalanges of the animal, as seen by the grooves that run the length of each specimen. Pictured at right is the complete distal end of a white-tailed deer metatarsal for comparison.

DID YOU KNOW? From 1913 to 1915 fossils were excavated from the La Brea Tar Pits, with permission from the Hancock family, who owned the land. L. E. Wyman led the workers, and each was paid $3.50 a day, a fair wage for the time. The Hancocks originally granted the Natural History Museum of Los Angeles County two years of exclusive excavation rights. That arrangement was later made permanent, and remains in effect today.

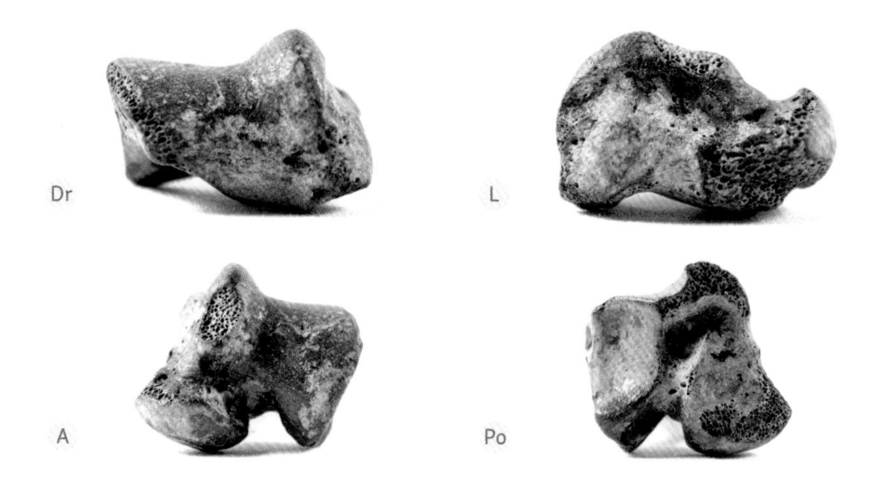

ASTRAGALUS

Castoroides dilophidus

Ankle bone from the extinct Pleistocene giant beaver, *Castoroides dilophidus*. Named for its teeth with two enamel lophs (dilophid), *C. dilophidus* is a southeastern species of giant beaver. It is distinct from *C. ohioensis*, though it was previously described as the subspecies *Castoroides ohioensis dilophidus*. The *C. dilophidus* astragalus is more broadly grooved than those from capybaras (*Neochoerus*) and armadillos (*Holmesina*).

SIZE

31 × 33 × 22 mm

1.2 × 1.3 × 0.9 in

GEOLOGIC AGE

Pleistocene

2.6 Ma–11 ka

IDENTIFIERS

Shallow articulation

Broad dorsal end

Square form

DENSITY

DID YOU KNOW? Roll the dice! The astragalus is a bone in the ankle joint of animals, including humans. Astragali have been used by many cultures worldwide in games of chance. From the Babylonians to the Native Americans of the American Southwest, bags of astragali were carried for quick pickup games. The Flemish artist Pieter Bruegel the Elder painted young women playing "knucklebones" with 16 astragali in his masterpiece *Children's Games* (1560).

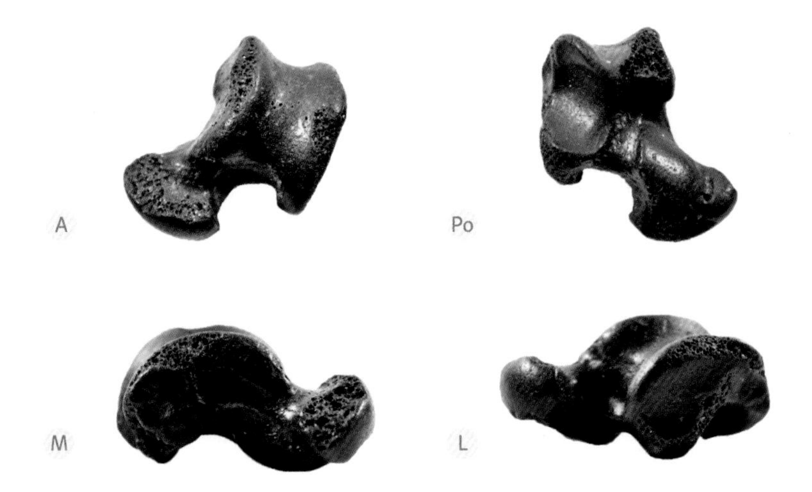

SIZE

23 × 18 × 13 mm

0.9 × 0.7 × 0.5 in

GEOLOGIC AGE

Pleistocene

2.6 Ma–11 ka

IDENTIFIERS

Medial articulation

Single-pulley design

Mammalian form

DENSITY

ASTRAGALUS *Procyon lotor*

Left ankle bone from the extant raccoon, *Procyon lotor*. Following the form of most mammalian astragali, the raccoon astragalus has a single pulley with an offset medial articulation. As with other modern species, unfossilized remains are useful for aiding the identification of fossil elements. Compare the articular surfaces above to the neighboring calcaneum (page 154), where the two bones articulated.

DID YOU KNOW? Raccoons are opportunistic freeloaders when choosing a residence. They like trees and logs with hollowed-out cavities, but won't say no to a warm, cozy attic. Inside, females give birth to cubs in early summer; after a couple of months, mom moves them to the ground to begin exploring. Nothing is more endearing than a family of young coon faces peering curiously out of vertically stacked tree holes.

ASTRAGALUS *Bison antiquus*

Ankle bone from the late Pleistocene bison, *Bison antiquus*. As with deer, camels, and other artiodactyls (even-toed ungulates), bison have the diagnostic double-pulley design to their astragali. The anterior side has a central depression, and the posterior side is broad and smooth in order to articulate with the calcaneum. Distally, the astragalus articulates with the cubonavicular (page 462), which has accommodating grooves for easy inline joint movement.

SIZE

79 × 55 × 43 mm

3.1 × 2.1 × 1.7 in

GEOLOGIC AGE

Pleistocene

2.6 Ma–11 ka

IDENTIFIERS

Double-pulley design

Proximal grooves

Curved posterior side

DENSITY

DID YOU KNOW? Pleistocene humans created art with what was available to them in their environment. Early artists at Tuc d'Audoubert Cave in the French Pyrenees cut a meter-wide slab from a clay deposit and sculpted, in high relief, a bison bull and cow. The sculpture is estimated at 14,000 years old. The artists had to walk and crawl nearly a kilometer underground to reach this site.

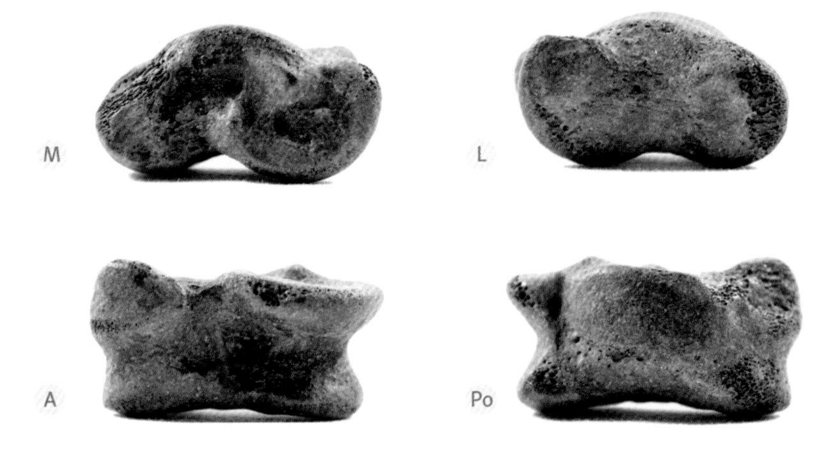

SIZE

39 × 23 × 22 mm

1.5 × 0.9 × 0.9 in

GEOLOGIC AGE

Pleistocene

2.6 Ma–11 ka

IDENTIFIERS

Double-pulley design

Oblique ridges

Elongated shape

DENSITY

ASTRAGALUS

Mylohyus nasutus

Left ankle bone from the extinct Pleistocene peccary *Mylohyus nasutus*. While the artiodactyl double-pulley design is present, the pulley ridges are oblique to the length of the bone and directed off center (seen in anterior view). These astragali are easily confused with those from deer species; accurate identification can require having two comparative specimens from each species (page 463).

DID YOU KNOW? Flat-headed peccaries lived on the coastal plains of Florida and as far north as New York. These short, stout peccaries were at home in scrubby brushland and open areas of wind-blown sand. These peccaries lived in herds, and large numbers of them have been found where they huddled for wind protection against towering dunes. Periodically, the upper dunes would collapse, burying and preserving peccaries found as fossils 20,000 years later.

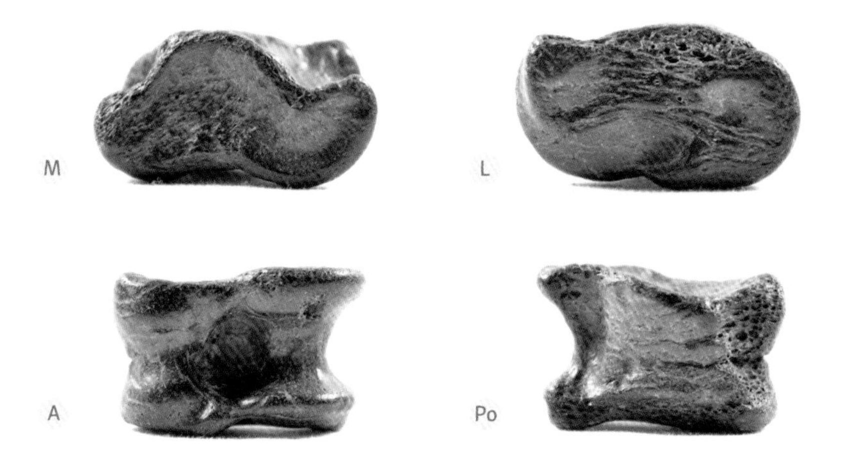

ASTRAGALUS

Odocoileus virginianus

Left ankle bone from a white-tailed deer, *Odocoileus virginianus*. Slightly smaller than astragali from peccary species, deer astragali show the artiodactyl double-pulley design, with the pulley ridges aligned with the length of the bone. Compare the inline shape of this astragalus to that of a peccary, whose more oblique pulley ridges can be seen in an anterior view (page 463).

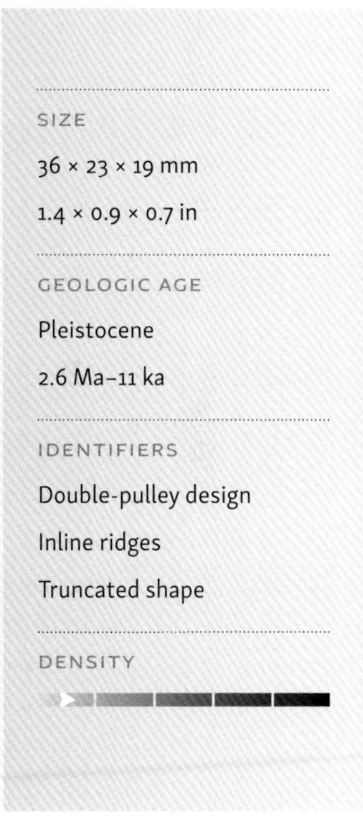

SIZE

36 × 23 × 19 mm

1.4 × 0.9 × 0.7 in

GEOLOGIC AGE

Pleistocene

2.6 Ma–11 ka

IDENTIFIERS

Double-pulley design

Inline ridges

Truncated shape

DENSITY

DID YOU KNOW? A doe takes special care of her newborn fawn, just as any mother would do. She finds a special hiding place for the fawn deep in the woods and comes to feed it two to three times a day. She also takes care of its daily hygiene. After each visit, she relocates the fawn to another secluded spot in order to minimize the chance of predators picking up its scent.

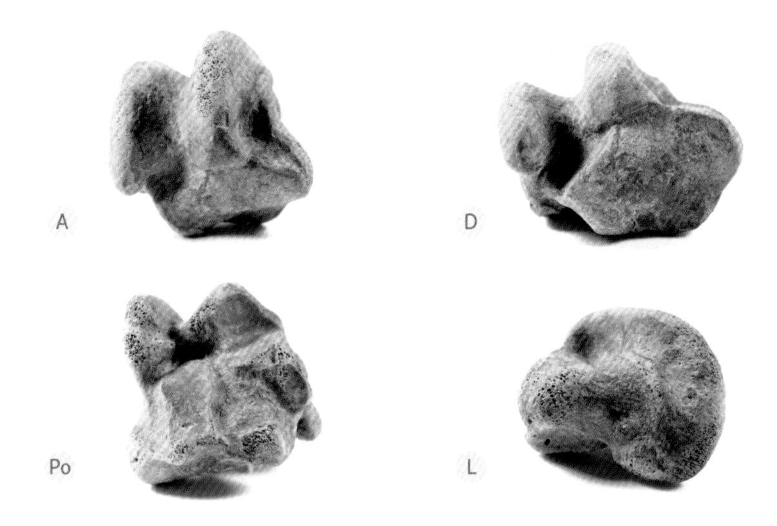

SIZE

60 × 60 × 48 mm

2.3 × 2.3 × 1.9 in

GEOLOGIC AGE

Pleistocene

2.6 Ma–11 ka

IDENTIFIERS

Single-pulley shape

Concave distal end

Articular surfaces

DENSITY

ASTRAGALUS *Equus* sp.

Left ankle bone from the extant genus of horses, *Equus*. Astragali of horses (and other perissodactyls, or odd-toed ungulates) are relatively easy to distinguish from those of artiodactyls because they lack the double-pulley design of artiodactyl astragali. The distal end is slightly concave from articulation with the navicular—one of three tarsals located beneath the astragalus.

DID YOU KNOW? *Equus* ankles and wrists are higher off the ground than the hooves. Imagine if your wrists and ankles were higher up on your arms and legs. The single digit, or hoof, which is a remnant from ancestral species, bears the horse's entire weight as it gallops. In humans, this would be like putting all your weight on the middle finger and toe of each hand and foot while running at top speed.

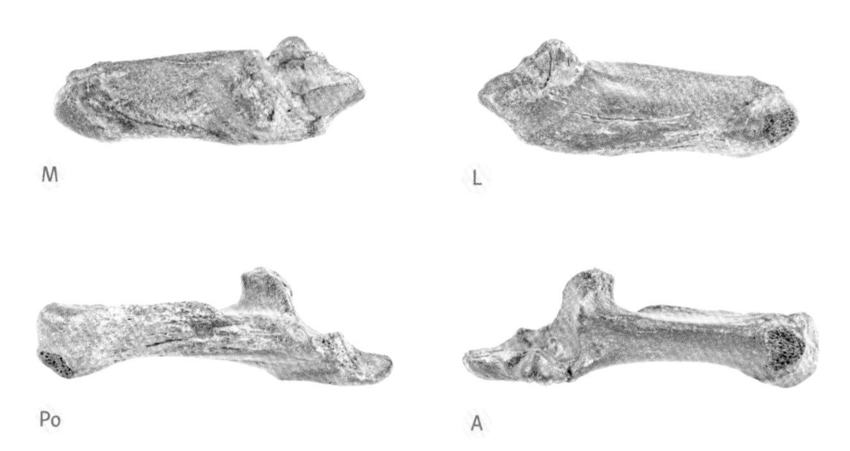

CALCANEUM

Odocoileus virginianus

Heel bone from the extant white-tailed deer, *Odocoileus virginianus*. The calcaneum is oddly shaped from its articulation with the astragalus. See page 151 for the astragalus. Deer have specialized inline movement of their legs, which is aided by the double-pulley ankle bones and their articulation with the calcaneum, tibia, and cubonavicular. Such articulations allow for great flexibility of the ankles. Peccary calcanea are similar, but shorter in length, around 70 millimeters long.

SIZE

85 × 28 × 24 mm

3.3 × 1.1 × 0.9 in

GEOLOGIC AGE

Pleistocene

2.6 Ma–11 ka

IDENTIFIERS

Oddly shaped form

Single articulation

Thin posterior end

DENSITY

DID YOU KNOW? "Heel and toe" is a common polka dance call. When many humans walk, their heel hits the ground slightly before the toes of the same foot do. That motion would be physically impossible for deer. Their heels are about two feet off the ground, and they walk not on their feet, but on their toes. All ungulates have evolved lengthened foot bones for speed, and as that happened, the heel, or calcaneum, migrated higher up the leg, along with the ankle. Needless to say, our modern deer haven't quite yet mastered the polka!

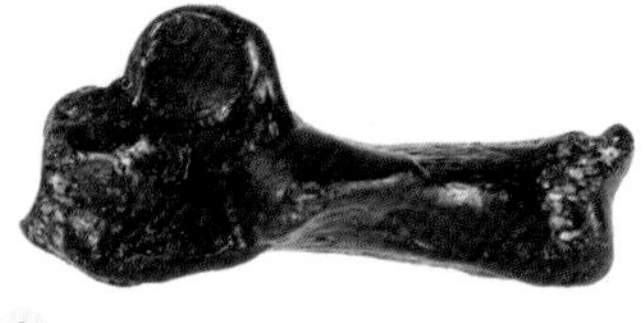

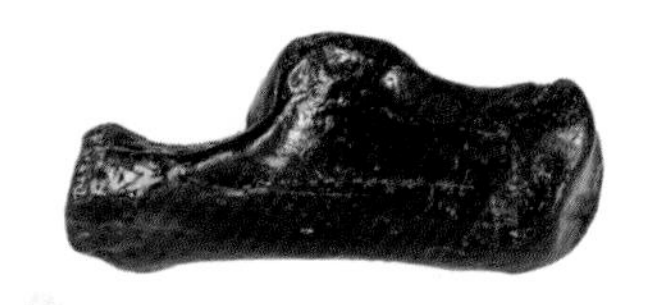

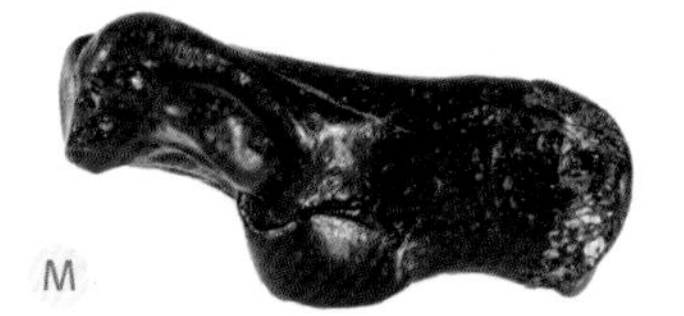

SIZE

30 × 12 × 13 mm

1.2 × 0.5 × 0.5 in

GEOLOGIC AGE

Pleistocene

2.6 Ma–11 ka

IDENTIFIERS

Oddly shaped form

Circular articulation

Thin posterior end

DENSITY

CALCANEUM *Procyon lotor*

Right heel bone from the extant raccoon, *Procyon lotor*. The calcaneum is oddly shaped from its articulation with the astragalus. See page 148 for the astragalus. Note the circular point of articulation (at left in the anterior view). The calcaneum is an important bone, sometimes bearing an animal's weight and sometimes providing the strength for jumping and running.

DID YOU KNOW? Do raccoons wet their food because they lack salivary glands? This long-standing myth probably arose from the raccoon's habit of foraging near water and kneading its food—and also from Linnaeus identifying raccoons as *Ursus lotor*, meaning "washer bear." (Raccoons aren't bears, and *Ursus* was later corrected to *Procyon*.) The raccoon's dexterous, sensitive palms and fingers enable it to feel food for sharp bones and foreign bits before eating.

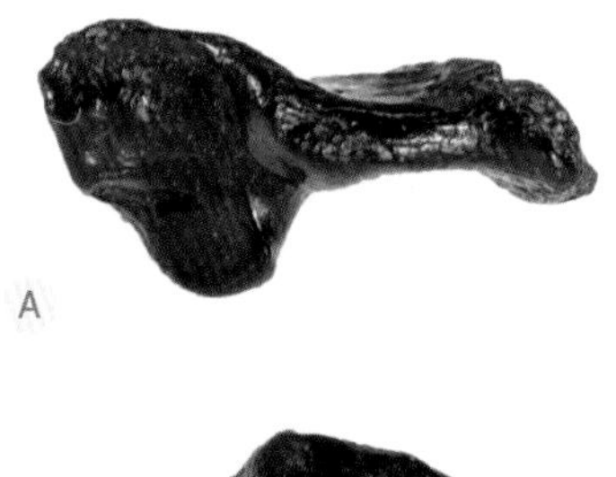
A

Po

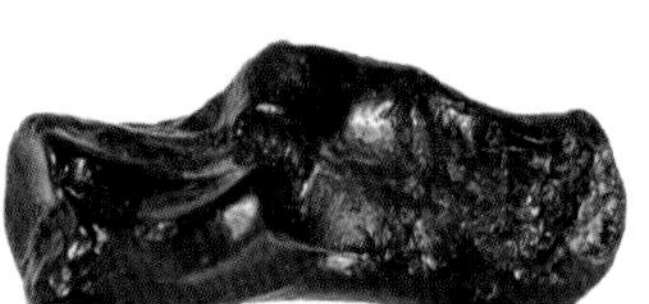
M

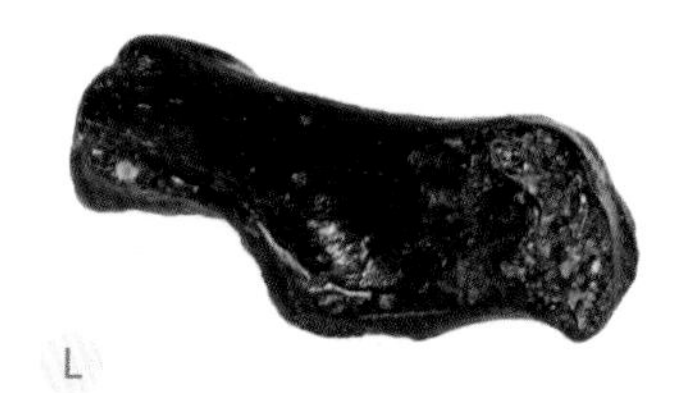
L

CALCANEUM *Mustela vison*

Left heel bone from the extant brown mink, *Mustela vison*. One of the tarsals, calcanea are oddly shaped from their articulation with the astragalus. Note the oval-to-circular point of articulation (at right in anterior view). Of all mustelids, *M. vison* has the most gracile bone structure.

SIZE

13 × 7 × 6 mm

0.5 × 0.3 × 0.2 in

GEOLOGIC AGE

Pleistocene

2.6 Ma–11 ka

IDENTIFIERS

Oddly shaped form

Circular articulation

Thin posterior end

DENSITY

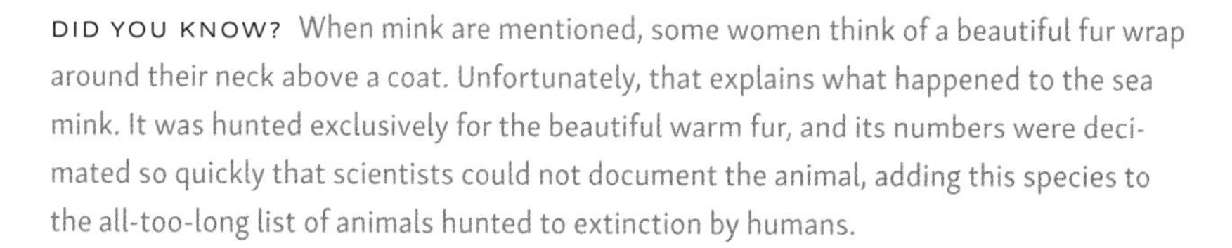

DID YOU KNOW? When mink are mentioned, some women think of a beautiful fur wrap around their neck above a coat. Unfortunately, that explains what happened to the sea mink. It was hunted exclusively for the beautiful warm fur, and its numbers were decimated so quickly that scientists could not document the animal, adding this species to the all-too-long list of animals hunted to extinction by humans.

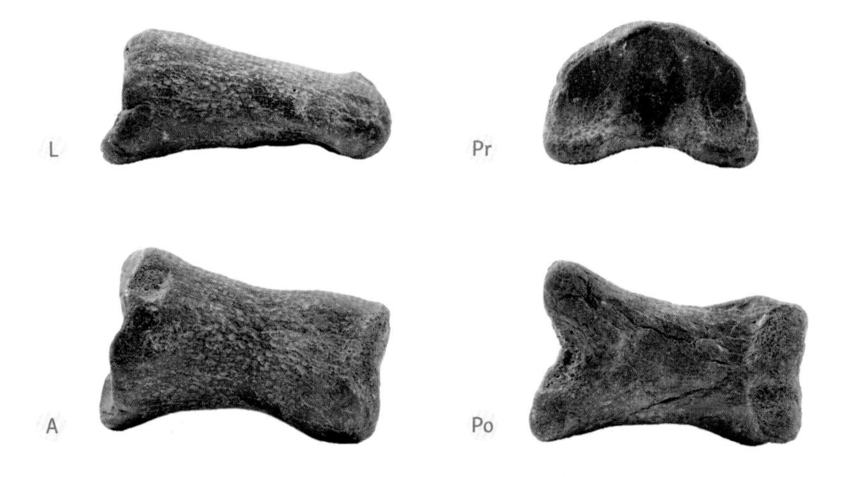

SIZE

90 × 56 × 35 mm

3.5 × 2.2 × 1.4 in

GEOLOGIC AGE

Pleistocene

2.6 Ma–11 ka

IDENTIFIERS

Grooved proximal end

Narrowed middle

Rounded distal end

DENSITY

PHALANX *Equus* sp.

Proximal (first) toe bone from the extant genus of horses, *Equus*. Morphologically, this digit is the third phalanx, but during the evolution of horses, the middle digits became enlarged to their current size, and the first, second, fourth, and fifth digits were reduced and eventually lost. The proximal articular surface is grooved in the middle, and the distal end is lobed in order to articulate with the medial phalanx (page 163).

DID YOU KNOW? How many hands high was the *Mesohippus* horse? A hand is 4 inches, and *Mesohippus* was about 2 feet tall (measured from ground to shoulder), so this early horse was 6 hands high. That is a tiny horse! (He could have used a helping hand.)

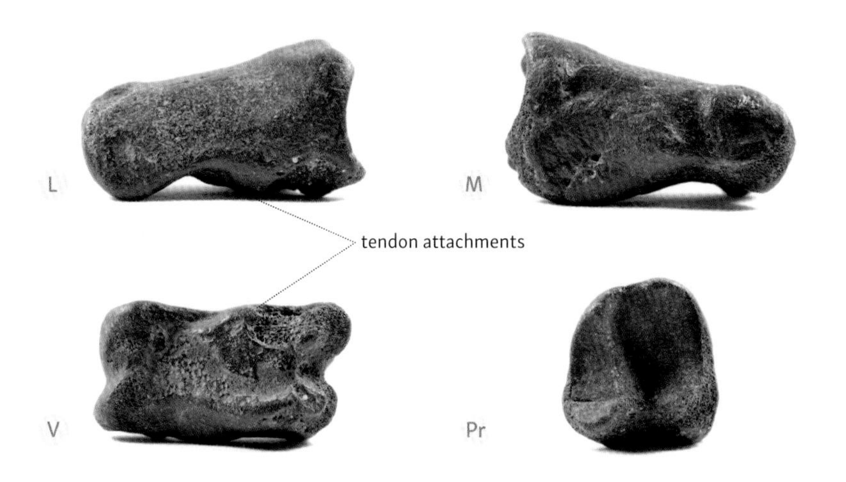

PHALANX *Bison antiquus*

Proximal (first) toe bone from the extinct Pleistocene bison, *Bison antiquus*. Reflecting the bison's robust build, the phalanges are extremely stout and thick to assist in bearing the weight of such massive creatures. There are two grooves on the proximal end where the bone articulated with the fused metatarsal or metacarpal bones. As with other phalanges, note the prominent points of attachment for tendons (indicated).

SIZE

73 × 38 × 41 mm

2.8 × 1.5 × 1.6 in

GEOLOGIC AGE

Pleistocene

2.6 Ma–11 ka

IDENTIFIERS

Grooved proximal end

Tapering form

Tendon attachments

DENSITY

DID YOU KNOW? Look at the end, or masticating surface, of a bison tooth, and you can see remarkable patterns. There is a curved outside layer of enamel, and on the inside is a crescent or U-shaped layer mimicking the outside of the tooth. This is an easy way to differentiate between the fossilized molars of bison and horses, the latter having a distinctly different pattern.

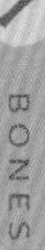

SIZE

46 × 15 × 17 mm

1.8 × 0.6 × 0.7 in

GEOLOGIC AGE

Pleistocene

2.6 Ma–11 ka

IDENTIFIERS

Tapered form

Proximal groove

Flattened medial side

DENSITY

PHALANX

Odocoileus virginianus

Proximal (first) toe bone from the extant white-tailed deer, *Odocoileus virginianus*. Note the flattened right side, where a mirroring phalanx would rest. This symmetry follows in two subsequent phalanges, the third being the hoof core (page 167). Deer phalanges are characteristically straight, lacking any arch on the underside of the bone, and tapering distally. The proximal surface bears a groove to articulate with the metapodials.

DID YOU KNOW? The white-tailed deer roamed most of North America in moderate numbers during the Pleistocene, probably because predators thrived then. Dire wolves hunted in packs of 3–20 animals, which likely limited Pleistocene deer populations. Human alterations to the landscape over the last 500 years have resulted in habitat more favorable to deer.

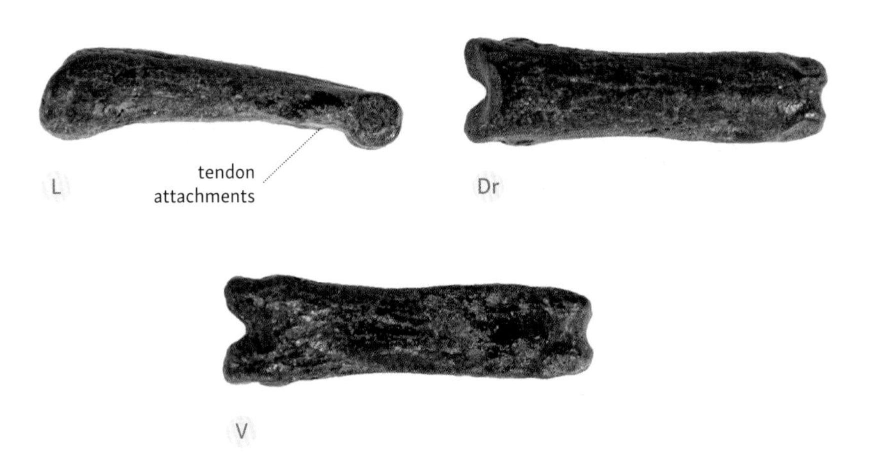

PHALANX *Procyon lotor*

Proximal (first) toe bone from the extant raccoon, *Procyon lotor*. These small phalanges are similar in form to other mammalian and reptilian toe bones, with wide proximal articulation, distally narrowing form, and small distal articulation. In lateral view, the tendon attachments (indicated) are visible to the left of the distal end. Modern skeletons are helpful for comparing the shape and form of similar fossils, especially with smaller specimens.

SIZE

17 × 5 × 3 mm

0.7 × 0.2 × 0.1 in

GEOLOGIC AGE

Pleistocene

2.6 Ma–11 ka

IDENTIFIERS

Tapering form

Wide proximal end

Small distal end

DENSITY

DID YOU KNOW? Christopher Columbus encountered raccoons when he landed on Hispaniola in 1492. Over 100 years later, English colonists at Jamestown attempted several spellings of a vocalization they heard from the Powhatans, "ab-rab-coon-um," which Captain John Smith recorded as "rabaugbcums." No doubt Europeans and Native Americans were fascinated by raccoons, but Daniel Boone never wore a coonskin cap—he preferred the Quaker's beaver felt hat, popular at the time!

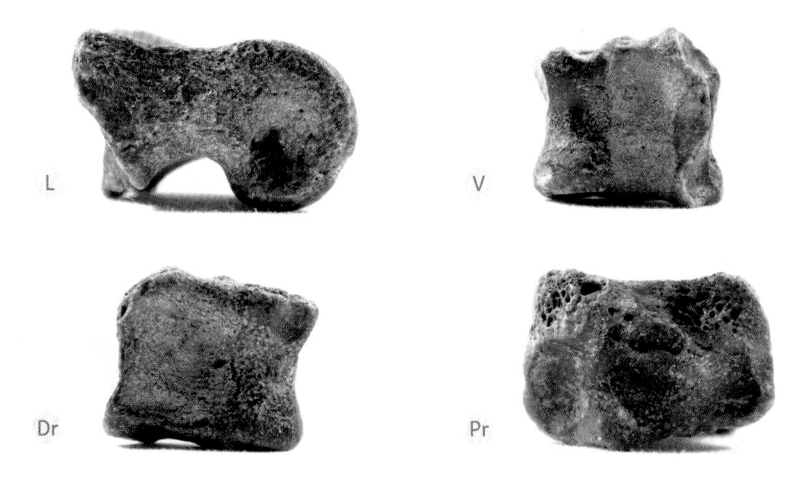

SIZE

26 × 24 × 16 mm

1.0 × 0.9 × 0.6 in

GEOLOGIC AGE

Pleistocene

2.6 Ma–11 ka

IDENTIFIERS

Angular shape

Large distal head

Stout form

DENSITY

PHALANX

Holmesina septentrionalis

Proximal (first) phalanx from the extinct giant armadillo, *Holmesina septentrionalis*. Living up to their classification as oddly jointed xenarthrans, the members of *Holmesina* have phalanges that are stubby, sharply curved, and angular. The distal end is smooth, with a broad depression for articulating with the medial phalanx, while the proximal end is scalloped, appearing irregular.

DID YOU KNOW? *Holmesina septentrionalis* was a virtual armored tank. Bony osteoderms protected its head, and its body was covered with immovable osteoderms called bucklers. Three bands of flexible, overlapping plates separated its anterior and posterior sections, allowing its back to bend. The now extended bucklers covered the back, and the curled position protected a fleshy underside. An armored, rigid tail completed this indestructible shield.

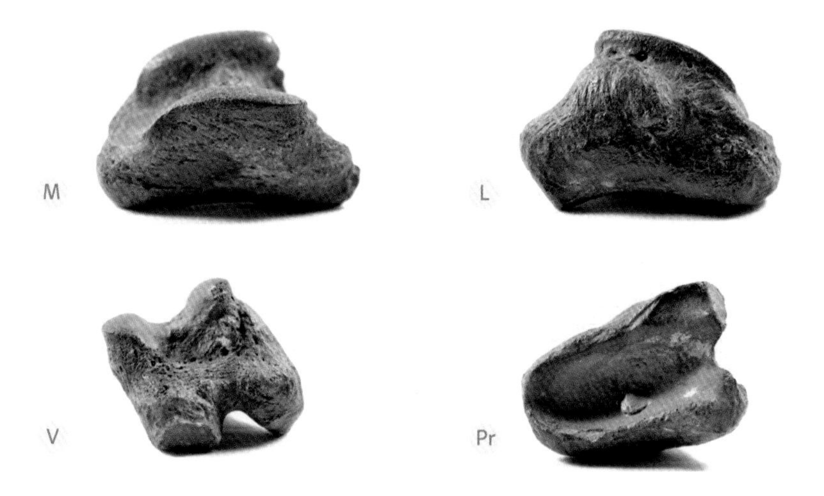

PHALANX *Megalonyx jeffersonii*

Proximal (first) toe bone from the extinct giant ground sloth *Megalonyx jeffersonii*. Unlike the proximal phalanges of other animals, those of the ground sloths are often drastically shorter, reduced to carpal- or tarsal-like elements. Similar in size to those of a black bear, the bones of *M. jeffersonii* are easily distinguished from those of other sloths based on size and the geologic date range of the deposit. The above specimen came from a late Pleistocene deposit.

SIZE

66 × 41 × 33 mm

2.6 × 1.6 × 1.3 in

GEOLOGIC AGE

Pleistocene

2.6 Ma–11 ka

IDENTIFIERS

Two distal ridges

Proximal depression

Short curved form

DENSITY

DID YOU KNOW? Humans have long hair on our heads and short hair on our legs. But what if that was reversed? A giant ground sloth fossil discovered in a South American cave had well preserved hair. Its skull hair was about 2 inches long, but the hair on its hind legs was nearly 9 inches long. Do you suppose ground sloths ever had "bad leg hair" days?

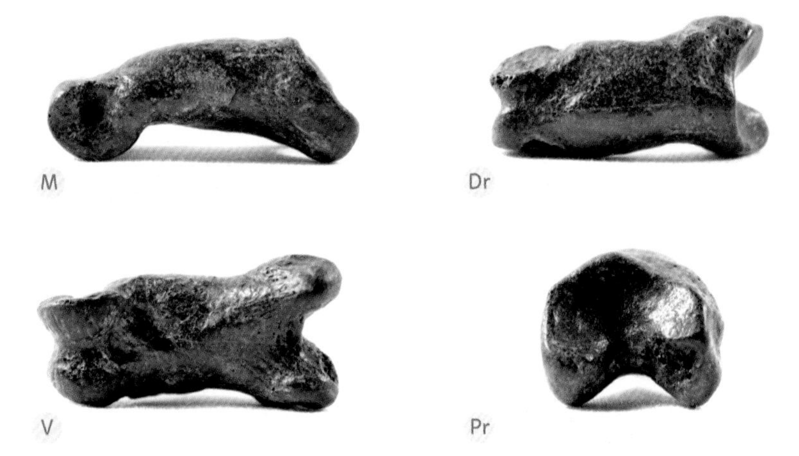

PHALANX *Smilodon* sp.

SIZE

45 × 16 × 17 mm

1.8 × 0.6 × 0.7 in

GEOLOGIC AGE

Pleistocene

2.6 Ma–11 ka

IDENTIFIERS

Arched form

Concave proximal end

Tendon attachments

DENSITY

Medial (middle) toe bone from a Pleistocene saber-toothed cat in the *Smilodon* genus. Saber-toothed cats had a relatively robust build, often mirrored in their bone structure. The rough points of attachment for tendons on the ventral sides of the phalanges are key identifiers to distinguish among species, genera, or even other animals. These areas are right behind the distal end, located on the lateral and medial sides. Phalanges of bears (*Ursus*, *Arctodus*, and *Tremarctos*) can appear identical, but are larger.

DID YOU KNOW? Saber-toothed cats were about the size of present-day lions. They had short strong legs and heavy-duty shoulders, which were advantageous for quickly attacking and surprising their prey. The aptly named canine teeth were curved, flat, and up to 7 inches long. The cat's jaws were therefore adapted to open extremely wide so that it could sink its teeth into prey.

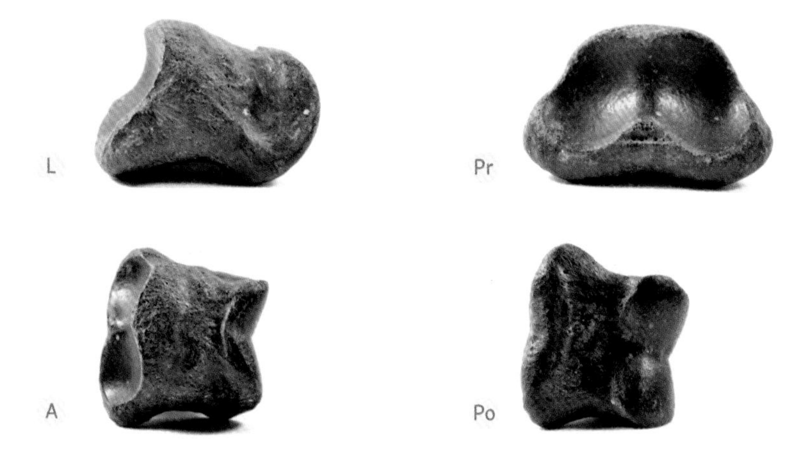

PHALANX *Equus* sp.

Medial (middle) toe bone from the extant genus of horses, *Equus*. Generally, medial phalanges are compressed in comparison with the much longer proximal phalanges. The distal end (at right in the anterior and posterior views) articulates with the hoof core, or ungual phalanx. Note the crisp articular surfaces on this specimen, indicating little wear from ocean tumbling.

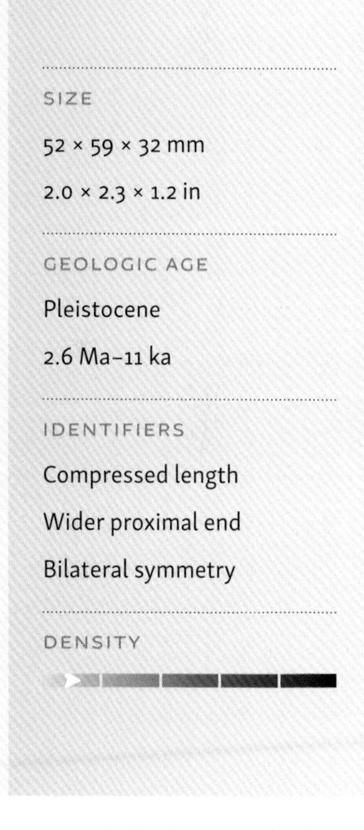

SIZE

52 × 59 × 32 mm

2.0 × 2.3 × 1.2 in

GEOLOGIC AGE

Pleistocene

2.6 Ma–11 ka

IDENTIFIERS

Compressed length

Wider proximal end

Bilateral symmetry

DENSITY

DID YOU KNOW? A horse's ability to stand on its legs for long periods of time evolved about 5 million years ago. Starting with *Dinohippus*, a bony dimple formed on one of the tendons, which fit over a crest projecting from the humerus bone as it connected to the adjacent bone. This dimple-crest matchup serves to lock the leg in place and relieve muscle tension when the horse stands for extended periods.

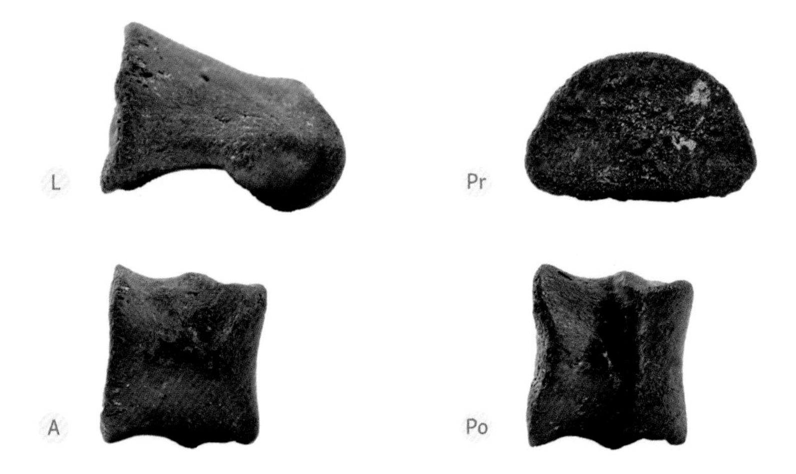

SIZE

28 × 26 × 18 mm

1.1 × 1.0 × 0.7 in

GEOLOGIC AGE

Pleistocene

2.6 Ma–11 ka

IDENTIFIERS

Mostly square shape

Tendon attachments

Flat proximal end

DENSITY

PHALANX *Tapirus* sp.

Medial (middle) toe bone from an extinct Pleistocene tapir, in the genus *Tapirus*. Since tapirs are perissodactyls, many of their bones resemble those from other members of the group, such as horses. Tapir medial phalanges are compressed, with prominent areas of attachment for tendons. The above phalanx most likely is from the second or third toe on a front foot; these digits are the two middle-most toes, which bear most of the animal's weight.

DID YOU KNOW? Tapirs, which are good swimmers, stay close to water to cool themselves off. Considering their hooves and toes, it is hard to imagine the swimming stroke they would use to avoid predators—dog paddle or backstroke? Okay, maybe not backstroke.

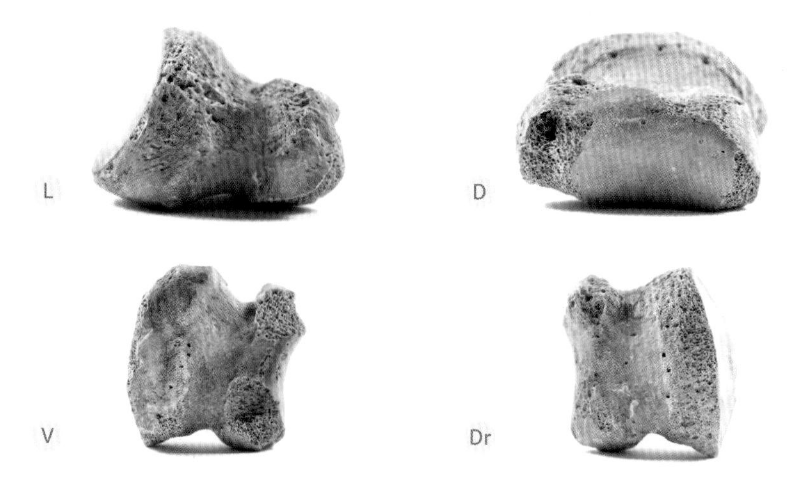

PHALANX

Mammuthus columbi

Toe bone from the Columbian mammoth, *Mammuthus columbi*. Reflecting the mammoth's large build, their phalanges are stout and robust in form. Also because of the animal's size, the holes for blood vessels are prominent (seen especially in the dorsal view). The proximal articulating surface is smooth, wide, and flat, lacking any distinct features.

SIZE

58 × 62 × 41 mm

2.3 × 2.4 × 1.6 in

GEOLOGIC AGE

Pleistocene

2.6 Ma–11 ka

IDENTIFIERS

Robust form

Large foramina

Flat proximal end

DENSITY

DID YOU KNOW? What constituted a Pleistocene "megafauna"? Scientists aren't in agreement about that. Some define the megafauna as any animal weighing more than 5 kg (11 pounds), which means that 90% of megafauna species became extinct at the end of that epoch. Others use 44 kg (100 pounds) as the cutoff, in which case 75% became extinct. Today, only about a dozen native North American land mammals typically exceed that weight, including bison, moose, polar bears, Kodiak bears, wapiti, and muskoxen. During the Pleistocene, there were nearly three times that number!

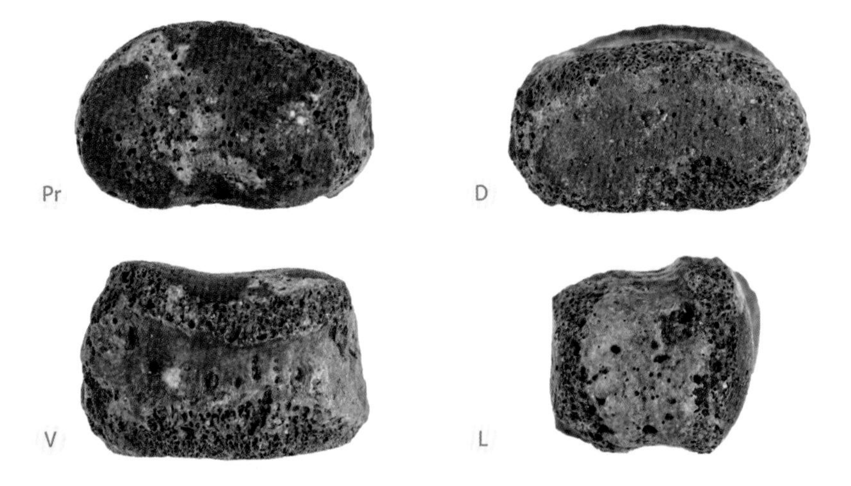

SIZE

19 × 12 × 11 mm

0.7 × 0.5 × 0.4 in

GEOLOGIC AGE

Pleistocene

2.6 Ma–11 ka

IDENTIFIERS

Scattered foramina

Flat proximal side

Curved distal side

DENSITY

PHALANX

Hesperotestudo crassiscutata

Toe bone from an extinct giant tortoise, *Hesperotestudo crassiscutata*. Unlike other phalanges, those of giant tortoises are rather reduced, stump-like, and nondescript. Note the relatively flat proximal side and the gently curved distal side, which articulates with other phalanges. These gentle articular surfaces are mirrored on the proximal side of the hoof cores. Foramina are prominent, visible above in the ventral and lateral views.

DID YOU KNOW? Galapagos Island tortoises have managed to survive exploitation by man and an endemic rice rat invasion. (Most of the rice rat species eventually became extinct.) Ironically, it was the tortoises' ability to live without food or water for upward of a year that nearly led to their demise by pirates. During long voyages, these unscrupulous seafarers sacrificed countless tortoises on board for food and for oil to light their lanterns.

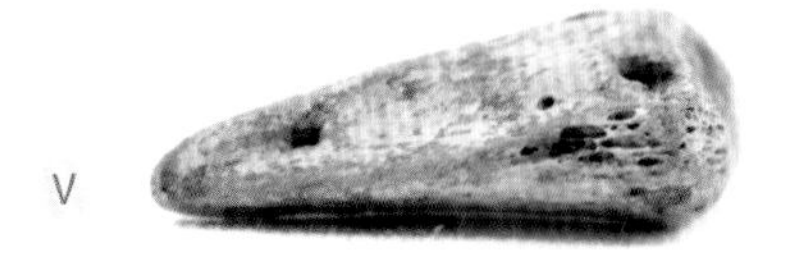

PHALANX

Odocoileus virginianus

Ungual phalanx (hoof core) from the extant white-tailed deer, *Odocoileus virginianus*. One of two cores in the hoof, the ungual phalanx is the bone within the hoof of a deer. The above specimen, the left phalanx, continues the symmetry seen in the other phalanges (page 462). The proximal end has two shallow depressions where it articulated with the medial phalanx. Note the large foramina to allow blood vessels to supply nutrients to the bone (visible in lateral and medial view).

SIZE

33 × 18 × 10 mm

1.3 × 0.7 × 0.4 in

GEOLOGIC AGE

Pleistocene

2.6 Ma–11 ka

IDENTIFIERS

Foramina

Grooved articulation

Triangular form

DENSITY

DID YOU KNOW? Deer tracks are well known by the two-toed impressions left in dirt or mud. Like horses, deer walk on their tiptoes. Their toes are attached to a hoof, or ungula, and so this group of animals is called the unguligrades. Sounds like a good name for a rock band!

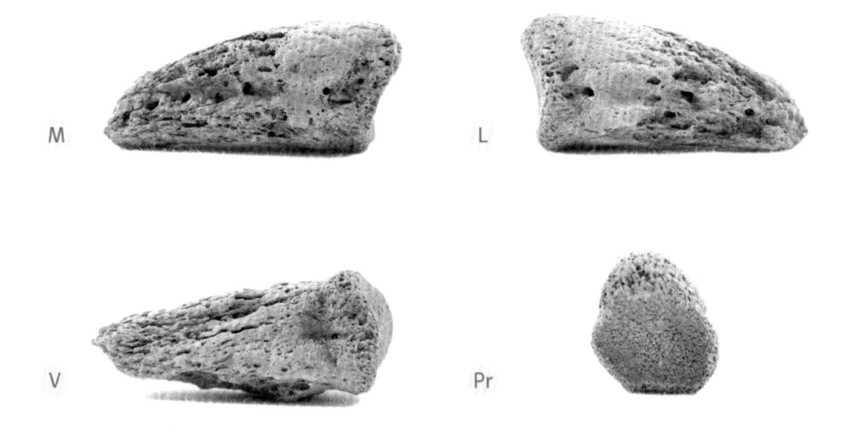

SIZE

35 × 14 × 14 mm

1.4 × 0.5 × 0.5 in

GEOLOGIC AGE

Pleistocene

2.6 Ma–11 ka

IDENTIFIERS

Porous bone

Foramina

Flat proximal end

DENSITY

PHALANX

Macrochelys temminckii

Ungual phalanx (claw core) from the extant alligator snapping turtle, *Macrochelys temminckii*. Similar to other claw cores, those of alligator snappers contain foramina, allowing the passage of blood vessels to supply nutrients and tendons to move the digits. The proximal end of the ungual phalanx is flattened and curves dorsally. Overall, these cores taper distally and laterally, and they lack the prominent point of attachment for tendons present on ground sloth claw cores.

DID YOU KNOW? The very name "alligator snapping turtle" conjures up images of prehistoric creatures. But these reptiles live today, mainly in the southeastern United States, and they have characteristics of both turtles and alligators. They are clearly turtles, but their large heads with pointed beaks are intimidating. This ferocious impression is reinforced by rows of large upraised knobs on top of their shells, which closely resemble the osteoderms lining an alligator's back.

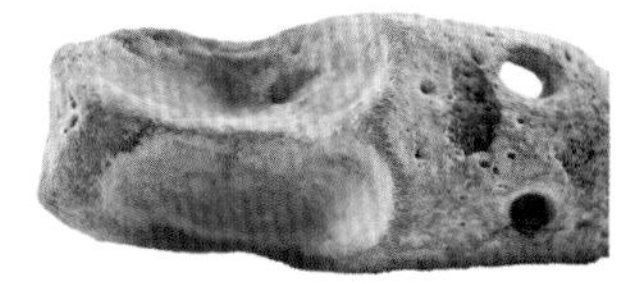

RL LL V Pr

CLAW CORE Folivora

Nearly intact claw core belonging to an undetermined species of Pleistocene giant ground sloth. While the tip of this specimen is missing, the dually grooved proximal end is intact, showing the unique articulation of these cores with the phalanges. Also present are the nutrient foramina—the two holes seen in the ventral and proximal views. The other main characteristic of sloth claw cores is the coarsely textured bone, where blood vessels and tendons were present.

SIZE

142 × 73 × 40 mm

5.5 × 2.8 × 1.6 in

GEOLOGIC AGE

Pleistocene

2.6 Ma–11 ka

IDENTIFIERS

Coarsely textured bone

Tendon attachment

Blood vessel grooves

DENSITY

DID YOU KNOW? During the Pleistocene, trees developed ways to discourage their consumption by herbivorous megafauna. Osage oranges, locusts, mesquites, and hawthorns developed sharp thorns along their trunks and limbs to ward off voracious sloths and mastodons. Mammals like modern deer and goats have evolved smaller jaws and tougher mouths that tolerate thorny obstacles.

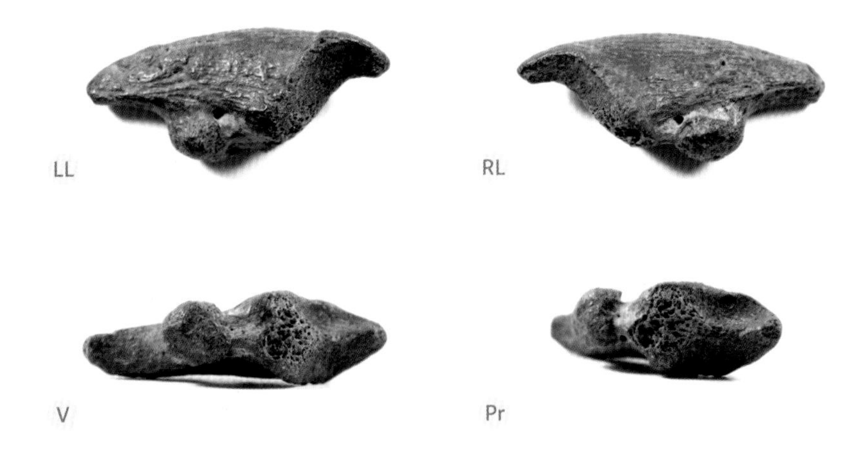

CLAW CORE Folivora

SIZE

55 × 23 × 17 mm

2.1 × 0.9 × 0.7 in

GEOLOGIC AGE

Pleistocene

2.6 Ma–11 ka

IDENTIFIERS

Coarsely textured bone

Tendon attachment

Blood vessel grooves

DENSITY

Claw core belonging to an undetermined species of Pleistocene giant ground sloth. Ground sloths have a dually grooved proximal end on their claw cores, which shows the unique articulation with the other phalanges. This claw's small size means that it was most likely from a juvenile or from the first digit of an adult. Note the prominent point of attachment for the tendons present in the toes (visible on the ventral side). Coarse texturing on the bone surface indicates where blood vessels and tendons ran across it.

DID YOU KNOW? Scientists assume that the huge claws of the giant ground sloth were used for digging up tubers as well as for defense, depending on the species. But defense against what? Ground sloths weighed 550–2,400 pounds! What predator was bigger than the sloth or would have taken on such a creature? This question remains a mystery.

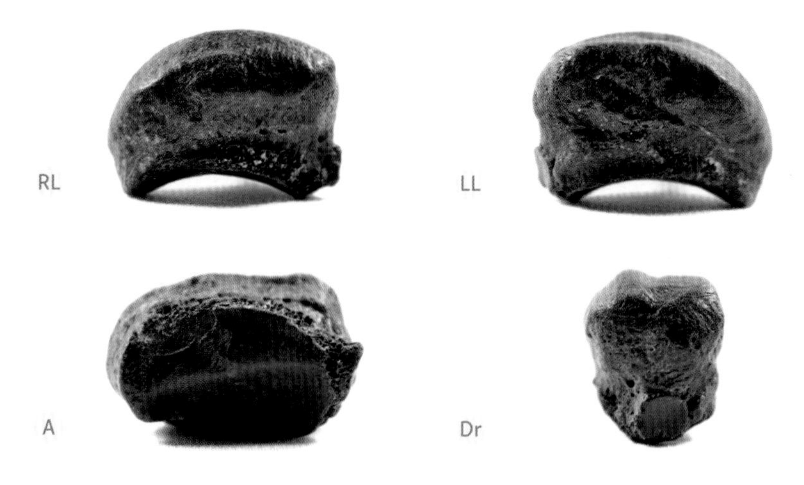

SESAMOID *Bison* sp.

Sesamoid bone from an extinct Pleistocene bison of the genus *Bison*. In vertebrates, the best-known sesamoid bone is the kneecap (patella). Sesamoids are embedded within tendons in areas where physical stress occurs. Aside from the patella, sesamoids are occasionally found at the ends of metapodials, as the above specimen demonstrates, located at the distal end of the metacarpals and metatarsals. In other species, smaller sesamoids can be found, similar in shape to the above fossil.

SIZE

36 × 18 × 23 mm

1.4 × 0.7 × 0.9 in

GEOLOGIC AGE

Pleistocene

2.6 Ma–11 ka

IDENTIFIERS

Few articulations

Dense structure

Curved form

DENSITY

DID YOU KNOW? Sesamoid bones are small calcium formations that assist in the movement of tendons and muscles around finger, foot, and knee joints. Much like a rope sliding over a pulley, a tendon glides easily over the smooth surface of a sesamoid. The human kneecap is the largest sesamoid. Horses have two sesamoid bones behind the fetlock on all four limbs.

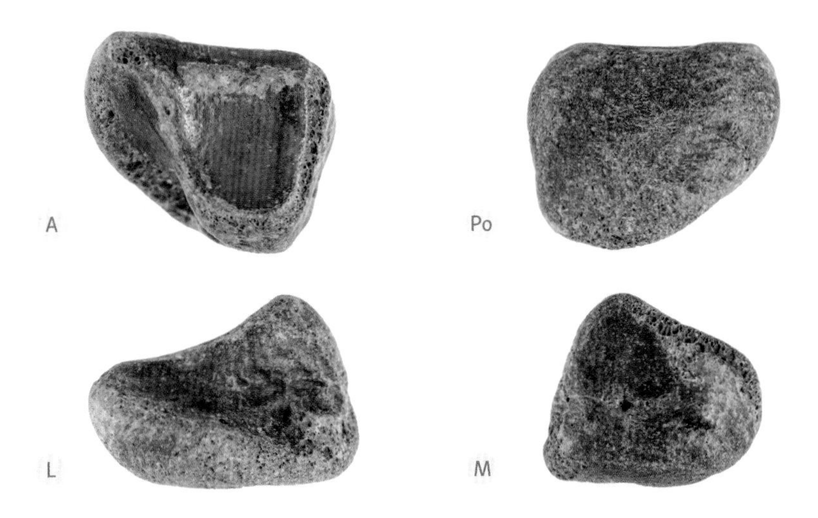

SESAMOID *Equus* sp.

SIZE

27 × 22 × 15 mm

1.1 × 0.9 × 0.6 in

GEOLOGIC AGE

Pleistocene

2.6 Ma–11 ka

IDENTIFIERS

Triangular form

Medially flattened surface

Laterally curved surface

DENSITY

Sesamoid bone from the extant genus of horses, *Equus*. Also known as the proximal sesamoids, a pair of these bones are located within the tendons of a horse's leg, posterior to the metapodial and proximal phalanges. Medially, each sesamoid is flattened to accommodate the adjacent sesamoid.

DID YOU KNOW? A horse's skull is longer than that of other perissodactyls such as peccaries and tapirs. The jaws of early horse ancestors held 44 teeth, 4 more than found in today's larger horses. Unlike their artiodactyl (even-toed) counterparts, which frequently lost incisors, prehistoric horses were "stingy" with their teeth and tended to hang onto most of them throughout life.

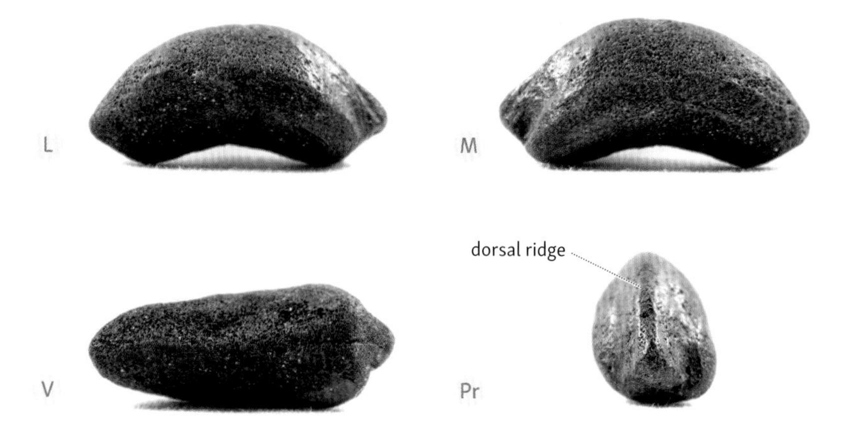

PISIFORM *Smilodon* sp.

A sesamoid bone from the extinct saber-toothed cat from the genus *Smilodon*. Pisiforms are sesamoid bones suspended in muscles in the wrist. Dorsally, a main ridge runs along the top of the pisiform (indicated), parallel to the sides of the bone. This ridge then extends out on either end. Functionally, pisiforms protect important tendons in the wrist, a feature found in the human wrist as well.

SIZE

28 × 11 × 12 mm

1.1 × 0.4 × 0.5 in

GEOLOGIC AGE

Pleistocene

2.6 Ma–11 ka

IDENTIFIERS

Curved form

Dorsal ridge

Fairly slender shape

DENSITY

DID YOU KNOW? Saber-toothed cats are second to dire wolves in the number of skeletons pulled from the La Brea Tar Pits. Over 1,200 representative specimens from this site have been preserved for posterity.

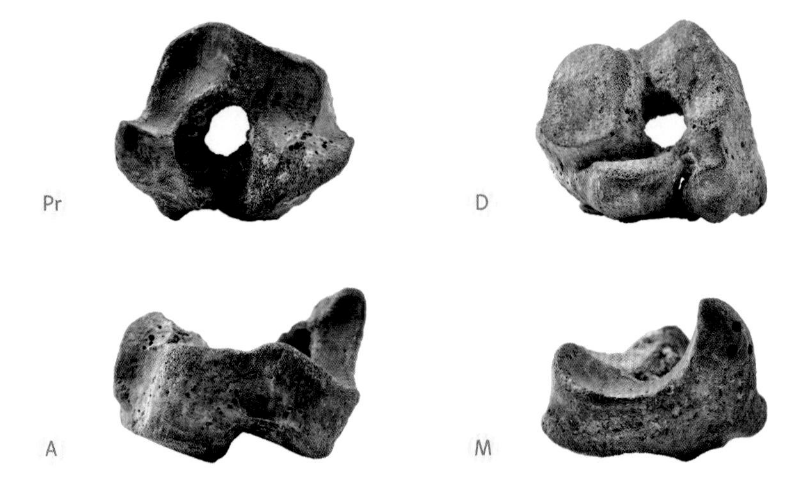

SIZE

74 × 71 × 56 mm

2.9 × 2.8 × 2.2 in

GEOLOGIC AGE

Pleistocene

2.6 Ma–11 ka

IDENTIFIERS

Articular surfaces

Puzzle-piece shape

Curved proximal side

DENSITY

CUBONAVICULAR *Bison* sp.

Tarsal element from an extinct Pleistocene bison, genus *Bison*. The cubonavicular represents a fusion of the cuboid and navicular bones, occasionally called the cuboid navicular bone or the naviculocuboid. Intact specimens do not bear a hole in the middle, but continue the concave contour of the proximal side. (See page 175 for an intact deer cubonavicular.) In addition to the calcaneum, the cubonavicular articulates with the astragalus (ankle bone).

DID YOU KNOW? *Bison antiquus* was widely nomadic between North America and Asia throughout the Pleistocene. During this epoch, sea levels changed many times, exposing land connections between the two continents. Along with the bison came such predators as saber-toothed cats (*Smilodon* spp.), American lions (*Panthera leo atrox*), and, possibly, dire wolves (*Canis dirus*).

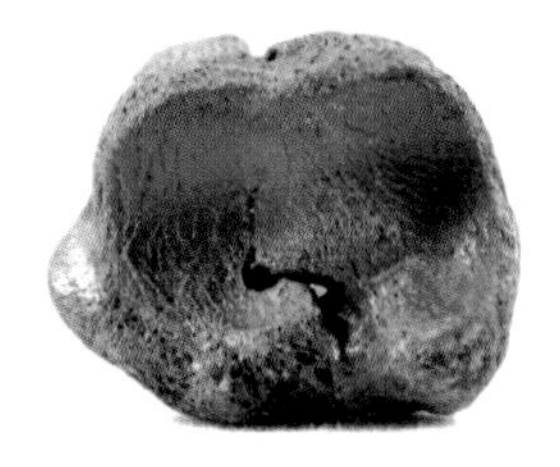

Pr

D

A

L

CUBONAVICULAR

Odocoileus virginianus

Tarsal bone from the extant white-tailed deer, *Odocoileus virginianus*. Cubonaviculars are found only in ruminants (cows, bison, deer, camels). These oddly shaped bones interlock with other tarsal elements in the hind limbs, analogous to the carpals of the front limbs. Proximally, they articulate with the astragalus, allowing for smooth movement of the ankle.

SIZE

30 × 22 × 16 mm

1.2 × 0.9 × 0.6 in

GEOLOGIC AGE

Pleistocene

2.6 Ma–11 ka

IDENTIFIERS

Concave dorsal side

Angular shape

Blood vessel holes

DENSITY

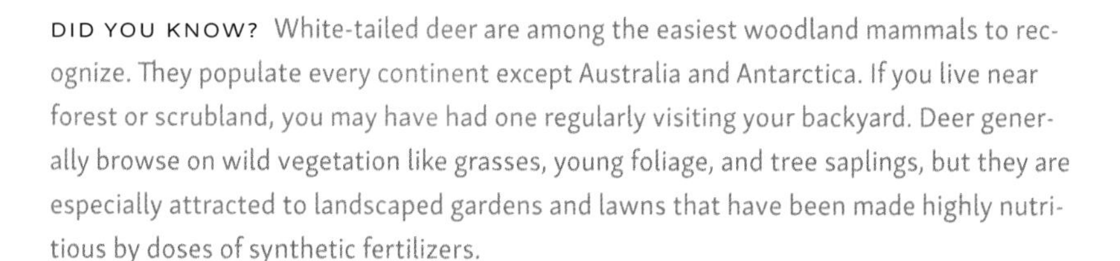

DID YOU KNOW? White-tailed deer are among the easiest woodland mammals to recognize. They populate every continent except Australia and Antarctica. If you live near forest or scrubland, you may have had one regularly visiting your backyard. Deer generally browse on wild vegetation like grasses, young foliage, and tree saplings, but they are especially attracted to landscaped gardens and lawns that have been made highly nutritious by doses of synthetic fertilizers.

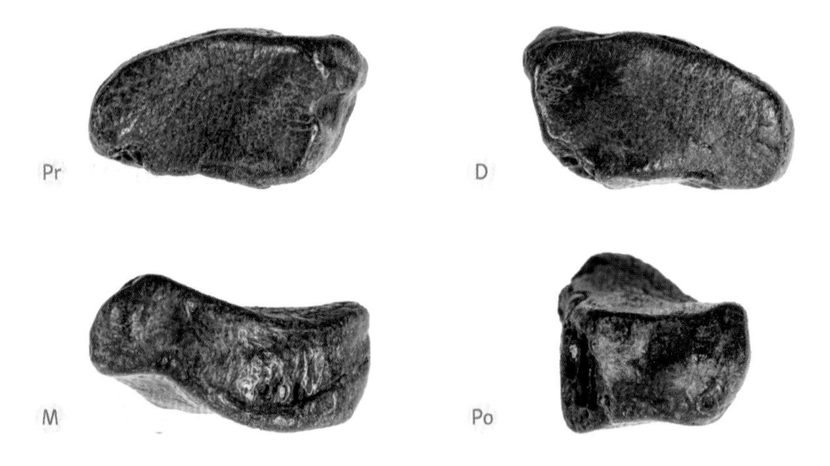

SIZE

20 × 10 × 7 mm

0.8 × 0.4 × 0.3 in

GEOLOGIC AGE

Pleistocene

2.6 Ma–11 ka

IDENTIFIERS

Articular surfaces

Kidney bean shape

Block-like form

DENSITY

INTERMEDIATE CUNEIFORM

Odocoileus virginianus

Intermediate cuneiform from the extant white-tailed deer, *Odocoileus virginianus*. Also known as the lateral cuneiform, this bone is a tarsal element located in the hind limb. The intermediate cuneiform articulates with the cubonavicular dorsally and the metatarsal ventrally. The intermediate cuneiform is shaped like a kidney bean. Other artiodactyls have similarly shaped tarsals.

DID YOU KNOW? Tarsals are leg bones in deer and other mammals. Deer also have tarsal glands, which secrete an oily, sebaceous substance that is activated when the buck rubs and urinates against trees and brush. Bucks and does both leave scents on vegetation year-round; males, however, do so more often in mating season. The complex interaction of bacteria and urine gives each deer its individual scent.

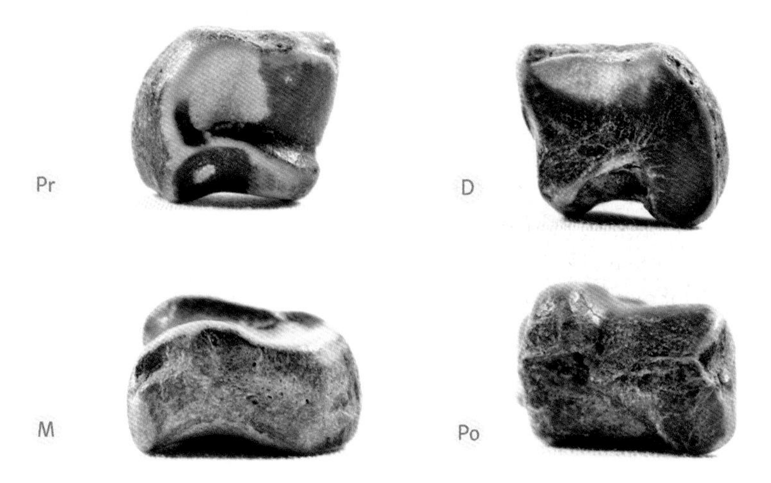

MAGNUM

Odocoileus virginianus

Left magnum from the extant white-tailed deer, *Odocoileus virginianus*. The magnum, also known as the trapezoid-magnum, is one of five carpal elements in the wrist of a deer. Like puzzle pieces, the angular bones interlock to form a variable junction between the metacarpal and the radius and ulna. The other interlocking bones include the unciform, cuneiform, scaphoid, and lunar. Note the foramina (blood vessel holes) in the medial view.

SIZE

20 × 20 × 12 mm

0.8 × 0.8 × 0.5 in

GEOLOGIC AGE

Pleistocene

2.6 Ma–11 ka

IDENTIFIERS

Flat distal side

Raised proximal side

Square form

DENSITY

DID YOU KNOW? Can you think of a setting that deer don't find habitable? The highly adaptable white-tailed deer can live alongside waterways, on mountain oak ridges, in pine forests, on farmland, and even in suburbia. All these locations provide some type of food that can sustain deer populations. Without predators, deer can overpopulate and consume all available food, even all of a forest's saplings, so wildlife management has become necessary.

SIZE

42 × 39 × 26 mm

1.6 × 1.5 × 1.0 in

GEOLOGIC AGE

Pleistocene

2.6 Ma–11 ka

IDENTIFIERS

Flat distal end

Curved proximal end

Angular articulations

DENSITY

CARPAL *Bison* sp.

Fused second and third carpal bone from an extinct Pleistocene bison, genus *Bison*. This carpal articulates with six other block-like bones in the wrist of a bison. Like the carpals and tarsals of other animals, these pieces interlock within the wrists and ankles to provide the joint's flexibility. Large comparative collections are required for precise identification. Out of all bison carpals, the fused one above is the flattest.

DID YOU KNOW? Paintings in the Lascaux Caves, dated to 17,000 years ago, document the animals that lived alongside man in present-day France. The local inhabitants, called Magdalenians, were observant and skilled painters. In one image, they used heated minerals to paint the details of a pregnant horse. Manganese and ocher, two minerals prized for their colors, were applied with sculptor's picks and stone burins (chisel-edged tools used for carving or engraving).

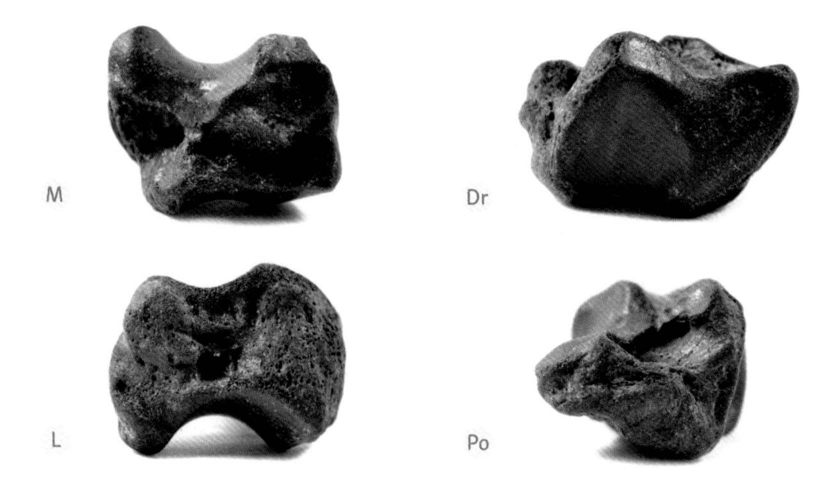

SCAPHOID *Bison* sp.

Right carpal from an extinct Pleistocene bison, genus *Bison*. The scaphoid is situated within the wrist of the bison, located proximally to the metacarpal and distally to the radius and ulna. The scaphoid is occasionally referred to as the radial carpal because of its direct articulation with the radius. There are six carpals in each front leg, interlocking like puzzle pieces to allow for the flexibility of the joints.

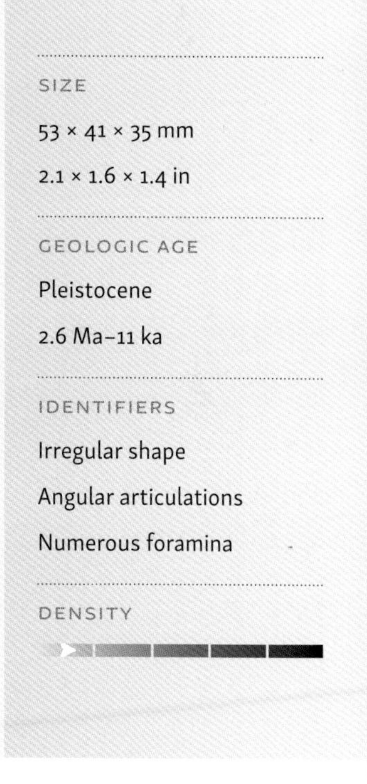

SIZE

53 × 41 × 35 mm

2.1 × 1.6 × 1.4 in

GEOLOGIC AGE

Pleistocene

2.6 Ma–11 ka

IDENTIFIERS

Irregular shape

Angular articulations

Numerous foramina

DENSITY

DID YOU KNOW? With their heavy, thick fur, prehistoric bison, like their modern descendants, were adapted to living in cold climates. They used their huge heads to bulldoze snow aside to reveal grass, their main food source. They also gleaned water from snow, which kept them hydrated during the long winter months.

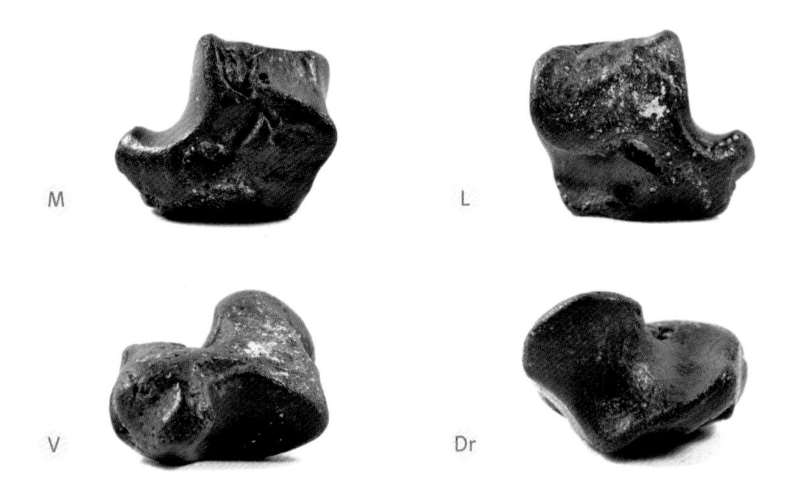

SIZE

58 × 47 × 32 mm

2.3 × 1.8 × 1.2 in

GEOLOGIC AGE

Pleistocene

2.6 Ma–11 ka

IDENTIFIERS

Irregular shape

Angular articulations

Numerous foramina

DENSITY

PYRAMIDAL *Bison* sp.

Right carpal from an extinct Pleistocene bison, genus *Bison*. The pyramidal is situated within the wrist of the bison, located proximally to the metacarpal and distally to the radius and ulna. The pyramidal is occasionally called the ulnar carpal, in reference to its direct articulation with the ulna. There are six carpals in each front leg, interlocking like puzzle pieces to allow for flexibility of the joints.

DID YOU KNOW? Fossilized bison teeth are used in determining the animal's age at death. From birth to five years old, a bison's age can be established to within a month, based on the number of teeth showing or beginning to show. After age five, the then-complete set of teeth begins to show wear from the chewing of grassland vegetation, and measurements between the worn dentine and the crown offer a good indication of age.

RIB *Trichechus manatus*

Rib from the extant species of manatee, *Trichechus manatus*. Unlike the bones of terrestrial mammals, those of the manatee are quite dense, lacking the inner spongy bone. Manatee ribs are characteristically broad and sharply curved inward and are occasionally described as banana-shaped. Ribs from Miocene dugongs (*Dugong dugon*) are similar, though squarer in cross section. Manatee rib bones exhibit an oval-to-suboval cross section.

SIZE

246 × 63 × 31 mm

9.6 × 2.5 × 1.2 in

GEOLOGIC AGE

Pleistocene

2.6 Ma–11 ka

IDENTIFIERS

Sharply curved shape

Dense bone structure

Narrow tip and base

DENSITY

DID YOU KNOW? Manatees' lips are prehensile (grasping), the upper ones having independently moving right and left sides. They use their flippers to push vegetation toward their lips, which use seven muscles to pull apart plants and move them into the mammals' mouths.

SIZE

200 × 28 × 15 mm

7.8 × 1.1 × 0.6 in

GEOLOGIC AGE

Pleistocene

2.6 Ma–11 ka

IDENTIFIERS

Laterally thin structure

Gentle curvature

Narrow form

DENSITY

RIB Ungulata

Rib from an undetermined Pleistocene mammal. Ribs have a characteristic lateral flattening and a gentle curvature. Based on the size of the specimen and faunal representation from the fossil assemblage, this specimen most likely belonged to a white-tailed deer. While fragments are easy to identify, rib bones are of little value to paleontologists unless isotopic dating of a specimen is desired, in which case the bone would be ground into a powder for analysis.

DID YOU KNOW? In 1875, William Denton of Wellesley College was given a saber-toothed cat canine from the La Brea Tar Pits. In 1901, John Merriman of the University of California, Berkeley, began the first scientific excavations of the pits. In 1969, part of the site was reopened for study of all the species, not just the famous large mammals. Today, over 600 species have been identified there.

SPECIES HIGHLIGHT

Giant Ground Sloths

Calling these creatures slow would have been risky!

Giant ground sloths are among the most unusual extinct mammals. Some were as large as bison and others were bear-sized. They had powerful limbs and giant claws and were primarily herbivores, though recent research suggests that a few species may have been omnivorous scavengers.

These animals had blunt snouts with long molar-like teeth, and the fossilized hip bones of some species show that they were adapted to walk upright. Ground sloths generally had three claws on their hind feet, but a differing number on their forelimbs, depending upon the species. Fossilized bones indicate that most walked with their feet turned inward and their giant claws turned upward, to prevent them from snagging on soil, roots, and rocks.

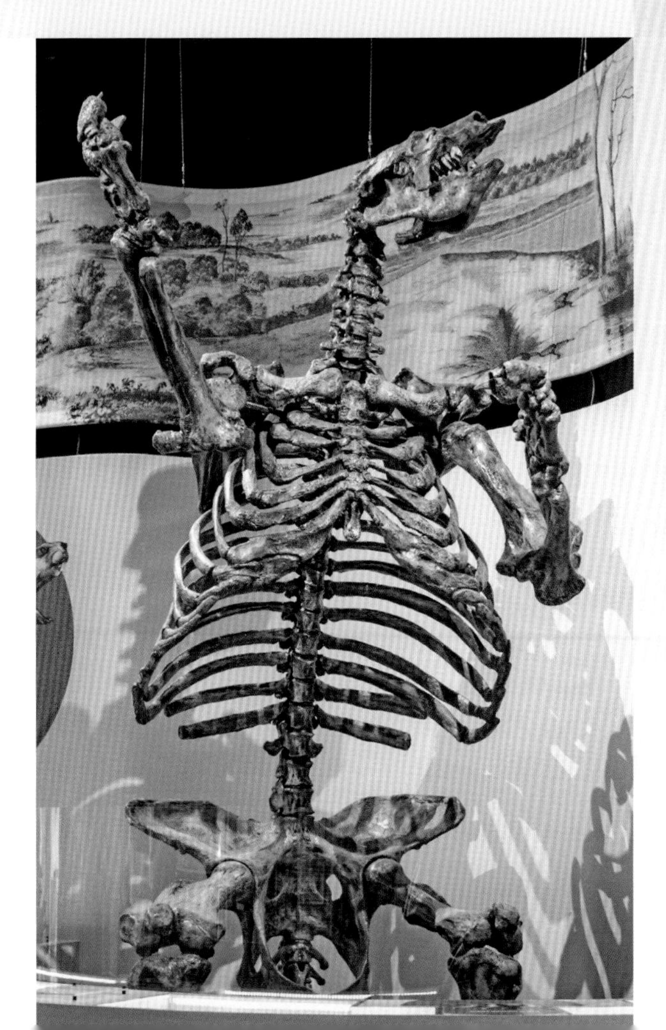

Towering profile of *Eremotherium laurillardi*, Laurillard's ground sloth, standing over 12 feet tall in the natural history hall at the Charleston Museum, Charleston, South Carolina.

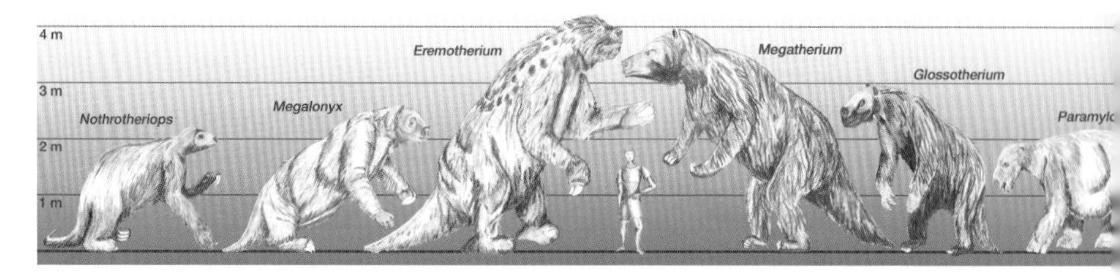

Ground sloth size chart, with a six-foot-tall human for comparison. *Left to right: Nothrotheriops, Megalonyx, Eremotherium, Megatherium, Glossotherium,* and *Paramylodon.*

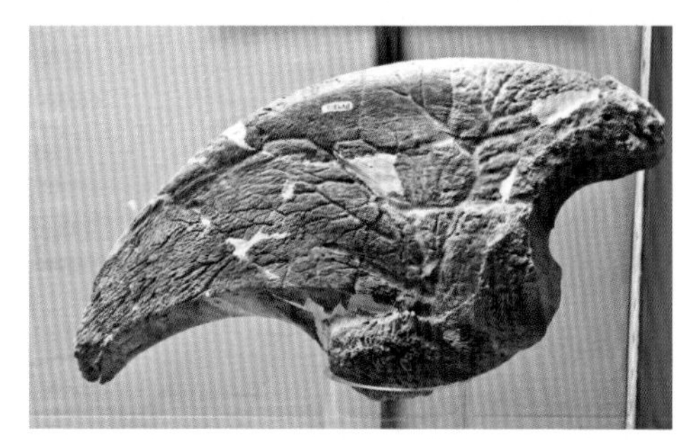

Eremotherium laurillardi claw core on display at the Charleston Museum, Charleston, South Carolina.

All ground sloths are extinct, and only two genera of sloth descendants remain today. The present-day species are about the size of a small dog, and rather than being ground-based, they spend their lives within the tree canopy. The oldest known fossils of a sloth species come from the family Megalonychidae, dating to the Late Eocene (about 35 Ma), and were recorded from the south polar regions of Patagonia and Seymour Island. The earliest fossils found in North America come from the Miocene, about 9 Ma, and were discovered in Florida. These are fossils of the sloth *Pliometanastes protistus.*

From the Miocene through the Pliocene, ground sloth diversity increased tremendously throughout South America and the West Indies and, following the Great American Biotic Interchange, over most of North America. At their height, sloths numbered about 100 species. This diversity declined, and by the close of the Pleistocene epoch, giant ground sloths had become extinct. At the end of the last glaciation, four families had spread through North America and were represented by seven species.

Laurillard's ground sloth, *Eremotherium laurillardi*, and *E. eomigrans* (no common name exists) are the largest-known sloths and were truly giants, growing up to 20 feet in length and weighing up to 3 tons, or about the same size and weight as two and a half bison. Both species were unique in the number and

Giant ground sloth skeleton on display at the Florida Museum of Natural History, Gainesville.

size of their claws. While most ground sloth species had three claws on fore- and hind feet, *E. laurillardi* had only one claw on its hind limbs and two on its forefeet, which grew to over 17 inches in length. *E. eomigrans* had four claws on its forelimbs, more than any other species identified to date.

Laurillard's ground sloth was widely distributed in North and South America, and in the United States from coast to coast, mostly in the South. *E. eomigrans* is known only from Florida and, more recently, South Carolina.

Jefferson's ground sloth, *Megalonyx jeffersonii*, is the best-known species because Thomas Jefferson became greatly interested in this sloth after being shown some *Megalonyx* fossils. He wrote an extensive paper describing *Megalonyx* and speculating on its characteristics. Unlike mammoths and mastodons, which entered North America from Siberia via the Bering Land Bridge, *M. jeffersonii* came onto the continent from South America after the Panamanian Land Bridge was established, and it was the only giant ground sloth to have spread as far north as the Alaska-Yukon region. Recently, two other species, *M. leptostomus* and *M. wheatleyi*, have been reported from South Carolina.

Harlan's ground sloth, *Paramylodon harlani*, a strict herbivore and mostly a grazer, is believed to have used its strong forearms and claws also for digging roots and tubers. Such foraging would have involved chewing abrasive grasses and large amounts of soil grit, so the unusually high tooth crowns of *P. harlani* are presumed to be an adaptation to reduce wear. This species had two claws on its forelimbs and three on its hind feet. At 10 feet long, it was smaller than *Eremotherium*, and it contained numerous osteoderms within its skin, which might have provided some armoring for defense.

The Shasta ground sloth, *Nothrotheriops shastensis*, was the smallest of the species found in the United States, measuring only up to 9 feet long, about the size of a black bear. The most abundant giant sloth collected from the La Brea Tar Pits, it was mostly a southwestern species, but fossils have also been reported from Florida.

Why did the giant ground sloths disappear? As with other megafauna of that time, climate change and hunting by the humans recently arrived on the scene have been proposed as explanations, but the reason is not fully understood. Fortunately, these creatures still exist in the form of beach fossils. No matter how unlikely, it is always possible that you might one day dig the claw of a giant ground sloth out of the sand!

OSTEODERMS

TRAITS OF OSTEODERMS

Osteoderms are defined as bony (osteo-) plates located within the skin (-derm) of an animal. Many times, patterns appear on osteoderms as a result of keratinous scutes that overlay the bony plates. From this nomenclature, people often incorrectly label osteoderms as scutes, which do not fossilize. Other features of some osteoderms are hair follicle holes (foramina) located on the dorsal side, and nerve or blood vessel foramina on the ventral side. On intact edges, the sutured appearance of the articular surfaces is evident.

COMMON TERMS

Articulate, buckler, carapace, denticle, dermal, dorsal, flex, follicle, ganoid, immovable, keratin (keratinous), leg spur, neural, nuchal, ossicle, peripheral, plastron, pygal, scute, stationary, ventral

COMMONALITY

On fossiliferous beaches, osteoderms, particularly turtle shell fragments, are prevalent. Other carapacial elements and osteoderms (gar fish scales, armadillo osteoderms, sturgeon scales) are less abundant but still common.

INCLUSIONS AND EXCLUSIONS

The greatest number of specimens in this section are turtle carapace and plastron elements. We recognize that, anatomically, these elements are bones; however, these bones armor turtles and provide the same protective function as osteoderms do in other animals. For that reason, they are included in this section. Scales from fishes are also included, along with their opercular coverings.

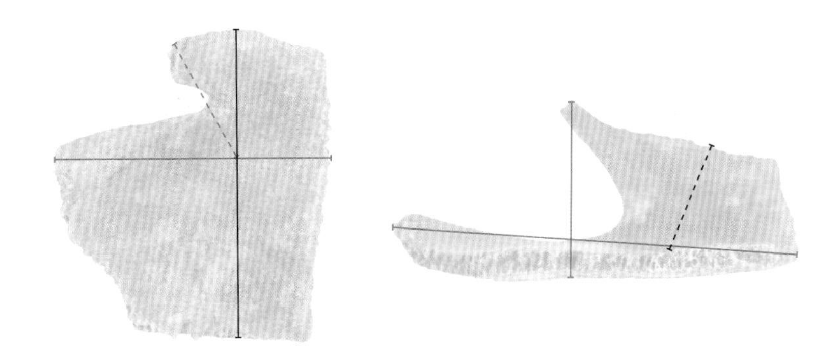

MEASUREMENTS

All osteoderms have measurements displayed in a three-part system:

(longest side × next longest × shortest side)

The longest side comes first, regardless of position. If this side is ambiguous in the photos, it is delineated in the Item Description. The second-longest side is measured perpendicular to the longest side and at its thickest part, and the shortest side is usually the thickness of the osteoderm. (Dashed lines indicate the third dimension.)

SUPPLEMENTARY IMAGES AND TERMS

See page 461 for a graphic of the positional terms in relation to the body.

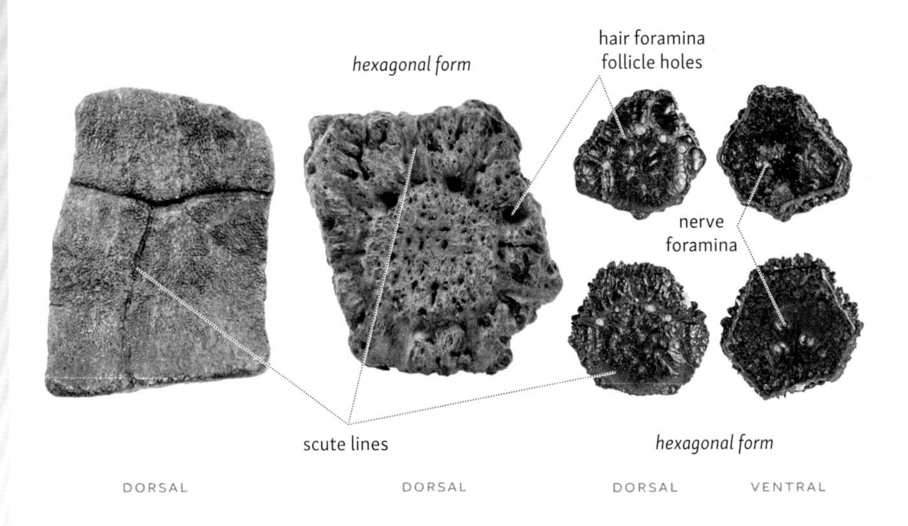

Dr

V

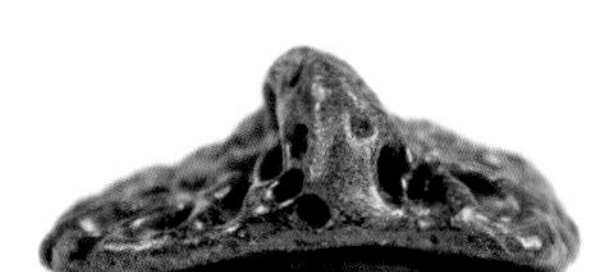
Po

L

OSTEODERM

Alligator mississippiensis

Square dermal plate from the extant American alligator, *Alligator mississippiensis*. Alligators have some of the most distinct osteoderms of any animal. Plates have a prominent ridge along the dorsal side, with a webbed pattern extending down to the edges of the plate. Similar osteoderms include crocodile osteoderms, which lack the dorsal ridge, and sturgeon (*Acipenser* sp.) scales, which have a finer webbed pattern than alligator osteoderms. The ventral side has a woven appearance and foramina (page 469).

SIZE

55 × 52 × 20 mm

2.1 × 2.0 × 0.8 in

GEOLOGIC AGE

Pleistocene

2.6 Ma–11 ka

IDENTIFIERS

Dorsal ridge

Webbed dorsal surface

Concave base

DENSITY

DID YOU KNOW? Osteoderms are common alligator fossils. These bony plates beneath the skin on the backs of alligators give them their "knobby" appearance. Osteoderm fossils are squarish plates that resemble a mountain, having a pinched high ridge in the center surrounded by numerous valley-like pits and holes. These plates were used for temperature regulation and, most importantly, for armored protection.

Dr

V

SIZE

25 × 23 × 9 mm

1.0 × 0.9 × 0.4 in

GEOLOGIC AGE

Pleistocene

2.6 Ma–11 ka

IDENTIFIERS

Orange-peel texture

Polygonal shape

Ventral nerve holes

DENSITY

PLATE

Holmesina septentrionalis

Osteoderm from the head of the extinct giant armadillo, *Holmesina septentrionalis*. Like other plates on *Holmesina*, cranial osteoderms are patterned with a porous texture on the dorsal side. Also present on the dorsal side is a raised ridge or bump, plus a similar ridge paralleling the sides of each plate. These osteoderms can be differentiated from stationary plates by their smaller size. As with other armadillos, foramina are visible on the ventral side.

DID YOU KNOW? *Holmesina septentrionalis*, the giant armadillo, is one of the members of the families of armadillo-like creatures that reached North America by way of the Panamanian Land Bridge. This migration began during the late Pliocene epoch. *H. septentrionalis* must have liked the Florida region, because many more armadillo fossils are found there than in any other part of the continent.

Dr

V

PLATE

Holmesina septentrionalis

Stationary plate from the extinct giant armadillo, *Holmesina septentrionalis*. Osteoderms like these, shaped like irregular polygons, are located on the armadillo's shoulders (anterior shield) and hind section (posterior shield). Note the unique texture present on the dorsal side, similar in appearance to an orange peel. Also present on the dorsal side is a raised ridge (seen above running from the one to seven o'clock positions); a similar ridge parallels the edges. As with other armadillos, foramina are visible on the ventral side.

SIZE

35 × 32 × 11 mm

1.4 × 1.2 × 0.4 in

GEOLOGIC AGE

Pleistocene

2.6 Ma–11 ka

IDENTIFIERS

Orange-peel texture

5- to 6-sided polygons

Ventral foramina

DENSITY

DID YOU KNOW? George Gaylord Simpson, assistant curator of vertebrate fossils at the American Museum of Natural History in 1927, became fascinated by a collection of Pleistocene fossils donated by the Florida businessman and fossil hobbyist Walter Holmes. Simpson documented the collection and surveyed the sites where they had been collected. To honor the museum's benefactor, Simpson named an extinct giant armadillo after him, *Holmesina septentrionalis*.

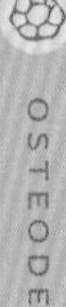

Dr

V

SIZE

35 × 28 × 8 mm

1.4 × 1.1 × 0.3 in

GEOLOGIC AGE

Pleistocene

2.6 Ma–11 ka

IDENTIFIERS

Orange-peel texture

Rectangular polygons

Ventral foramina

DENSITY

PLATE *Holmesina septentrionalis*

Stationary plate from the extinct giant armadillo, *Holmesina septentrionalis*. The pre- and post-flex osteoderms located closer to the armadillo's flexible bands are more rectangular than the other stationary osteoderms. A broad elevated ridge runs down the middle of the plate, and the ventral side shows the holes (foramina) for vessels that supplied blood and nutrients to this armor. Note the unique texture present on the dorsal side, similar in appearance to an orange peel.

DID YOU KNOW? What did the 600-pound "giant armadillos" eat? The modern nine-banded armadillo digs for insects and other invertebrates to sustain its 8- to 17-pound body weight. But the mighty *Holmesina* took a leaf out of Popeye's playbook and instead chose to eat his greens! Paleontologists studying *Holmesina* tooth microwear patterns and jaw morphology (shape) have determined that it consumed coarse vegetation, rather than insects like its smaller, modern cousin.

Dr

V

L

FLEX PLATE

Holmesina septentrionalis

Moveable osteoderm from the extinct giant armadillo, *Holmesina septentrionalis*. Four bands of these plates articulated together, providing some flexibility in the middle of the body and allowing the armadillo to curl its body slightly. Osteoderms from *H. septentrionalis* have a dorsal texture similar to that of an orange peel, and the ventral side is mottled with holes at irregular intervals. The anterior is wedge-shaped and angled to articulate with the adjacent flexible band.

SIZE

76 × 40 × 11 mm

3.0 × 1.6 × 0.4 in

GEOLOGIC AGE

Pleistocene

2.6 Ma–11 ka

IDENTIFIERS

Orange-peel texture

Scalloped ridge

Wedge-shaped base

DENSITY

DID YOU KNOW? *Holmesina septentrionalis* measured over two meters (six and a half feet) in length, much larger than the other armadillo species, and weighed approximately 600 pounds. The much smaller "beautiful armadillo," *Dasypus bellus*, another extinct species, was nevertheless twice as large as today's nine-banded species.

Dr

V

SIZE

14 × 13 × 5 mm

0.5 × 0.5 × 0.2 in

GEOLOGIC AGE

Pleistocene

2.6 Ma–11 ka

IDENTIFIERS

Dorsal follicle holes

Ventral foramina

4-, 5-, or 6-sided shape

DENSITY

PLATE *Dasypus bellus*

Stationary osteoderm from the extinct "beautiful armadillo," *Dasypus bellus*. Immovable osteoderms were located on the head, shoulders, and rump of the armadillo. These plates have four to six sides, and five to eight large holes for hair follicles on the dorsal side. Ventrally, up to five foramina allowed nerves or blood vessels to supply nutrients to the bone.

DID YOU KNOW? The most commonly found fossilized parts of *Dasypus bellus* are the osteoderms. The hard bony material is recognizable because of a four-, five-, or six-sided pattern with small holes that held the animal's hair follicles. This hexagonal stationary osteoderm is known as the buckler.

Dr

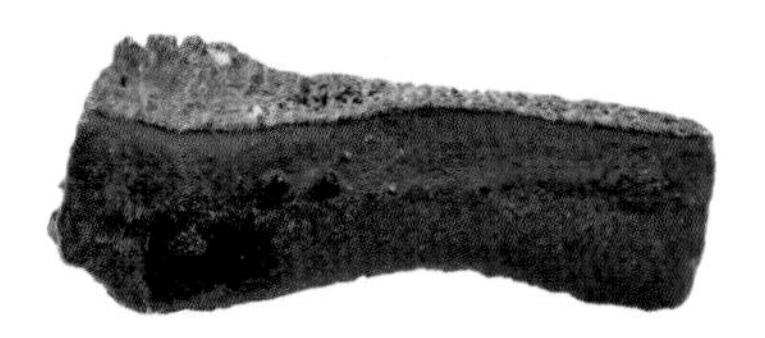

V

FLEX PLATE *Dasypus bellus*

Movable osteoderm from the extinct beautiful armadillo, *Dasypus bellus*. These plates are marked with numerous holes (foramina) both dorsally (for hair follicles) and ventrally (for nerves and blood vessels). On intact specimens, the foramina for the nerves consist of one to three large holes. *Dasypus bellus* is an ancestor of the modern armadillo found in the Southeast today and was approximately twice as large.

SIZE

38 × 10 × 4 mm

1.5 × 0.4 × 0.2 in

GEOLOGIC AGE

Pleistocene

2.6 Ma–11 ka

IDENTIFIERS

Dorsal follicle holes

Ventral nerve holes

Shingle-like form

DENSITY

DID YOU KNOW? In 2013, researchers compared bones of the extinct *Dasypus bellus* with those of the similar, extant *D. novemcinctus*, the nine-banded armadillo. *D. bellus* lacked the bony adaptations that enable the smaller *D. novemcinctus* to burrow underground. Since *D. bellus* ranged farther north than its modern descendant, its larger size may have allowed it to better conserve heat and wait out cold winter months in caves, where fossil remains have been found.

SIZE

45 × 32 × 15 mm

1.8 × 1.2 × 0.6 in

GEOLOGIC AGE

Pleistocene

2.6 Ma–11 ka

IDENTIFIERS

"Daisy" pattern

Porous exterior

Ventral foramen

DENSITY

CARAPACIAL ELEMENT

Glyptotherium sp.

Stationary osteoderm from the carapace of an extinct glyptodont, genus *Glyptotherium*. Glyptodonts had a large, rigid carapace made up of hundreds of thick osteoderms. The pattern on each was made from several keratinous scales, or scutes, and so these fossils are given such nicknames as "daisies." Note the single foramen on the ventral side.

DID YOU KNOW? The glyptodont, whose name means "carved tooth," was an herbivore that ate by shearing and tearing off plants with the front of its mouth and transferring them to the back, where peg-like molar teeth were located.

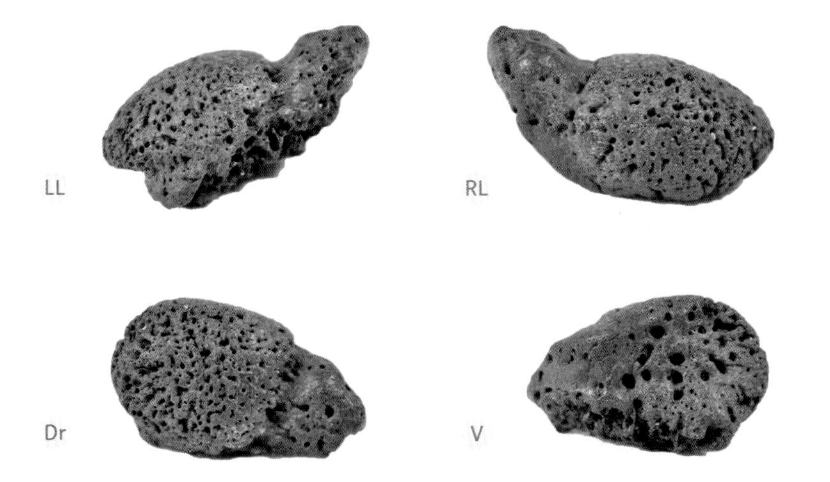

MARGINAL PLATE

Glyptotherium sp.

Peripheral osteoderm from an extinct, armadillo-like glyptodont, genus *Glyptotherium*. Marginal elements are rarer than carapacial elements because of the layout of the glyptodont's shell. The high-domed carapace was fringed with these osteoderms along the head, rear, and sides of the giant animal. Note the large porous exterior, typical of glyptodont osteoderms. Such holes are often confused with shell or rock material eaten away by a boring sponge (*Cliona* spp.).

SIZE

50 × 31 × 27 mm

2.0 × 1.2 × 1.1 in

GEOLOGIC AGE

Pleistocene

2.6 Ma–11 ka

IDENTIFIERS

Porous holes

Thick form

Rounded edge

DENSITY

DID YOU KNOW? Early human hunters may have advanced the decline of the glyptodonts. Though the glyptodont's armored shell posed a challenge, humans devised a tool with a sharp hook that could strike the animal's soft belly and kill it. Paleo-Indians used all parts of a glyptodont, including its hard armored shell, for specific purposes.

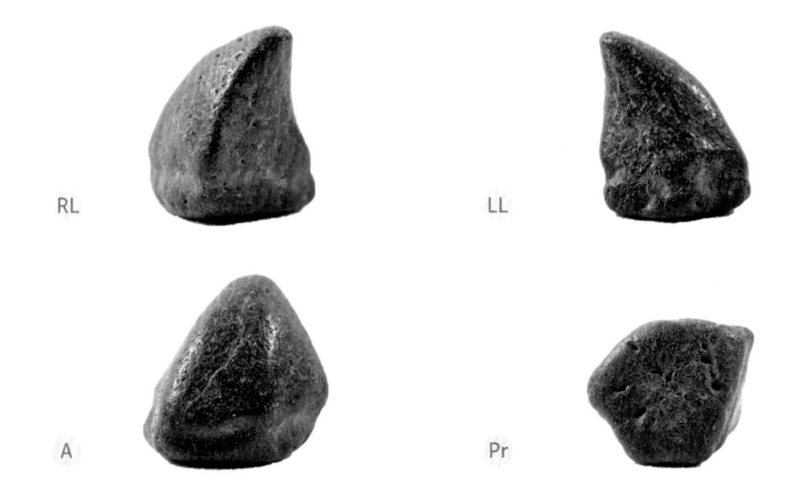

SIZE

26 × 21 × 24 mm

1.0 × 0.8 × 0.9 in

GEOLOGIC AGE

Pleistocene

2.6 Ma–11 ka

IDENTIFIERS

Radiating foramina

Chocolate-drop shape

Tip ventrally skewed

DENSITY

LEG SPUR

Hesperotestudo crassiscutata

Leg spur from the extinct Pleistocene giant tortoise, *Hesperotestudo crassiscutata*. Collectors often refer to these specimens as "Hershey's Kisses" or "chocolate drops" because of their shape. Likewise, older texts erroneously called them foot pads, when in fact these spurs projected off the legs, not the feet, of the tortoise. The proximal side usually displays foramina radiating from the center, and the tops are skewed ventrally. See page 467 for other shapes of spurs.

DID YOU KNOW? With modern technology, scientists can use photography to realistically reconstruct or reconnect the missing bones of megafauna fossils, such as the giant tortoise. Three-dimensional modeling, combined with such photography, provides a remarkable skeletal likeness, which can give us a glimpse into the prehistoric past.

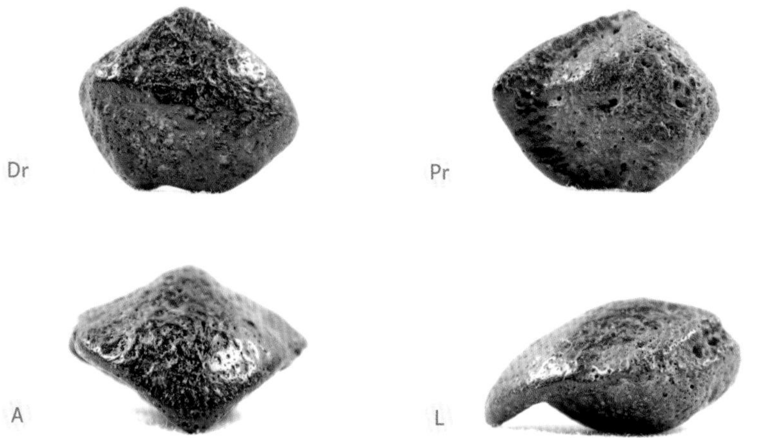

LEG SPUR

Holmesina septentrionalis

Leg spur from the extinct giant armadillo, *Holmesina septentrionalis*. As with the other *Holmesina* osteoderms, the leg spurs have a porous texture. Unlike giant tortoise leg spurs, the spurs on *H. septentrionalis* hook down on the anterior side (seen at left in lateral view). The middle of each spur is ridged, deflecting down to the left and right. Note the foramina on the bottom (seen in proximal view).

SIZE

24 × 19 × 11 mm

0.9 × 0.7 × 0.4 in

GEOLOGIC AGE

Pleistocene

2.6 Ma–11 ka

IDENTIFIERS

Orange-peel texture

Diamond shaped

Hooked anterior side

DENSITY

DID YOU KNOW? The best-preserved giant armadillo fossil was found in 1955 near Houston, Texas, by a teacher, Florence Dawdy, her school-age son, and his friend. Recognizing the importance of the find, she and her family informed the University of Houston's Department of Geology about the discovery. Students and volunteers carefully excavated the specimen, and it forms the centerpiece of the university's museum collection.

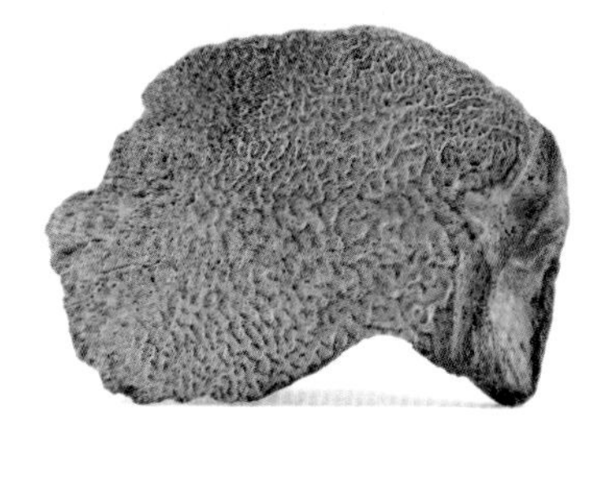

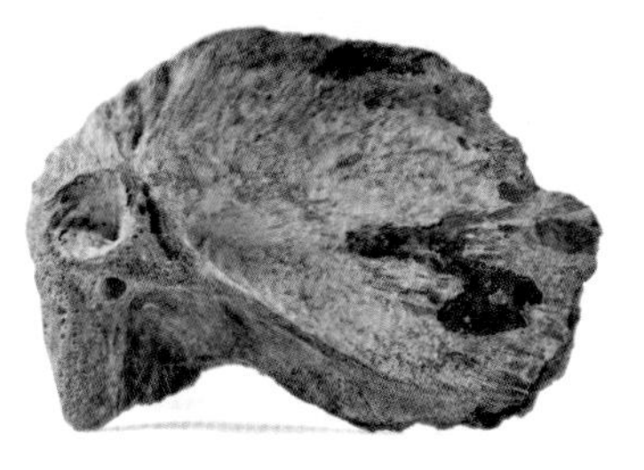

SIZE

41 × 27 × 2 mm

1.6 × 1.1 × 0.1 in

GEOLOGIC AGE

Pleistocene

2.6 Ma–11 ka

IDENTIFIERS

Stippled pattern

Thin form

Raised articulation

DENSITY

OPERCULAR Actinopterygii

The opercular bony gill covering of an undetermined Pleistocene fish. In medial view, the point of articulation can be seen at left. The articulation joint is much thicker than the rest of the plate. In lateral view, note the intricate patterns that are typical of many bony fish. Smaller fragments of opercular bones and cranial elements bear a similarly stippled or striated design (page 466).

DID YOU KNOW? Fish have a way of opening and closing their sensitive gills by activating the bony skin flap called the operculum. This "lid" helps the oxygen-rich water circulate. Water is taken in through the mouth and pushed out through the gills, which collect oxygen. The operculum then closes as water is again drawn into the mouth and the cycle is repeated.

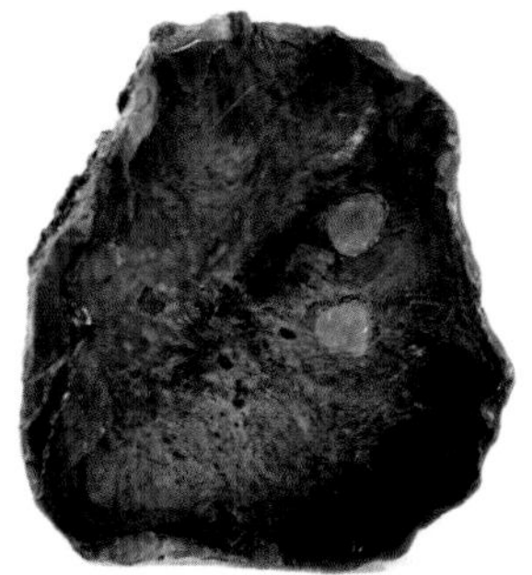

Dr

V

OSTEODERM *Acipenser* sp.

Osteoderm from a Pleistocene sturgeon, genus *Acipenser*. Sturgeon plates have a distinct layered appearance, similar to filo dough, which is apparent in the peeling observed in ventral view above. Osteoderms either are flat or rise up at sharp angles, depending on body placement. The topmost, dorsally located osteoderms are characterized by a prominent ridge (page 204) with an elongated webbed texture.

SIZE

49 × 44 × 6 mm

1.9 × 1.7 × 0.2 in

GEOLOGIC AGE

Pleistocene

2.6 Ma–11 ka

IDENTIFIERS

Tightly webbed pattern

Layered texture

Occasionally curved form

DENSITY

DID YOU KNOW? What do a sturgeon and a vacuum cleaner have in common? They both suck, but you probably won't see a sturgeon on the shelves of your local appliance store! The sturgeon, which is toothless, uses a mouth inhalation technique to draw in shrimp, polychaete worms, and other small organisms. Two pairs of "whiskers," called barbels, dangle from the sturgeon's mouth to help it locate food to suck into its toothless maw.

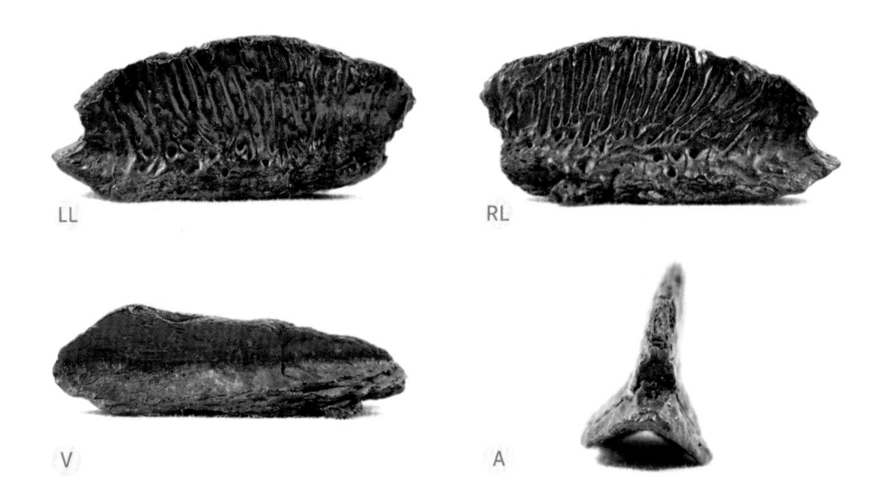

SIZE

57 × 16 × 25 mm

2.2 × 0.6 × 1.0 in

GEOLOGIC AGE

Pleistocene

2.6 Ma–11 ka

IDENTIFIERS

Stretched web pattern

Layered texture

Enamel-like appearance

DENSITY

OSTEODERM RIDGE *Acipenser* sp.

Ridge from one of the dorsal osteoderms of a Pleistocene sturgeon, genus *Acipenser*. The main ridge shows an extension of the pattern observed on lateral osteoderms, with the webbed holes elongated into stretched depressions. The enamel-like appearance comes from alternating layers of bone, ganoine (a shiny material like enamel), and dentine, a structure typical of primitive chondrostean fishes.

DID YOU KNOW? Sturgeons appeared around 225 million years ago, during the Triassic period. They followed an evolutionary pattern similar to that of today's sharks. Like sharks, these fish have a cartilaginous backbone. Sturgeons differ, however, in that they have five rows of external osteoderms, located along the head and top of the body. This armoring provides some protection from predators.

Dr

V

SCALE *Atractosteus spatula*

Ganoid scale from the extant alligator gar, *Atractosteus spatula*. Scales from alligator gars are much larger than those of their slimmer counterparts, *Lepisosteus*. Visible on the dorsal side is an enameloid pattern that radiates out from the middle of the scale. This enameloid often fossilizes as a different color from the main body of the scale. Because of the estuarine and marine range of *A. spatula*, their scales are often more common than those of the freshwater *Lepisosteus* species.

SIZE

36 × 18 × 5 mm

1.4 × 0.7 × 0.2 in

GEOLOGIC AGE

Pleistocene

2.6 Ma–11 ka

IDENTIFIERS

Large size

Diamond shape

Rugose enameloid

DENSITY

DID YOU KNOW? The elongated bodies of gar fish have diamond-shaped scales with a ganoid covering that gives the scales an iridescence or shiny quality. Each scale is very dense and often exhibits a rugose pattern, resembling tiny ridges and valleys, on one side.

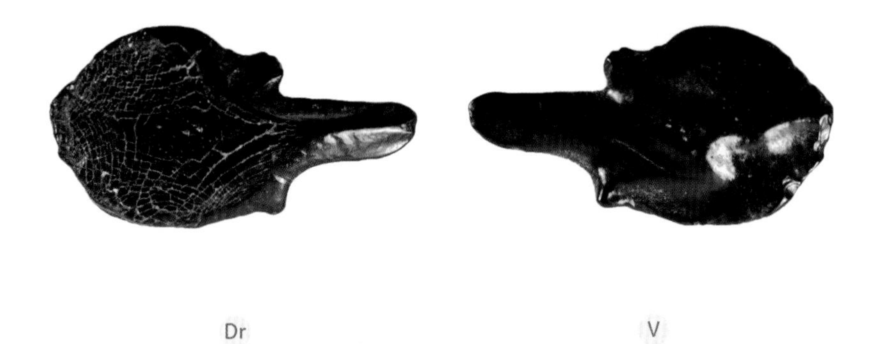

SIZE

16 × 9 × 2 mm

0.6 × 0.4 × 0.1 in

GEOLOGIC AGE

Pleistocene

2.6 Ma–11 ka

IDENTIFIERS

Crackled appearance

Diamond shape

Peg-shaped base

DENSITY

SCALE *Lepisosteus osseus*

Isolated scale from the extant gar fish, *Lepisosteus osseus*. Flat diamond-shaped scales have a narrow extension (often broken off) on the proximal end, where scales attach to the skin; radial grooves are sometimes visible inside the diamond. The dorsal side of the scale often has a crazed or cracked look. Gar fish scales are made of an enamel-like substance called ganoine, so their appearance is very much like tooth enamel: shiny and fairly dense. The scales interlock to create a protective armor. These scales can be differentiated from alligator gar (*Atractosteus* sp.) scales by their smaller size.

DID YOU KNOW? Alligator gars have two rows of teeth, with the inner row longer than the outer row. The teeth are long, slender, and fang-like, allowing them to stab and hold tightly to their prey.

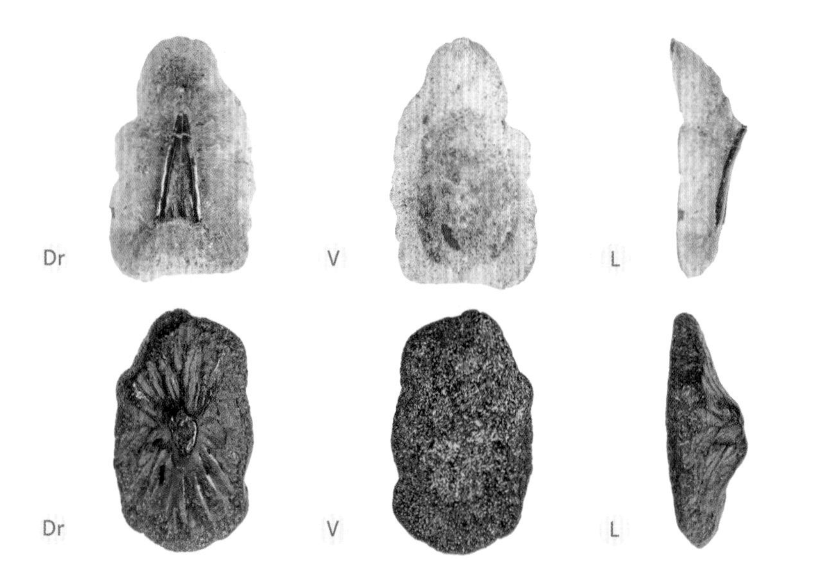

DERMAL DENTICLE

Dasyatis centroura

Dermal denticles from the extant roughtail stingray species, *Dasyatis centroura*. Similar to teeth, dermal denticles are composed of a dentine base and an enameloid tip. These tips, which are exposed, act as protection for the cartilaginous creatures. The bases are broad and flare out on all edges. Enameloid tips are triangular to conical and can be found preserved in groups of adjoining denticles. Radial grooves extend from the denticle margins to the apex.

SIZE

26 × 16 × 6 mm

1.0 × 0.6 × 0.2 in

GEOLOGIC AGE

Pliocene

5.3–2.6 Ma

IDENTIFIERS

Enameloid spine

Broad base

Striated base

DENSITY

DID YOU KNOW? Stingray and shark dermal denticles are similar in structure to human teeth. An inner core of pulp, composed of blood vessels and nerves, is covered with dentine and then solidified with vitrodentine, an extra-hard enamel. These dermal denticles face to the rear of the animal and are smooth to the touch when rubbed with the grain. But don't go against the grain of these creatures, or you will get "roughed up"!

SIZE

96 × 18 × 55 mm

3.7 × 0.7 × 2.2 in

GEOLOGIC AGE

Pleistocene

2.6 Ma–11 ka

IDENTIFIERS

Scute lines

Smooth top and bottom

Spongy-bone interior

DENSITY

CARAPACE

Terrapene carolina putnami

Carapace fragment from the extinct giant box turtle, *Terrapene carolina putnami*. We like to refer to fragments of turtle shell as the "Oreo cookies" of the fossil world. Fragments are smooth on the top and the bottom, with a "filling" of trabeculae where bone marrow would travel through the shell. The dorsal side bears lines where the keratinous scutes were located.

DID YOU KNOW? What are the odds? Two halves of a turtle humerus bone were reunited after 163 years. One part had been found and stored at Drexel University in or before 1849. The other half was discovered in 2012 on a creek bank in Monmouth County, New Jersey. From the size of the rejoined humerus, scientists were able to approximate the turtle's length at 9.8 feet, making it one of the largest sea turtles ever known.

Dr

V

NUCHAL ELEMENT *Trachemys* sp.

Nuchal bone from an extinct Pleistocene slider turtle, genus *Trachemys*. One of the most diagnostic elements of a turtle shell, the nuchal has bilateral symmetry and is fairly diamond-shaped. The scute lines on a nuchal element differ by species. *Trachemys* turtles have rugose (rippled) shells, in contrast with the smoother shells of other aquatic or terrestrial turtles. As with other Pleistocene megafauna, extinct sliders were much larger than extant species.

SIZE

59 × 53 × 17 mm

2.3 × 2.1 × 0.7 in

GEOLOGIC AGE

Pleistocene

2.6 Ma–11 ka

IDENTIFIERS

Scute lines

Bilateral symmetry

Rugose pattern

DENSITY

DID YOU KNOW? The nuchal element is the anterior-most bone of a turtle carapace. Generally, the turtle's neck comes out at that point of the shell, and the nuchal part is slightly curved so that the neck can crane to find food or look for predators.

Dr

V

SIZE

25 × 20 × 6 mm

1.0 × 0.8 × 0.2 in

GEOLOGIC AGE

Pleistocene

2.6 Ma–11 ka

IDENTIFIERS

Smooth dorsal side

Distinct scute lines

Bilateral symmetry

DENSITY

NUCHAL ELEMENT *Pseudemys* sp.

Nuchal bone from the carapace of a Pleistocene cooter, genus *Pseudemys*. Since the nuchal element is the only such bone in a turtle's carapace, the arrangement of scute lines is of great importance when identifying a fragment to the genus or species level. Some *Pseudemys* species differ from other aquatic turtles by having a smooth carapace (compare to page 209). *Pseudemys* shell fragments are also thinner than those of some other turtle species. Note: anterior is to the bottom of the pictured specimen.

DID YOU KNOW? The earliest known turtles are from sea turtle fossils discovered in 220-million-year-old Triassic deposits near Guizhou, China. *Odontochelys semitestacea* lacked a carapace (upper shell), but did have the lower plastron, which offered protection from predators attacking from below. *Odontochelys* jaws had upper and lower teeth, so it probably fed on softer marine prey, whereas some present-day sea turtles have strong, shell-crushing jaws and beaks, but no teeth.

Dr

V

NEURAL ELEMENT Emydidae

An isolated neural element from an undetermined turtle species, family Emydidae. Neural elements are located in the middle of the carapace, where the vertebrae fuse to the shell. These symmetrical bones run the length of the carapace, preceded by the nuchal element and followed by the pygal element. While neural elements are unique within each species, they are not always identifiable to the species level. Nuchal elements are much more helpful in distinguishing species, aided by the pattern and arrangement of the scute lines.

SIZE

32 × 33 × 19 mm

1.2 × 1.3 × 0.7 in

GEOLOGIC AGE

Pleistocene

2.6 Ma–11 ka

IDENTIFIERS

Occasional scute lines

Bilateral symmetry

Ventral vertebra joint

DENSITY

DID YOU KNOW? Turtles are fascinating creatures. The spine of a turtle is fused to the upper inside of the carapace throughout the torso section, but free in the cervical and caudal (neck and tail) regions. This allows the turtle to withdraw into the protected space between the armored upper carapace and lower plastron sections. Fortunately, turtles frequently gather the courage to "come out of their shells" and forage or bask in the sun.

SIZE

59 × 17 × 6 mm

2.3 × 0.7 × 0.2 in

GEOLOGIC AGE

Pleistocene

2.6 Ma–11 ka

IDENTIFIERS

Scute lines

Lateral projection

Curved form

DENSITY

COSTAL ELEMENT

Malaclemys terrapin

Costal, or rib bone, from a Pleistocene diamondback terrapin, *Malaclemys terrapin*. Costal elements articulate with the neural and peripheral bones to form the carapace of a turtle shell. The shallow curve of the above specimen indicates the semiaquatic nature of *Malaclemys*, as opposed to the high-domed carapace of a terrestrial turtle. Turtle costals show scute patterns on the dorsal side and have a projection on the end for articulation with the peripherals.

DID YOU KNOW? In 2015, researchers announced an evolutionary link between turtles and a lizard, *Pappochelys*, whose blocky trunk section shows the beginnings of rib-like pieces fusing together on the belly side. The fossil, discovered in Germany, is striking in its similarity to modern turtles, previously thought to have evolved from a different extinct reptile group. The 240-million-year-old fossil corroborates the discoveries of two similar creatures of around the same age found in China and South Africa.

Dr

V

COSTAL ELEMENT *Apalone ferox*

Rib bone fragment from a Pleistocene softshell turtle, *Apalone ferox*. Trionychid (softshell) turtle costal bones, unlike those of other species, do not attach to peripheral elements. Though similar in texture to emydid (slider) turtle shells, softshell turtle shells have a dimpled or rugose texture. Common fragments of softshell turtle fossils often have the rib projection attached (missing on the above specimen, at bottom on the right).

SIZE

65 × 58 × 7 mm

2.5 × 2.3 × 0.3 in

GEOLOGIC AGE

Pleistocene

2.6 Ma–11 ka

IDENTIFIERS

Dimpled texture

Lack of scute lines

Smooth ventral side

DENSITY

DID YOU KNOW? New fossil evidence from China provides clues about turtle shell evolution. The 220-million-year-old turtles have no upper shell, or carapace, but do have a protective plastron below, lending credence to the theory that the ribs and the carapace developed from the turtle's underside. Another theory has the carapace developing from the fusion of osteoderms in the skin, but the recently discovered turtles have no osteoderms.

Dr

V

SIZE

33 × 22 × 12 mm

1.3 × 0.9 × 0.5 in

GEOLOGIC AGE

Pleistocene

2.6 Ma–11 ka

IDENTIFIERS

Scute lines

Tapering to margin

Sutured edges

DENSITY

PERIPHERAL ELEMENT

Terrapene carolina putnami

A marginal (peripheral) bone from the extinct giant box turtle, *Terrapene carolina putnami*. The carapace and plastron of turtles are made of numerous elements that grow together, in the same way that human skulls fuse from multiple bones during infancy. Peripheral elements, which line the edge of a turtle's carapace, come in a variety of shapes, but complete specimens have three edges that show the bone sutures, and taper down to the marginal edge, which is closed.

DID YOU KNOW? Loggerhead sea turtles are toothless, yet their strong jaws and hooked beaks can crush whelks and other shelled creatures. On the other hand, they don't need very much force to feed on jellyfish, another favorite prey. Such meals are important nourishment for sustaining loggerheads during their nearly three-decade journey along the Gulf Stream to the North Atlantic Ocean, down to southern Europe, and back to their East Coast nesting grounds in the Americas.

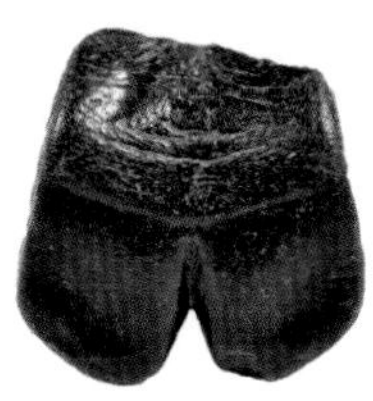

PYGAL ELEMENTS Emydidae

Posterior-most carapacial elements of an undetermined Pleistocene turtle species, family Emydidae. The above element is the last peripheral bone on a turtle's carapace, following the dorsally located neural bones. Because of its position, the pygal is the last bone to ossify (harden) in a turtle's body. Most pygals have a posterior notch on the margin, although those from cooters (*Pseudemys* spp.) have smooth margins.

SIZE

32 × 29 × 12 mm

1.2 × 1.1 × 0.5 in

GEOLOGIC AGE

Pleistocene

2.6 Ma–11 ka

IDENTIFIERS

Bilateral symmetry

Notched margin

Tapering to margin

DENSITY

DID YOU KNOW? Hawaiian green sea turtles, or *honu*, were hunted almost to extinction for their skins and their edible meat, which was considered a delicacy. This changed when, in 1973, the scientist George Balazs surveyed their nesting grounds and counted only 67 nests. Following public pressure for *honu* protection, the U.S. Fish and Wildlife Service classified this species as federally threatened, and it became illegal to kill a *honu*.

SIZE

89 × 63 × 11 mm

3.5 × 2.5 × 0.4 in

GEOLOGIC AGE

Pleistocene

2.6 Ma–11 ka

IDENTIFIERS

Grooved hinge

Anterior curve

Scute lines

DENSITY

PLASTRAL HINGE

Terrapene carolina putnami

Plastral "trapdoor" element from the extinct subspecies of the giant box turtle, *Terrapene carolina putnami*. This hinge, anteriorly located on the plastron, allowed for full closure of the plastron, which helped protect the box turtle from predators. A complete specimen would mirror the portion displayed, with little variation. Fragments of shell near the hinge are common beach finds, and they show a deep groove with a slight lip. The anterior edge would have arced up to nest against the curvature of the carapace when the turtle closed its shell.

DID YOU KNOW? Scientists have long wondered about the lives of sea turtles between the ages of seven and twelve. Tiny transmitters have provided new data. Avoiding the predator-ridden continental shelf, the tagged turtles primarily ride the Gulf Stream around the circular North Atlantic Gyre. Many turn off into the gyre's calm center to feed in the Sargasso Sea, where *Sargassum* seaweed occurs. *Sargassum* also warms surface temperatures, speeding the young turtles' metabolism.

ENTOPLASTRON Cryptodira

Plastral element from an undetermined turtle species, suborder Cryptodira. One of the most readily identifiable bones from a turtle shell, the entoplastron is located in the middle-anterior portion of a turtle's plastron. Complete elements (such as the one above) show distinct suture marks on all edges where the bone articulated with other elements of the shell. The "peace sign" seen in the ventral view was made by keratinous scutes covering the turtle's shell. Scutes do not fossilize well, leaving only their impressions.

SIZE

46 × 36 × 13 mm

1.8 × 1.4 × 0.5 in

GEOLOGIC AGE

Pleistocene

2.6 Ma–11 ka

IDENTIFIERS

"Peace sign" design

Rounded or 4-sided shape

Depressed center

DENSITY

DID YOU KNOW? The largest turtles of both prehistoric and modern times are the giant tortoises. Their huge carapaces are made up of much thicker scutes than those of smaller terrestrial or marine turtles. They also have additional armoring to protect their exposed legs. These take the form of numerous bony osteoderms, or leg spurs. These rounded, off-center bony knobs somewhat resemble leaning pyramids (page 200).

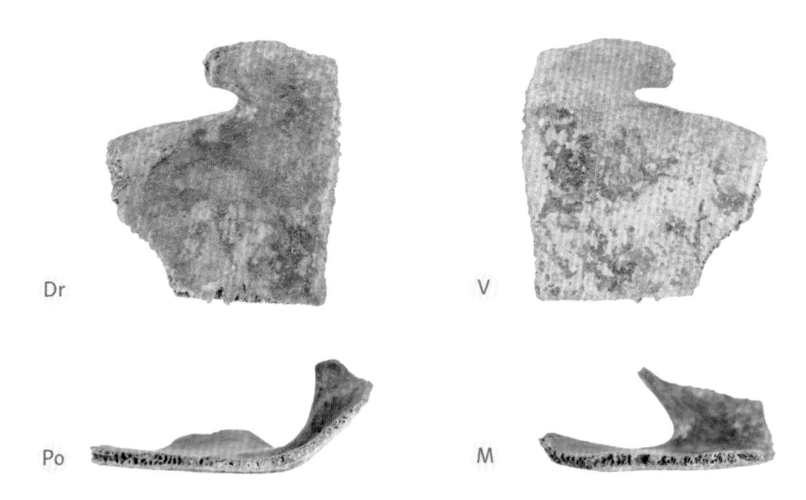

SIZE

45 × 45 × 22 mm

1.8 × 1.8 × 0.9 in

GEOLOGIC AGE

Pleistocene

2.6 Ma–11 ka

IDENTIFIERS

Scute lines

Articular sutures

Dorsal projection

DENSITY

HYOPLASTRON Emydidae

Hyoplastron from an undetermined Pleistocene turtle species, family Emydidae. The hyoplastron is one of nine elements that make up the plastron, or underside, of a turtle. The hypo- and hyoplastra are elements that make up the connecting bridge between the plastron and carapace; those elements allow the turtle's legs and head to come out of the shell. Fewer scute lines are present on the plastron than on the carapace (visible on the ventral side).

DID YOU KNOW? *How the Turtle Got Its Shell* is a popular children's book that retells folktales based on turtles. Native cultures on every continent except Antarctica have ancient stories portraying turtles in positive roles. Many Native American tribes refer to Earth as Turtle Island. In Iroquois and Lenape creation legends, the Great Spirit chose the turtle to carry the homeland island, Earth, on its back.

Dr

V

LL

RL

CARAPACE *Hesperotestudo* sp.

Peripheral fragment of a carapace from a giant tortoise, genus *Hesperotestudo*. As with other elements from giant tortoise shells, the carapace is extremely thick, much more so than in other turtle species. Note the broad scute line running along both sides of the above fragment (seen in the dorsal and ventral views). While this element is incomplete, the lower-right image shows the characteristic sutures present at the edges of each element, where bone growth occurred.

SIZE

85 × 70 × 40 mm

3.3 × 2.7 × 1.6 in

GEOLOGIC AGE

Pleistocene

2.6 Ma–11 ka

IDENTIFIERS

Scute lines

Spongy cross section

Extremely thick

DENSITY

DID YOU KNOW? The Galapagos Islands were named from the old Spanish word "galapago," meaning "saddle." Explorers noticed that some tortoises there had saddle-shaped carapaces that were higher in front. These carapaces had evolved on drier islands, where food was scarce, enabling tortoises to extend their necks to reach higher vegetation. Tortoises with dome-shaped carapaces were adapted to islands with a more humid climate, open spaces, and ample food.

V

Dr

PLASTRON *Hesperotestudo* sp.

SIZE

102 × 78 × 15 mm

4.0 × 3.0 × 0.6 in

GEOLOGIC AGE

Pleistocene

2.6 Ma–11 ka

IDENTIFIERS

Broad scute lines

Thinner than carapace

Flatter shape than carapace bones

DENSITY

Plastral fragment from an extinct giant tortoise, genus *Hesperotestudo*. In contrast with the relatively thin plastrons of terrestrial and aquatic turtles, those of the giant tortoises are thick, with heavy sutures between each plate. Though *Hesperotestudo* leg spurs (page 200) are commonly found, shell fragments—rarely large ones—turn up occasionally. The key identifier for giant tortoise specimens is the shell's thickness.

DID YOU KNOW? The Galapagos Islands were preserved as a national park with the help of the Charles Darwin Foundation in 1959. Scientists studied the remaining species of tortoises on the islands and found that 11 of the 14 species were alive, although some were close to extinction. "Lonesome George," the last member of a species from Pinta Island, lived the last forty years of his life at the Tortoise Center in Puerto Ayora, Santa Cruz Island, dying in June 2012 at the approximate age of 101.

SPECIES HIGHLIGHT

Giant Armadillos and Glyptodonts

Go west, young man! Go north, young mammal!

The nine-banded armadillo, which inhabits the southern United States, is a familiar creature even to those who have never seen one. Considered cute by most, and a huge annoyance by those car drivers who encounter unfortunate armadillos that are too slow in crossing the highway, these unusual animals are repeating a migration pattern their ancestors followed three million years ago. Today's armadillo has expanded its range north of Mexico and Florida since 1850, appearing in South Carolina in the 1980s and the southern Appalachian Mountains in 2014. Nine-banded armadillos extend into southern Illinois and Indiana and west to New Mexico. In 2015, the U.S. armadillo population was estimated at 30–50 million.

Articulated osteoderms from the extinct armadillo *Dasypus bellus*, collected from the Pleistocene Wando Formation in Charleston, South Carolina. Specimen number CCNHM-3496, housed in collections at the Mace Brown Museum of Natural History in Charleston.

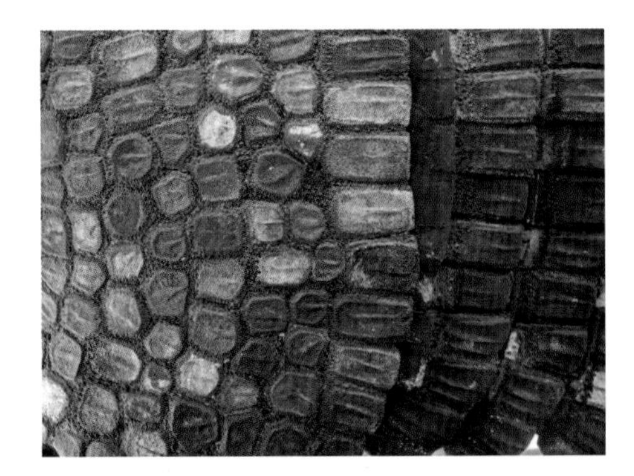

Lateral view of the interlocking osteoderms of the extinct giant armadillo *Holmesina septentrionalis* on display at the Mace Brown Museum of Natural History in Charleston, South Carolina.

Carapacial fragment from the extinct glyptodont, *Glyptotherium* sp.

As recently as 10,000 years ago, three early predecessors of today's armadillo had successfully settled throughout much of this same range before disappearing almost completely from North America. Their migration began in the Pampas region of Argentina before North and South America became connected by the Panamanian Land Bridge. The order of mammals known as Cingulata gave rise to three families—Glyptodontidae, Pampatheriidae, and Dasypodidae—each of which generated armadillo-like relatives that made their way to what is now the United States. Dasypodidae has survived to the present.

The Glyptodontidae family included *Glyptodon*, which made it as far as Guatemala, and *Glyptotherium floridanum*, which migrated as far north as South Carolina. The Pampatheriidae family produced the giant armadillo, *Holmesina septentrionalis*, which measured over 6 feet in length and weighed up to 600 pounds. Both families, and the species they contained, became extinct by the end of the Pleistocene epoch, 11,000 years ago.

Only the Dasypodidae family persisted. Its early species, *Dasypus bellus*, the beautiful armadillo, disappeared 11,000 years ago. Though twice as large as *Dasypus novemcinctus*, today's nine-banded species, this huge armadillo was nearly identical in appearance.

The major trait shared by all these creatures is an armored covering of countless bony plates, or "osteoderms," which create a formidable protection against potential predators. Earlier species had largely rigid or immobile plates and simply tucked their legs and heads in, leaving only the armor exposed. But some later developed movable plates, enabling them to curl their bodies to some degree. This design reached its greatest advancement with the beautiful and nine-banded species, both of which have nine rows of flexible plates (thus the common name of today's species). The immovable plates of both species have hexagonal shapes (shown below), while the flexible plates are in the form of long rectangles. Interestingly, only the diminutive southern three-banded armadillo, which occurs in South America, can curl up into a protective ball.

The nine-banded armadillo is able to run very fast and dig quickly into the soil, leaving only its protective armor exposed. The beautiful armadillo presumably used a similar defensive posture, though its much larger size may have prevented it from retreating from danger as rapidly as its present-day cousin. Another helpful feature of this design is that it makes it difficult for predators to grasp the armored shell. When a person tries to pick up an armadillo, the animal instinctively curls its back, causing a sudden spreading of flexible plates that enables it to pop out of one's grasp and hit the ground running, leaving a very astonished human behind.

Immovable osteoderms from the extinct armadillo *Dasypus bellus*.

All the armadillo-like creatures evolved from a grouping that included sloths and anteaters, which feed primarily on insects, plants and fruits, and small vertebrates such as frogs and lizards. Because of this soft diet, armadillos have neither molars nor incisors, but just a few peg-shaped teeth.

How far north will today's nine-banded armadillo be able to expand its range? That cannot be determined with any certainty. Since the species cannot survive extended cold winters, its range is currently limited. But climate models predict a continued increase in global temperatures, so it is not inconceivable that this historically southern species may someday claim Canada as part of its habitat.

MOUTHPARTS

TRAITS OF MOUTHPARTS

Mouthparts include mandibles, dentaries, maxillae (bones which house teeth), grinding plates, flattened teeth, crushing palates, and dental batteries (apparatuses used to process food). Crushing palates and dental batteries are similar to teeth in being made of enamel or an enameloid substance. Often, many mouthparts resemble the mouths of the creatures that once housed these bones, the anatomy of which are influenced by the teeth and jaw structure.

COMMON TERMS

Anterior, articulate, dentary, dentition, dorsal, grinding plate, labial, lingual, mandible, maxilla, occlusal, palate, posterior, ventral

COMMONALITY

Most mouthparts are relatively common on beaches, especially individual ray teeth. Complete elements and some fragments such as ratfish palates (above) are rarer to find whole.

INCLUSIONS AND EXCLUSIONS

Any fragment of a mandible, maxilla, or dentary is found in this section, regardless of whether it possesses teeth. While individual plates from stingray and eagle ray grinding plates are classified as teeth, they are included here as well. Unless a specimen is marked as an upper plate or tooth, all position icons are oriented as if the mouthpart was located in the bottom jaw (e.g., an occlusal view marked as a dorsal view).

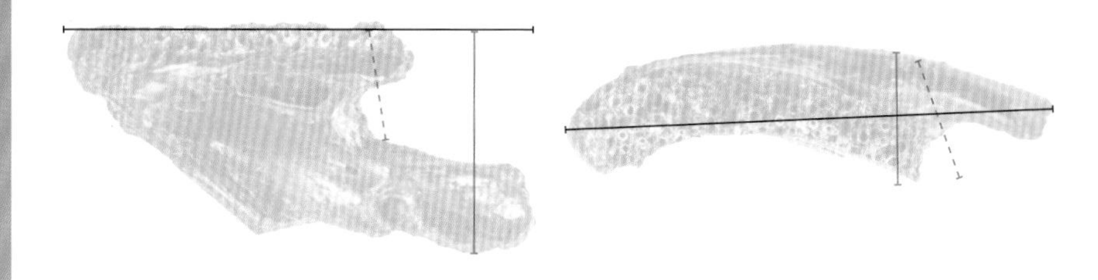

MEASUREMENTS

All mouthparts have measurements displayed in a three-part system:

(longest side × next longest × shortest side)

The longest side always comes first, regardless of position. If this side is ambiguous in the photos, it is delineated in the Item Description. The second-longest side is measured perpendicular to the longest side and in its thickest part. The shortest side is similarly measured perpendicular to the second-longest side. (Dashed lines indicate the third dimension.)

SUPPLEMENTARY IMAGES AND TERMS

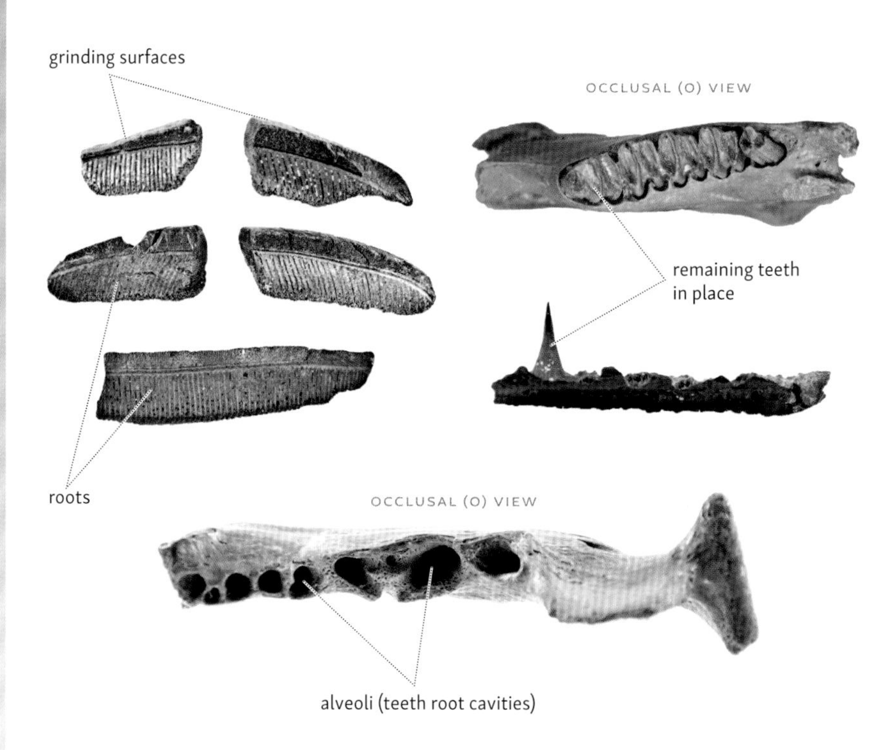

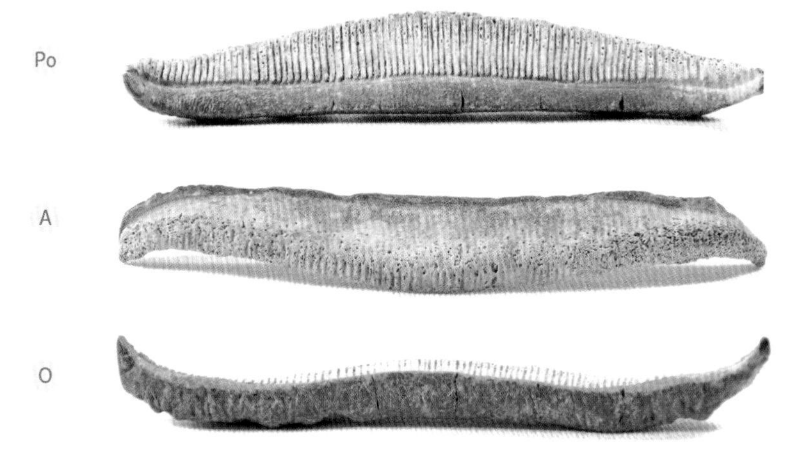

GRINDING PLATE

Aetobatus narinari

Upper tooth from the extant spotted eagle ray, *Aetobatus narinari*. Upper teeth are flat, tapering plates with a solid ridge along the occlusal length and perpendicular grooves running to the bottom. The edges of each plate are curved posteriorly, toward the back of the mouth. It is rare to find intact teeth in beach settings unless the specimen is contained in the matrix.

SIZE

85 × 14 × 7 mm

3.3 × 0.5 × 0.3 in

GEOLOGIC AGE

Pleistocene

2.6 Ma–11 ka

IDENTIFIERS

Occlusal surface

Grooved articulations

Curved tips

DENSITY

DID YOU KNOW? The spotted eagle ray eats a wide variety of marine invertebrates, including spine-covered sea urchins. You might think that chewing such prey would hurt, but the ray uses its platelike teeth to crush food. The crushing motions of the top and bottom teeth plates facilitate the separation of hard spines and shells from soft flesh.

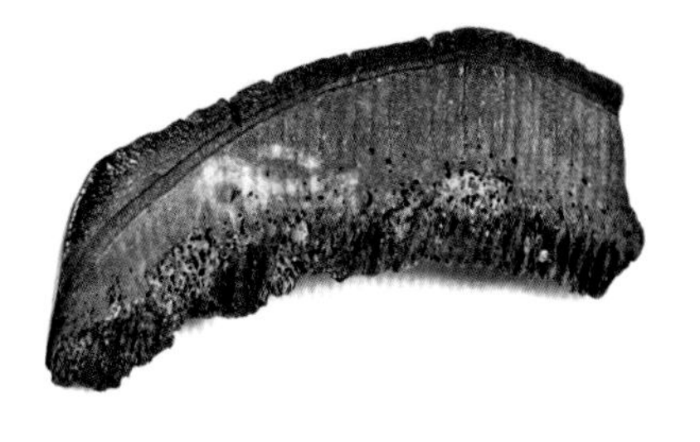

V

O

SIZE

39 × 12 × 6 mm

1.5 × 0.5 × 0.2 in

GEOLOGIC AGE

Pleistocene

2.6 Ma–11 ka

IDENTIFIERS

Occlusal surface

Slanted root grooves

V shape

DENSITY

GRINDING PLATE

Aetobatus narinari

Lower tooth from the extant spotted eagle ray, *Aetobatus narinari*. Lower teeth are angled, tapering plates with a solid ridge along the occlusal length and slanted grooves running to the bottom of each root. The complete form of lower plates is V-shaped, but often only the left or right side is found. These fragments can be differentiated from upper teeth by the angle made by the grooved articulations with the occlusal surface. All fragments of upper teeth are at 90-degree angles.

DID YOU KNOW? Rays are found throughout the world along its warm, equatorial midsection. Living along the edges of coral reefs and the continental shelf, manta rays feed on the tiny young of shrimp, fish, lobsters, octopuses, and other creatures. All these items on the ray's dinner menu are so small (no larger than your thumbnail) that they are crystal clear.

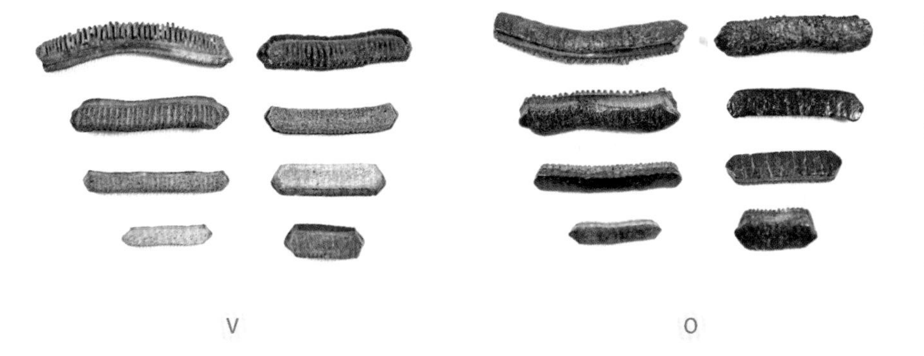

GRINDING PLATES *Rhinoptera* sp.

Isolated teeth of a Pleistocene cownose ray, genus *Rhinoptera*. On each tooth, one side is smooth (occlusal), while the roots on the opposite side are seen as vertical ribbing perpendicular to the tooth length. Tooth ends are often angled at 120 degrees where they articulate with adjoining teeth. Finding joined teeth is extremely rare (see pages 235–236), since this occurs only through the death of an individual. Single teeth are shed during a ray's lifetime, thus accounting for the large volume of isolated teeth that can be found during a hunt. (Measurements provided for the largest specimen above.)

SIZE

39 × 7 × 5 mm

1.5 × 0.3 × 0.2 in

GEOLOGIC AGE

Pleistocene

2.6 Ma–11 ka

IDENTIFIERS

Hexagonal junctions

Vertical ridges

Occasionally curved shape

DENSITY

DID YOU KNOW? Sharks, rays, and skates are cartilaginous fish and considered more primitive than sturgeons, gar fish, puffers, and porcupinefish. They have no true bones, and so material from this class of fishes usually decomposes before it can undergo fossilization. But shark teeth and ray teeth are easily fossilized, and they are abundant on beaches if one looks hard enough. The calcified cartilage of shark vertebrae can also sometimes be found.

SIZE

35 × 11 × 11 mm

1.4 × 0.4 × 0.4 in

GEOLOGIC AGE

Paleocene

66–56 Ma

IDENTIFIERS

Convex crown

Perpendicular roots

Thick crown

DENSITY

GRINDING PLATE *Myliobatis* sp.

Isolated tooth from a Paleocene eagle ray, genus *Myliobatis*. As with other ray species, eagle rays had large flat grinding plates to crush and reduce their prey. The above specimen is an isolated upper tooth. In lateral view, upper teeth are convex, while the lowers are practically flat. While relatively weathered from the ocean, this specimen had not been worn down much before being shed from the ray's mouth, as seen by the thicker middle at the crown (in lateral view).

DID YOU KNOW? While mantas and other ray species benefit from cleaner fishes eating parasites off their skin, are there any other benefits to the rays? Yes! These fish are likely helping maintain ray health by preventing the buildup of algae that can cause life-threatening infections, and the cleaner fishes get a free meal.

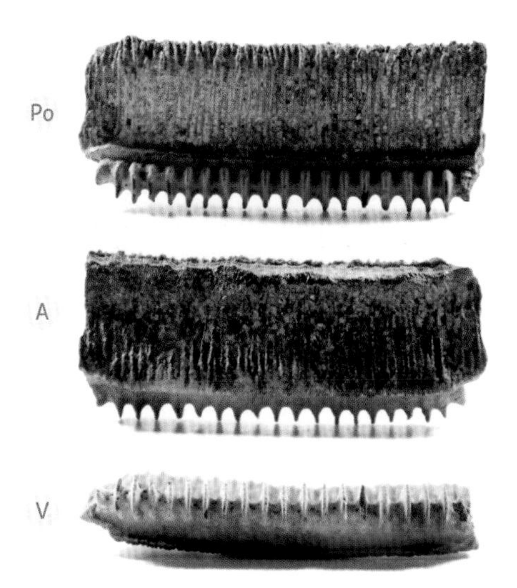

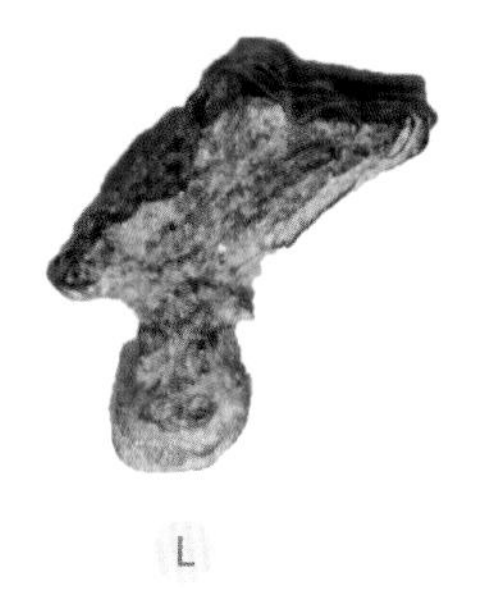

GRINDING PLATE

Plinthicus stenodon

Isolated tooth from a grinding plate of the extinct devil ray, *Plinthicus stenodon*. This tooth, which is of a "U4" elongated design, is the less common of *Plinthicus* teeth. Similar to myliobatid teeth (page 232), devil ray teeth have ridged roots, and those of the U4 design have 20 lobelets. Another distinct trait of these teeth is the 45-degree angle at which they interlock with the other teeth making up the mouth plate.

SIZE

23 × 9 × 3 mm

0.9 × 0.4 × 0.1 in

GEOLOGIC AGE

Oligocene

33.9–23 Ma

IDENTIFIERS

20 lobelets

Thin and fragile form

45-degree articulation

DENSITY

DID YOU KNOW? The name "devil ray" conjures wild images of horns, pitchforks, and red suits. But that is not the case with the mild-mannered *Mobula hypostoma*. Atlantic devil rays' "horns" are actually fleshy forward-facing cephalic fins, and these rays have no stinging spines or teeth with which to "attack" humans. Instead, they feed on plankton and small crustaceans.

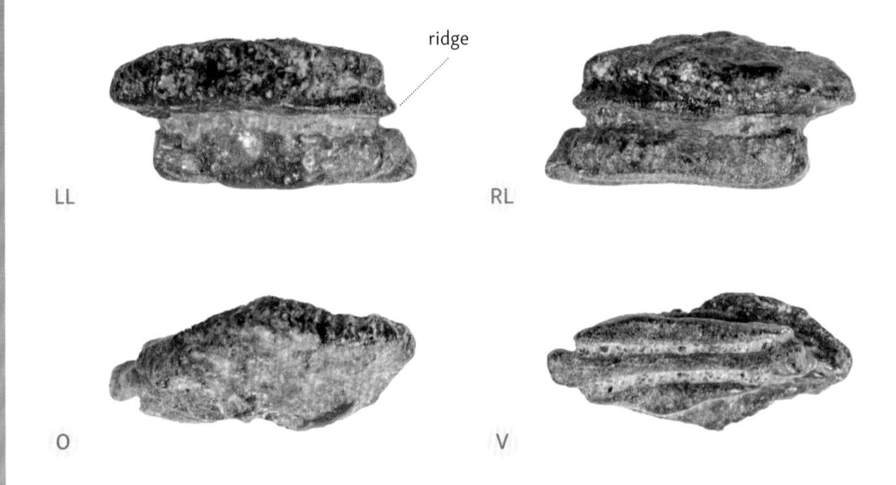

SIZE

10 × 5 × 5 mm

0.4 × 0.2 × 0.2 in

GEOLOGIC AGE

Paleocene

66–56 Ma

IDENTIFIERS

Lateral angles

Lingual shelf

Root design

DENSITY

LATERAL TOOTH *Myliobatis* sp.

Lateral tooth from a Paleocene eagle ray, genus *Myliobatis*. The lateral teeth are found on the sides of the middle teeth (page 236), and much smaller than them. Although these teeth are small, the angle on them is diagnostic for identifying certain genera. The roots of myliobatid teeth extend moderately back into the mouth (seen in the lateral view). Note the ridge that extends around the tooth between the occlusal surface and the root, right above the lingual shelf, where the individual teeth interlocked (indicated).

DID YOU KNOW? Stingrays have eyes on the top of the body, but their mouth, nostrils, and gill slits are located on the underbelly. Scientists believe that the eyes are not involved in hunting. Like their cousins the sharks, stingrays have mouth areas outfitted with electrical-impulse-sensing ampullae that alert the stingray to the presence of prey such as clams, oysters, and mussels.

O

V

GRINDING PLATE *Rhinoptera* sp.

Nearly complete grinding plate from a Pleistocene cownose ray, genus *Rhinoptera*. Rays did, and still do, have two grinding palates, one each on the top and bottom of their mouths. The smooth occlusal surface was used to crush and grind up food like snails and small crustaceans. Shown here in ventral view, the roots have vertical ribbing that is perpendicular to the length of each plate. Since this plate is fully articulated, it came from a dead individual that was fossilized. Note the matrix attached to the ventral side, along with the single lateral tooth (indicated).

SIZE

35 × 31 × 8 mm

1.4 × 1.2 × 0.3 in

GEOLOGIC AGE

Pleistocene

2.6 Ma–11 ka

IDENTIFIERS

Hexagonal articulation

Ridged roots

Smooth occlusal side

DENSITY

DID YOU KNOW? Cownose rays have a distinctive brownish forehead with symmetrical lobes on their snouts. These features give the ray a strong resemblance to a cow's head, and hence its name; they also make this one of the easiest ray species to identify.

GRINDING PLATE Myliobatidae

SIZE

30 × 25 × 8 mm

1.2 × 1.0 × 0.3 in

GEOLOGIC AGE

Paleocene

66–56 Ma

IDENTIFIERS

Curved form

Articulated teeth

Smooth occlusal view

DENSITY

Mostly intact upper grinding plate from a Paleocene eagle ray, family Myliobatidae. Upper plates can be distinguished from lowers by their broad curve (seen in the lateral view). Lower plates are flat, lying horizontally in the lower jaw's cartilage. The above plate was fossilized in the dead individual, explaining the full articulation of the teeth. Individual teeth are shed throughout a ray's lifetime, explaining their prevalence as fossils on many beaches.

DID YOU KNOW? Spotted eagle rays display a dramatic contrast of white spots against a black background, and a body twice as wide as it is long. During swimming, the pectoral fins essentially act as wings that allow the ray to "fly" through the water. Beware, however! These benign traits are accompanied by several stinging spines located behind the dorsal fin, which can inflict painful and serious wounds.

O

V

GRINDING PLATE *Diodon* sp.

Tooth battery from a Pleistocene porcupinefish, genus *Diodon*. These layered grinding plates often display a wear pattern extending down the occlusal surface (indicated). The tooth batteries of *Diodon* are posteriorly distant from the front teeth, and therefore the two are rarely preserved together. Larger porcupinefish have tooth batteries that are massive and high-domed, in contrast with the lower profile of similarly sized *Chilomycterus* (burrfish) tooth batteries. *Diodon* batteries also display 9–24 parallel dental sheets (21 on the above specimen); a lower count is seen in burrfish.

SIZE

25 × 13 × 10 mm

1.0 × 0.5 × 0.4 in

GEOLOGIC AGE

Pleistocene

2.6 Ma–11 ka

IDENTIFIERS

Layered plates

Enameloid surface

Semicircular shape

DENSITY

DID YOU KNOW? The porcupinefish, unsurprisingly, displays numerous rows of spines over most of its body. These spines are folded flat against its skin until the fish is threatened. Then it quickly inhales water, changing from a normal flat-sided fish into a ball of protruding spikes that makes the fish larger than life! No predator wants to tangle with this porcupine.

O

Dr

SIZE

41 × 17 × 16 mm

1.6 × 0.7 × 0.6 in

GEOLOGIC AGE

Pleistocene

2.6 Ma–11 ka

IDENTIFIERS

Layered plates

Enameloid

Football-shaped

DENSITY

GRINDING PLATE *Chilomycterus* sp.

Upper tooth battery from a Pleistocene burrfish, genus *Chilomycterus*. The upper tooth batteries of *Chilomycterus* are highly arched, with tile-like frontal teeth attached to the grinding surface. Unlike those of porcupinefish (*Diodon*), the tooth batteries of *Chilomycterus* are extremely close to the frontal teeth and nearly surrounded by the teeth on the upper and lower jaws. Occlusally, only 2–7 parallel dental sheets are visible on the battery itself, in contrast with the 9–24 seen in *Diodon*. Lower tooth batteries have gently arched frontal teeth and grinding surfaces that are ovoid to subrectangular, and flat to slightly concave.

DID YOU KNOW? Porcupinefish are among the 360 species within the order Tetraodontiformes. These fish include spiny boxfish, toadfish, puffers, blowfish, and burrfish. Porcupinefish swim slowly along the sea bottom, squirting small jets of water to uncover crustaceans, echinoderms, and corals hiding in the sand. Their fused teeth and ribbed mouth plates are used together in a crushing motion that easily separates the needed flesh from its prey.

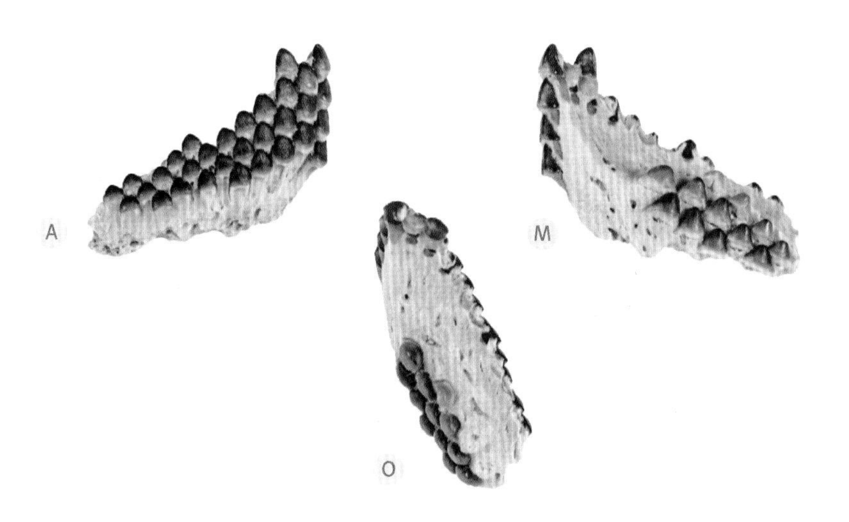

DENTARY Scaridae

Dentary "beak" from an Oligocene parrotfish, family Scaridae. In contrast with the tooth series of burrfish and porcupinefish, those of parrotfish bear small conical teeth growing in series up to the functional row. Scaridae possess two jaws, the front teeth (shown), and a pharyngeal set, and all are used in concert to process coral, seagrass, and calcified algae for eating. Coral-eating Scaridae have rounded teeth cemented together and arranged in diagonal rows; replacement teeth move into position before functional teeth are shed. Note: Older texts erroneously labeled the tooth batteries of burrfish and porcupinefish as belonging to parrotfish.

SIZE

10 × 5 × 3 mm

0.4 × 0.2 × 0.1 in

GEOLOGIC AGE

Oligocene

26–24 Ma

IDENTIFIERS

Unfused dentaries

Conical teeth

Layered tooth series

DENSITY

DID YOU KNOW? Like teenagers, parrotfish love browsing the net, though our scaly friends down under aren't watching cat videos! Parrotfish love browsing the seafloor for algae, sponges, sea grasses, and coral. With their strong jaws and pharyngeal teeth, parrotfish efficiently pulverize any hard material they ingest. Studies have shown this process is so effective that large colonies of parrotfish excreting fine carbonate silt can harm the reefs they live in. You can go learn more by diving in and doing a little browsing yourself.

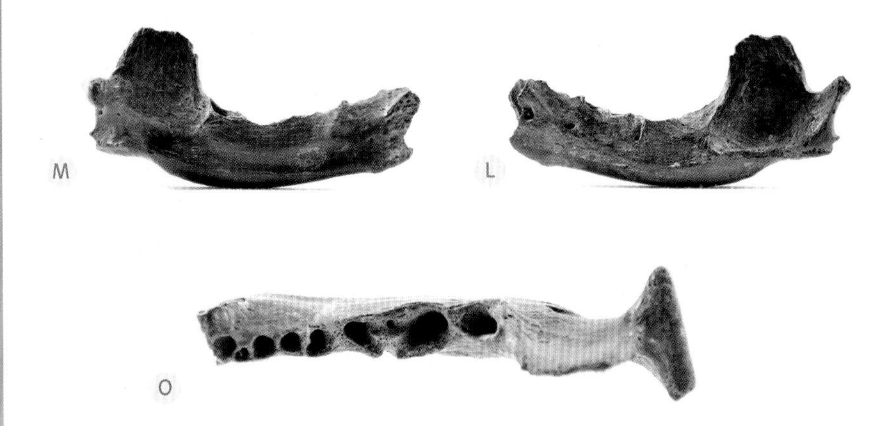

SIZE

61 × 31 × 16 mm

2.4 × 1.2 × 0.6 in

GEOLOGIC AGE

Pleistocene

2.6 Ma–11 ka

IDENTIFIERS

Large alveoli

Oblique root angles

Curved posterior

DENSITY

MANDIBLE *Procyon lotor*

Left mandible (lower jawbone) from the extant raccoon, *Procyon lotor*. As with other specimens from modern animal species, identification is aided by comparison with recent material. Raccoon mandibles can be distinguished from those of opossums by the relatively large alveoli, which are directed at oblique angles; opossum jaws have much narrower alveoli that are in line with the jaw. Note the missing anterior portion, which is broken off where the bone thinned at the lower canine.

DID YOU KNOW? The mask of a raccoon makes it appear cuddly and loveable, and so children often want them as pets. But young raccoons grow more aggressive with age, they are susceptible to carrying rabies, and they often shed parasites in their droppings. Therefore, enjoy these "masked bandits" from afar and prevent them from coming into contact with children and pets.

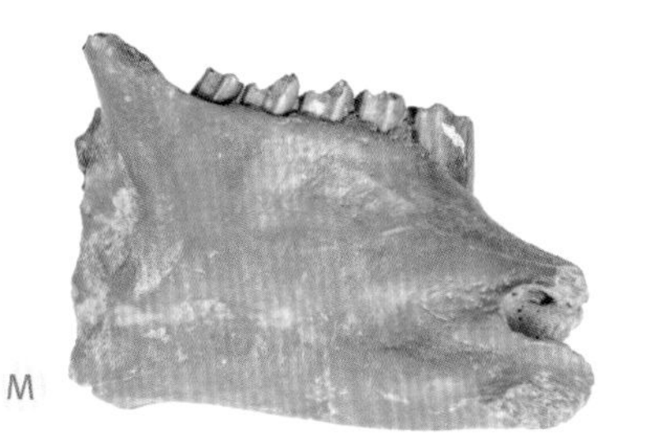

M

L

O

MANDIBLE *Sylvilagus floridanus*

Lower-right jaw from the extant cottontail rabbit, *Sylvilagus floridanus*. Medially, the bone rises closer to the occlusal surface than it does laterally. Note the large foramen at the anterior end of the jaw (seen in lateral view), where a blood vessel supplied nutrients to the anterior portion. In medial view, the alveolus for the lower incisor is evident at right. Compare the structure of an isolated tooth (page 311) to that of the jaw above.

SIZE

25 × 21 × 5 mm

1.0 × 0.8 × 0.2 in

GEOLOGIC AGE

Pleistocene

2.6 Ma–11 ka

IDENTIFIERS

Deep teeth cavities

Blunt shape

Tall posterior

DENSITY

DID YOU KNOW? Bugs Bunny chews on carrots with his showy incisors. In reality, rabbits use their molars to grind up food with a side-to-side masticating motion. This makes rabbits different from rodents. So don't be surprised if you see a rabbit chewing on a carrot with its back teeth instead of in Bugs's "Eh, (chomp-chomp-chomp), what's up, Doc?" style.

SIZE

221 × 27 × 52 mm

8.6 × 1.1 × 2.0 in

GEOLOGIC AGE

Pleistocene

2.6 Ma–11 ka

IDENTIFIERS

Oblique foramina

Round root sockets

Grooves for muscles

DENSITY

MANDIBLE

Alligator mississippiensis

A repaired left jawbone from the extant alligator, *Alligator mississippiensis*. One of the key characteristics of alligator jawbones is the presence of oblique foramina coming out of the bone at regular intervals (page 468). These holes are traces of nerve sensors that were positioned along the alligator's jaw. When their mouths are underwater, alligators use these sensors to detect movements of fish and other prey around them.

DID YOU KNOW? Alligators and crocodiles are often confused because they are similar in appearance. To differentiate between them, look at (but not in!) an alligator's mouth. The mouth and nose are bluntly rounded, and the entire head, from snout to skull, is much wider than a crocodile's. When a crocodile's mouth is closed, most of its top and bottom teeth are visible; however, only a few top teeth can be seen on a close-mouthed alligator.

DENTARY Testudines

Dentary from an indeterminate Late Pleistocene turtle. Since turtles lack teeth, a protective layer of keratin originally covered the jaws. Oblique foramina run through the length of the lower jawbone to allow vital nutrients to be supplied to the keratinous sheath. Holes seen in the dorsal view are from foramina and not alveoli. In the medial view, one large foramen is visible, along with dorsally located sutures from attachment to another bone.

SIZE

48 × 16 × 5 mm

1.9 × 0.6 × 0.2 in

GEOLOGIC AGE

Pleistocene

2.6 Ma–11 ka

IDENTIFIERS

Posterior hinge

Anterior suture

Curved form

DENSITY

DID YOU KNOW? A turtle's mouth has no teeth. The upper and lower jaws are covered with a tough layer of keratin, a structural protein found in horns, claws, and hooves. When a turtle closes its jaws, using strong muscles in its head, the force is powerful enough to break other turtles' shells. With that ability, who needs teeth?

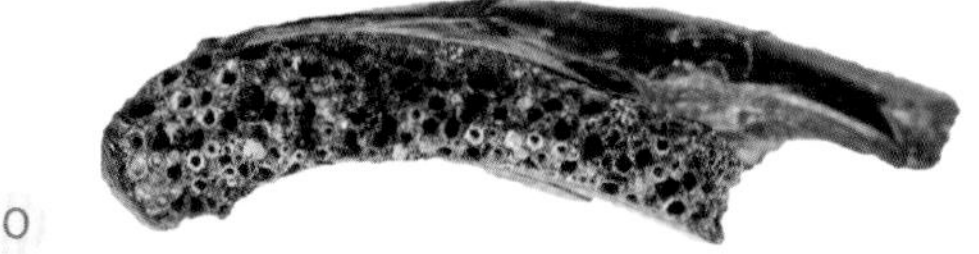

SIZE

22 × 10 × 4 mm

0.9 × 0.4 × 0.2 in

GEOLOGIC AGE

Pleistocene

2.6 Ma–11 ka

IDENTIFIERS

Curved form

Low bone density

Porous occlusal view

DENSITY

DENTARY *Pogonias cromis*

Right dentary from the extant black drum, *Pogonias cromis*. Distinctly different from the pharyngeal grinding mill (page 470), the dentary is the lower jaw located at the front of a fish's mouth. Small teeth were located where the holes are visible in the occlusal view. Other members of the Sciaenidae (drum and croaker) family have similar dentaries.

DID YOU KNOW? When bony fish species feed, two sets of jaws come into play. Oral jaws, located in the front of the mouth, are composed of the maxilla and premaxilla. These are involved in opening and closing the mouth, and in biting and killing the prey. Pharyngeal jaws, farther back in the throat, help mash and process food and then push it to the stomach.

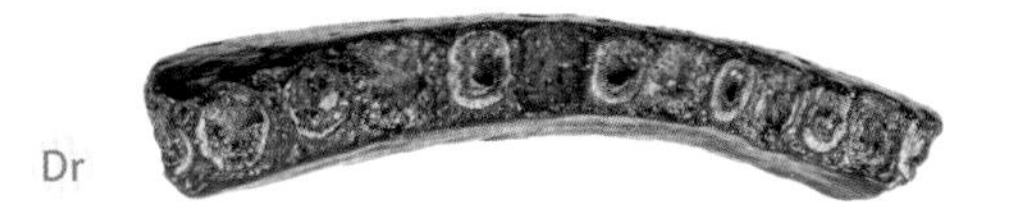
Dr

M

L

DENTARY *Amia calva*

Lower-left jaw (dentary bone) from a bowfin, *Amia calva*, the sole living species of the order Amiiformes. Tooth sockets are comfortably spaced at the rear of the mouth, becoming progressively more bunched together anteriorly. *A. calva* is a predatory freshwater species found in lakes and rivers with low flow rates. Such a restricted habitat indirectly contributes to the scarcity of these fossils on beaches.

SIZE

26 × 9 × 5 mm

1.0 × 0.4 × 0.2 in

GEOLOGIC AGE

Pleistocene

2.6 Ma–11 ka

IDENTIFIERS

Clustered tooth bases

Tapering curvature

Unique bone texture

DENSITY

DID YOU KNOW? There are fishes with names like ghost sharks, ratfish, and spook fishes. Hollywood could produce an imaginative horror movie with such material. In fact, the poorly received film *Ghost Shark* (2013) was such an attempt, but it featured the "ghost" of a great white shark, not a true ghost shark. The "scarily" named creatures above are actually mostly benign, spending their days simply trying to survive, as they have for thousands of years.

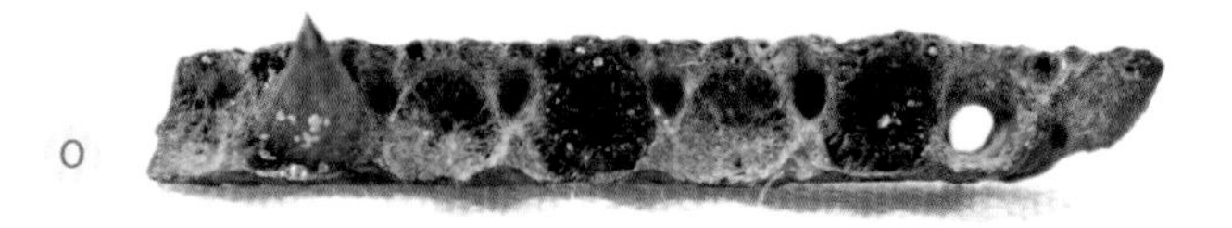

SIZE

27 × 4 × 8 mm

1.1 × 0.2 × 0.3 in

GEOLOGIC AGE

Pleistocene

2.6 Ma–11 ka

IDENTIFIERS

Thin, elongate bones

Conical teeth

Sutured tooth bases

DENSITY

DENTARY *Lepisosteus osseus*

Mandible fragment bearing one tooth from the extant gar fish, *Lepisosteus osseus*. Bases where other teeth attached to the jaw are seen at right. Such mandibular fragments are called infraorbital bones; a series of these bones unite to form the rostrum. Teeth are fragile points jutting irregularly out of the jaw. The ventral side (not shown) of the infraorbital bones is angled, showing the interlocking structure of each bone with another in the jaw.

DID YOU KNOW? Five of the seven species of gar live in North American waters. Gar have remained virtually unchanged for 50 million years and therefore, like a number of other animal species that closely resemble their prehistoric ancestors, are referred to as "living fossils."

Dr

V

DENTAL PLATE *Ischyodus dolloi*

Dental plate from the extinct ratfish, *Ischyodus dolloi*. Ratfish, which are in the same family as chimaeras (Callorhynchidae), use these dental plates to crush the small fish, crabs, and clams they feed on. The ovoid white patches are called tritors (grinding surfaces), several of which occur on the inside of the mouth plates. Note the grooves located on the anterior end in the ventral view (indicated).

SIZE

38 × 26 × 12 mm

1.5 × 1.0 × 0.5 in

GEOLOGIC AGE

Paleocene

66–56 Ma

IDENTIFIERS

Multiple tritors

Grooved anterior end

Chalky appearance

DENSITY

DID YOU KNOW? Chimaeridae fish species almost seem to be a link between the cartilaginous fish and bony fishes, though they belong to the former group. They reproduce like sharks and have similar cartilaginous skeletons, but have the gill structures of bony fish. Their mouths are unusual, containing three plates that protrude from the snout, similar to a rodent's incisors. Thus, they have been given names such as "rabbitfish" or, for species with a very long whip-like tail, "ratfish."

Open jaws of the fierce *Gavialosuchus americanus*, on display at the Charleston Museum, Charleston, South Carolina. *G. americanus* grew in excess of 20 feet long.

SPECIES HIGHLIGHT

Reptiles

Reptiles, scary? No! Come out of your carapace and get acquainted!

The earliest-known reptiles appeared about 315 million years ago, during the Carboniferous period. Reptiles arose from early amphibians and proliferated on land, branching out to form not only other reptile species, but also birds and mammals.

Traditionally, these groups were divided into three classes: Reptilia (reptiles), Aves (birds), and Mammalia (mammals). This classification, long accepted in both scientific and common circles, has come under question with the rise of cladistics, a 20th-century form of biological classification that defines a group of organisms based on traits shared with a common ancestor, but not shared with more distant ancestors. The major issue raised by cladistics is that the class Reptilia excludes Aves and Mammalia, when, in fact, the three classes came from an ancestor with traits shared by all three.

In cladistical taxonomy, these three classes would all be clades within the series Amniota. Amniotes are the major group that split off from the amphibians and that differ from them by sharing the common trait of an amnion, a series of protective layers around these species' embryos. In many reptiles and in all birds, amnions appear in the form of eggshells and membranes, while in most mammals, as an amniotic sac.

There is still controversy among taxonomists about the exact arrangement of orders and families within the series Amniota, and placement of the turtles and tortoises (order Testudines) is one example of such disagreement.

There is little disagreement when looking at the family, genus, and species levels, however. And the crocodiles, alligators, snakes, and turtles are worth noting, since all have left fossils that appear randomly today among beach sediments.

Most fascinating, perhaps, are the alligators and crocodiles, within the order Crocodilia. They fuel the imagination both because of their appearance, which implies a direct connection with creatures from the age of dinosaurs, and because of their notorious reputation as scary predators posing a potential danger to humans.

Crocodilians include alligators, crocodiles, caimans, and herbivorous gavials, but only the first two occur in North America. Both alligators and crocodiles live in the southeastern United States, but crocodiles are tropical creatures, requiring warm temperatures for their survival. Therefore, the one species that lives in North America—the American crocodile, *Crocodylus acutus*—is found only in the southern, tropical portion of Florida.

Alligators, on the other hand, range from southern Florida westward along the Gulf Coast to Texas and southern Arkansas. In the East, they occur in coastal environments and within rivers of the Atlantic coastal plain northward through the Carolinas, nearly to the Virginia border. *Alligator mississippiensis* is the sole species occurring in the United States.

Osteoderm from the American alligator, *Alligator mississippiensis*.

Extinct Oligocene loggerhead sea turtle, *Carolinachelys wilsoni*, on display at the Mace Brown Museum of Natural History, Charleston, South Carolina.

The earliest fossils from the order Crocodilia date to the Late Cretaceous period, around 80 million years ago. The gigantic *Deinosuchus* was to land mammals what *Carcharocles megalodon* was to sea creatures—an apex predator. Whereas the largest-known modern alligator measured in at 19.2 feet in length, *Deinosuchus*, incredibly, reached to at least 35 feet. While its habitat among coastal wetlands and along inland rivers indicates that sea turtles and fish species likely made up most of its diet, this reptile easily could have killed and eaten a *Tyrannosaurus rex*.

In fact, some fossil tail vertebrae from another large dinosaur, *Hadrosaurus*, show evidence of *Deinosuchus* teeth marks. *Hadrosaurus* reached heights of 15–20 feet and were up to 40 feet long, but were likely no match for *Deinosuchus*. Today's alligators differ very little in appearance from their giant ancestor, though they are only half as big. Common fossils found from these reptiles are osteoderms, the knobby bony structures visible on an alligator's back but lying beneath its skin. Less common, but still occasionally found, are alligator teeth. Though modern alligator teeth vary from blunt and dull to sharp and pointed, fossil teeth found on the beach will likely be blunt and worn.

The most common reptile fossils found on many southeastern beaches come from the order Testudines, which includes turtles or, as some prefer to call them, tortoises, or even terrapins. Each name is correct, but their use depends on the country or region where one lives. In the United States, "turtle" generally refers to those species that live in the water, plus some land dwellers, such as the eastern box turtle. "Tortoise" is usually associated with the huge reptiles found in distant lands, such as the Galapagos Islands tortoise. Nevertheless, the small (less than a foot long) gopher tortoise is native to Florida, Georgia, and Mississippi, extending slightly into South Carolina and Louisiana. And "terrapin" is most often associated with the native diamondback terrapin, which occurs along the Gulf and eastern U.S. coasts.

The variety of turtle fossils is remarkable, and finding them is fun, since they are readily identifiable by comparing them with the analogous parts of modern turtles. Most fossils come from the turtle's carapace, commonly called the turtle's shell. A turtle's shell comes in two main parts, the carapace (upper shell) and the plastron (lower shell). These are joined by bridge plates. The pattern seen on a carapace is a reflection of the outline of its many scutes, which are joined together. The lines and patterns found on these scutes, along with their junctures with adjacent scutes, are often well preserved in fossil parts. Each scute has a different name, depending on its location in the carapace.

Pond turtle scutes differ from those of land-dwelling species in the rugose relief patterns they contain. Shell remnants from the giant tortoise that once roamed the coastal plain are noticeably different from any others (page 219). They are clearly giant-sized in comparison with the same parts from smaller pond and land species. These huge tortoises also had legs covered with knobby hard armor called leg spurs, and careful searching will turn these up on occasion.

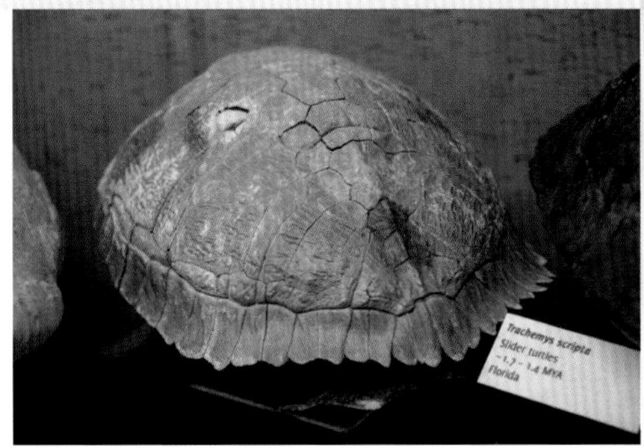

left Pleistocene slider turtle shell on display at the Mace Brown Museum of Natural History, Charleston, South Carolina. The predation puncture holes are from a crocodilian.

right Posterior view of a *Trachemys* slider turtle shell on display at the Mace Brown Museum of Natural History, Charleston, South Carolina.

The third grouping of reptiles worth noting is found within the order Squamata, which includes the lizards and snakes. Lizard bones are so tiny that they rarely survive the ocean's pummeling action. The skeletal fossils of snakes (suborder Serpentes) are also unlikely to survive intact. Snake skull plates, which are held together relatively weakly, tend to deteriorate quickly, usually before becoming fossilized, but it is not uncommon to encounter fossil vertebrae from many species of snakes.

The earliest evidence of snakes comes from fossils found in the United States, England, and Portugal that date to 143–167 million years ago, during the Late Jurassic period, though Serpentes species likely evolved much earlier. The biggest snake fossil ever found came from an open-pit coal mine in Colombia, and was dated to about 60 million years ago. This was the monstrous *Titanoboa cerrejonensis*, which reigned for 10 million years after the extinction of the dinosaurs. It is estimated to have been nearly 50 feet in length and to have weighed 2,500 pounds. In addition to vertebrae, a rare fossilized skull was unearthed, revealing jaws that could separate widely, as is the case with modern boa constrictors and anacondas. *Titanoboa* was a constrictor capable of exerting an extreme crushing force on crocodiles and other large reptiles.

The snakes that evolved later did so in much cooler climates, which do not allow for such incredible proportions. Boas and anacondas do not occur naturally in the United States, but many species of much smaller snakes lived and hunted in the Southeast. Most intact fossils are found in inland sites such as quarries. In Florida, such fossils go back to the Eocene epoch and become more common through the Oligocene, Miocene, Pliocene, and Pleistocene. Most of those found on southeastern beaches are of Pleistocene origin.

Snake vertebrae have intricate and fascinating shapes, and it is always exciting to discover one among the items picked up from beach deposits. Nevertheless, reptiles typically aren't spoken of with affection. William Blake certainly didn't describe them in glowing terms when he scrolled: "The man who never alters his opinion is like standing water, and breeds reptiles of the mind."

Maybe. But by moving at a turtle's pace and sidewinding your way from the dunes to the water, you might discover an alligator osteoderm or a snake vertebra. See you later, alligator!

TEETH

TRAITS OF TEETH

Teeth are the most studied and most useful elements for the identification of current and fossil animals. As a result, the terminology and classification of teeth are fairly complex, with many terms devoted solely to their study. Most teeth are composed of a crown with an enamel covering that sits on a dentine core and a root covered in cement. In vertebrates other than mammals, teeth are shed continuously throughout the organism's life. Mammals, however, start life with deciduous premolars and molars (milk teeth), shedding only one set before reaching adulthood. Mammalian teeth follow a specific numbering system (see Measurements) based on a primitive tooth state, determined by the position within the mouth.

COMMON TERMS

Anterior, brachyodont, bunodont, canine, cement, crown, cusp, cuspule, dentine, dentition, enamel, fossette, heterodonty, homodonty, hypselodont, hypsodont, incisor, labial, lingual, loph, lophodont, molar, occlusal, oreodont, posterior, premolar, root, selenodont, tusk

Additional terms may be used to describe the complex folds of enamel on the teeth of different animals.

COMMONALITY

At localities with numerous vertebrate fossils, fragments of enamel and root dentine are fairly common. Herbivore teeth are more abundant than carnivore teeth, and finding complete teeth is less common than finding their fragments.

INCLUSIONS AND EXCLUSIONS

Mammalian, reptilian, and fish teeth are contained in this section, from incisors to molars. Also included are rostral denticles from sawfish, despite their anatomical identification as denticles rather than teeth. Isolated teeth from ray grinding plates are not included in this section; refer to the chapter Mouthparts for such specimens.

MEASUREMENTS

All teeth have measurements displayed in a three-part system:

(longest occlusal side × shorter occlusal side × tooth height)

The occlusal dimensions are always listed first, followed by the total tooth height or the crown height if no root is present. (Dashed lines indicate the third dimension.) If possible, the position of a tooth is provided. This is indicated by the following system:

I2	Second upper incisor
P4	Fourth upper premolar
M3	Third upper molar
DP2	Second deciduous premolar (upper)

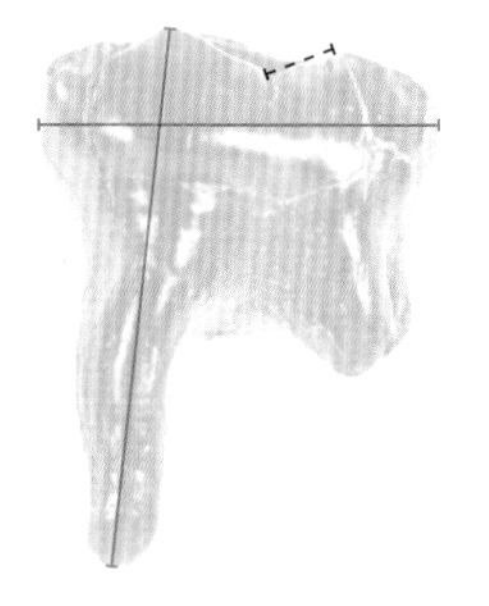

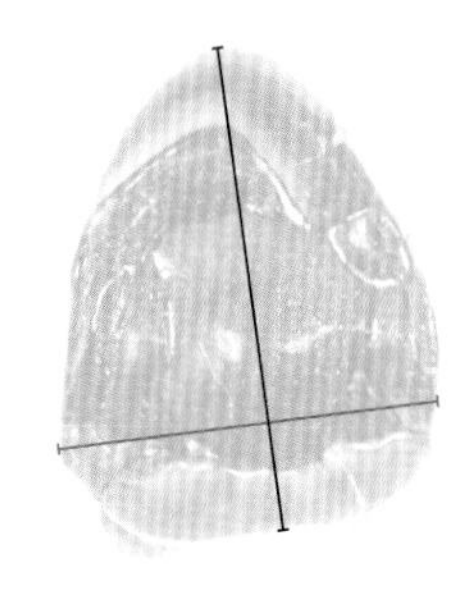

All upper teeth positions are capitalized, while lowers are lowercase. Deciduous teeth bear the prefix "D/d" before the tooth type. Numbers represent the location of the tooth, as numbered by its ancestral position in the mouth. Teeth designated by lower numbers are more anteriorly located, while those with higher numbers are more posterior. (See diagram, page 470.)

SUPPLEMENTARY IMAGES AND TERMS

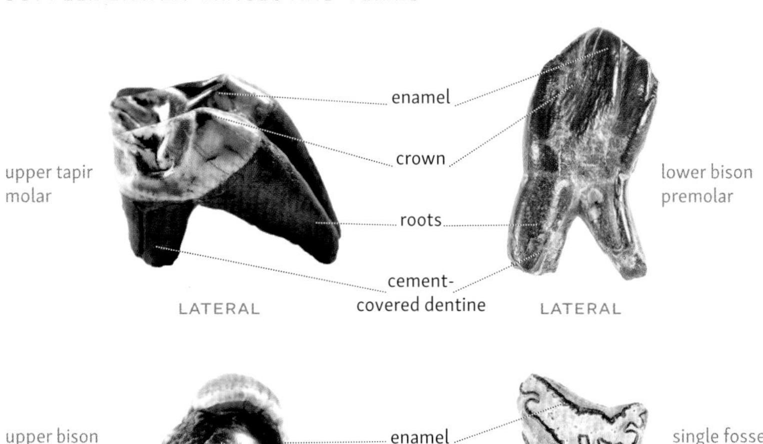

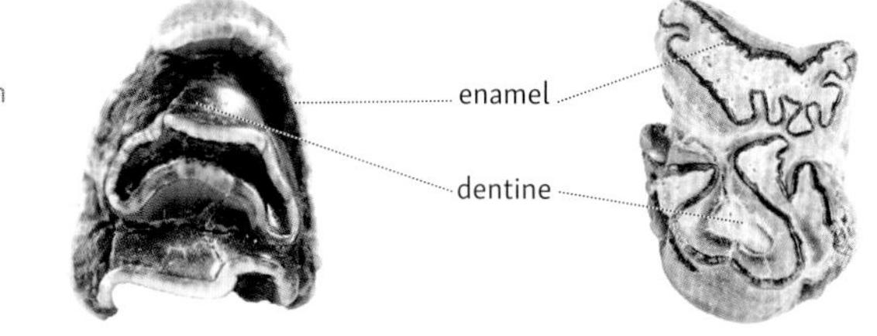

INCISOR *Tapirus veroensis*

Incisor from the common Pleistocene tapir, *Tapirus veroensis*. Tapir incisors are similar to chisels in the way that they come to a sharp edge on the occlusal surface. Others describe the teeth as having the form of a spatula. Unlike *Equus* incisors, tapir incisors have roots that are straight and in line with the exposed crown.

SIZE

11 × 11 × 47 mm

0.4 × 0.4 × 1.8 in

GEOLOGIC AGE

Pleistocene

2.6 Ma–11 ka

IDENTIFIERS

Chisel-like crown

Straight root

Spatulate shape

DENSITY

DID YOU KNOW? Imagine shrinking an elephant down to the size of a large pig. You would have the rough image of a tapir. A tapir's mini trunk is useful in snuffling out food and then easing it into its mouth.

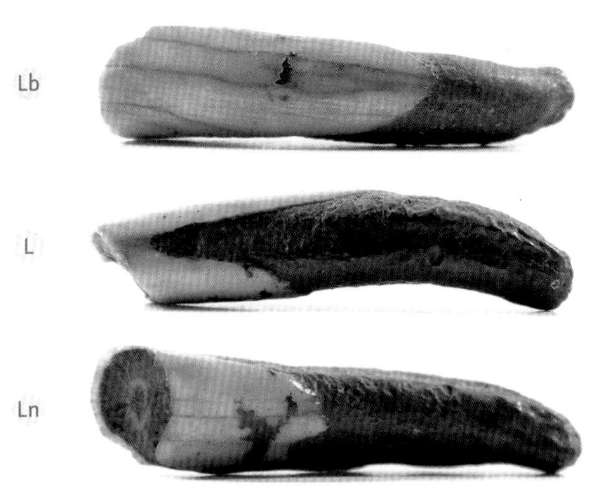

SIZE

10 × 8 × 42 mm

0.4 × 0.3 × 1.6 in

GEOLOGIC AGE

Pleistocene

2.6 Ma–11 ka

IDENTIFIERS

Round form

Long anterior enamel

Curved root

DENSITY

INCISOR *Palaeolama mirifica*

Incisor from the Pleistocene camelid *Palaeolama mirifica*. *Palaeolama* incisors are distinctly round in form, with an acute wear angle. The occlusal surface, in lingual view, bears a unique radiating pattern from the center of the tooth outward to the enamel. In lateral view, the enamel is greatly reduced because of the bunched nature of the incisors and their proximity to each other.

DID YOU KNOW? Camels had snowshoes? Pleistocene camelids living in the cold Canadian climate had wide feet, somewhat resembling snowshoes, that didn't sink down into softer ground material like snow and sand. Their humps may have originated as places to store fat to help keep them warm in the cold, but eventually became a method of storing fat for use as food during lengthy travels across the desert.

INCISOR *Equus* sp.

Curved incisor from the extant genus of horses, *Equus*. A horse has six upper and six lower incisors. Patterns in the enamel seen in the occlusal view vary based on the age of the individual—some may have simple rings of enamel, while others may have an interior enamel ring or a fold in the outer enamel (seen above). Teeth taper to laterally compressed roots, enabling the teeth to fit in the jaw.

SIZE

18 × 10 × 56 mm

0.7 × 0.4 × 2.2 in

GEOLOGIC AGE

Pleistocene

2.6 Ma–11 ka

IDENTIFIERS

Curved shape

Wavy occlusal enamel

Narrow root

DENSITY

DID YOU KNOW? *Merychippus* was the first of the early equines to have the classic horse-shaped head of today's *Equus* species. The longer muzzle and widely separated eyes, together with a longer neck and long legs, enabled these animals to lower their heads for grazing as well as to look up high above the grasses and keep a wary eye out for predators.

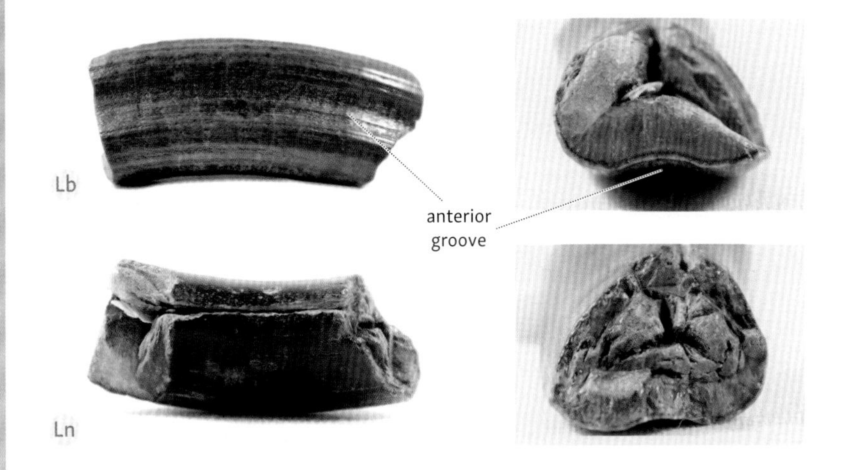

SIZE

17 × 12 × 42 mm

0.7 × 0.5 × 1.6 in

GEOLOGIC AGE

Pleistocene

2.6 Ma–11 ka

IDENTIFIERS

Anterior groove

Anterior enamel

Hypselodont form

DENSITY

INCISOR *Neochoerus pinckneyi*

Partial incisor from the extinct giant capybara, *Neochoerus pinckneyi*. Incisors from both the giant capybara and the Pleistocene capybara (*Hydrochoerus holmesi*) have an anterior groove running the length of the incisor (indicated). *H. holmesi* and *N. pinckneyi* incisors appear nearly identical, but the former are smaller—around 10 mm in diameter. Capybaras have two upper and two lower incisors. Complete incisors form a curved semicircular shape, typical of all rodents.

DID YOU KNOW? "Capybara" means "master of the grass," and the word comes from Tupi, a language spoken by a native people of Brazil. The specific name of the giant capybara was named after Charles Pinckney Jr., who owned the Magnolia Phosphate Mine near Charleston, South Carolina.

INCISOR *Castoroides dilophidus*

Incisor fragment from the extinct giant beaver, *Castoroides dilophidus*. Fragments of these incisors are occasionally confused with those of capybaras (*Neochoerus* and *Hydrochoerus*); however, giant beaver incisors lack the broad anterior groove in the middle of the tooth and have much deeper, thicker enamel grooves. See the comparison on page 467. Enamel covers only the anterior portion of the incisors. Intact uppers span a sharp 180 degrees, while lowers curve at a much shallower angle.

SIZE

27 × 20 × 61 mm

1.1 × 0.8 × 2.4 in

GEOLOGIC AGE

Pleistocene

2.6 Ma–11 ka

IDENTIFIERS

Deep enamel grooves

No anterior groove

Anterior enamel

DENSITY

DID YOU KNOW? Beavers are well known for their prominent incisors; the extinct giant beaver's front teeth were six inches long. The texture of the teeth is longitudinally ridged, with blunt, curved cutting edges, unlike the chisel-shaped incisors of modern beavers. Their cheek teeth resembled a capybara's, with an S-shaped enamel chewing surface for grinding tough vegetation (page 314).

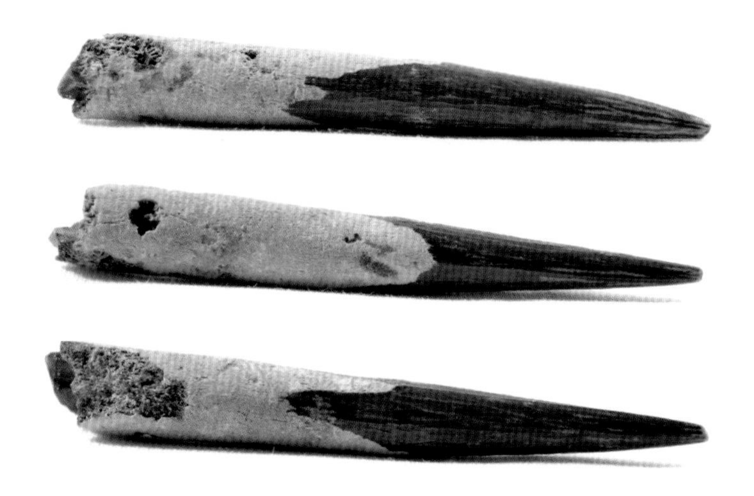

INCISOR Waipatiidae

SIZE

8 × 8 × 63 mm

0.3 × 0.3 × 2.5 in

GEOLOGIC AGE

Oligocene

33.9–23 Ma

IDENTIFIERS

Wavy enamel base

Conical shape

Striated enamel

DENSITY

Isolated incisor from an unnamed whale species in the Waipatiidae family. This odontocete used these pointed front teeth to spear and cage fish in its mouth. After the conical incisors and premolars come a series of double-rooted serrated teeth (page 330) similar to those of *Xenorophus*, *Squalodon*, and other heterodont echolocating whales from the Oligocene.

DID YOU KNOW? Whale skulls have evolved for over 50 million years. Early whales had large cavities behind their eyes with specialized muscles for snapping their jaws shut on prey. Through time, some whales evolved an efficient method of using their tongues to suck in large amounts of water containing prey. Therefore, in such species, the tongue muscles became larger and more important, and the jaw muscles and cavities became smaller.

CANINE · C *Ursus americanus*

Upper canine from the extant American black bear, *Ursus americanus*. Identification of isolated canines is difficult; knowledge of the geologic deposit helps greatly. Florida cave bear (*Tremarctos floridanus*) canines have a broader enamel base and are more robust than *U. americanus* canines. Note the smooth transition between the enamel base and the root.

SIZE

21 × 12 × 66 mm

0.8 × 0.5 × 2.6 in

GEOLOGIC AGE

Pleistocene

2.6 Ma–11 ka

IDENTIFIERS

Thick root

Thin enamel crown

Sharply curved crown

DENSITY

DID YOU KNOW? Black bears of the eastern United States are black with brown muzzles. But black bears of the western states, Alaska, and British Columbia vary in coloration from cinnamon brown or blonde to creamy white and even bluish gray. That is not exactly black, but it provides a good example of the wide variety in color within a species.

SIZE

13 × 9 × 56 mm

0.5 × 0.4 × 2.2 in

GEOLOGIC AGE

Pleistocene

2.6 Ma–11 ka

IDENTIFIERS

Robust size

Lateral compression

Thick crown

DENSITY

CANINE · c *Canis dirus*

Lower canine from the extinct Pleistocene dire wolf, *Canis dirus*. Lower canines curve slightly to the lateral side of the tooth, and the overall curve is within the anterior-posterior plane. In all carnivoran canines, the roots in the lower teeth have a sharper curve than the roots in the uppers. Medially, the crown has a distinct elevated ridge of enamel called the mesial tubercle and ridge (indicated). In the posterior view, note the wear facet on the inside of the canine where the upper canine occluded with the lower.

DID YOU KNOW? Dire wolf skeletons are the commonest large-animal fossils found in the La Brea Tar Pits, where over 4,000 individual specimens have been found.

CANINE · C *Lynx rufus*

Upper canine from the extant bobcat, *Lynx rufus*. Unlike the more conical teeth of canids and ursids (bears), canines from bobcats are more laterally compressed, showing their function for tearing meat. Note the ridge of enamel (carina) that runs along the anterior and posterior sides of the crown. Overall, the form of bobcat upper canines is straight, in contrast to the more curved canid or raccoon canines.

SIZE

5 × 3 × 27 mm

0.2 × 0.1 × 1.1 in

GEOLOGIC AGE

Pleistocene

2.6 Ma–11 ka

IDENTIFIERS

Straight form

Lateral compression

Ridged enamel crown

DENSITY

DID YOU KNOW? The manes of male lions are a distinguishing feature between the sexes. Manes offer protection during interspecies fighting, provide recognition at a distance, and indicate a male's physical and reproductive fitness. Manes develop with climate and testosterone production. For a male lion, the "main" thing is to grow "manely" hair!

CANINE · C *Palaeolama mirifica*

SIZE

16 × 8 × 46 mm

0.6 × 0.3 × 1.8 in

GEOLOGIC AGE

Pleistocene

2.6 Ma–11 ka

IDENTIFIERS

Lateral compression

Angled interior

Bladelike crown

DENSITY

Upper canine from the extinct common Pleistocene camelid, *Palaeolama mirifica*. Note the laterally compressed nature of this canine, which is in contrast with the width of those from bears, peccaries, and raccoons. The interior side (in the posterior view) has a thin, bladelike edge, while the outer (anterior) side is broad and smooth. The anterior side also curves more smoothly than the interior, which is angled, especially once the enamel crown begins.

DID YOU KNOW? Fossils of a 100,000-year-old giant camel were reported from a site in Syria in 2003, and the find was later confirmed when more of its bones were discovered there. Paleontologists also found the remains of paleo humans and their stone weapons at the site. The wide savanna there had springs that attracted many animals, and the early humans may have killed the giant camel when it came to drink.

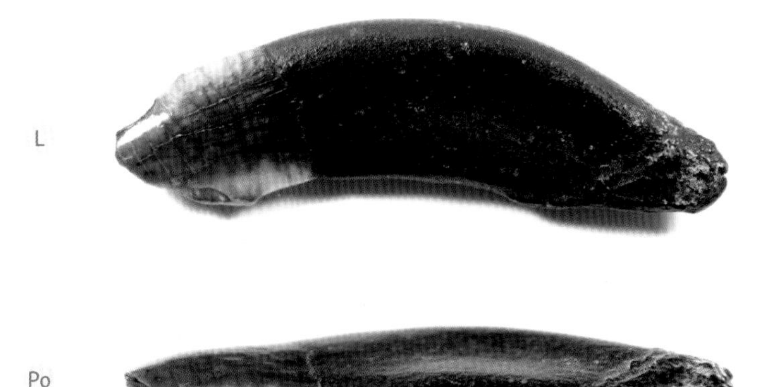

CANINE · c Lamini

Lower canine tooth from an undetermined species of Pleistocene lamine camelid. As with other camel canines, this lower tooth is compressed laterally, with a narrow root and a much narrower crown. Note the bladelike enamel projecting inward, or posteriorly. The straightness of lower canines contrasts with the sharply curved uppers.

SIZE

8 × 4 × 32 mm

0.3 × 0.2 × 1.2 in

GEOLOGIC AGE

Pleistocene

2.6 Ma–11 ka

IDENTIFIERS

Lateral compression

Bladelike enamel

Narrow root

DENSITY

DID YOU KNOW? Camels originally evolved around 44 million years ago in North America, not in Asian deserts. Not until the relatively recent Pliocene–Pleistocene time span did camels, which were then sheep-sized animals, migrate to Eurasia, Africa, and South America. As camels evolved, they became slender and gazelle-like (*Stenomylus*) or long-legged and long-necked (*Oxydactylus*). A few species, such as *Camelops hesternus*, were the last known camels in North America—probably similar to today's llamas.

SIZE

15 × 9 × 64 mm

0.6 × 0.4 × 2.5 in

GEOLOGIC AGE

Pleistocene

2.6 Ma–11 ka

IDENTIFIERS

Beveled tip

Tapering root

Oval cross section

DENSITY

CANINE · C *Platygonus compressus*

Upper canine (also referred to as a tusk) from the extinct Pleistocene peccary *Platygonus compressus*. Flat grooves mark where this canine ground against the lower canine. On the beveled edge, the interior structure of the canine can often be seen (page 469). From their saber-like appearance, peccary tusks can occasionally be mistaken as canines from saber-toothed cats, though they are much shorter and lack an enamel covering. Lower *Platygonus* canines are beveled on the concave side.

DID YOU KNOW? How can peccary tusks make sounds? Modern peccaries rub their tusks together to make a chattering sound, and, likely, so did their extinct ancestors. These very audible sounds warn potential predators to stay away.

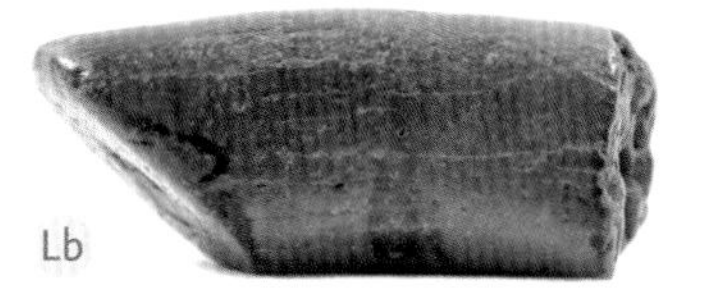

CANINIFORM

Paramylodon harlani

Upper first cheek tooth from the extinct Harlan's ground sloth, *Paramylodon harlani*. Distinct from the other cheek teeth, the anterior-most upper tooth became worn to a chiseled edge, since it did not occlude well with the first lower tooth. Sloth teeth are ever-growing (hypselodont) and lack the enamel characteristic of most vertebrate teeth.

SIZE

18 × 16 × 44 mm

0.7 × 0.6 × 1.7 in

GEOLOGIC AGE

Pleistocene

2.6 Ma–11 ka

IDENTIFIERS

Lack of enamel

Chiseled edge

Hypselodont form

DENSITY

DID YOU KNOW? North America was home to many species of ground sloths during prehistoric times. *Megalonyx* was prevalent throughout all of North America, and its fossils have been found at over 150 sites. *Nothrotheriops* specimens were located mainly in the Southwest, although some fossils have been collected from Florida. *Paramylodon* was well dispersed through the United States from lower altitudes up to an elevation of about 8,000 feet.

O

L

SIZE

25 × 18 × 11 mm

1.0 × 0.7 × 0.4 in

GEOLOGIC AGE

Pleistocene

2.6 Ma–11 ka

IDENTIFIERS

Small size

Thin, rippled enamel

Button-like shape

DENSITY

PREMOLAR *Mammuthus columbi*

The small deciduous premolar (dp2/DP2) from a Columbian mammoth, *Mammuthus columbi*. Just like humans, mammoths are born with deciduous premolars that are shed between the ages of two and five years old. Because these teeth appear in the very young, they are often referred to as "milk molars." Though small, these teeth show the layers of enamel present on adult molars.

DID YOU KNOW? Mammoth calves began growing milk tusks at around 6 months of age. These deciduous "baby teeth" were the precursors of the large asymmetrical tusks that replaced them at 18 months and that slowly grew (1–6 inches per year) throughout the rest of the mammoth's life. Paleo humans, close observers of the animals living around them, left cave paintings showing some mammoths with small tusks or no tusks at all.

O

Po

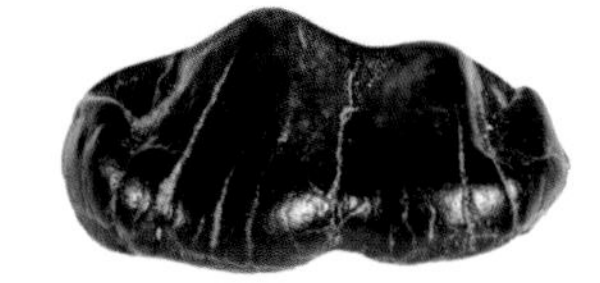
Lb

Ln

PREMOLAR · DP1 *Tapirus veroensis*

Deciduous upper-right premolar (DP1) from the late Pleistocene tapir, *Tapirus veroensis*. Tooth morphology in tapirs shows that the premolars were heavily molarized, which assisted in processing vegetation; this can be seen in the broad occlusal surfaces of the P1–P4. Unique among mammals is tapirs' retention of the first premolar (P1) once the deciduous premolar is shed, giving the animals seven upper cheek teeth, compared with the usual six (P2–M3) of other mammals.

SIZE

17 × 15 × 8 mm

0.7 × 0.6 × 0.3 in

GEOLOGIC AGE

Pleistocene

2.6 Ma–11 ka

IDENTIFIERS

Triangular shape

Molarization

Multiple cusps

DENSITY

DID YOU KNOW? Maturing to adulthood involves many rites of passage, including losing the teeth you have known for your first six or so years of life. The same is true for today's tapir species. Tapirs lose their baby premolars for the better-developed grinding premolars that ensure a happy future of browsing and grinding up the leaves of shrubs, bushes, and small trees.

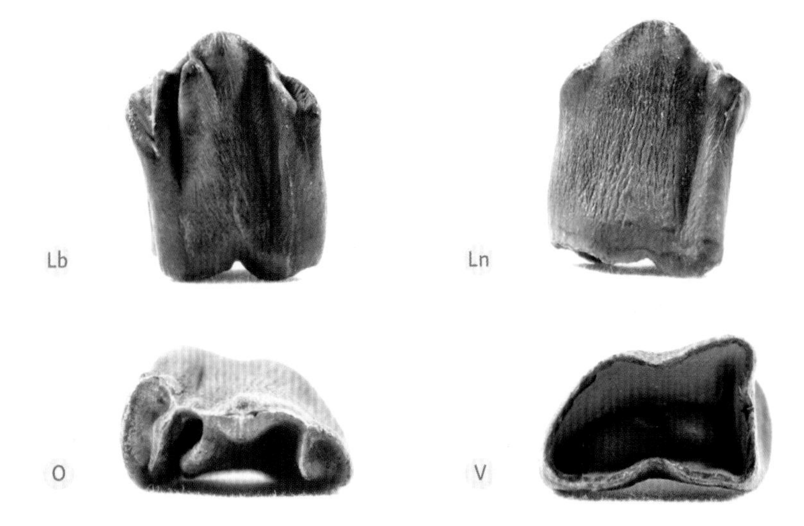

SIZE

23 × 13 × 30 mm

0.9 × 0.5 × 1.2 in

GEOLOGIC AGE

Pleistocene

2.6 Ma–11 ka

IDENTIFIERS

Hollow root

Unworn crown

Crenulated enamel

DENSITY

PREMOLAR · dp3 *Bison antiquus*

Deciduous lower-left premolar (dp3) from a juvenile *Bison antiquus*. Deciduous teeth have two features: crowns that are seldom worn down (seen in occlusal view) and hollow roots (seen in ventral view). Because of these characteristics, deciduous teeth are often mistaken for teeth belonging to other animals. As the animal matures, the adult tooth displaces the deciduous premolar. During this stage, the deciduous premolar appears as a cap on the emerging adult tooth; if the mandible associated with the above tooth was present, the permanent premolar (p3) would be situated within the cavity present in ventral view.

DID YOU KNOW? Did the bison migrate from Asia to North America twice during the Pleistocene epoch? Yes, and they made back-and-forth crossings too. At least twice in geologic history, the Bering Land Bridge was accessible by Paleo-Indians and animals when glacial ice grew substantially, tying up ocean water and lowering sea levels.

"PREMOLAR"

Holmesina septentrionalis

N1 tooth from the extinct giant armadillo, *Holmesina septentrionalis*. (See tooth classification system, page 47). This would have been the first tooth located in the armadillo's mouth. Posterior teeth become elongated and pinched in the middle, forming a bilobate, peanut shape. Armadillo teeth do not have enamel but, rather, alternating dentine bands of varying hardness. Because this lack of enamel results in rapid tooth wear, armadillo teeth are ever-growing (hypselodont).

SIZE

9 × 9 × 22 mm

0.4 × 0.4 × 0.9 in

GEOLOGIC AGE

Pleistocene

2.6 Ma–11 ka

IDENTIFIERS

Cylindrical shape

Hollow root

Hypselodont form

DENSITY

DID YOU KNOW? The immovable bony plates of armor, or osteoderms, of *Holmesina* are typically hexagonal, an easily recognized shape for those hunting beach fossils, and their osteoderms are more common than their teeth. Osteoderms have small holes (foramina) that once housed the hair follicles of these animals. The density of these osteoderms makes them feel heavier in your hand than many similar-sized fossils.

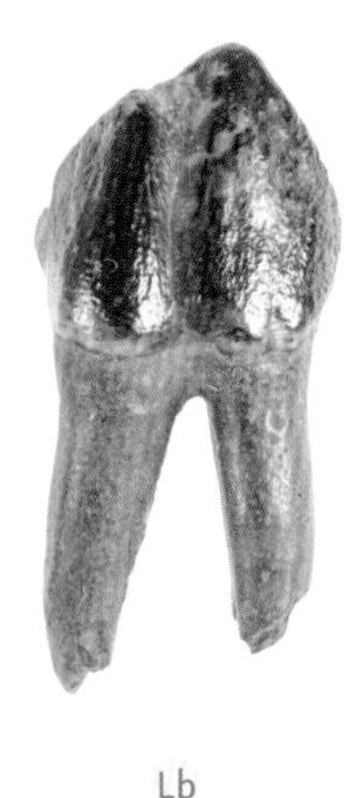

Lb

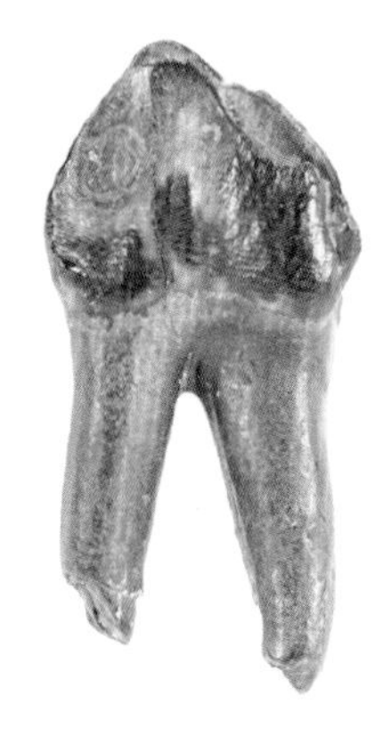

Ln

SIZE

12 × 6 × 25 mm

0.5 × 0.2 × 1.0 in

GEOLOGIC AGE

Pleistocene

2.6 Ma–11 ka

IDENTIFIERS

Round roots

Medium size

Crenulated enamel

DENSITY

PREMOLAR · p3 *Palaeolama mirifica*

Lower-right third premolar (p3) from the Pleistocene camelid, *Palaeolama mirifica*. *Palaeolama* premolars are larger than deer teeth and smaller than bison teeth. As with all *Palaeolama* teeth, the premolars do not have the cement covering typical of teeth from *Hemiauchenia*, another camelid genus. Look for crenulations on both sides of the crown. These premolars also have round roots, as opposed to the angular roots of bison teeth.

DID YOU KNOW? Skeletal elements help determine the age, size, and habitat of camels. Young *Camelops* are identified by their unfused vertebrae, while older individuals typically show age-related wear and tear and arthritic bones. Measurements of the foot and hand bones are taken to determine the size of the individual, and the two splayed toes of *Camelops* provided increased support when the animals traveled on uneven terrain.

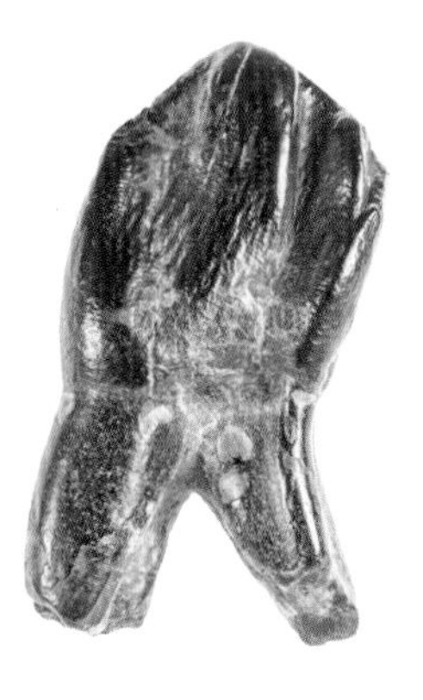

Ln

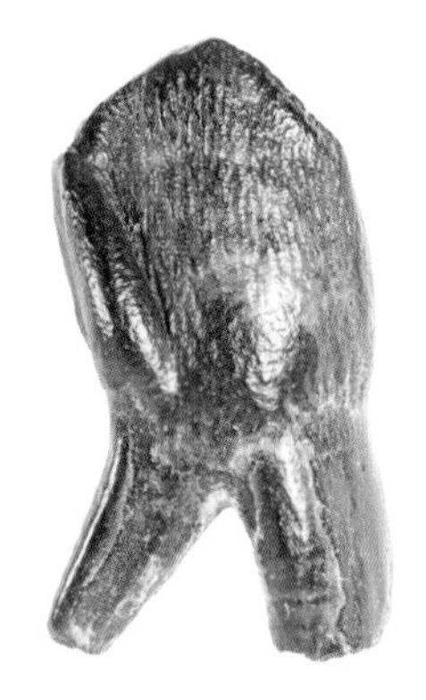

Lb

PREMOLAR · p2 *Bison antiquus*

Lower second premolar (p2) from the extinct species of bison, *Bison antiquus*. While the dentition of bovids (including modern cows) varies little between species, the age of the deposit supports the identification of *B. antiquus* for this tooth. The p2 is the first premolar in the line of cheek teeth in a bison. (See page 471 for clarification.) This premolar shows little to no wear on the occlusal surface, indicating that this individual died soon after the tooth erupted. Worn specimens show folded enamel and no interior crescents (isolated pockets of enamel).

SIZE

14 × 9 × 28 mm

0.5 × 0.4 × 1.1 in

GEOLOGIC AGE

Pleistocene

2.6 Ma–11 ka

IDENTIFIERS

Angular roots

Lack of crescents

Crenulated enamel

DENSITY

DID YOU KNOW? Bison are generally thought of as animals from the western United States, which is true today. But European settlers documented the presence of bison in their early travels to the southeastern part of the country, and in fact bison once roamed over most of the East from Pennsylvania to Florida.

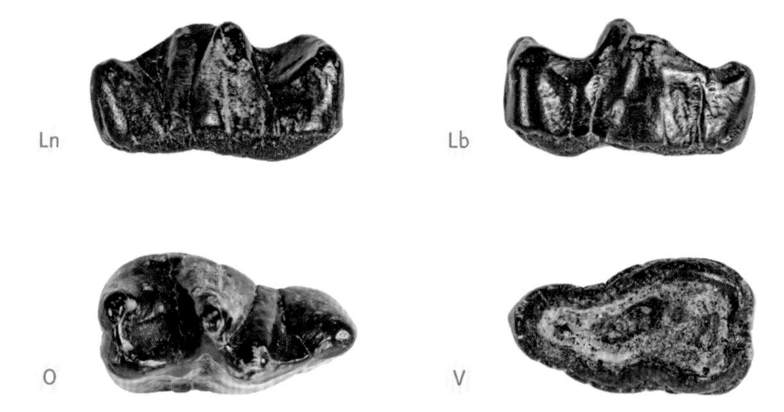

SIZE

24 × 13 × 12 mm

0.9 × 0.5 × 0.5 in

GEOLOGIC AGE

Pleistocene

2.6 Ma–11 ka

IDENTIFIERS

Triangular shape

Molarization

Brachyodont form

DENSITY

PREMOLAR · p2 *Tapirus veroensis*

Enamel cap from the lower-right premolar (p2) of a Pleistocene tapir, *Tapirus veroensis*. Upper premolars are much more squared off, and not triangular, as is the p2. Other tapir species (*T. haysii, T. simpsoni, T. polkensis*) have similarly shaped p2 teeth, so a working knowledge of the geologic age of the deposit is needed to determine the species. The robust nature of the p2 demonstrates the evolutionary molarization of tapir premolars.

DID YOU KNOW? Wishbones aren't just found in a Thanksgiving turkey. They are also found inside a tapir's mouth. A tapir jaw narrows extremely at the snout and widens and curves like a wishbone toward the throat. When viewed from above, the arrangement of teeth reflects this wishbone shape, which has evolved only minimally over the millennia.

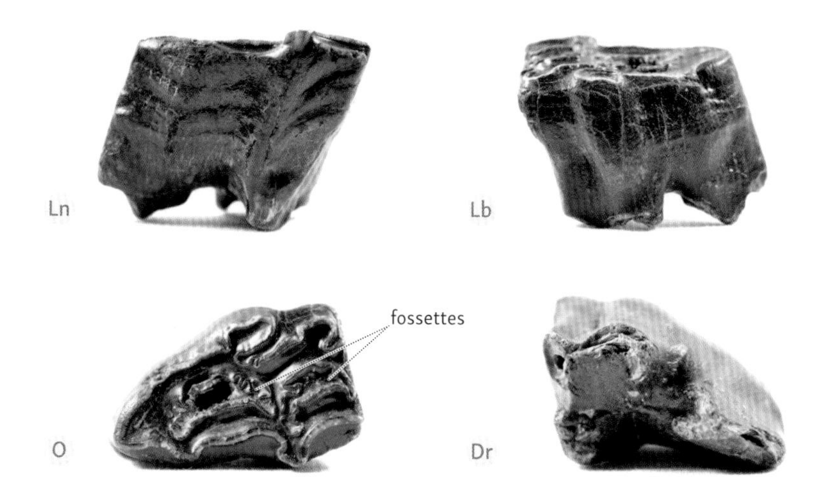

PREMOLAR · P2 *Equus* sp.

Upper-right premolar (P2) from the extant genus of horses, *Equus*. Of the upper cheek teeth in *Equus*, the second premolars are the only ones that are triangular. Compare it to the last molar (page 286), which has a more rounded form in occlusal view. As with the other upper teeth, the above specimen bears two fossettes (indicated), which show the classic sinusoidal curves of enamel found in horse teeth. This tooth is from an older individual; the short height indicates a lifetime of wear.

SIZE

39 × 23 × 42 mm

1.5 × 0.9 × 1.6 in

GEOLOGIC AGE

Pleistocene

2.6 Ma–11 ka

IDENTIFIERS

Fossettes

Sinusoidal enamel

Hypsodont form

DENSITY

DID YOU KNOW? Horse hooves are composed of keratin, the same substance found in animal horns and human fingernails. Hooves have been adapted to provide traction over natural ground, but are not well suited to hard, wet surfaces, so domesticated horses are fitted with horseshoes. Like human sneakers, they are designed to provide balance, cushioning, corrective support, and hoof alignment. Lightweight aluminum is used for racing horseshoes to enhance speed.

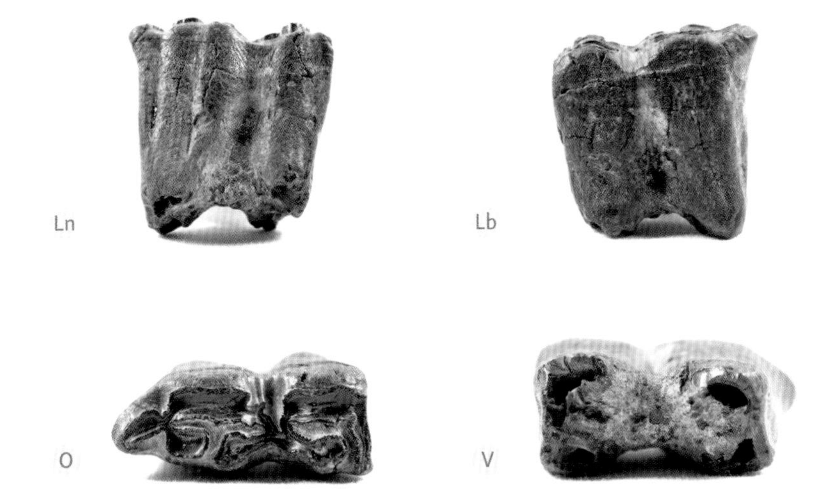

SIZE

37 × 15 × 33 mm

1.4 × 0.6 × 1.3 in

GEOLOGIC AGE

Pleistocene

2.6 Ma–11 ka

IDENTIFIERS

Tapered anterior end

Squared posterior end

Four roots

DENSITY

PREMOLAR · p2 *Equus* sp.

Lower-right premolar (p2) of a Pleistocene horse from the genus *Equus*. The p2 is the first premolar after the lower incisors. As with all *Equus* teeth, the occlusal view and enamel pattern are the most important features in determining the tooth placement and genus (or family) of the animal. Premolars are narrowed at the anterior end and squared off on the posterior end. Note the four roots and the enamel pattern, which is simpler than the similarly shaped third molar, page 287

DID YOU KNOW? All wild horses, including zebras, have short manes, while the domesticated *Equus ferus caballus* breeds of today have long, flowing manes.

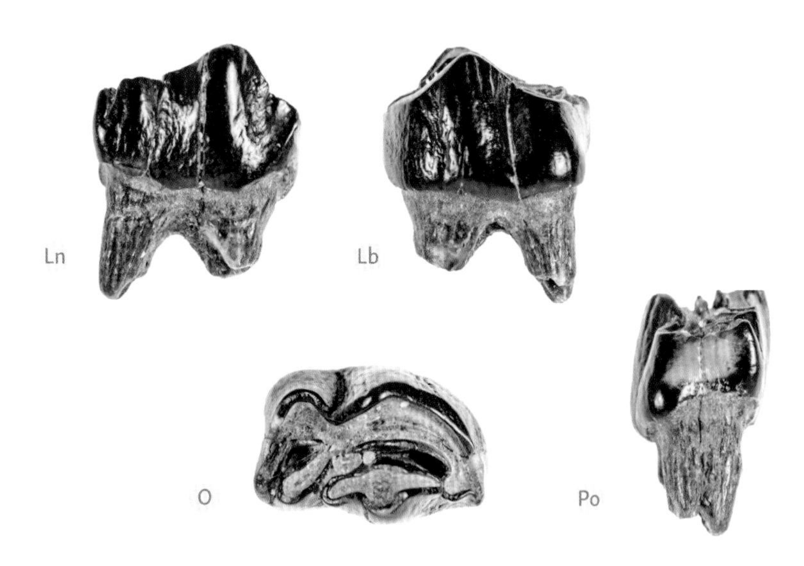

PREMOLAR · p4

Odocoileus virginianus

Lower fourth premolar (p4) from the extant white-tailed deer, *Odocoileus virginianus*. The p4 is the third cheek tooth in the row of lower teeth in a deer's mouth. The above specimen is a permanent premolar from a middle-aged deer (see below). A unique aspect of the p4 of a deer is the worn, off-center cusp.

SIZE

11 × 7 × 15 mm

0.4 × 0.3 × 0.6 in

GEOLOGIC AGE

Pleistocene

2.6 Ma–11 ka

IDENTIFIERS

Enamel folds

Two roots

Single main cusp

DENSITY

DID YOU KNOW? Deer ages can be estimated by looking at their teeth. Fawns have fewer than six teeth. By 19 months, deer have acquired all three permanent premolars, which, unlike older teeth, are chalky white. At 6.5 years old, deer show excessive wear on the second and third premolars, with the infundibulum on the latter beginning to show as a triangular space.

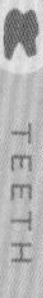

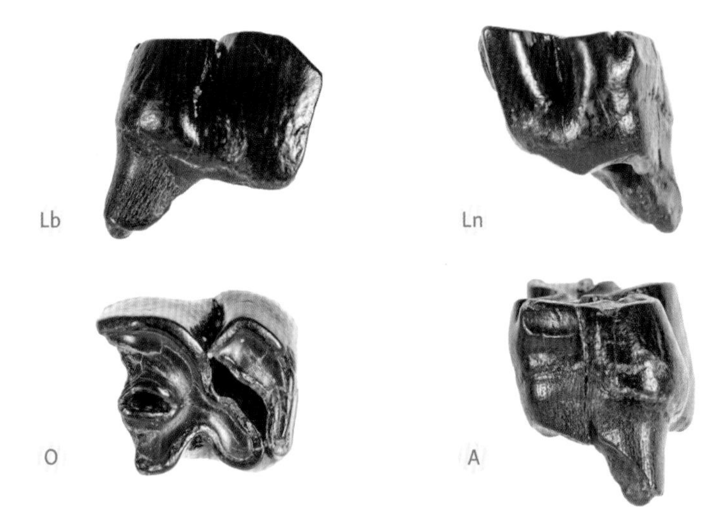

SIZE

13 × 9 × 15 mm

0.5 × 0.4 × 0.6 in

GEOLOGIC AGE

Pleistocene

2.6 Ma–11 ka

IDENTIFIERS

Narrow crescents

Blunt and flattened shape

Selenodont form

DENSITY

PREMOLAR • p4

Odocoileus virginianus

Broken lower premolar (p4) from the extant white-tailed deer, *Odocoileus virginianus*. While this premolar is incomplete, it is included here to demonstrate the difference in appearance between worn and relatively unworn teeth. In this worn tooth, the crests are extremely blunt and flattened, and the crescents have become much narrower than those on unworn teeth.

DID YOU KNOW? Fawns are born with spotted fur that resembles dappled sunlight filtering through the tree canopy, causing them to blend in with the forest floor. Does periodically lead their young to the herd for peer "play dates." The fawns chase one another in and out of the trees, exercise that helps them grow stronger and gives them the skills to evade predators.

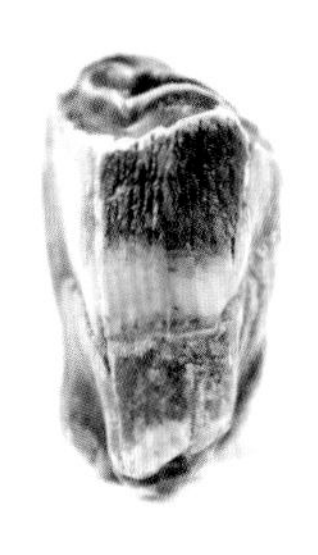
Ln

Lb

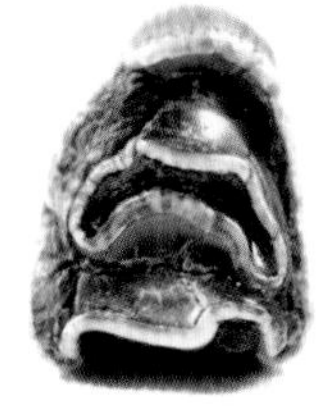
O

L

PREMOLAR · P4 *Bison antiquus*

Upper fourth premolar (P4) from the extinct Pleistocene bison, *Bison antiquus*. Unlike the upper and lower molars, M1–M3 and m1–m3, premolars lack the isolated stylid (accessory pillar of enamel) and have only one enamel crescent. Lower premolars (p2–p4) are much more laterally compressed, with wrinkled enamel and no inner enamel crescent.

SIZE

22 × 18 × 34 mm

0.9 × 0.7 × 1.3 in

GEOLOGIC AGE

Pleistocene

2.6 Ma–11 ka

IDENTIFIERS

Single enamel crescent

Lack of stylid

Crenulated enamel

DENSITY

DID YOU KNOW? Extinct bison were very similar in appearance to modern bison, with the exception of size. The greater body mass and extreme horns, spanning up to 2 meters, of ancient bison led to the development of stronger shoulder muscles to support the weight of the bison's huge head and heavy horns. In bison skeletons, the spine contains very tall neural spikes, which form the base of attachment for these muscles.

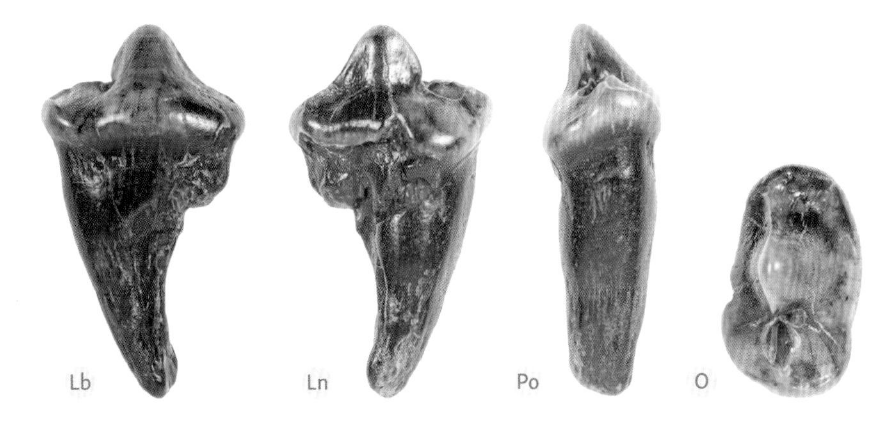

SIZE

14 × 8 × 24 mm

0.5 × 0.3 × 0.9 in

GEOLOGIC AGE

Pleistocene

2.6 Ma–11 ka

IDENTIFIERS

Ridged crown

Two roots

Stout form

DENSITY

PREMOLAR · P4 Felidae

Upper premolar (P4) from an undetermined Pleistocene felid. While it is relatively easy to recognize a tooth as belonging to a felid or other carnivore, isolated teeth (especially premolars) are more difficult to pin to a specific species. A ridge runs the length of the crown top. Complete specimens have two roots. Most modern large cats have lost the first and second lower premolars, and occasionally the third, as is the case with *Smilodon* and some other extinct felid species. For teeth of the above size, comparative material useful for identification would come from *Smilodon*. It is possible this tooth is an upper third premolar (P3) from *Smilodon* spp.

DID YOU KNOW? Bobcats might seem like introverted night-loving loners. These nocturnal felids avoid others of their species during most of the year in order to prevent fighting and injury. But when it is winter and mating time, things change. The male, in marking his territory, includes the dens of several females with whom he will mate. And the formerly solitary females are equally generous with their affections. And then it is back to the solitary life.

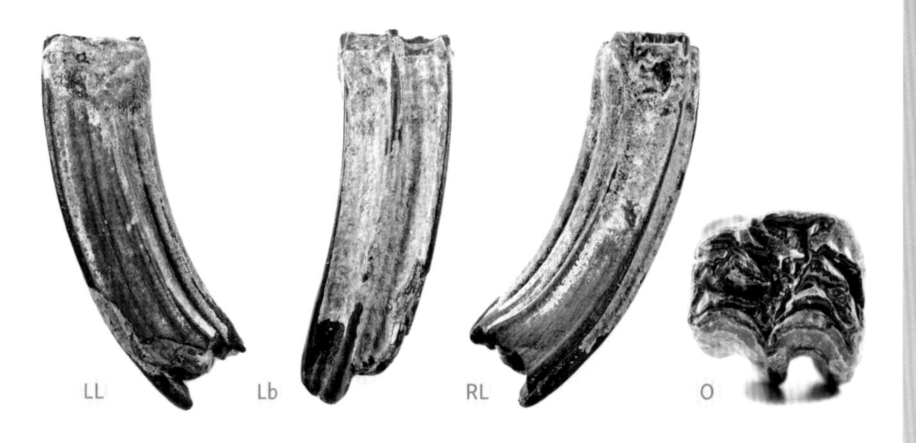

CHEEK TOOTH *Equus* sp.

Upper cheek tooth from the extant genus of horses, *Equus*. Aside from the P2 and M3, the P3–M2 can be difficult to distinguish from one another without in-depth enamel analysis. Upper cheek teeth curve lingually, in toward the mouth, and have roughly square forms in the occlusal view. Teeth from younger individuals are longer (seen above), and shorter and more worn down in older individuals (page 277). Note the two enamel fossettes visible in the occlusal view.

SIZE

31 × 27 × 99 mm

1.2 × 1.1 × 3.9 in

GEOLOGIC AGE

Pleistocene

2.6 Ma–11 ka

IDENTIFIERS

Enamel fossettes

Lingual curvature

Hypsodont form

DENSITY

DID YOU KNOW? Majestic Arabian horses have existed for 4,500 years. Attributed to the Bedouins, who have long been deeply engaged in horse breeding, Arabians differ from other horses. They have thicker, stronger ribs (though one fewer than other breeds), and fewer lumbar and tail vertebrae. Missing bones haven't hurt the Arabians. They are among the animals with the greatest endurance, capable of running up to 100 miles without rest.

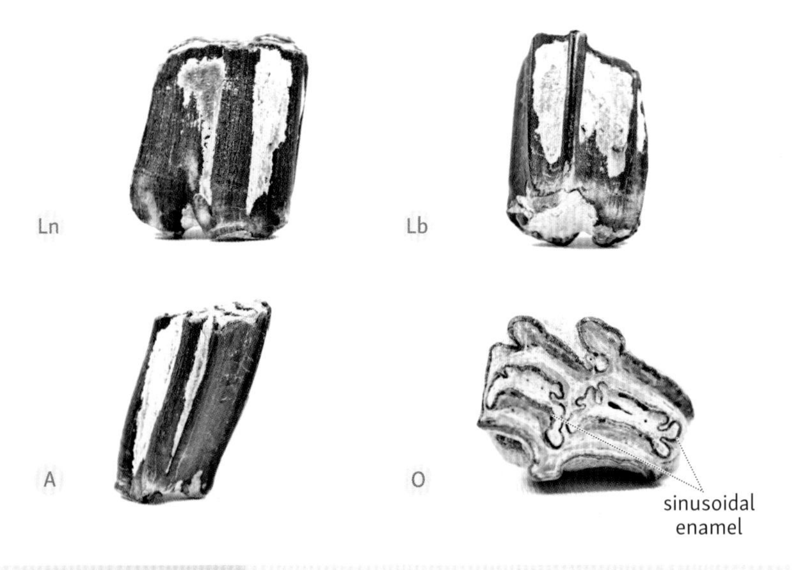

CHEEK TOOTH *Equus* sp.

SIZE

30 × 21 × 50 mm

1.2 × 0.8 × 2.0 in

GEOLOGIC AGE

Pleistocene

2.6 Ma–11 ka

IDENTIFIERS

Enamel fossettes

Sinusoidal enamel

Hypsodont form

DENSITY

Upper right tooth from the extant genus of horses, *Equus*. The square form of this tooth indicates that it is one of the P3–M2 cheek teeth. Lower teeth are more rectangular in occlusal view. Seen in occlusal view, the sinusoidal patterns in the enamel of the fossettes are readily visible (indicated). This curving and recurving of the inner enamel, similar to the winding of the Mississippi River, is seen in both modern and fossil equid teeth. Enamel in uppers is thinner and more complex than in lower teeth.

DID YOU KNOW? Horses have the largest eyes of any land mammal, two inches in diameter. Also, horses have three eyelids—two that are like ours, and a nictitating membrane that travels sideways across the surface of the eye to wipe away debris. In addition, the bottom half of horses' eyes sees things at a distance, and the upper half views close-up objects.

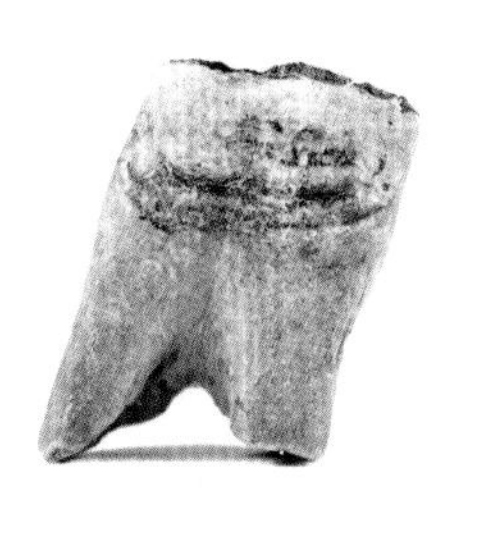

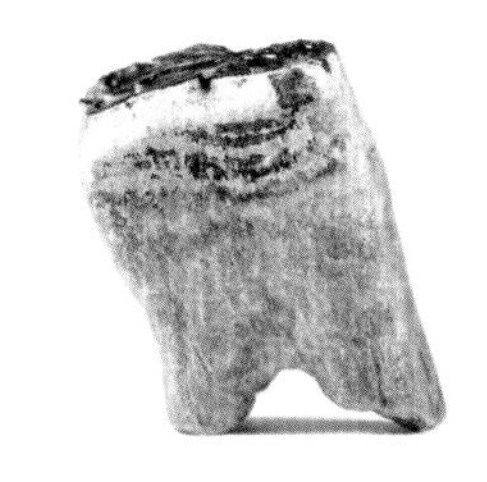

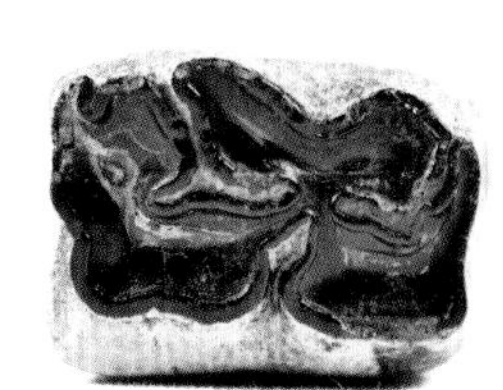

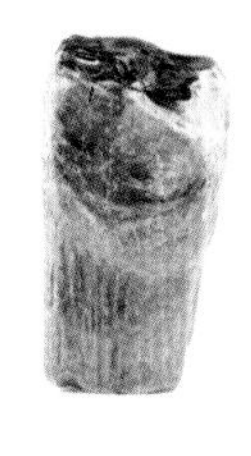

CHEEK TOOTH *Equus* sp.

Lower-right cheek tooth from the extant genus of horses, *Equus*. This tooth, which could be the p3, p4, m1, or m2, shows the classic enamel pattern of *Equus*. The high amount of intraspecific variation in horse teeth does not allow for further species identification. The large size and late Pleistocene age of the deposit that this specimen came from help determine it belongs to *Equus*. Predecessors to *Equus* have similar lower teeth, but the size is greatly reduced.

SIZE

27 × 19 × 45 mm

1.1 × 0.7 × 1.8 in

GEOLOGIC AGE

Pleistocene

2.6 Ma–11 ka

IDENTIFIERS

Enamel patterns

Rectangular shape

Hypsodont form

DENSITY

DID YOU KNOW? Johann Wolfgang von Goethe (1749–1832) is remembered as a famous German poet, writer, and philosopher. But few are aware of his fascination with fossils. After being invited to serve as a member of Duke Carl August's court in Weimar, Germany, Goethe studied the nearby Mesozoic limestone land formations. He built a collection of 718 fossils, including notable horse molars from *Equus taubachensis*.

SIZE

26 × 24 × 62 mm

1.0 × 0.9 × 2.4 in

GEOLOGIC AGE

Pleistocene

2.6 Ma–11 ka

IDENTIFIERS

Narrow posterior

Lateral curvature

Posterior curvature

DENSITY

MOLAR · M3 *Equus* sp.

Upper-right molar (M3) from the extant genus of horses, *Equus*. Reflecting its terminal position within the jaw, the M3 is tapered at the posterior end, setting it apart from teeth in the P3–M2 set. Compare the M3 to the more triangularly shaped P2 (page 277). Another distinguishing feature of the M3 is its curvature both laterally and posteriorly, whereas the P3–M2 curve laterally only.

DID YOU KNOW? Have you ever seen a horse wrinkle its nose, show its teeth, and appear to be laughing? When it does that, it is using its upper-lip muscles to direct scents into the olfactory region of its nose. This flehmen response—which is exhibited by many types of mammals, including cats (large and small), giraffes, tapirs, and hedgehogs—is useful in distinguishing different scents, both good and bad.

Lb

Ln

O

ectoflexids

V

MOLAR · m3 *Equus* sp.

Lower-right molar (m3) of a Pleistocene horse from the genus *Equus*. The m3 is the last tooth in the series of lower teeth. Third molars are squared off at the anterior end and tapered on the posterior end—the opposite shape of premolars. The m3 has slightly more complex enamel than the p2, with two deep ectoflexids (indicated). An ectoflexid is a deep infolding of enamel on the labial side of the tooth opposite the linguaflexid, present in equine tooth morphology; see page 465.

SIZE

32 × 15 × 43 mm

1.2 × 0.6 × 1.7 in

GEOLOGIC AGE

Pleistocene

2.6 Ma–11 ka

IDENTIFIERS

Squared anterior end

Tapered posterior end

Deep ectoflexids

DENSITY

DID YOU KNOW? Horses attend every classical orchestral performance! Never seen a horse at the symphony? Look in the string section. Every bow of every string player in a symphony orchestra is strung with hair from a horse tail. The hairs are stretched and treated with rosin, which enhances the string vibrations that form those beautiful violin, viola, cello, and double bass sounds. Only the stronger, thicker hair of horses from cold climates like Siberia is of high enough quality for this use.

Ln

Lb

O

A

SIZE

24 × 19 × 24 mm

0.9 × 0.7 × 0.9 in

GEOLOGIC AGE

Pleistocene

2.6 Ma–11 ka

IDENTIFIERS

Enamel lacking cement

Uneven enamel waves

Selenodont form

DENSITY

MOLAR *Palaeolama mirifica*

Molar from the Pleistocene camelid, *Palaeolama mirifica*. Unlike molars from *Hemiauchenia*, *Palaeolama* molars lack the cement covering the outer portion of the tooth. Enamel bears minute crenulations, and the inner enamel pockets are much more open than those of *Hemiauchenia*. The above specimen is relatively unworn, which can significantly alter the appearance of the occlusal view.

DID YOU KNOW? Camels developed long legs early in their evolution. This feature enabled the animals to use a pacing gait, in which both legs on one side of the animal move at the same time. This gait allowed for long strides, which used much less energy when the camels traversed great distances across grassy plains. These early camels have been called the first "prairie schooners" for their ability to travel efficiently.

Ln

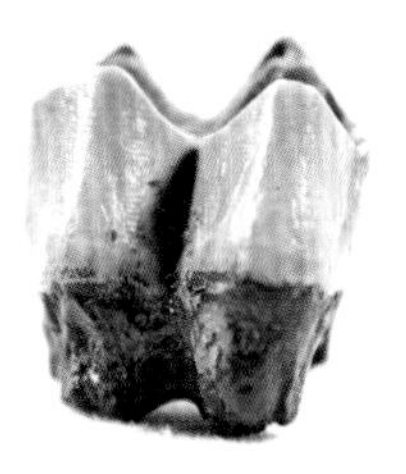

Lb

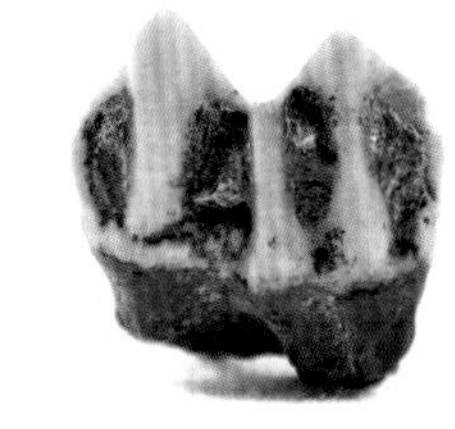

O

Po

MOLAR *Hemiauchenia* sp.

Upper molar from the extinct long-legged camelid, genus *Hemiauchenia*. The black substance seen in lingual view is the characteristic cement that covers *Hemiauchenia* teeth. This trait alone aids greatly in identification. Center enamel folds are much more angular than those seen in *Palaeolama*, page 288.

SIZE

22 × 20 × 22 mm

0.9 × 0.8 × 0.9 in

GEOLOGIC AGE

Pleistocene

2.6 Ma–11 ka

IDENTIFIERS

Cement on enamel

Angled enamel crests

Selenodont form

DENSITY

DID YOU KNOW? The Pleistocene camels, known as *Camelops*, were adapted to the climate in North America. They first evolved here, not in the Asian Mideast, and their evolution coincided with a drying period and the appearance of early savanna ecosystems. It is not known whether these camels evolved the ability to go without water for long periods while still on this continent, or whether that trait developed after their migration to Asia.

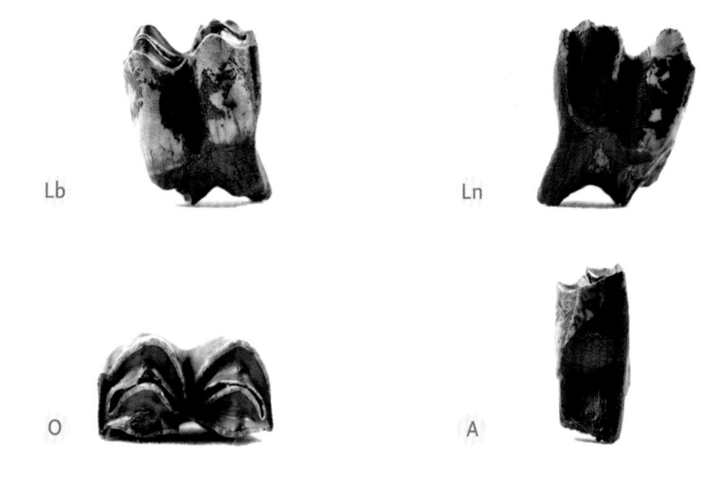

MOLAR *Hemiauchenia* sp.

SIZE

25 × 14 × 35 mm

1.0 × 0.5 × 1.4 in

GEOLOGIC AGE

Pleistocene

2.6 Ma–11 ka

IDENTIFIERS

Cement covering

Thin enamel crescents

Hypsodont form

DENSITY

Lower molar from the Pleistocene camelid genus, *Hemiauchenia*. On greatly worn specimens such as this one, a key characteristic that distinguishes *Hemiauchenia* teeth from those of *Palaeolama* is the coating of cement on the outside of the tooth enamel, seen here as black. Other traits include sharp, pointed enamel crescents inside a molars, and labial styles (enamel folds; seen on the top of the occlusal view).

DID YOU KNOW? Camels are usually associated with hot and arid desert environments, rather than subzero climates. But in 2013, fossil bone fragments from prehistoric camels were found in the northernmost island in the territory of Nunavut, Canada. This camel species, which lived 45 million years ago, was adapted to the boreal forests of the Arctic region, some 3,300 miles north of the warmer environments they inhabit today.

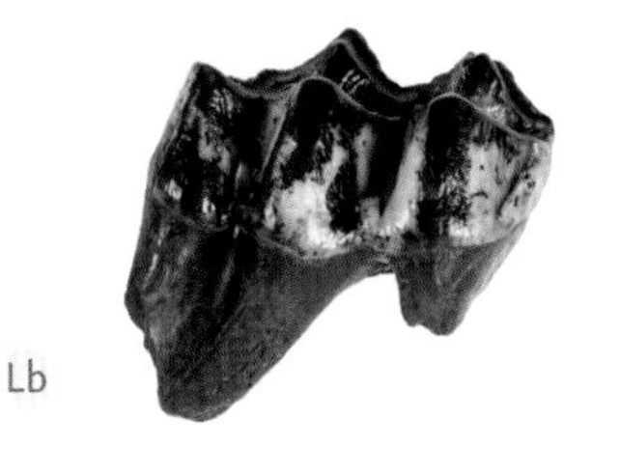
Lb

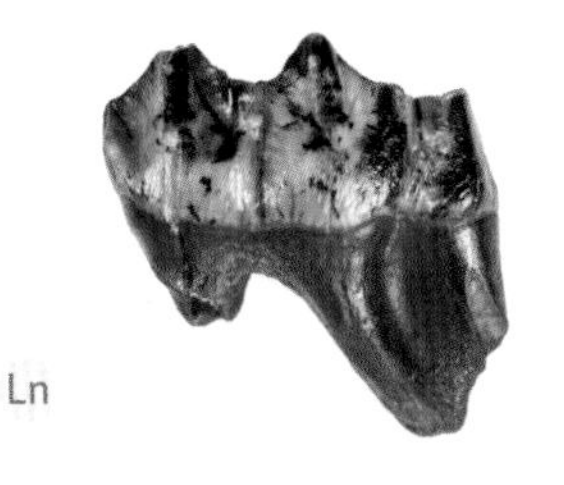
Ln

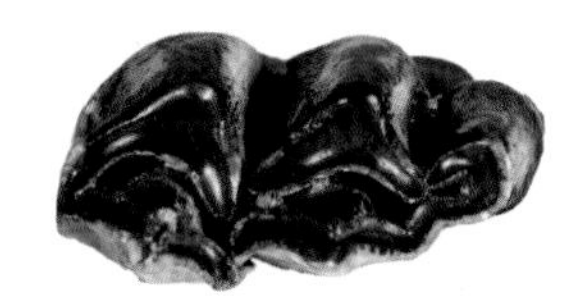
O

A

MOLAR · m3 *Odocoileus virginianus*

Lower third molar (m3) from the extant white-tailed deer, *Odocoileus virginianus*. This specimen shows little wear. Deer molars are similar to camel molars in having four crescent-shaped enamel lophs, but relatively smaller. Lower molars will occasionally show a small stylid between the lophs on the labial side.

SIZE

15 × 8 × 11 mm

0.6 × 0.3 × 0.4 in

GEOLOGIC AGE

Pleistocene

2.6 Ma–11 ka

IDENTIFIERS

High crests

Occasional stylid

Selenodont form

DENSITY

DID YOU KNOW? Deer were immortalized by early human artists in the cave paintings of Lascaux, France. In one image, a red deer drawn in profile has an impressive nine-point antler rack. Over a dozen black ovals are painted beneath the image. Do these signify the number of hunting conquests, or do they hold some other meaning? The cave paintings provide insight into prehistoric artistry and also leave unanswered questions.

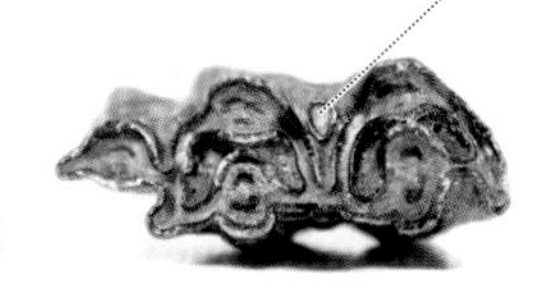

SIZE

50 × 17 × 70 mm

2.0 × 0.7 × 2.7 in

GEOLOGIC AGE

Pleistocene

2.6 Ma–11 ka

IDENTIFIERS

Two roots

Isolated stylid

U-shaped crescents

DENSITY

MOLAR · m3 *Bison antiquus*

Third lower-left molar (m3) from the late Pleistocene bison, *Bison antiquus*. Third molars are large, distinct teeth, with the typical crenulate enamel of bovids. Note the isolated stylid (indicated) between the two main cusps. This stylid is a distinguishing trait between similarly isolated bison and camelid teeth. Present on the m3 is a posterior stylid of enamel (seen at left in occlusal view), which is absent from the first two molars.

DID YOU KNOW? James Earl Fraser designed the much-loved buffalo, nickel in 1913. He used three American Indian models and a bison from the Central Park Zoo named "Black Diamond." Fraser was a student of the famous sculptor Augustus Saint-Gaudens. Two coins were struck, the first with a bison standing on a mound. But because the raised design and print wore down too quickly, the nickel was reminted with the design in lower relief, and the bison moved from a mound to a plain.

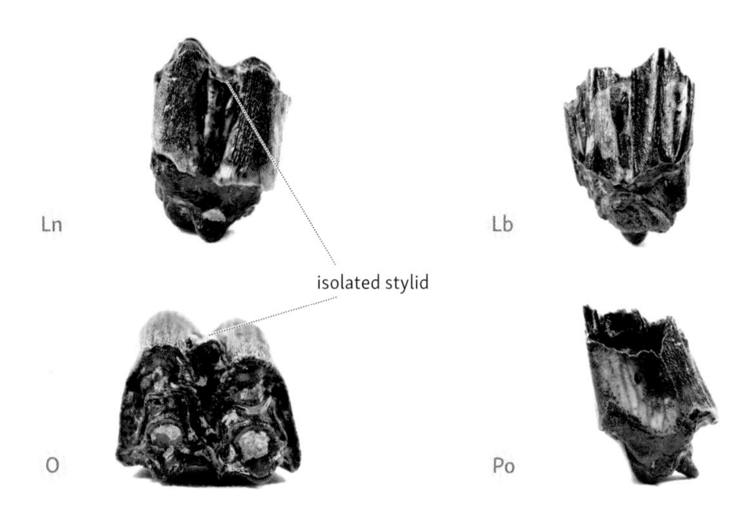

MOLAR *Bison antiquus*

Upper second or third molar from an extinct species of bison, *Bison antiquus*. Most southeastern deposits from the Late Pleistocene contain only *B. antiquus* fossils, while those of *B. latifrons* can be found in deposits farther west and north. The isolated stylid (indicated) is diagnostic of bison and bovid dentitions. As the tooth wears, the shape of the enamel circle changes and ultimately separates from the lingual wall of enamel.

SIZE

36 × 26 × 53 mm

1.4 × 1.0 × 2.1 in

GEOLOGIC AGE

Pleistocene

2.6 Ma–11 ka

IDENTIFIERS

Isolated stylid

U-shaped crescents

Crenulated enamel

DENSITY

DID YOU KNOW? *Bison antiquus* and *Bison latifrons* were contemporaries, but lived in different habitats. *B. antiquus* frequented wide-open woodlands and savannas, while *B. latifrons* found security within interior forests. *B. antiquus* dined on low-growing shrubs and herbs, while *B. latifrons* didn't eat anything it had to bend down for, feeding instead on tree and shrub foliage growing at eye level.

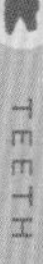

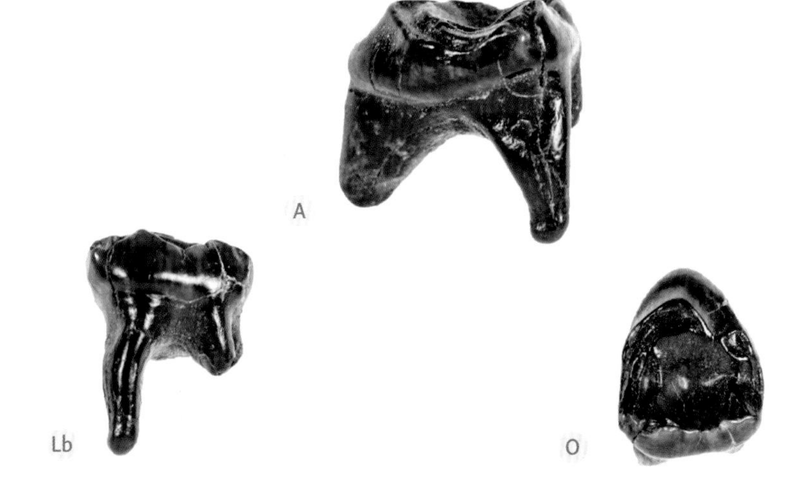

MOLAR · M3 *Procyon lotor*

SIZE

8 × 6 × 8 mm

0.3 × 0.2 × 0.3 in

GEOLOGIC AGE

Pleistocene

2.6 Ma–11 ka

IDENTIFIERS

Triangular shape

Three roots

Bunodont form

DENSITY

Upper-right third molar from the extant raccoon, *Procyon lotor*. Raccoon molars are bunodont, aiding in the chewing of their omnivorous diet. The M3 molars are three-rooted and roughly triangular in occlusal view. The interior (lingual) root is much broader than the labial roots. The above specimen lacks the posterior labial root. Lower molars, m1–m3, are two-rooted, less broad than uppers, and more laterally compressed to fit within the narrow jaws (page 240).

DID YOU KNOW? Raccoons, often considered nocturnal marauders, have long, dexterous fingers that can access almost anything from garbage cans to birdfeeders. Unlike squirrels, they seldom do damage, choosing to untie or unlatch obstacles rather than chewing their way to their target.

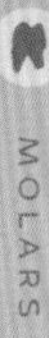

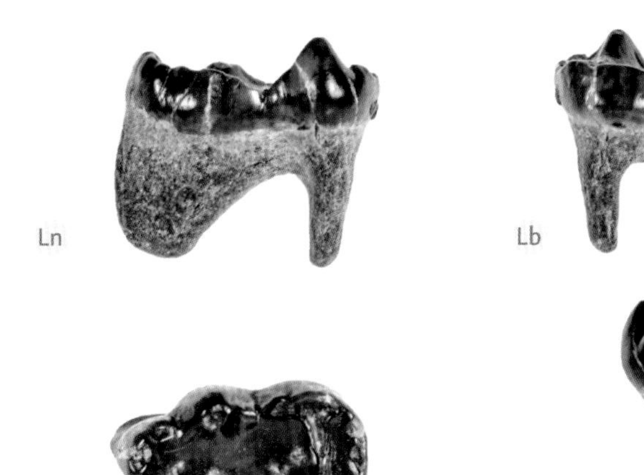

MOLAR · m3 *Procyon lotor*

Lower-left third molar (m3) from the extant raccoon, *Procyon lotor*. A teardrop- or oval-shaped tooth, the last molar in a raccoon's mouth is anteriorly broad to accommodate the processing of their omnivorous diet. Multiple rounded cusps on the crown make up the bunodont dentition. The roots are two-parted, broader posteriorly, with a thin root at the anterior end.

SIZE

10 × 6 × 9 mm

0.4 × 0.2 × 0.4 in

GEOLOGIC AGE

Pleistocene

2.6 Ma–11 ka

IDENTIFIERS

Two roots

Multicusp crown

Bunodont form

DENSITY

DID YOU KNOW? In the wild, raccoons feed at night by bodies of water, catching crayfish, frogs, and small fish. Coastal coons follow receding tides to catch still-open mussels, even during daylight hours. Away from water, they seek out insects and sleeping mice for midnight snacks. With their ambidextrous hands and feet, they easily climb trees to find eggs in nests.

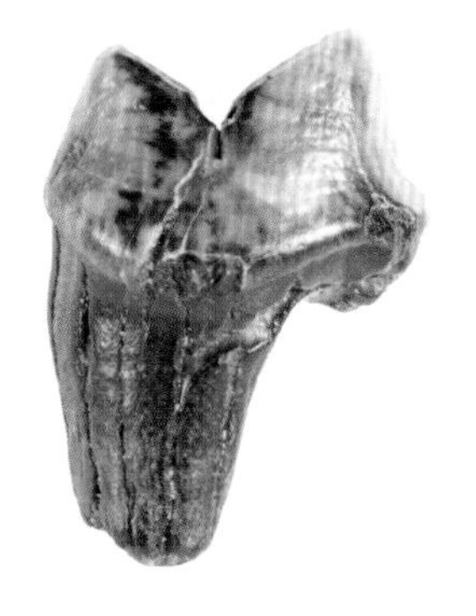

Lb

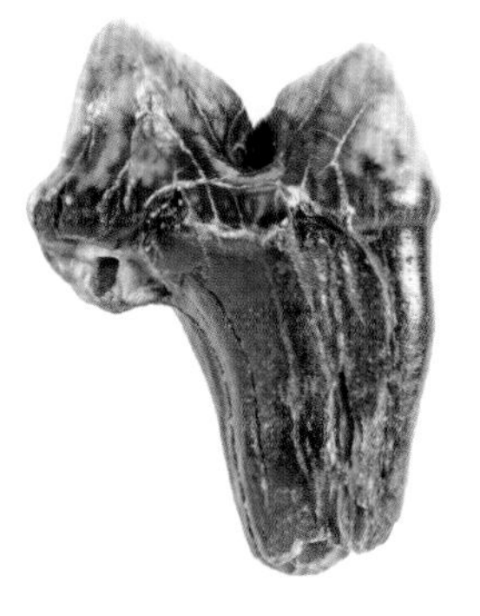

Ln

SIZE

18 × 6 × 25 mm

0.7 × 0.2 × 1.0 in

GEOLOGIC AGE

Pleistocene

2.6 Ma–11 ka

IDENTIFIERS

Carnassial notch

Two roots

Lateral compression

DENSITY

MOLAR · m1 Felidae

Lower-right molar (m1) from a cat in the Felidae family. The m1, also known as the carnassial, is the most prominent tooth of the felid and canid cheek teeth. Carnassial teeth are used like scissors to cut and slice flesh from prey. The notch in the crown is called the carnassial notch. To fit within the jaw, the lower teeth are laterally compressed. This carnassial likely belongs to a jaguar (*Panthera onca*) or a large puma (*Puma* sp.).

DID YOU KNOW? Roughly 30,000 years ago, Cro-Magnons in present-day France noted many details of lions from afar and then drew the animals on cave walls. Observant artists crept close enough to lions to see the dark dots at the base of the whiskers, and then included them in their paintings.

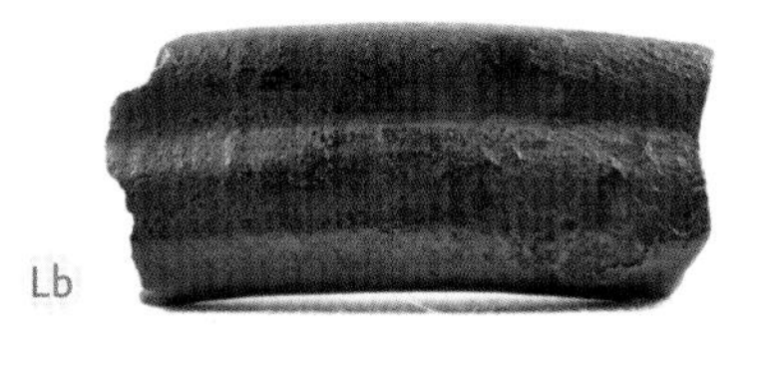

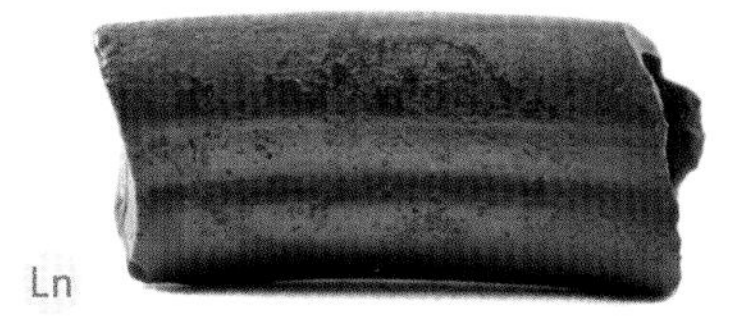

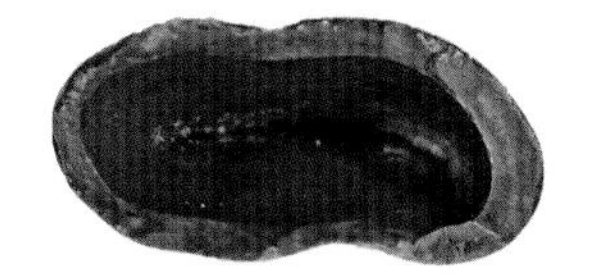

"MOLAR"

Holmesina septentrionalis

A middle-to-rear tooth from the extinct giant armadillo, *Holmesina septentrionalis*. Based on their dental structure, the teeth of xenarthrans (sloths, armadillos, and anteaters) cannot be classified as molars, premolars, canines, and so forth. In place of that system, scientists merely number the teeth (N1, N2, . . .), starting at the front of the mouth. Without the original jaw or maxilla, it is difficult to accurately place this tooth's location in the mouth. It should be noted that pampatheres, such as *Holmesina*, were herbivores and not insectivores like extinct and extant members of Dasypodidae.

SIZE

17 × 8 × 41 mm

0.7 × 0.3 × 1.6 in

GEOLOGIC AGE

Pleistocene

2.6 Ma–11 ka

IDENTIFIERS

Peg-like shape

Hollow root

Hypselodont form

DENSITY

DID YOU KNOW? The study of *Holmesina septentrionalis* skulls by paleontologists indicates that the armadillo had a thick tongue and flexible lips for gathering the kind of softer vegetation commonly growing in humid southern climates. Their teeth, though dull and peg-shaped, were adequately adapted for chewing this food.

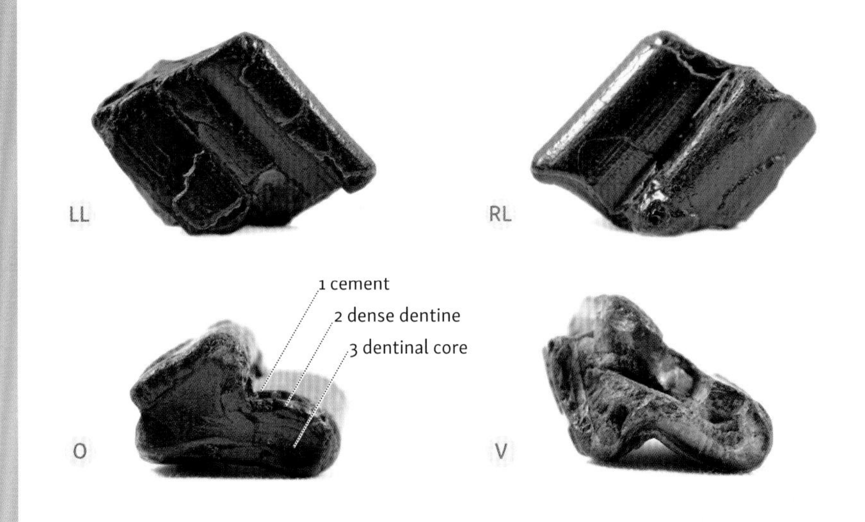

SIZE

29 × 20 × 30 mm

1.1 × 0.8 × 1.2 in

GEOLOGIC AGE

Pleistocene

2.6 Ma–11 ka

IDENTIFIERS

Lobate shape

Layered components

Hypselodont form

DENSITY

MOLARIFORM

Paramylodon harlani

Upper-right molariform tooth from the extinct giant ground sloth *Paramylodon harlani*. Teeth of *Paramylodon* have three distinct parts: an outer coating of cement, a thick layer of dense dentine, and an inner dentinal core (all indicated). This multilayered style of tooth allowed for unique wear patterns, accommodating the sloth's varied diet. As with other xenarthran teeth, *Paramylodon* teeth were hollow-rooted and grew continuously.

DID YOU KNOW? Giant ground sloths fed on upward of 300–500 pounds of vegetation daily. Their giant tails helped steady these large animals upright as they ate. Sloths had block-shaped teeth, with V-shaped grooves on the surfaces. This enabled the upper and lower teeth to fit perfectly together, facilitating the munching of the tasty leaves, twigs, and woody herbs they foraged in swamps and wooded areas.

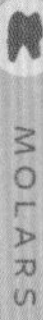

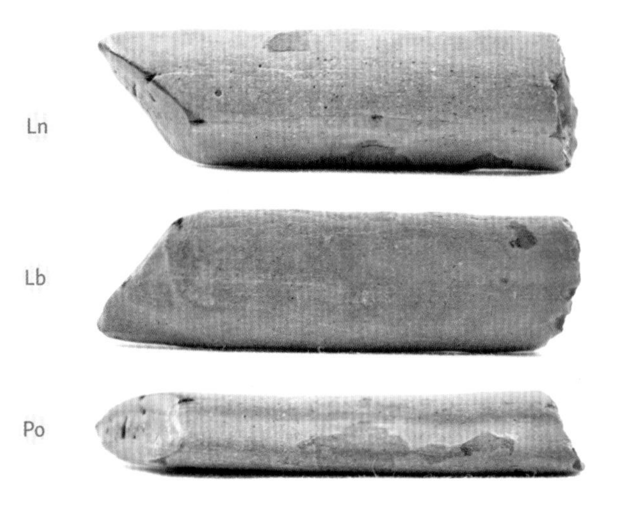

MOLARIFORM

Paramylodon harlani

Tooth from the extinct giant ground sloth *Paramylodon harlani*. As seen on page 298, *Paramylodon* teeth are made of three layers of cement and dentine, varying in thickness. These layers resulted in the teeth occluding at variable angles, which aided in the shearing of twigs, leaves, and other debris included in the sloth's diet. Note the hollow root at right (in the lingual view), indicating that this specimen is a complete tooth. Incomplete specimens lacking the root are even, flush with the broken end.

SIZE

77 × 21 × 12 mm

3.0 × 0.8 × 0.5 in

GEOLOGIC AGE

Pleistocene

2.6 Ma–11 ka

IDENTIFIERS

Lobate shape

Hollow root

Hypselodont form

DENSITY

DID YOU KNOW? The French zoologist Georges Cuvier (1769–1832) firmly established vertebrate paleontology as a legitimate science. Through detailed comparisons of fossils with modern species, Cuvier provided proof that animals that had lived on Earth long ago had become extinct, an unpopular idea at the time. He theorized that there was a time before mammals, when megafauna dominated the living environment. Cuvier first identified mammoths as extinct elephants, and *Megatherium* as an extinct giant sloth.

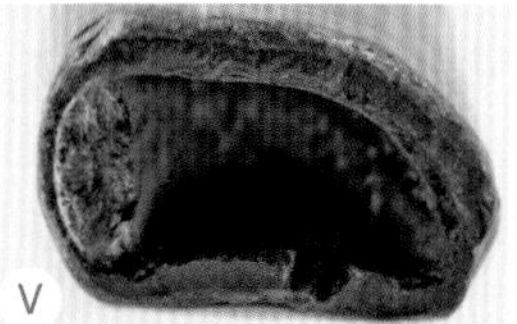

SIZE

21 × 14 × 51 mm

0.8 × 0.5 × 2.0 in

GEOLOGIC AGE

Pleistocene

2.6 Ma–11 ka

IDENTIFIERS

Lobate shape

Hollow root

Hypselodont form

DENSITY

MOLARIFORM

Megalonyx jeffersonii

Molariform tooth from the moderately sized extinct ground sloth *Megalonyx jeffersonii*. Most of the lobate teeth from *M. jeffersonii* range in shape from ovate to rectangular and have the characteristic hollow roots of hypselodont teeth. As with *Paramylodon*, *Megalonyx* had teeth that were concave and wore in unique ways to aid in the shearing of woody vegetation. *Megalonyx* teeth also follow the three-layered structure of cement, dentine, and dentinal tubules (page 298) found in *Paramylodon*.

DID YOU KNOW? Unlike mammoths and mastodons, which entered North America from Siberia via the Bering Land Bridge, the giant ground sloth *Megalonyx jeffersonii* came onto the continent from South America after the Panamanian Land Bridge was established. It is the only giant ground sloth to have spread as far north as the Alaska-Yukon region. More recently, fossils from two other species of giant ground sloths, *M. leptostomus* and *M. wheatleyi*, have been reported from South Carolina.

Po

L

V

MOLAR *Eremotherium laurillardi*

Cheek tooth from the Late Pleistocene giant ground sloth *Eremotherium laurillardi*. Teeth are square to rectangular, with anterior and posterior ridges worn high on the occlusal surface, and a deep V-shaped valley separating the two peaks. Note that N5 (the last upper cheek tooth) is rounder than the other teeth. Intact roots are hollow, following xenarthran dentition, and teeth are composed of dentine and cement, lacking any enamel. The ventral view shown above is from a different specimen, to more clearly highlight the tooth structure.

SIZE

50 × 36 × 69 mm

1.9 × 1.4 × 2.7 in

GEOLOGIC AGE

Pleistocene

2.6 Ma–11 ka

IDENTIFIERS

Squared teeth

Two tall ridges

Hypselodont form

DENSITY

DID YOU KNOW? There is great morphological variation among giant ground sloth hands and feet. Primitive species of *Eremotherium* had five digits, like humans, although the thumb was short and the fifth digit had only one phalanx. But the more advanced *E. laurillardi* evolved with three digits, the third, fourth, and fifth. No matter the number of digits, sloth claws of all species were versatile in either digging to find roots and tubers (mylodontids) or pulling down vegetated limbs (Megalonychidae).

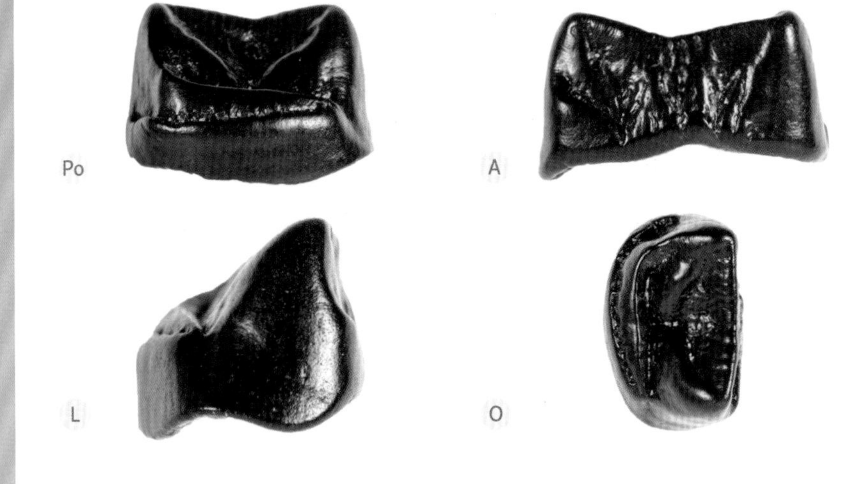

SIZE

16 × 11 × 10 mm

0.6 × 0.4 × 0.4 in

GEOLOGIC AGE

Pleistocene

2.6 Ma–11 ka

IDENTIFIERS

Halved crown

Distinct ridges

Brachyodont form

DENSITY

PARTIAL MOLAR CAP

Tapirus veroensis

Broken lower tooth from the extinct Pleistocene tapir, *Tapirus veroensis*. These fragments, in which the molar has cleaved down the "valley" of the tooth, are a common beach discovery. Compared with upper molars, lowers are far simpler, lacking the ectoloph (connection of the outer cusps). Because of this simplification, lower molars, especially the enamel caps, break quite frequently.

DID YOU KNOW? Tapir hooves evolved over time, with three back toes (or hooves) and four front toes (or hooves). These spreading toes allowed the tapir to walk in the marshy, wet soils where they lived and searched out tasty plants.

MOLAR CAP *Tapirus veroensis*

Enamel cap from an upper molar of the extinct Pleistocene tapir, *Tapirus veroensis*. Because tooth roots are quite fragile, enamel caps or molar caps are some of the most common forms of fossil teeth found on beaches—especially for larger specimens. Upper molars are distinguished from lowers by the ectoloph (indicated), a ridge connecting the two main cusps on the labial side of each tooth.

SIZE

26 × 20 × 15 mm

1.0 × 0.8 × 0.6 in

GEOLOGIC AGE

Pleistocene

2.6 Ma–11 ka

IDENTIFIERS

Ectoloph

Separate ridges

Brachyodont form

DENSITY

DID YOU KNOW? Tapirs use their watery environments for several purposes. They can hold their breath for 60–90 seconds, which allows them to completely submerge and hide from pests and predators. They use water to combat parasites. They also sleep in the water—but just in a few inches. When they are awake, they often wallow in the mud. Both sleeping and wallowing help keep them cool.

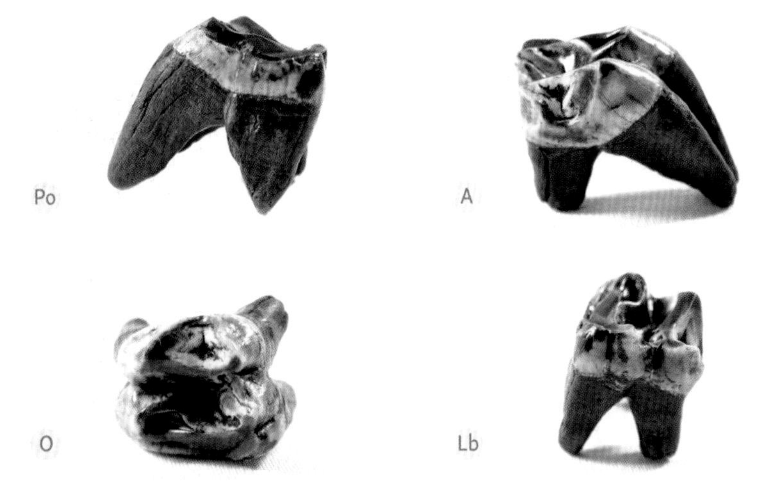

MOLAR *Tapirus veroensis*

SIZE

40 × 30 × 33 mm

1.5 × 1.2 × 1.3 in

GEOLOGIC AGE

Pleistocene

2.6 Ma–11 ka

IDENTIFIERS

Separate ridges

Three large roots

Brachyodont form

DENSITY

Upper molar from the extinct Pleistocene tapir, *Tapirus veroensis*. These tapirs had distinct, three-rooted upper molars, with large enamel lophs. This molar shows the classic dentition of an herbivore; the tooth assisted in browsing on vegetation collected by tapirs' prehensile snouts. Notice the sharp wear facets on each loph of enamel, indicating that this tooth had been erupted for a significant portion of the tapir's life before it died. Of the three roots, the bilobate lingual root has a broad groove running down the exterior.

DID YOU KNOW? *Tapirus veroensis* was first identified in 1918 at Vero Beach, Florida, by E. H. Sellards. These relatives of horses and rhinoceroses survived for about 55 million years before becoming extinct at the end of the Pleistocene, around 11,000 years ago. Four tapir species survive today, though none within the United States. Modern tapirs measure about 7 feet long and can weigh up to 700 pounds, though *T. veroensis* was even larger than that.

O 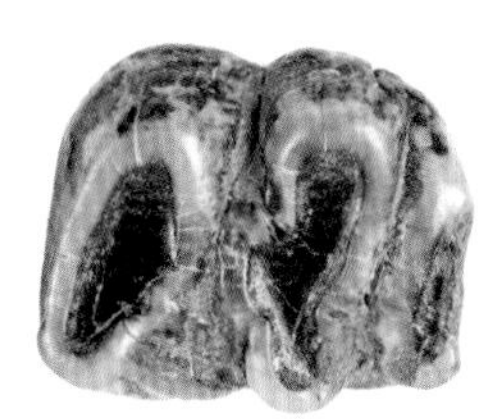

V 

Ln

A 

MOLAR *Trichechus manatus*

Lower-molar enamel cap from the extant manatee, *Trichechus manatus*. Manatees have a method of horizontal tooth replacement similar to that used by the proboscideans (elephants). In the occlusal view, posterior is to the right. Though it looks broken, the third fold of enamel is complete; it is called the posterior cingulum, a ridge or shelf of enamel on a tooth. Upper molars from manatees appear heart-shaped, as do their vertebrae (page 367).

SIZE

18 × 14 × 9 mm

0.7 × 0.5 × 0.4 in

GEOLOGIC AGE

Pleistocene

2.6 Ma–11 ka

IDENTIFIERS

Square shape

Posterior cingulum

Trilophodont form

DENSITY

DID YOU KNOW? Modern manatees are being studied to learn about the small hairs on their bodies. Each hair follicle is specialized, with compact nerves that transmit information about movement directly to the brain. This sensation is more precise at farther distances. Sadly, manatees can't move fast enough to get out of the way of speeding boats—many suffer or die from collisions with boat hulls and propellers.

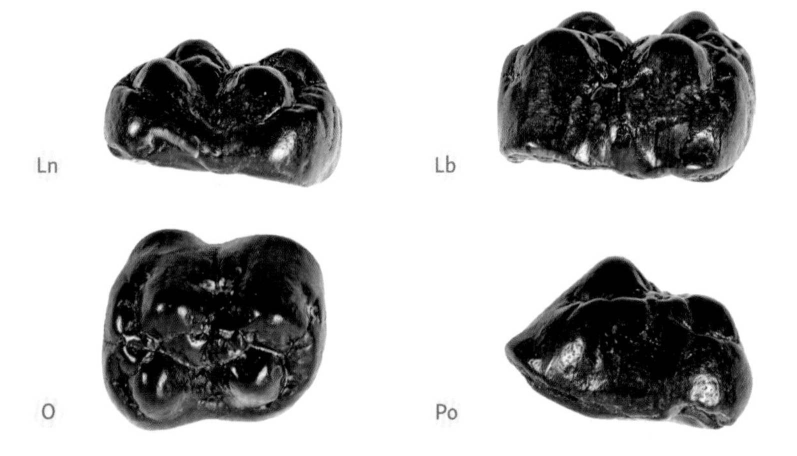

SIZE

16 × 13 × 9 mm

0.6 × 0.5 × 0.4 in

GEOLOGIC AGE

Pleistocene

2.6 Ma–11 ka

IDENTIFIERS

Low crown

Multiple cuspules

Bunodont form

DENSITY

MOLAR *Mylohyus nasutus*

Molar enamel cap from the extinct Pleistocene peccary *Mylohyus nasutus*. The low-crowned teeth demonstrate that this peccary's diet most likely consisted of soft vegetation such as fruits, succulents (similar to cacti but without spines), and, most likely, nuts. Most molars have four main cusps, but can bear multiple smaller cuspules, depending on the species.

DID YOU KNOW? *Mylohyus nasutus*, or the long-nosed peccary, has ancestry going back to a Pliocene genus, *Prosthenops*, and is a distant cousin of today's white-lipped peccary of Central and South America. It is one of several extinct North American peccary species. As with many species, prehistoric peccaries were bigger and heavier than modern species. The elongated skull of *M. nasutus* led to its common name; *nasutus* is a Latin word meaning "large-" or "long-nosed."

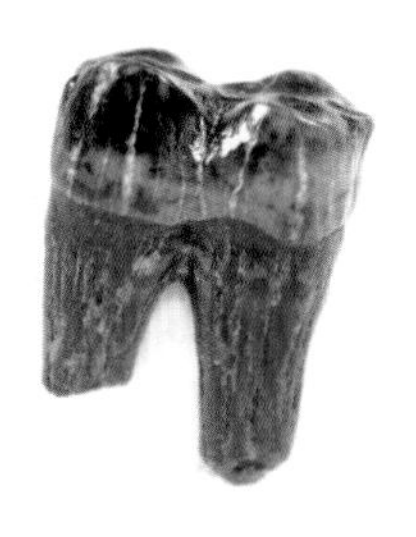

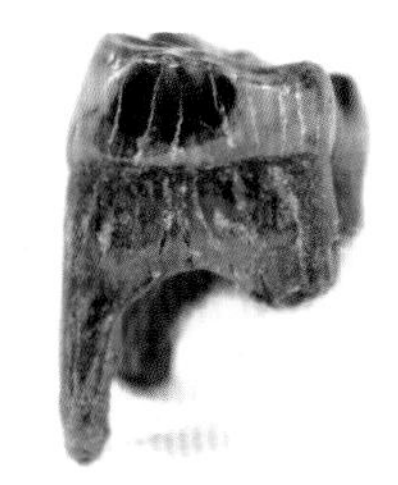

MOLAR *Mylohyus nasutus*

Worn molar from the Pleistocene peccary *Mylohyus nasutus*. Finding a mammal molar with most of the roots intact is a rare occurrence, even for river specimens. This molar shows considerable wear, so it likely came from an older individual in the population. Less abraded specimens have four highly domed cusps (page 306).

SIZE

14 × 12 × 19 mm

0.5 × 0.5 × 0.7 in

GEOLOGIC AGE

Pleistocene

2.6 Ma–11 ka

IDENTIFIERS

Four roots

Worn cusps

Square form

DENSITY

DID YOU KNOW? Peccaries are related to modern pigs, but are classified separately because of their teeth and vertebrae. Peccary molars are generally smooth, while pig molars have more wrinkles and indentations. Peccary molars also have four distinct surfaces, or crowns. In addition, peccaries have 6–9 tail vertebrae, whereas pigs have 20 or more caudal vertebrae in their curly tails.

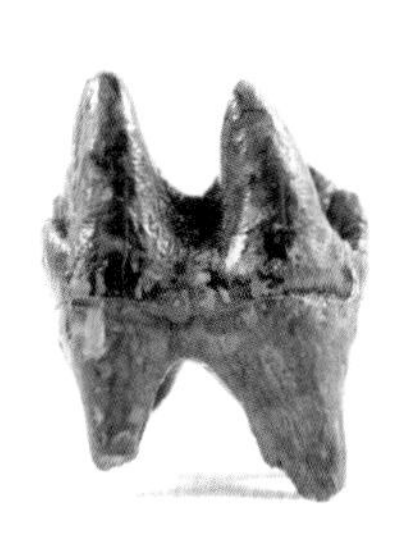
LL

RL

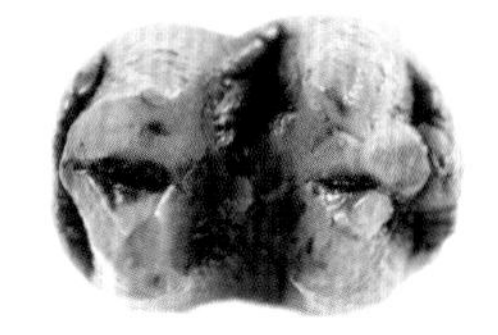
O

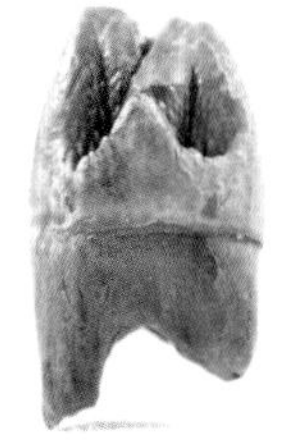
Po

SIZE

17 × 12 × 22 mm

0.7 × 0.5 × 0.9 in

GEOLOGIC AGE

Pleistocene

2.6 Ma–11 ka

IDENTIFIERS

High crowns

Four roots

Bilophodont form

DENSITY

MOLAR *Platygonus compressus*

Molar of the Pleistocene peccary *Platygonus compressus*. All *Platygonus* teeth are high-crowned, with steep angles to the sides of each cusp. Comparison with the other peccary common during the Pliocene and Pleistocene, *Mylohyus*, with its low-crowned teeth, makes clear their dietary differences. Similar to a mastodon's diet of twigs and rough leaves, the *Platygonus* diet most likely consisted of cacti and rough vegetation. Their high-crowned teeth enabled them to process tougher food than *Mylohyus* could.

DID YOU KNOW? The long-nosed peccary, which was as large as a deer, was at home in a wide range of habitats, from woodlands to open plains. This species was found throughout North America, from glacial edges to warm areas of the South. This range closely overlapped with that of its shorter but bulkier cousin, the flat-headed peccary. That species favored scrubby open areas, while the long-nosed peccary spent more of its time browsing in woodlands.

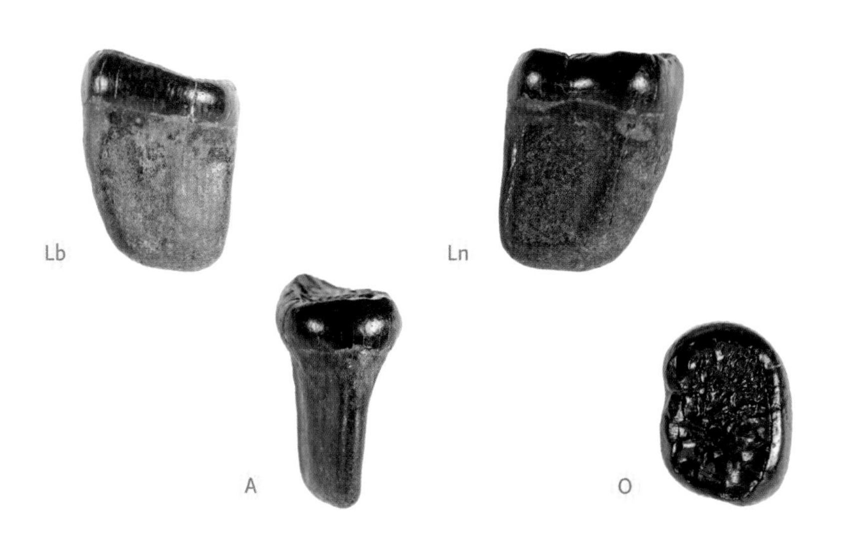

MOLAR · m3 *Tremarctos floridanus*

Last lower molar (m3) from the extinct spectacled (short-faced) bear, *Tremarctos floridanus*. Molars show the flat masticating surface typical of bear teeth, similar to those of such extant species as the European cave bear and the spectacled bear of South America. The enamel forms a relatively small part of the tooth when compared with the root, and can be heavily abraded on specimens from older individuals. The above specimen is most likely from a young adult or a juvenile, based on the lack of such enamel wear.

SIZE

14 × 10 × 20 mm

0.5 × 0.4 × 0.8 in

GEOLOGIC AGE

Pleistocene

2.6 Ma–11 ka

IDENTIFIERS

Thin root

Warped crown

Dimpled crown

DENSITY

DID YOU KNOW? The short-faced bear was one of the most powerful bears that lived during the last ice age. It had elongated legs with feet facing forward, traits that enhanced the bear's speed and its ability to run greater distances than other Pleistocene bears. As a hypercarnivore, the short-faced bear consumed a diet consisting of 70%–100% animal tissue. Rather than being a picky eater, this bear fed on many animals, possibly scavenging rather than hunting.

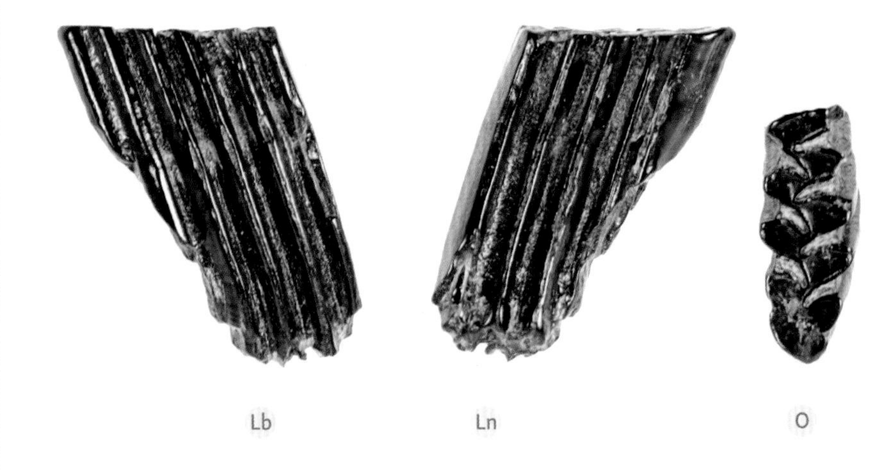

SIZE

6 × 2 × 10 mm

0.2 × 0.1 × 0.4 in

GEOLOGIC AGE

Pleistocene

2.6 Ma–11 ka

IDENTIFIERS

Triangular enamel

Alternating patterns

Hypselodont form

DENSITY

MOLAR *Neofiber deluvianus*

Lower molar from the extinct round-tailed muskrat, *Neofiber deluvianus*. Muskrats are arvicoline rodents, whose teeth are readily identifiable by the rows of alternating triangles that pattern their enamel (seen in the occlusal view). A good comparative collection is crucial for identifying isolated molars from many animals, especially small rodents.

DID YOU KNOW? When trading with Europeans, Native Americans used items from nature in place of currency, and animal skins were a logical choice. Muskrat skins were valued at a quarter of a dollar; raccoon skins, a third of a dollar; doeskins, half a dollar; and buckskins, one dollar. As a result, from the mid-1800s to the present, the nickname "buck" has been given to the almighty dollar.

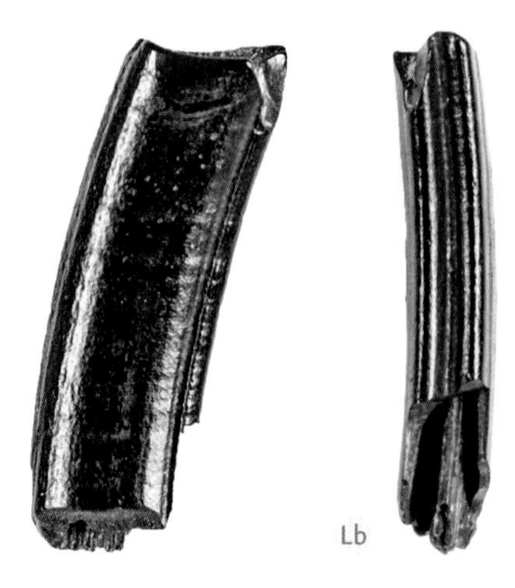

Po Lb O

MOLAR *Sylvilagus floridanus*

Molar from the extant cottontail rabbit, *Sylvilagus floridanus*. The cheek teeth of *Sylvilagus* are all fairly similar, and identification of position is difficult if the teeth are not housed in the mandibles or maxillae. An enamel ridge divides the occlusal surface into two equally sized ovals, rounded on one side and pointed on the other (bottom and top above). Under magnification, the middle enamel ridge is distinctly folded, with two sinusoidal ridges of enamel.

SIZE

3 × 2 × 12 mm

0.1 × 0.08 × 0.5 in

GEOLOGIC AGE

Pleistocene

2.6 Ma–11 ka

IDENTIFIERS

Thin and fragile

Oval occlusal view

Folded enamel ridge

DENSITY

DID YOU KNOW? Rabbit mandibles house razor-sharp upper and lower incisors. Unlike rodents, rabbits have an additional, smaller pair of upper incisors behind the main front set. This tooth arrangement allows them to cleanly snip off tiny leaves of clover, grasses, and the other herbs that make up their diet. Given their long, hearing-sensitive ears, their lightweight bones, which allow for speedy escapes, and their double row of incisors, rabbits are highly specialized creatures.

MOLAR *Neochoerus pinckneyi*

SIZE

13 × 19 × 30 mm

0.5 × 0.7 × 1.2 in

GEOLOGIC AGE

Pleistocene

2.6 Ma–11 ka

IDENTIFIERS

Thin enamel plates

Acute wear angle

Hypselodont form

DENSITY

Molar fragment from the extinct giant capybara, *Neochoerus pinckneyi*. These molars are distinguished by their plates of thin vertical enamel, often worn at an acute angle from chewing. (Rodents chew in an anterior-posterior direction.) Cement is fairly thick between the enamel layers, compared with the size of the molar. On complete specimens, V-shaped ridges of enamel form the molar's edge. Apart from geographic distribution, the number of enamel plates is used to determine genus and species.

DID YOU KNOW? Capybaras are the largest rodents in the world. They can measure up to 2 feet tall and 4 feet long, and weigh a hefty 100 pounds! Most rodents, like mice and rats, are significantly smaller, thankfully. In size, modern capybaras can't hold a candle to their prehistoric counterparts, which weighed in at 800 pounds. Rodent teeth never stop growing, constantly being worn down by the rough vegetation that they chew.

MOLAR *Castor canadensis*

Lower molar from the extant genus of beaver, *Castor canadensis*. The m1–m3 of beaver teeth have an isolated circle of enamel inside one of the three buccal infoldings of enamel (indicated), whereas the p4 lacks this feature. The cheek teeth of both jaws curve in an anteroposterior direction and have a roughly square occlusal surface. *Castor* teeth are rooted and high-crowned (hypsodont), in contrast with those of the giant beaver (*Castoroides*), which are ever-growing (hypselodont).

SIZE

11 × 8 × 26 mm

0.4 × 0.3 × 1.0 in

GEOLOGIC AGE

Pleistocene

2.6 Ma–11 ka

IDENTIFIERS

Rooted molars

Folded enamel

Hypsodont form

DENSITY

DID YOU KNOW? How would you like to carry around a wood-carving set in your mouth, ready at a moment's notice to fell a tree or shred smaller limbs for a home project? Well, a beaver's teeth function like a carpenter's set. The incisors are sharp chisels for carving away at trees for home or nourishment, while the molars are like rasps, smoothing pieces of woody fibers for food.

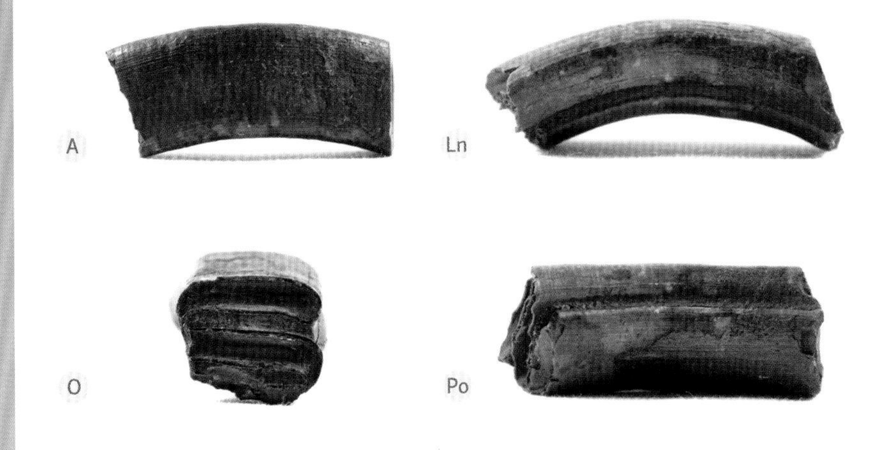

SIZE

16 × 13 × 45 mm

0.6 × 0.5 × 1.8 in

GEOLOGIC AGE

Pleistocene

2.6 Ma–11 ka

IDENTIFIERS

Curving shape

Rounded enamel

Hypselodont form

DENSITY

MOLAR *Castoroides dilophidus*

Molar from the extinct Pleistocene giant beaver, *Castoroides dilophidus*. Unlike the modern beaver (*Castor*), the giant beaver had continuously growing, or hypselodont, molars. The above molar was determined to be from C. *dilophidus* because it was found in a Late Pleistocene deposit in Florida. Fragments can be identified by the curving lophs of enamel with rounded edges, which contrast with the angular enamel of capybara teeth.

DID YOU KNOW? The giant beaver's scientific name, *Castoroides dilophidus*, comes from the Latin roots *castor*, meaning "beaver," and *oides*, meaning "-like." The extinct giant beaver did look like the modern beaver, based on its skeletal framework. It grew to about 8 feet long and weighed up to 220 pounds—the size of a modern black bear.

RL

LL

O

V

MOLAR *Mammuthus* sp.

Molar from a Pleistocene mammoth, genus *Mammuthus*. Mammoths had large flat molars composed of numerous vertical enamel plates (lophs). Each loph contains an elliptical plate of enamel filled with dentine and held to the other plates with cement. Determining the age and species of a mammoth from its teeth depends greatly on the enamel thickness and number of enamel plates, especially on the third molars. *Mammuthus columbi* molars have 20–30 enamel plates.

SIZE

190 × 95 × 220 mm

7.4 × 3.7 × 8.6 in

GEOLOGIC AGE

Pleistocene

2.6 Ma–11 ka

IDENTIFIERS

Vertical enamel plates

Flat occlusal surface

Number of plates

DENSITY

DID YOU KNOW? Imagine swimming with a mammoth 47,000 years ago. Mammoths were good swimmers. During the times of the Pleistocene land bridges, California's Channel Islands were never connected to the mainland. *Mammuthus columbi* reached them by swimming through shallow waters. After rising oceans halted this two-way migration, *M. columbi* adapted to the limited island resources, eventually evolving into the smaller *M. exilis*.

SIZE

147 × 83 × 136 mm

5.7 × 3.2 × 5.3 in

GEOLOGIC AGE

Pleistocene

2.6 Ma–11 ka

IDENTIFIERS

Ridged crown

Multiple roots

Lophodont form

DENSITY

Mammut americanum

Third molar from the extinct American mastodon, *Mammut americanum*. To consume a diet composed primarily of leaves, twigs, spiny fruit, and woody debris, mastodons had lophodont teeth, with high cusps for chewing the plant matter. The first and second molars are trilophodont, with three main lophs (ridges), and the third molars are tetralophodont, with four main lophs (seen above). Note the distinct separation between the enamel crown and the root; mammoth (*Mammuthus*) and modern elephant molars, by contrast, lack a defined boundary.

DID YOU KNOW? Compared to mammoths, mastodons were shorter, broader, and stronger. Shorter, stronger legs formed a foundation for their broad, spreading hips, and together these supported the great weight of *Mammut americanum*. Mastodons' skulls were longer than those of the mammoth and were carried more horizontally outward, thanks to this strong skeleton. In addition, the massive body design enabled the mastodons to carry their enormous ivory tusks.

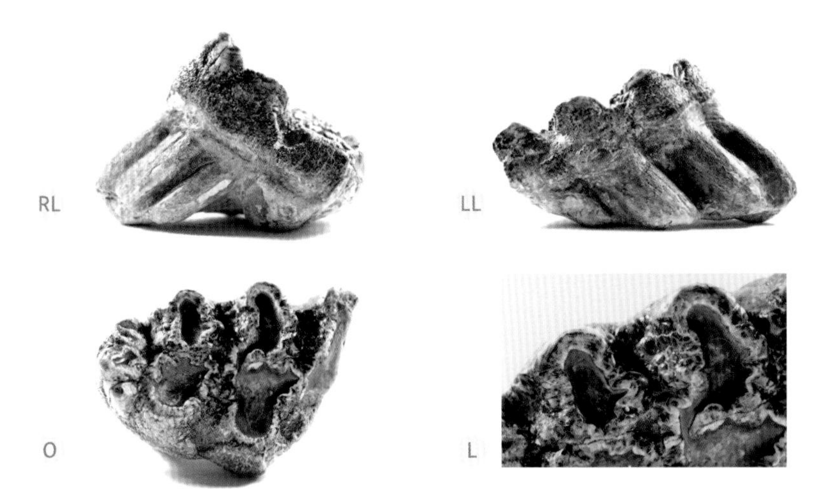

MOLAR *Cuvieronius tropicus*

Well-worn molar from the extinct gomphothere *Cuvieronius tropicus*. As seen in all gomphotheres, molars from *Cuvieronius* exhibit a cloverleaf (trefoil) enamel pattern, a system of complex folds present on each cusp. This molar came from a Late Pleistocene deposit, supporting the specific identification. *Cuvieronius* was the only gomphothere still alive in the Southeast during that time.

SIZE

134 × 90 × 111 mm

5.2 × 3.5 × 4.3 in

GEOLOGIC AGE

Pleistocene

2.6 Ma–11 ka

IDENTIFIERS

Trefoil pattern

Complex enamel

Rooted molar

DENSITY

DID YOU KNOW? Most people view the dentist's office with some apprehension, fearing a possibly painful experience if a tooth needs extracting or filling. For human babies, even teething is painful as each new tooth cuts through the gum. Now consider the extinct *Cuvieronius*. Those poor gomphothere youngsters must have really cried out in pain, because all their cheek teeth erupted at the same time.

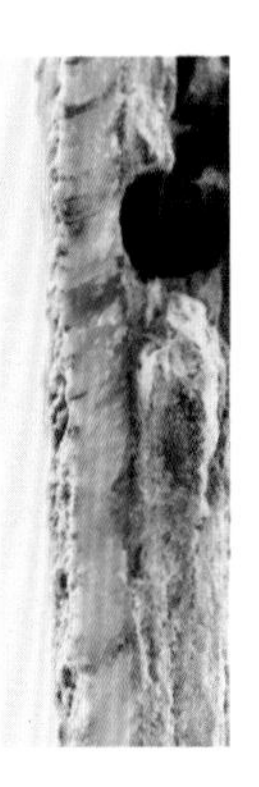

L

ENAMEL *Mammuthus columbi*

SIZE

35 × 13 × 42 mm

1.4 × 0.5 × 1.6 in

GEOLOGIC AGE

Pleistocene

2.6 Ma–11 ka

IDENTIFIERS

Crenulation

Wispy growth lines

Cement-dentine coat

DENSITY

Tooth enamel from the extinct Pleistocene mammoth *Mammuthus columbi*. Mammoth enamel is heavily crenulated, with ridges extending vertically along the plates. In lateral view, the growth patterns of the enamel are visible, characterized by thin, curving "wisps" (called Hunter-Schreger bands) where enamel was added as the individual grew. An isolated fragment of enamel will have dentine on one side and cement on the other. A complete plate comprises two enamel plates, an inner dentine core, and an outer cement layer.

DID YOU KNOW? "Zed" is the name of a Columbian mammoth unearthed at the La Brea site in California. His fame consists of being the biggest, best-preserved mammoth yet found, one still possessing a well-kept set of tusks.

ENAMEL PLATE

Mammuthus columbi

An isolated enamel plate from the Columbian mammoth, *Mammuthus columbi*. Since plates of mammoth enamel were originally embedded in a molar containing up to 30 plates (M3/m3), isolated fragments are often unfamiliar to fossil collectors. The lobed occlusal surface (at bottom, above) shows the growth centers, called plate tubercles, for each plate of enamel. The teeth of each species of mammoth differed in the number of plates, their texture (crenulation), and the thickness of the enamel. *M. columbi* had the thinnest enamel, a moderate amount of crenulation, and the most plates.

SIZE

34 × 5 × 35 mm

1.3 × 0.2 × 1.4 in

GEOLOGIC AGE

Pleistocene

2.6 Ma–11 ka

IDENTIFIERS

Wrinkled texture

Plate tubercles

Oval cross section

DENSITY

DID YOU KNOW? Animal tooth shapes reflect their uses. In the case of mammoth molars, many flat enamel ridges were grouped together to form a masticating (chewing) surface that allowed mammoths to graze on the many types of grasses found during the Pleistocene. At that time, the eastern coastal plain extended 50 miles to what is now the Gulf Stream, and grassland savannas could be found there.

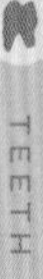

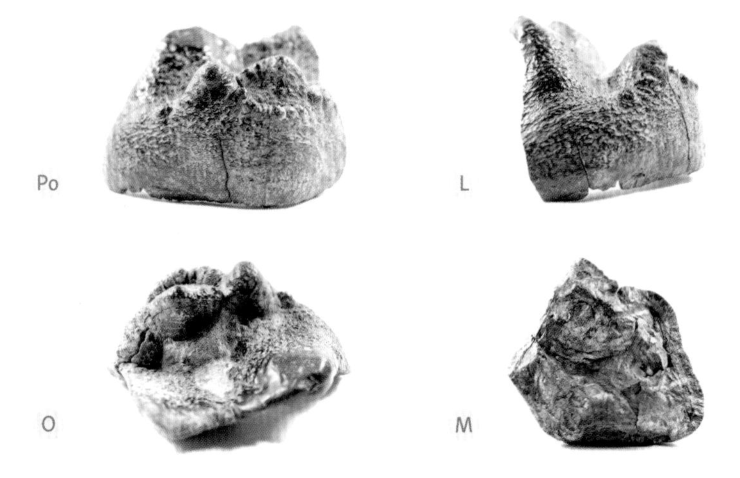

SIZE

80 × 45 × 54 mm

3.1 × 1.8 × 2.1 in

GEOLOGIC AGE

Pleistocene

2.6 Ma–11 ka

IDENTIFIERS

Thick enamel

Enamel growth lines

Trilophodont form

DENSITY

MOLAR *Mammut americanum*

Molar fragment from the Pleistocene mastodon, *Mammut americanum*. Mastodons ate woody debris (leaves, twigs, shrubs, hard fruits), and their tooth morphology reflects the consumption of such a coarse diet. Mastodon tooth enamel fragments are distinctly thicker than enamel from other vertebrates; for example, mastodon enamel averages 5 mm thick, while Columbian mammoth enamel is around 2–3 mm thick. Intact molars typically have three lophs (trilophodont), but the M3/m3 can have five or more.

DID YOU KNOW? The word "mastodon" means "nipple teeth." *Mastos* is Greek for "breast," and *dont* is Latin for "tooth." Mastodon teeth have sharp conical cusps with high relief, making them appear breast-like. They were adapted for chewing (masticating) woody vegetation. As herbivores, mastodons chomped on conifer tree limbs as well as tree bark and shrubs within the wetlands and swamp forests where they lived.

MOLAR *Cuvieronius tropicus*

Fragment of a molar from the extinct Late Pleistocene gomphothere *Cuvieronius tropicus*. Compare this fragment to the nearly complete specimen, page 317. Gomphotheres had a diet similar to that of mastodons, feeding on shrubs, herbs, and woody debris. The thick enamel on their molars (and the accessory cusps in *Cuvieronius*) helped them chew up this tough food. The enamel is extremely thick, around 5 millimeters.

SIZE

32 × 30 × 25 mm

1.3 × 1.2 × 1.0 in

GEOLOGIC AGE

Pleistocene

2.6 Ma–11 ka

IDENTIFIERS

Bumpy enamel

Trefoil pattern

Thick enamel

DENSITY

DID YOU KNOW? *Cuvieronius* is one of two proboscideans that lived in the southern United States and then migrated to South America. The tusks of *Cuvieronius* were unique in their spiraling, curving shape. Sometimes these tusks are described as narwhal-like. But the tight spirals within a narwhal tusk result in a straight, spear-like projection that is a modified tooth lacking enamel.

SIZE

10 × 10 × 6 mm

0.4 × 0.4 × 0.2 in

GEOLOGIC AGE

Pleistocene

2.6 Ma–11 ka

IDENTIFIERS

Flattened-pebble shape

Ventral foramen

Thin enamel coating

DENSITY

TOOTH *Pogonias cromis*

Isolated tooth from a fish in the drum family, most likely the black drum, *Pogonias cromis*. Similar in appearance to palmetto berries or rounded phosphate pebbles, intact drum teeth have a foramen on the bottom for the nerve ending. Broken specimens reveal the thin enamel ring that makes up the top and sides of the teeth. Drum teeth come in a variety of shapes and sizes, demonstrating the mosaic arrangement of the teeth in the back of the throat. The tooth plate is called a pharyngeal grinding mill.

DID YOU KNOW? Drum fish species include red drum, star drum, sea trout, spot perch, and silver perch. A typical drum fish has a short deep body with a flat belly and a highly arched back, and weighs 20–40 pounds. Their method of chewing is unusual: along with pointed jaw teeth located in the front of the mouth, another set of teeth is found inside the throat, where large, flat, cobblestone-like teeth (seen above) are used to crush the hard parts of shellfish.

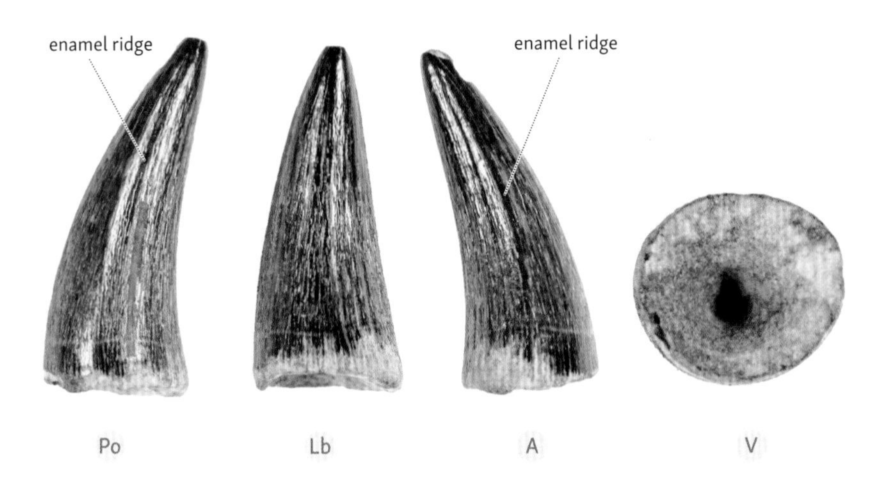

TOOTH Crocodilia

Tooth from an extinct species of Paleocene crocodile, found along the Potomac River in Maryland. Isolated teeth from crocodiles are extremely hard to identify to the genus level because of the wide variation in tooth shapes and sizes. Crocodile genera from the Paleocene Aquia Formation include *Eosuchus*, *Crocodilius*, *Thecachampsa*, and *Thoracosaurus*. Note the conically hollow root, crenulated enamel, and anterior-posterior enamel ridge running the length of the tooth (indicated).

SIZE

10 × 8 × 21 mm

0.4 × 0.3 × 0.8 in

GEOLOGIC AGE

Paleocene

66–56 Ma

IDENTIFIERS

Crenulated enamel

Enamel ridge

Conically hollow root

DENSITY

DID YOU KNOW? A well-known Beatles tune made living "in a yellow submarine" sound fun, but life for a "brown submarine" is quite different. When submerged for long periods, crocodiles accumulate an acidic buildup of carbon dioxide in their bloodstreams. Luckily, their bony osteoderms secrete alkaline minerals like magnesium and calcium into the bloodstream, which neutralizes this acidic buildup, so it isn't a problem for them.

SIZE

19 × 19 × 32 mm

0.7 × 0.7 × 1.3 in

GEOLOGIC AGE

Pleistocene

2.6 Ma–11 ka

IDENTIFIERS

Enamel growth rings

Hollow root

Enamel ridge

DENSITY

TOOTH *Alligator mississippiensis*

Isolated tooth from the extant species of American alligator, *Alligator mississippiensis*. Distinct layers of enamel are visible in most tooth specimens, showing the enamel growth patterns. The outer layer of enamel is covered in fine striations running the length of the crown. A ridge (carina; indicated) runs anteroposteriorly along the crown. On broken specimens, such as the one above, a conical depression is visible where the tooth was rooted in the jaw.

DID YOU KNOW? Alligator teeth are similar to one another in shape and internal structure. They exhibit polyphyodontism, the process of continually replacing lost or broken teeth. On average, alligators shed 50 teeth a year. Over their lives, alligators can produce thousands of teeth, many of which may become fossilized.

TOOTH *Alligator mississippiensis*

Nearly complete tooth from the extant species of American alligator, *Alligator mississippiensis*. Alligators (and other crocodilians) exhibit polyphyodontism, or the shedding and re-growing of multiple teeth throughout their lifetime. On average, each tooth is replaced each year, up to 50 times during the alligator's life. Since the root is attached in the above specimen, this tooth was not shed, but fell out of the jaw after death and fossilization. Alligator teeth, especially small ones, are laterally compressed.

SIZE

8 × 7 × 31 mm

0.3 × 0.3 × 1.2 in

GEOLOGIC AGE

Pleistocene

2.6 Ma–11 ka

IDENTIFIERS

Lateral compression

Lateral crown ridges

Hollow root

DENSITY

DID YOU KNOW? It is well known that Spanish explorers searched the wetland landscape of Florida for the Fountain of Youth. They found alligators and other animals of the New World fascinating and described them in their writings. It is assumed that the name "alligator" is a modification of the Spanish *el largarto*, meaning "the lizard."

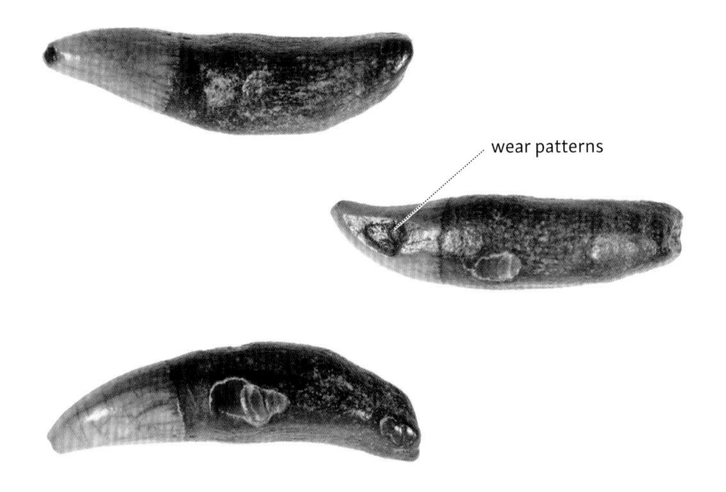

SIZE

6 × 6 × 26 mm

0.2 × 0.2 × 1.0 in

GEOLOGIC AGE

Pleistocene

2.6 Ma–11 ka

IDENTIFIERS

Crenulated enamel

Wear patterns

Homodont form

DENSITY

TOOTH Odontoceti

Tooth from an undetermined echolocating toothed whale. Isolated teeth from many modern odontocetes usually cannot be assigned a specific place in the mouth, because of their homodont structure. Teeth often show wear patterns (indicated) where they occluded with other teeth during feeding. The above tooth likely came from a delphinid, or dolphin-sized, whale.

DID YOU KNOW? Dolphins have 80–100 cone-shaped teeth, which are mainly used for grasping, since these marine mammals lack the jaw muscles for chewing. These teeth extend all the way out into the dolphin's snout, or beak. Teeth lost during a dolphin's lifetime are not replaced with new ones.

TOOTH Odontoceti

Isolated tooth from an Oligocene toothed whale, or echolocating odontocete. The bottlenose dolphin is a modern example of an echolocating odontocete, an endothermic marine mammal that feeds primarily on fish. Isolated, the teeth are hard to identify to the family level, let alone to genus. Note the relatively smooth enamel crown and the sharp bend between the crown and the root. Many odontocetes had teeth angled inward for catching fish.

SIZE

23 × 8 × 5 mm

0.9 × 0.3 × 0.2 in

GEOLOGIC AGE

Oligocene

33.9–23 Ma

IDENTIFIERS

Smooth enamel

Angled crown

Thick root

DENSITY

DID YOU KNOW? The name "dolphin" comes from the Greek word *delphis*, meaning "womb." In ancient Greece, dolphins were revered as *hieros ichthys*, which means "sacred fish," and the act of killing a dolphin was punishable by death. According to Greek mythology, Apollo took the form of a dolphin when founding his oracle at Delphi.

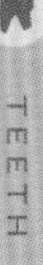

SIZE

5 × 3 × 16 mm

0.2 × 0.1 × 0.6 in

GEOLOGIC AGE

Miocene

23–5.3 Ma

IDENTIFIERS

Striated enamel

Conical crown

Peg shape

DENSITY

TOOTH Eurhinodelphinidae

Isolated tooth from an unidentified Miocene dolphin, family Eurhinodelphinidae. Modern odontocetes have peg-shaped teeth, used primarily for grasping prey as opposed to chewing. Some odontocete species have over 100 of these teeth. The conically tapering crown is often worn at an angle from occluding with the opposite jaw's teeth. Eurhinodelphinids typically have narrow conical teeth set in an elongated rostrum.

DID YOU KNOW? The order Odontoceti, toothed whales, includes porpoises and dolphins, which can be identified by the shape of their teeth. Porpoises have spade-like teeth, and dolphins have round teeth. Odontocetes hunt in packs and don't feed randomly. Working as a team, some dolphin species herd fish together and create a huge wave that strands their prey on the edge of the shore for easy dining.

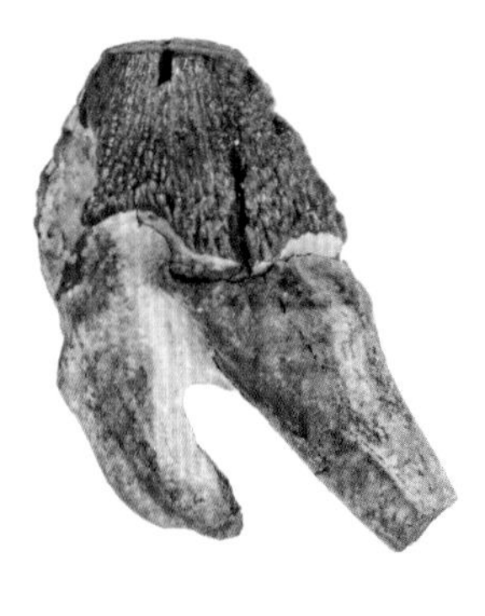

Ln

Lb

REAR TOOTH *Squalodon* sp.

Rear tooth from the Miocene shark-toothed whale, *Squalodon*. Teeth from *Squalodon* have deeply crenulated enamel, anterior-posterior cusps, with two roots on rear teeth. Note the sharply curved root lobes. On older individuals, the crown becomes worn down, as it is above; younger individuals have less worn, sharply pointed cusps. Most *Squalodon* fossils have a distribution from Maryland to North Carolina.

SIZE

22 × 11 × 43 mm

0.9 × 0.4 × 1.7 in

GEOLOGIC AGE

Miocene

23–5.3 Ma

IDENTIFIERS

Two roots

Crenulated enamel

Serrations and cusps

DENSITY

DID YOU KNOW? *Squalodon* was an extinct whale that occurred after earlier whales like *Basilosaurus*, but before *Orcinus orca*, today's killer whale. *Squalodon* was a successful predator of marine organisms, possibly even mammals. But it was also a contemporary of predatory sharks, which were increasing in size. One such "new kid on the block," *Carcharocles megalodon*, eventually became the ocean's top predator.

Ln

Lb

SIZE

10 × 4 × 17 mm

0.4 × 0.2 × 0.7 in

GEOLOGIC AGE

Oligocene

33.9–23 Ma

IDENTIFIERS

Two roots

Crenulated enamel

Serrations and cusps

DENSITY

REAR TOOTH Waipatiidae

Rear cheek tooth from an echolocating odontocete, family Waipatiidae. Previously misclassified as *Squalodon* teeth, these small double-rooted cheek teeth are frequently found in Oligocene marine deposits in the Southeast. Members of the Waipatiidae family have relatively small cheek teeth. These dolphins are heterodont, exhibiting single-rooted conical teeth at the front of their mouth to grasp prey, and double-rooted serrated teeth in the back of their mouth to slice captured prey. Note the wear facet from an occluding tooth (seen at left in the lingual view).

DID YOU KNOW? Around 30 million years ago, whales were going through their "awkward teenage years" of evolution. Some whales, such as the pint-sized *Inermorostrum xenops*, lacked teeth and scoured the seafloor like vacuum cleaners, sucking up squid and soft-bodied fare. Others, such as *Coronodon havensteini*, had huge teeth, but they were used for filter feeding as the whales pushed water through their teeth to strain out small fish and krill. Snaggle-toothed grins and toothless maws—now *those* would have been some yearbook photos worth seeing!

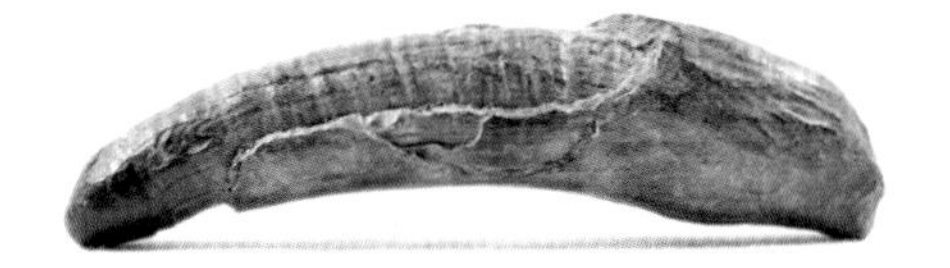

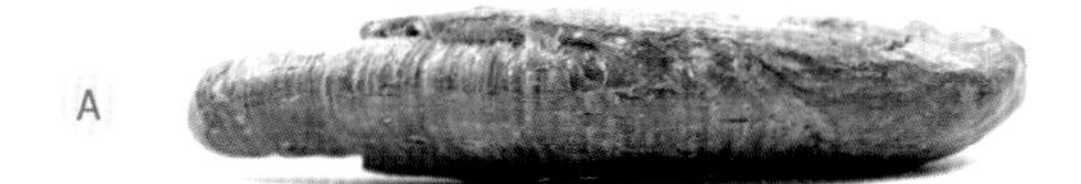

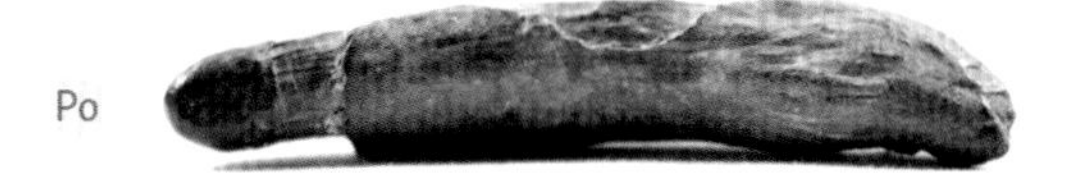

TOOTH Kogiidae

Isolated tooth from an undetermined genus of Miocene sperm whale, family Kogiidae. While some sperm whales have teeth with enamel crowns, other genera, such as *Physeterula* and *Kogiopsis*, have only a dentinal core covered by cement (seen above). These cylindrical teeth curve slightly and have wear facets resulting from occluding with other teeth. Note the distinct parallel growth bands on the dentinal core.

SIZE

17 × 14 × 78 mm

0.7 × 0.5 × 3.0 in

GEOLOGIC AGE

Miocene

23–5.3 Ma

IDENTIFIERS

Lack of enamel crown

Slightly curved shape

Wear facets

DENSITY

DID YOU KNOW? Blue whales are a collection of superlatives. They are the largest mammals on Earth. In fact, they are the largest animals that have ever lived. Reaching lengths of up to 100 feet, these magnificent whales can weigh up to 300,000 pounds, or 150 tons. A blue whale's tongue can weigh as much as an elephant.

SIZE

33 × 26 × 65 mm

1.3 × 1.0 × 2.5 in

GEOLOGIC AGE

Miocene

23–5.3 Ma

IDENTIFIERS

Bulbous root

Crenulated enamel

Cement-covered root

DENSITY

TOOTH Physeteroidea

Isolated tooth from a Miocene sperm whale in the stem Physeteroidea superfamily. As with many other odontocetes, isolated teeth are difficult to assign to a genus or a species. The above tooth has a crown with crenulated enamel; the crown is dwarfed by a bulbous dentine root covered in cement. Historically, many texts identified any enameled, thick-rooted tooth as belonging to *Scaldicetus*, but these assignments were often incorrect. Therefore, it is best labeled as a *Scaldicetus*-grade sperm whale tooth.

DID YOU KNOW? Ambergris is a valuable substance used in the production of perfume as a fixative to the skin; that is, it helps the scent last longer. Sperm whales produce this mixture of waxy stomach juices that hardens and has a varying musky scent. Ambergris is found floating on the water or on beaches. American perfumeries do not use it, since it is illegal to use products from an endangered species, but other nations still allow its use.

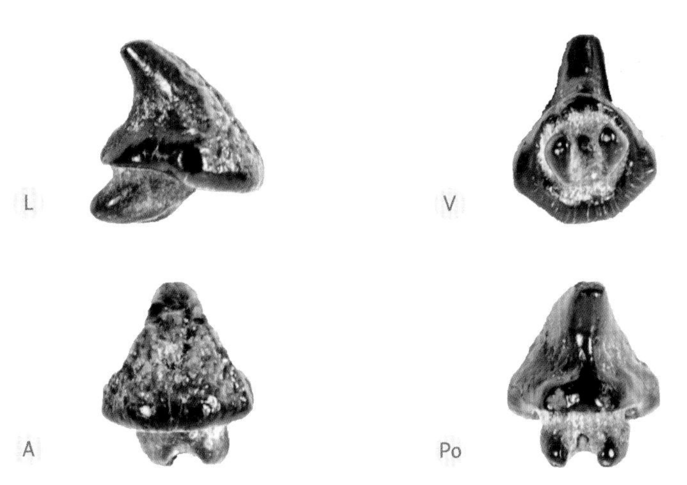

TOOTH *Raja* sp.

Tooth from a male Miocene skate, genus *Raja*. As with the teeth of myliobatids (rays), *Raja* teeth interlock to form a wide system of teeth used to grind and swallow prey. The root of each tooth has two lobes divided in the middle. Pointed male teeth contrast with the flatter and dorsally compressed teeth of females. Note the crenulations visible in the anterior view. (Matrix was left on the root to provide a better image of the two lobes.)

SIZE

3 × 3 × 4 mm

0.1 × 0.1 × 0.2 in

GEOLOGIC AGE

Miocene

23–5.3 Ma

IDENTIFIERS

Pointed crown

Bilobate root

Crenulated enamel

DENSITY

DID YOU KNOW? Manta rays fly! They are regularly observed leaping out of the ocean and using their wing-shaped fins to glide briefly over the surface before plunging back into the sea. This may be one of the ways that rays attempt to rid themselves of parasites. Or they may just be having fun!

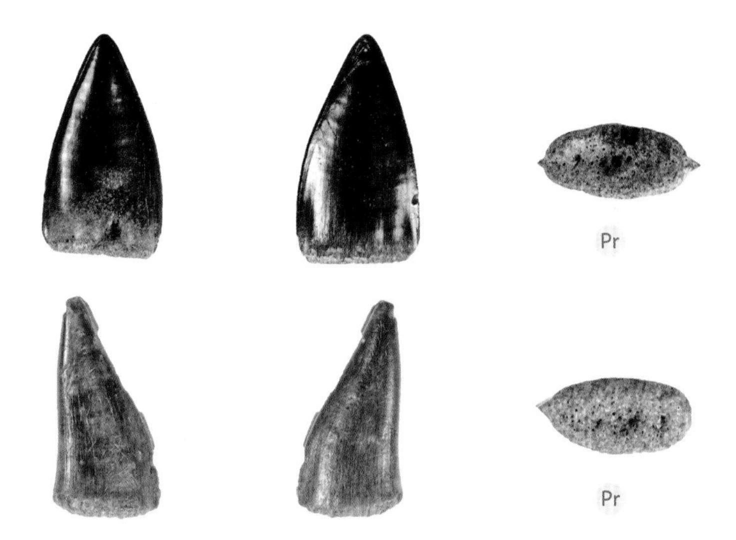

TEETH *Sphyraena* sp.

SIZE

9 × 5 × 16 mm

0.4 × 0.2 × 0.6 in

GEOLOGIC AGE

Miocene

23–5.3 Ma

IDENTIFIERS

Triangular shape

Sharp edges

Striations

DENSITY

Teeth from an extinct barracuda, genus *Sphyraena*. Barracuda teeth are extremely sharp, and not unlike knife blades when used by their owner. Most lateral teeth are symmetrical (black specimen), while anterior teeth are asymmetrical and fang-like (tan specimen). Many collectors confuse barracuda teeth with broken shark teeth, and vice versa. *Sphyraena* teeth are porous, with a stippled texture at their points of attachment to the jaw.

DID YOU KNOW? Barracudas have an extreme underbite that an orthodontist would love to correct! But their jaws are efficiently designed. Tiny razor-sharp triangular teeth are backed up by an inside row of long dagger-like teeth, all designed for tearing apart large prey. Opposing jaws contain sockets aligned to hold the longer teeth so that the barracuda can fully close its mouth, leaving no chance for smaller prey (swallowed whole) to escape.

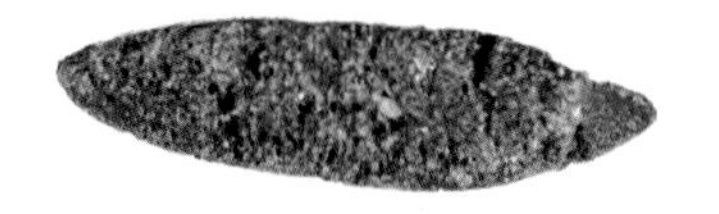

Pr

ROSTRAL DENTICLE

Anoxypristis sp.

Rostral denticle from an Oligocene sawfish, genus *Anoxypristis*. These "teeth" are actually modified dermal denticles. Sawfish do have oral teeth, which are similar in shape and size to those of *Raja*. Rostral denticles of *Anoxypristis* lack the posterior groove seen in *Pristis*. Rostral denticles are oval in cross section and display vertical bands where they were rooted in the rostrum. The shape of rostral denticles varies with the size and age of the sawfish as well as from abrasion due to feeding practices (see below). Several extant species are recognized, contained in two genera (*Anoxypristis* and *Pristis*).

SIZE

38 × 14 × 4 mm

1.5 × 0.5 × 0.2 in

GEOLOGIC AGE

Oligocene

33.9–23 Ma

IDENTIFIERS

Banded denticle base

Elliptical cross section

Stippled bottom

DENSITY

DID YOU KNOW? Sawfish are amazing for their unusual snout-like rostra (something like a hedge-trimmer blade), with "teeth" protruding along them. A sawfish uses this rostrum to stir up invertebrates from bottom sediments or to slash side to side while swimming into a school of fish, wounding prey before devouring it. The spined rostrum also acts as a defensive weapon against sharks and other predators.

SPECIES HIGHLIGHT

Felids

My, *Smilodon*, what big teeth you have!

The saber-toothed tiger is ingrained into most peoples' minds from sensational stories in books and the media as one of the most formidable predators that roamed the prehistoric world. And indeed, it must have been so, as one look at the remarkably long canine teeth of this felid makes clear.

The "tiger" common name is misleading, however, since this animal was not related to modern tigers. Both are classified as cats of the Felidae family, but the saber-toothed species of *Smilodon* belonged to an extinct subfamily called Machairodontinae. *Panthera*, the tigers, are classified within the modern subfamily Pantherinae, which also includes lions, jaguars, and leopards. The other extant Felidae subfamily is Felinae, made up of cougars, cheetahs, lynxes, bobcats, ocelots, and domestic cats.

Worldwide, the big cats are in trouble. The most endangered are the jaguars, whose former range from the Grand Canyon south throughout South America has shrunk and become fragmented. Cheetahs' ranges have been reduced to isolated portions of Africa and a tiny area of Iran, and lions, which once ranged

Skull of the formidable Late Pleistocene saber-tooth cat, *Smilodon*. This cast is modeled after a preserved specimen from the La Brea Tar Pits.

Upper canine from *Smilodon fatalis*; specimen CCNHM 413.1, courtesy of the Mace Brown Museum of Natural History, Charleston, South Carolina.

Serrated tooth margins on a canine from *Smilodon fatalis*; specimen CCNHM 413.1, courtesy of the Mace Brown Museum of Natural History, Charleston, South Carolina.

over all of Africa, India, the Mideast, and Greece, are now found only in parts of Africa.

Tigers are seriously endangered as well. Where once nine subspecies occurred throughout Asia, only five remain, and the overall number is less than 2,000. The Siberian tiger has only about 450 surviving individuals; the South Chinese tiger is extinct in the wild; and the Caspian, Bali, and Javan tigers have joined the saber-toothed cat in extinction.

Two smaller cat species, by contrast, are doing well. Bobcat (*Lynx rufus*) populations have rebounded in recent decades and are considered stable; the species is widespread in North America. *Felis catus*, the domestic cat, is estimated to number more than 100 million worldwide and is also the most common household pet. Ironically, as big cats have become increasingly threatened with extinction, the overpopulation of predatory feral and domestic cats has become a threat to wild bird species.

A surprising number of unrelated felid species bearing distinctively long canine teeth have appeared and disappeared over the eons. The first such creatures known were not mammals but mammal-like members of a group called the Synapsids. *Gorgonops* in this group lived between 260 and 254 million years ago (Ma) and had canines that were nearly five inches long. A later mammal, *Machaeroides*, that lived during the Eocene epoch bore saber-like teeth despite being only about the size of a small dog.

A third group included *Hoplophoneus* species, which were active from the late Eocene to the early Oligocene. These were bobcat-sized and had moderately long canines. After these came a fourth long-toothed species, *Barbourofelis*, a lion-sized animal that inhabited North America from the mid to late Miocene epoch.

Yet another saber-tooth-bearing family evolved within a different branch of animals from the Late Miocene to the Late Pliocene. These were members of the Metatherian group—which were more closely related to marsupial mammals (modern kangaroos, opossums, and so forth) than to placental mammals. *Thylacosmilus* species were members of this group. Although these species came from different families and different time spans, each evolved the similar trait of elongated canines, a pattern known as "convergent evolution."

Finally, there came *Smilodon*, the "poster child" saber-toothed cat. *Smilodon*'s direct ancestor was *Megantereon*, known from Florida fossils from 6 Ma. Much is known about the *Smilodon* genus, since over 1,200 saber-toothed cat fossils have been analyzed from the La Brea Tar Pits. *Smilodon* lived during most of the Pleistocene, becoming extinct 13,000 years ago, just before the end of that epoch. Three species of *Smilodon* evolved: *S. gracilis*, which lived mainly in North America; *S. populator*, from South America; and the widespread *S. fatalis*, found on both continents.

From the La Brea collection it is known that *Smilodon fatalis* was about a foot shorter than modern lions, but had a bearlike build and weighed nearly twice as much as today's big felids. Analysis of the hyoid bones within *Smilodon*'s throat indicates that it likely had a powerful roar.

The species may have operated in social groups in both friendly and unfriendly ways. *Smilodon* bones have been found with wounds attributed to other saber-toothed cats. But other bones show wounds that have healed, which enabled those individuals to live on. This has led to speculation that such animals were cared for by other cats or at least allowed to feed on others' prey while they healed. If *Smilodon* had been a solitary hunting species, it is unlikely that such victims would have survived these nearly fatal wounds.

It took about 8 million years for a new saber-toothed species to take over the ecological niche of its predecessor. The elongated canines were useful in subduing the megafaunal prey of the day, such as giant sloths and camels, and the teeth certainly proved to be effective weapons. But they may also have contributed to the periodic demise of the cats during times of megafaunal species extinctions. The bulky saber-toothed cats could not keep up with smaller, faster species, and their teeth would have been a disadvantage in trying to grab more diminutive prey. Thus, the disappearance of the last of the giant Pleistocene creatures also signaled the final deathblow to *Smilodon*, their fearsome predator.

What will be the fate of today's big cats, whose survival is directly tied to the activities of humans? Will *Homo sapiens* use its advanced intelligence, a charac-

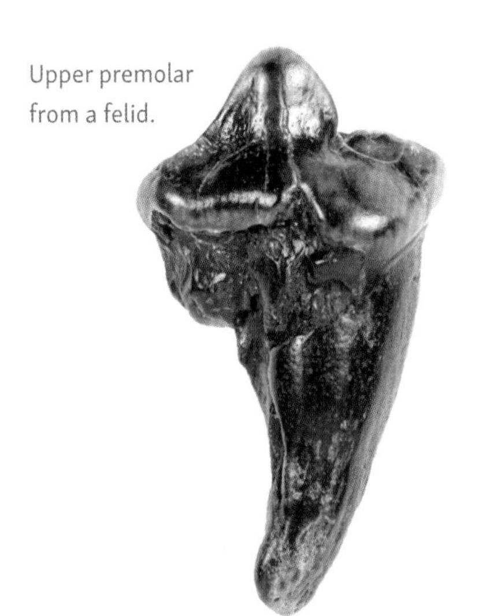

Upper premolar from a felid.

Carnassial from a large cat in the Felidae family.

teristic unique among all living species, to prevent any further felid extinctions? The answer to that question will be a part of our own species' legacy.

One thing is certain. The mighty *Smilodon* has left its legacy through fossil bones preserved in locations from the La Brea Tar Pits to the ocean sediments of the Southeast. Preserved as well are those magnificent seven-inch-long saber teeth. These treasures are rare, but one may be waiting to be found on a beach near you!

Mandible from the extinct dire wolf, *Canis dirus*, with p2–m2 present. Specimen CCNHM 378, courtesy of the Mace Brown Museum of Natural History, Charleston, South Carolina.

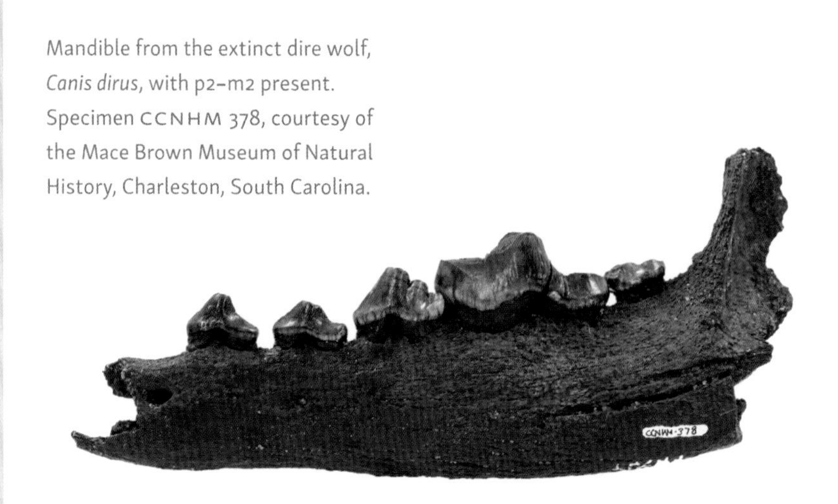

SPECIES HIGHLIGHT

Canids

Who's afraid of Virginia wolf? Or Colorado wolf?
Or Florida, or Texas . . . ?

Despite thousands of years of superstition, fear, trapping, and hunting, wolves have managed to persist to the present day. Because of extremely rare attacks on humans, now attributed to rabies rather than aggression, and because wolves periodically prey on livestock, the wolf is an object of animosity for some people. But thanks to informative scientific field studies, most of the public now views this creature favorably, and efforts by many have brought it back from a path to extinction.

Because the wolf evolved as an apex predator, it has characteristics that enable it to successfully attack and bring down any species it can overtake. Since it can bring harm to humans, it is natural that the wolf has gotten a fearsome reputation, in the same way that sharks, bears, snakes, bats, and many other animals have done. But like these animals, wolves serve an important role within a healthy ecosystem.

The oldest fossils of carnivorous species connected with wolves are from a group of small animals, both terrestrial and arboreal, called miacids, from the Paleocene and Eocene epochs. The miacids are believed to have evolved into mammals within the order Carnivora in North America about 42 million years ago. This order soon split into the suborders of doglike Caniformia and catlike Feliformia. The caniforms gave rise to a number of genera, including the Canidae family, whose surviving members include wolves. The genus *Canis* appeared in North America during the Miocene epoch about 9 to 10 million years ago. Its early species migrated across the Bering Land Bridge into Eurasia around 8 million years ago and diversified into two tribes: Canini, which includes domestic dogs, wolves, jackals, coyotes, and some foxes, and Vulpini, the true foxes. Hyenas, once classified as caniforms, are now known to have evolved within the feliforms, and though doglike in some ways, they actually share more traits with the felids.

The gray wolf, *Canis lupus*, evolved from the early Eurasian *Canis* species and crossed into North America during the mid to late Pleistocene. The earliest gray wolf fossils known are from the Middle Pleistocene Beringia region.

The extinct dire wolf, *Canis dirus*, is nearly as well known as the modern gray wolf. One of the top Pleistocene mammalian predators, whose closest ancestor is believed to be *C. armbrusteri* (also the close ancestor of *C. lupus*), the dire wolf appeared at least 252,000 years ago, as shown by fossils from Salamander Cave in the Black Hills of South Dakota. Dire wolves account for the most numerous fossil remains (over 4,000) of any large animal found in the La Brea Tar Pits. This suggests that the species hunted in packs, and many individuals became trapped at the site while preying on megafauna mired in the tar.

Largest of the canids, dire wolves were about 25% heavier than the modern gray wolf and had larger upper carnassial teeth. It is estimated that their strong

A close look at the interior of a dire wolf (*Canis dirus*) carnassial tooth.

jaws could exert around 30% more force than gray wolves' bites. Because such a large number of the dire wolf teeth found in La Brea are broken, it has been suggested that *C. dirus* may not have been as well adapted to crushing bones as are gray wolves. But these samples may also reflect the intense feeding competition among many wolves trying to quickly devour as much flesh as possible.

Dire wolves coexisted with *C. armbrusteri* across North America, and then outcompeted that species, pushing its remnant population southeastward to Florida. Dire wolves coexisted with gray wolves, too, for about 100,000 years, but were finally replaced by their longer-legged and swifter competitors. The disappearing megafauna left *Canis dirus* with only smaller animal prey to feed on. But this mighty predator wolf, having a heavy body and short legs, was too slow to successfully pursue such prey and became extinct by the end of the Pleistocene.

Dire wolves have left their legacy, however. For those not "afraid of the big bad wolf," bones or teeth may be found, preserved for millennia among river and ocean sediments that subsequently wash ashore. What beach might you luckily be exploring when finding yourself in such "dire" circumstances?

VERTEBRAE

TRAITS OF VERTEBRAE

Vertebrae, the interlocking puzzle pieces making up the spine, consist of three main parts: the middle portion, known as the centrum; the external protrusions, known as the processes; and the center archway, known as the neural arch. The placement of vertebrae along the spine from head to tail (cervical, thoracic, lumbar, sacral,* caudal) determines their morphology. Likewise, the animal of origin can also be determined based on a variety of vertebral features. Differences in the centrum structure (acoelous, opisthocoelous, amphicoelous, procoelous) can reflect the animal type; for instance, amphicoelous vertebrae are typical of fishes, while reptiles have procoelous vertebrae. Scientists are not particularly interested in isolated vertebrae when making specific determinations, because of the difficulty of identifying them at the species level.

COMMON TERMS

Acoelous, amphicoelous, anterior, articular, caudal, centrum, cervical, dorsal, epiphyseal, epiphysis, heterocoelous, lateral, lumbar, neural arch, opisthocoelous, posterior, process, procoelous, sacral, thoracic, ventral, zygapophysis

COMMONALITY

Fish vertebrae and processes are commonly found on beaches. Complete mammalian vertebrae are uncommon, and when found, they tend to lack processes.

INCLUSIONS AND EXCLUSIONS

Typical mammalian, avian, reptilian, and fish vertebrae as well as vertebral growth plates are included. Because of the high morphological variability of vertebrae, extensive species coverage is not addressed—only the most common beach finds.

*In some animals, the sacral vertebrae are fused to form the sacrum, while in others, such as birds, the sacral vertebrae are fused with the lumbar, and some thoracic and caudal vertebrae, to form the synsacrum.

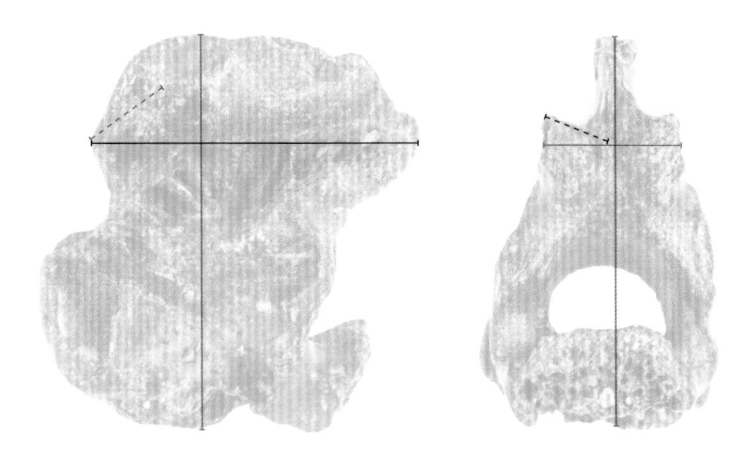

MEASUREMENTS

All vertebrae have measurements displayed in a three-part system:

(AP length × lateral width × DV height)

The first measurement is the anteroposterior (AP) length, measured from head to tail, followed by the width, measured laterally from left to right. The third measurement is the dorsoventral (DV) height, from the back side of the torso to the front. (Dashed lines indicate the third dimension.)

SUPPLEMENTARY IMAGES AND TERMS

See page 476 for an explanation of the vertebral centrum classification system.

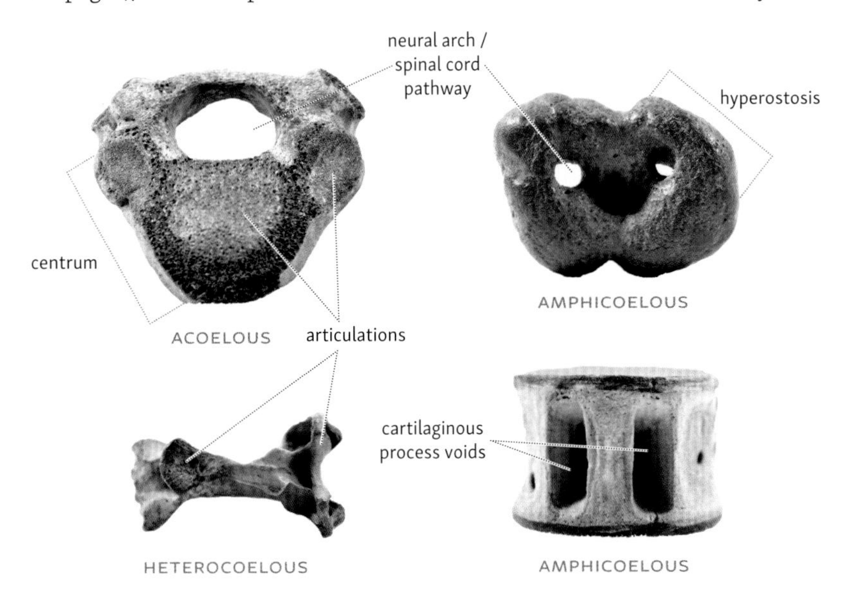

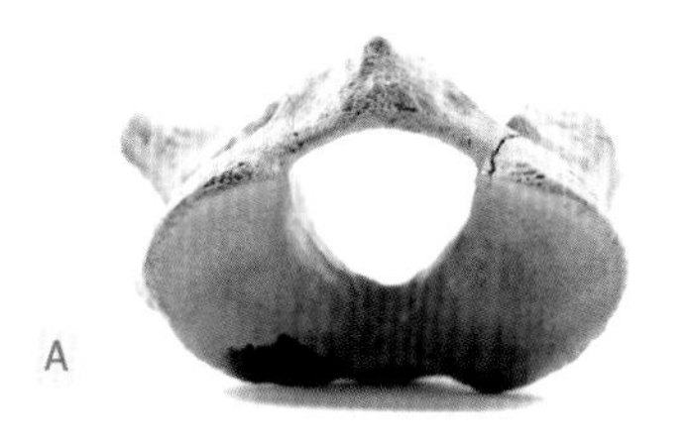
A

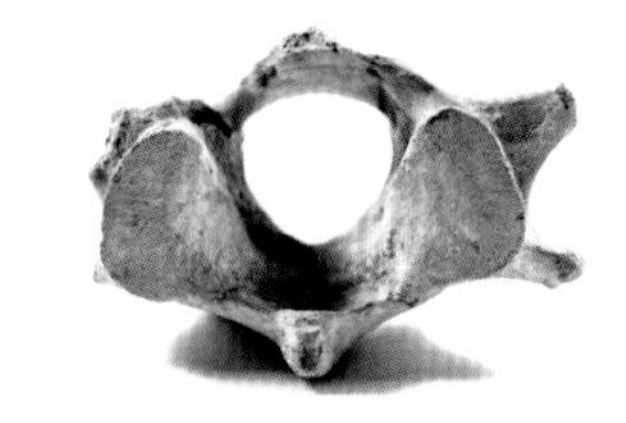
Po

V

L

ATLAS Odontoceti

Atlas vertebra from a dolphin-sized Miocene odontocete. The atlas is the first vertebra, situated right behind the base of the skull. Anteriorly, the atlas articulates with the occipital condyles, and posteriorly with the axis vertebra. Because the spinal column passes through the middle of the atlas, the overall shape of the vertebra is ringlike, lacking a centrum. The axis vertebra has slightly more processes than the atlas and a developed centrum with a strong anterior protuberance.

SIZE

46 × 89 × 59 mm

1.8 × 3.5 × 2.3 in

GEOLOGIC AGE

Miocene

23–5.3 Ma

IDENTIFIERS

Ring-like shape

Lack of centrum

Lack of neural arch

DENSITY

DID YOU KNOW? Some vertebrae have specialized functions. The cervical atlas and axis vertebrae are connected by a lubricated synovial joint. The atlas assists in nodding the head, and the axis allows for movement from side to side. Dolphins make maximum use of these vertebrae in swimming, twisting, jumping, and hunting for food.

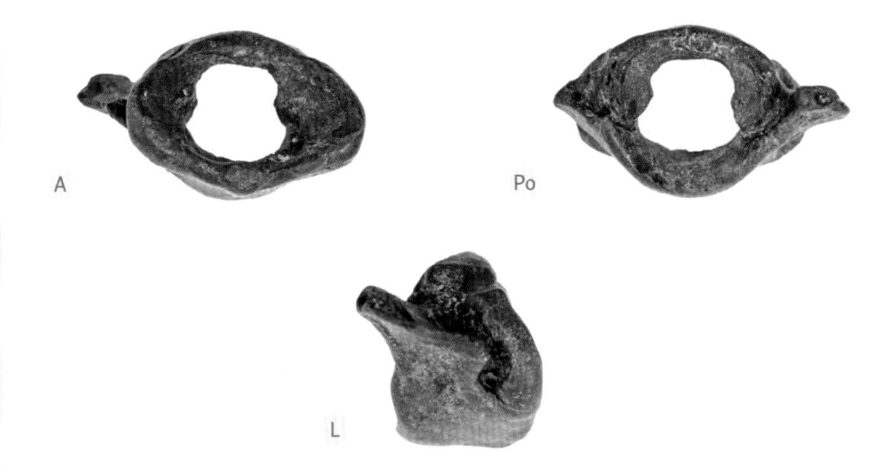

ATLAS *Procyon lotor*

SIZE

22 × 12 × 12 mm

0.9 × 0.5 × 0.5 in

GEOLOGIC AGE

Pleistocene

2.6 Ma–11 ka

IDENTIFIERS

Wide anterior

Ringlike form

Simple processes

DENSITY

Atlas vertebra from the extant raccoon, *Procyon lotor*. The atlas is the first vertebra in all animals. The wide anterior portion articulates with the occipital condyles found at the base of the skull (page 472). The two arches that form this ringlike vertebra encase the spinal cord; in other vertebrae, the neural arch above the centrum performs this function. The processes are simple in form (one is missing from the above specimen).

DID YOU KNOW? The Barbados raccoon, a subspecies of the common North American species, is the only raccoon to have become extinct in modern times. The raccoon's small body size and small population were due to the limited space and resources of its island environment. Habitat destruction and increased stress from the growing tourism and hotel industry brought about its extirpation in 1964.

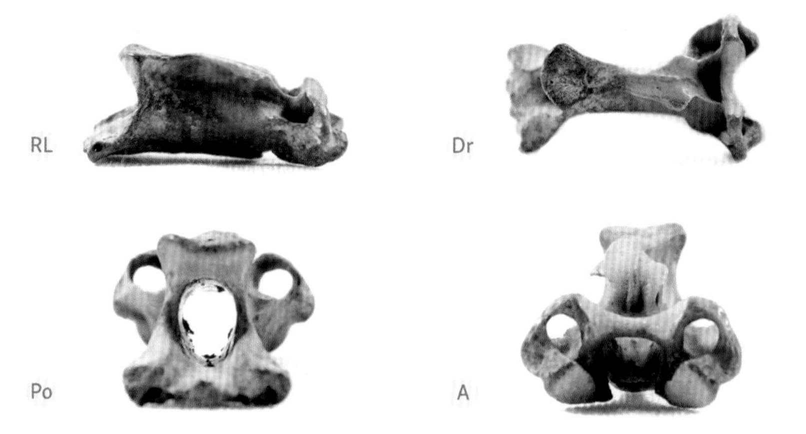

CERVICAL Aves

Neck vertebra from an indeterminate Pleistocene wading bird species. This specimen shows the classic heterocoelous form found in bird vertebrae—a centrum with saddle-shaped articular surfaces, which allow for great flexibility of the neck. Note the delicate bone structure typical of avian species.

SIZE

23 × 9 × 4 mm

0.9 × 0.4 × 0.2 in

GEOLOGIC AGE

Pleistocene

2.6 Ma–11 ka

IDENTIFIERS

Delicate structure

Saddle shape

Heterocoelous form

DENSITY

DID YOU KNOW? Specialized vertebrae evolved in the necks of birds. The cervical vertebrae match and interlock, being concave on one surface and convex on the adjacent matching surface. Some vertebrae bend forward and others bend backward. This allows for a wide range of motion for cleaning and preening and enables wading birds to snap their heads suddenly forward to snag underwater prey.

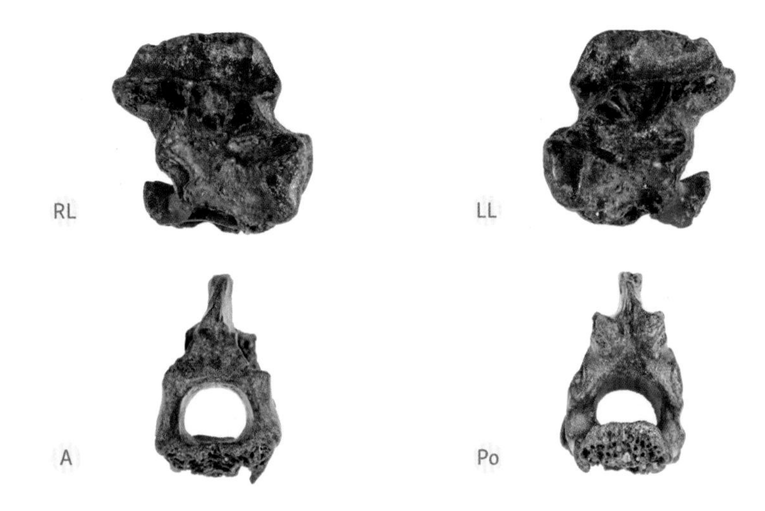

SIZE

17 × 12 × 18 mm

0.7 × 0.5 × 0.7 in

GEOLOGIC AGE

Pleistocene

2.6 Ma–11 ka

IDENTIFIERS

Dorsal ridge

Large neural arch

Multiple processes

DENSITY

CERVICAL C3 Carnivora

Third cervical vertebra (C3) from an undetermined species of Pleistocene carnivore. Unlike the other vertebrae in the neck, the C3 has a tall ridge extending along the dorsal side. Processes are located on the dorsal and ventral sides, both anteriorly and posteriorly. Note the large neural arch for the spinal column—typical of cervical vertebrae. The centrum of the above specimen is worn down and incomplete.

DID YOU KNOW? Fossils from creatures previously unknown to science continue to be found. Bones from *Dahalokely tokana*, a 9- to 14-foot-long carnivorous dinosaur, were unearthed among 90-million-year-old rocks in Madagascar in 2013. The paleontologists Andrew Farke and Joseph Sertich found the ribs and vertebrae, which led to identification of the new species. They named it from words in the Malagasy language meaning "lonely small bandit."

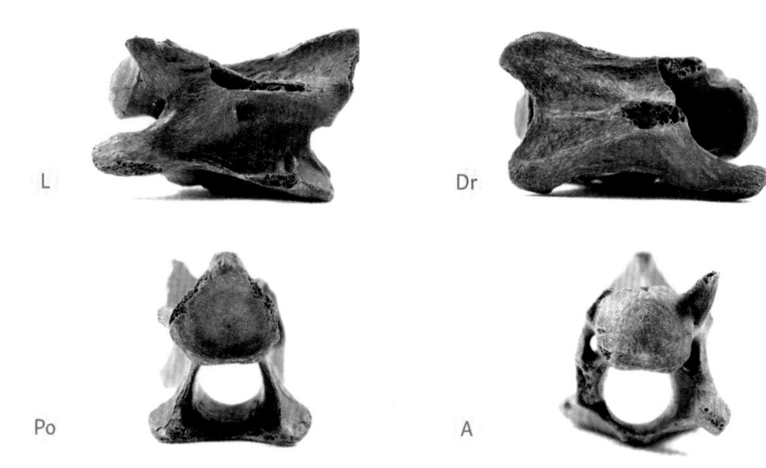

CERVICAL *Canis* sp.

Vertebra from the neck of a Pleistocene wolf, genus *Canis*. Fairly cylindrical in form, canid cervical vertebrae have round neural arches that are near equal in proportion to the centrum. Two holes for nerves and blood vessels run parallel to the neural arch (seen in the anterior view). Processes are streamlined within the cervical vertebrae to allow for smooth movement of the neck. Note that this specimen is anatomically inverted in the anterior and posterior views.

SIZE

57 × 28 × 38 mm

2.2 × 1.1 × 1.5 in

GEOLOGIC AGE

Pleistocene

2.6 Ma–11 ka

IDENTIFIERS

Large neural arch

Streamlined processes

Anteroposterior foramina

DENSITY

DID YOU KNOW? Members of the Canidae family (canines, including wolves, dogs, and foxes) have vertebrae that are similar in number and location. Thirteen dorsal, 7 lumbar, 3 sacral, and 15 caudal vertebrae support these mammals. Dog and wolf species have an identical number, but the fox has 22 caudal vertebrae. Maybe foxes need more of these to show off their elegant, bushy tails.

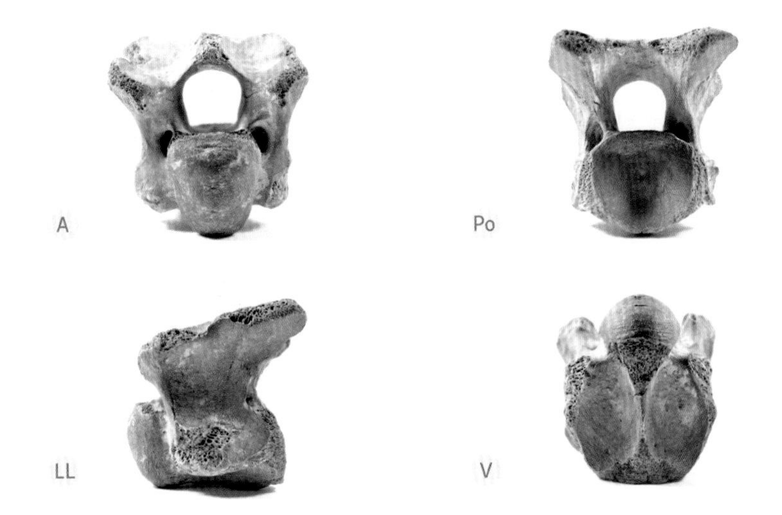

SIZE

98 × 84 × 80 mm

3.8 × 3.3 × 3.1 in

GEOLOGIC AGE

Pleistocene

2.6 Ma–11 ka

IDENTIFIERS

Numerous processes

D-shaped centrum

Large neural arch

DENSITY

CERVICAL *Bison* sp.

Cervical vertebra from an extinct Pleistocene bison, genus *Bison*. On intact specimens, seven main processes project from the centrum. Note the sideways D-shaped centrum and large neural arch. The posterior side of the centrum is deeply concave. Bison vertebrae rigidly interlock to support the massive weight of the head and back.

DID YOU KNOW? The bison species name "*antiquus*" comes from Latin for "old" or "ancient." But some bison apparently didn't get the chance to live to old age, at least not in good health. DNA testing of *B. antiquus* fossils has found osteoarthritis caused by *Mycobacterium tuberculosis*. Osteoarthritis affects the entire joint: cartilage, joint lining, ligaments, and underlying bone. The condition would have had a crippling effect on a bison's mobility.

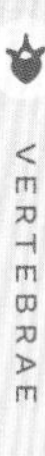

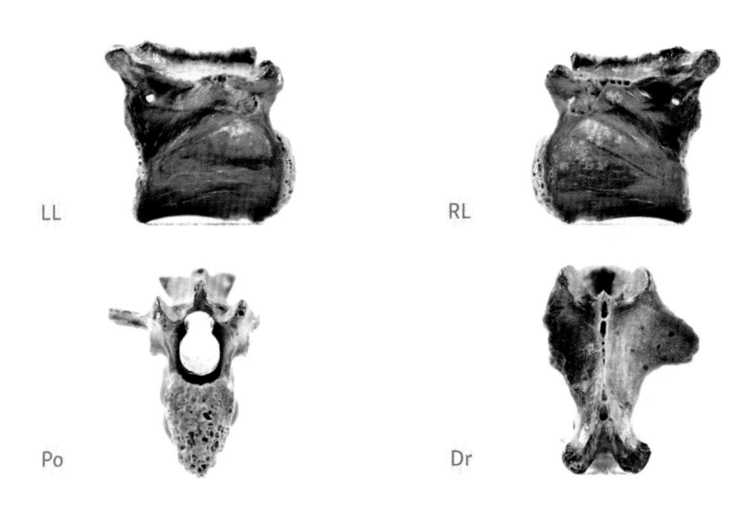

THORACIC Aves

Thoracic vertebra from an indeterminate Pleistocene bird species. Most likely belonging to a wading bird, such as a heron or an egret, this specimen shows the procoelous form of centrum, being anteriorly concave and posteriorly convex. The ventral side of the centrum attenuates to a sharp ridge narrowly extending down the body. The neural arch, which has the appearance of two joined circles, held the spinal cord and associated blood vessels.

SIZE

20 × 14 × 18 mm

0.8 × 0.5 × 0.7 in

GEOLOGIC AGE

Pleistocene

2.6 Ma–11 ka

IDENTIFIERS

Thin form

Sharp ventral side

Procoelous form

DENSITY

DID YOU KNOW? Bird necks are flexible, allowing movement for preening, catching prey, and watching for predators, but their pelvic regions are designed for stability. The six vertebrae below the pelvis and the three lumbar vertebrae of the trunk are fused to create the synsacrum (essentially, the bird's rump). These fused bones create a stronger pelvis than that of mammals and play an important role in respiration, locomotion, and flight.

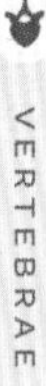

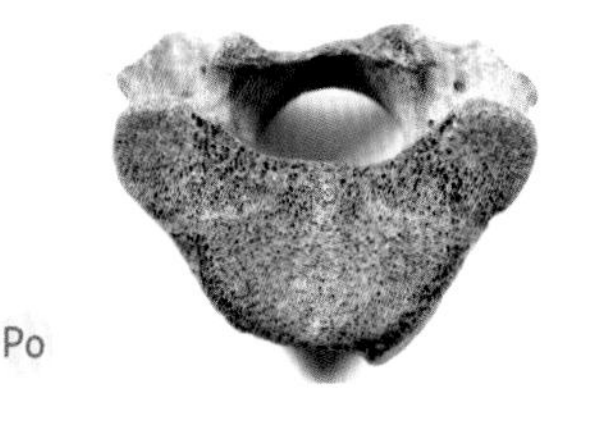
Po

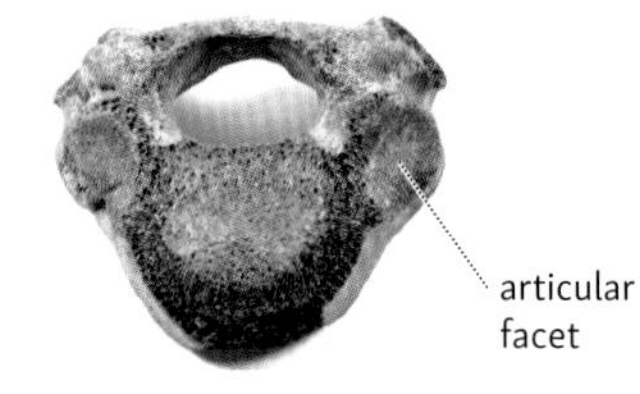

A

Dr

L

THORACIC *Tapirus veroensis*

Thoracic vertebra from the extinct Pleistocene tapir, *Tapirus veroensis*. The above vertebra, which is missing the dorsal process, shows the articular facets where the ribs articulated (indicated). The neural arch is fairly circular, and the dorsal process would have projected posteriorly from the centrum. Tapir centra are acoelous, lacking any concavity or convexity.

SIZE

25 × 60 × 47 mm

1.0 × 2.3 × 1.8 in

GEOLOGIC AGE

Pleistocene

2.6 Ma–11 ka

IDENTIFIERS

Round, flat centrum

Rounded neural arch

Acoelous form

DENSITY

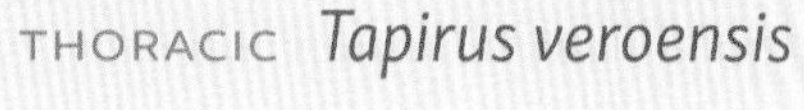

DID YOU KNOW? People in the northern United States have migrated south to Florida's warm climate for decades. But tapirs migrated north to Florida after the Panamanian Land Bridge formed, and they lived there until around 11,000 years ago. Their skeletons abound in Florida's Haile 7G site, a limestone quarry near the town of Newberry believed to hold more tapir fossils than any other place in the world.

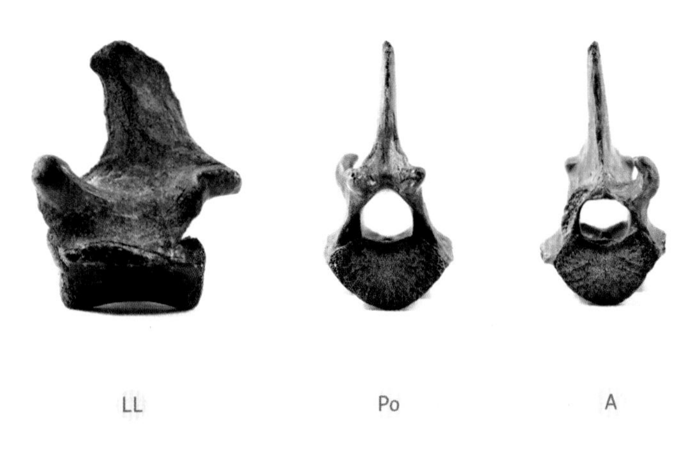

LL Po A

LUMBAR *Odocoileus virginianus*

Lumbar vertebra from the extant white-tailed deer, *Odocoileus virginianus*. Note the curved articular process(es) on the anterior side and the knob-like processes on the posterior side. The transverse processes are missing on the lateral sides, but sat at roughly 120 degrees, spanning the ventral side. This vertebra is from a juvenile deer; the centrum shows the radiating lines where the epiphyses had not yet fused.

SIZE

50 × 30 × 64 mm

2.0 × 1.2 × 2.5 in

GEOLOGIC AGE

Pleistocene

2.6 Ma–11 ka

IDENTIFIERS

Curved processes

Tall dorsal process

Acoelous form

DENSITY

DID YOU KNOW? The largest deer species ever known lived in Europe and Asia. *Megaloceros*, commonly called the Irish elk, was actually a deer species. Many of their fossil skeletons have been found preserved in Irish bogs. The deer stood 7 feet tall with antlers that spanned an amazing 12 feet. Unable to survive in the changing subarctic climate, this deer had become extinct by the end of the Pleistocene.

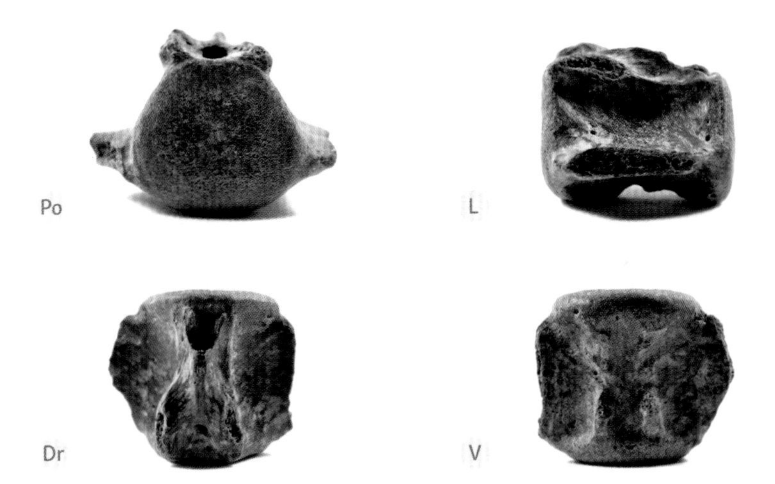

SIZE

43 × 50 × 36 mm

1.7 × 2.0 × 1.4 in

GEOLOGIC AGE

Pleistocene

2.6 Ma–11 ka

IDENTIFIERS

Minimized neural arch

Extra articulation

Acoelous form

DENSITY

CAUDAL *Holmesina septentrionalis*

Caudal (tail) vertebra from the extinct giant armadillo *Holmesina septentrionalis*. Note the reduced neural arch, which is often observed on tail vertebrae. These vertebrae are also acoelous, meaning that the centrum faces are neither concave nor convex. See *Dasypus bellus* vertebra (page 363) for the classic xenarthran articulation, which would be visible on the above specimen if the processes were attached.

DID YOU KNOW? The oldest ground sloth fossils, which are from the family Megatheriidae, date from the Late Oligocene epoch and were found in South America. At 4.5 feet long, the megatheriids were quite a bit smaller than the Late Pleistocene ground sloths. They lived in Central and South America during the Miocene epoch, 23–5.3 Ma, and began to spread throughout the West Indies and southern United States. How, you might ask? Some scientists think the animals could have rafted across the sea on floating debris.

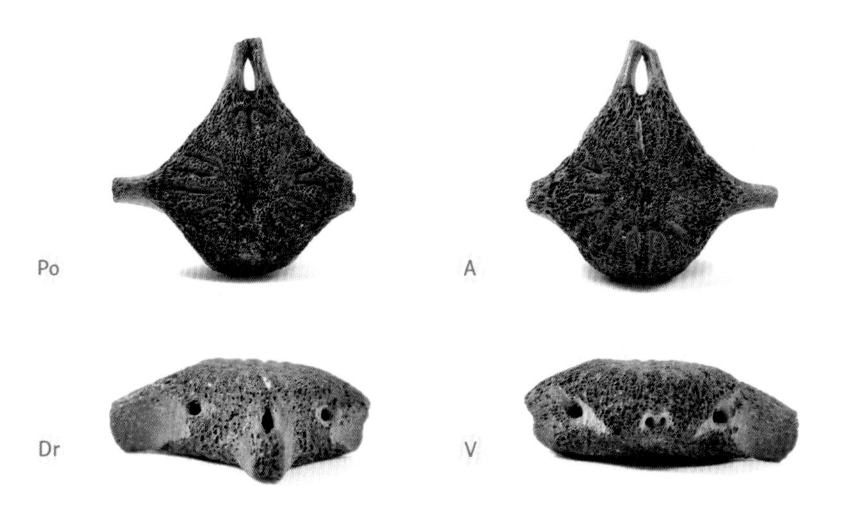

CAUDAL Odontoceti

Caudal vertebra from an undetermined toothed echolocating whale. Cetacean caudal vertebrae have reduced neural arches and are generally smaller than other vertebrae, excluding the thin-walled cervical vertebrae. This particular vertebra came from an immature cetacean, as shown by the epiphyseal lines, where the growth plates (page 376) separated after death.

SIZE

15 × 47 × 43 mm

0.6 × 1.8 × 1.7 in

GEOLOGIC AGE

Pleistocene

2.6 Ma–11 ka

IDENTIFIERS

Thin form

Narrow neural arch

Acoelous form

DENSITY

DID YOU KNOW? Dolphins have 41–98 vertebrae. Each is characterized by a large neural arch, a structure at the top of the vertebra for muscle attachment and for housing the spinal cord. The caudal, or tail, section of a dolphin's spine comprises many bones that descend in size until they are replaced by muscle. The caudal section is an important part of "Flipper," since he uses his tail for locomotion and spectacular leaps above the water.

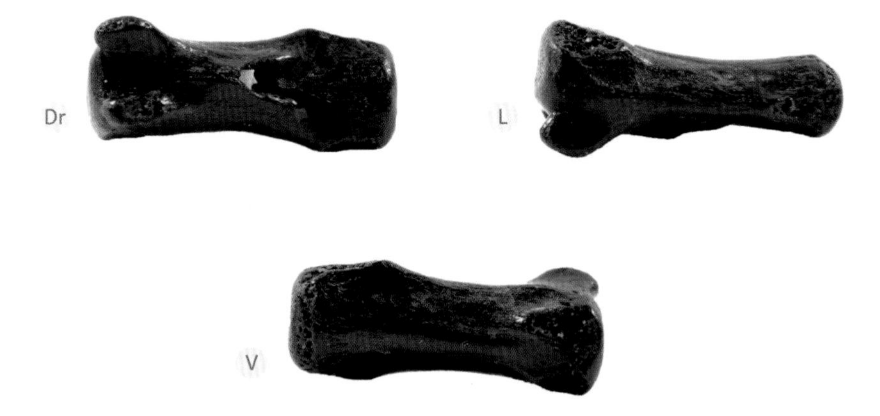

SIZE

22 × 8 × 8 mm

0.9 × 0.3 × 0.3 in

GEOLOGIC AGE

Pleistocene

2.6 Ma–11 ka

IDENTIFIERS

Reduced neural arch

Small processes

Streamlined shape

DENSITY

CAUDAL Mammalia

Tail vertebra from an undetermined species of Pleistocene vertebrate. Caudal vertebrae are characteristically slimmer, more elongated, and simpler than other vertebrae. The neural arch is reduced or lost, and the processes are similarly modified.

DID YOU KNOW? *Spinosaurus* is believed to be the largest carnivorous dinosaur to have lived—perhaps up to 23 feet high, 60 feet long, and weighing 20 tons—even larger than *T. rex* or *Gigantosaurus*. Its name, meaning "spine lizard," refers to the long spines extending from its vertebrae, which supported a skin-covered sail. *Spinosaurus* is believed to be the first dinosaur to swim and to spend a majority of its time in the water.

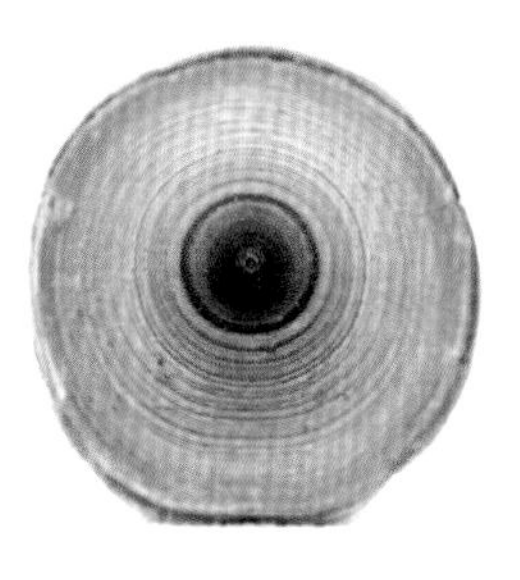

A

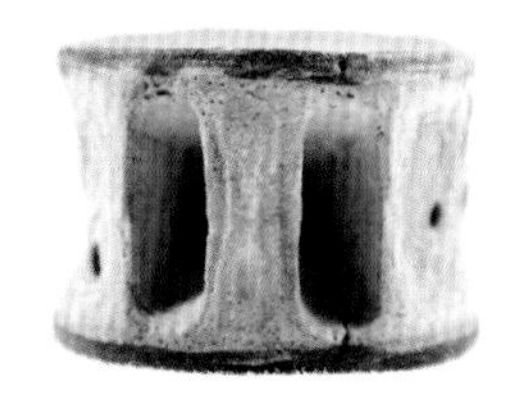

V

SCYLIORHINOID

Carcharhiniformes

Distinct vertebra from an undetermined Pleistocene shark species. Shark vertebrae are broken down into two categories, the lamnoid and scyliorhinoid designs. Representing the carcharhiniform sharks, the scyliorhinoid design is disc-shaped and conically depressed on both ends (amphicoelous) and has two hollows ventrally and dorsally. These hollows are where cartilaginous processes attached to the centrum. Being composed of noncalcified cartilage, the processes do not fossilize. The plates of the centra are rigidly held together by thick cartilage. (Compare with the more fragile lamnoid design, page 362.)

SIZE

17 × 24 × 24 mm

0.7 × 0.9 × 0.9 in

GEOLOGIC AGE

Pleistocene

2.6 Ma–11 ka

IDENTIFIERS

Disc shape

Growth rings

Amphicoelous form

DENSITY

DID YOU KNOW? Shark vertebrae have a concave depression on each side of a round disk. Look closely and you can see concentric circles too. Scientists originally thought that the circles were like tree growth rings and that one could age the shark by counting these rings. Additional research has shown that is not necessarily the case. Species and size need to be considered first, since some sharks deposit two growth rings a year as they mature.

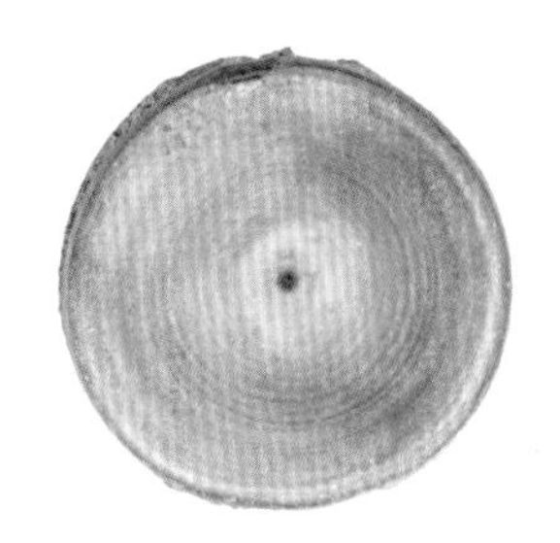

SIZE

27 × 27 × 10 mm

1.1 × 1.1 × 0.4 in

GEOLOGIC AGE

Oligocene

33.9–23 Ma

IDENTIFIERS

Septae

Growth rings

Amphicoelous form

DENSITY

LAMNOID Lamniformes

Vertebra from an undetermined Oligocene shark species. Shark vertebrae are separated into two categories: those from the Lamniformes order and those from the Carcharhiniformes order. Shark species in the Lamniformes include makos, great whites, threshers, sand tigers, goblins, crocodile sharks, and megamouth sharks. Between the ends of the centrum are multiple thin bridges, or septae, that connect each vertebral plate. These vertebrae are therefore fragile and often found broken; the teeth of Lamniformes sharks, by contrast, are quite robust.

DID YOU KNOW? Many teenagers have taken tetracycline to fight acne. Sharks are injected with the same drug to record rings on their vertebrae. It is absorbed into the vertebra and retained, marking that point in time. When the shark is recaptured, ultraviolet light highlights that tagged spot, and scientists can figure how much the vertebra and the shark have grown since being tagged.

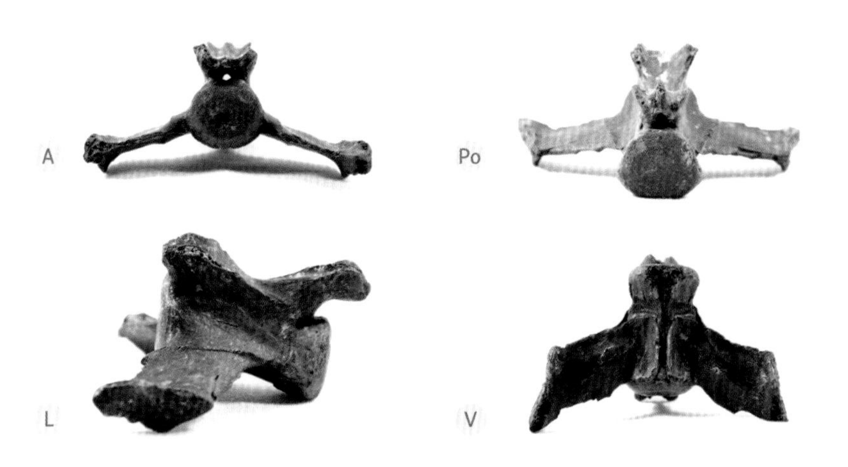

VERTEBRA *Dasypus bellus*

Vertebra from the extinct "beautiful armadillo," *Dasypus bellus*. Armadillos are in a class of mammals called xenarthrans, which means "strange joints." Oddly jointed vertebrae occasionally have extra points of articulation (xenapophyses), which aid in identification. Note the reduced neural arch (above) and the flat, acoelous centrum.

SIZE

37 × 62 × 27 mm

1.4 × 2.4 × 1.1 in

GEOLOGIC AGE

Pleistocene

2.6 Ma–11 ka

IDENTIFIERS

Wide, thin processes

Minimized neural arch

Grooved ventral side

DENSITY

DID YOU KNOW? Armadillos are good swimmers, even with their heavy armor. They swallow air and push it into their intestines, increasing their buoyancy. This maneuver helps them float while they swim, which looks something like dog-paddling. An armadillo can hold its breath for up to six minutes, allowing it to walk along the bottoms of streams or rivers. In this way, armadillos have moved from the mainland to nearby islands and have enlarged their range, which today extends to Illinois.

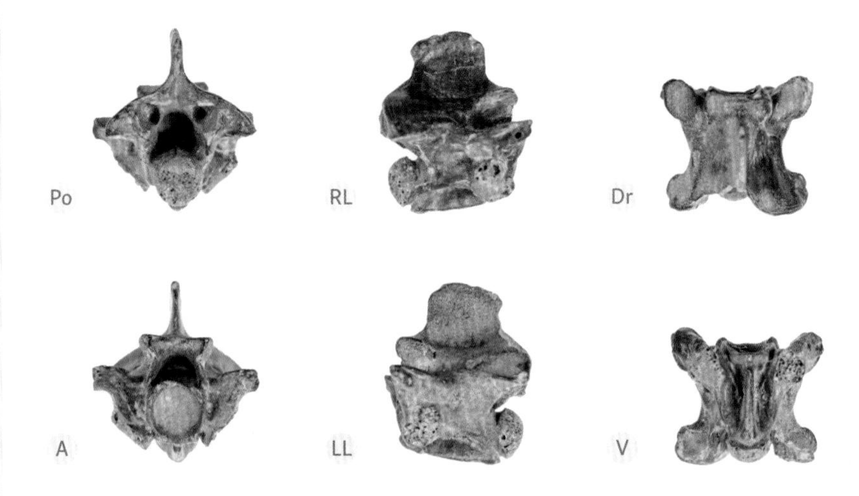

SIZE

13 × 15 × 14 mm

0.5 × 0.6 × 0.5 in

GEOLOGIC AGE

Pleistocene

2.6 Ma–11 ka

IDENTIFIERS

Complex articulations

Domed neural arch

Procoelous form

DENSITY

VERTEBRA Serpentes

Trunk vertebra from an undetermined Pleistocene snake species. Snake vertebrae are difficult to identify, even to the genus level, without a large comparative collection and years of expertise. For the most part, Pleistocene snake genera reflect those alive today. The ball-and-socket (procoelous) articulation of reptile vertebrae makes distinguishing them from mammal vertebrae relatively easy.

DID YOU KNOW? Snake skull fossils are rare, since the skull bones are weakly attached to one another by connective tissue. Therefore, these bones usually disarticulate before fossilizing. Snake vertebrae, however, are more common, thanks in part to their structure, but largely because of their abundance. Some snake species have vertebral counts as high as a few hundred!

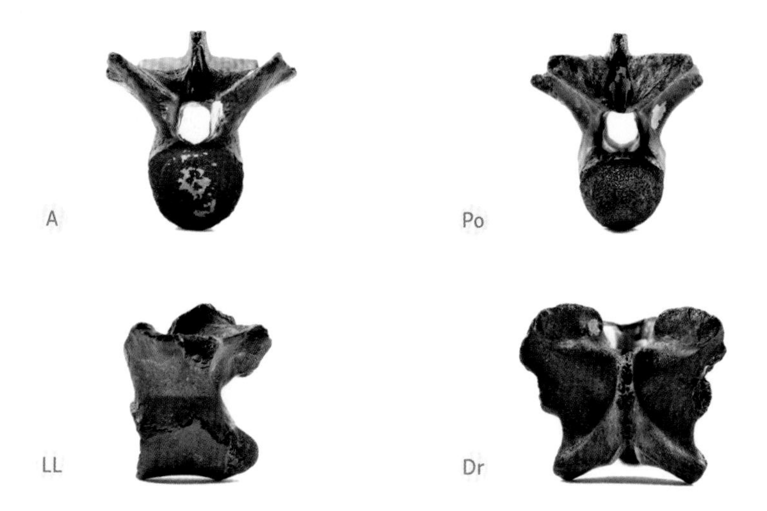

VERTEBRA

Alligator mississippiensis

Vertebra from the extant American alligator, *Alligator mississippiensis*. Like other reptilian vertebrae, those from the alligator are procoelous, concave on the anterior end. The neural arch is round to ovate, with a wide platform of processes on the dorsal side. The processes attach to the centrum relatively close to one another and are primarily restricted to the dorsal side.

SIZE

40 × 55 × 55 mm

1.6 × 2.2 × 2.2 in

GEOLOGIC AGE

Pleistocene

2.6 Ma–11 ka

IDENTIFIERS

Round neural arch

Dorsal processes

Procoelous form

DENSITY

DID YOU KNOW? Alligators travel across land, sometimes for great distances, to find bodies of freshwater, since they are not very saltwater-tolerant. Their fossils thus may end up in places far from their usual habitats.

CENTRUM Odontoceti

SIZE

45 × 35 × 25 mm

1.8 × 1.4 × 1.0 in

GEOLOGIC AGE

Pleistocene

2.6 Ma–11 ka

IDENTIFIERS

Dorsal process lines

Lateral process lines

Acoelous form

DENSITY

Water-worn vertebra from an undetermined toothed echolocating whale. This specimen represents one of the most commonly found states of cetacean vertebrae: all the processes are broken off, and the centrum is tumbled and water-worn. Note the two areas of attachment in dorsal view (indicated), which would have connected to the neural arch, and the similar lateral processes. This vertebra came from an immature cetacean, based on the epiphyseal lines (visible in the anterior view).

DID YOU KNOW? Would you ever describe someone as a "dolphin in wolf's clothing"? Dolphins once lived on land and were similar in appearance to wolves, though they walked on five hoof-like toes instead of paws with claws. Eventually, dolphins and some other mammals returned to the ocean, where they evolved into the cetaceans. Dolphins, whales, and porpoises retain some terrestrial skeletal elements, such as the phalanges in modern dolphin flippers.

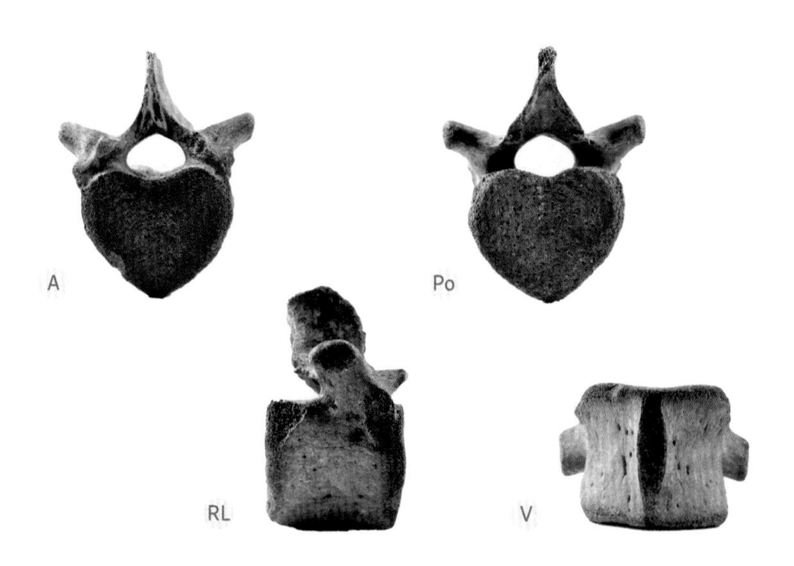

VERTEBRA *Trichechus manatus*

Vertebra from the extant manatee, *Trichechus manatus*. One of the main characteristics of manatee vertebrae is their heart-shaped centra. Like their ribs and other bones, the vertebrae are fairly dense compared with those of other vertebrates. Processes are simple for the most part and restricted to the dorsal portion.

SIZE

60 × 93 × 108 mm

2.3 × 3.6 × 4.2 in

GEOLOGIC AGE

Pleistocene

2.6 Ma–11 ka

IDENTIFIERS

Heart-shaped centrum

Simple processes

Acoelous form

DENSITY

DID YOU KNOW? Manatee bones are particularly interesting for their structure and density. The heavy rib bones act as ballast, allowing manatees to submerge easily to find herbaceous food on the bottom of rivers and bays. All the plant material that a manatee eats is converted to gas, which counteracts the heaviness of the ribs.

SIZE

17 × 15 × 15 mm

0.7 × 0.6 × 0.6 in

GEOLOGIC AGE

Pleistocene

2.6 Ma–11 ka

IDENTIFIERS

Curved ends

Webbed sides

Opisthocoelous form

DENSITY

VERTEBRA *Lepisosteus osseus*

Vertebra from the extant longnose gar species, *Lepisosteus osseus*. Unlike other fish, gars have opisthocoelous vertebrae, meaning they are convex on the anterior side and concave on the posterior. As with other fish vertebrae, the sides are webbed with deep sinuses. Compare the above specimen to the more prevalent articulation of fish vertebrae, page 370.

DID YOU KNOW? Gar fish skeletons are interesting combinations of bones and cartilage. Thus, gars are believed to be a curious link with cartilaginous sharks (order Chondrichthyes) and with bony fish (order Osteichthyes), with which they are classified. Spines of these long skinny fish have evolved a ball-and-socket arrangement for each vertebra, which allows for great freedom of movement when attacking prey or escaping predators.

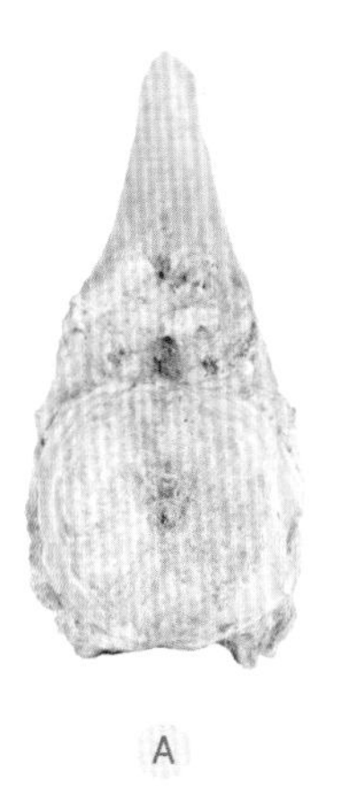

A

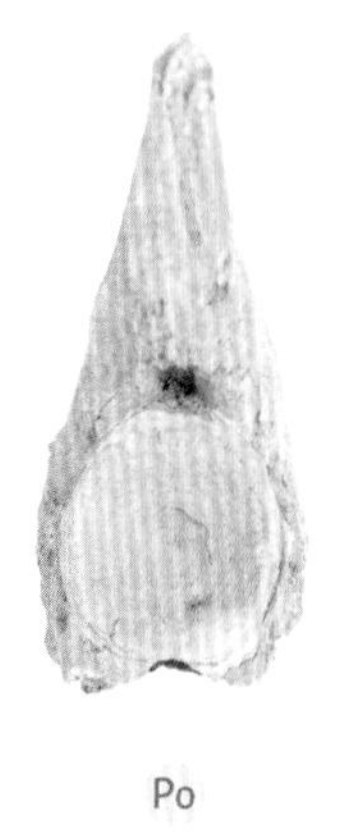

Po

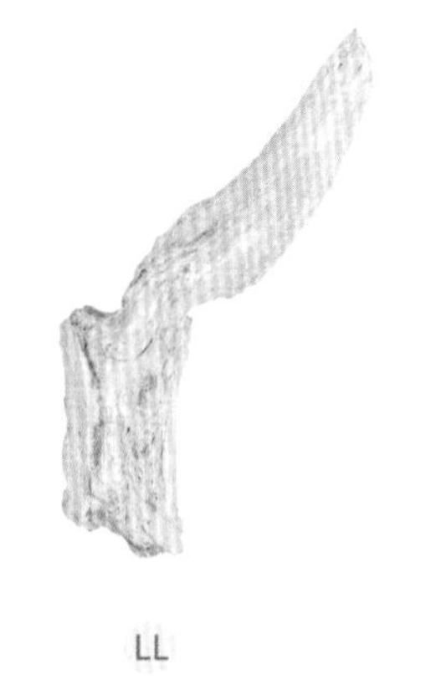

LL

VERTEBRA *Thunnus* sp.

Caudal vertebra from the hypural complex of a tuna, genus *Thunnus*. This specimen retains one of two processes (neural and hemal arches) that project off the centrum. These processes interlock with adjacent ones to provide support at the base of the tuna's tail (see hypural bone, page 374). Some fish species retained a center hole that evolved to allow passage of the notochord—a thin rod that provided for skeletal flexibility and also rigidity. This hole is obscured above by matrix left on the specimen.

SIZE

14 × 10 × 31 mm

0.5 × 0.4 × 1.2 in

GEOLOGIC AGE

Miocene

23–5.3 Ma

IDENTIFIERS

Notochord hole

Two processes

Amphicoelous form

DENSITY

DID YOU KNOW? *Saurichthys* was a Triassic fish genus whose members were similar to modern eels and gar fish. Some species, such as *S. grignae* from the Ladinian of Europe, could grow to four feet long. Unlike any other fish known to science, this species had twice the usual number of vertebral arches, which allowed for a long skeleton, but at the cost of both flexibility and speed over long distances.

A

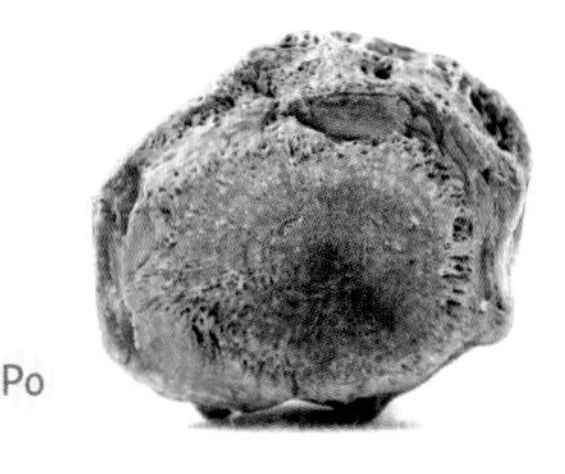
Po

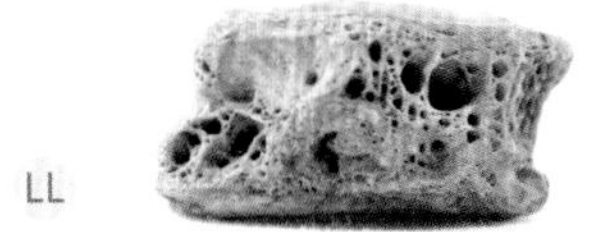
LL

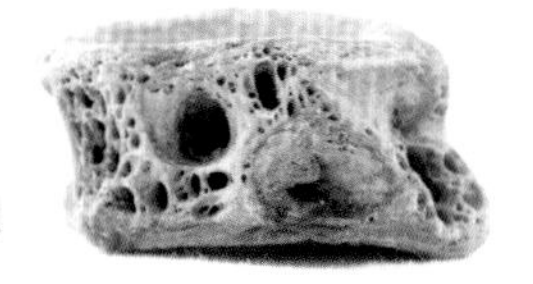
RL

SIZE

15 × 29 × 34 mm

0.6 × 1.1 × 1.3 in

GEOLOGIC AGE

Pleistocene

2.6 Ma–11 ka

IDENTIFIERS

Medial septae

Process voids

Amphicoelous form

DENSITY

VERTEBRA Osteichthyes

Vertebra from an undetermined species of Pleistocene fish. The most readily identifying trait of fish vertebrae (with the exception of those from gar fish) is their concave centrum, which is funnel-shaped on each end. Most fish have two processes extending dorso-ventrally off the centrum, as seen on page 115. These processes are called the neural arch (dorsally) and the hemal arch (ventrally).

DID YOU KNOW? Resourceful islanders of the South Pacific once used inflated and dried puffer fish or burrfish skins with spines still attached to make war helmets. If you want to try this, some tourist stores sell the puffed-up dried skins of puffer fish. But it would take a number of them to cover your head.

A

Po

LL

RL

HYPEROSTOTIC Osteichthyes

Swollen vertebra from an undetermined fish species. Because of hyperostosis, or above-average bone growth, many features of this vertebra can be hard to distinguish. It retains the amphicoelous centrum found in fishes, along with the neural and hemal arch pathways. Vertebrae exhibiting abnormal bone growth take on many shapes and sizes. Fragments of them can be distinguished from phosphate pebbles by some form of bilateral symmetry left in the bone or by traces of cancellous bone structure. Note that all views are turned 90 degrees from the original body orientation.

SIZE

19 × 36 × 25 mm

0.7 × 1.4 × 1.0 in

GEOLOGIC AGE

Pleistocene

2.6 Ma–11 ka

IDENTIFIERS

Excessive growth

Two nerve holes

Amphicoelous form

DENSITY

DID YOU KNOW? Hyperostosis in fish occurs in several bone regions, including skulls, clavicles, and hemal and neural arches. This thickening of the bones is not considered a disease, but an abnormality. The irregular forms are pear-shaped, spherical, and oblong. It does not seem as if the presence of extra calcified bone material hinders the fish's movement.

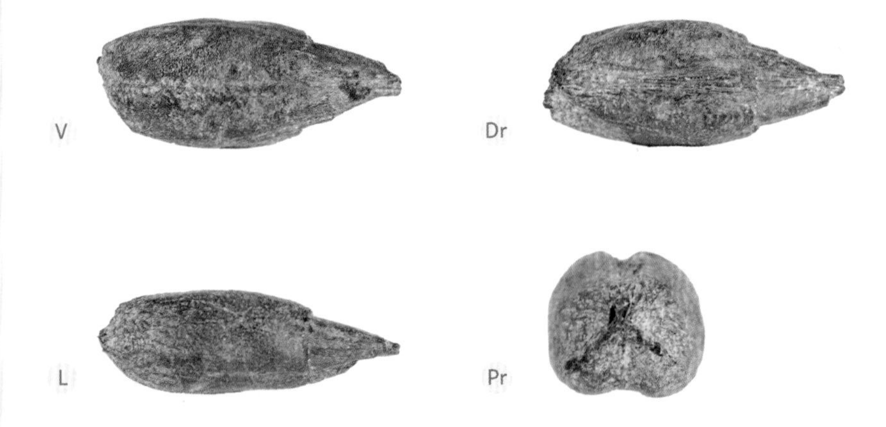

PTERYGIOPHORE Osteichthyes

SIZE

31 × 19 × 13 mm

1.2 × 0.7 × 0.5 in

GEOLOGIC AGE

Pleistocene

2.6 Ma–11 ka

IDENTIFIERS

Trigonal symmetry

Inflated appearance

Tapered distal end

DENSITY

Base of a dorsal fin ray (pterygiophore) from an undetermined fish species. This gall-like structure is a result of bone expansion and above-normal bone growth (hyperostosis). These fin rays, in particular, are occasionally mislabeled "ballast bones" by collectors, yet their function is not to provide ballast, which is indicated by their anterodorsal position within the fish's body. Pterygiophores can be found in both the dorsal and anal fins.

DID YOU KNOW? "Tilly bones" are abnormal growths along the spines of some fish species. These bones have no specific location, but may appear randomly along the spine. X-rays of fish have revealed three to six "Tilly bones" from the caudal section to the thoracic area. The bones were named for the female paleontologist Tilly Edinger (1897–1967), who founded the field of paleoneurology.

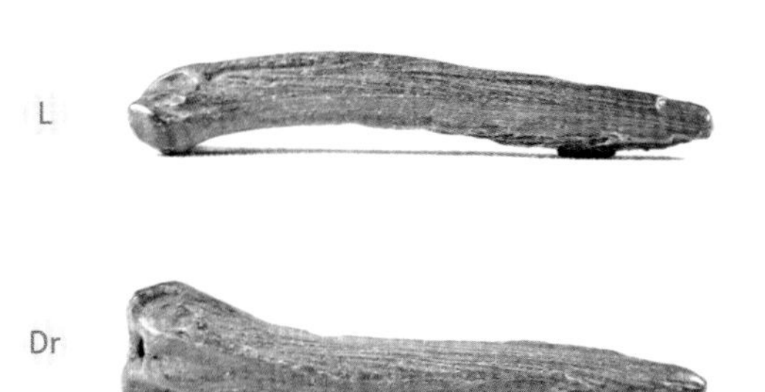

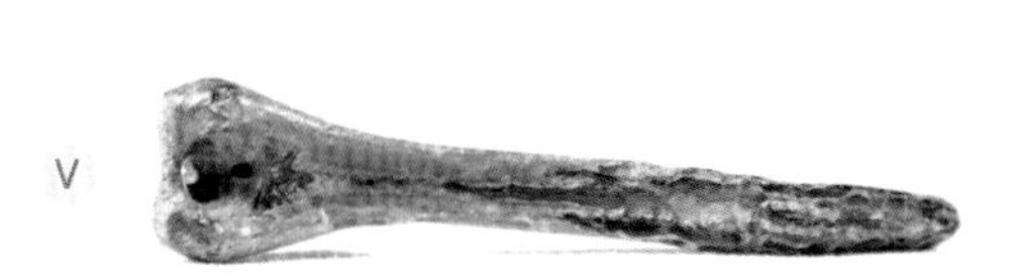

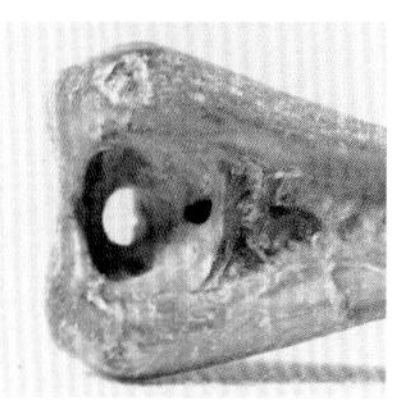

DORSAL SPINE *Centropomus* sp.

Fin spine from an extinct species of snook fish, genus *Centropomus*. These spines articulated dorsally above the vertebra. Classified as a pinna, this spine would have held up the dorsal fin in the snook's body. Note the holes centered in the middle of the spine, located both dorsally and ventrally. The ventral side is concave, coming to a keeled groove at the deepest point, while the dorsal side, with the same keeled form, is convex.

SIZE

60 × 6 × 8 mm

2.3 × 0.2 × 0.3 in

GEOLOGIC AGE

Pleistocene

2.6 Ma–11 ka

IDENTIFIERS

Centered holes

Concave ventral side

Convex dorsal side

DENSITY

DID YOU KNOW? Members of the Centropomidae family, commonly called "snook," are commercially valuable fish that range from the southeastern United States to Brazil. They have a slender body with a long, sloping, narrow head and high, separated dorsal fins with small spines. Commercial snook fishing is banned in Florida and Texas in favor of recreational sportfishing—which is popular because snook put up an exciting fight.

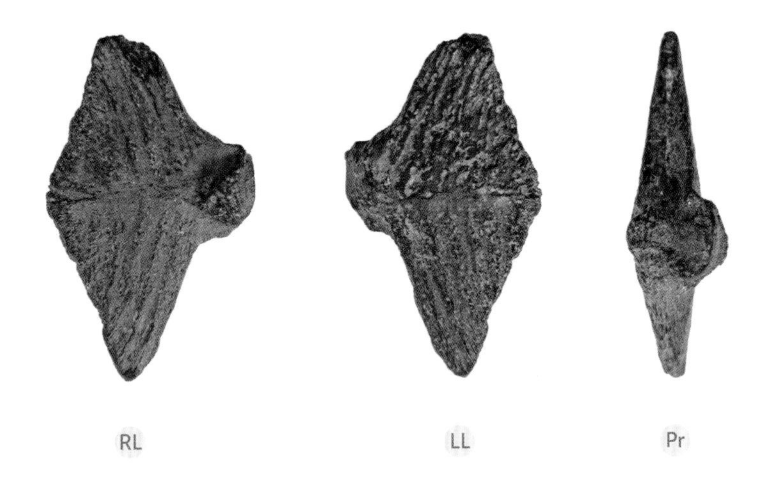

HYPURAL *Thunnus* sp.

Hypural bone from a tuna, genus *Thunnus*. The hypural bone, the last vertebra in a fish's spinal column, is the vertebral element that directs tail movement. The ray-shaped design of the hypural demonstrates how the caudal fin rays attach to the bone, enabling fin movement. The amphicoelous centrum is retained, visible on the proximal articulation.

SIZE

24 × 11 × 39 mm

0.9 × 0.4 × 1.5 in

GEOLOGIC AGE

Miocene

23–5.3 Ma

IDENTIFIERS

Thin posterior

Fan shape

Amphicoelous form

DENSITY

DID YOU KNOW? Ever use a fan to stay cool on a hot summer day? Well, fish have a fan in their vertebrae. The fan-shaped hypural vertebra is positioned vertically and works in concert with the spiny rays that fan outward to form the caudal fin, commonly known as the tail. The word "hypural" comes from the Greek roots *hypo* (under) and *oura* (tail). While fish might not be keeping cool with their fans, these bones are certainly "cool"!

EPIPHYSIS Cetacea

Fragment of a vertebral epiphysis from a whale. Also called vertebral growth plates, these bones sandwich cartilage against the main body of the centrum, where bone growth occurs. Once an animal reaches adulthood, bone growth ceases and these plates fuse to the bone, to be replaced by an epiphyseal line. This epiphysis was determined to belong to a whale by its size, shape, and thickness.

SIZE

9 × 63 × 40 mm

0.4 × 2.5 × 1.6 in

GEOLOGIC AGE

Pleistocene

2.6 Ma–11 ka

IDENTIFIERS

Curved outer edge

Articulating surface

Bumpy growth side

DENSITY

DID YOU KNOW? Whale fossils, including ribs, vertebrae, ear bones, jaws, and teeth, are frequently found in shore sediments. But you won't find teeth from one group of whales, the Mysticeti, which have toothless jawbones. These whales (humpbacks, blue whales, and bowhead whales among them) evolved baleen, a comblike structure for filtering out krill, which is the main diet of these whales. Baleen bristles are made of keratin, just like your fingernails.

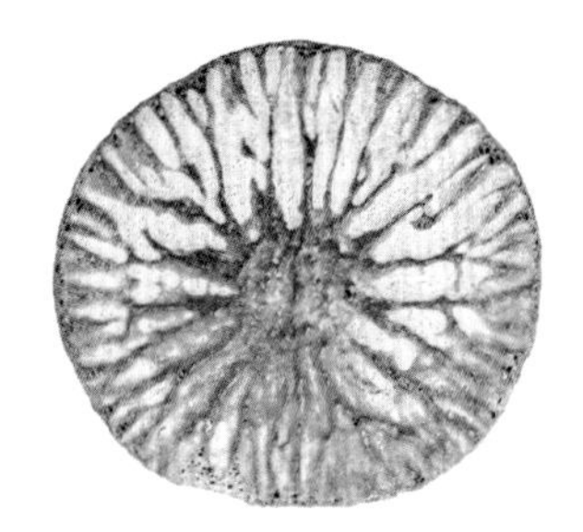

SIZE

3 × 40 × 37 mm

0.1 × 1.6 × 1.4 in

GEOLOGIC AGE

Pleistocene

2.6 Ma–11 ka

IDENTIFIERS

Thin form

Radiating pattern

Visible growth rings

DENSITY

EPIPHYSIS Odontoceti

Vertebral growth plate from a dolphin-sized odontocete. Epiphyses are plates found on the ends of all bones in vertebrates. Vertebral epiphyses are frequently found after separating from the centrum. These thin bones serve as the functional ends of bones in juveniles, and cartilage separates the centrum and the growth plate. As the animals mature, bone growth occurs between the plate and the main bone. Once the animal reaches adulthood, the epiphyses fuse to the bone—to the centrum in this case. Centra lacking the epiphyses look like the one at right above, with the radiating growth pattern visible.

DID YOU KNOW? Dolphins are social animals that live in groups called pods. They can communicate with others in the pod by emitting whistles and clicks simultaneously. For a person, it would be like carrying on two conversations, in two voices, at two pitches. Dolphins have a highly organized social structure and can apparently communicate a wide range of expressive states—even humor!

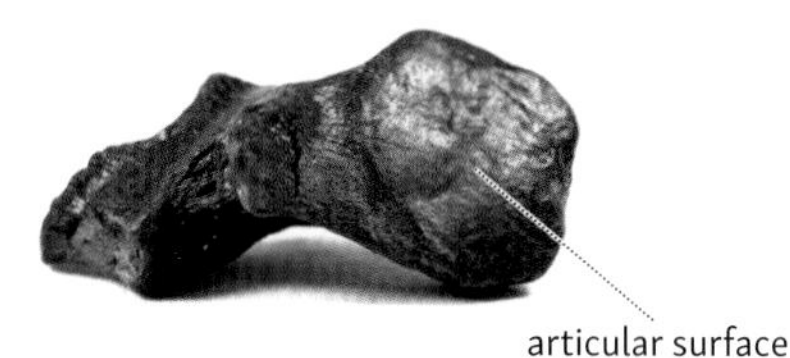

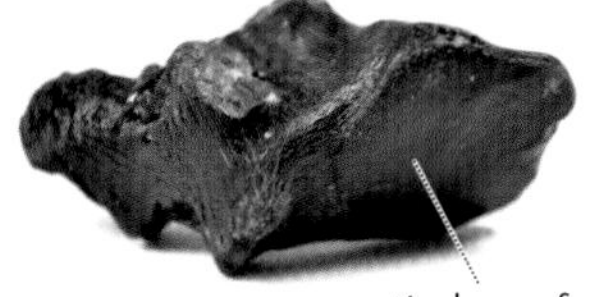

ZYGAPOPHYSIS Mammalia

Spinous process from an undetermined Pleistocene land mammal. Projecting from a vertebra's centrum, the zygapophyses are the processes that articulate with adjoining vertebrae rather than the ribs. At right in the first three photos above are two main articular surfaces (indicated) where this process interlocked with another. The zygapophysis is distinguished from the neural spine by these surfaces, since the neural spine lacks articulations.

SIZE

75 × 25 × 34 mm

2.9 × 1.0 × 1.3 in

GEOLOGIC AGE

Pleistocene

2.6 Ma–11 ka

IDENTIFIERS

Articular surfaces

Complex shapes

Sharp angles

DENSITY

DID YOU KNOW? Assembling a spinal column is like putting together a 500-piece puzzle. Each end shape of one vertebra perfectly fits with the corresponding end of an adjacent vertebra, and this sculptural edge is called a zygapophysis. If you work on jigsaw puzzles by first connecting a single row of pieces along one side of the frame, you're in effect building a spine with matching zygapophyses.

SPECIES HIGHLIGHT

Tapirs

What is it—a pig? An elephant? No, it's a tapir!

One of the oddest-looking animals in the world today is the tapir. It could humorously be described as a pig that is trying to be an elephant. Tapirs are similar to pigs in that they have fat bodies with short legs, but the comparison stops there. Tapir snouts are, indeed, adapted from extended noses and elongated lower lips to form short elephant-like trunks, and they are used similarly to grab leaves and fruits and place them into tapirs' mouths.

Even the great Linnaeus misclassified these animals, labeling them a type of hippopotamus, *Hippopotamus terrestris*, though he was familiar only with the Brazilian species of tapir, now known as *Tapirus terrestris*. Tapirs are related neither to hippos nor to pigs, but are, instead, within the group of odd-toed ungulates, which includes horses and rhinoceroses.

The earliest tapir fossils, *Protapirus obliquidens*, were found on Ellesmere Island, Canada, in Eocene rocks from 50 million years ago. Unlike many animal species whose prehistoric ancestors were much larger than their modern forms, tapirs have changed little in size over the eons. Although tapirs originated in North America, no tapir species remain there today. All five extant species occur in South America and Asia, and all are either endangered or threatened.

Together with *Protapirus obliquidens*, 11 other species of tapirs have been identified from fossilized remains, most of which are known from North America. One

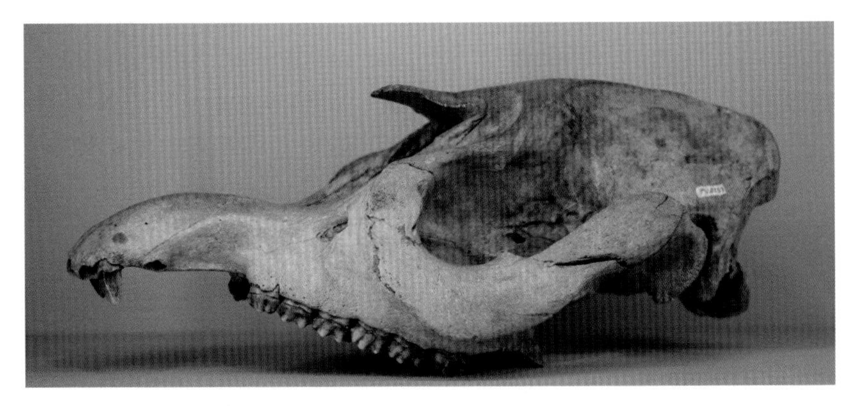

Tapir (*Tapirus veroensis*) skull on display at the Charleston Museum, Charleston, South Carolina.

of these, *Tapirus veroensis*, was thought to be rare when E. H. Sellards discovered it in 1918 at Vero Beach, Florida. But it has become one of the most commonly found tapir fossils, and many samples exist of its teeth, jaws, skulls, and other bones. Evidence of the species has been found in Georgia, South Carolina, Tennessee, Missouri, and Kansas. Other tapirs known to have lived in the southeastern U.S. are *Tapirus simpsoni, T. polkensis, T. webbi, T. lundeliusi,* and *T. haysii.*

Of these six species, *T. simpsoni, T. polkensis,* and *T. webbi* are known from the late Miocene epoch. *T. webbi* is a recent discovery, reported by Richard Hulbert Jr. in 2005; it lived around 7.5–9.5 Ma. *T. polkensis*, commonly known as the pygmy tapir, is the smallest of all tapirs, both extinct and extant, except for the little black tapir, *T. kabomani*, identified in 2009 and discovered living among the forests and savannas of Brazil and Colombia.

The other three tapirs among those listed above became extinct during the Pleistocene-Holocene boundary, around 11,700 years ago. They were placed in the subgenus *Helicotapirus* by Hulbert in 2010, based on strong evidence indicating their close relationship. Their scientific names are now represented as *Tapirus* (*Helicotapirus*) *veroensis*, *T.* (*Helicotapirus*) *lundeliusi*, and *T.* (*Helicotapirus*) *haysii*. The last of these is known commonly as the giant tapir because it is one of the largest tapirs known from available fossil evidence, and the largest in the Eastern Hemisphere. Today, the largest species is the Malayan tapir, which can grow to nearly 8 feet in length and can weigh over 1,100 pounds.

Given their similar skeletal frameworks and dental characteristics, it is possible to get an idea of the living habits of Pleistocene tapirs by observing those surviving today. Modern tapirs have more or less teardrop-shaped bodies, smaller in

Upper molar from the extinct tapir *Tapirus veroensis*.

front and larger toward the rear, and they are covered by a very tough skin. These characteristics, combined with short muscular legs, make them well adapted to their habitats, mainly forests and thick brushy areas adjacent to bodies of water.

When confronted by predators, tapirs are capable of inflicting serious damage, but they usually choose to avoid such showdowns. Instead, they can speedily slip through thick brush, making it difficult for enemy pursuers (large feline predators) to hold onto them, until they reach water. They can remain submerged for up to a minute and a half.

Despite this "home field" habitat advantage, there is concern about the survival of today's species. Unless their habitat is protected, and the poaching of the tapirs halted, it is likely that they, too, will become extinct. Unlike their ancestors, however, which evolved new species to replace those that didn't adapt to changing conditions, modern tapirs may be extirpated by *Homo sapiens*, a predator against which they have no defense.

SPECIES HIGHLIGHT

Mammoths, Mastodons, and Gomphotheres

Our homes were their STOMPING grounds!

It is commonly assumed that today's African and Asian elephants are direct descendants of the mastodons and mammoths, which became extinct around 10,000 years ago. But in fact, mastodons and mammoths arose separately from modern elephants, from an ancestral line of elephant-like proboscideans that entered North America via the Bering Land Bridge.

The group called mastodonts formed one branch of the proboscidean line, which then split into several families: Mammutidae, Elephantidae, and Gomphotheriidae. The first of these families gave rise to the American mastodon (*Mammut americanum*). The Elephantidae, or elephant family, produced two present-day species, the African elephant (*Loxodonta africana*) and Asian elephant (*Elephas maximus*), as well as the now extinct line of mammoths (*Mammuthus* species).

The third group, Gomphotheriidae, or gomphothere family, contained many species, some of whose classification is still being worked out. Gomphotheres were unusual in that they had four tusks, two upper and two lower, instead of just two upper tusks, as seen in other extinct and present-day elephant-like animals. Their two lower tusks were oval-shaped or shovel-shaped, depending on the species. Five gomphotheres were present in the southern United States, and of these, *Cuvieronius* and *Stegomastodon* species migrated as far as South America after the Panamanian Land Bridge was established.

Mammoths originated from the ancestral Eurasian species *Mammuthus meridionalis*, which crossed the Bering Land Bridge about 1.5 million years ago. This mammoth gave rise to the well-known woolly mammoth (*Mammuthus primigenius*), which populated the uppermost part of North America, as well as the Columbian mammoth (*Mammuthus columbi*). The latter species spread throughout most of the United States and as far south as Mexico City. It was this species, not the woolly mammoth, that inhabited the southeastern coastal plain, so mammoth fossils found there today are from *M. columbi*.

A major difference between mastodons and mammoths is seen in their molars. While the molars of both are enormous, those of mastodons have distinctly separated roots and noticeably ridged crowns. Mammoth molars, on the other hand, are clusters of flat enamel layers sandwiched together vertically, forming a more even crown, or "masticating surface," and containing shorter, more connected

above The manus (front foot) bone structure of an American mastodon (*Mammut americanum*), on display at the Florida Museum of Natural History, Gainesville.

left Anterior view of an American mastodon (*Mammut americanum*) skeleton on display at the Florida Museum of Natural History, Gainesville.

roots. Beach fossils from mammoths are almost always in the form of pieces of these molars, often with several enamel layers still together.

The tusks of mastodons and mammoths are formed by concentric growth layers, similar to the growth rings of a tree. They also display unique cross-hatching lines called Schreger patterns. Both rings and cross-hatching are visible when tusk pieces are viewed in cross section, though this may be harder to see on worn-down beach fossils.

There is ample evidence that early North American humans lived among and

Columbian mammoth skeleton on display at the Florida Museum of Natural History, Gainesville.

Molar Morphology

MASTODONS

High, pointed lophs allow consumption of leaves and twigs

MAMMOTHS

Flat, ridged plates enable consumption of fibrous grasses

hunted mammoths and mastodons. Fossils with piercing marks and embedded arrowheads or spear points have been found. Fossilized bones inscribed with etchings of mammoths have also been recovered. Until recently, it was believed that the gomphotheres had become extinct several thousand years before humans arrived. But in 2010 in New Mexico, arrow points from one of the earliest human cultures in North America, the Clovis people, were mixed in with a gomphothere skull, tusks, and other bones. This evidence indicates that humans lived among gomphotheres, and also hunted them, as recently as 13,400 years ago.

It seems hard to believe that giant elephant ancestors once grazed over a much-expanded coastal plain that, along the Atlantic Ocean, extended all the way to the Gulf Stream. But it fires the imagination to stop and think about what their life must have been like, and there is nothing quite like finding a molar, tusk part, or large piece of tooth enamel from one of these creatures to bring this world to life in the mind's eye!

MISCELLANEOUS

TRAITS

"Miscellaneous" is a broad term for a broad category. Individual opinions vary on what should be classified in specific groups, and in an effort to keep the number of sections in this book low, many different fossils and artifacts have been grouped here. These fossils include trace fossils, specimens preserved by different means of fossilization, and artifacts from Indian civilizations—all of which washed up on coasts.

COMMON TERMS

Bivalve, cast, conchoidal, flint, gastropod, limestone, mold, permineralization, recrystallization, replacement, steinkern, trace fossil

COMMONALITY

Occurrence varies with the specimen type. Recrystallized shell fragments are fairly uncommon. Native American artifacts can be common—especially pottery shards—on some beaches if local rivers cut through old middens.

INCLUSIONS AND EXCLUSIONS

Fossils that we classified as miscellaneous include invertebrate remains; trace fossils such as coprolites, casts, and preserved burrows; materials that did not come from animals (permineralized wood); and artifacts from Paleo-Indians. Unique skeletal elements from some fish species are included, as are modified bones and osteoderms such as antlers and stingray spines.

CLASSIFICATION

Scientific nomenclature is omitted in this section except where known.

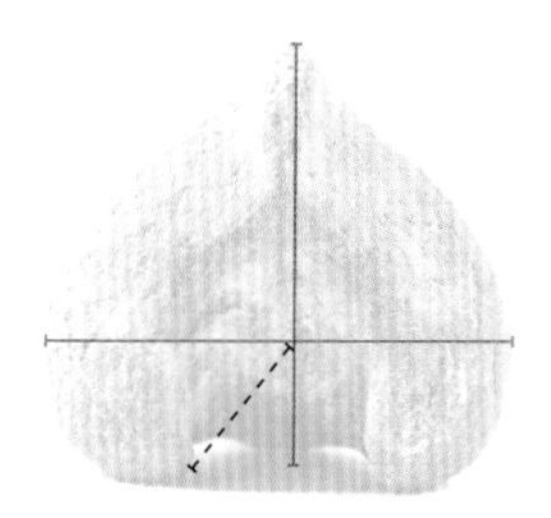

MEASUREMENTS

All miscellaneous items have measurements displayed in a three-part system:

(longest side × next longest × shortest side)

The longest side will always come first, regardless of position. If this side is ambiguous in the photos, it is delineated in the Item Description. The second longest side is measured perpendicular to the longest side and in its thickest part, and the shortest side is similarly perpendicular. (Dashed lines indicate the third dimension.)

SUPPLEMENTARY IMAGES AND TERMS

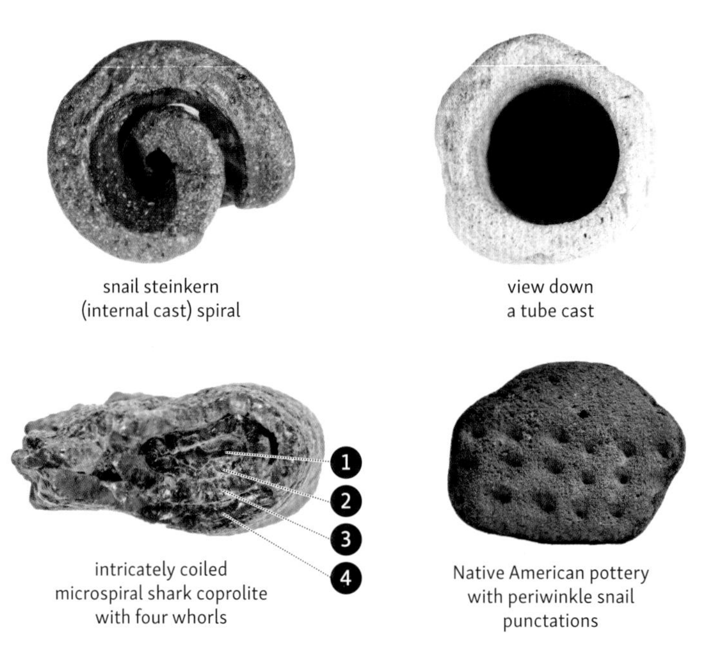

snail steinkern (internal cast) spiral

view down a tube cast

intricately coiled microspiral shark coprolite with four whorls

Native American pottery with periwinkle snail punctations

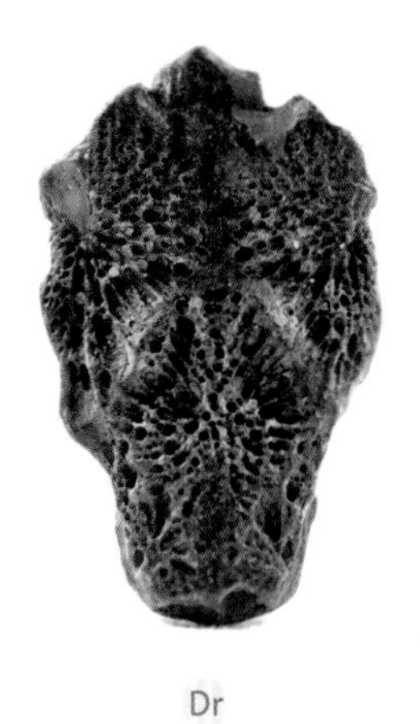

Dr

V

FRONT PLATE Triglidae

Front skull plate from a Pleistocene sea robin fish, family Triglidae. These skull elements are symmetrical arrowhead-shaped plates. The dorsal side has intricate, radially symmetric designs, and the ventral side has foramina running the length of the skull. Nearly all beach specimens are broken, since the full frontal plate is made up of one large plate connected to a smaller plate by a thin rib of skull (page 472). Depending on the species, these fossils are also affectionately called fish noses.

SIZE

40 × 24 × 7 mm

1.6 × 0.9 × 0.3 in

GEOLOGIC AGE

Pleistocene

2.6 Ma–11 ka

IDENTIFIERS

Radial patterns

Ventral foramina

Porous texture

DENSITY

DID YOU KNOW? A sea robin's entire head is encased with bony plates. This feature distinguishes the fish from the sculpin, a close relative. Sea robins grow calcium plates to protect their skulls. As bottom feeders, they also burrow into the sand both to ambush prey and to hide from predators.

Dr

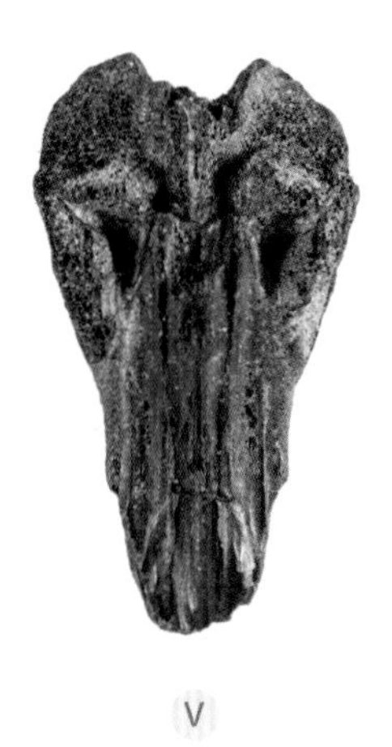

V

SIZE

29 × 17 × 5 mm

1.1 × 0.7 × 0.2 in

GEOLOGIC AGE

Pleistocene

2.6 Ma–11 ka

IDENTIFIERS

Ventral grooves

Dorsal patterns

Blood vessel holes

DENSITY

FRONT PLATE *Prionotus* sp.

Anterior-most skull element of a Pleistocene sea robin species, genus *Prionotus*. This plate articulates with the rear plate (page 391), but the two rarely make it to shore in one piece. The top (posterior) portion of this plate is where the fish's eyes were located. The pattern seen in dorsal view was mirrored on the skin of the fish and can be seen on freshly caught specimens. As a cranial element, this piece exhibits bilateral symmetry. Note the ventral grooves that run the length of the plate.

DID YOU KNOW? Have you ever heard of flying fish? The sea robin doesn't fly, but its large wing-like pectoral fins are used for swimming in the ocean in the way that a bird uses its wings. Sea robins do occasionally leap from the water and glide through the air for short distances before diving back into the sea. The sea robins' "flying" method of swimming and the bright orange underbellies on the Atlantic species earned them their nickname.

Dr

V

REAR PLATE *Prionotus* sp.

Posterior-most front skull element from a Pleistocene sea robin species, genus *Prionotus*. Normally articulated with the frontal plate (page 390), the above element commonly washes ashore separated from the anterior skull plate. The narrowest part of this specimen is where the eyes were located, nestled between both plates. The pattern seen in dorsal view was mirrored on the skin of the fish and can be seen on freshly caught specimens. As a cranial element, this piece exhibits bilateral symmetry. Note the two foramina (nerve holes) that run the length of the plate.

SIZE

23 × 19 × 7 mm

0.9 × 0.7 × 0.3 in

GEOLOGIC AGE

Pleistocene

2.6 Ma–11 ka

IDENTIFIERS

Bilateral symmetry

Dorsal patterns

Blood vessel holes

DENSITY

DID YOU KNOW? Some fish have personal cleaners. Rays employ a number of personal cleaners. By hanging out above coral, rays invite three-inch-long fish called wrasses to dine on edible material found in their gill arches. Larger fish such as jacks and orange clarion angelfish pick bits of dead skin, parasites, and marine growth from rays' fins and may hide from predators under these giant "wings."

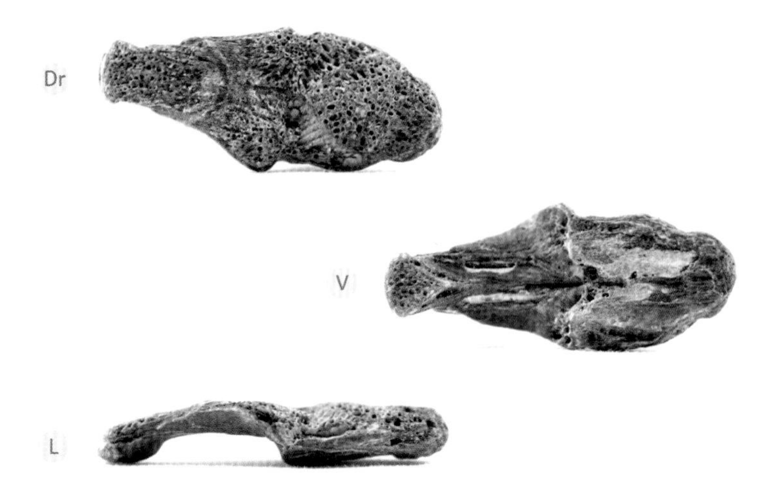

SKULL PLATE Triglidae

SIZE

54 × 21 × 9 mm

2.1 × 0.8 × 0.4 in

GEOLOGIC AGE

Pleistocene

2.6 Ma–11 ka

IDENTIFIERS

Bilateral symmetry

Dorsal patterns

Ventral foramina

DENSITY

Nearly complete skull plate from a Pleistocene sea robin fish, family Triglidae. As a complete specimen, this skull plate resembles the composite skull on page 472. Seen at left, the narrowest part of this specimen is where the eyes of the sea robin were located. The dorsal sides of sea robin bone elements are often adorned with intricate, radially symmetric patterns. As a cranial element, this piece exhibits bilateral symmetry.

DID YOU KNOW? The common sea robin, *Prionotus carolinus*, which inhabits Atlantic coastal waters of the United States, can be extremely vocal. By vibrating their swim bladders, sea robins can produce a loud drumming sound. It is often thought of as a grunting sound, which has earned them another common name, gurnards, derived from the Latin *grunnire*, "to grunt."

Dr

V

Po

L

SKULL Triglidae

Hyperostotic frontal skull element from an Oligocene sea robin fish, family Triglidae. A dramatic swelling of the bone, hyperostosis occurs in many of the teleost fishes, members of the class of ray-finned fish. Even with the swelling, this skull plate retains the bilateral symmetry observed in unaffected bones. Elements that undergo hyperostosis are often irregular and asymmetrical.

SIZE

27 × 27 × 14 mm

1.1 × 1.1 × 0.5 in

GEOLOGIC AGE

Oligocene

33.9–23 Ma

IDENTIFIERS

Bilateral symmetry

Swollen form

Irregular shapes

DENSITY

DID YOU KNOW? How does freshly fried flying fish sound for dinner? You can pan fry the sea robin. Tasty recipes abound for cooking its firm white flesh. Commercial fishing vessels that net gurnards often discard them as bycatch, but sustainable-living advocates have found uses for them as substitutes for popular but threatened species of food fish. Can you fathom freshly fried fat flying fish for your future fare?

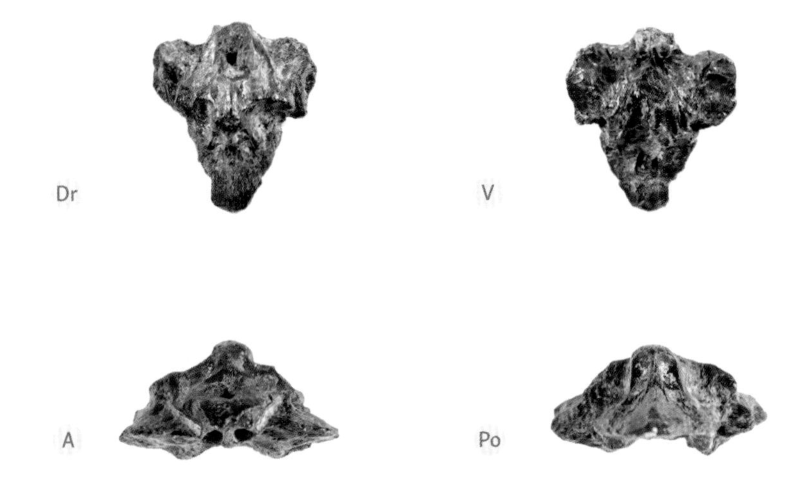

SIZE

23 × 21 × 10 mm

0.9 × 0.8 × 0.4 in

GEOLOGIC AGE

Pleistocene

2.6 Ma–11 ka

IDENTIFIERS

Bilateral symmetry

Nerve holes

Triangular form

DENSITY

CRANIAL ELEMENT Acanthuridae

Skull fragment from an undetermined member of the Acanthuridae family, possibly a surgeonfish. Similar to elements from sea robins, these cranial fragments have foramina that run anteroposteriorly (front to back) along the skull. As with other cranial and vertebral fish elements, these fossils exhibit bilateral symmetry. Members of the Acanthuridae family include surgeonfishes, unicornfishes, and tangs.

DID YOU KNOW? Some sea robins are heavily armored with scales and prominent spines. They also have elaborate barbels, whisker-like features on their mouths that serve as taste buds to sample food bits while scavenging along the ocean floor. These armored sea robins are closely related to the common sea robins of the family Triglidae, but are enough different that some taxonomists classify them in their own family.

Dr

V

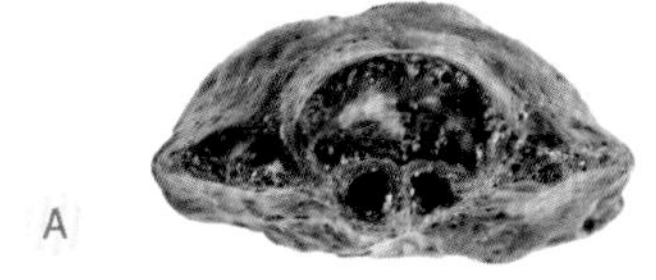

A

Po

CRANIAL ELEMENT Acanthuridae

Water-worn skull fragment from an undetermined member of the Acanthuridae family, possibly a surgeonfish. This specimen has been subjected to ocean tumbling and water wear. Such tumbling can make a fossil appear much different from the original element (see previous page). Foramina run the length of the specimen, front to back. Members of the Acanthuridae family include surgeonfishes, unicornfishes, and tangs.

SIZE

18 × 17 × 9 mm

0.7 × 0.7 × 0.4 in

GEOLOGIC AGE

Pleistocene

2.6 Ma–11 ka

IDENTIFIERS

Bilateral symmetry

Nerve holes

Rounded form

DENSITY

DID YOU KNOW? Sea robins have blue eyes, and they are the only feature that can be seen when the fish have burrowed under the sediments on the ocean bottom. Their eyes have to stay visible so that the sea robin can determine when it is safe to come out, either to play or to prey.

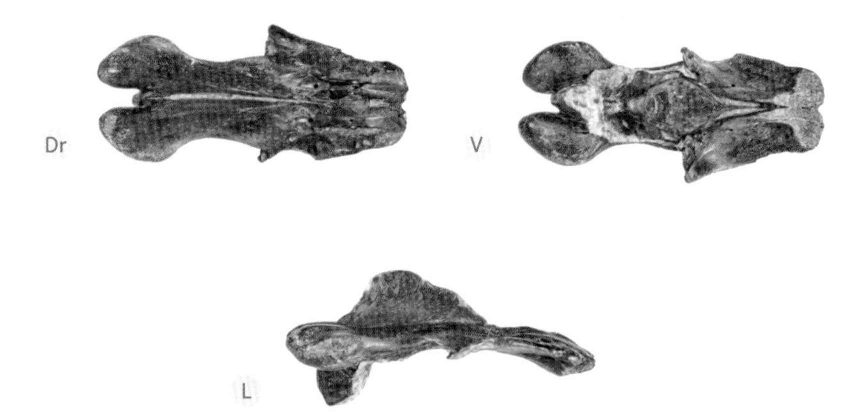

SIZE

39 × 17 × 17 mm

1.5 × 0.7 × 0.7 in

GEOLOGIC AGE

Pleistocene

2.6 Ma–11 ka

IDENTIFIERS

Bilateral symmetry

Swollen posterior

Arched form

DENSITY

NEUROCRANIUM Osteichthyes

Hyperostotic neurocranium element from an indeterminate Pleistocene fish species. As with hyperostotic fish vertebrae (page 371), this cranial bone—likely a frontal—underwent a cancerous rate of growth, swelling to the point of obscuring generic identification. Bilateral symmetry indicates placement along the sagittal plane (body midline). The arch present at right shows the eye placement of the fish. Posteriorly, two nodes are equally inflated. These are the pieces preserved most frequently, as seen on the next page.

DID YOU KNOW? "Neuro" comes from the Greek word for nerves, and "cranium" from *kranion*, the Greek term for the part of the skull enclosing the brain. The neurocranium can generally be thought of as a rectangular box with three major bones making up its sides and many smaller bones forming the rest. Nerves thread through holes in the sides of the bones, and while they do not function to tie these bones together, their presence is easily inferred from the many grooves and holes left behind on the bone (page 395).

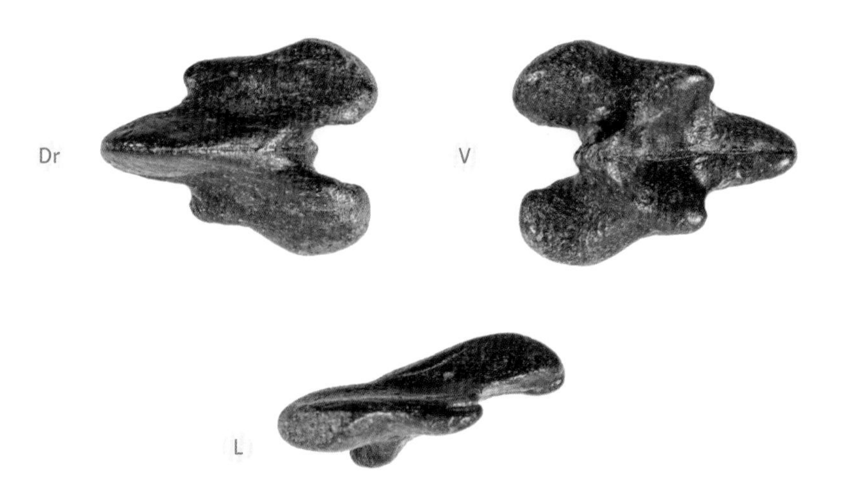

NEUROCRANIUM Osteichthyes

Hyperostotic neurocranium element from an indeterminate Pleistocene fish species. An extremely water-worn posterior-most fragment of the swollen frontal shown on the preceding page. Though the specimen is worn, bilateral symmetry is still apparent. Hyperostosis caused both an uncontrolled rate of bone growth and a hardening of the bone. As a result, these worn elements are the most common portion of the frontal bone found by beachcombers.

SIZE

19 × 15 × 6 mm

0.8 × 0.6 × 0.2 in

GEOLOGIC AGE

Pleistocene

2.6 Ma–11 ka

IDENTIFIERS

Bilateral symmetry

Swollen posterior

Ventral arch

DENSITY

DID YOU KNOW? When you send a meticulously crafted email, the message is sent in one quick electrical pulse through the Internet. In fish, warning messages from the brain to the body are sent via a specialized pathway. Scientists have identified a set of neurons called Mauthner cells, which are located at the base of the brainstems of fish (and amphibians) and are involved in quick escapes. Axons (the threadlike parts of neurons that conduct signals away from the cell) crossing over to these cells activate neurons that send a message down the spine, which in turn activates a fish's escape reflex and propels the fish away from the mouths of hungry predators.

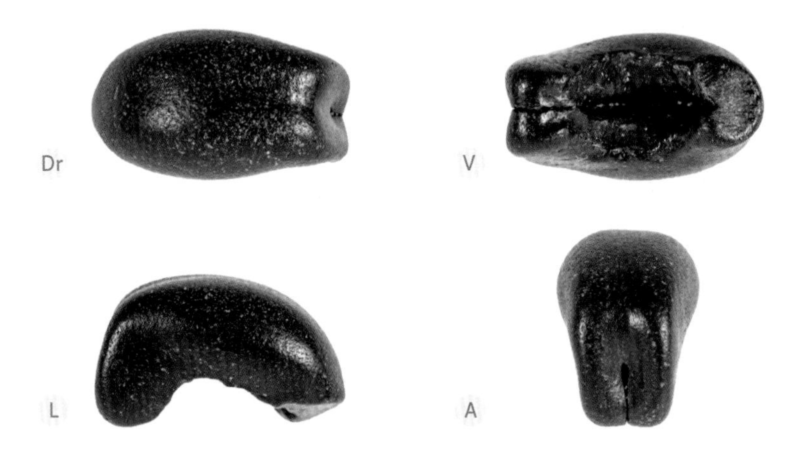

SIZE

17 × 10 × 9 mm

0.7 × 0.4 × 0.4 in

GEOLOGIC AGE

Pliocene

5.3–2.6 Ma

IDENTIFIERS

Bilateral symmetry

Bean shape

Small size

DENSITY

Emmons Fish Tooth

Hyperostotic bone from an undetermined Pliocene fish species. Originally described in 1858 as fish teeth, fossils of this kind are swollen bone elements from fish, similar in nature to "Tilly bones" and the hyperostotic vertebrae of other fishes. Specimens are all bilaterally symmetrical and curved, with a deep line (sulcus) down the middle. This groove, and the foramen seen at bottom right, allowed blood vessels and nerves to supply nutrients to the bone.

DID YOU KNOW? Ebenezer Emmons couldn't be faulted for mistakenly proclaiming a fossil in Edgecombe County, North Carolina, to be a fish tooth. It was a find new to science, and he based his claim on experience and state-of-the-art paleontology. Later scientists, using newer evidence, corrected the error. And that is science at its best. Findings are often questioned until cumulative evidence and sufficient consensus establish them as fact.

L

M

Pr

Ivory

Tusk ivory from an extinct Pleistocene proboscidean. The most reliable identifier of ivory is the unique cross-hatching pattern seen in the cross section (shown above in the proximal view). This pattern, the Schreger pattern, is made of bundles of dentine within the inner core of tusks. Numerous studies of the angles of Schreger lines have shown them to be helpful in distinguishing fossil from modern ivory; however, these angles vary greatly among individuals, and there is further variation along different cross sections of a single tusk. Therefore, Schreger lines are not of much use in determining genera from isolated fragments of ivory.

SIZE

92 × 30 × 18 mm

3.6 × 1.2 × 0.7 in

GEOLOGIC AGE

Pleistocene

2.6 Ma–11 ka

IDENTIFIERS

Schreger pattern

Extremely dense

Smooth exterior

DENSITY

DID YOU KNOW? During the Pleistocene, Osage orange trees grew commonly in Canada, but are now found mainly in the south-central United States. Modern animals spurn their tough, seedy spheres, so why did such large fruit evolve? Research suggests that mastodons and other prehistoric tree-browsing megafauna easily digested these fruits, spreading their seeds. Despite shrinking habitat, the tree grows on, unaware that its original benefactors have, sadly, become extinct.

Ivory "Bark"

SIZE

33 × 24 × 4 mm

1.3 × 0.9 × 0.2 in

GEOLOGIC AGE

Pleistocene

2.6 Ma–11 ka

IDENTIFIERS

Longitudinal banding

Growth rings

High density

DENSITY

Fragments of the cementum layer of tusk ivory from Pleistocene proboscideans. On such tusks, the outermost layer is composed of cementum, and the inner core is dentine, which makes up 95% of the composition of proboscidean tusks. If concentric growth rings are present in cross section, then it is likely the specimen belonged to a mammoth (*Mammuthus* spp.). Fragments from areas closer to the dentine-cementum boundary can occasionally have Schreger lines (page 472).

DID YOU KNOW? Mammoth tusks are covered with layers of ivory bark, or cementum. Cementum layers, which are especially thick in extinct proboscidean species, absorb minerals from surrounding sediments as fossilization occurs. This adds to ivory bark's beauty, making it especially attractive to knife makers, who carve it into blade handles. Because of current elephant population declines from poaching, it is illegal to possess modern elephant ivory.

L

M

TUSK ENAMEL

Cuvieronius tropicus

Section of enamel from the ivory tusk of a gomphothere. Based on the locality where this fragment was collected, it most likely belonged to the Late Pleistocene gomphothere *Cuvieronius tropicus*. Gomphotheres had enamel on either the upper tusks or the lower tusks. Most of these bands were straight and ran the length of the entire tusk. By contrast, enamel on the upper tusks of the Miocene-Pliocene *Gomphotherium* spiraled around the tusk like a candy-cane stripe. Note the section of ivory present (indicated) in medial view, which obscures most of the enamel.

SIZE

75 × 51 × 13 mm

2.9 × 2.0 × 0.5 in

GEOLOGIC AGE

Pleistocene

2.6 Ma–11 ka

IDENTIFIERS

Enamel on ivory

Thin, smooth enamel

Slightly opaque enamel

DENSITY

DID YOU KNOW? *Amebelodon britti*, shovel-tusked gomphotheres, were among the largest species in the elephant family. Upper and lower tusks were distinctly different. The flattened, shovel-like lower tusks exhibited shafts of dentine, hard calcareous tissue denser than bone. The upper tusks, more like those of elephants, grew slightly curved and had a 2- to 3-inch-wide enamel surface covering their length.

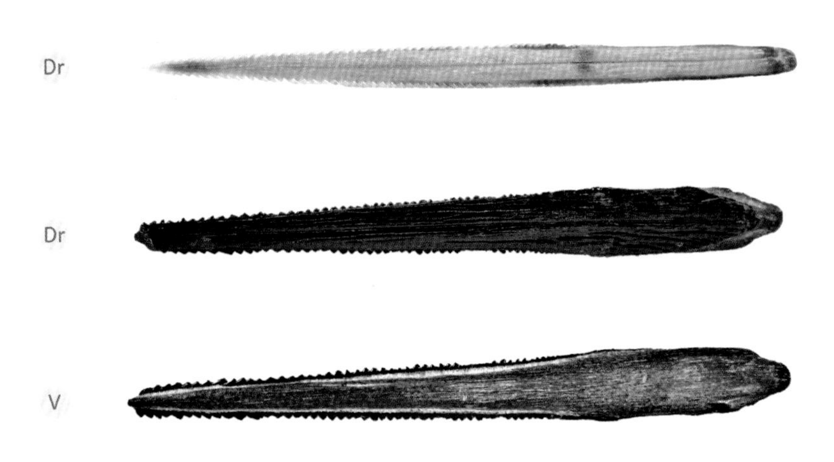

TAIL SPINE Myliobatiformes

SIZE

103 × 9 × 4 mm

4.0 × 0.4 × 0.2 in

GEOLOGIC AGE

Pleistocene

2.6 Ma–11 ka

IDENTIFIERS

Crenulation

Single point at end of taper

Barbed sides

DENSITY

Tail spine from a Pleistocene species of eagle ray (family Myliobatidae) or stingray (family Dasyatidae). Identical in appearance to modern stingray spines (at top), these specimens taper to a sharp point with barbs on each side except at the base. Some specimens have a main line running down the middle of the dorsal side, while others are deeply crenulated. Tail spines are modified dermal denticles covered in enameloid.

DID YOU KNOW? According to one version of the story of the Greek hero Odysseus, a prophecy revealed that his death would come from the sea. Years later, his son Telegonus sailed to find him. Landing tired and hungry on Ithaca, Odysseus's island, Telegonus killed some sheep for dinner. Thinking him a pirate, Odysseus and his eldest son, Telemachus, attacked. Telegonus unknowingly killed his own father with a poisoned stingray spine, thus fulfilling the prophecy.

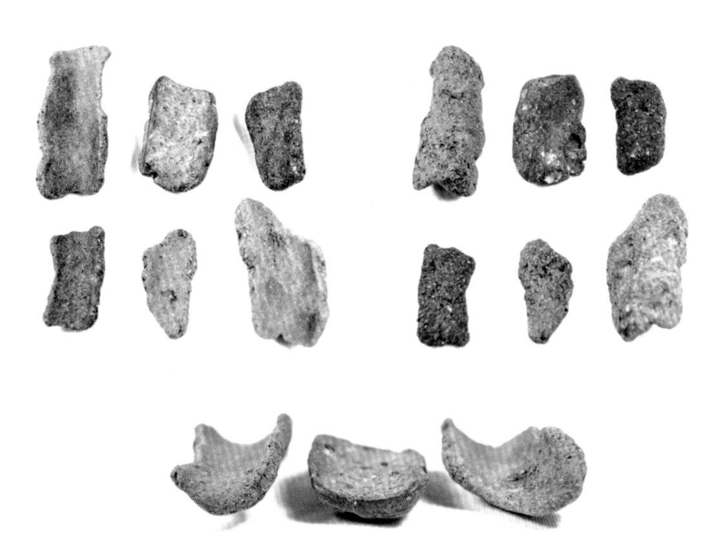

Tube Casts

Fragments of external burrow casts from Pleistocene animals. As trace fossils from animals' burrows, these specimens are evidence of past burrowing activity. Beach specimens are often broken, with only half of the tube left, rarely whole (see the following page). Many specimens are made of glauconitic sediment, similar to the composition of mollusk steinkerns. Unlike the smooth feel of bone and tooth enamel, tube casts feel gritty to the touch, from sand and other concreted particles.

SIZE

60 × 25 × 16 mm

2.3 × 1.0 × 0.6 in

GEOLOGIC AGE

Pleistocene

2.6 Ma–11 ka

IDENTIFIERS

Curved shape

Rock-like appearance

Gritty feel

DENSITY

DID YOU KNOW? Unusual tube-forming worms were discovered in 1900 when deep-water sediments were dredged around Indonesia. These strange creatures, named *Pogonophora*, resemble annelid tube worms. But there are major differences between the groups. The Indonesian tube worms lack a mouth, gut, and anus, and only their posterior end is segmented. Mineral-rich water taken in through hairlike tentacles is turned into food by bacteria living in the worm host.

Tube Casts

SIZE

101 × 22 × 22 mm

3.9 × 0.9 × 0.9 in

GEOLOGIC AGE

Pleistocene

2.6 Ma–11 ka

IDENTIFIERS

Tube shape

Hollow interior

Spiral shape on occasion

DENSITY

External casts of burrows from Pleistocene marine creatures. Classified as trace fossils, these specimens represent the burrows of animals; they are not the fossilized remains of biological creatures. Scientists study trace fossils such as these to infer the habits of crabs, ghost shrimp, worms, and other burrowing animals that lived in the past. Note how the bottom specimen became filled with sediment after being preserved. Measurements given are for the longest specimen (top).

DID YOU KNOW? Soft-bodied marine animals lived in or near soft, muddy environments. As they went about daily life, they left behind impressions that, if covered quickly by sediments, became trace fossils. These casts help paleontologists answer questions about their prehistoric activities. Was the burrowing creature a worm, crustacean, fish, or mammal? Why was it there? Was it stalking prey or running from a predator? Migrating or searching for a body of water?

Coprolites

Three heteropolar coprolites from Oligocene sharks. The intricate whorls of these permineralized feces are best attributed to the complex structure of the small intestines of sharks. The heteropolar microspiral (scroll-like) structure is best seen in the cross section at right, displaying three complete whorls, and in the specimen at top left, in which four whorls are visible. The intact nature and shape of these coprolites indicate that their preservation occurred while in the small intestine of a dead shark buried by sediment.

SIZE

39 × 15 × 11 mm

1.5 × 0.6 × 0.4 in

GEOLOGIC AGE

Oligocene

33.9–23 Ma

IDENTIFIERS

Layered folds

Scroll-like structure

Ellipsoidal shape

DENSITY

DID YOU KNOW? "Coprolite" is a fancy word for fossilized poop. The Greek *kopros* means "dung," and *lithikos* means "stone." Fossilized waste represents a fascinating and intimate piece of an animal's life history. Scientists can determine what an animal ate, whether it was an herbivore or a carnivore, and even what its habitat might have been, simply by studying the plants it digested.

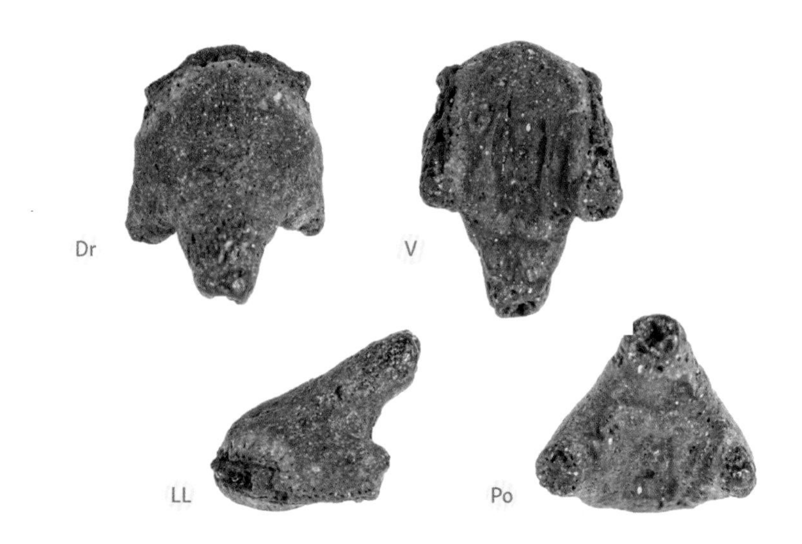

Shark Rostral Node

SIZE

14 × 11 × 10 mm

0.5 × 0.4 × 0.4 in

GEOLOGIC AGE

Pleistocene

2.6 Ma–11 ka

IDENTIFIERS

Blunt tip

Bilateral symmetry

Posterior protrusions

DENSITY

Rostral node from an undetermined shark species. As with the vertebrae and other "bones" in a shark's body, these nodes are made of cartilage, and therefore seldom fossilize. Note the bilateral symmetry, blunt tip, and three protrusions directed posteriorly.

DID YOU KNOW? The entertainer Jimmy Durante was known for his big schnoz, and sharks are famous for their rostral nodes, or snouts. Beneath the skin and dermal denticles of a shark's nose area is a mass of cartilage that protects pathways for respiration and nerves connecting to the brain and eyes. These rostral nodes give sharks their own characteristic pointy schnozzes.

Prismatic Cartilage

Fragments of prismatic cartilage from undetermined Oligocene shark species. The most rarely preserved elements of sharks are pieces of their cartilaginous skulls and gill arches. Cartilage fossils are identified by their tightly packed hexagonal prisms (tesserae), which are preserved through hydroxyapatite mineralization. These tesserae are usually 2 millimeters in width, and sometimes smaller. Most cylindrical fragments of cartilage are filled with phosphate or other sediments (seen at left). The rostral cartilage of sawfish is similar in appearance, although the tesserae are more elliptical.

SIZE

36 × 19 × 11 mm

1.4 × 0.8 × 0.4 in

GEOLOGIC AGE

Oligocene

33.9–23 Ma

IDENTIFIERS

Hexagonal tesserae

Thin structure

Honeycomb appearance

DENSITY

DID YOU KNOW? Bones, which are composed of calcium, are not particularly flexible. Shark cartilage, however, is skeletal tissue that is both firm and elastic. The chemical compound chondroitin sulfate and the elastic protein collagen bind with water to aid in this flexibility.

Permineralized Sticks

SIZE

41 × 6 × 5 mm

1.6 × 0.2 × 0.2 in

GEOLOGIC AGE

Pleistocene

2.6 Ma–11 ka

IDENTIFIERS

Branched pattern

Growth rings

Bark texture

DENSITY

Fossilized remains from trees alive during the Pleistocene epoch. As in modern trees, fossilized twigs show the branched pattern of limbs, growth rings in cross section, and the texture of bark. These specimens, which are easy to spot, can be identified as fossils when they do not break. Fossilized sticks should ping or make a clinking noise when tapped against a hard surface.

DID YOU KNOW? Volcanoes can freeze entire ecosystems in place by the sheer volume of ash that settles out from their eruptions. This happened during the time of Pangaea, over 300 million years ago, in what is now Inner Mongolia. A primal forest was buried beneath 39 inches of ash. As this organic plant material was subjected to heat and pressure during the succeeding eons, large coal deposits were created, which are mined today in China.

L

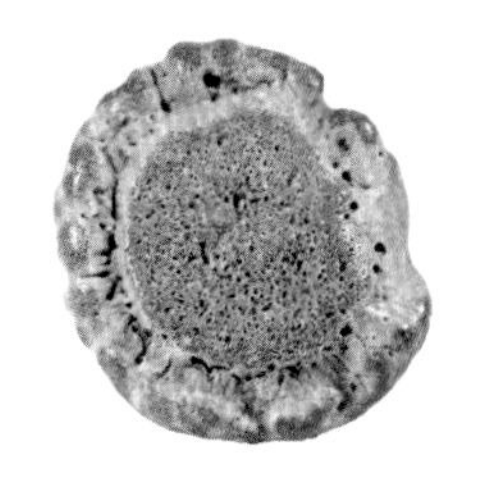

V

ANTLER *Odocoileus virginianus*

Fragment of antler from the extant white-tailed deer, *Odocoileus virginianus*. Fossil antler fragments appear identical to their modern, unfossilized counterparts. Specimens are often of the tines, branched joints, or knobbed bases (above). The interior of an antler has a fine, spongy appearance, distinctly different from the cancellous bone present in the interior of most vertebrate skeletons. See page 462 for comparisons. Likewise, the walls of antlers are thicker than those of most bones, and relatively dense.

SIZE

22 × 27 × 25 mm

0.9 × 1.1 × 1.0 in

GEOLOGIC AGE

Pleistocene

2.6 Ma–11 ka

IDENTIFIERS

Knobbed bases

Spongy interior

Branched form

DENSITY

DID YOU KNOW? Theories abound about why *Megaloceros*, the Irish elk, grew such huge (12-foot span) antlers. Proposed uses such as defending against predators and killing prey have given way to considerations of natural selection in mating: bucks with the biggest racks attracted more females than others did, perhaps because a buck's ability to thrive despite having such unwieldy headgear suggested its superior fitness. The genes of successful elk were passed on to large numbers of offspring, guaranteeing continued generations of healthy, impressive bucks.

WORMSTONE *Dodecaceria* sp.

SIZE

90 × 58 × 26 mm

3.5 × 2.3 × 1.0 in

GEOLOGIC AGE

Pleistocene

2.6 Ma–11 ka

IDENTIFIERS

Curving holes

Porous texture

Fused mass

DENSITY

Fossil remnant from a colony of tube worms in the genus *Dodecaceria*. These polychaete worms live in large colonies, depositing calcium carbonate and other compounds as they grow. *Dodecaceria*, which first evolved at the beginning of the Pleistocene, can be found in shallow marine environments today. The worms grow to be 2 inches long. Holes in these stones often run from one side to the other. (Note: The hole at the left was made by a drilling bivalve such as a mollusk in the Pholadidae family.)

DID YOU KNOW? Johann von Goethe's studies of Weimar stratigraphy and fossils might have remained unknown but for the amateur geologist Christien Kieferstein, who wanted to document Goethe's findings. Goethe was too busy to answer Kieferstein's queries, so his son, August, collected records on the rock formation layers and, following further analysis and corrections made with his father, sent the information to Kieferstein. Only in 2003, 180 years later, was this information finally published.

CORAL *Balanophyllia* sp.

Two specimens of solitary coral in the genus *Balanophyllia*. These corals have flat, occasionally concave bases and show radiating grooves that attenuate at the top of each specimen. The top coral is from an unphosphatized limestone formation and shows the actual coral; the lower specimen is a phosphatic steinkern. In contrast to the ovoid coral *Flabellum*, *Balanophyllia* are circular to subcircular. Solitary corals are not found in large colonies, as are the grouped and branching corals. *Balanophyllia*, a genus known from the Cretaceous, is still extant.

SIZE

16 × 12 × 15 mm

0.6 × 0.5 × 0.6 in

GEOLOGIC AGE

Oligocene

33.9–23 Ma

IDENTIFIERS

Radial symmetry

Conical shape

Flat or concave bases

DENSITY

DID YOU KNOW? Some corals inflate themselves with water, which changes them into mushroom-like shapes. Inhaling the surrounding water brings in additional nutrients to supplement the food being provided by algae living inside the coral. It also enlarges the surface area exposed to light, likely stimulating this algal production.

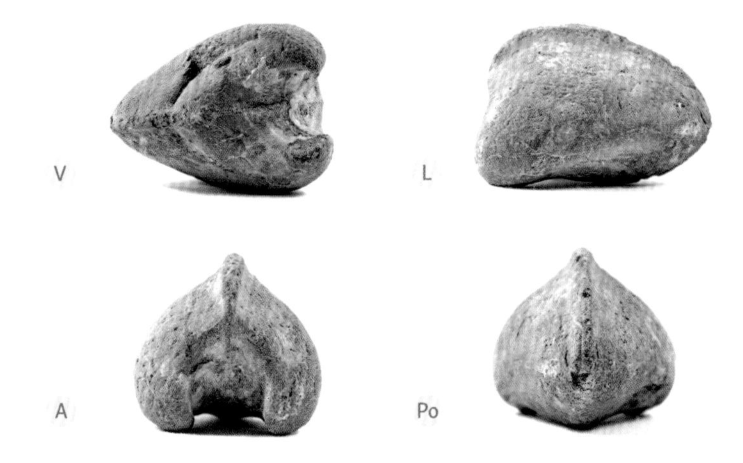

SIZE

67 × 50 × 42 mm

2.6 × 2.0 × 1.6 in

GEOLOGIC AGE

Cretaceous

145–66 Ma

IDENTIFIERS

Large size

Heart shape

Bilateral symmetry

DENSITY

STEINKERN *Cucullaea* sp.

Internal cast from an extinct Cretaceous bivalve, recovered from a beach renourishment project at Myrtle Beach, South Carolina. Affectionately called turtle heads because of their shape, these steinkerns are all that remains after the original shell filled with sediment. Once the sediment solidified, the shells dissolved or eroded away, leaving an internal cast of the original bivalve.

DID YOU KNOW? Paleomagnetism is one method used to date fossils. As molten rock cools below the Curie temperature (1,060°F), the magnetite within it solidifies in alignment with Earth's magnetic poles. The north and south poles have flipped back and forth through the eons, as is well documented by scientists, so it is possible to estimate the age of a fossil by the orientation of its magnetite and that of the surrounding rock formation.

L

V

STEINKERN Bivalvia

Internal cast of an undetermined bivalve. Steinkerns of bivalves and gastropods are formed when marine sediments fill the empty shells after the creature dies or is eaten. After the sediments harden, the original shell is dissolved or eroded away by the ocean, leaving only the internal cast. Since this specimen came from a bivalve, it has the bilateral symmetry of bivalves and a ridge running the circumference of the cast where the two halves of the shell met.

SIZE

23 × 22 × 13 mm

0.9 × 0.9 × 0.5 in

GEOLOGIC AGE

Oligocene

33.9–23 Ma

IDENTIFIERS

Rock-like appearance

Circumferential ridge

Bilateral symmetry

DENSITY

DID YOU KNOW? Bivalves are the builders of their own homes. They possess an organ called the mantle, which produces calcium carbonate, the same mineral compound that makes up limestone. The calcium carbonate forms the bivalves' hard protective shells. As the animals grow, the mantle secretes more calcium carbonate, enabling them to add onto their homes.

STEINKERN *Turritella* sp.

SIZE

40 × 13 × 13 mm

1.6 × 0.5 × 0.5 in

GEOLOGIC AGE

Paleocene

66–56 Ma

IDENTIFIERS

Elongated form

Conical taper

Spiral shape

DENSITY

Internal cast of a common Paleocene gastropod, *Turritella*, found along the Potomac River. Two species of *Turritella* snails (*T. mortoni* and *T. humerosa*) occur in the Aquia Formation. It is difficult to make a specific determination from only a steinkern. The overall form of these fossils is conical and elongate. In some deposits, it is possible to find intact shells; however, most common are the steinkerns, since they are more durable. *Turritella* limestone consists of entire pieces of limestone filled with these specimens.

DID YOU KNOW? The name of the genus *Turritella* comes from the Latin word *turritus*, meaning "turreted" or "towered," since these gastropods somewhat resemble turrets or towers. The mineral matrix of this shell cast reflects the size and shape of the snail that once lived inside the shell. It is the negative image and form of the inside of this snail's home.

STEINKERN Gastropoda

Internal cast of an undetermined species of gastropod from the Pleistocene epoch. Steinkerns are the internal casts of dead organisms, preserved by sediments. In this specimen, glauconitic muds from the continental shelf filled the shell of a snail. When the shells break away or disintegrate, these steinkerns are left behind.

SIZE

42 × 16 × 14 mm

1.6 × 0.6 × 0.5 in

GEOLOGIC AGE

Pleistocene

2.6 Ma–11 ka

IDENTIFIERS

Spiral forms

Varying shapes

Conical taper

DENSITY

DID YOU KNOW? Gastropods (snails and slugs) make up a class of animals whose species have successfully populated three environmental settings. Of the 65,000 species that make up this class, 30,000 are marine species, 30,000 are terrestrial animals, and 5,000 are freshwater species. Fossil records indicate that the gastropod lineage goes back to the Late Cambrian period, 500 million years ago.

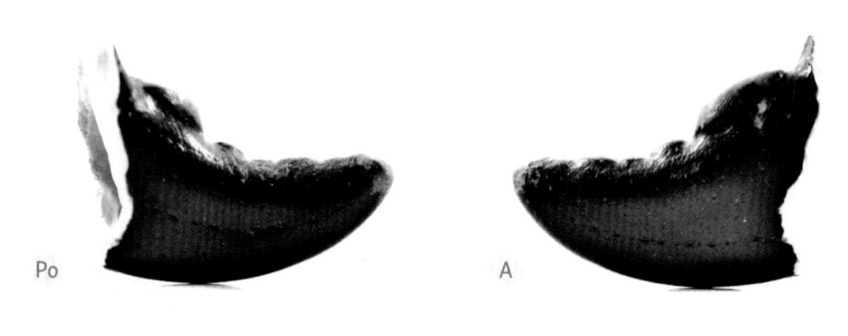

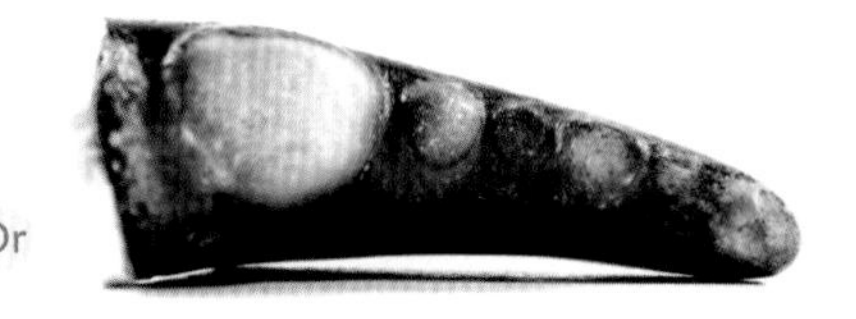

SIZE

30 × 22 × 10 mm

1.2 × 0.9 × 0.4 in

GEOLOGIC AGE

Pleistocene

2.6 Ma–11 ka

IDENTIFIERS

Hollow form

White interior

Lumps and nodes

DENSITY

CLAW Crab

Lower-left claw from an undetermined Pleistocene crab species. As with modern species, nodes or lumps are located on the interior curve of the claw, seen here in dorsal view. Despite being mineralized, some fossilized claws can be bleached white on the inside, leading many beachcombers to think the specimen is not a fossil. Claws from many different species of crabs have similar characteristics.

DID YOU KNOW? Have you seen the shells of horseshoe crabs on the beach? These "living fossils" have changed very little over 450 million years; like other chelicerates, they are descended from trilobites, their Cambrian ancestors. The North American species of horseshoe crab, *Limulus polyphemus*, is generally found in the Gulf of Mexico and on the North Atlantic coast. Horseshoe crabs are not true crabs, but are closely related to arachnids such as spiders, scorpions, and mites. Like starfish, horseshoe crabs can regrow lost limbs.

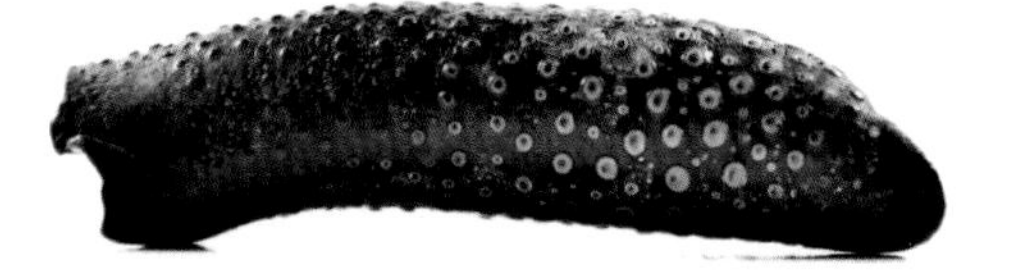

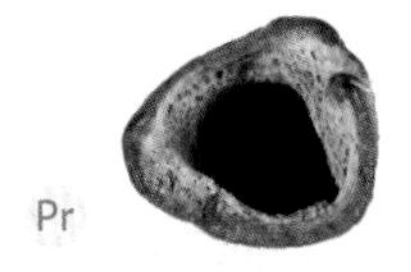

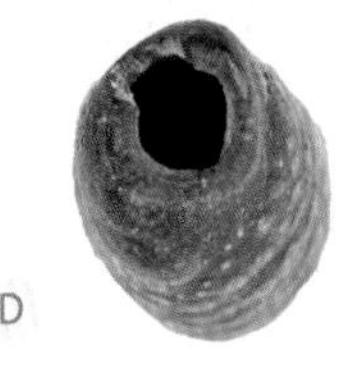

LEG Crab

Leg from an extinct Pleistocene crab species, found on the shores of South Carolina. Crab legs are small hollow tubes, occasionally bulbous on one end, and triangular in cross section, especially on the proximal end. Fossil legs often retain markings from the living creature, and can be adorned with white circles or dots.

SIZE

28 × 6 × 6 mm

1.1 × 0.2 × 0.2 in

GEOLOGIC AGE

Pleistocene

2.6 Ma–11 ka

IDENTIFIERS

Hollow tubes

White dots

Slightly bulbous shape

DENSITY

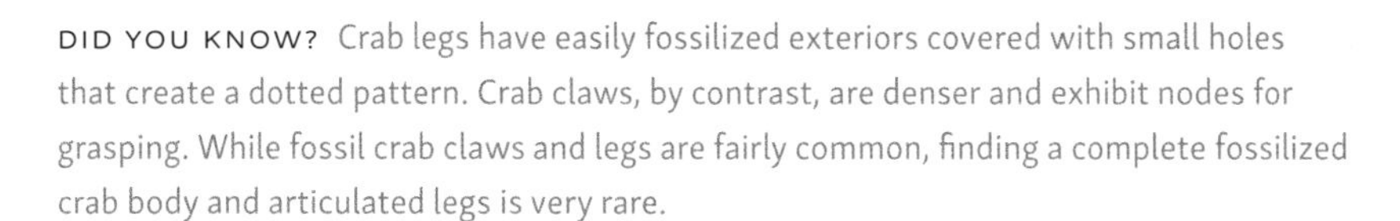

DID YOU KNOW? Crab legs have easily fossilized exteriors covered with small holes that create a dotted pattern. Crab claws, by contrast, are denser and exhibit nodes for grasping. While fossil crab claws and legs are fairly common, finding a complete fossilized crab body and articulated legs is very rare.

Dr

V

SIZE

94 × 88 × 29 mm

3.7 × 3.4 × 1.1 in

GEOLOGIC AGE

Paleocene

66–56 Ma

IDENTIFIERS

Growth rings

Two main halves

Round form

DENSITY

SHELL

Mansfieldostrea compressirostra

Fossil oyster, *Mansfieldostrea compressirostra*, commonly found along the banks of the Potomac River. Compared to the eastern oyster (*Crassostrea virginica*), this specimen is more rounded. Such fossil oysters are usually encased in matrix (visible on the ventral side). Oysters are bivalves, so complete specimens have two shell halves, one slightly domed (dorsal) and one flattened (ventral). Note the growth rings present on the dorsal side.

DID YOU KNOW? "He was a bold man that first eat an oyster," said Jonathan Swift. The oyster's rough-looking, tightly glued shells are hard to crack open, and once inside, the diner is greeted by a slimy, brainy-looking blob of flesh. Not exactly inviting. But loaded with minerals and protein, oysters are delicious when steamed, smoked, or eaten raw. And oyster roasts are fun social events, even for the not very bold.

Recrystallized Oyster Shell

An excellent example of a completely recrystallized Pleistocene oyster, genus *Crassostrea*. In recrystallization, minerals in the original shell, especially calcite, re-form (recrystallize) into larger forms or turn into different compounds. This specimen was primarily recrystallized with calcite. Such specimens appear nearly identical to their modern counterparts, but have a more crystalline appearance. Similarly, as with limestone, drops of hydrochloric acid will make a recrystallized fossil fizz and bubble.

SIZE

71 × 32 × 20 mm

2.8 × 1.2 × 0.8 in

GEOLOGIC AGE

Pleistocene

2.6 Ma–11 ka

IDENTIFIERS

Original form retained

Crystalline appearance

Fizz response to acid

DENSITY

DID YOU KNOW? The tasty edible oysters in the Ostreidae family, true oysters, occur worldwide and are capable of producing pearls. But pearls of commercial quality come from oysters within family Pteriidae, the feather oysters. Two species are popular for pearls. The eastern American oyster is found in the Atlantic Ocean from Canada to Argentina, and the Pacific oyster occurs from the U.S. Pacific Northwest to Japan and south to Australia.

Dr

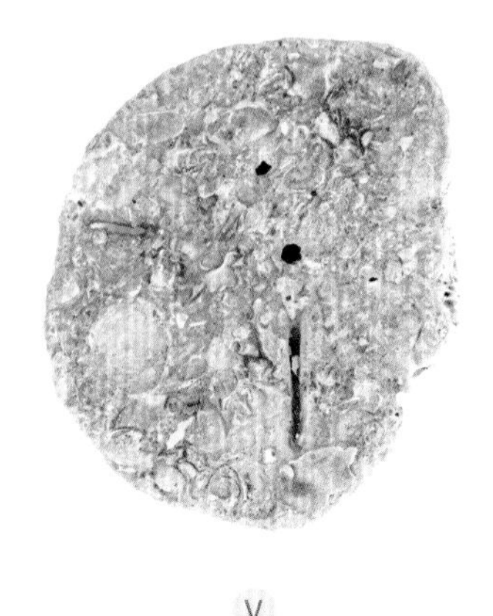

V

Recrystallized Sand Dollar

SIZE

48 × 35 × 7 mm

1.9 × 1.4 × 0.3 in

GEOLOGIC AGE

Pleistocene

2.6 Ma–11 ka

IDENTIFIERS

Pentagonal symmetry

Webbed interior

Slim, tapering form

DENSITY

Fragment of a recrystallized sand dollar, genus *Mellita*. Similar in shape to modern keyhole sand dollars (*Mellita quinquiesperforata*), this specimen is disk-shaped, tapering from the raised center to the edges. Crystallization of calcite is visible on the interior of many such fossils (page 464). On the exterior, the gluing of other sand particles and bivalves is evident. Fragments of modern sand dollars are not as dense and lack calcite crystals and the attachment points of other sediments or shells.

DID YOU KNOW? Sand dollars are prized by beginning seashell collectors. They live on the bottom of the ocean in water at least chest-deep, eating plankton, crab larvae, and detritus. On a sand dollar's lower (oral) side are hundreds of tiny hairlike spines. These are used to move food along five grooves to a central mouth, to propel the animals over the sand, or to burrow beneath the sand.

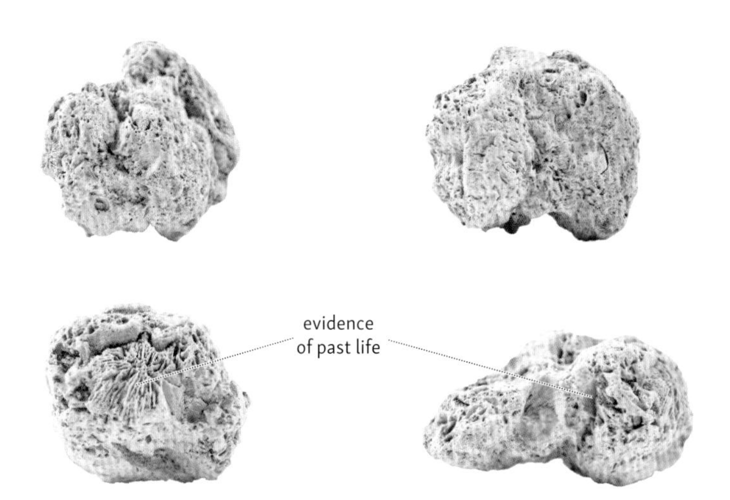

Coral-Bearing Limestone

Ocean-tumbled limestone from an Oligocene formation near Charleston, South Carolina. Like other fossiliferous limestone, this specimen shows evidence of past life, for example, the *Balanophyllia* coral (indicated), seen here on many sides. To test whether a specimen is limestone, place a couple of drops of hydrochloric acid or white vinegar (acetic acid) on the rock to look for fizzing.

SIZE

55 × 49 × 27 mm

2.1 × 1.9 × 1.1 in

GEOLOGIC AGE

Oligocene

30–28 Ma

IDENTIFIERS

Presence of coral

Presence of shells

Fizz response to acid

DENSITY

DID YOU KNOW? While working as an engineer constructing canals in Italy, Leonardo da Vinci witnessed the unearthing of fossils. He understood and described the connection between sedimentary deposition and marine animals buried within layers of the ocean floor. Da Vinci knew that shells in alpine rock formations could not have gotten there from the biblical flood, as many believed, but only via uplift, which raised sedimentary layers up to those elevations.

Fossil-Bearing Limestone

SIZE

65 × 54 × 27 mm

2.5 × 2.1 × 1.1 in

GEOLOGIC AGE

Paleocene

66–56 Ma

IDENTIFIERS

Presence of shells

Presence of coral

Fizz response to acid

DENSITY

Fossiliferous limestone found on the shores of Ponte Vedra Beach, Florida. Present in fossil-bearing limestone are impressions and casts of ancient marine mollusks. Those visible in this specimen are primarily bivalves—animals with two hard shells. To test whether a specimen is limestone, place a couple of drops of hydrochloric or acetic acid on the rock and look for fizzing. Such fossiliferous rocks are quite interesting on their own and can add character to a collection.

DID YOU KNOW? Limestone is at least 50% calcium carbonate, a material that forms in warm shallow waters on continental shelves. A sedimentary rock, limestone is formed from the piling up of layer on layer of shells, corals, algae, and poop detritus. These materials become compressed over the millennia into rock formations. Because the layers incorporate numerous dead animals, limestone is one of the richest marine-fossil-bearing rock types.

Calcarenite

Tumbled fragment of a common sedimentary rock, calcarenite. Found on many East Coast beaches, calcarenite is medium- to fine-grained and varies in color from buff green to paler yellows and tans. Fragments of shells, foraminifera, and sand are often visible. Specimens fizz under hydrochloric acid, since calcarenite is a form of limestone and contains calcite. A coarser, more shell-rich limestone called coquina can also be found. It is especially common off the coasts of Florida and North Carolina.

SIZE

107 × 73 × 27 mm

4.2 × 2.8 × 1.1 in

GEOLOGIC AGE

Pleistocene

2.6 Ma–11 Ka

IDENTIFIERS

Presence of shells

Varying colors

Fizz response to acid

DENSITY

DID YOU KNOW? Calcarenite is an animal hodgepodge. It is derived mostly from pieces of shells and the skeletal material of marine organisms. They become pulverized and cemented together in sedimentary layers, much as sandstone does, but may be white, yellow, or orange because of their shell origins.

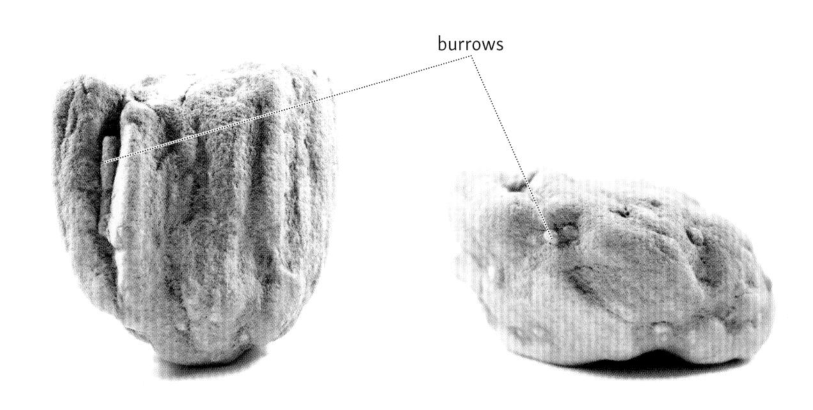

SIZE

105 × 100 × 45 mm

4.1 × 3.9 × 1.8 in

GEOLOGIC AGE

Cambrian

541–485 Ma

IDENTIFIERS

Vertical alignment

Straight tubes

Long traces

DENSITY

BURROW TRACES

Skolithos linearis

Trace fossil of an Upper Cambrian vermiform (worm-shaped) organism, *Skolithos linearis*. Though this is a trace fossil, scientists assign the Latin name of the organism to its trace. These burrows are often long, especially in the original deposit, and are similar in color and texture to the surrounding matrix. *Skolithos*, a filter feeder, lived in burrows (indicated) where it excavated and backfilled the sediment, as seen in this quartzose sandstone. This is a common fossil found on the shores of the Potomac River.

DID YOU KNOW? Biochronology is a way of estimating fossil ages when paleomagnetic and radioactive dating methods are not practical. Fossils are compared with fossil remains from the same species that have been successfully dated, from youngest to oldest, at other fossil sites.

Whelk Operculum

Unfossilized operculum from a knobbed, channeled, pear, or lightning whelk. Whelks produce the beautiful spiral shells found on many beaches along the East Coast (page 1), and opercula are the lids or trapdoors to these mollusks. Attached to the foot of a whelk, the operculum grows as the whelk grows, which can be seen in the growth lines of increasing size, from right to left. Though these unusual remains are not fossils, many fossil collectors stumble across them in the search for unique beach artifacts.

SIZE

52 × 26 × 1 mm

2.0 × 1.0 × 0.04 in

GEOLOGIC AGE

Holocene

11 ka–Present

IDENTIFIERS

Growth lines

Teardrop shape

Thin, delicate form

DENSITY

DID YOU KNOW? Whelks are one of the loggerhead turtle's favorite foods. Using their powerful jaws, loggerheads are able to crunch through whelk shells for a mouthful of slimy snail. Whelks can live up to 40 years. They start off as males, and once they reach a certain age, male whelks can become females and lay and fertilize their own eggs. This reproductive strategy is called protandric hermaphroditism. Now, that's a mouthful!

Arrowheads

SIZE

60 × 25 × 8 mm

2.3 × 1.0 × 0.3 in

GEOLOGIC AGE

Holocene

11 ka–present

IDENTIFIERS

Triangular shape

Conchoidal fractures

Historical context

DENSITY

Arrowheads from the Late Archaic to Woodland period. Regardless of origin, worked spear points share similar features with one another, such as material, general shape, size, and locality. Projectile points are usually made from flint, chert, or quartz—materials that, like glass, break in conchoidal fractures. Shapes are regularly triangular and vary in width, with a broad base that terminates in a point at the top. The point of origin determines whether artifacts wash up on beaches after eroding out of stream banks next to old settlements or middens.

DID YOU KNOW? Arrowheads reflect the quality of humans' touch from the past. Flint knapping involved striking a piece of flint with a hard roundish rock to chisel it into a rough projectile shape. Then the point and edges were finely sharpened with a tool such as an antler point to remove even smaller flakes. Finally, notches were abraded into the blunt end where leather strips would secure the arrowhead to the shaft.

Native American Pottery

Fragments of pottery from Late Archaic Indians, 4,000 years old. Shards of pottery have many characteristics that can aid in identification: incorporated sand grains, incorporated fiber patterns (page 470), convex and concave forms, and patterned designs. Measurement indicated at right is an average. The lower-right fragment shows where a cracked pot was mended by threading rawhide through two holes on opposite sides of the crack.

SIZE

46 × 36 × 6 mm

1.8 × 1.4 × 0.2 in

GEOLOGIC AGE

Holocene

11 ka–present

IDENTIFIERS

Gritty texture

Concave or convex forms

Exterior patterns

DENSITY

DID YOU KNOW? Horsehair has such fine characteristics that it has been incorporated into Native American pottery design. Bisque ware (unglazed pottery fired one time) is refired to 1,000°F and then withdrawn from the kiln with metal tongs and placed on the ground. Horsehairs are immediately placed on the hot object, which absorbs carbon from the hair. This process results in myriad fine dark lines of design on the finished piece.

Soapstone Pendant

SIZE

36 × 27 × 10 mm

1.4 × 1.1 × 0.4 in

GEOLOGIC AGE

Holocene

7.5–2.5 ka

IDENTIFIERS

Slippery feel

Human-drilled hole

Historical context

DENSITY

Man-made pendant from a Late Archaic Indian tribe in South Carolina. Soapstone, as its name suggests, is soapy or slippery to the touch. Soapstone is far smoother and slicker than river-worn pebbles. As with shark teeth and other fossils that require geologic context for precise identification, Native American artifacts can usually be dated with similar accuracy by correlating them with tribes that historically lived in the area. This artifact came from a beach area inhabited by humans as far back as 7,500 years ago.

DID YOU KNOW? Soapstone is a metamorphic rock that both withstands and retains heat for a long time. Native Americans used soapstone to make large boiling stones with holes drilled through their centers. The stone was placed in a fire until it was extremely hot. Then it was transferred to soups prepared in pits lined with animal skins. The soup was cooked by one or more boiling stones until ready to serve. Smaller stones with drilled holes were used as adornments.

SPECIES HIGHLIGHT

Rodents

Eh, what's up, Doc? Rodents? (Yes, but *not* rabbits!)

Rabbits were once considered rodents, but they are now classified within the order Lagomorpha. Order Rodentia, however, includes such commonly known mammals as mice, rats, squirrels, beavers, porcupines, and capybaras.

Rodents descended from a group of ancestral mammals called multituberculates, so named for the bumpy projections, or tubercles, on their back teeth. These early rodent-like creatures were unique because they had extremely flexible ankles, allowing them to scurry quickly over the ground. In addition, they appeared before the first dinosaurs, lived throughout the dinosaurs' reign, and then outlived them by about 30 million years. Overall, their time on Earth lasted about 130 million years, ending with their extinction during the Oligocene epoch.

Though fossil remnants of multituberculates are plentiful, it wasn't until the recovery of a complete skeleton of *Rugosodon eurasiaticus* that paleontologists had a complete picture of this group. This mouse-sized species, like other mammals then alive, was tiny, unlike the many Pleistocene animals that dwarfed their modern descendants. During the time of giant dinosaurs, mammal species survived by remaining small and filling an ecological niche much lower in the food web. They likely remained out of sight of these huge predators, living underground and foraging during the relative safety of night.

Skull size comparison of a giant beaver (*Castoroides dilophidus*) and a North American beaver (*Castor canadensis*). Specimens courtesy of the Mace Brown Museum of Natural History, Charleston, South Carolina.

North American beaver, *Castor canadensis*.

Another notable rodent ancestor, from about 93 million years ago, was *Cronopio dentiacutus*, which has the sensational common name saber-toothed squirrel. They did have unusually long canine teeth, but their 8-inch-long body was hardly intimidating to other mammals, and they probably ate insects and plants.

Rodents differ from other mammals in that their incisor teeth grow continuously throughout life, a condition known as hypselodonty. Therefore, they must be constantly chewing in order to keep their teeth worn down. The incisors have a thick enamel layer on the front surface but very little on the reverse side, where softer dentine wears down to maintain a sharp, chisel-like tooth edge.

Rodents have powerful jaws and cheek molars for grinding food. They lack canines and anterior premolars, which leaves a gap, or diastema, between the incisors and molars. This allows them to suck their cheeks inward to prevent undesirable material, such as wood shavings, from entering the throat, and further allows for this material to be ejected from the side of the mouth, all while chewing continues.

Today's largest rodent is a South American capybara, *Hydrochoerus hydrochaeris*. The smallest is *Salpingotulus michaelis*, the Baluchistan pygmy jerboa, measuring only 1.7 inches in body length. Capybaras crossed the Panamanian Land Bridge into North America during the Pliocene, around 3.5 million years ago, and fossils of one species, *Neochoerus pinckneyi*, attest to its occurrence in South Carolina, Florida, Texas, and California during the Pleistocene epoch.

The largest rodent ever known, *Josephoartigasia monesi*, was discovered in

Uruguay. It weighed 2,200 pounds and measured 10 feet in length. This species lived from two to four million years ago. The only surviving member of this family today is the pacarana (*Dinomys branickii*), a rare species inhabiting South American tropical forests.

Another Pleistocene rodent of interest was the giant beaver, two species of which are notable. *Castoroides ohioensis* occurred throughout the northern United States and Canada, and *C. dilophidus* fossils have been found throughout Florida and South Carolina. (*C. dilophidus* is the senior synonym of *C. leiseyorum*, as described in texts published before 2014.) These were the largest Pleistocene rodents, measuring from 6 to 7 feet in length and weighing 198–276 pounds. Similar in appearance to modern beavers, they differed in that their incisors had conspicuously ridged sides and blunt, rounded cutting edges rather than chisel-shaped tips.

While *Rugosodon* and saber-toothed squirrel fossils aren't found on southeastern beaches or in offshore sediments, don't worry. It is possible to find fossilized bones and teeth from beavers, capybaras, and any number of different kinds of small rodents. Even these are rare, but stay alert while collecting. It will be an exciting day when you run across one!

An unexpected treasure: the beachcomber doesn't just collect fossils and other physical items but memories of clear skies, calm walks, and enjoyable times with friends and family.

LOOK-ALIKES

TRAITS OF LOOK-ALIKES

Look-alikes, or pseudofossils, are undoubtedly the bane of every fossil hunter's search. Pseudofossils are defined as any object that looks like a fossil but is not one. Concretions, shell fragments, man-made waste, and driftwood are all culprits in fooling the eye. Pseudofossils take on many forms and confuse even the most proficient amateurs and learned professionals. To stay ahead of the curve, study the more intricate bones and teeth from animals; ear bones, carpals, tarsals, and mammalian molars are all oddly shaped. Look for distinct patterns and symmetry in such fossils and learn the irregular tendencies of their look-alikes.

COMMON TERMS

Banded, canal, concretion, conglomerate, ferrous, opaque, pitted, porous, pseudofossil, rust-colored, sandstone, slag

COMMONALITY

Unfortunately, look-alikes are extremely common on every beach.

INCLUSIONS AND EXCLUSIONS

Man-made waste and naturally occurring items are included. Darker shell fragments are also included, based on the frequency with which new fossil hunters often pick them up. While people mistake many objects for fossils, the following represent a decent cross section of what can be found along the Atlantic and Gulf Coasts. Because of the irregular appearance of look-alikes and their lack of diagnostic anatomical positions, the position indicators have been omitted unless their use would aid in identification.

MEASUREMENTS

All look-alikes have measurements displayed in a three-part system:

(longest side × next longest × shortest side)

The longest side always comes first, regardless of position. If this side is ambiguous in the photos, it is delineated in the Item Description. The second-longest side is measured perpendicular to the longest side and in its thickest part. The shortest side is similarly measured on the perpendicular. (Dashed lines indicate the third dimension.)

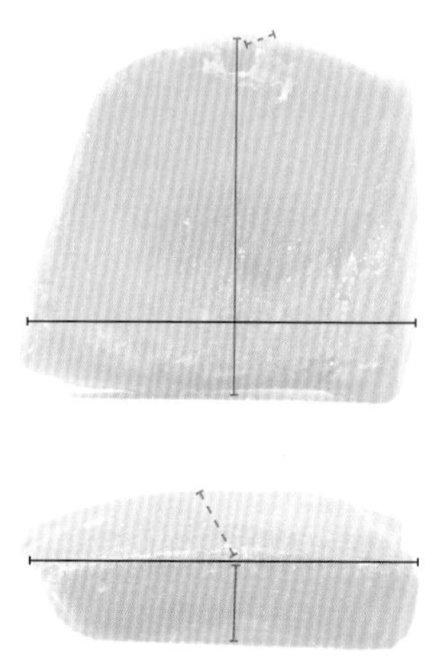

SUPPLEMENTARY IMAGES AND TERMS

Phosphate

Three nodules of phosphate, a rock that often contains fossils from Early Cretaceous–Pleistocene deposits. Phosphate pebbles are some of the trickiest pseudofossils, taking on the appearance of bones, ear bones, and all manner of fossils. The surface is often pitted with pockets and occasionally banded in layers. When dry, these rocks appear duller than most fossils, a feature than can aid in the identification of ambiguous specimens. Note the distinct lack of symmetry in any of the above nodules.

SIZE

48 × 19 × 32 mm

1.9 × 0.7 × 1.2 in

GEOLOGIC AGE

Early Cretaceous–Pleistocene

145 Ma–11 ka

IDENTIFIERS

Pitted surface

Irregular shapes

Occasional banding

DENSITY

DID YOU KNOW? Phosphorus is a mineral whose name comes from the Greek for "bringer of light." Phosphate is a sedimentary rock that forms in anaerobic (nonoxygenated) environments. It is dark black in color and appears in a variety of shapes. Pieces of this rock can mimic many types of fossils, causing frustration for collectors who pick them up in great anticipation of finding a new fossil.

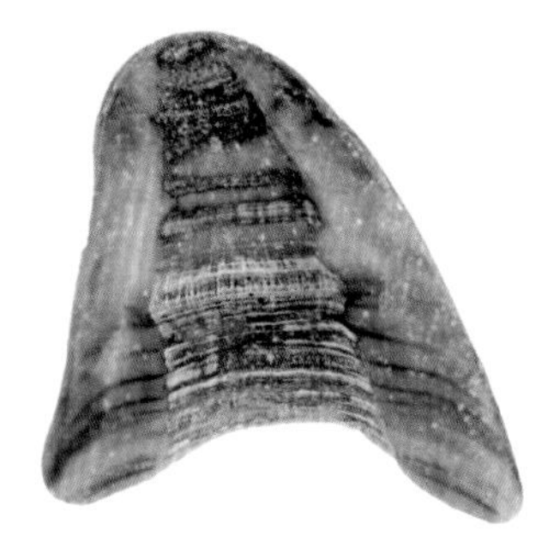

SIZE

25 × 20 × 8 mm

1.0 × 0.8 × 0.3 in

GEOLOGIC AGE

Holocene

11 ka–present

IDENTIFIERS

Growth layers

Dark gray color

Triangular shape

DENSITY

SHELL BASE *Crassostrea virginica*

Bottom knob from the extant eastern oyster, *Crassostrea virginica*. On oyster shell beaches such as those found throughout South Carolina, oyster fragments, especially the bases, are commonly collected pseudofossils. Look for the characteristic growth lines as alternating layers of gray and white (seen above at left). Once dry, these specimens turn a dull gray, in contrast with shiny fossilized enamel and bone in varying shades of black, brown, and blue-gray (page 22). An easy test to distinguish an oyster fragment from a fossil is to try to break the fragment with two fingers; oysters usually snap in half with little effort.

DID YOU KNOW? Oysters are efficient filters. A single oyster can process 30–50 gallons of water per day. Large colonies of oysters can filter many thousands of gallons daily. Oysters are nutritious and high in zinc. Their crushed shells contain calcium, which, when added to a garden with acidic soil, balances the soil pH for stronger and brighter plants, and potentially faster harvest times. Now, that's efficient *and* nutritious!

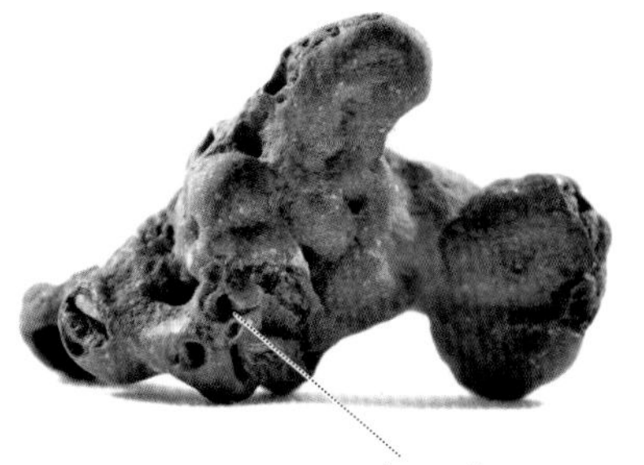

Iron Concretion

Iron concretion commonly found in the Chesapeake Bay region. These irregular specimens come in a variety of shapes, colors, and sizes, confusing many beachgoers. Look for areas of thin walls (indicated), often a different color from the rest of the concretion. Iron shapes frequently appear bloated, as if inflated with air. The exterior is gritty to the touch, contrasting with the smooth feel of fossil material. Concretions are represented in many geologic deposits and have even been known to form around World War II–era military shrapnel.

SIZE

54 × 33 × 24 mm

2.1 × 1.3 × 0.9 in

GEOLOGIC AGE

Cretaceous–Holocene

145 Ma–present

IDENTIFIERS

Thin walls

Irregular shape

Multiple colors

DENSITY

DID YOU KNOW? Iron concretions are an art form of geology. These naturally occurring concretions come in many shapes. The chemical weathering of iron oxide in rocks results in shapes and patterns such as hollow pipes, concentric rings or circles, layered slabs, cross-hatched slabs, fossil slabs, and botryoidal textures, which resemble, and are commonly called, "melted chocolate."

Iron-Bearing Sandstone

SIZE

43 × 30 × 15 mm

1.7 × 1.2 × 0.6 in

GEOLOGIC AGE

Pleistocene

2.6 Ma–11 ka

IDENTIFIERS

Rusty red color

Gritty texture

Irregular shapes

DENSITY

Typical fragment of iron-rich sandstone. Fragments of these rocks exhibit a rusty red color, deep pockets, and numerous holes. Such specimens have no true form and come in a variety of sizes. Once they are dry, it becomes easier to distinguish these stones from fossils. In addition to the rusty color, they generally have a gritty texture, feeling rough to the touch. These specimens are also denser than most rock material. The geologic age of the above specimen is undetermined, though it most likely formed during the Pleistocene.

DID YOU KNOW? Radioactivity is an important property of rocks and rock formations. From the earliest point in a rock's igneous or metamorphic history, its radioactive components begin to decay, and this happens at a steady, predictable rate. In carbon 14 dating, argon dating, and uranium-series methods, scientists use this radioactive decay "clock" to determine the age of fossils and the rock formations in which they are found.

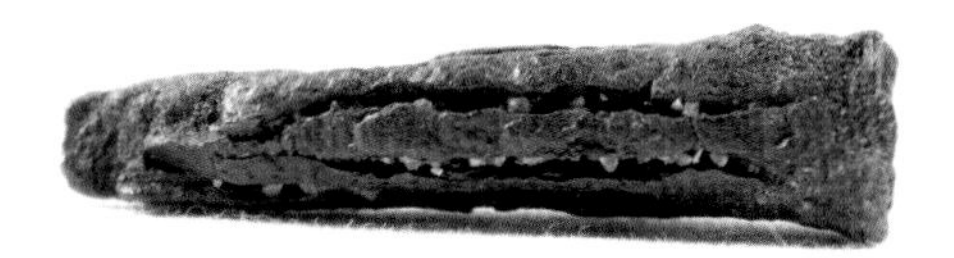

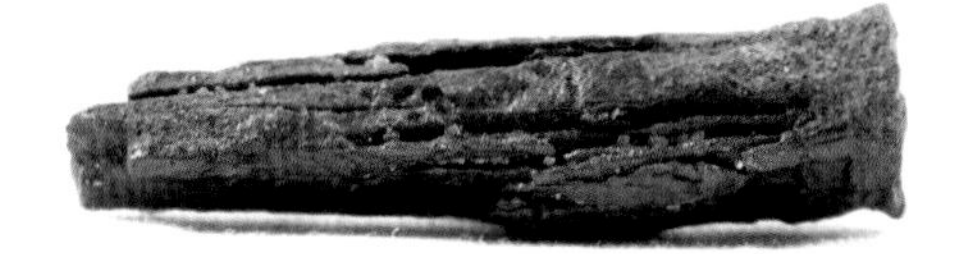

Iron Nail

A forged square nail from the 1800s. Saltwater is harsh on all artifacts, though it is especially tough on iron. Fragments of iron begin to peel, crack, and flake off from the original object, rendering many artifacts unrecognizable. Just like terrestrial fragments of iron, iron objects that spend time in saltwater show the classic rusty red color that is key in identifying old fragments of iron.

SIZE

35 × 9 × 6 mm

1.4 × 0.4 × 0.2 in

GEOLOGIC AGE

Holocene

1500–present

IDENTIFIERS

Rusty red color

Square or circular shape

Flaked exterior

DENSITY

DID YOU KNOW? Bronze Age man fashioned nails by heating iron ore to its melting point and shaping it into square plates from which nails were then cut. After reheating, the tips were hammered into points and the top end was hammered into a flattened rosehead. In the 1600s, a machine simplified the process, and further improvements led to today's round-diameter wire nails. Many rusted, older, cut nails still wash up on today's beaches.

Industrial Slag

SIZE

49 × 40 × 20 mm

1.9 × 1.6 × 0.8 in

GEOLOGIC AGE

Holocene

1800–present

IDENTIFIERS

Metallic luster

Bubble pockmarks

Metal shavings

DENSITY

Fragment of "rock" from industrial by-products (see below). Slag ranges in density from extremely light to quite dense, based on its origin. Regardless, all fragments exhibit the same bubbles (often observed as pockmarks), metallic luster, and occasional metal shavings. Its presence on beaches is likely from fill gravel for nearby construction projects.

DID YOU KNOW? Industrial slag is a man-made waste product from smelting plants, metal mine tailings, or older landfills. It lacks crystals, tarnishes easily, and breaks readily under pressure. Slag exhibits a metallic appearance; it is sometimes sharp-edged and sometimes has globular bumps. No part of slag resembles bones, osteoderms, teeth, or pottery. If you happen to pick up a piece to inspect it more closely, you will probably discard it quickly.

M

L

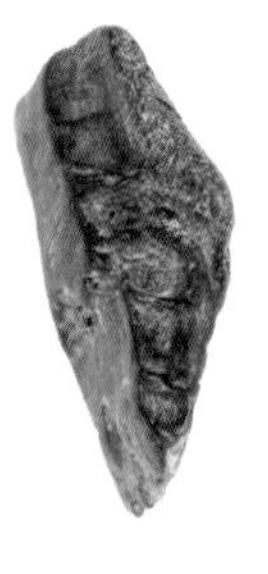

A

LIGAMENT Bivalvia

Shell hinge (ligament) from a modern bivalve. The ligament, along with the hinge plates and teeth, is responsible for holding bivalve shells shut. The hinge pictured is stained black-gray from estuarine muds. Note the growth lines of the bivalve, occasionally present on the lateral sides, curving down the shell.

SIZE

23 × 20 × 10 mm

0.9 × 0.8 × 0.4 in

GEOLOGIC AGE

Holocene

11 ka–present

IDENTIFIERS

Growth lines

Ligament grooves

Lateral curve

DENSITY

DID YOU KNOW? Bivalves can leap. The shell halves are held together by tension from adductor muscles, and a ligament opens the halves when the adductors are relaxed. Once open, a clam, mussel, or other bivalve extends a foot to dig in the sand or to project the bivalve up as a means of locomotion. A cockle can bend its foot and straighten it suddenly to leap a short distance and escape predators such as starfish.

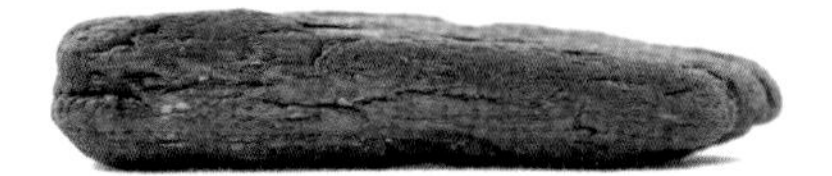

Bituminous Coal

SIZE

91 × 36 × 17 mm

3.5 × 1.4 × 0.7 in

GEOLOGIC AGE

Carboniferous

359–299 Ma

IDENTIFIERS

Layered structure

Shiny fractures

Relatively light weight

DENSITY

Section of ocean-worn bituminous coal. Because of how coal is formed, many fragments of it, especially of bituminous coal, appear layered. Coal is often difficult to break in half, but easier to peel off in layers when in the field. Look for shiny faces reflecting sunlight where the specimen has chipped recently. Another way to test a fragment is to take a hammer or screwdriver and knock off a couple of pieces. If the broken surfaces have an oily sheen or show alternating bright and dull layers, then the specimen is coal.

DID YOU KNOW? Lumps of coal often fool the fossil hunter, so you have to look closely at these black objects. Coal is made of carbon, hydrogen, oxygen, nitrogen, and sulfur. It forms when plant material decays and then becomes buried, compressed, and metamorphosed. Anthracite coal becomes very hard and shiny after this transformation, and its appearance can mimic that of fossils. Don't be fooled! Look closely for biological indicators: symmetry, enamel, and bone textures.

BERRY *Sabal palmetto*

Fruit from the cabbage palmetto tree, *Sabal palmetto*. Palmetto trees are found from Cape Fear, North Carolina, to southern Florida. A disjunct population occurs at Cape Hatteras, North Carolina. Once dried, palmetto berries become hard and extremely difficult to dent or depress. Most often, these berries are confused with the teeth of drum fish (page 322), being similar in size and shape. Note the wrinkled point of attachment (at right), where the berry was connected to the stem. The same location on a drum fish tooth bears a comparably puckered look, but drum teeth cave inward where the nerve endings were attached.

SIZE

7 × 7 × 5 mm

0.3 × 0.3 × 0.2 in

GEOLOGIC AGE

Holocene

Present

IDENTIFIERS

Perfectly round

Wrinkled base

Hardness when dried

DENSITY

DID YOU KNOW? Looking for certain fossils along the southeastern coast can be frustrating because of South Carolina's state tree. The dark palmetto berries resemble drum fish teeth in outline and luster. The fleshy, single, stone-like seeds of these drupes are covered with shiny black skin. So as you are searching the upper beach–dune interface for drum fish teeth, look up occasionally to make sure that you aren't under a palmetto tree.

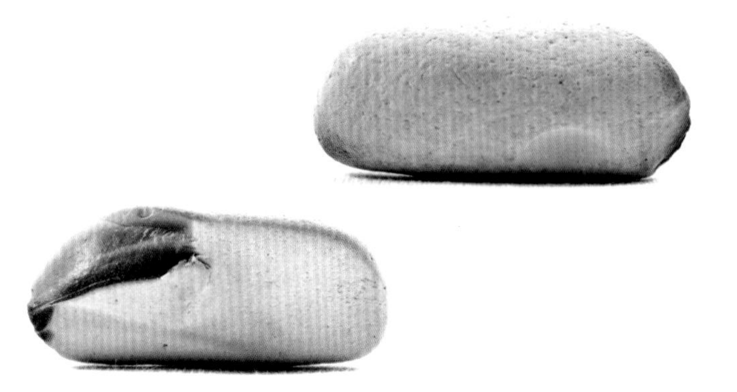

Chert

SIZE

37 × 15 × 7 mm

1.4 × 0.6 × 0.3 in

GEOLOGIC AGE

Miocene

23–5.3 Ma

IDENTIFIERS

Conchoidal fractures

Milky colors

Absorbency

DENSITY

Pebble of the microcrystalline sedimentary rock chert. Made up of silicon dioxide, chert is a rock best known for its conchoidal fractures. From such breaks, chert, along with flint and quartz, was one of the commonly used rocks for spear points. In the ocean, chert has a tendency to gradually degrade to silica. Such samples, which are very absorbent, appear to dry immediately after water is applied. Beach specimens are smooth and rounded, in contrast with inland specimens, which are sharp and angular.

DID YOU KNOW? Chert was a valued material for making arrowhead points, which early humans used in hunting animals. The rock's uniform consistency, along with the ease with which shards can be chipped off, made it possible to fashion points with extremely sharp, scalloped edges that proved deadly for hunted prey. Chert was not found everywhere, so skilled craftsmen who located this material could trade their valuable points for other items, making them early entrepreneurs.

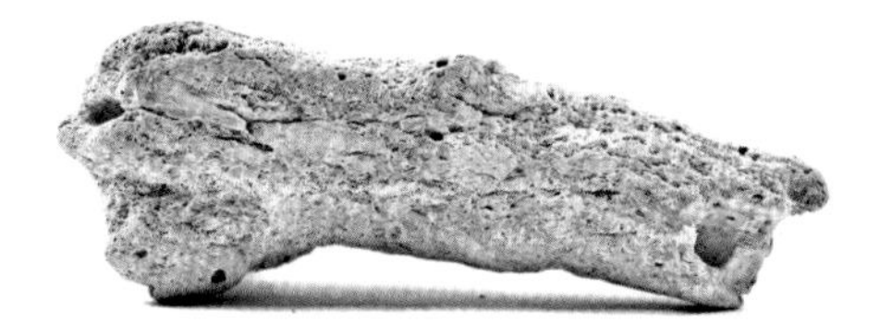

Calcareous Conglomerate

Oddly shaped piece of conglomerate rich in shell fragments and sand particles. Conglomerates are sedimentary rocks made up of particles of varying sizes, from sand grains to pebbles and larger rocks. Look for uneven layers in these specimens as well as chunks and pieces of shell fragments. Ocean tumbling can cause them to take on many different shapes, such as the bone-shaped specimen above. Test the rocks for calcareous content by dropping hydrochloric acid on them and looking for any fizzing.

SIZE

90 × 31 × 20 mm

3.5 × 1.2 × 0.8 in

GEOLOGIC AGE

Miocene–Pleistocene

23 Ma–11 ka

IDENTIFIERS

Uneven layers

Shell fragments

Fizzing response to acid

DENSITY

DID YOU KNOW? Conglomerates form distinctive sedimentary rock formations. Large stones are the first to settle to the bottom of water bodies following severe precipitation or erosion events. Smaller rocks then settle over the larger ones, followed by pebbles and sand grains, which fill in voids around the "early settlers." Mixed into all this material, and forming a final layer, a liquidy sand-cement seals the remaining voids. The whole mass eventually hardens into a conglomerate.

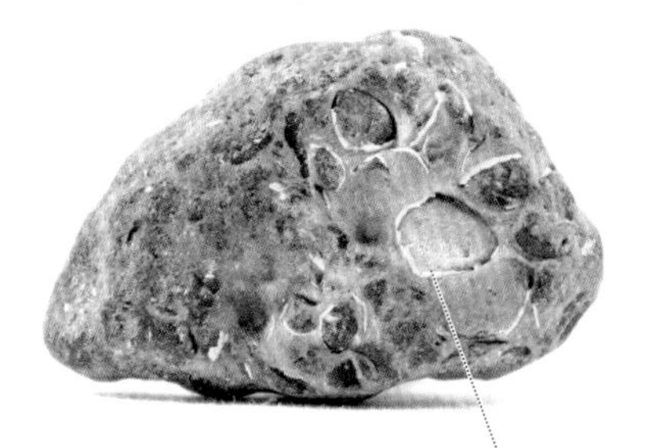

SIZE

49 × 31 × 7 mm

1.9 × 1.2 × 0.3 in

GEOLOGIC AGE

Miocene–Pleistocene

23 Ma–11 ka

IDENTIFIERS

Inclusion of shells

Presence of pebbles

Glued-together look

DENSITY

Stony-Shell Conglomerate

Worn stone fragment from a formation rich in smaller pebbles and coquina shells. To the untrained eye, conglomerates appear to be the mouthparts or grinding plates of some large fishes. In distinguishing rock from fossil, look for the outlines of old shell fragments (indicated) and other rocks that may be present in the specimen. Conglomerates are sedimentary rocks that are made up of sand particles, pebbles, shells, and other minerals deposited in riverbeds or offshore.

DID YOU KNOW? Conglomerate rocks are sedimentary, meaning they formed from multiple layers. Conglomerates have little value to industry; the rock does not break cleanly and may shatter easily. They can be attractive, though, combining many variously colored rocks that have pleasantly rounded, rather than sharp or angular, shapes from years of downstream travel. This makes them popular for landscape borders and rock gardens. And, fortunately, some contain fossils.

L

M

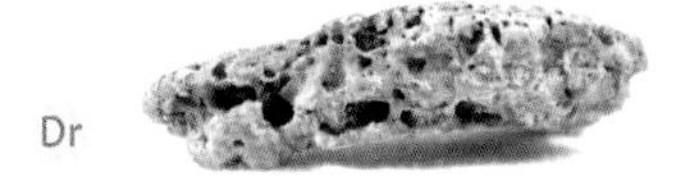
Dr

V

SHELL FRAGMENT

Mercenaria mercenaria

Shell fragment from the extant quahog clam, *Mercenaria mercenaria*. The above specimen demonstrates how unrecognizable shells can become; this one was drilled through by a boring sponge (*Cliona* spp.). Such bored-through shells often resemble armadillo or glyptodont osteoderms. Note the lateral grooves and growth lines, which help identify this fragment as a shell.

SIZE

56 × 38 × 14 mm

2.2 × 1.5 × 0.5 in

GEOLOGIC AGE

Holocene

11 ka–present

IDENTIFIERS

Growth lines

Dorsal grooves

Relative thickness

DENSITY

DID YOU KNOW? "Money money money money!" The O'Jays weren't singing about the quahog clam in their 1973 hit, but they could have been. When Carolus Linnaeus named the quahog clam, he used the Latin term for wages or money because of this clam's famed use. Native Americans used pieces of these shells as currency with distinct values. Most of the shell is white, so white pieces were of lower value. But purple areas, which make up around 10% or less of the clam, were worth more.

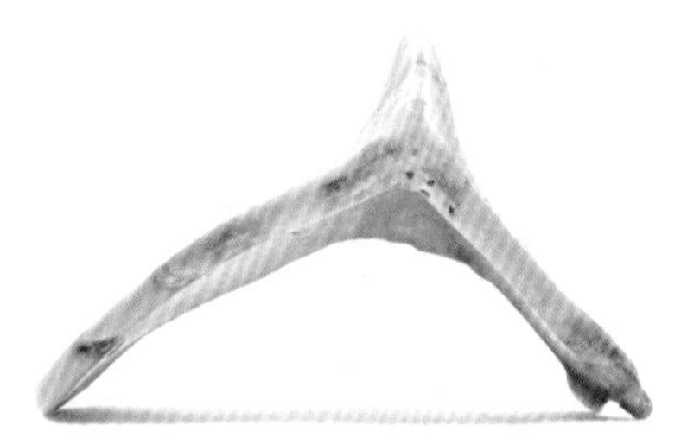

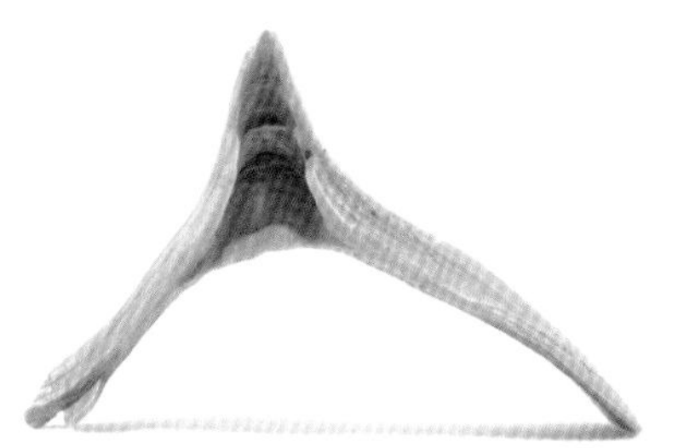

SIZE

58 × 21 × 15 mm

2.3 × 0.8 × 0.6 in

GEOLOGIC AGE

Holocene

11 ka–present

IDENTIFIERS

Growth layers

Exterior knob

Multiple colors

DENSITY

WHELK KNOB *Busycon* spp.

Exterior knob from an extant whelk species, genus *Busycon*. Fragments of whelks often show the growth layers where calcium carbonate was deposited while the whelk grew (visible above, inside the knob at right). Depending on such shell fragments' final resting place, their color can vary; fragments deposited in darker marine muds are often a deep gray-black. Novices can mistake smaller, darker specimens for shark teeth.

DID YOU KNOW? In recent years, entrepreneurial businesses and coastal scientists alike have learned the importance of offering environmental outings. Ecotourism revenue earned through activities such as whale watching, observing sea turtles nesting, or snorkeling among coral reefs contributes millions of dollars to local economies. Once participants have personally experienced the natural lives of threatened or endangered animals, they often become proponents of laws to protect these species.

Dr

V

WHELK KNOBS *Busycon* spp.

Whelk shell fragment with two complete knobs, or spines. These knobs are located on the spiraled shells that wash up on southeastern and mid-Atlantic beaches (page 1). The interior portion of shell fragments (seen in the ventral view) is often opaque or off-white compared with the shell in dorsal view. The above fragment most likely came from a shell encased in old estuarine muds, which stained the shell a dark gray.

SIZE

23 × 21 × 7 mm

0.9 × 0.8 × 0.3 in

GEOLOGIC AGE

Holocene

11 ka–present

IDENTIFIERS

Arched knobs

Opaque interior

Curved form

DENSITY

DID YOU KNOW? Whelks are gastropods—a word meaning "stomach foot." These aquatic snails hunt other gastropods and bivalves, using their powerful feet to open shells with suction. A whelk wedges the rim of its shell between a bivalve's shell halves and pries open the shell farther. The whelk then uses its spiny tongue to drill out the mollusk's flesh.

SIZE

42 × 41 × 10 mm

1.6 × 1.6 × 0.4 in

GEOLOGIC AGE

Holocene

1500–present

IDENTIFIERS

Translucence

Curved fragments

Conchoidal fractures

DENSITY

Sea Glass

Sea glass comes in many different shapes, sizes, colors, and thicknesses. In fact, many beachcombers specifically search for these surf-worn pieces of man-made glass. Fragments from bottles are curved and, depending on age, may contain bubbles, like the specimen pictured. Like all glass, these fragments chip and exhibit conchoidal fractures when broken. The above fragment is from the mid-1800s. Translucence is apparent when the glass is held up to a light.

DID YOU KNOW? Untreated beach sand that is made into glass turns dark green, like the specimen above. Early settlers made glass bottles from the sand they found on the beaches, and the resulting bottles were a very distinct dark green. If you look closely on some bottles, you can see air bubbles from the glass-blowing process.

SPECIES HIGHLIGHT

Horses

"Hello, I'm Mr. *Equus*." (A horse, of course!)

Members of the Equidae, or horse family, have been closely intertwined with humankind for at least 5,000 years. This family encompasses horses, zebras, asses (including donkeys), tapirs, and rhinoceroses as well as extinct ancestors of these species. The family falls within the Perissodactyla order, commonly known as odd-toed ungulates, which are hoofed mammals having an odd number of toes on each foot.

Within Equidae, modern horses are classified within the genus *Equus*, and only two species, *Equus ferus caballus* and *Equus ferus przewalskii*, exist today. These are commonly referred to, respectively, as the domestic horse and Przewalski's horse, the latter being the only true untamed horse surviving in the wild today. Horses have an interesting evolutionary history, biologically, taxonomically, and culturally.

The horses that roamed North America during the ice age were identical at the genus level, *Equus*, to those found in North America today.

The most significant ancestor of *Equus* was *Hyracotherium*, a dog-sized animal that appeared around 52 million years ago. This species had multiple spreading toes on its feet, making it well adapted to walking on soft tropical-forest soils. *Hyracotherium* was notable because it showed the first adaptation toward supporting its body weight on the middle toe of each foot. This change was in response to a climatic shift that prompted these species to move away from forests toward a life of grazing among the firm, drier grassy plains.

Over the next 50 million years of equine evolution, single-toe support became increasingly important, and equids' adjacent toes became reduced to vestigial appendages before disappearing altogether. Similarly, the front teeth evolved into long incisors, and the molars became more advanced, with crowns suited to grinding the coarse grasses of the Pliocene–Pleistocene steppes of North America. In this open and exposed habitat, early horses grew taller, allowing them to see predators at greater distances, and developed long powerful legs, enabling them to run at a fast clip to escape their foes.

Paleontologists of the 19th and early 20th centuries developed a simple, straight-line taxonomy of the evolution from early to modern horses, seemingly confirming the gradualism implied by natural selection. Based on the fossil record of the time, a series of generic names attached to the horse species

Two horses that are descendants from ones reintroduced to North America by the Spaniards in the 16th century.

Intricate enamel pattern on an upper P2 from a horse. Such patterns are found on many equine cheek teeth.

hinted at this idealized progression. Beginning with *Hyracotherium* (originally named *Eohippus*), these generic labels translated into romantic common names that complemented the neat hypothesis of horse evolution.

Thus, *Eohippus* ("dawn horse") was proposed to have evolved into *Orohippus* ("mountain horse"), then to *Mesohippus* ("middle horse"), *Miohippus* ("lesser horse"), *Epihippus* ("marginal horse"), *Parahippus* ("almost horse"), *Merychippus* ("ruminant horse"), *Hipparion* ("like a horse"), *Hippidion* ("like a pony"), and, ultimately, *Equus*. The English scientist Thomas Huxley embraced this progression, and it was widely accepted until 1951, when George Gaylord Simpson showed the story to be more complicated.

To be fair, the transition from *Hyracotherium*/*Eohippus* to *Equus* was mostly orderly, but many lines branched off this progression, and abrupt appearances and disappearances of new species occurred along this multimillennium journey as well.

Culturally, the development of human society owes much to horses. *Equus*, first domesticated around 10,000 years ago, has been selectively bred into over 300 varieties, including giant agricultural draft horses, sleek racers, high-jumping show horses, and small ponies. Throughout preindustrial history, horses were pressed into service in countless military battles and were used to herd cattle across western U.S. plains.

From the Eocene to the present, horses have also left their legacy in buried sediments as fossilized bones and teeth. Encountering such remnants today, one might pause to wonder about the life of their former owner. Did it have a special connection with some Paleo-Indian? Perhaps.

And perhaps someday while perusing the detritus along a southeastern beach, you might excitedly pick up what looks like a fossil incisor. What creature could this fossil have come from? Well, it was a horse, of course!

Exhibit showing a modern bison and a bison's internal skeletal structure, on display at the Charleston Museum, Charleston, South Carolina.

SPECIES HIGHLIGHT

Bison

Shuffle off to Buffalo with bison, America's megafauna legacy

The United States has had a deep and lasting relationship with the American plains bison. Most people refer to this animal as a buffalo, a name that was ultimately derived from a Greek word for an African gazelle. While this name is extensively used and acceptable, "bison" is considered more proper. Indeed, the American plains bison is most closely related to the European wood bison, which, like its New World counterpart, was once threatened with extinction. True buffalos, the Asian water buffalo and the African Cape buffalo, are only distantly related to *Bison* species.

Around 2 to 5 million years ago, the *Bison* group split off from the lineage that gave rise to today's cattle species. The earliest known bison species, *Bison priscus*, commonly known as the steppe bison, became widespread throughout Eurasia; it is the bison depicted in southern Europe's famous Paleolithic cave paintings. Like the mammoths and mastodons, steppe bison arrived in North America by crossing over the Bering Land Bridge as a changing climate led to the lowered sea levels that created this connection. But the bison arrived almost a million years later than those mastodont species. The bison migration began at least 500,000 years ago and involved back-and-forth crossings for the next 280,000 years. This early species inhabited the northern part of North America throughout the Pleistocene epoch and into the Holocene, eventually becoming extinct 4,000–8,000 years ago.

Scientists believe that the giant bison or long-horned bison, *Bison latifrons*, which evolved from *B. priscus*, first appeared in central North America about 500,000 years ago, as shown by the fossil record. This was the largest bison to inhabit the continent, measuring over 8 feet tall at the shoulder, up to 15.5 feet in length, and weighing as much as 4,400 pounds. But the most notable feature was its set of horns, which curved gently upward and spanned a distance of 7–8 feet. The long-horned bison gave rise to another species, *Bison antiquus*, about 250,000 years ago, and the two coexisted until the disappearance of *B. latifrons* during the late part of the Wisconsin glaciation, 21,000–30,000 years ago.

Another bison, *Bison occidentalis*, appeared soon after *B. antiquus* and was either a subspecies of that bison or, as some taxonomists propose, the transition from *B. latifrons* to today's *Bison bison*. Unlike all other megafauna from the ice ages, *B. antiquus* survived well into the Holocene, becoming extinct only 5,000 years ago as the American bison became the dominant species. It is remarkable to think that early Native American generations witnessed the evolutionary transition from the Pleistocene *Bison antiquus* to today's *Bison bison*.

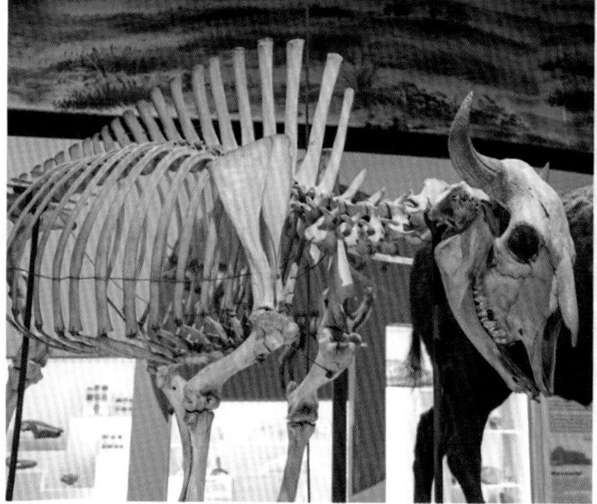

left Bison found in North America during the ice age were similar in appearance to those found across the Great Plains today.

right Bison skeleton on display at the Charleston Museum, Charleston, South Carolina. Note the high dorsal processes ascending from the thoracic vertebrae. Such high processes allowed for the attachment of the large neck muscles needed to support the bison's massive head.

Bison antiquus teeth in occlusal view. Note the isolated stylid on the two leftmost teeth.

The most recent evolution of the *Bison* genus resulted in the two North American subspecies seen today. One is the well-known American plains bison, with the scientific name *Bison bison bison*. The other is the American wood bison, *Bison bison athabascae*, which is native to Alaska and northwestern Canada. Like the plains bison, this animal almost became extinct in recent times, with only 200 surviving in 1957. A successful breeding recovery program has increased that population to 2,500 (as of 2014).

Fortunately, similar protection in the United States has ensured a stable, though historically reduced, population of plains bison in the 21st century. By chance, reminders of their Pleistocene–Holocene ancestors, though much fewer in number, can still be found around the United States, too. These exist in the form of fossilized bones and teeth from *Bison antiquus* and *Bison latifrons*, many of which await your discovery on southeastern beaches today.

Illustrated Glossary

This illustrated glossary is intended to be used in conjunction with the written glossary and the Identification Pages. The following images relate to common fossil terminology used throughout the text. Each page consists of plates, often close-up views, showing small details and subtle differences in some of the fossils featured in this guide. A subject title is at the top of each plate, followed by an explanatory caption. By referring to these images, the written glossary, and Identification Pages, readers can increase their familiarity with terminology, which will help them catalogue their collections.

Anatomical Directions Two views of the anatomical directions used in identifying bone, osteoderm, mouthpart, and vertebrae placement within the body. Abbreviations: A—*anterior*, D—*distal*, Dr—*dorsal*, L—*lateral*, LL—*left lateral*, M—*medial*, Po—*posterior*, Pr—*proximal*, RL—*right lateral*, V—*ventral*.

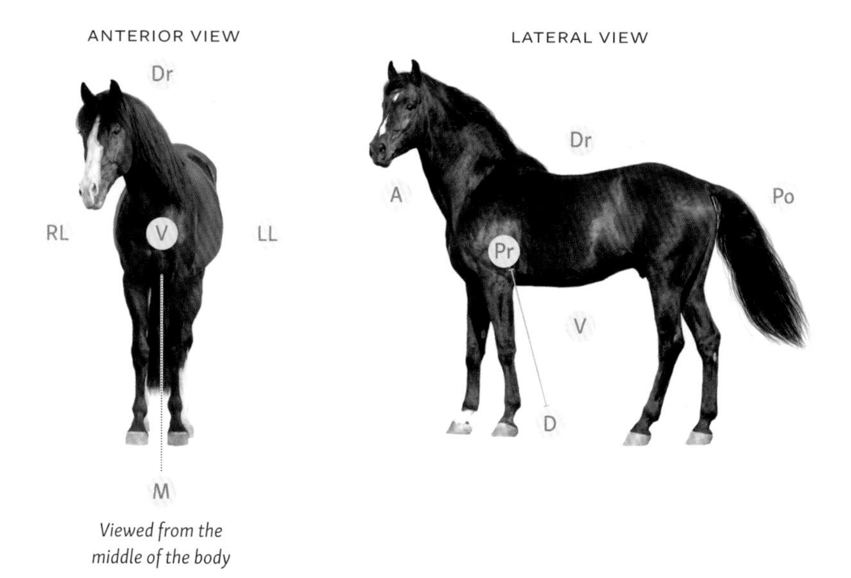

Viewed from the middle of the body

Antler Fragments Fragments of white-tailed deer (*Odocoileus virginianus*) antlers. The unique texture inside antlers comes from a much finer spongy bone than the cancellous bone found in limbs and vertebrae.

Articulation: Astragalus to Cubonavicular Anterior view of a bison astragalus articulating with the cubonavicular. Posteriorly, the astragalus articulates with the calcaneum, and dorsally with the tibia.

Articulation: Metapodial to Phalanges Articulation of the metapodial with the proximal phalanges. *Top*: horse (*Equus* sp.); *bottom*: white-tailed deer (*Odocoileus virginianus*).

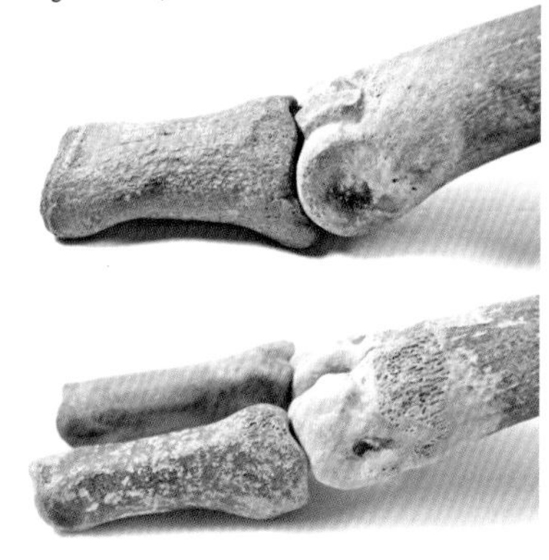

Astragalus Forms: Single Pulley and Double Pulley *Top*: single-pulley form of astragalus (*Equus* sp.). *Bottom*: double-pulley form (*Odocoileus virginianus*). The double-pulley design is unique to the artiodactyl group.

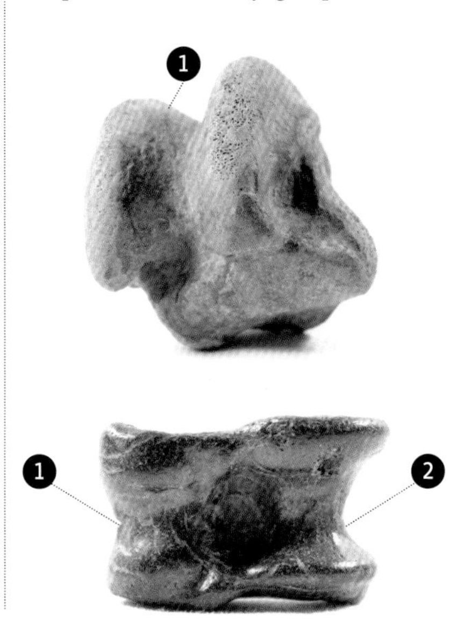

Astragalus: Deer and Peccary Comparison. 1 white-tailed deer (*Odocoileus virginianus*); 2 peccary (*Mylohyus nasutus*).

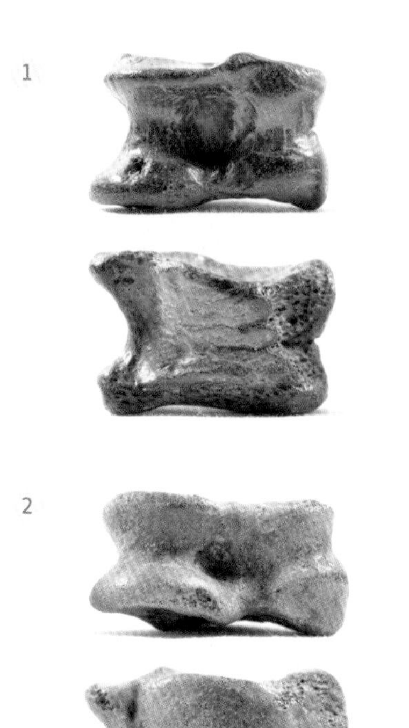

Billfish Rostrum Detail Detail of the rostrum from an extinct billfish species. Note the grainy pattern of the bone and the three main grooves running parallel to the length of the rostrum.

Bone Textures

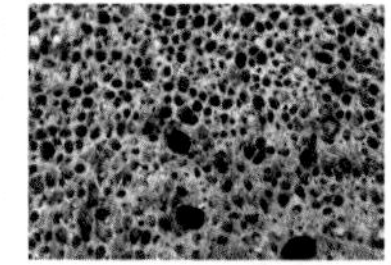

Cancellous | *Unworn*

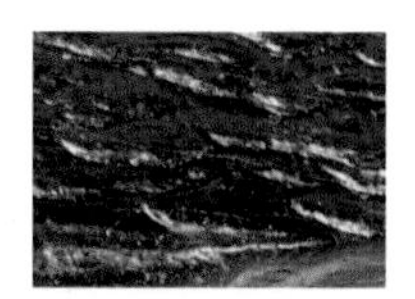

Cancellous | *Worn*

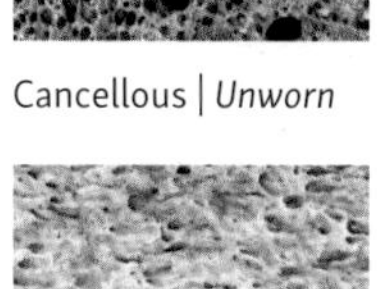

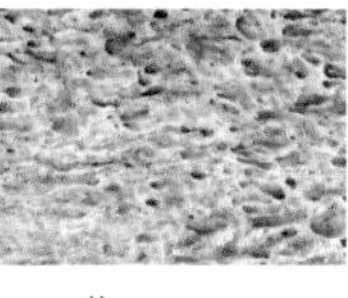

Cancellous
Medium wear

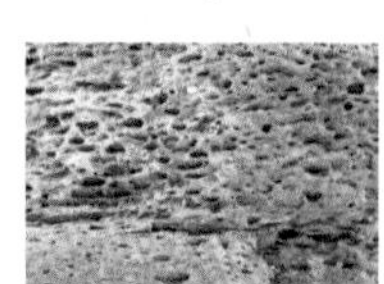

Cancellous
Moderate wear

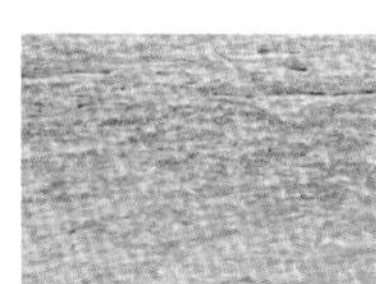

Cortical
Unworn

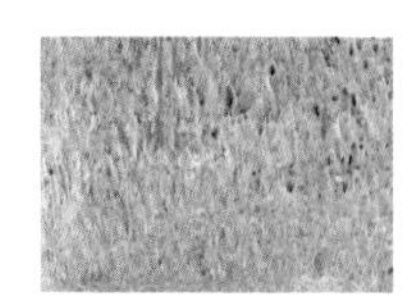

Vertebral centrum
Cross section

Bony Fish Skeletons X-ray of the skeletal framework found in bony fishes. Note the funnel-shaped amphicoelous vertebrae and the neural and hemal processes projecting off the vertebrae dorsally and ventrally, respectively. Specimen courtesy of Edisto Beach State Park, South Carolina.

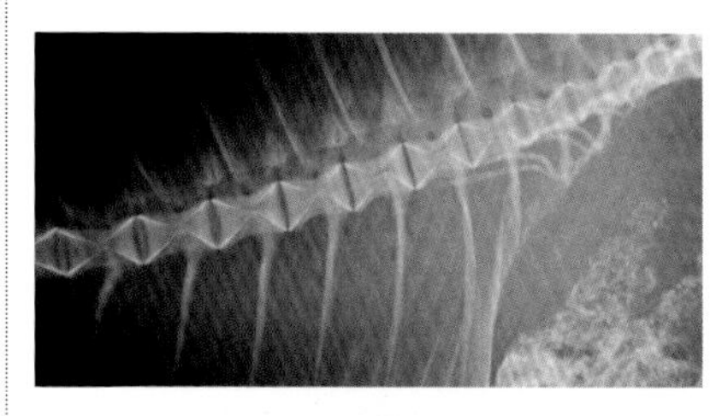

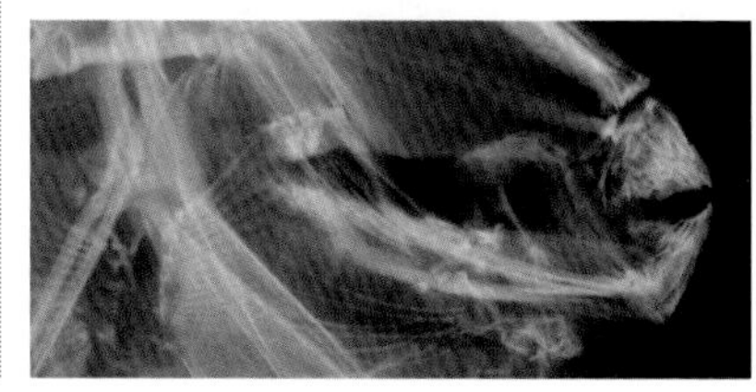

Bourlette Detail Close-up of the dental band (bourlette) present on a *Carcharocles megalodon* tooth.

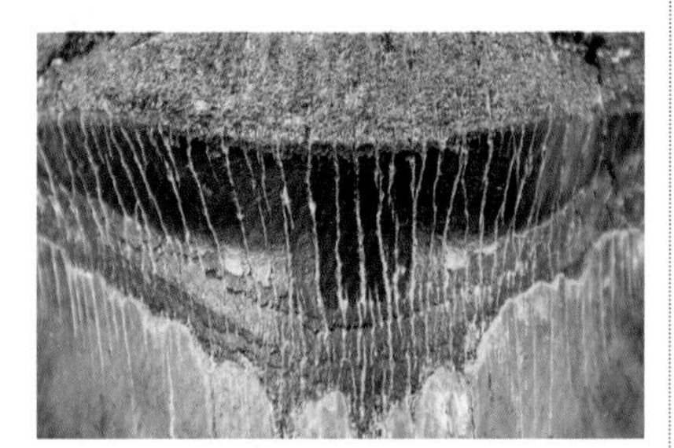

Calcite Crystallization Composite cross section of a bone with calcite-rich groundwater intrusion. Excess groundwater filled the interior of the bone, allowing crystals (indicated) to form slowly as the calcite precipitated out of solution.

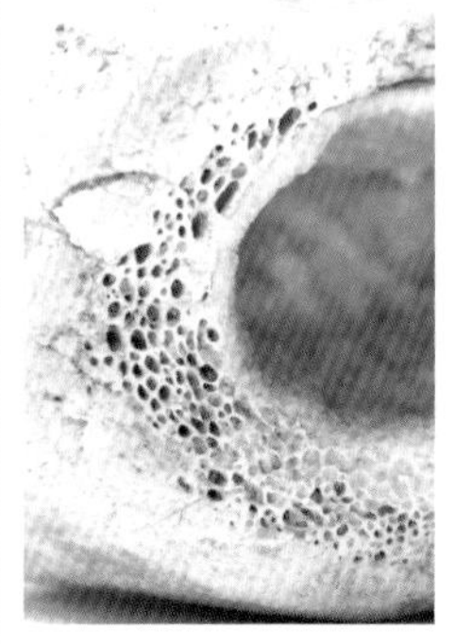

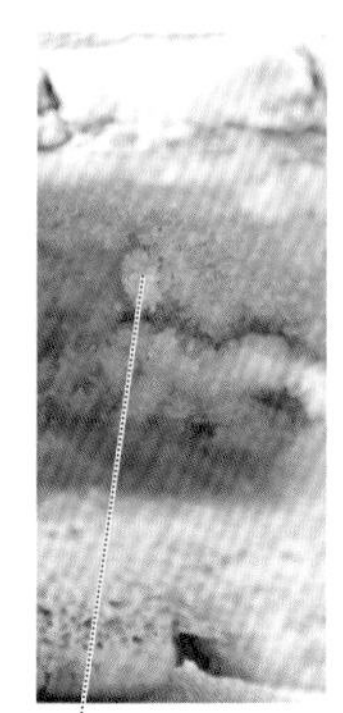

Diodontidae Upper and Lower Tooth Batteries Tooth batteries of porcupinefish and burrfish. The tooth projections on upper batteries are anteriorly angled with straight sides, while lowers arc smoothly along the anterior side. The lower-right image shows the difference between ***Chilomycterus*** (left) and ***Diodon*** (right) tooth batteries.

Distal Notch, Hammerhead Teeth
Distal notch on a hammerhead (*Sphyrna* spp.) shark tooth. Note the lack of serrations along the cutting edges and the sharp angle of the notch. Compare to the gradual distal curve of *Carcharhinus* teeth, pages 85–87, which have serrated edges.

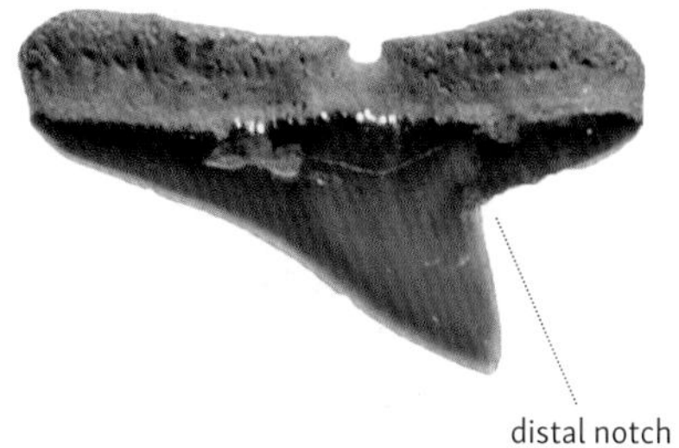

Dolphin Humerus, Articular Ends
Proximal (*top*) and distal (*bottom*) articular surfaces of a Miocene eurhinodelphinid humerus. The corresponding specimen can be seen on page 134.

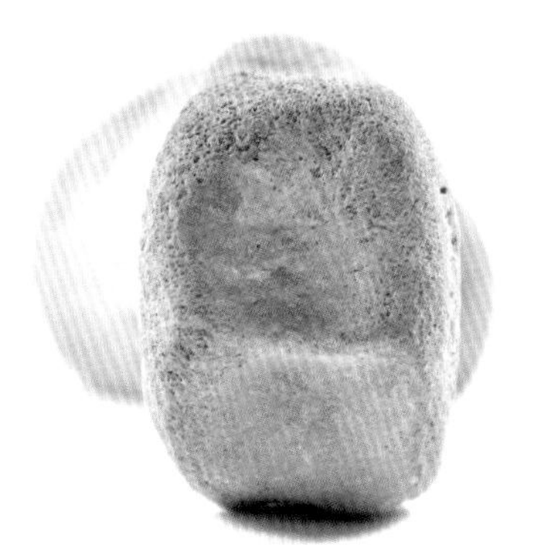

Ectoflexid: *Equus* sp. Teeth Three ectoflexids observed in lower cheek teeth of a horse, genus *Equus*. The ectoflexid is a fold in the enamel, pointing inward on the occlusal surface, from the labial side of the tooth.

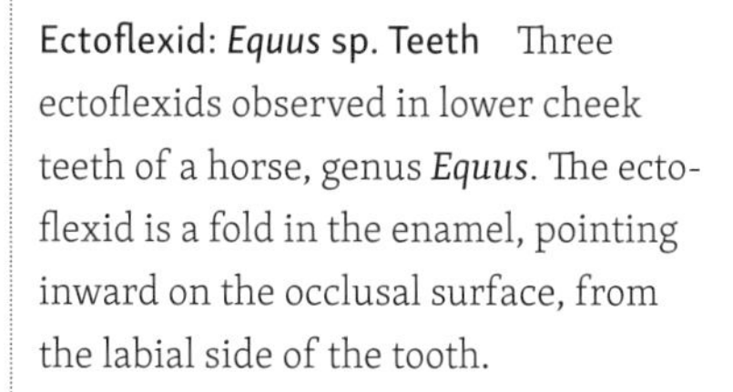

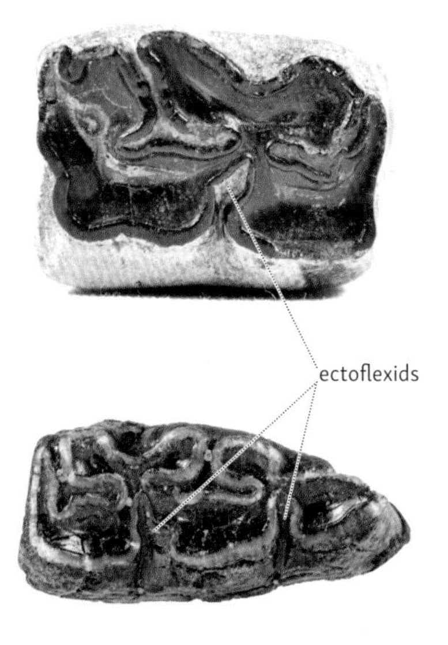

Enamel Patterns: *Bison* and *Equus* Comparison Occlusal view of bison (B) molars and premolars, and horse (E) cheek teeth. Note the simple shapes of bison enamel and the intricate, sinusoidal patterns on horse (*Equus* sp.) teeth.

Enamel: Crenulated Two views of mammoth (*Mammuthus* sp.) tooth enamel showing the crenulated pattern. The crenulations are the vertical lines and ripples in the enamel.

Fish Skeletal Material Fragments of fish opercular and cranial material.

Gar Fish Cranial Material Detail of the cranial bones and scales on a modern gar fish (*Lepisosteus* sp.) skeleton.

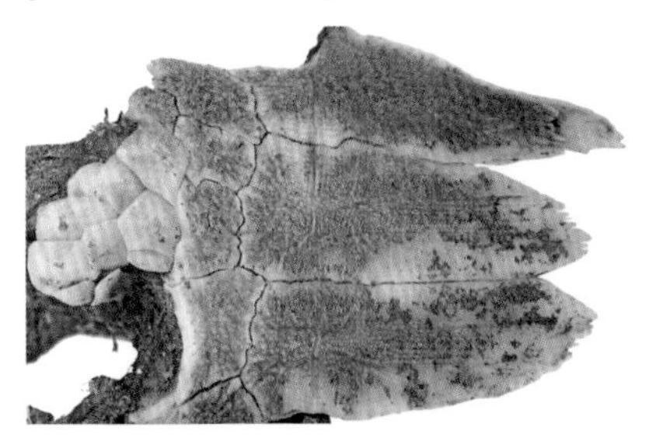

Gar Fish Scale Articulation Articulated scales on a living gar fish (*Lepisosteus osseus*).

Giant Tortoise Leg Spurs Giant tortoise (*Hesperotestudo* spp.) leg spurs.

Hyperostosed Neurocrania Shapes Four swollen cranial bones in multiple views. The images in each column are of one bone. See page 396 for a complete specimen.

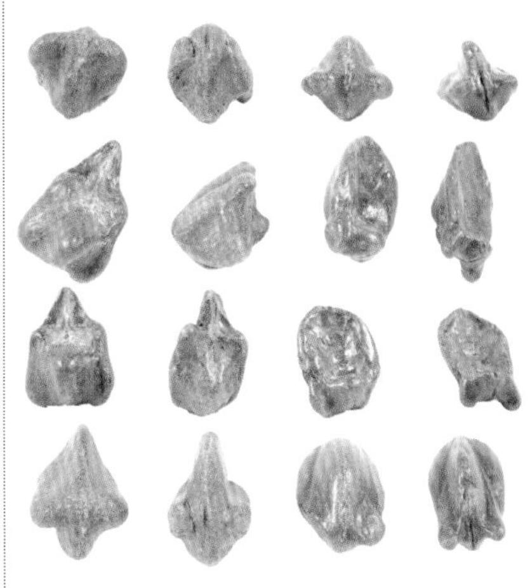

Incisors: Capybara and Giant Beaver Comparison *Top* Detail of a capybara (*Neochoerus* sp.) incisor. *Bottom* Detail of a giant beaver (*Castoroides* sp.) incisor.

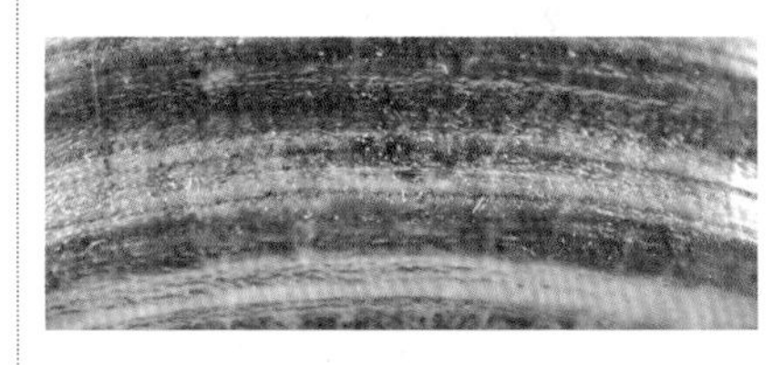

Interactions between Species: After Fossilization *Left, middle* water-worn bone fragment with holes made by drilling bivalves (Pholadidae), which are capable of boring through rock. *Right* bone fragment colonized by northern star coral (*Astrangia poculata*).

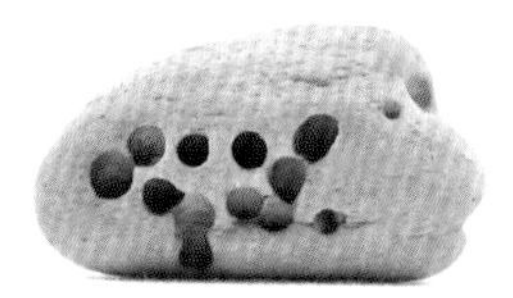
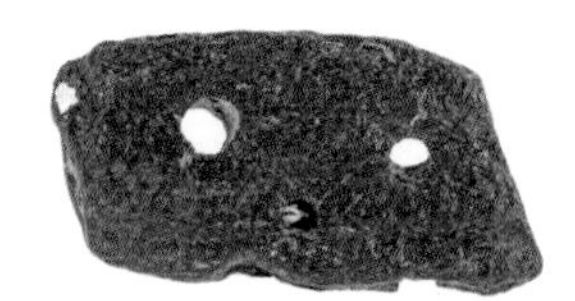

Interactions between Species: Before Fossilization Evidence of interactions between extinct animals before death or fossilization.

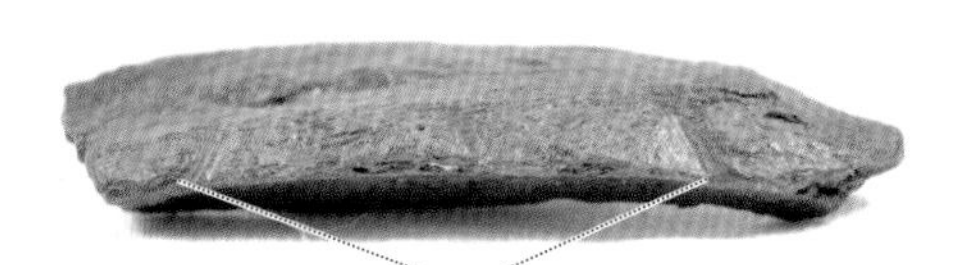

Carving by Paleo-Indians

Predation puncture holes

Predation scrapes

Rodent gnawing

Mandible: Alligator Fragment of an alligator (*Alligator mississippiensis*) mandible. It can be identified by the oblique foramina (holes) along the length of the dentary. These holes allowed for passage of sensors through the bone to the outer skin.

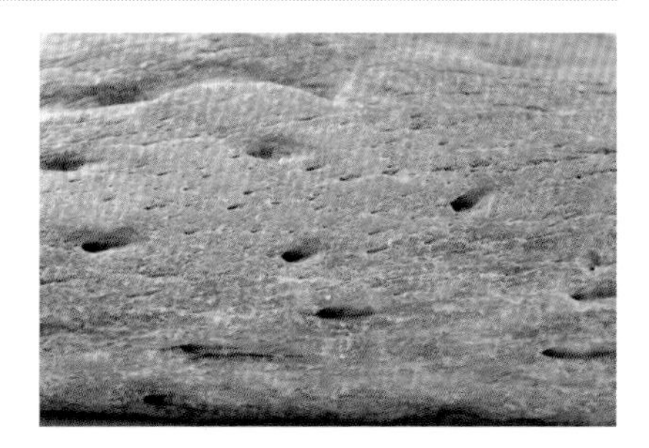

Matrix-Encased Specimens *Left* sea robin (*Prionotus* sp.) skull contained in coquina. *Right* Extinct megatoothed shark (*Carcharocles megalodon*) tooth in the original conglomerate where fossilization took place.

Metapodial: *Equus*, Proximal End Proximal view of a horse (*Equus*) metapodial. See page 144 for the corresponding specimen.

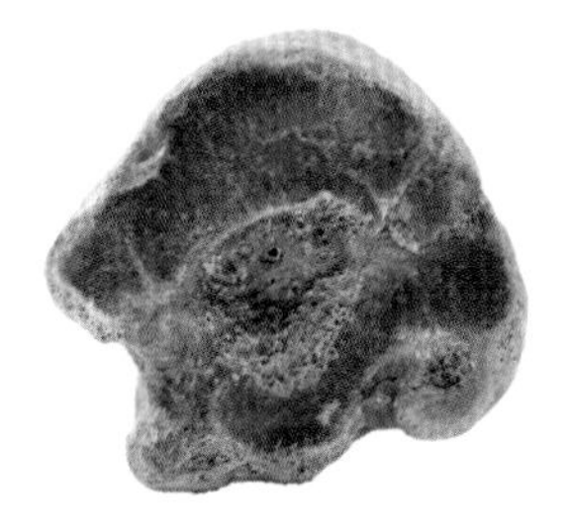

Osteoderm: Alligator, Ventral Design Detail of the ventral side of an alligator (*Alligator mississippiensis*) osteoderm. Fragments can be identified by the woven, fiberglass-like appearance on the ventral surface. These woven marks are the remnants of former fascia attachment sites.

Pathological Deformities When a bone, tooth, or other anatomical part has an altered morphology (shape) caused by malnourishment, disease, illness, genetics, or injury, the specimen is considered "pathological." The *Carcharocles auriculatus* tooth (*top*) has a kinked cutting edge, possibly from overcrowding in the jaw, an injury incurred while the tooth formed, or a birth defect. The *Squalicorax* tooth (*bottom two*) is almost buckled in on itself, likely from overcrowding.

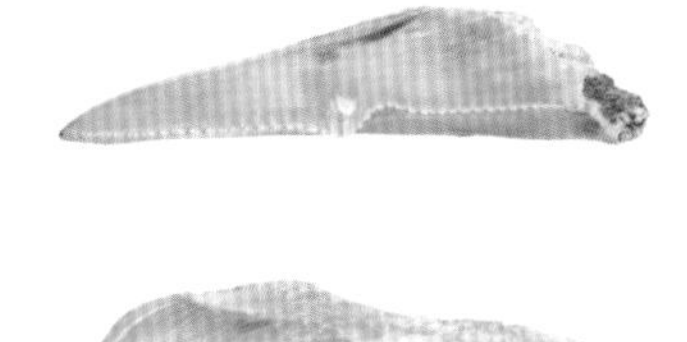

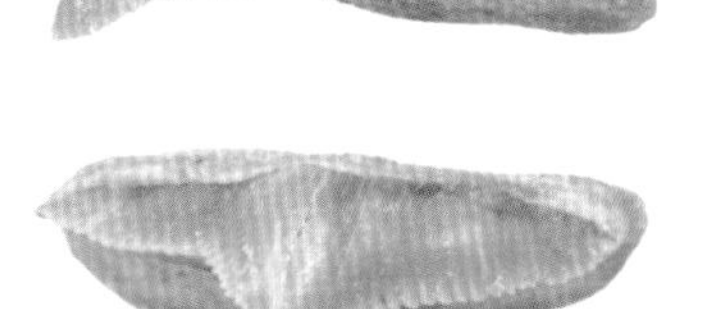

Peccary Tusk Detail Detail of the occluding surface of a peccary (*Platygonus compressus*) upper canine. Note the dual beveled edges (indicated) where the lower tusk and incisors abraded against the upper tusk.

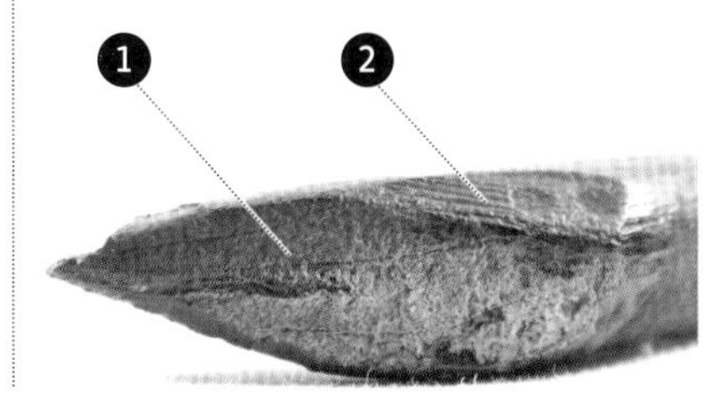

Pharyngeal Grinding Mill Unfossilized grinding mill from the extant black drum, *Pogonias cromis*, in occlusal view (anterior to left).

Pottery: Embedded Fiber Detail of Native American pottery showing evidence of incorporated Spanish moss, used to strengthen the clay.

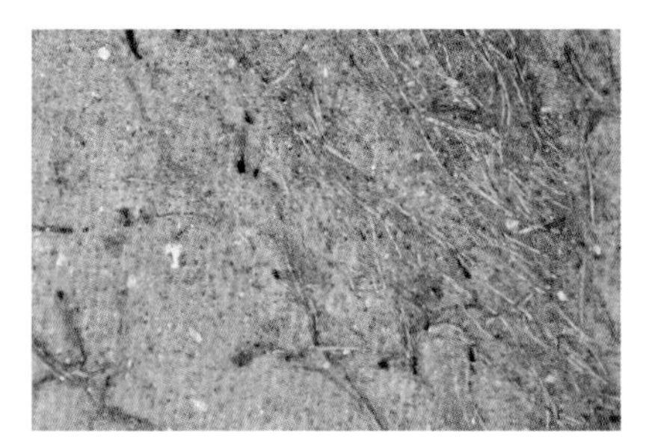

Primitive Dentition State Occlusal view of the dentition of the extant raccoon, *Procyon lotor*. See the note about primitive dentition in the next entry.

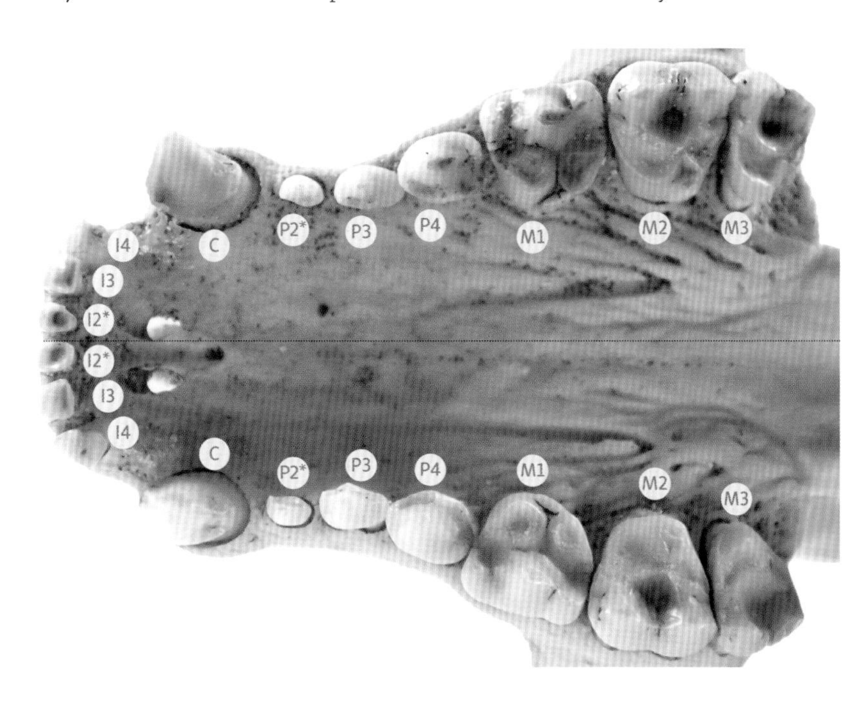

Primitive Dentition State (*cont.*) Unfossilized left mandible from the extant white-tailed deer, *Odocoileus virginianus*.

The primitive mammalian dentition had a fourth incisor classified as the *first* incisor (I1 upper and i1 lower), and a fourth premolar classified as the *first* premolar (P1/p1), both lost in later evolutionary groups. Instead of reclassifying all mammalian dentition (I1, I2, I3, or P1, P2, P3), the primitive state is used, and the original assignments (I2, I3, I4, and P2, P3, P4) are retained without shifting the numbering of the teeth.

In animals such as sloths and armadillos, the numbering system is modified. Since these creatures do not have teeth classifiable as premolars, molars, incisors, or canines, the letter prefixes I, C, P, and M are replaced with N, and the numbering starts with the anterior-most tooth and continues posteriorly (N1, N2, N3, N4 . . .).

Such a system is also applied to digit numbering. For example, modern horses have one metapodial, which they stand on; evolutionarily, this digit is the third (middlemost) metapodial. Rather than labeling this retained metapodial as the first digit, scientists maintain the continuity of evolutionary history by calling it the third metapodial.

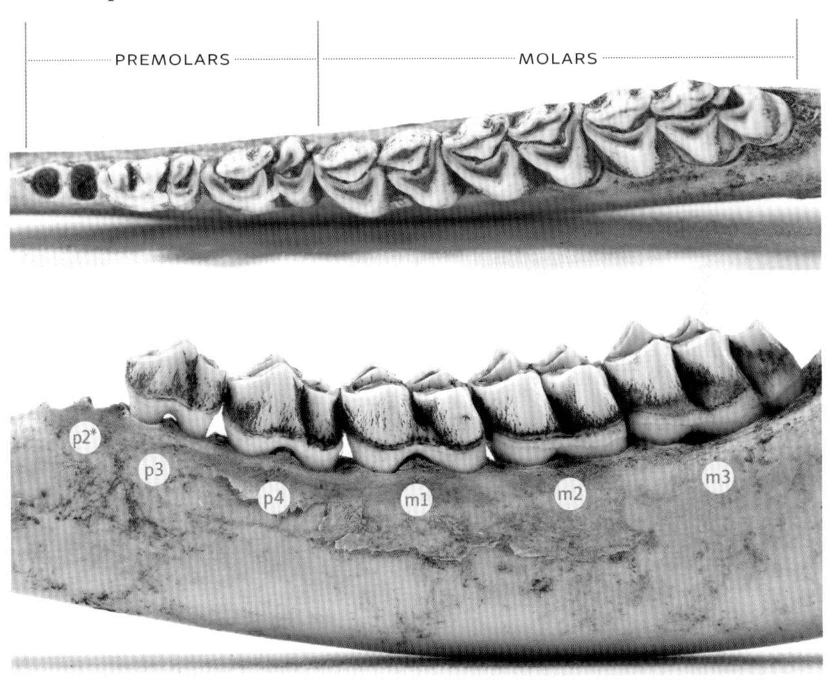

***Procyon lotor* Occipital Condyles** Oblique ventral (*left*) and posterior (*right*) views of a raccoon (*Procyon lotor*) skull. The occipital condyles (indicated) in the center of the skull are the points of articulation for the atlas vertebra (page 348).

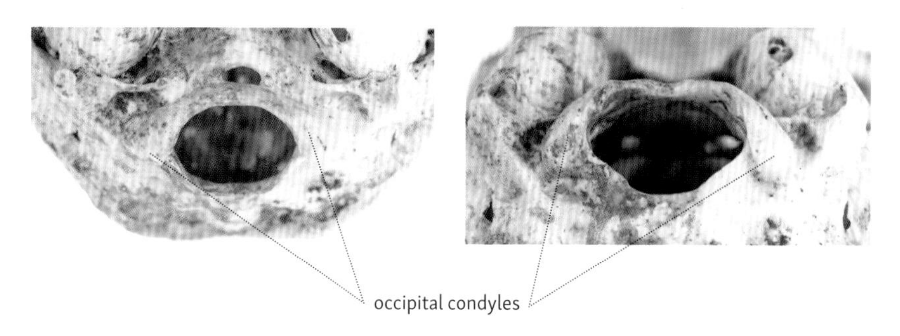

Ratfish Tritors Detail of the tritors on ratfish (*Ischyodus dolloi*) mouth plates.

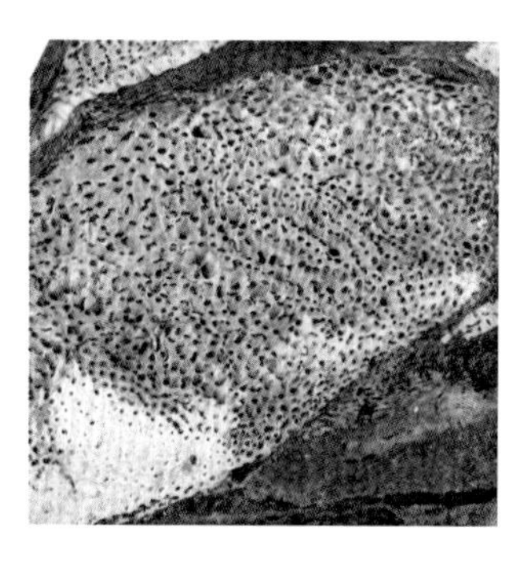

Sea Robin Skull Composite complete skull plate from a sea robin (*Prionotus* sp.). *Left*: frontal plate; *right*: rear plate.

Schreger Pattern Unique cross-hatching pattern observed on ivory from proboscideans. This pattern is formed by the growth rings of dentinal tubules in ivory tusks. Lines are included to help with visualization of the pattern.

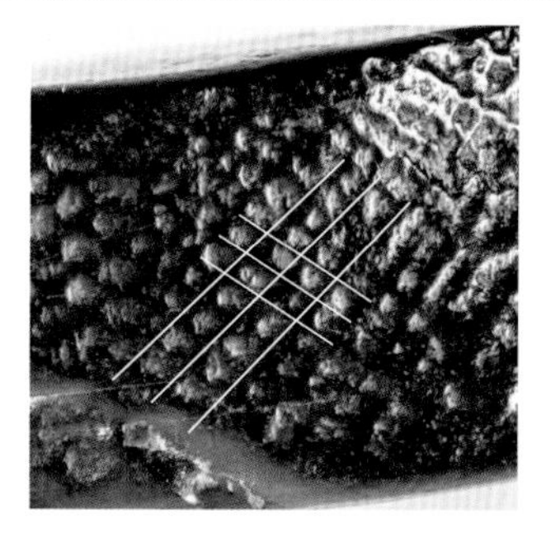

Shark Teeth Serrations Degrees of serrations found on shark teeth. *From top to bottom*: no serrations (0 serrations / mm), extremely fine (4+ serrations / mm), fine (3–4 serrations / mm); medium (2–3 serrations / mm), coarse (1–2 serrations / mm), extremely coarse (0–1 serrations / mm).

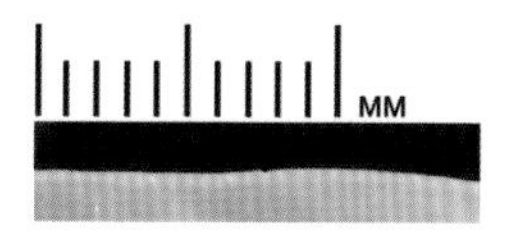

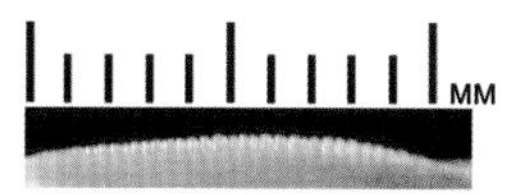

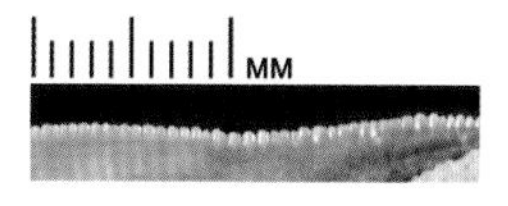

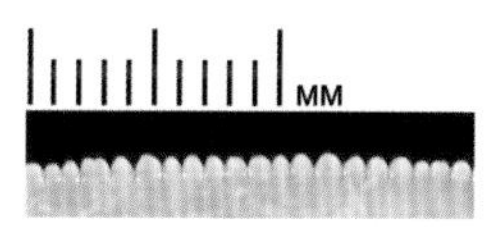

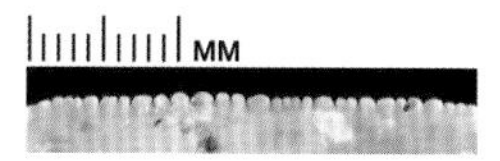

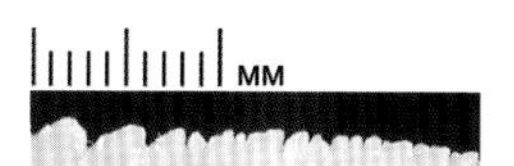

Shark Teeth Serrations: Doubly Serrate Distal shoulder of a modern tiger shark (*Galeocerdo cuvier*) tooth. Note the predominant serrations, with finer serrations visible in the valley of each serration.

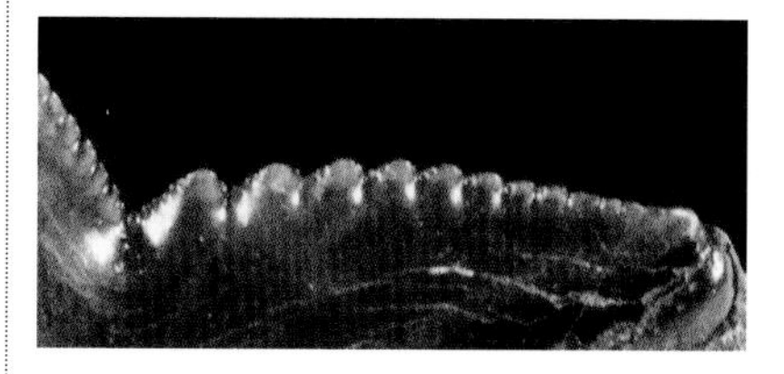

Shark Teeth: Great White and Megalodon Comparison Comparison of two similarly sized shark teeth. *Left*: great white (*Carcharodon carcharias*); *right*: megalodon (*Carcharocles megalodon*). Note the wide dental band (bourlette) on the *C. megalodon* tooth (indicated).

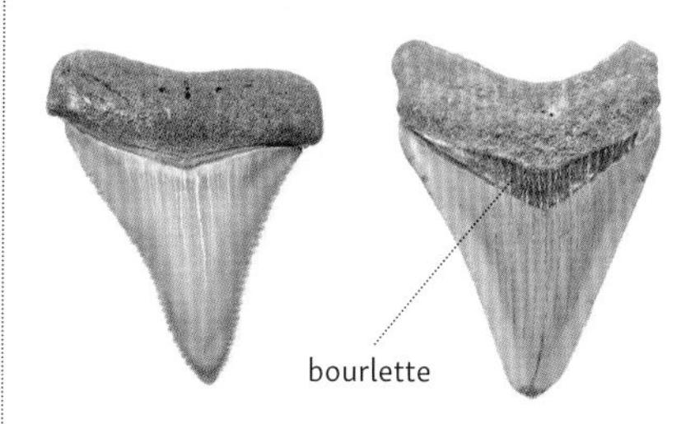

Shark Teeth: Megalodon Size Range
Not all *Carcharocles megalodon* teeth were large. Posterior teeth (*far right*) were small, to accommodate closure of the jaw. Lateral teeth ranged in size between the anterior and posterior teeth.

Shark Teeth: *Striatolamia striata* and *Carcharias taurus* Comparison

Extinct mackerel shark | *Striatolamia striata*

Extant sand tiger shark | *Carcharias taurus*

Shark Tooth: Cow Shark Upper lateral tooth of a cow shark (*Notorynchus primigenius*) (page 100) in lateral view, displaying the raised ridge (indicated) at the crown base, which tapers to the base of the root.

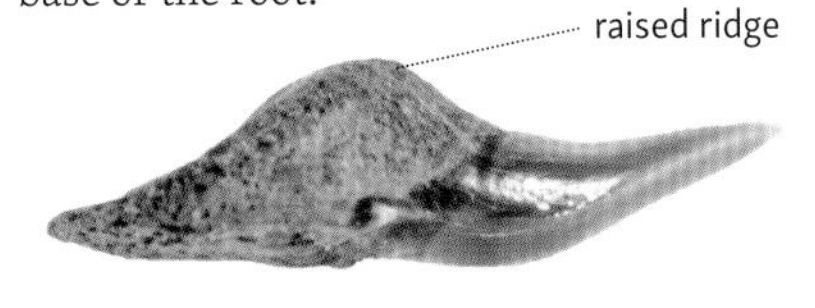

Shark Tooth: Extinct Pygmy White
Intact tooth from the extinct pygmy white shark, *Palaeocarcharodon orientalis*, showing extremely coarse serrations, a thin dental band, and the crude lateral cusplets, characteristic of the species. This specimen is from Morocco.

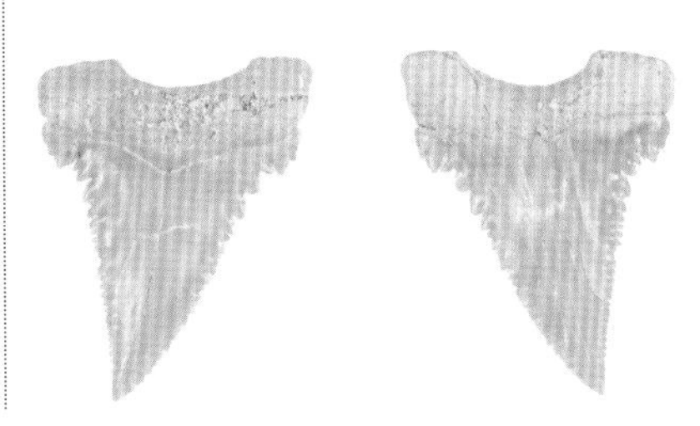

Shark Tooth: ***Physogaleus contortus*** Lateral views of a longtooth tiger shark tooth, displaying the contorted mesial edge, from which the species name was derived.

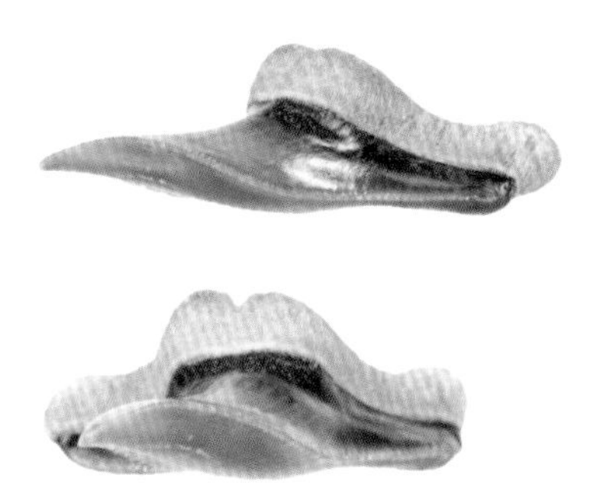

Shell Patterns: Aquatic Turtle and Land Turtle Aquatic turtle shell (*top, middle*) bearing a rippled, rugose pattern; the smooth land turtle shell (*bottom*) has only occasional scute lines visible on fragments.

Sperm Whale Teeth Both observed types of sperm whale teeth. Some genera have reduced enamel crowns and large, bulbous roots (*top*), while whales in the *Physeterula* and *Kogiopsis* genera have narrow teeth made of dentine and cement (*bottom*).

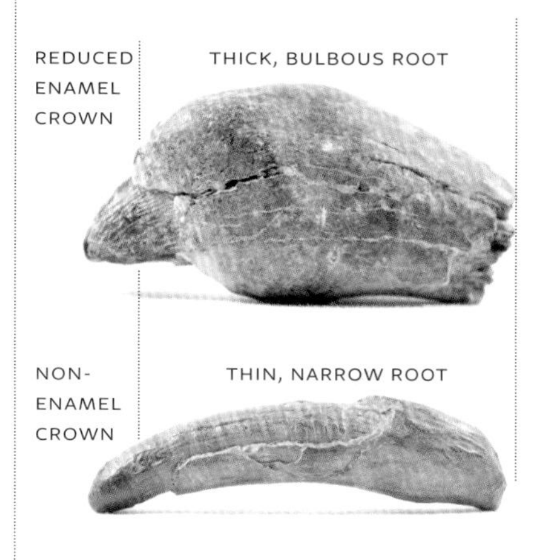

Sutured Edges Sutured turtle bone edges (1 and 2) compared with a fractured piece (3) showing the trabeculae inside the bone.

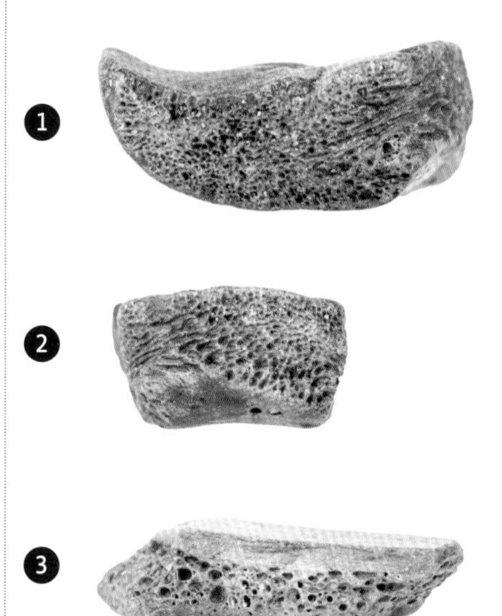

Tooth Morphology: Mammalian
Tooth morphologies referred to in this book. See the Glossary for explanations.

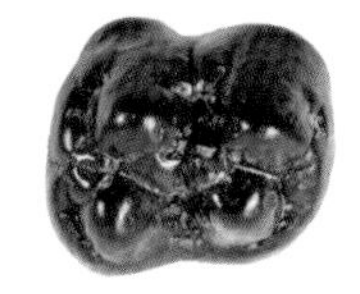
Bunodont

Brachyodont

Selenodont

Hypselodont

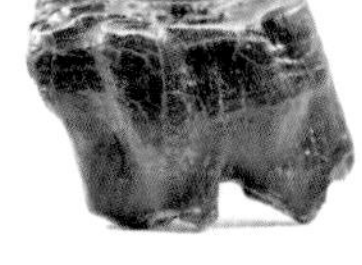
Hypsodont

Lophodont

Trefoil Pattern Occlusal detail from a gomphothere (*Cuvieronius*) molar displaying the cloverleaf trefoil pattern found in most gomphothere molars. Specimen courtesy of the South Carolina Department of Natural Resources, Botany Bay Plantation Wildlife Management Area, Edisto Island, South Carolina.

Vertebral Centrum Classifications
Acoelous: lacking any concavity or convexity; amphicoelous: concave on both sides; procoelous: anteriorly concave, posteriorly convex; opisthocoelous: anteriorly convex, posteriorly concave; heterocoelous: saddle-shaped articulations. Note: anterior is to the right in all images.

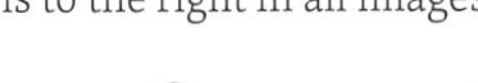

POSTERIOR

Acoelous

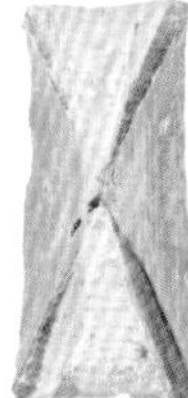
Amphicoelous

Procoelous

Opisthocoelous

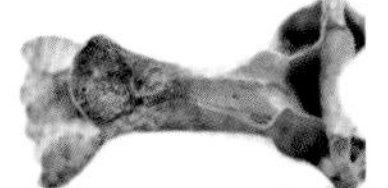
Heterocoelous

ANTERIOR

Water Wear Heavily water-worn *Bison antiquus* astragalus. See page 149 for a more complete specimen. Note the areas of exposed cancellous bone, where higher ridges were present on the original bone surface.

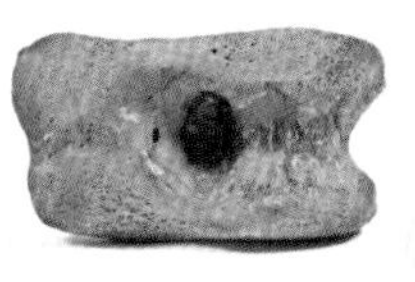

Glossary

acetabulum The cup-shaped socket in a pelvic bone that articulates with the proximal end of the femur.

acoelous A vertebral centrum with anterior and posterior surfaces that are flat rather than convex or concave; compare *amphicoelous* and *procoelous*.

amphicoelous A vertebral centrum with anterior and posterior surfaces that are concave rather than convex or flat.

analogous structure A structure in different organisms that provides the same function, even though the species do not share a common ancestor (e.g., dolphin flippers and fish fins, the jointed legs of vertebrates and arthropods); compare *homologous structures*.

anterior Forward section or front end of an organism; compare *posterior*.

anteroposterior 1. Relating to both the front and the rear of an anatomical part. 2. Area extending from front to back along an axis, such as a spinal column.

anuran Pertaining to the order Anura, which includes the frogs and toads.

apatite A mineral that makes up the teeth of extinct and modern sharks; also called *calcium phosphate*.

apex predator A species at the top of the food pyramid, particularly one that is not preyed on by any other organism (e.g., wolves, lions, crocodilians); also called an *alpha predator*.

apical Referring to the tip of a rounded or pyramidal structure of an anatomical part such as a bone or a tooth.

appendicular Pertaining to the cartilage and bones that make up the limbs, or appendages, of a skeleton; compare *axial*.

archaeocete Primitive cetacean of the suborder Archaeoceti, whose members lived from the Early Eocene to the Late Oligocene Epoch.

articular surfaces The points where adjacent bones meet.
articulation The interlocking of adjoining bones (e.g., vertebra to vertebra, astragalus to tibia, phalanx to phalanx).
artiodactyls Even-toed ungulates, which compose the order Artiodactyla (e.g., pigs, camels, peccaries, deer, bison, and llamas).
astragalus One of the proximal bones of the tarsus; commonly known as the ankle bone in higher vertebrates.
atlas The first cervical (C1) vertebra, which supports the skull and enables forward and backward movement of the neck; named for the Greek god Atlas, who supported the Earth on his shoulders.
auditory bulla A hollow, bulbous bone that receives sound waves; located on the rear ventral side of an animal's skull.
axial Pertaining to the central skeletal region (as opposed to the pelvis and extremities), which includes the skull, its internal bones, the sternum, the rib cage, and the vertebral column.
axis The second cervical (C2) vertebra, which articulates with the atlas (C1). The axis enables side-to-side rotation of the neck.

bilateral symmetry The arrangement of an organism's body parts in which each part, right and left of a line bisecting the organism, is a mirror image of the other.
bilobate Divided into two halves or lobes.
bilophodont Pertaining to the crown of a tooth molar that has two ridges; see *cusp*.
bivalve A mollusk made up of two shells that are connected by a hinge and that protect soft internal tissues (e.g., arks, mussels, clams, and oysters).
bourlette A strip of thin enamel on a shark tooth, often V-shaped and located just above the main cusp.
brachyodont Describing permanent teeth that have short crowns, often shorter than the roots; also called brachydont.
bulla See *auditory bulla*.
bunodont Describing a tooth with rounded cusps or cones.

calcaneum The heel bone. Largest of the tarsal bones, it articulates proximally with the astragalus and distally with the cuboid.
calcareous Consisting of calcium, calcium carbonate, or limestone.
calcium phosphate See *apatite*.
callosity A raised area appearing as a lobe or bump on an anatomical part such as a bone or tooth.
cancellous Having a porous structure of cells forming a spongy or mesh-like matrix in the center of bones.
carapace The dorsal section of an animal shell structure, usually of a turtle, made up of the dermal bone, ribcage, and spine.
carbonization Process by which soft animal parts and plant leaves decompose in

water and oxygen; the hydrogen and nitrogen within them are driven off, but the carbon remains.

carnassial Pertaining to the paired set of upper and lower molars, and sometimes premolars, in some carnivoran species. These teeth meet in a scissor-like manner in order to shear through, rather than bite down on, prey. The abrading action caused by this shearing motion results in the self-sharpening of the teeth in some species.

carnivoran Any member of the order Carnivora, which includes placental mammals that feed entirely or mostly on meat.

carpal Any one of the eight bones of the carpus; commonly known as the wrist bones in higher vertebrates.

cartilage Soft connective tissue often found between bones in joints. Sharks, rays, and other fish have skeletons made of cartilage. In humans, noses and ears are made of this soft tissue.

cartilaginous Of or pertaining to cartilage.

cast A type of fossil in which a shell or other hollow part is filled with sediment and minerals, leaving a solid form of the original structure after it erodes or dissolves away.

caudal Pertaining to the tail or to the tail bones, as in caudal vertebrae.

cementum Calcified material made mostly of collagen that covers teeth (especially the roots) and attaches them to the jawbone; also called *cement*. Cementum is softer than dentine and enamel.

Cenozoic era The geologic age beginning 66 million years ago (Ma) and extending to the present day.

centrum The main body of a vertebra. The vertebral processes are outwardly projected from it.

cephalic Pertaining to the head.

cervical Pertaining to the first seven vertebrae, which form the neck portion of a spinal column.

cetacean A member of the order Cetacea, marine mammals such as whales, dolphins, and porpoises. This order has been proposed as an infraorder in recent discussions of scientific classification.

chondrostean Pertaining to the class of ray-finned fishes of two orders, Acipenseriformes (sturgeons and paddlefish) and Polypteriformes (reedfishes and bichirs). Chondrosteans have mostly cartilaginous skeletons but also some bony parts.

cingulum An enamel ridge found on the crown of teeth (cuspids or incisors); it may be either V-shaped or W-shaped.

cladistics Biological classification system that defines a group of organisms based on traits shared with a common ancestor but not the preceding ancestor.

cladogram A diagram displaying the relationships of living organisms to one another; from the Greek *clados* (branch).

conchoidal A type of fracture found in rocks with small crystal sizes (quartz, chert, flint, glass). The fractures are curving, arced, C-shaped breaks that often produce flakes with extremely sharp edges.

concretion A buildup of hard mineral composition derived from an aqueous deposition within a rock material dissimilar from the mineral. Spheroid or irregular in shape, concretions form around a nucleus, which may be made up of a variety of materials.

coprolite Fossilized excrement; from the Greek *kopros* (dung) and *lithikos* (stone).

coracoid In mammalian skeletons, a process extending from the scapula to the sternum. In reptiles and birds, the coracoid bone is separate from, but articulates with, the sternum and scapula.

cosmoid scales Fish scales found on prehistoric lobe-finned fishes, such as early lungfishes, and on extant but rare coelocanths. These scales have alternately dense and spongy inner bone layers covered by an outer layer of cosmine.

costal Pertaining to the ribs or to a rib-like part.

crazed Containing a pattern or network of fine cracks.

crenulations Wavy or rounded ridges and valleys appearing on some molar teeth, such as those of mammoths, bison, camelids, and deer.

ctenoid scales Fish scales with a comblike pattern at the outer, nonoverlapping edge. "Ctenoid" comes from the Greek root *kten-*, meaning "comb."

cubonavicular A fused pair of tarsal bones: the cuboid, located on the outer side of the foot, and the navicular, toward the inside; found only in ruminants, such as deer, cows, and bison.

cuneiform Any of three bones located side by side and toward the inside of the foot; they articulate with the metatarsals anteriorly and the cuboid and navicular bones posteriorly.

cusp A pointed or rounded projection on the chewing surface of a tooth. Molars may have two or more cusps.

cusplet 1. A small cusp. 2. A small sharp or rounded projection at the base of a shark tooth.

cuspule A small tubercule occurring on the occlusal end of molars, such as those of peccaries.

cycloid scales Fish scales with concentric circular lines parallel to the outer, nonoverlapping edge of the scale. Their pattern is reminiscent of the elevation lines on a contour map.

deciduous Pertaining to the primary teeth (also known as temporary, baby, or milk teeth) in young diphyodont mammals. These teeth are lost and replaced by permanent teeth as the animal matures.

dental band See *bourlette*.

dental battery See *tooth battery*.

dentary 1. Pertaining to teeth. 2. The anterior bone of the lower jaw, which bears the teeth.

denticle 1. A small tooth or tooth-like projection. 2. A placoid scale.

dentine The primary component of most teeth, made up of apatite crystals (calcium and phosphate); harder than cementum but softer than enamel; also called *dentin*.

dermal bone A bone formed by ossification of the skin; also called *ossicle*.

dermal denticles See *placoid scales*.

diastema The space separating teeth having different functions, such as incisors, canines, and molars.

dignathic Pertaining to variation in teeth in the upper and lower jaws; generally used in relation to sharks; compare *monognathic*.

diphyodont Pertaining to animals that grow two successive sets of teeth. The early, deciduous teeth are later replaced by permanent teeth.

distal 1. Farthest from the point of origin; used primarily in reference to limb bones. The origin refers roughly to the center of the body (e.g., the tibia is distal to the pelvis in comparison with the femur, which is closer to that point of origin); compare *proximal*. 2. Regarding shark teeth, the side of the tooth facing toward the rear of the mouth; compare *mesial*.

dorsal Pertaining to the upper side or back; compare *ventral*.

ectoflexid See the Illustrated Glossary.

elasmobranch A cartilaginous fish of the subclass Elasmobranchii. This group includes sharks and rays.

elasmoid scales Thin fish scales overlapping in the manner of shingles. These scales are composed of lamellar bone covered by a layer of tubercles, or bumps, usually derived from bone.

electroreception The ability of animals, particularly saltwater species, to detect weak electric impulses from other marine animals.

enamel The hardest and densest organic tissue in the body, making up the cusps (or crowns) of most teeth. Like dentine, enamel contains mostly hydroxyapatite crystals and very little protein.

enameloid A hypermineralized structure found in some fish scales and teeth; it may have evolved into modern tooth enamel. The enameloid condition, though still not clearly understood, is somewhat different from enamel.

entoplastron The median plate of the plastron (lower shell) of a turtle; considered homologous with the interclavicle of other reptilian species.

Eocene The geologic epoch extending from 56 million years ago (Ma) to 33.9 Ma.

epiphysis A bone disc separated from the ends of developing bones by cartilage. Once an individual reaches maturity, these discs fuse with the ends of the developed bones.

epiphyseal Pertaining to an epiphysis.

epoch A unit of geologic time smaller than a period (e.g., the Pleistocene epoch is contained within the Quaternary period).

Equus The genus of horses, zebras, and donkeys; the only extant genus within the family Equidae.

era A unit of geologic time smaller than an eon but larger than a period (e.g., the Cenozoic era is part of the Phanerozoic eon).

estuarine Relating to the lower or coastal part of a river body where it meets with tidally influenced waters.

extant Referring to currently living species; compare *extinct*.

external auditory meatus The tubular passage in mammals that runs from the outer ear to the tympanic membrane of the middle ear. This tube is often visible as a hole in the petrous (densest) portion of fossilized temporal bones.

extinct Referring to species that no longer exist. Extinction usually occurs from drastic environmental changes such as rapid cooling or warming events, food source losses, or changes in predator-prey dynamics; compare *extant*.

file A row of teeth in a shark's jaw from the medial position at the symphysis to the distal position at the back of the jaw. One file refers to a row on either the left side or the right side of a shark's jaw, but not both.

flex plate Moveable osteoderms in the armor of extinct and extant armadillo-like species of the superorder Xenarthra.

foramen See *nutrient foramen*.

fossette 1. An inner pocket of enamel observed to plicate, or fold, in the upper molars, especially in equine genera. 2. A depression in a bivalve shell to which the chitinous hinge ligament is anchored.

fossil The naturally preserved remains or trace of an animal or plant that lived in the geologic past.

fossiliferous Containing or yielding fossils; often used to refer to rock layers, as in fossiliferous limestone.

fossilization Generally, the process of organic tissues being preserved or replaced by minerals over time; see also *casts*; *molds*; *permineralization*; *recrystallization*.

ganoid Pertaining to primitive fish scales derived from bones and containing ganoine, a substance giving a shiny, enamel-like appearance to the outer surface.

ganoine Enamel-like substance found in the scales of some ray-finned fishes such as gar fish. The multiple layers of apatite microcrystals in ganoine give the scales and bones of such fishes a glassy appearance.

gastropod A mollusk having one shell protecting a soft-tissue body (e.g., snails, whelks, conchs).

genus Plural: *genera*. The classification division that is below family or subfamily and made up of one or more lower ranks called species.

glauconite A marine mineral making up the steinkerns of some trace fossils, gastropods, and bivalves. Glauconite muds are characteristic of the sediments on the continental shelf.

Great American Biotic Interchange An exchange of fauna between North and South America made possible by the formation of the Panamanian Land Bridge. The height of the exchange occurred around 3 million years ago.

grinding plate A dental palate that stingrays, spotted eagle rays, and parrotfish, puffer fish, burrfish, and porcupinefish use to crush and grind food.

groin Also spelled *groyne*. A wall or jetty built from rocks or concrete and extending out into a river, bay, or ocean to prevent the movement of sediment by currents or wave action.

hemal arch The opening formed by several V-shaped bones growing from the ventral portion of a vertebral centrum. These bones project from the third to sixth coccygeal (tail) vertebrae to form the arch, which encloses the caudal blood vessels.

heterocoelous A vertebral centrum that has saddle-shaped articular surfaces.

heterodonty Referring to animals having more than one type of tooth, such as incisors, premolars, and molars.

Holocene The current epoch of geologic time, extending from 11,700 years ago to the present. It is defined by the warming period that has followed since the last glaciation event.

homodonty Referring to animals having teeth that are all of one type, such as molars.

homologous structures Organs or features in different animals that suggest a common ancestor or evolutionary origin based on their physical similarity, even if their function or appearance may be different (e.g., bat wings and human arms); compare *analogous structures*.

homoplasy A feature or characteristic shared by two or more organisms that do not share a common ancestor (e.g., eyes, which have repeatedly evolved but at separate times).

humerus The upper arm bone of vertebrates. It articulates proximally with the scapula and distally with the radius and ulna of the lower arm.

hyoplastron The second lateral bony plate making up the plastron (lower shell) of a turtle.

hyperostosis An excessive growth of bone giving the bone an uncharacteristic appearance, as in the hyperostotic vertebrae called "Tilly bones" in some fish.

hypoplastron The third lateral bony plate making up the plastron (lower shell) of a turtle.

hypselodont Cheek teeth found in lagomorphs and some rodents that grow continuously throughout the animal's life. Specialized stem cells at the tooth base constantly mineralize enamel to create the ever-growing teeth, which lack roots.

hypsodont Pertaining to teeth that have high crowns of enamel and low, short roots attached to the jawbone.

hypural bone The posterior-most bone at the end of a fish spine; the caudal fin rays are attached to it.

incisor A sharp-edged, angled tooth located at the front of the mouth; its primary function is for biting and cutting.

infraorbital Referring to an area or structure beneath (inferior to) the orbit, or eye socket (e.g., the infraorbital artery, infraorbital nerve, and infraorbital sinus).

infundibulum A usually funnel-shaped anatomical opening, passage, or structure. In premolars or molars, the infundibulum appears as an opening in a tooth crown as its cusps become greatly worn down.

inner ear bone Common name for a structure within the petrous portion of the temporal bone in an animal ear.

insectivoran Any member of the order Insectivora, which includes mammals that feed on insects (e.g. moles, shrews, and hedgehogs).

in situ Latin for *on site* or *at the site of*.

intraspecific variation Dissimilarities among individuals of the same species.

ivory An extremely dense, modified form of dentine that composes the tusks of elephants, gomphotheres, and walruses.

keratin A protein that makes up hair, fingernails, and scutes.

labial Pertaining to the forward face of a tooth, directed away from or out of the mouth.

lagomorph Any member of the order Lagomorpha, which includes rabbits, hares, and pikas.

lamniform Pertaining to sharks of the order Lamniformes, which includes the mackerel sharks.

lamnoid design Having the shape or other characteristics of sharks in the order Lamniformes or family Lamnidae; compare *scyliorhinoid design*.

lateral Referring to either the left or the right side, often in regard to the location of skeletal or dental parts an animal.

lateral cusplet A small toothlike projection occurring on either side of the crown base of a shark tooth.

leptoid scales Scales occurring in the group of fish known as teleosts. The scales, which increase in size through the growth of concentric rings, overlap each other like roof shingles in a manner that reduces drag as the fish move through water. Leptoid scales occur in two forms, cycloid and ctenoid.

lingual Pertaining to the rear face of a tooth, directed toward the inner, or throat, portion of the mouth.

lobate Having lobes; lobed.

loph A single ridge or plate projecting from the crown of a molar.

lophodont Pertaining to the molars of ungulates having two or more transverse ridges along the tooth crown; see also *bilophodont*, *trilophodont*, and *tetralophodont*.

lumbar Refers to the lower spinal region.

Ma (abbr.) Million years ago.

mandible The lower jaw or jawbone in a vertebrate skull.

marginal Occurring along the margin or edge of a bone, tooth, or other structure.

marl A loose, easily pulverized mix of lime-rich muds that may be derived from marine or lake sediments. Its calcium carbonate component usually comes from calcite, but may also come from dolomite, aragonite, or siderite.

marsupial Member of the infraclass Marsupialia, which includes mammals that are born in a relatively undeveloped form and finish developing while being carried in a pouch (e.g., opossums, kangaroos, and wallabies). Once considered an order, this classification has been broken down by scientists into several subdivisions.

masticate To crush or grind food through the use of teeth.

matrix The fine-grained background material in rocks within which larger grains, pebbles, or mineral crystals are embedded.

maxilla The upper jawbone or cheekbone. (Though also a structure of insects, maxilla when used in this book refers only to the vertebrate jawbone.)

medial Referring to the middle or to an area close to the middle.

megalodon Common name for the prehistoric megashark *Carcharocles megalodon*, whose generic name is still under discussion by paleontologists.

mesial Regarding shark teeth, the side of a tooth facing the front of the mouth; compare *distal*.

metacarpal One of five long bones in the upper extremities (hands or forefeet) of vertebrates; they articulate with the wrist bones (carpals) and finger bones (phalanges).

metapodial Referring to both the metatarsal and metacarpal bones.

metatarsal One of five long bones in the lower extremities (feet or hind feet) of vertebrates; they articulate with the cuneiform and cuboid bones near the middle of the foot and with the toe bones (phalanges).

mineralization 1. Anatomy: the process of bone formation by the calcification of soft tissue. 2. Paleontology: the process in which an organic material from a dead animal is quickly covered by sediment and eventually replaced by waterborne minerals.

Miocene The geologic epoch extending from 23 million years ago (Ma) to 5.3 Ma.

molar The rearmost cheek tooth in mammals; used to grind food.

molariform Like a molar; having the design of a molar.

mold A distinctive impression remaining when an organism's body leaves a void in rock or sediment but is not preserved.

mollusk Invertebrate animal in the phylum Mollusca, with soft body parts usually enclosed by a shell.

monognathic Pertaining to variation in teeth within a single jaw; usually used in reference to sharks; compare *dignathic*.

mouth plate A structure in the throat of rays and some fish to which are anchored specialized teeth for grinding food.

neural Relating to nerves or nervous system.

neural arch A structure behind the vertebral centrum that provides passage for the spinal cord.

notochord A flexible rodlike structure in early fauna that became the defining structure of chordates; it gave rise to the vertebral and spinal columns. Notochords are visible in the embryonic development of chordates and are still present in some primitive fishes.

nuchal bone The first carapace element, located at the anterior end and immediately behind the cervical bone of a turtle carapace (or shell).

nutrient foramen Plural: *nutrient foramina*. Small opening within a bone (jaw bones, phalanges, carpals, tarsals, osteoderms, and roots of shark teeth) that serves as a passage for blood vessels and nerves.

nutrient groove A narrow indentation or channel at the center of the root of a shark tooth.

obovoid Having an asymmetric oval or egg-like shape.

occipital bone The large trapezoidal plate forming the lower-rear part of the skull. Shallowly curved like a saucer, it contains a large hole through which the brain stem (medulla) narrows and enters the spinal column.

occipital condyles Bony protuberances on the occipital bone beneath the skull that articulate with the first (atlas) cervical vertebra.

occlusal Relating to the masticating (grinding or biting) surfaces of teeth.

odontocetes Dolphins, porpoises, and toothed whales in the parvorder Odontoceti.

operculum A thin, hard partition that serves as the protective cover to the opening on the shells of snails and other marine gastropods.

opisthocoelous A vertebral centrum with a convex anterior surface and a concave posterior surface.

ossicle A bone formed by ossification of the skin; also called *dermal bone*.

ossification The transformation of soft tissue into bone-like material through calcification.

osteoderm Bony structures below the skin that develop into scales, plates, or other types of protective armoring in animal species.

Paleocene The geologic epoch extending from 66 million years ago (Ma) to 56 Ma.

paleontology The study of surviving evidence and fossils to gain an understanding of the prehistoric past. Paleontology can focus on microscopic organisms, invertebrates, vertebrates, botany, ecology, climate, or animal tracks and other trace fossils.

pectoral Pertaining to the pair of fins located on either side of a fish just behind the head.

periotic Pertaining to the inner ear; also, a bone in the inner ear of whales.

peripheral Pertaining to areas away from the center (e.g., a bone or body part located away from the center of the body).

perissodactyls Odd-toed ungulates; they make up the order Perissodactyla, which includes horses, rhinoceroses, and tapirs.

permineralization The process of replacing organic tissues and bones with minerals present in groundwater; for this process to occur, burial must take place soon after death.

petrification The replacement of all hard or soft organic matter of an organism by minerals and its resulting conversion to stone.

petrosal The very dense portion of the temporal bone that occurs at the base of the skull in mammals and that surrounds the inner ear.

petrous Pertaining to the petrosal bone.

phalanx Plural: *phalanges*. A finger or toe bone.

pinna The visible part of the ear projecting on the outside of the head in mammals.

piscivorous Relating to fish-eating organisms.

pisiform One of the small sesamoid bones located within tendons of the feet, wrists, or knees of most vertebrates.

placoid scales Scales on cartilaginous fish. These scales are considered equivalent to denticles, or dermal denticles, since they are homologous with teeth (i.e., they contain pulp, blood vessels, dentine, and enamel).

plastron The ventral, "breastplate" portion of a turtle shell; it is characteristically flat and made up of nine bones.

Pleistocene The geologic epoch extending from 2.58 million years ago (Ma) to 11,700 years ago.

plication A furrow-and-ridge combination extending longitudinally along the tooth crowns of some shark species; plications run in parallel, giving the enamel surface a slightly wrinkled appearance.

Pliocene The geologic epoch extending from 5.3 million years ago (Ma) to 2.58 Ma.

polychaete worm Member of a class of annelid worms found worldwide in many different ocean-floor habitats and depths.

polyphyodontism The condition of having several sets of teeth or having a succession of teeth, as seen in reptiles and fishes.

posterior The rear section or back end of an organism; compare *anterior*.

premolar Tooth forming a transition between the canines at the front of the mouth and the molars at the back in vertebrate species; also called *bicuspid*.

proboscidean Any of the elephant-like species of the order Proboscidea, which includes one living family (Elephantidae) and several extinct families.

process A structure projecting off a bone and serving as a place of attachment and leverage for muscles (e.g., a transverse process of a vertebra).

procoelous A vertebral centrum with a concave anterior surface and a convex posterior surface; compare *acoelous* and *amphicoelous*.

proximal 1. Closest to the point of origin; used primarily in reference to limb bones. The origin refers roughly to the center of the body (e.g., the humerus is proximal to the shoulder in comparison with the radius, which is farther away from that point of origin); compare *distal*. 2. Regarding shark teeth, the side of the tooth facing toward the front of the mouth, synonymous with *mesial*.

pygal The final element, or bone, located at the posterior end of a turtle carapace (or shell).

pyramidal Of or shaped like a pyramid.

quartzose sandstone A sedimentary rock made of more than 90% quartz grains, with the remaining matrix composed of feldspar or rock detritus.

radioulna A bone in the forelimbs of frogs and other amphibians that represents a fusion of the separate radius and ulna in higher tetrapod species.

radius The smaller of two large bones in the forearms or forelegs of tetrapods.

recrystallization The process of transforming the original compounds in an organism (primarily shells) into another form (e.g., carbonate shells becoming calcified).

rodent Any member of the order Rodentia, which includes mammals with continuously growing incisors in their upper and lower jaws (e.g., mice, rats, squirrels, beavers, porcupines, and capybaras).

root The supportive base of a tooth, anchored in the jawbone.

root lobe A rounded end or corner of the root of a shark tooth.

rostral Positioned near the front end of the body; in particular, near the nose or mouth.

rostrum For the purposes of this book, a beak-like extension of the skulls of billfish and sawfish.

rugose Describing a tooth or bone surface that is wrinkled or rough like the shallow rounded valleys and ridges of a landscape.

sacral Referring to the lower (lumbar) region of the spinal column in vertebrates. The sacral vertebrae are located between the thoracic vertebrae of the middle spine and the coccygeal, or caudal, vertebrae of the lower spine.

scaphoid One of the bones in the wrists and feet of vertebrates; they articulate with several other bones in each structure; also called *navicular*. From the Greek *skaphos*, "boat," referring to the bone's boatlike shape.

Schreger pattern Lines visible in the ivory tusks of proboscideans that appear as cross-hatching patterns. These lines form angles of less than 90 degrees in extinct mammoths, and greater than 115 degrees in modern elephants.

scute Keratinous plate on the top of bones and osteoderms of animals.

scyliorhinoid design Having the shape or other characteristics of the family Scyliorhinidae, or cat sharks, which have catlike eyes and dorsal fins set far back toward the posterior end; compare *lamnoid design*.

selenodont Cheek teeth found in artiodactyls—especially ruminants—that display crescent-shaped ridges of enamel in occlusal view, with exposed interiors of dentine and cement.

septum Plural: *septa*. A wall or partition dividing two chambers, spaces, or tissues in plants and animals.

serration Pointed or rounded projection along the outer edge of a tooth, especially a shark's tooth; often visible as tiny sawteeth lining part or all of the edge of a tooth.

sesamoid Referring to a group of bones in the extremities of tetrapods.

sexual dimorphism The condition in which the sexes of a species display differences in characteristics such as weight, size, color, or markings.

shell hash Surface layers of beach detritus dominated by loose shell material of particles 2–64 millimeters in size.

sinusoidal Pertaining to sinuses or cavities; also, curving in the shape of a mathematical sine curve or curving sharply.

sirenian Any member of the order Sirenia, which includes the herbivorous marine mammals (e.g., manatees and dugongs).

spatulate Describing a wide, flattened surface of a bone.

species In scientific binomial classification, the final defining term in the name of an organism, sometimes followed by a subspecies name. In common usage, a plant or animal type (e.g., a bass species, sloth species, reptile species).

spinous Relating to or having spines, such as stingray spines or the rays in a fish fin.

steinkern A fossil infilling from a hollow organism or body part, such as a shell. Steinkerns form when mud or sediment fills a chamber and preserves the shape of the original animal or body part long after the organism is gone.

stylid A ridge running down the side of some bovine molars and forming part of the masticating surface. They are especially diagnostic for bovid species.

substrate An underlying material, such as a rock formation beneath a soil layer.

sulcus A groove or fissure between the convolutions (folds) on the surface of a bone or an organ.

suture The union or articulation of two bones that forms a seamlike, immovable junction.

symphyseal Pertaining to two structures that have grown together, such as an intervertebral disk attached to the end of a vertebra.

taphonomy The scientific study of the processes that preserve animal and plant remains during the time between death and fossilization.

tarsal Any of the group of seven bones of the hind foot and ankle that articulate with the distal end of the tibia and the metatarsals of the midfoot.

teleost fish A member of the infraclass Teleostei, which includes most fish today. In these fish, the maxilla and premaxilla are fully movable in a way that enables the jaw to project forward during predation. They also have homocercal, or symmetrically lobed, tail fins.

tetralophodont 1. A member of any of three species of the *Tetralophodon* genus within the Gomphotheriidae family, characterized by having four tusks. The early elephant-like species lived from the Late Miocene to Early Pliocene Epochs. 2. A third molar with four main lophs, or ridges, like those found in gomphothere species.

thoracic Pertaining to the middle- to upper-back area below the cervical and above the lumbar regions.

tibia The posterior lower leg bone parallel to the fibula; in humans, this is often called the shinbone.

tooth battery An arrangement of teeth in an interlocking or mosaic pattern that creates a larger surface used for grinding. Dental batteries are seen in durophagous fishes and in dinosaurs such as triceratopsids and hadrosaurines.

trabeculae Partitions in the structure of bones, especially in cancellous bone. This calcareous connective tissue is spongy in appearance and occurs most often at the ends of limb bones, vertebral centra, and the inner bone of a turtle shell.

transverse Appearing crosswise or extending across the surface of a bone, tooth, or other fossil.

trefoil A folded cloverleaf-like pattern; apparent on the occlusal surface in molars of *Cuvieronius* gomphotheres.

trilophodont First and second molars having three main lophs, or ridges, like those found in gomphothere species.

tritor The grinding surface that forms on the crowns of teeth.

trochlear notch A deep depression on the proximal end of the ulna that articulates with the trochlea of the humerus.

tubercle A small bump or rounded projection on the surface of a structure such as a bone, tooth, or osteoderm.

tubule A small tube or tubular structure.

tympanic bulla A bony structure in the ear of a marine mammal that responds to incoming sound waves by producing vibrations, which are passed on through the auditory nerve to the brain.

ulna One of the two major bones closest to the hand or forefoot and making up the forelimbs of a tetrapod.

ungulate A member of the superorder Ungulata, animals defined by having hoofed feet.

ventral Pertaining to the underside or belly; compare *dorsal*.

vertebra A bone that is a component of the spine.

vertebrate An animal with an internal skeleton and a spinal column.

xenapophyses Extra surfaces for articulation found in the vertebrae of xenarthrans. The word *xenarthran* comes from Greek roots meaning “strange joints.”

Xenarthra The superorder of placental mammals that includes both extinct and extant species of anteaters, glyptodonts, armadillos, pampatheres, and sloths.

zygapophysis One of the four processes of a vertebra. Occurring in pairs, the zygapophyses interlock with each of the adjoining vertebrae in the spinal column.

Suggested Reading

PRINT SOURCES

Additions to the Pleistocene Mammal Faunas of South Carolina, North Carolina, and Georgia, by Albert E. Sanders. Philadelphia: American Philosophical Society, 2002. | A useful text for identifying minute features of specific vertebrate fossils. Since this is a scientific publication aimed at those adding species to a recorded fossil assemblage, much of the text is technical and not geared toward the beginning collector. Black-and-white images.

Florida's Fossils: Guide to Locations, Identification, and Enjoyment, by Robin C. Brown. Sarasota, Fla.: Pineapple, 1988. | A good Florida-specific text on fossil-hunting locations. Useful primarily for finding locations. There are some identification plates in the back, with multiple fossils, which are identified in the captions. Black-and-white images.

Fossil Sharks of the Chesapeake Bay Region, by Bretton W. Kent. Columbia, Md.: Egan Rees & Boyer, 1994. | Good introduction to teeth placement in the jaw as well as to identifying many common teeth found in Maryland. Line drawings. Out of print.

Fossil Shark Teeth of the World: A Collector's Guide, by Joe Cocke. Torrance, Calif.: Lamna, 2002. | A short guide that covers some of the common shark teeth from around the world. Geared toward beginning collectors who are buying teeth. Terminology and descriptions are simple. Small black-and-white images.

The Fossil Vertebrates of Florida, edited by Richard C. Hulbert Jr. Gainesville: University Press of Florida, 2001. | An 8.5" × 11" text on the fossil vertebrate history of Florida. Excellent line drawings of skeletons and enamel patterns on teeth. The information is readable without sacrificing scientific integrity. Line drawings and black-and-white images.

Osteology for the Archaeologist, by Stanley J. Olsen. Cambridge, Mass.: Peabody Museum, 1979. | An excellent comparison of individual skeletal elements of mammoths and mastodons. The second half of the book features bird skeletons. Each anatomical viewing angle is presented and featured in a neat, organized manner. Black-and-white images.

Seal/Dolphin—Phoca/Stenella: A Skeletal Comparison of Two Marine Mammals, by John R. Timmerman. Durham: North Carolina Fossil Club, 1997. | A simple text with well drawn images of individual skeletal elements of seals and dolphins. Fairly basic, with labeled anatomical views. Line drawings.

Teeth, 2nd ed., by Simon Hillson. Cambridge: Cambridge University Press, 2005. | Though geared toward archaeologists, this text has a fairly comprehensive coverage of Pleistocene fauna dentition. The occlusal views of teeth are well drawn, and the correct anatomical positions are labeled. Digital line drawings.

Vertebrate Fossils: A Neophyte's Guide, by Frank A. Kocsis Jr. Palm Harbor, Fla.: IBIS Graphics, 1997. | A simple text that mainly provides images and identifications of fossil specimens, predominantly bones. Several scientific names are outdated, and some pages can appear cluttered. Overall, a fair coverage of many vertebrates. Black-and-white images. Out of print.

Vertebrate Fossils: Beach and Bank Collecting for the Amateur, by M. C. Thomas. Gainesville: Florida Paleontological Society, 1968. | A classic that hooked many people on beach fossil hunting. A short introductory text for identification; its usefulness is somewhat limited by its old photographs. Black-and-white images.

ONLINE SOURCES

Elasmo.com: The Life and Times of Long Dead Sharks, elasmo.com | An excellent resource for shark tooth hunters; especially good for Paleocene material. Color photographs supply detailed views of small shark teeth. The site is slightly tricky to learn to navigate.

The Fossil Forum, thefossilforum.com | A community of amateur fossil hunters and professional paleontologists who share finds and help with the identification of specimens. A valuable resource for those who don't have a state museum or university nearby.

PaleoEnterprises, http://paleoenterprises.com | A site that sells vertebrate fossils, predominantly from the Miocene–Pleistocene epochs. The anatomical identifications are sound, and multiple color photos are displayed of each specimen. Useful for obscure bone identifications.

Bibliography

ANONYMOUS WORKS

"Alligator Biology and Behavior: *Alligator mississippiensis*." Louisiana Alligator Advisory Council. https://www.louisianaalligators.com/alligator-biology-and-behavior.html.

"Alligator Snapping Turtle." *National Geographic*. https://www.nationalgeographic.com/animals/reptiles/a/alligator-snapping-turtle.

"American Alligator." *National Geographic Kids*. https://kids.nationalgeographic.com/animals/reptiles/american-alligator.

"Amphibia." *Encyclopædia Britannica*. 9th ed. 1878.

Animal Diversity Web. University of Michigan Museum of Zoology. http://animaldiversity.org.

"Canis Dirus." Florida Museum of Natural History, March 11, 2015. flmnh.ufl.edu/florida-vertebrate-fossils/species/canis-dirus.

"*Carcharocles/Carcharodon auriculatus*." Prehistoric Wildlife, 2015. prehistoric-wildlife.com/species/c/carcharocles-auriculatus.html.

"*Carcharocles/Carcharodon chubutensis*." Prehistoric Wildlife, 2015. prehistoric-wildlife.com/species/c/carcharocles-chubutensis.html.

"Chert and Flint." *Encyclopædia Britannica Online*. britannica.com/EBchecked/topic/109569/chert-and-flint.

"Chimaera." *Encyclopædia Britannica Online*. britannica.com/EBchecked/topic/111552/chimaera.

"*Cuvieronius*." Prehistoric Wildlife. prehistoric-wildlife.com/species/c/cuvieronius.html.

"*Dasypus bellus*: Beautiful Armadillo Fossil Facts and Photos." Fossil-Treasures-of-Florida.com. fossil-treasures-of-florida.com/dasypus-bellus.html.

"Dusky Shark." *National Geographic*. https://www.nationalgeographic.com/animals/fish/d/dusky-shark.

"The End of the Super Predator?" Endangered Species International. 2011. endangeredspeciesinternational.org/superpredator.html.

"Extinct American Lion (*Panthera atrox*) Fact Sheet: Summary." San Diego Zoo Global Library. Updated October 15, 2019. https://ielc.libguides.com/sdzg/factsheets/extinctamericanlion.

"Extinct California Tapir (*Tapirus californicus*) Fact Sheet: Summary." San Diego Zoo Global Library. Updated October 15, 2019. http://ielc.libguides.com/sdzg/factsheets/extinctcaliforniatapir.

"Extinct Columbian (*Mammuthus columbi*) and Channel Island (*M. exilis*) Mammoths Fact Sheet: Summary." San Diego Zoo Global Library. Updated October 15, 2019. http://ielc.libguides.com/sdzg/factsheets/extinctmammoth.

"Extinct Ground Sloths (*Paramylodon harlani*, *Nothrotheriops shastensis*, and *Megalonyx jeffersoni*) Fact Sheet: Summary." San Diego Zoo Global Library. Updated October 15, 2019. https://ielc.libguides.com/sdzg/factsheets/extinctgroundsloths.

"Extinct Long-horned Bison & Ancient Bison Fact Sheet (*Bison latifrons* and *B. antiquus*): Summary." San Diego Zoo Global Library. Updated October 15, 2019. http://ielc.libguides.com/sdzg/factsheets/extinctlonghorned-ancientbison.

"Fossil Shark Teeth." Florida Museum of Natural History. https://www.floridamuseum.ufl.edu/discover-fish/sharks/fossil/shark-teeth.

"Giant Armadillo Fossil Images and Information." Fossil-Treasures-of-Florida.com. http://www. fossil-treasures-of-florida.com/giant-armadillo.html.

"Giant Eremotherium Ground Sloth." Fossil-Treasures-of-Florida.com. http://www.fossil-treasures-of-florida.com/eremotherium.html.

"Giant Tortoise." World Wildlife Fund. https://www.worldwildlife.org/species/giant-tortoise.

"Hearing." In *Encyclopedia of Marine Mammals*, edited by W. F. Perrin, Vernd Vursig, and J. G. M. Thewissen, 555. 2nd ed. San Diego: Academic Press, 2002.

"The History of Nail Making." Glasgow Steel Nail. 2002. http://www.glasgowsteelnail.com/nailmaking.htm.

"Homology: From Jaws to Ears—An Unusual Example of a Homology." Understanding Evolution. https://evolution.berkeley.edu/evolibrary/article/0_0_0/homology_06.

"How to Age a Whitetail Deer." Dane County Conservation League. Updated September 18, 2017. http://www.dccl.org/information/deer/deerage.htm.

"Jack." *Encyclopædia Britannica Online*. http://www.britannica.com/EBchecked/topic/298681/jack.

"Jefferson's Ground Sloth." Yukon Beringia Interpretive Centre. https://www.beringia.com/exhibit/ice-age-animals/jeffersons-ground-sloth.

"Leonardo da Vinci (1452–1519)." University of California Museum of Paleontology. https://ucmp.berkeley.edu/history/vinci.html.

"Mako Shark." Sharks-World. https://www.sharks-world.com/mako_shark.

"Maryland Fish Facts." Maryland Department of Natural Resources. https://dnr.maryland.gov/Fisheries/Pages/fishfacts-index.aspx.

"Mastodon Ivory? Interesting Read." Online discussion at BladeForums.com, September

26, 2008. https://www.bladeforums.com/threads/mastodon-ivory-interesting-read.712872.
"Megatherium: Extinct Mammal." *Encyclopædia Britannica Online*. Updated October 10, 2018. https://www.britannica.com/animal/Megatherium.
"More Geologic Goodies on South Carolina." Overview of SC Geology. https://www.sciway3.net/2001/sc-geology/Overview_of_SC_Geology.htm.
"Native American Turtle Mythology." Native Languages of the Americas. http://www.native-languages.org/legends-turtle.htm.
"North American Mammals and the American Black Bear, *Ursus americanus*: A Guide to Sources." *Reference and User Services Association* 51, no. 3 (2012). https://journals.ala.org/index.php/rusq/article/view/3136/3260.
"Northern Sea Robins, *Prionotus carolinus*." MarineBio Conservation Society. https://marinebio.org/species/northern-sea-robins/prionotus-carolinus.
"No Smooth Sailing for the Smooth Hammerhead." *Defenders of Wildlife* blog. May 13, 2015. https://defenders.org/blog/2015/05/no-smooth-sailing-smooth-hammerhead.
"Odysseus." *Wikipedia*. Updated October 17, 2019. https://en.wikipedia.org/wiki/Odysseus.
"Oysters." *National Geographic*. http://animals.nationalgeographic.com/animals/invertebrates/oyster.
"Permineralization." Fossils—Window to the Past. University of California Museum of Paleontology. https://ucmp.berkeley.edu/paleo/fossilsarchive/permin.html.
"Prehistoric Sharks." Sharks-World. https://www.sharks-world.com/prehistoric_sharks.
"Prehistoric Sharks through the Ages." Prehistoric Wildlife. prehistoric-wildlife.com/articles/prehistoric-sharks-through-the-ages.html.
Prehistoric Wildlife. http://prehistoric-wildlife.com.
"Raccoon." *National Geographic*. http://animals.nationalgeographic.com/animals/mammals/raccoon.
"Raccoon Nation: Raccoon Fact Sheet." PBS, February 7, 2012. pbs.org/wnet/nature/raccoon-nation-raccoon-fact-sheet/7553.
"Raccoons." Birds Amoré. https://www.birdsamore.com/critters/raccoons.htm.
"Raccoons." Washington Department of Fish and Wildlife. https://wdfw.wa.gov/species-habitats/species/procyon-lotor.
"Sand Dollar." Monterey Bay Aquarium. https://www.montereybayaquarium.org/animal-guide/invertebrates/sand-dollar.
"Sea Robin." *Encyclopædia Britannica Online*. britannica.com/EBchecked/topic/530708/sea-robin.
"Sharks and Rays." Defenders of Wildlife. https://defenders.org/wildlife/sharks-and-rays.
"Skeletal Anatomy (Marine Mammals)." What-when-how. http://what-when-how.com/marine-mammals/skeletal-anatomy-marine-mammals.
"Skull Science." New York State Department of Environmental Conservation. dec.ny.gov/docs/wildlife_pdf/skullscience.pdf.

"Sperm Whale." *National Geographic*. https://www.nationalgeographic.com/animals/mammals/s/sperm-whale.

"Stingrays." *National Geographic*. https://www.nationalgeographic.com/animals/fish/group/stingrays.

"UF Researchers Find Oldest Bones of New Giant Ground Sloth Species." University of Florida News, June 20, 2000. https://news.ufl.edu/archive/2000/06/uf-researchers-find-oldest-bones-of-new-giant-ground-sloth-species.html.

"Unusual Bones to Identify." TreasureNet: The Original Treasure Hunting Website, June 12, 2011. Discussion thread started by Harry Pristis. treasurenet.com/forums/fossils/242840-unusual-bones-identify.html.

"White Tail Deer." Deer Trail. www.deertrail.us/minnesotawildlife/minnesotawildlife/whitetaildeer.html.

"Woolly Mammoth Facts." Extinct Animals Facts. http://extinct-animals-facts.com/Extinct-Prehistoric-Animal-Facts/Woolly-Mammoth-Facts.shtml.

AUTHORED WORKS

Ábelová, M. "Schreger Pattern Analysis of *Mammuthus primigenius* Tusk: Analytical Approach and Utility." *Bulletin of Geosciences* 83, no. 2 (2008): 225–32. DOI:10.3140/bull.geosci.2008.02.225 .

Alden, Andrew. "A Fossil Picture Gallery." ThoughtCo. Updated January 29, 2018. thoughtco.com/fossil-picture-gallery-4122830.

———. "How to Identify the 3 Major Types of Rocks." ThoughtCo. Updated December 23, 2018. https://www.thoughtco.com/rock-type-identification-4147694#step-heading.

Alroy, John. Fossilworks: Gateway to the Paleobiology Database. http://fossilworks.org.

Alteir, Nuran. "Free Entrance Monday to La Brea Tar Pits for 100th Anniversary." Southern California Public Radio, October 26, 2013. https://www.scpr.org/news/2013/10/26/40028/free-entrance-monday-to-la-brea-tar-pits-for-100-y.

Andrianavalona, Tsiory H., Tolotra N. Ramihangihajason, Armand Rasoamiaramanana, David J. Ward, Jason R. Ali, and Karen E. Samonds. "Miocene Shark and Batoid Fauna from Nosy Makamby (Mahajanga Basin, Northwestern Madagascar)." *PLoS One* 10, no. 6 (2015): e0129444.

Anglen, John, and Thomas M. Lehman. "Habitat of the Giant Crocodilian *Deinosuchus*, Aguja Formation (Upper Cretaceous), Big Bend National Park, Texas." *Journal of Vertebrate Paleontology* 20, supplement to no. 3 (2000): 1–86.

Argyriou, Thodoris, Todd D. Cook, Ahmed M. Muftah, Paris Pavlakis, Noel T. Boaz, and Alison M. Murray. "A Fish Assemblage from an Early Miocene Horizon from Jabal Zaltan, Libya." *Journal of African Earth Sciences* 102 (2015): 86–101. DOI:10.1016/j.jafrearsci.2014.11.008.

Azzaroli, A. "Ascent and Decline of Monodactyl Equids: A Case for Prehistoric Overkill." *Annales Zoologici Fennici* 28 (1991): 151–163.

Balter, Michael. "What Killed the Great Beasts of North America?" *Science*, January 28, 2014. https://www.sciencemag.org/news/2014/01/what-killed-great-beasts-north-america.

Bargo, M. Susana, and Sergio F. Vizcaino. "Paleobiology of Pleistocene Ground Sloths (Xenarthra, Tardigrada): Biomechanics, Morphogeometry and Ecomorphology Applied to the Masticatory Apparatus." *Ameghiniana* 45, no. 1 (2008): 175–196.

Barnett, Ross, Ian Barnes, Matthew J. Phillips, et al. "Evolution of the Extinct Sabretooths and the American Cheetah-like Cat." *Current Biology* 15, no. 15 (2005): PR589–R590. DOI:10.1016/j.cub.2005.07.052.

Baskin, Jon A. "The Pleistocene Fauna of South Texas." South Texas Pleistocene Fossils. texasturtles.org/Pleistocene_Fauna_of_South_Texas.pdf.

Bearzi, Maddalena, and Craig B. Stanford. *Beautiful Minds: The Parallel Lives of Great Apes and Dolphins*. Cambridge, Mass.: Harvard University Press, 2008.

Bellairs, A. d'A. Review of *Crocodiles: Their Natural History, Folklore, and Conservation*, by C. A. W. Guggisberg. *Oryx* 11, no. 6 (2011): 478–479.

Benton, Michael J. *Vertebrate Palaeontology*. London: Chapman and Hall, 1997.

———. *Vertebrate Palaeontology*. 3rd ed. Oxford: Blackwell Science, 2005.

———. *Vertebrate Palaeontology*. 4th ed. Chichester, UK: Wiley-Blackwell, 2014.

Bester, Cathleen. "*Aetobatus narinari*: Spotted Eagle Ray." Florida Museum of Natural History, Ichthyology Department. https://www.floridamuseum.ufl.edu/discover-fish/species-profiles/aetobatus-narinari.

———. "*Notorynchus cepedianus*: Sevengill Shark." Florida Museum of Natural History, Ichthyology Department. https://www.floridamuseum.ufl.edu/discover-fish/species-profiles/notorynchus-cepedianus.

———. "*Parmaturus xaniurus*: Filetail Catshark." Florida Museum of Natural History, Ichthyology Department. https://www.floridamuseum.ufl.edu/discover-fish/species-profiles/parmaturus-xaniurus.

Bester, Cathleen, Henry Mollet, and Jim Bourdon. "*Pteroplatytrygon violacea*: Pelagic Stingray." Florida Museum of Natural History, Ichthyology Department. https://www.floridamuseum.ufl.edu/discover-fish/species-profiles/pteroplatytrygon-violacea.

Bigelow, Henry B., and William C. Schroeder. "Common Sea Robin *Prionotus carolinus* (Linnaeus) 1771." In *Fishes of the Gulf of Maine*. Fishery Bulletin of the Fish and Wildlife Service 53:468–470. U.S. Department of the Interior, Fish and Wildlife Service. Washington, D.C.: Government Printing Office, 1953.

———. "Cow-nosed Ray *Rhinoptera bonasus* (Mitchill) 1815." In *Fishes of the Gulf of Maine*. Fishery Bulletin of the Fish and Wildlife Service 53:76–77. U.S. Department of the Interior, Fish and Wildlife Service. Washington, D.C.: Government Printing Office, 1953.

Blanco, Rudemar Ernesto, Washington W. Jones, and Joaquín Villamil. "The 'Death Roll' of Giant Fossil Crocodyliforms (Crocodylomorpha: Neosuchia): Allometric and Skull Strength Analysis." *Historical Biology* 27, no. 5 (2015): 514–524.

Boisvert, Catherine A., Elga Mark-Kurik, and Per E. Ahlberg. "The Pectoral Fin of Panderichthys and the Origin of Digits." *Nature* 456 (2008): 636–638.

Bressan, David. "Poet and Paleontologist: Johann Wolfgang Von Goethe."*History of*

Geology (blog). *Scientific American*, August 28, 2014. https://blogs.scientificamerican.com/history-of-geology/poet-and-paleontologist-johann-wolfgang-von-goethe.

Brochu, C. "King of the Crocodylians: The Paleobiology of Deinosuchus." *Palaios* 18, no. 1 (2003): 80–82.

Bronaugh, Whit. "The Trees That Miss the Mammoths." *American Forests*, Winter 2010, 38–43. https://www.americanforests.org/magazine/article/trees-that-miss-the-mammoths.

Bryner, Michelle. "How Long Does It Take to Make Petrified Wood?" *LiveScience*, November 30, 2012. https://www.livescience.com/32316-how-long-does-it-take-to-make-petrified-wood.html.

Canadian Museum of Nature. "Remains of Extinct Giant Camel Discovered in High Arctic by Canadian Museum of Nature." EurekAlert! press release, March 5, 2013. https://www.eurekalert.org/pub_releases/2013-03/cmon-roe030113.php.

Chambers, Steven M., Steven R. Fain, Bud Fazio, and Michael Amaral. "An Account of the Taxonomy of North American Wolves from Morphological and Genetic Analyses." *North American Fauna* 77 (2012): 1–67.

Cicimurri, David J., and James L. Knight. "Late Oligocene Sharks and Rays from the Chandler Bridge Formation, Dorchester County, South Carolina, USA." *Acta Palaeontologica Polonica* 54, no. 4 (2009): 627–647. DOI:10.4202/app.2008.0077.

Cocke, Joe. *Fossil Shark Teeth of the World: A Collector's Guide*. Torrence, Calif.: Lamna, 2002.

Cohen, K. M., S. Finney, and P. L. Gibbard. "International Chronostratigraphic Chart" (PDF). International Commission on Stratigraphy. International Union of Geological Sciences. 2013. http://www.stratigraphy.org/ICSchart/ChronostratChart2013-01.pdf.

Colbert, Edwin H., and Roland T. Bird. "A Gigantic Crocodile from the Upper Cretaceous Beds of Texas." *American Museum Novitates*, no. 1688 (1954).

Compagno, L. J. V. "Endoskeleton." In *Sharks, Skates, and Rays: The Biology of Elasmobranch Fishes*, edited by William C. Hamlett, 75–79. Baltimore: Johns Hopkins University Press, 1999.

Cushman, Abi. "Capybara Facts for Kids." Animal Fact Guide. Updated August 24, 2014. https://animalfactguide.com/animal-facts/capybara.

Diedrich, Cajus D. "Evolution of White and Megatooth Sharks, and Evidence for Early Predation on Seals, Sirenians, and Whales." *Natural Science* 5, no. 11 (2013): 1203–1218. DOI:10.4236/ns.2013.511148.

Donati, Annabelle. *Animal Camouflage*. New York: Golden Book, 1995.

Drew, Joshua, Christopher Philipp, and Mark W. Westneat. "Shark Tooth Weapons from the 19th Century Reflect Shifting Baselines in Central Pacific Predator Assemblies." *PLoS One* 8, no. 4 (2013): e59855.

Espinoza, Edgar O., and Mary-Jacque Mann. "Identification Guide for Ivory and Ivory Substitutes." 1991. Reprint, CITES [Convention on Trade in International Species], 1999. https://www.cites.org/sites/default/files/eng/resources/pub/E-Ivory-guide.pdf.

Evans, Howard E., and Alexander de Lahunta. *Guide to the Dissection of the Dog*. 8th ed. St. Louis: Elsevier, 2017.

Feirstine, Harry L. "Fossil History of Billfish (Xiphioidei)." *Bulletin of Marine Science* 79, no. 3 (2006): 433–453.

Fields, Steven E., H. Gregory McDonald, James L. Knight, and Albert E. Sanders. "The Ground Sloths (Pilosa) of South Carolina." *PalArch's Journal of Vertebrate Paleontology* 9, no. 3 (2012): 1–19.

Foronda, Marco. "Skull of Extinct Animal Reveals More about Prehistoric Mammals." *China Topix*, November 10, 2014. chinatopix.com/articles/21475/20141110/skull-of-ancient-critter-could-reveal-better-mammalian-history.htm.

Garcia, Frank A., and Donald S. Miller. "Vertebrate Fossils." In *Discovering Fossils: How to Find and Identify Remains of the Prehistoric Past*, 153. Mechanicsburg, Pa.: Stackpole, 1998.

Gauthier, Franzen, and Jenz Lorenz. *The Ancestral Horses of the Dawn*. New York: Oxford University Press, 2007.

Geggel, Laura. "Image Gallery: Ancient Beast Fossils Leap into 3D World." Live Science, December 31, 2014. https://www.livescience.com/48681-photos-3d-turkana-fossils.html.

Gentry, Andrew D., James F. Parham, Dana J. Ehret, and Jun A. Ebersole. "A New Species of *Peritresius* Leidy, 1856 (Testudines: Pan-Cheloniidae) from the Late Cretaceous (Campanian) of Alabama, USA, and the Occurrence of the Genus within the Mississippi Embayment of North America." *PLoS One* 13, no. 4 (2018): e0195651.

Ghose, Tia. "Found: Whale Thought Extinct for 2 Million Years." Live Science, December 18, 2012. Available at nbcnews.com/id/50242411/ns/technology_and_science-science/t/found-whale-thought-extinct-million-years/#.XauNfi-ZPUI.

Gillis, J. Andrew, Randall D. Dahn, and Neil H. Shubin. "Shared Developmental Mechanisms Pattern the Vertebrate Gill Arch and Paired Fin Skeletons." *Proceedings of the National Academy of Sciences* 106, no. 14 (2009): 5720–5724. https://www.pnas.org/content/106/14/5720.

Glick, Daniel. "Back from the Brink." *Smithsonian*, September 2005. https://www.smithsonianmag.com/science-nature/back-from-the-brink-73104693.

Gonzaga, Shireen. "Unique Spine Found in 240-Million-Year-Old Fish Fossil." EarthSky, October 14, 2013. https://earthsky.org/earth/unique-spine-found-in-240-million-year-old-fish-fossil.

Gradstein, Felix M., James G. Ogg, Mark D. Schmitz, and Gabi Ogg, eds. *The Geologic Time Scale 2012*. Vol. 1. Oxford: Elsevier, 2012.

Greenfieldboyce, Nell. "How the Turtle Got Its Shell." NPR, June 24, 2015. https://www.npr.org/sections/thetwo-way/2015/06/24/416657576/how-the-turtle-got-its-shell.

Griffiths, Sarah. "Baby Mammoth under the X-RAY: Scans Reveal 42,000-Year-Old Lyuba in Unprecedented Detail." *Mail Online*, July 11, 2014. https://www.dailymail.co.uk/sciencetech/article-2687341/Baby-mammoth-X-RAY-Newly-released-images-reveal-42-000-year-old-Lyuba-unprecedented-detail.html.

Hallett, Mark. "Dire Wolf." Personal webpage. 1987. https://faculty.evansville.edu/ck6/bstud/direwolf.html.

Handwerk, Brian. "Oldest Turtle Found; May Crack Shell-Evolution Mystery." *National Geographic News*, November 26, 2008. http://english.ivpp.cas.cn/ns/es/200812/t20081201_31391.html

Harris, J. M., and G. T. Jefferson, eds. *Rancho La Brea: Treasures of the Tar Pits*. Los Angeles: Natural History Museum of Los Angeles County, 1985.

Harrison, Jessica A. "Giant Camels from the Cenozoic of North America." *Smithsonian Contributions to Paleobiology* 57 (1985): 1–29.

Hartigan, Chris, Scott Osborne, and Evin Stanford. "White Tailed Deer." North Carolina Wildlife Resources Commission, June 2009. Available at http://locavore.guide/sites/default/files/resources/files/whitetaildeer.pdf.

Havens, Kat. "Paper to Predator: Making Your Own Shark with Sandpaper!" *Beyond Bones* (blog), December 18, 2014. Houston Museum of Natural Science. http://blog.hmns.org/2014/12/paper-to-predator-making-your-own-shark-with-sandpaper.

Head, Jason J., Jonathan I. Bloch, Alexander K. Hastings, et al. "Giant Boid Snake from the Palaeocene Neotropics Reveals Hotter past Equatorial Temperatures." *Nature* 457 (2009): 715–717.

Heckel, Claire E. "Physical Characteristics of Mammoth Ivory and Their Implications for Ivory Work in the Upper Paleolithic." *Mitteilungen der Gesellschaft für Urgeschichte* 18 (2009): 71–91.

Helfman, Gene S., Bruce B. Collette, and D. E. Facey. *The Diversity of Fishes*. Malden, Mass.: Blackwell Science, 1997.

Henry, Leigh, and Tom Dillon. "Whale." World Wildlife Fund. worldwildlife.org/species/whale.

Hillson, Simon. *Teeth*. New York: Cambridge University Press, 2005.

———. "Tooth Forms in Mammals." In *Teeth*, 118. Cambridge: Cambridge University Press, 1986.

Holland, Christina, and Richard C. Hulbert Jr. "*Ambelodon britti*." Florida Museum of Natural History. Updated February 25, 2015. https://www.floridamuseum.ufl.edu/florida-vertebrate-fossils/species/amebelodon-britti.

Hulbert, Richard C., Jr. "A New Early Pleistocene Tapir (Mammalia: Perissodactyla) from Florida, with a Review of Blancan Tapirs from the State." *Florida Museum of Natural History Bulletin* 49, no. 3 (2010): 67–126.

Hulbert, Richard C., Jr., Andreas Kerner, and Gary S. Morgan. "Taxonomy of the Pleistocene Giant Beaver Castoroides (Rodentia: Castorae) from the Southeastern United States." *Florida Museum of Natural History Bulletin* 53, no. 2 (2014): 26–43.

Itano, Wayne M. "Function of the Symphyseal Tooth Whorls of *Edestus*." Paper presented at the Society of Vertebrate Paleontology Annual Meeting, October 18, 2012. https://www.academia.edu/2445892/Function_of_the_symphyseal_tooth_whorls_of_Edestus.

Jacques, Arnold, G. Kluge, Timothy Rowe. "Amniote Phylogeny and the Importance of Fossils." *Cladistics*, 2008, 105–209.

Jansen, Thomas, Peter Forster, Marshal A. Levine, et al. "Mitochondrial DNA and the Origins of the Domestic Horse." *Proceedings of the National Academy of Sciences* 99, no. 16 (2002): 10905–10910.

Jasinski, Steven E., and Steven C. Wallace. "Investigation into the Paleobiology of *Dasypus bellus* Using Geometric Morphometrics and Variation of the Calcaneus." *Journal of Mammalian Evolution* 21, no. 3 (2014): 285–298. DOI:10.1007/s10914-013-9239-0.

Jawad, Laith A. "Hyperostosis in Three Fish Species Collected from the Sea of Oman." *Anatomical Record* 296, no. 8 (2013): 1145–1147.

Kennedy, Jennifer. "What Is a Dermal Denticle?" ThoughtCo, March 7, 2019. https://www.thoughtco.com/what-is-a-dermal-denticle-2291706.

Key, Marcus M., Jr. "*Skolithos* in the Lower Cambrian Antietam Formation at South Mountain, Pennsylvania." In *Guidebook for the 79th Annual Field Conference of Pennsylvania Geologists*, edited by D. Hoskins and N. Potter Jr., 13–26. Harrisburg: Field Conference of Pennsylvania Geologists, 2014.

Kiger, Patrick J. "Could You Dig a Hole All the Way to the Earth's Mantle?" HowStuffWorks.com, November 12, 2012. https://science.howstuffworks.com/environmental/earth/geophysics/dig-hole-to-earths-mantle.htm.

King, Heather M., Neil H. Shubin, Michael I. Coates, and Melina E. Hale. "Behavioral Evidence for the Evolution of Walking and Bounding before Terrestriality in Sarcopterygian Fishes." *Proceedings of the National Academy of Sciences* 108, no. 52 (2011): 21146–21151.

King, Hobart. "Coal." Geology.com. https://geology.com/rocks/coal.shtml.

———. "Limestone." Geology.com. https://geology.com/rocks/limestone.shtml.

———. "Soapstone." Geology.com. https://geology.com/rocks/soapstone.shtml.

Kirkpatrick, Karen. "What's the Difference between a Mammoth and a Mastodon?" HowStuffWorks.com. https://animals.howstuffworks.com/extinct-animals/difference-between-mammoth-mastodon.htm.

Klappenbach, Laura. "The Basics of Vertebrate Evolution." ThoughtCo, October 16, 2019. https://www.thoughtco.com/basics-of-vertebrate-evolution-130033.

Kocsis, Frank A. *Vertebrate Fossils: A Neophyte's Guide*. Palm Harbor, Fla.: IBIS Graphics, 1997.

Koerper, Henry C., and Nancy A. Whitney-Desautels. "Astragalus Bones: Artifacts or Ecofacts?" *Pacific Coast Archaeological Society Quarterly* 35, nos. 2–3 (Spring and Summer 1999): 69–80. pcas.org/Vol35N23/3523Koerper.pdf.

Kurtén, Björn, and Elaine Anderson. "Order Artiodactyla." In *Pleistocene Mammals of North America*, 295–339. New York: Columbia University Press, 1980.

Kurtén, Björn, and Lars Werdelin. "Relationships between North and South American Smilodon." *Journal of Vertebrate Paleontology* 10, no. 2 (1990): 158–169.

Kwok, Roberta. "Scientists Find World's Biggest Snake." *Nature*, February 4, 2009. https://www.nature.com/news/2009/090204/full/news.2009.80.html.

Lacurci, Jenna. "Snaggletooth Shark Skeleton Discovered in Maryland Backyard." *Nature World News*, November 10, 2014. https://www.natureworldnews.com/articles/10186/20141110/snaggletooth-shark-skeleton-discovered-in-maryland-backyard.htm.

Larson, Jack. "Fun Facts about Alligator Gar." *Field & Stream*, January 1, 2009.

Laurin, Michel, and Robert R. Reisz. "A Reevaluation of Early Amniote Phylogeny." *Zoological Journal of the Linnean Society* 113 (1995): 165–223.

Leidy, Joseph. "Article XXIII." In *On the Extinct Species of American Ox . . .; Description of an Extinct Species of American Lion: Felis Atrox: A Memoir on the Extinct Dicotylinæ of America*, 337. Philadelphia: Smithsonian, 1852.

Lenhardt, Karin. "69 Interesting Dolphin Facts." FactRetriever. Updated April 14, 2019. https://www.factretriever.com/dolphin-facts.

Liszewski, Erica. "Basic Animal Anatomy." *EMG-Zine*. 2015. http://emg-zine.com/item.php?id=729.

MacFadden, Bruce J. "Systematics and Phylogeny of Hipparion, Neohipparion, Nannippus, and Cormohipparion (Mammalia, Equidae) from the Miocene and Pliocene of the New World." *Bulletin of the American Museum of Natural History* 179, no. 1 (1984): 1–195.

Malde, Harold E. "Geology of the Charleston Phosphate Area, South Carolina." Geological Survey Buelletin 1079. Washington, D.C.: Government Printing Office, 1959.

Marquez, Laura. "Rising Demand for Fins Contributes to Decline in Shark Population, Critics Charge." ABC News, October 30, 2006. Available from the Internet Archive, https://web.archive.org/web/20071102230904/http://www.flmnh.ufl.edu/fish/sharks/InNews/critics2006.html.

Martin, R. Aiden. "A 'Quick & Dirty' Guide to Fossil Shark Teeth." Biology of Sharks and Rays. ReefQuest Centre for Shark Research. elasmo-research.org/education/evolution/guide_f.htm.

———. "Do Sharks Feel Pain?" Biology of Sharks and Rays. ReefQuest Centre for Shark Research. elasmo-research.org/education/topics/s_pain.htm.

Matthew, William D. "Climate and Evolution." *Annals of the New York Academy of Sciences* 24, no. 1 (1914): 171–318.

Maxwell, Erin, Carlo Romano, Feixiang Wu, and Heinz Furrer. "Two New Species of *Saurichthys* (Actinopterygii: Saurichthyidae) from the Middle Triassic of Monte San Giorgio, Switzerland, with Implications for Character Evolution in the Genus." *Zoological Journal of the Linnean Society* 173, no. 4 (2015): 887–912.

Mehrtens, John M. *Living Snakes of the World in Color*. New York: Sterling, 1987.

Mestel, Rosie. "Saber-toothed Tales." *Discover*, April 1993, 50–59.

Meyer, Peter K. "Stingray Injuries." *Wilderness & Environmental Medicine* 8, no. 1 (February 1997): 24–28.

Modesto, Sean, and Jason Anderson. "The Phylogenetic Definition of Reptilia." *Systematic Biology* 53, no. 5 (2004): 815–821.

Musick, J. A., R. D. Grubbs, J. Baum, and E. Cortés. "Dusky Shark: *Carcharhinus obscurus*."

The IUCN Red List of Threatened Species. Version 2015.2. 2009. DOI:10.2305/IUCN.UK.2009-2.RLTS.T3852A10127245.en.

Nelson, Bryan. "13 Animals Recently Hunted to Extinction: Sea Mink." Mother Nature Network, May 6, 2011. https://www.mnn.com/earth-matters/animals/photos/13-animals-hunted-to-extinction/sea-mink.

Nelson, Joseph S. *Fishes of the World*. 4th ed. Hoboken, N.J.: Wiley, 2006.

O'Leary, Maureen A. "An Anatomical and Phylogenetic Study of the Osteology of the Petrosal of Extant and Extinct Artiodactylans (Mammalia) and Relatives." *Bulletin of the American Museum of Natural History* 335 (2010): 1–206.

Olsen, Stanley John. *Osteology for the Archaeologist*. *Papers of the Peabody Museum of Archaeology and Ethnology* 56, nos. 3–5 (1972, 1979).

Orlando, Ludovic, Aurélien Ginolhac, Guojie Zhang, et al. "Recalibrating Equus Evolution Using the Genome Sequence of an Early Middle Pleistocene Horse." *Nature* 499 (2013), 74–78.

Orlando, Ludovic, Dean Male, Maria Teresa Alberdi, et al. "Ancient DNA Clarifies the Evolutionary History of American Late Pleistocene Equids." *Journal of Molecular Evolution* 66, no. 5 (2008), 533–538.

Osborn, H. F. "The Reptilian Subclasses Diapsida and Synapsida and Early History of Diaptosauria." *Anthropological Papers of the American Museum of Natural History* 1 (1903): 451–507.

Owen, Richard. "Skeleton of Carnivora." In *On the Anatomy of Vertebrates*, 2:487–510. London: Longmans, Green, 1866.

Parry, Wynne. "Fossilized, 'Pompeii' Forest Discovered under Ash." LiveScience, February 21, 2012. https://www.livescience.com/18569-ancient-forest-preserved-ash.html.

———. "Missing Half of Bone Reveals Prehistoric Sea Giant." LiveScience, March 25, 2014. https://www.livescience.com/44345-missing-fossil-reveals-giant-sea-turtle.html.

Paton, R. L., Tracy Smithson, and Jennifer A. Clack. "An Amniote-like Skeleton from the Early Carboniferous of Scotland." *Nature* 398 (1999): 508–513.

Pauly, Daniel, Villy Christensen, Rainer Froese, and Maria Lourdes Palomares. "Fishing Down Aquatic Food Webs." *American Scientist* 88 (2000): 46-51.

Peterson, Beth. "Horse Hair Pottery." The Spruce Crafts. Updated September 1, 2018. https://www.thesprucecrafts.com/horse-hair-pottery-2745844.

Poisuo, Pauli. "10 Fascinating Facts about Horses." Listverse. Updated February 16, 2019. https://listverse.com/2014/01/22/10-fascinating-facts-about-horses.

Prat, François, Françoise Delpech, Nicolas Cancel, Jean-Luc Guadelli, and René Slott-Moller. "Le Bison des steppes, *Bison priscus Bojanus*, 1827, de la grotte d'Habarra à Arudy (Pyrénées-Atlantiques)." *Paleo: Revue d'Archéologie Préhistorique* 15 (2003): 1–102. https://journals.openedition.org/paleo/1362.

Press, Michelle. "Common Snook." Florida Museum of Natural History, Ichthyology Department. flmnh.ufl.edu/fish/gallery/descript/snook/snook.html.

Prothero, Donald R., and Robert M. Schoch. "Cloven Hooves." In *Horns, Tusks, and Flippers: The Evolution of Hoofed Mammals*, 37. Baltimore: Johns Hopkins University Press, 2002.

Prothero, Donald R., and Neil Shubin. "The Evolution of Oligocene Horses." In *The Evolution of Perissodactyls*, edited by Donald R. Prothero and Robert M. Schoch, 142–175. New York: Oxford University Press, 1989.

Purdy, Robert. *A Key to the Common Genera of Neogene Shark Teeth*. Washington, D.C.: National Museum of Natural History, 1990. Revised March 2006.

Radinsky, Leonard, and Sharon Emerson. "The Late, Great Sabertooths." *Natural History* 91, no. 4 (1982): 50–56.

Ramel, Gordon. "The Fish's Skeleton." Earthlife Web. https://www.earthlife.net/fish/skeleton.html.

Ray, Clayton E., ed. *Geology and Paleontology of the Lee Creek Mine, North Carolina, I*. Smithsonian Contributions to Paleobiology 53. Washington, D.C.: Smithsonian Institution Press, 1983.

Ray, Clayton E., and David J. Bohaska, eds. *Geology and Paleontology of the Lee Creek Mine, North Carolina, III*. Smithsonian Contributions to Paleobiology 90. Washington, D.C.: Smithsonian Institution Press, 2001.

Raymond M. Alf Museum of Paleontology. "New Carnivorous Dinosaur from Madagascar Raises More Questions than It Answers." *Science Daily*, April 18, 2013. https://www.sciencedaily.com/releases/2013/04/130418214043.htm.

Reynolds, John Elliott, and Randall S. Wells. *The Bottlenose Dolphin: Biology and Conservation*. Gainesville: University Press of Florida, 2000.

Rieppel, Olivier, Hassam Zaher, Eitan Tchernov, and Michael J. Polcyn. "The Anatomy and Relationships of *Haasiophis terrasanctus*, a Fossil Snake by Well-Developed Hind Limbs from the Mid-Cretaceous of the Middle East." *Journal of Paleontology* 77, no. 3 (2003): 536–558.

Rincón, Ascanio D. "A First Record of the Pleistocene Saber-toothed Cat *Smilodon populator* Lund, 1842 (Carnivora: Felidae: Machairodontinae) from Venezuela." *Ameghiniana* 43, no. 2 (2006): 499–501.

Rizzo, Johnna. "What's Ambergris? Behind the $60K Whale-Waste Find." *National Geographic News*, August 30, 2012. https://www.nationalgeographic.com/news/2012/9/120830-ambergris-charlie-naysmith-whale-vomit-science.

Roach, John. "Jaws, Teeth of Earliest Bony Fish Discovered." *National Geographic News*, August 1, 2007.

Romer, Alfred Sherwood. *Vertebrate Paleontology*. 3rd ed. Chicago: University of Chicago Press, 1966.

Rowe, Timothy. Review of *Vertebrate Paleontology and Evolution, by Robert L. Carroll*. *Journal of Vertebrate Paleontology* 8, no. 2 (1988): 235–236.

Rutherford, David. "10 Facts about the Horsehair on a String Player's Bow." Colorado Public Radio, April 21, 2014. https://www.cpr.org/2014/04/21/10-facts-about-the-horsehair-on-a-string-players-bow.

Sander, Paul Martin. "Reproduction in Early Amniotes." *Science* 337 (August 2012): 806–808.

Sanders, Albert E. *Additions to the Pleistocene Mammal Faunas of South Carolina, North Carolina, and Georgia*. Transactions of the American Philosophical Society, n.s., 92, no. 5. Philadelphia: American Philosophical Society, 2002.

Sanzenbacher, Beth. "*Mammut americanum* (Kerr 1792)." Encyclopedia of Life. https://eol.org/pages/4454807/articles.

Schwimmer, David R. "The Early Paleontology of Deinosuchus." In *King of the Crocodylians: The Paleobiology of Deinosuchus*, 37–39. Bloomington: Indiana University Press, 2002.

———. "The Prey of Giants." In *King of the Crocodylians: The Paleobiology of Deinosuchus*, 167–192. Bloomington: Indiana University Press, 2002.

Shubin, Neil. "The Evolution of Paired Fins and the Origin of Tetrapod Limbs." *Evolutionary Biology* 28 (1995): 39–86.

Simpson, George Gaylord. "American Museum of Natural History, 1927–1930." In *Simple Curiosity: Letters from George Gaylord Simpson to His Family, 1921–1970*, 115–118. Edited by Leo F. Laporte. Berkeley: University of California Press, 1987.

———. *Horses: The Story of the Horse Family in the Modern World and through Sixty Million Years of History*. New York: Oxford University Press, 1970.

———. "Notes on Pleistocene and Recent Tapirs." *Bulletin of the American Museum of Natural History* 86, no. 2 (1945): 33–82.

Smart, Tamela S. "Carpals and Tarsals of Mule Deer, Black Bear and Human: An Osteology Guide for the Archaeologist." Master's thesis, Western Washington University, 2009. https://cedar.wwu.edu/wwuet/19.

Speers, Brian R., and Ben Waggoner. "Introduction to the Pogonophora." University of California Museum of Paleontology. https://ucmp.berkeley.edu/annelida/pogonophora.html.

Stains, Howard James, and Serge Lariviere. "Carnivore." *Encyclopædia Britannica Online*. http://www.britannica.com/EBchecked/topic/96384/carnivore/51538/Form-and-function.

Stocker, Michael. "Introduction to Odontocetes and Mysticetes." Ocean Conservation Research, 2011. https://ocr.org/sounds/intro-to-odontocetes-mysticetes.

Switek, Brian. "Josephoartigasia monesi, a True ROUS." *Laelaps* (blog). ScienceBlogs, January 16, 2008.

Taylor, Paul. Review of *King of the Crocodylians: The Paleobiology of Deinosuchus*, by David R. Schwimmer. *Journal of Natural History* 38, no. 14 (2004): 1850.

Thompson, Helen. "Where Do Newly Hatched Baby Sea Turtles Go?" *Smithsonian*, March 4, 2014. https://www.smithsonianmag.com/science-nature/where-do-newly-hatched-baby-sea-turtles-go-180949954.

Timmerman, John R. *Seal/Dolphin, Phoca/Stenella: A Skeletal Comparison of Two Marine Mammals*. North Carolina: North Carolina Fossil Club, 1997.

Toennies, Jamie. "Bison Aging Techniques." 2003. Personal web page. https://fossils.its.uiowa.edu/paleo/bison.htm.

Torrens, Hugh. "Mary Anning (1799–1847) of Lyme; 'The Greatest Fossilist the World Ever Knew.'" *British Journal for the History of Science* 28, no. 3 (1995): 257–284.

Tsuji, Linda A., and Johannes Müller. "Assembling the History of the Parareptilia: Phylogeny, Diversification, and a New Definition of the Clade." *Fossil Record* 12, no. 1 (2009): 71–81.

Turner, A. *The Big Cats and Their Fossil Relatives*. New York: Columbia University Press, 1997.

University of Chicago Medical Center. "Evolution of Fins and Limbs Linked with That of Gills." *ScienceDaily*, March 25, 2009. https://www.sciencedaily.com/releases/2009/03/090323212021.htm.

———. "A Small Step for Lungfish, a Big Step for the Evolution of Walking." *ScienceDaily*, December 13, 2011. https://www.sciencedaily.com/releases/2011/12/111212153117.htm.

van den Hoek Ostende, Lars W., Michael Morlo, and Doris Nagel. "Fossils Explained 52: Majestic Killers: The Sabre-Toothed Cats." *Geology Today* 22, no. 4 (July 2006): 150–157.

Vickery, Nancy, and Bob Brown. "Concretions of the Tibooburra Area." http://brovey.yolasite.com/resources/Concretions.pdf.

Vila, Carles, Jennifer A. Leonard, Anders Gotherstrom, et al. "Widespread Origins of Domestic Horse Lineages." *Science* 291 (2001): 474–477.

Walford, Lionel, and Douglas Long. "Chondrichthyan." *Encyclopædia Britannica Online*. britannica.com/EBchecked/topic/114261/chondrichthian/63401/Reproduction-and-development.

Walker, J. D., J. W. Geissman, S. A. Bowring, and L. E. Babcock, comps. *GSA Geologic Time Scale v. 4.0*. Geological Society of America, 2012.

Ward, H. Trawick, and R. P. Stephen Davis Jr. *Time before History: The Archaeology of North Carolina*. Chapel Hill: University of North Carolina Press, 1999.

Watson, D. M. S. "On Millerosaurus and the Early History of the Sauropsid Reptiles." *Philosophical Transactions of the Royal Society B: Biological Sciences* 240 (1957): 325–400.

Weinstock, Jaco, Eske Willerslev, Andrei Sher, et al. "Evolution, Systematics, and Phylogeography of Pleistocene Horses in the New World: A Molecular Perspective." *PLoS Biology*, June 28, 2005. https://journals.plos.org/plosbiology/article?id=10.1371/journal.pbio.0030241.

Welsh, Jennifer. "Frozen in Time: Removing an Ancient Whale from Limestone." LiveScience, November 7, 2011. https://www.livescience.com/16906-ancient-whale-limestone-fossil.html.

Whitley, John. "Extinct Tiger Shark: *Galeocerdo aduncus*." Fossils of New Jersey. http://fossilsofnj.com/shark/tiger_extinct.htm.

———. "Extinct Tiger Shark: *Galeocerdo latidens*." Fossils of New Jersey. http://www.fossilsofnj.com/shark/galeocerdo_latidens.htm.

Wilson, Don E., and DeeAnn M. Reeder, eds. *Mammal Species of the World: A Taxonomic and Geographic Reference*. 3rd ed. Baltimore: John Hopkins University Press, 2005. https://www.departments.bucknell.edu/biology/resources/msw3.

Wu, Ping, Xiaoshan Wu, Ting-Xin Jiang, Ruth M. Elsey, et al. "Specialized Stem Cell Niche Enables Repetitive Renewal of Alligator Teeth." *Proceedings of the National Academy of Sciences* 110, no. 22 (2013): 2009–2018. DOI:10.1073/pnas.1213202110.

Wyneken, Jeanette. *The Anatomy of Sea Turtles*. NOAA Technical Memorandum NMFS-SEFSC-470. Washington, D.C.: U.S. Department of Commerce, National Oceanic and Atmospheric Administration, 2001. Available at https://ufdc.ufl.edu/AA00012424/00001.

Index

Entries in bold indicate species and anatomical part identification pages.

May the thrill of discovery lead

to lasting memories and cherished keepsakes.

BOB, PAM, AND ASHBY GALE

About the Authors

Bob and Pam have collected fossils since 1986, when they enlisted the help of the naturalist Rudy Mancke to lead a guided beach walk at Edisto Island, South Carolina. He introduced them to the fossil world, and they were immediately hooked. Since then, they and their son, Ashby, have built a significant collection and added to their fossil expertise with countless field visits and research. Ashby has gone on to pursue paleontology as a profession.

Bob, who holds a bachelor of science in geology and biology from the University of South Carolina, is the ecologist and public lands director for MountainTrue, an environmental nonprofit organization in the mountain region of North Carolina. Much of this book's writing was artfully penned by Bob. He has a diverse professional background in wetland science, specializing in alluvial and rare wetland bog ecosystems. He also spent 15 years as a nature photojournalist, and his articles on forest, river, beach, and saltmarsh ecology, as well as on paleontology, have appeared in *South Carolina Wildlife, American Forests, Islander*, and other publications. He authored the natural history sections for the book *Highroad Guide to the North Carolina Mountains*. Bob has been involved in ecological protection and restoration for over 45 years through his engagement with a number of conservation organizations. He chaired the local Sierra Club groups in Columbia, South Carolina, and Asheville, North Carolina, and in 1980 he founded the Hilton Head Island Sierra Group. He was actively involved in the campaign that led Congress to establish Congaree National Park, an old-growth forest that contains the greatest diversity of bottomland tree species in North America.

Pam, a working professional artist, earned a bachelor of arts in art education from Limestone College, in Gaffney, South Carolina. She drew all the illustrations in this guide and researched the 300-plus "Did You Know?" features on the Identification Pages. Pam taught art for many years at elementary schools in North and South Carolina. She has conducted on-site teaching at the Hilton Hotel and Westin Resorts on Hilton Head Island, South Carolina, and she founded and directed Kreation Station, a full-time art-teaching studio on Hilton Head. In 2018, she expanded on this idea and founded Majik Studios in Asheville, where participants of all ages learn an art form from professional artists and create their own pieces. Pam is a frequent presenter at the prestigious John C. Campbell Folk School in the mountains of western North Carolina and was a contributor to the book *Earth Friendly Crafts for Kids.* Her art specialty skills include graphic illustrations, handmade papermaking, and fabric marbling.

Ashby, who dreamed of being a paleontologist from an early age, received a bachelor of science in environmental science from Appalachian State University, in Boone, North Carolina. True to his dream, Ashby is now a paleontologist and the principal of Charleston Fossil Adventures, LLC, a tour company he founded in 2016, in Charleston, South Carolina. CFA offers beach walks, kayaking, and boat tours to educate and assist the public in finding fossils, with an emphasis on contributing significant finds to the College of Charleston's Mace Brown Museum of Natural History. Ashby did much of the research and writing for the fossil classifications and identifications in this book. He took all the photographs in the field and in the studio. Before founding CFA, he spent three years as an interpretive ranger and a program specialist at Edisto Beach State Park, South Carolina, where he became the park's authority on coastal paleontology, curating its fossil exhibits and collections, and creating new displays. He has written multiple articles for the *Explore Edisto* magazine and provided photographs for its natural history segments. He has given paleontological presentations at annual conferences of the Southeastern Association of Vertebrate Paleontology (Aurora, N.C., 2018), the Southeastern Section of the Geological Society of America (Charleston, S.C., 2019), and the Society of Vertebrate Paleontology (Brisbane, Australia, 2019).